Time Out

Florence

& the best of Tuscany

timeout.com/florence

Penguin Books

PENGUIN BOOKS

Published by the Penguin Group
Penguin Books Ltd, 80 Strand, London WC2R ORL, England
Penguin Books USA Inc., 375 Hudson Street, New York, New York 10014, USA
Penguin Books Australia Ltd, 250 Camberwell Road, Camberwell, Victoria 3124, Australia
Penguin Books Canada Ltd, 10 Alcorn Avenue, Toronto, Ontario, Canada M4V 3B2
Penguin Books (NZ) Ltd, cnr Rosedale and Airborne Roads, Albany, Auckland, New Zealand

Penguin Books Ltd, Registered Offices: Harmondsworth, Middlesex, England

First published 1997
Second edition 1999
Third edition 2001

Fourth edition 2003
10 9 8 7 6 5 4 3 2 1

Colour reprographics by Icon, Crowne House, 56-58 Southwark Street, London SE1 1UN
Printed and bound by Cayfosa-Quebecor, Ctra. de Caldes, Km 3 08 130 Sta, Perpètua de Mogoda, Barcelona, Spain

PERICOLO
DI
MORTE

Edited and designed by
Time Out Guides Limited
Universal House
251 Tottenham Court Road
London W1T 7AB
Tel + 44 (0)20 7813 3000
Fax + 44 (0)20 7813 6001
Email guides@timeout.com
www.timeout.com

Editorial
Editor Sam Le Quesne
Deputy Editor Jessica Eveleigh
Consultant Editor Nicky Swallow
Listings Editor Helen Holubov
Proofreader Tamsin Shelton
Indexer Jackie Brind

Editorial/Managing Director Peter Fiennes
Series Editor Ruth Jarvis
Deputy Series Editor Lesley McCave
Guides Co-ordinator Anna Norman
Accountant Sarah Bostock

Design
Art Director Mandy Martin
Acting Art Director Scott Moore
Acting Art Editor Tracey Ridgewell
Senior Designer Averil Sinnott
Designers Astrid Kogler, Sam Lands
Digital Imaging Dan Conway
Ad Make-up Charlotte Blythe

Picture Desk
Picture Editor Kerri Littlefield
Deputy Picture Editor Kit Burnet
Picture Researcher Alex Ortiz
Picture Desk Trainee Bella Wood

Advertising
Sales Director Mark Phillips
International Sales Manager Ross Canadé
International Sales Executive James Tuson
Advertising Sales (Florence) MAD & Co. International
Advertising Assistant Sabrina Ancilleri

Marketing
Marketing Manager Mandy Martinez
US Publicity & Marketing Associate Rosella Albanese

Production
Guides Production Director Mark Lamond
Production Controller Samantha Furniss

Time Out Group
Chairman Tony Elliott
Managing Director Mike Hardwick
Group Financial Director Richard Waterlow
Group Commercial Director Lesley Gill
Group Marketing Director Christine Cort
Group General Manager Nichola Coulthard
Group Art Director John Oakey
Online Managing Director David Pepper

Contributors
Introduction Sarah Dunant. **History** Anne Hanley (*Roman ghosts* Nicky Swallow). **The Renaissance** Clare Gogerty (*Non-Renaissance Men* Julia Burdet). **Florence Today** Nicky Swallow. **Architecture** Richard Fremantle, Nicky Swallow. **Food in Tuscany** Kate Singleton, Kate Carlisle (*The out of towners* Nicky Swallow). **Tuscan Wine** Kate Singleton. **Accommodation** Nicky Swallow. **Sightseeing** Julia Burdet (Outside the City Gates, *The green scene* Nicky Swallow; *On the up and up* Sam Le Quesne). **Restaurants** Nicky Swallow. **Wine Bars** Nicky Swallow. **Cafés, Bars & *Gelaterie*** Julia Burdet. **Shops & Services** Julia Burdet. **Festivals & Events** Nicky Swallow. **Children** Natasha Garland. **Film** Julia Burdet. **Galleries** Julia Burdet. **Gay & Lesbian** Bruno Casini. **Music: Classical & Opera** Nicky Swallow. **Music: Rock, Roots & Jazz** Julia Burdet (*Plastic people* Julia Burdet and Rob Dean). **Nightlife** Julia Burdet. **Sport & Fitness** Mary Kristel Lokken. **Theatre & Dance** Nicky Swallow, Keith Ferrone. **Florence & Prato Provinces** Tim Cooper. **Pistoia Province** Tim Cooper. **Pisa** Tim Cooper. **Pisa & Livorno Provinces** Tim Cooper. **Siena** Kate Singleton. **Siena Province** Kate Singleton. **Lucca** Sam Le Quesne. **Massa-Carrara & Lucca Provinces** Sam Le Quesne. **Arezzo** Kate Singleton. **Arezzo Province** Kate Singleton. **Southern Tuscany** Tim Cooper. **Directory** Julia Burdet.

Maps J.S. Graphics (john@jsgraphics.co.uk).

Photography Gianluca Moggi, New Press Photo, except: pages 6, 11, 14, 15, 16, 17, 21, 23 AKG London; page 18 Corbis/Vittoriano Rastelli.

The Editor would like to thank: Giuseppe Cabras, Dibiarma Darmawan, Pippa Le Quesne and all contributors from the previous three editions.

Contents

Introduction 2

In Context 5

History 6
The Renaissance 20
Florence Today 24
Architecture 27
Food in Tuscany 34
Tuscan Wine 40

Accommodation 45

Accommodation 46

Sightseeing 63

Introduction 64
Duomo & Around 67
Santa Maria Novella 84
San Lorenzo 87
San Marco 90
Santa Croce 94
Oltrarno 98
Outside the City Gates 103

Eat, Drink, Shop 107

Restaurants 108
Wine Bars 123
Cafés, Bars & *Gelaterie* 126
Shops & Services 132

Arts & Entertainment 151

Festivals & Events 152
Children 157
Film 160
Galleries 162
Gay & Lesbian 164
Music: Classical & Opera 167
Music: Rock, Roots & Jazz 170
Nightlife 174
Sport & Fitness 181
Theatre & Dance 185

Tuscany 189

Introduction 190
Florence & Prato Provinces 193
Pistoia Province 197
Pisa 200
Map: Pisa 202
Pisa & Livorno Provinces 208
Siena 212
Map: Siena 214
Siena Province 224
Lucca 238
Map: Lucca 239
Massa-Carrara & Lucca Provinces 248
Arezzo 254
Map: Arezzo 255
Arezzo Province 261
Southern Tuscany 268

Directory 277

Getting Around 278
Resources A-Z 283
Italian Vocabulary 297
Art & Architecture Glossary 298
Further Reference 299
Index 300
Advertisers' Index 306

Maps 307

Tuscany 308
Greater Florence 311
Florence Overview 312
Street Maps 314
Street Index 316

Introduction

When Florence was under siege in the 1520s, Michelangelo designed the city's defences. They'd be useless now against an inexhaustible army of credit cards but, all things considered, Florence handles the onslaught of modern tourism with remarkable good grace. For the casual visitor, zen patience in the Uffizi queue and a phrase book for the restaurants will probably be enough to get by. But if you're looking for more, then (as with most things in life) you'll have to put out a bit.

The first trick is timing; Florentines are much more relaxed when the heat is off them. Mid October to mid March is optimum. Travel light, outside the herd, and keep your eyes on the people as much as the art. Botticelli's *Birth of Venus* and David's genitals are tea towel and mouse mat fodder now, but spend an afternoon with Benozzo Gozzoli's frescoed Medici Chapel and you can almost taste the flamboyant confidence of the moment, mid 15th century, when this city rewrote the rules of Western art and culture.

Inside the ring road that marks the old city walls nowhere is too far to walk, and the more lost you get the more you'll find: hidden gardens glimpsed through gateways; churches with ghostly, less-famous frescoes; mouth-wateringly beautiful houses; and the long cobbled road to the eastern gate where the condemned, their bodies broken by torture, were rolled on carts to the gallows. Today, resident Florentines walk part of it on their way back from the market at Sant' Ambrogio.

In any of the bars, English will get you a drink, but a little Italian will get you respect and a conversation at whatever level of proficiency you care to pitch it. It doesn't have to be hard work. Florentines like to play – and to flirt. Men to women, women to men, either to either. Machismo isn't dead but it's been leavened by generations of smart, stylish Italian women who give as good as they get. Relax and give it a go. Drink slowly, eat later and when the streets empty, get on your feet again. As you walk through moon shadows in the piazzale degli Uffizi (no queues now) or hear the echo of your feet on cobbles bouncing off the stone *palazzi* above, the city can start to feel very old indeed. Even the Ponte Vecchio, tourist honey-pot hell, is potent at 2am. Back in its heyday in the 15th century, when sin was a more serious business, the bridge was the centre of a thriving sex trade and the city was patrolled by a special 'night police', whose job it was to poke their noses into dark alleys with names like La Bocca (the mouth). Their records listed the names of so many prominent families that many of the cases were settled out of court.

But, while her past was indeed sometimes dark and bloody, Florence has none of that rank sweet decay of Venice. There are no Ian McEwan endings lurking here. The secret of this city is that she was always interested in having fun. She still is. Take your time and join in for a while.

Sarah Dunant, BBC Radio 3 broadcaster and author of Florence-based novel The Birth of Venus.

ABOUT THE TIME OUT CITY GUIDES

The *Time Out Guide to Florence & the best of Tuscany* is one of an expanding series of *Time Out* city guides produced by the people behind London and New York's successful listings magazines. Our guides are all written and updated by resident experts who have striven to provide you with all the most up-to-date information.

THE LOWDOWN ON THE LISTINGS

Above all, we've tried to make this book as useful as possible. Addresses, telephone numbers, websites, transport, opening times, admission prices and credit card details were all checked and correct at the time we went to press. However, owners can change their arrangements at any time. Before you go out of your way, we'd advise you to telephone and check opening times and other particulars. While every effort has been made to ensure the accuracy of the information contained in this guide, the publishers cannot accept responsibility for any errors it may contain.

PRICES AND PAYMENT

We have noted whether venues such as shops, hotels and restaurants accept credit cards but have only listed the major cards – American Express (**AmEx**), Diners Club (**DC**), Japanese credit cards (**JCB**), MasterCard (**MC**) – also known as EuroCard – and Visa (**V**). Many hotels and the more salubrious shops and restaurants will also accept travellers' cheques in all denominations; some also take pounds and US dollars.

THE LIE OF THE LAND

Florence has few easily identifiable areas. For convenient orientation, we have divided the city into six areas, most based around their principal church. These areas are clearly marked on the map on page 314 and echoed in the titles of our sightseeing chapters. Bear in mind, however, that central Florence is very compact and so it's often easy to walk between destinations. For this reason, we have given public transport only for addresses beyond the old city walls: in the central area, a combination of short walks and using the four electric bus circuits marked on the page 314 map should get you everywhere quickly.

Note that the city's famously complex street numbering system can be confusing. Residential addresses are 'black' numbers (nero) and take an 'n' suffix and most commercial addresses are 'red' (rosso), with an 'r' suffix. If, however, there is no suffix at all, you can then assume that it is a 'black' number. This system means that in any one street there can be multiple addresses that all have the same number (albeit in different colours) and are sometimes far apart.

TELEPHONE NUMBERS

The area code for Florence is 055; do not drop the zero when calling from outside the country (and do use the code when calling from within the city). The international code for Italy is 39. Numbers preceded by 800 can be called free of charge from Florence. For more details of phone codes and charges, *see p293*.

ESSENTIAL INFORMATION

For all the practical information you might need for visiting the city – including visa and customs information, disabled access, emergency telephone numbers, a list of useful websites and the lowdown on the local transport network – turn to the **Directory** chapter at the back of this guide. It starts on page 277.

Advertisers

We would like to stress that no establishment has been included in this guide because it has advertised in any of our publications and no payment of any kind has influenced any review. The opinions given in this book are those of *Time Out* writers and entirely independent.

TUSCANY

A third of this guide is devoted to the highlights of Tuscany. Again, phone numbers are given in their entirety as dialled locally and throughout Italy – when dialling from abroad, preface them with 39, leaving the initial zero. In the shorter listings, the accommodation rates are for a double room unless otherwise stated and the average price for a meal covers *antipasto* or *primo, secondo, contorno* and *dolce*, but not wine or water.

MAPS

We've included a series of fully indexed colour maps of the city at the back of this guide – they start on page 312. Where possible, we've printed a grid reference against all venues that appear on the maps. There's a map of Tuscany on page 308 and individual city maps in the relevant chapters.

LET US KNOW WHAT YOU THINK

We hope you enjoy the *Time Out Guide to Florence & the best of Tuscany*, and we'd like to know what you think of it. In addition, we also welcome tips for places that you consider we should include in future editions, and take notice of your criticism of our choices. There's a reader's reply card at the back of this book – or you can email us at the following address: guides@timeout.com.

There is an online version of this guide, and guides to over 35 international cities, at **www.timeout.com**.

In Context

History 6
The Renaissance 20
Florence Today 24
Architecture 27
Food in Tuscany 34
Tuscan Wine 40

Features

Taking an interest 11
Roman ghosts 13
Family fortunes: the Medici 14
Key events 19
Non-Renaissance men 22
Visual aids 30
The out of towners 36
Understanding the menu 38

Farinata degli Uberti, leader of the Ghibellines, as depicted by 19th-century painter Sabatelli.

History

Past glories and gory stories.

From around the eighth century BC, much of central Italy was controlled by the Etruscans, who may have been natives or may have drifted in from Asia Minor. Whatever their origins, they settled in Veio and Cerveteri close to Rome and further north – in what is now Tuscany – in Volterra, Populonia, Arezzo, Chiusi and Cortona. They entirely overlooked the site we now know as Florence, making hilltop Fiesole their northernmost stronghold.

Tantalisingly little evidence remains of Etruscan history and culture before they were clobbered out of existence by the Romans. One of the main reasons we can be sure of so little about them is that they constructed almost everything from wood. Everything, that is, except their tombs. Because of this, their tombs and the objects recovered from them constitute most of the evidence on their civilisation. With so little to go on, mythologisers have had a field day. Enchanting frescoes of feasts, dancing and hunting that adorn many of the tombs led DH Lawrence to conclude that 'death to the Etruscan was a pleasant continuance of life'. Others that the Etruscans were terrified of death, that the seemingly carefree paintings were a desperate plea for the gods to show mercy on the other side.

The historical bones of what we know about the Etruscans are as follows. They were certainly a spiritual people, but they were also partial to a good war, against either other tribes or rival Etruscan cities. Their civilisation reached its peak in the seventh and sixth centuries BC, when their loose federation of cities dominated much of what is now southern Tuscany and northern Lazio. Women played an unusually prominent role, apparently having as much fun as the lads; writing in the fourth century BC, Theopompos said: 'Etruscan women take particular care of their bodies and exercise often, sometimes along with the men, and sometimes by themselves. It is not a disgrace for them to be seen naked. They do not share their couches with their husbands but with other men who happen to be present… They are expert drinkers and very attractive.'

Etruscan cities grew wealthy on the proceeds of mining and trading copper and iron. Their art and superbly worked gold jewellery display distinctive oriental influences, adding credence to the theory that the Etruscans migrated to Italy from the East, though such influences could have been due to their extensive trading in the eastern Mediterranean.

At the end of the seventh century BC, the Etruscans captured the small town of Rome and ruled it for a century before being expelled. The next few centuries witnessed city against city, tribe against tribe, all over central Italy until the emerging Roman republic overwhelmed all-comers by the third century BC. As the virulently pro-Etruscan, anti-Roman Lawrence put it: 'The Etruscans were the people who occupied the middle of Italy in early Roman days and whom the Romans, in their usual neighbourly fashion, wiped out entirely in order to make room for Rome with a very big R.'

The Romans absorbed many aspects of Etruscan society, such as Etruscan gods and divination by entrails, but when the Etruscans were awarded Roman citizenship in 90 BC, all distinct signs of their civilisation had vanished.

ETRUSCAN TO TUSCAN

In 59 BC Julius Caesar established a colony for army veterans along the narrowest stretch of the Arno, and Florentia was born. Strategically located at the heart of Italian territory, it grew into a flourishing commercial centre, becoming the capital of a Roman province in the third century AD. In the fifth century the Roman Empire in the west finally crumbled before the pagan hordes (some of whom were no less cultured than the dissolute Romans they displaced). Italian unity collapsed as Ostrogoths, Visigoths, Huns then Lombards rampaged through the peninsula.

'By 1200 Tuscany had become a patchwork of self-ruling entities. The potential for conflict was huge.'

The Goths who swept into central Italy in the fifth century were dislodged by the Byzantine forces of the Eastern emperor in conflicts that left the area badly battle-scarred. The Goth King Totila seized Florence again in 552, only to be ejected two decades later when the Lombards stormed across the Alps and established a regional HQ at Lucca.

In the eighth century Charlemagne and his Frankish forces crushed the last of the Lombard kings of Italy. To thank him for his intervention and ensure his future support (a move that backfired badly, leading to centuries of conflict between pontiff and emperors), Pope Leo III crowned Charlemagne Holy Roman Emperor. Much of the country then came under (at least nominal) control of the emperor. In practice, local warlords carved out feudal fiefs for themselves and threw their weight around much as they pleased.

The imperial margravate of Tuscany began to emerge as a region of some promise during the tenth and 11th centuries, when it came under the control of the Canossa family. Initially, the richest city was Lucca, but it was Pisa's increasingly profitable maritime trade that brought the biggest impetus of ideas and wealth into the region.

As a prosperous merchant class developed in cities all over Tuscany, the region sought to throw off the constraints and demands of its feudal overlords. By 1200 the majority had succeeded (Florence, Siena and Lucca had been established as independent city states or *comuni* by the redoutable Matilda di Canossa on her death in 1115) and Tuscany had become a patchwork of tiny but increasingly self-confident and ambitious self-ruling entities. The potential for conflict was huge, and by the 13th century it crystallised into an intractable struggle between Guelph and Ghibelline.

GUELPH VS GHIBELLINE

The names Guelph and Ghibelline came from the Italian forms of Welf (the family name of the German emperor Otto IV) and Waiblingen (a castle belonging to the Welfs' rivals for the role of Holy Roman Emperor, the Hohenstaufen) respectively, but by the time the appellations crossed the Alps into Italy (probably in the 12th century) their significance had changed.

'Guelph' became attached primarily to the increasingly influential merchant classes. In their continuing desire to be free from imperial control, they looked around for a powerful backer. The only viable candidate was the emperor's enemy, the pope, who by this time had recognised the error of creating a rival ruler and was peddling the theory that the fourth-century Roman emperor Constantine (who sat by in his new Eastern capital at Constantinople as the Western Empire fell from the hands of the last Roman emperors into the ruthless ones of barbarian invaders) had assigned not just spiritual but also temporal power in Italy to the papacy. The Guelphs could thus add a patriotic and religious sheen to their own self-interest.

Anyone keen to uphold imperial power and opposed to papal designs and rising commercial interests – mainly the old nobility – became known as Ghibellines. That, at least, was the theory. It soon became clear, however, that self-interest and local rivalries were of far greater importance than theoretical allegiances to emperor or pope.

Although bad feeling had been simmering for decades, the murder of Florentine nobleman Buondelmonte dei Buondelmonti is traditionally seen as the spark that ignited flames across Tuscany. On his wedding day in 1215,

GSM
Make yourself at home.
TIM national coverage, Italy (March 2003) - GSM: 94.2% country, 99.8% population.

TIM
Living without borders

Buondelmonte was stabbed to death by a member of the Amidei family for having previously jilted an Amidei maiden. The subsequent trial dissolved into a test of wills (and soon of arms) between the pro-Empire Amidei and the pro-*comune* faction mourning the demise of the groom. The Ghibelline Amidei finally prevailed with help from Emperor Frederick II in 1248, but were ousted with Guelph aid two years later, when semi-democratic government by the merchant class known as the *piccolo popolo* was established.

Ten years on, Ghibellines from Siena had dislodged the *piccolo popolo* and came close to razing the town; a decade on, the Guelphs were back in the driving seat, with the major craft guilds running the show through an administration called the *secondo popolo*. In 1293 the body passed a regulation effectively banning the nobility from government in Florence, giving power to a *signoria* made up of representatives of the guilds.

The situation was no less complex in other Tuscan towns: Lucca was generally Guelph-dominated, while Siena and Pisa tended to favour the Ghibellines, but this had as much to do with mutual antagonisms as deeply held beliefs. Siena started off Guelph, but couldn't bear the thought of having to be nice to its traditional enemy, Florence, and so swapped to the Ghibelline cause. Similarly, the Guelph/Ghibelline splits within cities were more often class- and grudge-based than ideological.

Throughout the 14th century, power ebbed and flowed between the two (loosely knit) parties across Tuscany and from city to city. When one party was in the ascendant its supporters would tear down its opponents' fortified towers (the Guelphs' with their square crenellations, the Ghibellines' with swallow-tail ones), only to have its own towers levelled in turn as soon as the pendulum swung back.

Once firmly in command of Florence at the end of the 13th century, the Guelphs started squabbling internally. In around 1300 open conflict broke out between the virulently anti-Imperial 'Blacks' and the more conciliatory 'Whites'. After various toings and froings, the Blacks booted the Whites out for good. Among those sent into exile was Dante Alighieri.

Eventually, the Guelph/Ghibelline conflict ran out of steam. It says much for the energy, innovation, graft and skill of the Tuscans (or for the relative harmlessness of much medieval warfare in Italy) that throughout this stormy period, the region was booming economically.

By the beginning of the 14th century Florence was one of the five biggest cities in Europe, with a population of almost 100,000. It went through a rocky patch in the middle of the century, when England's King Edward III defaulted on his debts (1342), bankrupting several Florentine lenders, and a plague epidemic (1348) carried off an estimated half of the city's population. But it soon bounced back: its currency – the florin, first minted in 1252 – remained one of Europe's strongest; and with fewer illness-prone poor to employ and feed, Florence may even have benefited economically from the Black Death.

'Florence turned to a fire-and-brimstone monk and his Bonfire of the Vanities.'

The city's good fortune was due in no small part to its woollen cloth industry. Taxes to finance the costly conflict known as the War of the Eight Saints against Pope Gregory XI in 1375-8 hit the *ciompi* (wool carders) hardest, and they revolted, gaining representation in city government. By the mid 1380s, however, the three guilds formed in the wake of the uprising began to lose ground to the *popolo grasso*, a small group of the wealthiest merchant families, who had united with the Guelphs to form an oligarchy in 1382. The *popolo grasso* held sway in the *signoria* (government) for 40 years, during which time intellectuals and artists were becoming increasingly involved in political life.

Not all of Florence's business community backed the *popolo grasso*. Banker Cosimo de' Medici's stance against the extremes of the *signoria* gained him the support both of other dissenting merchants and the *popolo minuto* from the less influential guilds. Cosimo's mounting popularity alarmed the *signoria*, and the dominant Albizzi family clan had him exiled on trumped-up charges in 1433. A year later he returned to Florence by popular consent and with handy military backing from his allies in Milan, and he was immediately made first citizen, becoming 'king in all but name'. For most of the next 300 years, the Medici dynasty remained more or less firmly in Florence's driving seat (*see p14* **Family fortunes: the Medici**).

KINGS IN ALL BUT NAME

Cosimo's habit of giving large sums to charity and endowing religious institutions with artworks helped make Florence a centre of artistic production, while by persuading representatives of the Eastern and Western churches to try to mend their schism at a conference in Florence in 1439, he hosted Greek scholars who could sate his intellectual hunger for classical literature. This artistic and intellectual fervour gathered steam through the long 'reign' of his grandson Lorenzo il Magnifico.

Taking an interest

As international trade flourished in the 13th century, merchants were faced with two problems: finding capital for investments, and devising methods of moving money without having to haul bags of bullion with them. A major commercial centre, Florence was among the first European cities to come up with handy solutions, thus establishing itself a role as one of the Continent's biggest banking centres.

The first problem was partially solved by money lenders, many of whom were successful merchants themselves with cash to spare. But a papal ban on usury – charging interest on loans – meant that simply handing out money made little sense except to Jews, who were not affected by Church law. Florence's original bankers, therefore, hailed from the city's thriving Jewish community, with the Da Pisa, Da Rieti and Abrabanel families leading the pack.

It wasn't long before gentiles sought a way to get into this high-yielding field. By the mid 13th century the pope had come up with a handy cavil allowing Christians to charge a levy on loans where risk was involved – meaning practically any. Soon Florence's excellent bankers were handling the huge papal accounts and collecting taxes for the pope.

In the 1290s the Florentine Bardi and Peruzzi banking families set up offices around Europe, and in London in particular, overcoming that second problem, moving cash, by instituting the system of bankers' drafts that formed the basis of modern banking. By the 1320s these two, along with the Acciaiuoli (another Tuscan family), had become Europe's biggest bankers.

Twenty years later when Florence boasted more than 80 banks functioning internationally, the Bardi, Peruzzi and Acciaiuoli paid the price of over-concentrating their assets, in this case in England. Major financers of the Hundred Years' War, they were all bankrupted when Edward III defaulted on the debts accumulated over long periods of conflict fought by expensive mercenary soldiers.

The older banks' downfall provided a solid lesson for another up-and-coming banking dynasty, the Medici, who learned not to place all their florins in one basket. Firmly in charge of the papal account, and diversifying their operations around the Continent, they dominated the city's banking scene for well over a century.

Florence's downfall as a banking heavyweight came in the second half of the 15th century. He may have been Magnifico in many ways, but Lorenzo, the grandest of the Medici (*see p14* **Family fortunes: the Medici**), didn't have the Midas touch, and his family fortunes had been eroded well before his son Piero di Lorenzo sealed the fate of Florentine banking for good. The luckless Piero capitulated before the French king Charles VIII in 1494, the Medici bank effectively shut up shop, and the focus of the political, commercial and banking world shifted definitively to northern Europe.

Under his de facto leadership, Florence enjoyed a long period of relative peace, aided to some extent by Lorenzo's diplomatic skills in minimising squabbles between Italian states. Which isn't to say that all went smoothly: Lorenzo's relations with Pope Sixtus IV were famously bitter, resulting in excommunication and war; the pope also backed the Pazzi Conspiracy, an assault financed by rival banking clan the Pazzi in which Lorenzo was injured and his brother Giuliano killed during Easter Sunday mass in 1478. Moreover, Lorenzo was more scholar-prince than all-round leader: his lack of economic prowess was to bankrupt the family business and come close to doing the same to his city-state. Though his personal popularity endured until his death in 1492, it didn't spill over on to his son Piero di Lorenzo, who in 1494 handed Florence to the French king Charles VIII as he passed through on the way to conquer Naples, then fled.

In a violent backlash against the splendour of Lorenzo's times, Florence turned for inspiration and guidance to a fire-and-brimstone-preaching monk who railed against paintings that made the Virgin Mary 'look like a harlot' and against Humanist thought, which he said would prompt the wrath of the one true and very vengeful God. Girolamo Savonarola (1452-98) perfectly caught the end-of-century spirit, winning the fanatical devotion not only of the poor and uneducated but of the leading minds of Lorenzo's magnificent court. Artists and art patrons willingly threw their works and finery on to the monk's Bonfire of the Vanities in piazza della Signoria in 1497.

For Savonarola, Charles VIII represented the 'sword of the Lord': the city's capitulation was a just punishment. Savonarola set up a semi-democratic government, firmly allied to him, then allowed his extremist tendencies to get the better of him, alienating the Borgia pope Alexander VI and getting himself excommunicated. Had Florence been in a better economic state, the pope's gesture may have had little resonance; as it was, the region was devastated by pestilence and starvation. Resentment turned on Savonarola, who was summarily tried and burned at the stake in piazza della Signoria in May 1498.

The republic created after his death was surprisingly democratic but increasingly ineffective, making a stronger leadership look enticing to disaffected Florentines. In 1502 Piero Soderini, from an old noble family, was elected gonfalonier-for-life, along the model of the Venetian doge. His pro-French policies brought him into conflict with the pro-Spanish pope Julius II, who had Cardinal Giovanni de' Medici whispering policy suggestions in his ear. In 1512 Soderini went into exile. Giuliano de' Medici, Duke of Nemours, was installed as Florence's most prominent citizen, succeeded by his nephew Lorenzo, Duke of Urbino. Their clout was reinforced in 1513 when Giovanni became Pope Leo X.

The Medici clan got a second crack at the papacy in 1524, when Giulio, Lorenzo's illegitimate nephew, became Clement VII. Renowned for his vacillating nature, Clement withdrew his support from Europe's most powerful ruler, the Habsburg emperor Charles V, then dithered for months without reinforcing Rome's fortifications; in 1527 Charles dispatched some troops to show the Medici pope who was who, Rome was sacked and Clement was forced to slink back to Charles's side, crowning him Holy Roman Emperor in 1529. Meanwhile, back in Florence the local populace had exploited the Medici ignominy in Rome to reinstall the republic. It was short-lived: Clement had agreed to crown Charles in exchange for a promise of help to get Florence back into Medici hands. The city fell in 1530.

When Clement installed the frizzy-haired Alessandro in power in Florence in 1530 and Charles V made him hereditary Duke of Florence, the city entered one of its darkest and most desperate periods. Buoyed by support from Charles, whose daughter he had married, the authoritarian Alessandro trampled on Florentines' traditional rights and privileges while indulging in some shocking sexual antics.

'Napoleon's triumphant romp down the peninsula brought him possession of Tuscany.'

His successor Cosimo had different, though no less unpleasant, defects; nor was he much cop at reversing Tuscany's gentle slide into the economic doldrums. Still, this dark horse – whom the pope made the first Grand Duke of Tuscany in 1569 – at least gave the city a patina of action, extending the writ of the *granducato* to all of Tuscany save Lucca, and adorning the city with vast new *palazzi*, including the Uffizi and the Palazzo Pitti.

BACKWATER

Cosimo's descendants continued to rule for 150 years: they were fittingly poor rulers for what was a very minor statelet in the chessboard of Europe. The *granducato's* farming methods were backward; the European fulcrum of its core industry, wool-making, like that of its main service industry, banking, had shifted definitively to northern Europe, leaving it to descend inexorably into depression. Its glory – and a very dusty glory it was – hung on its walls and adorned its palaces, with only the occasional spark of intellectual fervour (such as Cosimo II's spirited defence of Galileo Galilei when the astronomer was accused of heresy) to recall what the city had once represented. One 17th-century visitor described Florence as 'much sunk from what it was [...] one cannot but wonder to find a country that has been a scene of so much action now so forsaken and so poor.'

The male Medici line came to a squalid end in the shape of Gian Gastone, who died in 1737. His frantically pious sister Anna Maria couldn't wait to offload the *granducato*, handing it over to the house of Lorraine, cousins of the Austrian Habsburgs. Grand Duke Francis I and his

Roman ghosts

In 59 BC Julius Caesar founded a community on the narrowest point of the River Arno thereby establishing the Roman colony of Florentia. The river was to play a significant part in the development of the city, which was enlarged during the Augustan period to a point when the population reached more than 10,000. In its early days, however, it was a modest place in an undeveloped area, which Caesar built as a retirement community for army veterans, and was dominated by the earlier and much more important Etruscan settlement of Faesulae, now Fiesole.

Florentia's street plan, like all the cities founded by the Romans, was characterised by straight roads crossed at right angles, which is currently visible between the Duomo and piazza della Signoria and between via Tornabuoni and via del Proconsolo. The two main roads led to four towered gates. The *decumanus maximus* ran from today's via del Corso, along via degli Speziali and via degli Strozzi, while the *cardo maximus* ran from the Baptistery down via Roma and along via Calimala. The two roads converged on a central square where the Forum was built and where piazza della Repubblica now stands. In spite of having relatively modest beginnings, however, Florentia was to lie on the via Cassia, which connected Rome to such new, thriving centres as Bononia (Bologna) and Mediolanum (Milan) in the north, and while it never played a significant role in the days of the Empire, it was to expand; its boundaries eventually reached via de' Fossi, via Sant' Egidio and via de' Benci. Commercial activity and trade thrived thanks to its strategic position for both land and water routes, and the city became the capital of the Regio Tuscia et Umbria and headquarters of the corrector or governor of the region.

Archeological finds over the years have made it possible to locate and identify the remains of various important public buildings and other structures: the Capitoline Baths, the Baths of Capaccio, the sewage system, the pavement of the streets, the Temple of Isis (in piazza San Firenze) and other lesser temples, the Theatre (an area now occupied by the back of the Palazzo Vecchio and Palazzo Gondi in piazza San Firenze) and, just west of piazza Santa Croce, the Amphitheatre, whose perimeter can still be seen in curved via Torta, via Bentaccordi and piazza Peruzzi. Some of these structures were built outside the original walls (the Theatre and the Amphitheatre, for example), which testifies to the urban development of the settlement, probably as early as the first century BC. The Arno also lay outside the walls (the city developed on the right banks) with a busy river port (between today's piazza Goldoni and via de' Castellani) that constituted an important infrastructure for the city, for in Roman times the river was navigable from its mouth to a point just upstream from Florence.

The earliest indications of Christianity in Florentia date from the construction of two churches outside the city walls: San Lorenzo (consecrated in 393) and Santa Felicità on the left bank of the Arno, which also dates from the fourth century. It is believed that the latter was founded by the Syrian Greek traders who first brought the religion to the city.

successors spruced up the city, knocked its administration into shape, introduced new farming methods and generally shook the place out of its torpor.

Napoleon's triumphant romp down the peninsula at the end of the 18th century brought him into possession of Tuscany in 1799, to the joy of liberals and the horror of local peasantry, who drove the French out in the Viva Maria uprising, during which they also wreaked their revenge on unlucky Jews and anyone suspected of Jacobin leanings.

But it wasn't long before the French returned, installing Louis de Bourbon of Parma as head of the Kingdom of Etruria in 1801. Napoleon's sister Elisa Baciocchi was made Princess of Piombino and Lucca in 1805, and Grand Duchess of Tuscany from 1809 to 1814 – a time that saw much constitutional reform and much pilfering from Florence's art collections. Many of the works spirited off to Paris were returned to Tuscany after the restoration of the Lorraine dynasty in the shape of Ferdinand III in 1816.

FLORENCE IN THE *RISORGIMENTO*

By the 1820s and 1830s, under the laid-back if not overly bright Grand Duke Leopold II, Tuscany enjoyed a climate of tolerance that attracted intellectuals, dissidents, artists and writers from all over Italy and Europe. They would meet in the Gabinetto Scientifico-Letterario in the Palazzo Buondelmonti in piazza Santa Trinità, frequently welcoming prominent foreigners such as Heine and Byron.

Family fortunes: the Medici

The name Medici (pronounced with the stress on the first 'e') is all but synonymous with Florence and Tuscany. It suggests that the family's origins probably lie in the medical profession, though their later wealth was built on banking.

Giovanni di Bicci (1360-1429)

The fortune Giovanni di Bicci quietly built up through his banking business – boosted immensely by the fact that it handled the papal account – provided the basis for the Medici's later clout. While filling the family coffers, Giovanni acted with the utmost discretion, wary of the Florentines' habit of picking on those who got above themselves.

Cosimo 'Il Vecchio' (1389-1464)

Cosimo ran Florence informally from 1434, presiding over one of its most prosperous and prestigious eras. An even more astute banker than his father, he pacified opponents and his conscience by spending lavishly on charities and public building projects, introducing a progressive income tax system and balancing the interests of the volatile Florentine classes relatively successfully. Cosimo was also an intellectual; he encouraged the new Humanist learning and developments in art that were sweeping Florence. He built up a wonderful public library (the first in Europe), financed scholars and artists, gave architectural commissions and founded a school along the lines of Plato's Academy. He was the epitome of the Renaissance *uomo universale*. The name *il Vecchio* ('The Elder') was a mark of respect. When he died, the Florentines inscribed on his tomb the words *Pater Patriae* ('father of the nation').

Piero 'Il Gottoso' (1416-69)

All the Medici suffered from gout, but poor Piero the Gouty's joints gave him such gyp that he had to be carried around for half his life. During his short spell at the helm he proved a surprisingly able ruler: he crushed an anti-Medici conspiracy, maintained the success of the Medici bank and patronised the city's best artists and architects.

Lorenzo 'Il Magnifico' (1449-92)

Cosimo's grandson Lorenzo was the big Medici, famous in his own time and legendary in later centuries. His rule marked the peak of the Florentine Renaissance, with artists such as Botticelli and the young Michelangelo producing superlative works. Lorenzo was a gifted poet, and gathered round him a supremely talented group of scholars and artists. The climate of intellectual freedom he fostered was a major factor in some of the Renaissance's greatest achievements.

For a time Leopold and his ministers kept the reactionary influence of the Grand Duke's uncle, Emperor Francis II of Austria, at arm's length while playing down the growing populist cry for Italian unification. But by the 1840s it was clear that the nationalist movement posed a serious threat to the status quo. Even relaxed Florence was swept up in nationalist enthusiasm, causing Leopold to clamp down on reformers and impose some censorship.

In 1848, a tumultuous year of revolutions, insurrections in Livorno and Pisa forced Leopold to grant concessions to the reformers, including a Tuscan constitution.

When news reached Florence that the Milanese had driven the Austrians out of their city, and that Carlo Alberto, King of Sardinia-Piedmont, was determined to push them out of Italy altogether, thousands of Tuscans joined the cause. In 1849 the pendulum seemed to be swinging back in favour of the better-trained Austrians. But radicals in Florence dug in and bullied the Grand Duke into appointing the activist reformer Giuseppe Montanelli, a professor of law at Pisa University, to head a new government. Montanelli went to Rome to attend a constituent assembly, but the alarmed Pope Pius IX threatened to excommunicate anyone attending such an assembly.

Lorenzo's reign was a time of relative peace, thanks in part to his diplomatic skills. As a businessman, however, he wasn't a patch on his predecessors and the Medici bank suffered a severe decline. Lorenzo maintained a façade of being no more than *primus inter pares* ('first among equals'), but he made sure he always got his way, and he could be ruthless with his enemies.

Piero di Lorenzo (1471-1503)

Piero couldn't live up to his father: ruthless, charmless and tactless, he had a violent temper, no sense of loyalty and a haughty wife. His father described him as foolish, and he certainly did nothing to help his cause when he surrendered the city to the French in 1494. He spent the rest of his days skulking around Italy, trying to persuade unenthusiastic states to help him regain power in a Florence that had no wish to see his mug again.

Giuliano, Duke of Nemours (1478-1516)

The third son of Lorenzo il Magnifico and an improvement on his brother Piero only in the sense that he was more nonentity than swine, Giuliano was ruler of Florence in name only, being little more than a puppet of his brother Cardinal Giovanni, later Pope Leo X.

Lorenzo, Duke of Urbino (1492-1519)

Son of Piero di Lorenzo, Lorenzo was puny, arrogant, high-handed and corrupt. No one was anything but relieved when he succumbed to tuberculosis, aggravated by syphilis. His only significant legacy was his daughter Catherine, who as wife then widow of Henri II wielded considerable power in France.

Giovanni; Pope Leo X (1475-1521)

Lorenzo il Magnifico's second son wasn't such a loser as his brothers, perhaps because the night before his birth his mother dreamed she would have not a baby but a huge lion. Lorenzo decided early on that Giovanni was destined for a glittering ecclesiastical career, and serious papal ear-bending ensured that he became a monk at eight and a cardinal aged 16. He elbowed his way into the papacy in 1513. Pope Leo (spot the lion reference) was a remarkably likeable, open character, and though lazy and fond of the good life ('God has given us the papacy so let us enjoy it,' he's reported to have said), he was a generous host and politically conciliatory. But his shameless exploitation of the sale of indulgences to ease his debts added fuel to the fires of critics of papal corruption. ▶

Leopold panicked, and fled in disguise to Naples. A provisional government was set up but, in the absence of armed support, collapsed. The Florentines invited Leopold back; he returned in July 1849 but brought Austrian troops to keep order. Grim times followed for a city just recovering from one of its worst ever floods. On his return, Leopold seemed content to be an Austrian puppet and clamped down on the press and dissent; his popularity vanished.

In April 1859 Piedmont's Count Camillo Cavour persuaded Napoleon III's France to join him in expelling the Austrians. The French and Piedmontese swept the Austrian armies before them, while in Florence nationalist demos forced the government to resign. On 27 April Leopold left Florence and his family for the last time, his former subjects watching in silence. The following year the Tuscan people voted for unification with the Kingdom of Piedmont.

CAPITAL OF ITALY

Five years later, with Rome holding out against the forces of unification, Florence was declared capital of Italy, much to the annoyance of the Piedmontese capital of Turin – 200 people died in riots there when the shift was announced. The Florentines greeted their new king with enthusiasm when he arrived in February 1865 to take up residence in the Palazzo Pitti, but the

Family fortunes: the Medici (continued)

Giulio; Pope Clement VII (1478-1534)

Lorenzo Il Magnifico's illegitimate nephew, Giulio had honours heaped on him by his cousin Pope Leo. Though this didn't endear him to other cardinals (his disagreeable personality didn't help much either), he swung the papacy in 1524. Pope Clement was notorious for his indecision, irresolution and disloyalty. He abandoned his alliance with Charles V only to regret it when the emperor's troops sacked Rome in 1527.

Alessandro (1511-37)

Thought to be Clement's illegitimate son, Alessandro proved to be a bastard by nature too, abandoning all pretence of respecting the Florentines' treasured institutions and freedoms. Increasingly authoritarian, he tortured and executed his opponents, while managing to outrage the good Florentine burghers by his appalling rudeness and sexual antics. He had a penchant for dressing in women's clothes and riding about town with his bosom buddy and distant cousin, the equally alarming Lorenzaccio. A deputation of senior figures complained to Charles V, to no avail. It was left to Lorenzaccio to put everyone out of their misery by luring Alessandro to bed and stabbing him to death.

Cosimo I (1519-74)

With no heir in the direct Medici line, the Florentines chose this obscure 18-year-old (grandson of Lorenzo il Magnifico's daughter Lucrezia), thinking they could manipulate him. But they could not have been more wrong: cold, secretive and cunning, Cosimo set about ruling with merciless efficiency. His unpleasantness, however, did not stop him from restoring stability in Florence and boosting the city's international image. He also found time to build up a navy and he succeeded in throwing off the dependence on imperial troops to maintain order. After relentless lobbying he was granted the title Grand Duke of Tuscany by Pope Paul V in 1569.

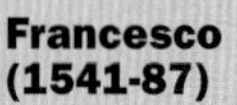

Francesco I (1541-87)

Short, skinny, graceless and sulky, Francesco had little in common with his father Cosimo. He retreated into his own little world at any opportunity, to play with his pet reindeer, dabble in alchemy and invent a new process for porcelain production.

Ferdinando I (1549-1609)

Ferdinando was a huge improvement on his brother Francesco. He reduced corruption, improved trade and farming, encouraged learning, and developed the navy and the

influx of northerners was met with mixed feelings: business boomed, but the Florentines didn't take to Piedmontese flashiness.

Huge changes were wrought in the city. Ring roads encircled the old centre, avenues, squares (such as piazza della Repubblica) and residential suburbs were built and parks were laid out. Intellectuals and socialites crowded the salons and cafés.

When war with Prussia forced the French (who had swapped sides) to withdraw their troops from Italy in 1870, Rome finally fell to Vittorio Emanuele's troops and Italy was united for the first time since the fall of the Roman Empire. Florence's brief reign as capital ended.

THE 20TH CENTURY

Florence began the 20th century much as it ended it – as a thriving tourist centre. In the early 1900s it drew an exclusive coterie of writers, artists, aesthetes and the upper-middle classes. An English-speaking industry sprang up to cater for the needs of these wealthy foreigners.

The city was neither occupied nor attacked in World War I, though it inevitably suffered the social repercussions. Post-war hardship inspired a fierce middle-class rage for order that found expression in the black shirt of Fascism. Groups of *squadristi* were already forming in 1919, organising parades and demonstrations in the streets of Florence.

port of Livorno. By staging lavish popular entertainments and giving dowries to poor girls, he became the most loved Medici since Lorenzo il Magnifico.

Cosimo II (1590-1621)

The son of Ferdinando I, Cosimo protected Galileo from a hostile Catholic Church – the only worthwhile thing he would ever do.

Ferdinando II (1610-70)

Porky, laid-back, moustachioed Ferdinando did little to pull Florence from the backwater into which it had sunk. He loved to hunt, eye up boys and collect bric-a-brac.

Cosimo III (1642-1723)

Though trade was drying up and plague and famine stalked the land, Cosimo – a joyless, gluttonous, anti-Semitic loner who hung out with monks (his sulky wife Marguerite-Louise must take some blame for this) – did nothing to improve Tuscany's lot during his 53 years at the helm. Instead, intellectual freedom took a nosedive, taxes soared and public executions were a daily occurrence.

Gian Gastone (1671-1737)

Cosimo's disaster of a son was forcibly married to a spectacularly offensive woman, Anna Maria Francesca of Saxe-Lauenberg, who dragged him off to her gloomy castle near Prague, where he drowned his sorrows in taverns, whoring about with stable boys before escaping back to Florence in 1708. He was shocked to find himself Grand Duke in 1723. In the surprisingly coherent early years of his rule, he tried to relieve the tax burden and reinstate citizens' rights but quickly lapsed into chronic apathy and dissolution. When his relations tried to get him back on the straight and narrow he disgraced himself by, for instance, vomiting into his napkin at a respectable dinner, then taking off his wig and wiping his mouth with it. Eventually, he wouldn't even get out of bed and was reduced to having troops of rowdy boys entertain him by cavorting about and shouting obscenities.

Anna Maria (died 1743)

Every visitor to Florence since the mid 18th century has reason to be grateful to the straight-laced, pious Anna Maria, who was Gian Gastone's sister and the very last surviving Medici. In her will she bequeathed all Medici property and treasures to the Grand Duchy in perpetuity, on the sole condition that they never leave Florence.

When Mussolini was elected in 1923, there began in Florence a campaign to expunge the city of foreign elements and influences. Hotels and shops with English names were put under pressure to sever their Anglo-Saxon affiliations. The Florence that had been described as a 'ville toute Anglaise' by the French social-historian Goncourt brothers was under threat.

When Italy entered the war at Germany's side on 10 June 1940 Florentines were confident that the Allies would never attack their city from the air: Florence was a museum, a testament to artistic evolution; its monuments were its best protection. Nevertheless, the Fascist regime, perhaps for propaganda reasons, began protecting the city's art. Photos of the period show statuary disappearing inside comically inefficient wooden sheds, while the Baptistery doors were bricked up and many of the main treasures from the Uffizi and the Palazzo Pitti, including Botticelli's *Allegory of Spring*, were taken to Castello di Montegufoni – owned by the British Sitwell family – in the Tuscan countryside for safekeeping.

The Germans occupied Florence on 11 September 1943, just weeks after Mussolini's arrest and the armistice was signed. Only when it became necessary to hinder the Nazis' communications line to Rome were aesthetic scruples set aside. In September 1943 a

The devastating flood of November 1966.

formation of American bombers swooped in to destroy Florence's Campo di Marte station: the operation was bungled, leaving 218 civilians dead while the station remained in perfect working order. Further air raids were banned by orders from the highest levels.

At the beginning of the war Florence had a Jewish population of more than 2,000. The chief rabbi saved the lives of many Jews in the city by advising them to hide in convents or little villages under false names.

Three raids were carried out by Nazis and Fascists on the night of 27 November 1943. The largest was on the Franciscan Sisters of Mary in piazza del Carmine, where dozens of Jews were concealed. The second train to leave Italy bound for the gas chambers set out from Florence, carrying at least 400 Jews from Florence, Siena and Bologna; not one of them is known to have returned.

By 1944 allied commanding officers had extracted permission from leaders to attack Florence using only the most experienced squadrons, in ideal weather conditions. On 11 March the Americans began unleashing their bombers on the city, causing casualties but leaving the *centro storico* and its art intact. On 1 August 1944 fighting broke out in various parts of the city, but poorly armed Florentine patriots couldn't prevent the Germans from destroying all the Arno bridges except the Ponte Vecchio. Along with the bridges, the old quarter around the Ponte Vecchio was razed to the ground.

The Val D'Orcia and Monte Amiata areas in southern Tuscany were key theatres for partisans, who held out with considerable loss of life until British and US infantry reinforced their lines on the Arno on 1 September 1944. The German army abandoned Fiesole a week later. When the Allies reached Florence they found a functioning government formed by the partisan Comitati di Liberazione Nazionale (CLN). Within hours of the Germans' departure, work started to put the bridges back into place – the Ponte Santa Trinità was rebuilt, stone by stone, in exactly the same location.

DAMAGED GOODS

Two decades later the Florentine skill at restoration was required again, this time for a calamity of an altogether different nature: in the early hours of the morning of 4 November 1966 citizens awoke to find their homes flooded by the Arno, which had broken its banks, and soon all the main *piazze* were under water. An estimated 15,000 cars were destroyed, 6,000 shops put out of business, and almost 14,000 families left homeless. Many artworks, books and archives were damaged, treasures in the refectory of Santa Croce were blackened by mud, and in the church's nave Donatello's *Cavalcanti Annunciation* was soaked with oil up to the Virgin's knees. As word of the disaster spread around the world, public and private funds were pumped into repairs and restoration.

The city's cultural heritage took another direct hit in 1993 when a bomb planted by the Mafia exploded in the city centre, killing five people. It caused structural damage to the Uffizi, destroying the Georgofile library and damaging the Vasari Corridor. Not that you'd know it now: in a restoration job carried out in record time, one of the world's most-visited art repositories was returned to its pristine state and tourists began queuing outside again, confirming the modern city's vocation for living off its past.

Florence solemnly commemorated the tenth anniversary of the Uffizi bomb in May 2003 and now seems to be looking to the future more than ever before, in spite of a general and alarming drop in tourist numbers post September 11. For a city that relies heavily on tourist revenue, this is bad news. However, new exciting urban planning and architectural projects are in the air (*see pp27-33*) and Florence would seem, on the face of it at least, to have a foot in the new millennium.

Key events

7th-6th centuries BC Height of Etruscan civilisation.
3rd century All Etruria under Roman control.
59 BC Foundation of Florentia by Julius Caesar.
56 BC Caesar, Crassus and Pompey form first triumvirate at Lucca.
AD 540s Tuscany contested in Goth vs Byzantine campaigns.
552 Florence falls to the Goths under Totila.
c800 New walls erected around Florence.
10th-12th centuries Pisa becomes wealthy port; Lucca, seat of margraves of Tuscany, is region's most important city.
1076 Matilda becomes Countess of Tuscany.
1115 Matilda bequeaths all her lands to the pope except Florence, Lucca and Siena, which become independent *comuni*.
1125 Florence captures Fiesole.
1173-5 More new walls for Florence.
1215 Murder of Buondelmonte ignites Guelph/Ghibelline conflict.
1252 First gold florin minted.
1289 Florence defeats Arezzo at Campaldino.
1293 Nobility excluded from government, *signoria* created.
1296 Foundations laid for new Duomo.
1329 Florence takes over Pistoia.
1342 Florence's biggest banks collapse when English king Edward III defaults on debts.
1348 Black Death ravages Tuscany.
1351 Florence buys Prato from Naples.
1375-8 War of the Eight Saints frees Florence from papal influence. Guelphs join with *popolo grasso* to exclude guilds from power.
1406 Florence captures Pisa.
1411 Florence gains Cortona.
1421 Florence buys Livorno from Genova.
1428 War between Florence and Lucca.
1432 Florence beats Siena at San Romano, immortalised by artist Paolo Uccello.
1433 Cosimo de' Medici exiled by Albizzi clan during unpopular Lucchese war.
1434 Return of Cosimo from exile; overthrow and exile of the Albizzi.
1436 Brunelleschi finishes the Duomo dome.
1437 Florence defeats Milan at Barga.
1452 Naples and Venice declare war on Milan and Florence.
1454 Threat of the Turks brings pope, Venice, Florence and Milan together in Holy League.
1466 Piero quashes conspiracy to oust Medici.
1478 Piero's son Lorenzo escapes murder in Pazzi conspiracy. Papacy and Naples declare war on Florence.
1479 Lorenzo goes alone to Naples to negotiate peace treaty with King Ferrante.
1494 Wars of Italy begin – France's Charles VIII invades Italy.
1512 Papal and Spanish armies sack Prato and force return of Medici to Florence.
1524 Giulio de' Medici becomes Pope Clement VII; continues to run Florence from Rome.
1527 Horrific sacking of Rome by Habsburg emperor Charles V's army. Medici expelled; new republic declared.
1529 Charles V, now allied with Clement VII, besieges and takes Florence.
1530 Alessandro de' Medici installed as head of government then Duke by Charles V.
1537 Alessandro murdered. Obscure Cosimo defeats Florentine rebels at Montemurlo.
1555 With imperial help, Cosimo crushes Siena after a devastating war.
1569 Cosimo buys the title Grand Duke of Tuscany from Pope Paul V.
16th-17th centuries Steady decline of Tuscan agriculture and industry overseen by succession of Medici Grand Dukes.
1723 Gian Gastone now the last Medici ruler.
1735 Grand Duchy of Tuscany given to Francis, Duke of Lorraine. Enlightened regime begins.
1737 Death of Gian Gastone's sister, Anna Maria, who leaves all Medici art and treasures to Florence in perpetuity.
1799 French troops enter Florence. Revival of interest in Tuscany, which becomes major stop on the 'Grand Tour'.
1801-7 Grand Duchy absorbed into Kingdom of Etruria.
1809 Napoleon installs his sister Elisa Bacciochi as Grand Duchess of Tuscany.
1816 Grand Duke Ferdinando III returns to Tuscany on defeat of Napoleon.
1824 Genial Leopold II succeeds father.
1859 Leopold allows himself to be overthrown in the *Risorgimento*.
1865-70 Florence becomes first capital of united Italy.
1943 Germans enter Florence, establish Gothic Line on the Arno.
1944 Germans blow up all Pisa's bridges and all but the Ponte Vecchio in Florence. Allies liberate Florence.
1966 The Arno floods, causing huge damage.
1993 Bomb destroys Georgofile library and damages Vasari Corridor.
2002 The lira is withdrawn, euro coins and notes come into circulation.

Cupid takes aim in **Botticelli**'s *Allegory of Spring*.

The Renaissance

When art and ideas changed forever.

For centuries, Florence has basked in the afterglow of this great event, and the world has basked with it. Florentines have learned to live alongside the perennial swarms of visitors and they have grown accustomed to the sight of tour guides marching about their city. In fact, part of them even welcomes this intrusion. It may have left them with little peace and quiet, but the legacy of the Renaissance has always been (and continues to be) a deep source of pride for Florentines. And for the visitor too it's a subject that is impossible to ignore. Even the most cursory overview of this seminal period in the city's past can substantially increase a visitor's understanding, not just of the history of Florence, but of its architecture, its culture and, above all, its citizens.

THE RENAISSANCE AND HUMANISM

The guiding doctrine of the Renaissance (*Rinascimento*, rebirth) was Humanism – the revival of the language and art of the ancient Greeks and Romans and the reconciliation of this pagan heritage with Christianity. Although the most visible manifestation of the Renaissance in Florence was the astonishing outpouring of art in the 15th century, it was classical studies that sparked the new age.

The groundwork had been done by a handful of exceptional men: **Dante** (1265-1321), **Petrarch** (1304-74) and **Boccaccio** (1313-75) had all collected Latin manuscripts, which shaped their approach to writing. But it was mounting Florentine wealth that paid for dedicated manuscript detectives such as **Poggio Bracciolini** (1380-1459) to dig through neglected monastery libraries across Europe.

A few classical works had never been lost, but those that were known were usually corrupted versions only available to clerics who forbade their dissemination or discussion. The volume of unknown works discovered was incredible. Their effect was intellectual dynamite, causing the Florentines to reassess the way they thought about almost every field of human endeavour. In the first few decades of the 15th century there came to light Quintilian's *The Training of an Orator*, which detailed the Roman education system, Columella's *De Re Rustica* on agriculture, key texts on Roman architecture by Vitruvius and Frontinus, and Cicero's *Brutus* (a justification of Republicanism). Very few Greek works were known in western Europe. Suddenly, almost simultaneously, most of Plato, Homer, the plays of Sophocles, Aeschylus, Euripides,

Aristophanes, histories by Herodotus, Xenophon and Thucydides, the speeches of Demosthenes and many other classics were discovered.

The Renaissance focus on a pre-Christian age didn't mean that God was under threat. Just as Renaissance artists had no compunction about enhancing the beauty of their forms and compositions with classical features and allusions, Renaissance Humanists sought explanations beyond the Scriptures that were complementary to accepted religion rather than a challenge to it. Much effort was made to present the wisdom of the ancients as a precursor to the ultimate wisdom of God. The main players of the Renaissance did not perceive it as 'recanting' when they went on to embrace the millennial rantings of Savonarola (*see p12*) with enthusiasm.

Nor did the Renaissance fascination with things semi-scientific (Leonardo's anatomical drawings or the widespread obsession with the mathematics of Pythagoras) mean that this was a scientific age. The 15th century was an era when ideas were still paramount and science, as a process of deduction based on observation and experimentation, didn't really get going until the 17th century. In medicine, the theory of the four humours still held sway. Astronomy and astrology were all but synonymous. Mathematics was an almost mystical art, while alchemy, the attempt to transform base metals into gold, flourished.

Magnificent while it lasted, Florence's pre-eminence in art and ideas was abruptly snuffed out on the death of Lorenzo il Magnifico in 1492 – the invasion by Charles VIII of France in the 1490s and Savonarola's Bonfire of the Vanities (*see p12*) saw to that. In the early 16th century the cutting edge switched to Rome, where **Michelangelo**, **Bramante** and **Raphael** were creating their finest works. Thence, after Emperor Charles V sacked Rome in 1527, to Venice, where masters such as **Palladio** and **Titian** practised.

THE RENAISSANCE AND ART

By the time **Giorgio Vasari** coined the expression *rinascita* ('rebirth') for the extraordinary flowering of art that took place in Tuscany in the 14th and 15th centuries, artistic primacy had passed to Rome. His seminal work *Lives of the Most Eminent Painters, Sculptors and Architects* (1550), the basis for much later assessment of the Renaissance, was as much a piece of propaganda for a declining city as a true reflection of the development of art in Italy. The Renaissance was not a spontaneous Florentine outburst, but a development in an unbroken tradition, the fulcrum of which shifted to Florence when the *caput mundi*, Rome, became so strife-ridden that the papacy fled into exile in Avignon (1305-78). The innovations of **Giotto** (so-called father of the Renaissance) owe as much to his contact with the great, but neglected, Romans **Pietro Cavallini** and his contemporary **Jacopo di Torriti** as they do to the stiff, Byzantine art of **Cimabue**, whom Vasari describes as Giotto's teacher.

There's no doubt, however, that events conspired to ensure that with Rome out of the artistic picture Florence was ready to fill the gap. With trade booming and enlightened leaders splashing their great wealth on beautifying their city, the arts bloomed. Civic pride was at its peak, and visual arts were considered an essential part of the city's rejuvenation. Spurred by Humanist studies into classical texts, rediscovered after being lost to the West for centuries, in which artists were lauded to the skies, the 'artisans' who had long been designing or daubing superlative works became highly regarded personages. This reached its apogee in the 15th century with **Michelangelo**, whose reputation as a divinely inspired genius was far removed from that of the jobbing artisans of yore. Rather than ordering decorations by the yard, patrons would seek the top names to create or decorate *palazzi* and churches worthy of their status. The 'artist' was reborn.

Although Vasari didn't give a name to the Renaissance until the 16th century, the Florentine people were aware much earlier on that they were living in a new age. The rebirth of the city was financial, social and intellectual. Slowly recovering from the economic depression of the mid 14th century, the city finally had the wealth and the confidence to study itself. Artists chose to do this by looking to classical models that placed man and human achievement at the centre of things. It's a testament to the spirit of the age that artists were not content to merely copy Antiquity but to draw inspiration from it and then transcend it with innovations so remarkable that they would change modern art.

In sculpture, follow this progress in the famous doors of the Baptistery: from **Nicolo Pisano**'s glorious Gothic quatrefoils to **Lorenzo Ghiberti**'s doors at the eastern end of the building (described by Michelangelo as worthy to stand at the Gates of Paradise). Ghiberti's student took his innovations to new heights in his free-standing statue of *David* and his wonderfully animated figure of *St George*, designed to fit a niche in the church of Orsanmichele. Both works are now in the Bargello. **Donatello**'s enormous confidence

Non-Renaissance men

In a city renowned as the seat of the greatest art revolution of all time, it would be easy to overlook the contribution of artists who didn't play a part in the Renaissance. At first the pickings may seem slim. But leave aside the impossibly high expectations of living up to the Great Event and take each non-Renaissance Florentine artist on their own merits, and it's a different story.

In his *Lives of the Artists*, Vasari writes, somewhat vaguely: '**Cimabue** was almost the first to give rise to the renovation of painting.' By opening his reputed anthology with Cimabue, Vasari rightly pays tribute to this late 13th-century artist who first showed signs of breaking with the formalism of Byzantine art and added a touch of Humanism to traditional subjects. With the same hand Vasari excludes him from the early Renaissance hall of fame that Cimabue's most famous protégé **Giotto** was the first to enter. Poor Cimabue's greatest claim would be as the artist who discovered a young shepherd, Giotto, sketching sheep on rocks. But his own efforts should not to be sniffed at. Cimabue's magnificent *Maestà di Santa Trinità* (Uffizi; *see p80*) counterposes a cool Byzantine style with an intensity of expression and a sense of volume and space that hinted at the Humanism and perspective that were to characterise Renaissance art for the next two centuries.

Michelangelo's high Renaissance style led directly to Mannerism. This occurred because of his insistence on an emphasis on human form, even to the extent that it could be exaggerated and distorted to order. Once again, Florence found itself at the vanguard of the major artistic movement of the time. **Giambologna**, the Flemish sculptor, adopted Florence as his spiritual home and did the movement proud by coming up with one of the best-known Mannerist sculptures, the spiralling *Rape of the Sabines* (Loggia dei Lanzi of piazza della Signoria; *see p73*), and with the fleet-of-foot bronze *Mercury* (Bargello; *see p94*). Despite his dislike of painting, it was again Michelangelo with his *Tondo Doni* (Uffizi; *see p80*) who set the scene for the brightly coloured, clearly delineated fishbowl forms of Mannerist painting. Meanwhile, **Rosso Fiorentino** and **Pontormo** were happy to pick up the painting baton. Rosso Fiorentino's most famous contribution, *Moses Defends the Daughters of Jethro* (Uffizi; *see p80*) and Pontormo's *Deposition* (church of Santa Felicità; *see p102*) epitomise the Mannerist spirit. But it is Pontormo's adopted son **Cosimo d'Agnolo**, known as Bronzino, who is heralded as the most prolific Mannerist portrait artist. His most famous work is the cold, detached *Eleonora of Toledo and Cosimo I* (Palazzo Vecchio; *see p79*).

A wander round the chronologically ordered Uffizi is an unforgiving reminder of the paucity of world-class Florentine art in the 17th, 18th and early 19th centuries. The Titian and Canaletto, Rembrandt and Vermeer rooms are testament to the fact that the smart money went north to Venice, Holland, and to London too where Turner and Constable were making waves. Only the follower of Venetian artist Correggio, **Cristofano Allori**,

in himself and his destiny marks him as a man of the Renaissance and anticipates the style of later masters Leonardo and Michelangelo.

Inspired by trips to Rome to study ancient buildings and texts, **Filippo Brunelleschi**'s (1377-1446) buildings with their centralised plans and pure geometrical spaces cogently express the leap from the late Gothic to the Renaissance. Nowhere is this illustrated more clearly than in his magnificent dome for the Duomo, which replaced the Gothic fanciness of Arnolfo di Cambio's with great aplomb.

Brunelleschi is also credited with another achievement of far-reaching effect: the invention of linear perspective. This method of suggesting distance in pictures by the introduction of a vanishing point at the viewer's eye-level was to revolutionise the art of painting, and elevated it to a science. One artist who quickly employed these new techniques was **Masaccio** (1401-28), a giant of the early Renaissance. His fresco *The Holy Trinity with the Virgin and St John* (in Santa Maria Novella) sees the artist place his figures in a deep, vaulted chamber wherein they could move freely about, if they so wished. This opening up of space was quite new and in marked contrast to the linear flatness of the late Gothic painters.

Another artist who readily adopted perspective was **Paulo Uccello**. His *Rout of San Romano*, painted for the walls of the Medici Palace, so thoroughly uses the new science that its figures and horses, monumental and decorative though they are, seem to exist with his *Judith, Magdalene* and *Adoration of the Magi* (all in Galleria del Palatina, Palazzo Pitti; *see p99*) and the Caravaggio-esque woman artist **Artemisia Gentileschi**, best known for her gruesome *Judith and Holofernes* (Uffizi; *see p80*), came up with the goods in the 17th century. The 18th century was singularly bleak, and Florentine art looked dead in the water.

Then came the reviving powers of coffee. In the mid 19th century Parisian café society was giving rise to an explosion of intellectual and artistic expression, and the Florentine artistic elite were not to be outdone. In the Caffè Michelangelo a group of painters formed a new anti-academic current inspired by the French Impressionists, the **Macchiaioli**, so-called because of their use of dots (*macchie*) of colour. Led to recognition by **Giovanni Fattori** (Galleria d'Arte Moderna, Palazzo Pitti; *see p99*), the movement may have made few ripples worldwide compared to Florence's European neighbours, but in Italy, the Macchiaioli kicked up a storm, and strongly influenced the most famous Florentine painter of the last century, **Ardengo Soffici** (*Tuscan Women*, *Procession*, both Galleria d'Arte Moderna, Palazzo Pitti; *see p99*). Soffici's Futurist tendencies in turn influenced Florence's best-known metaphysical painter, **Ottone Rosai**. It was left to sculpture to make the greatest non-Renaissance mark on the city. This was achieved in the equine mega-forms by **Marino Marini**, the only modern Florentine artist to have a museum dedicated entirely to his work (*see p85*).

Judith and Holofernes by **Artemisia Gentileschi**.

merely as an excuse to show off his technique. Outside Florence, a more successful exponent was **Piero della Francesca**, whose love of mathematics and reverence of the sacred combined to create works of great solemnity and profound human emotion that were reminiscent of Masaccio and became synonymous with Renaissance art.

Along with **Fra Angelico**, whose frescoes in the convent of San Marco used the new spatial awareness to illustrate biblical scenes with great dignity and directness, della Francesca laid the groundwork for a new generation, including **Domenico Ghirlandaio**, **Filippo Lippi** and **Andrea del Verrocchio**. His influence, plus a thorough understanding of perspective, can also be seen in the graceful, mythological paintings of Medici favourite **Sandro Botticelli** (1445-1510). From Verrocchio's workshop came Leonardo da Vinci, and from Ghirlandaio's, Michelangelo Buonarotti. The artistic heavyweights worked at the zenith of the high Renaissance, which was actually a remarkably short period, with all its key moments produced between 1495 and 1520. Both were fully aware of the cult of the genius, and it may have been this that spurred them on to tackle their own vast and ambitious goals.

They left their mark as much elsewhere as in this city: Leonardo in Milan and Michelangelo in his unforgettable works in Rome, which by then was picking up the pieces of its shattered glory, eclipsing Florence and becoming the world centre of art once more.

Florence Today

Little changes in the Tuscan capital.

Ask any Italian and they'll tell you: Florentines are famed for their tolerance. And why not? Life is sweet; anywhere you look, the eye alights on beauty and harmony. Though rather provincial, culture in Florence remains vibrant and the city's love of tradition has kept modern development at arm's length. And a similar desire for neatness colours the Florentine mentality: politics and personal compliments are favourite topics of conversation, while the uglier issues of city life are swept under the carpet.

In a country that has the seat of the Roman Catholic empire embedded in its capital, Florence has a remarkably easygoing relationship with the Church. The Vatican is another country. Religion is something depicted in Renaissance art, rather than an arbiter of contemporary morality. While the pope's proclamation that the pill is chemical abortion caused a moral dilemma in many areas of Italy, in Florence it was a distant furore.

The Mafia too has a low profile in Florence, and tales of bribery and corruption stand out against a backdrop of polite decency. Deputy mayor Cioni has been known to wire his office with listening devices to entrap contract-hunters offering bribes. Oiling palms just doesn't wash here. You're more likely to see genuine handshakes than funny ones. The suave mayor, or *sindaco*, Leonardo Domenici, pops up in the papers on matters of civic pride and does a good job of entertaining VIPs such as Kofi Anan and Tony Blair when they come to town. He is someone who likes to be seen to be out and about and is just as likely to appear at a Bruce Springsteen concert as at the opening night of the opera.

CONSERVE AND SURVIVE

Politics is constantly debated, particularly in the on-going period of Silvio Berlusconi's premiership. Florence, along with much of Tuscany and Emilia Romagna, is communist and vehemently opposed to the right-wing media tycoon's march to power. However, for a 'communist' city, Florence is deeply conservative, with a small 'c'. Conservation and preservation of museums and monuments are a priority, in no small part because of the money they bring in from the tourist trade. But leftist politics protects workers' family life, rather than seeking to maximise profits. Post may take three weeks (as part of a job creation programme, mail is diverted to southern Italy for sorting), but workers' rights are considered more important than efficiency. A fast food outlet staged a strike when staff insisted they should get an afternoon siesta like everyone else. That went down like a lead balloon in McBurger land.

NETWORKING

One of the biggest issues is the endless grumbles about the traffic and getting around in a city where private cars are restricted. Traffic-restricted areas collectively known as the ZTL were instated some years ago and continue to function in principal (although they are sorely abused) and there are now restrictions on traffic entering the city centre in the evenings too. But other initiatives have never got off the ground. A few years ago, cameras mounted on tall ugly poles were put up at strategic entry points to the *centro storico* designed to catch ZTL trespassers. They still haven't been switched on. There was a brief period when the *comune* supplied bicycles almost free of charge to allow people to move around free from pollution, but the scheme basically failed through lack of interest. Bikes, of course, would be a great way to cut down on traffic pollution; it's just that if there's nowhere to keep them without risk of them getting pinched (there aren't nearly enough bike racks in town) it can get a little discouraging.

The city's private and commercial sectors are locked in endless disputes on the subject of the ZTL. The former is basically in favour of traffic restrictions, the latter remains stoically against. Other 'anti-smog' initiatives include pilot schemes to make electric cars available at hotels and to introduce buses that run on gas. Tour buses are no longer allowed into the centre of town; they disgorge their passengers at a set-down point (where they have to pay a toll) and then go and park out of harm's way. There are bigger ideas too, though they often have credibility problems, partly because of failures in the past. The idea of a subway comes and goes, for example (at the moment it seems to be out of favour); meanwhile, a clutch of new projects may finally have gained enough momentum to make a significant impact. The new satellite town of Firenze Nova is well on its way to completion; the university is already in business. Work on the first phase of the *tranvia* (tramway), a line connecting Scandicci with the centre of town, has also begun, other lines will follow, and a whole host of lower-profile plans are in the pipeline too (*see pp27-33*).

PERSONAL COMFORTS

Florentines grow up surrounded by beauty, and perhaps vanity is the side effect. In Florence, it's believed that promotion goes to the best-groomed man. Not that promotion is taken too seriously. There is little overt ambition. A job that necessitates foreign travel is viewed as an infringement not a fringe benefit. Milan is perhaps the only city in Italy where the work ethic is as important as *divertimento* (having fun) so Florence continues to leave ample time for hedonistic pursuits. However, there are signs that this is changing. Whereas lunch used to be a sacrosanct three-hour affair, bar and café menus reveal a quick plate of pasta is becoming popular, and fewer shops now close for lunch.

Driving in Florence...

...it'll end in tears.

Another area where things have started to change is in the home. Property tends to stay in the family as the younger generation inherit a home from their grandparents and move directly there from their parents' homes; until recently, you'd never hear Notting Hill-style dinner party talk of house prices or property renovations. But changes in the finance markets have meant that mortgage rates have fallen to around UK levels, with a smaller deposit required: more young people are buying properties. Florence's brand new IKEA (which opened in November 2002 near Vespucci Airport at Peretola) is packed with homebodies on Sunday afternoons.

IMMORAL MINORITY

The pleasure industry has changed in the past few years. The wide leafy *viali* leading out of the city have long been a place where transvestite and transsexual 'ladies' of the night proudly displayed their designer plastic surgery. The city turned a blind eye – a generously liberal, broadly tolerant attitude in the spirit of the Venusian arts that define the city's mentality. The problem is, however, that it's no longer a carnival of individual vanity and fluttering false eyelashes, but a sleazy business allegedly organised by a criminal underworld.

The girls available for sale really are girls, with many as young as 13 or 14. They're procured to order for the city's wealthy indigenous and visiting businessmen. The polite response is still a faltering 'if that's how they want to live, let them get on with it'. But it would seem that the girls didn't choose to live that way, and now turning a blind eye seems more of an immoral weakness than a moral strength. And the official attitude has recently swung that way too, with a big clamp-down on prostitution resulting in a wave of arrests.

According to the newspapers, illegal immigration rackets, drugdealing and prostitution are being run by a new Albanian mafia. Inner-city problems are anathema to Florentines. Illegal immigration is a pressing human rights issue, but a public brought up in the bosom of its family is out of its depth when faced with harsh facts. The Church takes an active role in secular social issues while the local authorities look the other way. A priest, Don Benzi, has been raising awareness of the plight of girls whose asylum-seeking parents have been duped into selling them into sex slavery and has been attempting to rescue them from the streets. Not so much to save their souls as their bodies and their lives.

This change in tone has made Florentines uneasy, but rather than facing the awkward questions it raises about their own family men, who are apparently willing customers in this trade, they are directing their indignation into xenophobia. Immigrants aren't warmly welcomed in Florence. Italy is not a naturally multicultural society; it has a history not of colonies but of warring principalities, and regional insularity is deeply entrenched.

Racism towards the African street pedlars, who are often in the city as students or graduates, is covert. The pedlars live in cramped conditions, often with ten to a room, in tenements in the industrial hinterland outside the city. They are tolerated (grudgingly by businesses), but this doesn't mean they are welcomed with open arms by Florentines.

Hostility is reserved for Albanians, who are widely feared. There has been an upsurge in crimes such as knifings and violent encounters between opposing gangs of drug pushers (mostly North African and Albanian) as well as muggings and handbag snatches by thieves on scooters. Car crime is accelerating and elegant villas in the hills immediately surrounding the city are often in the news for having been burgled. Parents worry that their student children are being sold drugs. While cocaine has acceptance in clubbing and fashion circles, the feared drug is heroin. Police have attempted to clean up the action in bohemian left-bank piazza Santo Spirito and piazza Santa Maria Novella, near the station, where dealing was rife under the shadowy cloisters. Nowadays, tour guides complain that drug deals are conducted openly in front of the Duomo with dealers operating in the safety of numbers as thousands of tourists pass by.

SWEET NOTHINGS

Florentines solemnly marked the tenth anniversary of the Uffizi bomb (which killed five people and caused terrible damage to buildings and works of art in 1993). President Ciampi came up from Rome for the occasion and a commemorative concert was held in thePalazzo Vecchio. Also, during the 2003 war in Iraq, huge numbers of rainbow-coloured peace flags appeared on Florentine buildings; it was one of the highest turnouts anywhere in Italy. Otherwise, little really disturbs people going about their daily lives in this prosperous city. They spend much time complaining about the issues of the day but when it comes to action, lethargy or a kind of jaded scepticism ('why bother doing anything when nothing's going to change anyway…'), together with a lack of faith in the authorities, prevails. That's not to say there's a lack of social conscience, it's just a matter of whether or not Florentines are prepared to act. For now at least, *la dolce vita* goes on.

Plain and simple: Brunelleschi's **Santo Spirito**. *See p29.*

Architecture

Building the Renaissance city.

The roots of Florentine builders are primarily Etruscan. It was the Etruscans, in the third or fourth century BC, who first used the arch. And it was their sense of proportion and colour that reappeared during the Middle Ages as Florentine architecture found its form. The Romans were important too. But since some of the early kings of Rome were Etruscans, the distinction is somewhat blurred. Besides, Rome was located on the southern border of Etruria near many of the main Etruscan centres and may have originally been an Etruscan city. So when, during the Renaissance, Imperial Rome and Christian Rome infused Florentine architecture, it was to a great extent a rebirth.

Fiesole, the hill town just to the north of Florence, was the first major settlement in the area. It was one of the league of major Etruscan cities and, as such, would have been settled to protect the pass coming south out of the Apennines, and the crossing point over the Arno, more or less where the Ponte Vecchio now stands. Extensive sections of walls survive there (some with the massive blocks of stone for which the Etruscans were famous) and there are considerable remains from both Etruscan and later Roman times. The Roman theatre is still used for shows in the summer. Also worth a visit is the Badia Fiesolana cathedral (*see p106*), with its elegant green and white marble façade.

Only when the Romans began to absorb Etruscan civilisation was Roman Florence built, probably on the site of a razed Etruscan village. Laid out in the grid pattern still visible on any map, the town was apparently founded by Julius Caesar in 59 BC. Not much of Roman Florence remains above ground, but it is known that the theatre was just behind the Palazzo Vecchio, while the amphitheatre's shape can still be seen in the shape of the streets and buildings just west of piazza Santa Croce.

It was along one of the main axes of Roman Florence, now via dei Calzaiuoli, that medieval Florence grew up. At one end of the axis was the religious centre with the Baptistery and Santa Reparata, the church that once stood where the Duomo now stands. And, at the other, the civil centre of piazza della Signoria, where the Palazzo Vecchio stands. Between the two, just as today, was the commercial centre now called piazza della Repubblica.

There are a number of medieval towers still standing, the oldest of which is the round Torre della Pagliazza in via Santa Elisabetta, just off via del Corso. There are others in via Dante Alighieri, opposite Dante's house, in piazza di San Pier Maggiore, and in borgo San Jacopo, near the Ponte Vecchio.

As Florence expanded, new walls had to be built, principally between 1259 and 1333. The newly enclosed area came to include the *borghi*, which were service areas for industry and storage that grew up along the roads leading out of early medieval towns. The *borghi* suddenly became fairly straight, wide streets, and the owners of industrial property found themselves sitting on prime development land. Many of them moved their commercial premises outside the new walls, knocked down the old ones, now inside the city, and built large townhouses in their place (eventually to be called *palazzi*) with ample gardens behind.

IT STARTS HERE

Florentine architecture, as opposed to architecture in Florence, began in the 11th century with the completion of the Baptistery of San Giovanni, the green and white structure just in front of the Duomo. It's characterised by a search for harmony. The buildings are balanced and simple. They are sharp-edged, with wide, overhanging roofs. The almost black shadows they cast on to the hard stone streets have no gradation at all between light and dark. Any baroque that you may see in Florentine architecture is certainly an import from Rome.

Its distinct style partly arises from the fact that the prominent architects who worked in Florence were all local: Arnolfo di Cambio (c1245-1302); Giotto (1266/7-1337); Filippo Brunelleschi (1377-1446); Michelozzo di Bartolommeo Michelozzi (1396-1472); Leon Battista Alberti (1404-72); Giuliano da Sangallo (c1445-1535); Il Cronaca (1454-1508); Michelangelo Buonarroti (1475-1564); Giorgio Vasari (1511-74); Bartolommeo Ammanati (1511-92); Bernardo Buontalenti (1531-1608); and, in the 19th century, Giuseppe Poggi (1811-1901). Even one of the most notable modern buildings in Florence, the railway station at Santa Maria Novella, was built in the 1930s by a local fellow: Giovanni Michelucci (1891-1991) from Pistoia.

ROMANESQUE AND GOTHIC

Along with San Miniato al Monte – the wonderful green-and-white-faced church that looks down on the city from above piazzale Michelangelo – and Santissimi Apostoli, the **Baptistery** (*see p71*) is the main Romanesque church in Florence. It was built some time between the sixth and the 11th centuries. The stupendous mosaics inside and the marble decoration outside seem to have been finished in the late 12th or early 13th century, indicating that the building was completed by that time. **San Miniato al Monte** (*see p106*) is an 11th-century building, also finished at the beginning of the 13th century. With the Baptistery, it's among the finest Romanesque churches in Europe. **Santissimi Apostoli** (c1080; *see p82*) is hidden away on the north bank of the Arno, between Ponte Vecchio and Ponte Santa Trinità. It's also an early building and purely Romanesque in its plan and the way it conveys the beauty of medieval culture.

Gothic construction followed, using a pointed arch instead of the earlier half-moon Roman one that enabled builders to make higher and wider structures. There are five major Gothic churches in Florence, four of which were influenced by the one built slightly earlier: **San Remigio**, a French pilgrims' church of the 12th century, located just behind the Palazzo Vecchio. It retains, as does much Florentine building, an external simplicity that belies its interior. In 1278 the building of **Santa Maria Novella** (*see p86*) was started. This vast and beautiful Domenican church near the railway station is perhaps the loveliest structure ever put up by that order of monks.

The cathedral of Santa Maria del Fiore, better known as the **Duomo** (*see p67*), was begun in 1297, perhaps designed by Arnolfo di Cambio. It carried medieval construction to a yet higher and larger scale, while retaining the essential Gothic principles of construction. (The great size of the building's cupola was not actually envisaged in the original plan.)

The fourth major Gothic church in Florence is **Santa Croce** (1298; *see p97*), also attributed to Arnolfo. Although this Franciscan building has wide, pointed arches along both sides of the nave, springing diagonally across it, the flat, timber ceiling inside Santa Croce, supported on the two rows of parallel nave arches means that, upon entering the church, the eye is drawn along the nave to the main altar and to the wall of stained glass behind it, rather than upwards.

At the end of the 14th century, the grain market and store that was San Michele in Orto (now known as **Orsanmichele**; *see p79*) had its ground-floor loggia closed on all sides to create a small, rather gloomy church for the guilds of Florence. At the beginning of the 15th century each guild commissioned a statue to place in each of the 14 niches around the building's exterior. These statues, modelled as they were on humans rather than on traditional medieval Christian figures, were an important impetus to the development of the early Renaissance. Many of the originals are housed in the Museo di Orsanmichele and the Bargello and have been replaced here by replicas.

The stunning marble patterns of the **Badia Fiesolana**. *See p27.*

Another Gothic structure is the belltower of the Duomo, the **Campanile** (*see p69*). Designed and begun by Giotto in about 1330, it was completed only after his death. The **Bargello** (originally the Palazzo del Popolo, begun 1250; *see p94*) and the **Palazzo Vecchio** (begun 1299; *see p79*) are two more civil structures that were built in the Gothic period, this latter another structure apparently designed by Arnolfo di Cambio, Florence's early sculptor and architect.

EARLY RENAISSANCE

Brunelleschi, Michelozzo and Alberti are the three most important names of early Renaissance architecture in Florence. Brunelleschi not only gave the Duomo its cupola (the largest such construction since ancient Roman times) he also designed two of the city's finest churches: **San Lorenzo** (constructed 1422-69; *see p89*), including its especially fine, almost independent Old Sacristy (1422-9) and **Santo Spirito** (1444-81; *see p102*). He also built the **Cappella dei Pazzi** (begun 1442; *see p96*), a small private family building in the garden of Santa Croce. Breaking with the past, these buildings embrace human thought even more than Christian faith. They turn back to ideas and forms of the pagan world before Christianity. Their very roots spring from a new, lay Christianity centred on the individual. The cupola of the Duomo is really already the ideal Renaissance central-plan church, built on top of an earlier 14th-century structure. Many later churches, dating from the high Renaissance and even baroque periods, descend directly from this amazing structure. St Peter's cupola in Rome, begun about 100 years later by Michelangelo, has roughly the same interior diameter at 42 metres (546 feet). But both structures are marginally narrower than the dome of the Pantheon in Rome, built over 1,200 years earlier, a structure that itself descends from the still much earlier design of large Etruscan domed tombs.

> **'Michelangelo's creations were oriented toward man's emotional state, rather than his Christianity.'**

Michelozzo worked often for Cosimo de' Medici (Cosimo il Vecchio), the founder of the Medici family's fortunes. He built Cosimo's town residence, now called **Palazzo Medici-Riccardi** (1444; *see p89*), where he developed

Visual aids

Below are some visual aids illustrating six of the city's most common architectural features, along with some examples of where you might see them. For a more comprehensive glossary of architectural terms, *see p298*.

Spandrel: The triangular space between two arches in an arcade (loggia di Brunelleschi in piazza SS Annunziata, loggia dei Lanzi in piazza Signoria, cloister of Santa Croce).

Sporti: Overhang on a building (often an upper floor). Typical of Florentine medieval houses (Ponte Vecchio, south side of piazza Santa Croce).

Crenellations: Battlements or castellations (tower of the Palazzo Vecchio, Museo del Bargello).

Transenna: Open grille or screen often made of marble. Found in early churches (San Miniato al Monte).

Capital: The upper part of a column, often decorated with scenes, figures or leaves (cloister of Santa Maria Maddalena dei Pazzi, church of SS Apostoli).

Lunette: Semi-circular space above a window or door, often decorated with a painting or relief (church of Ognissanti, cloister of San Marco).

the traditional Florentine palazzo so that it had two façades, as well as strongly rusticated orders. He also built for Cosimo a number of castellated villas in 13th-century style.

Although Florentine, Alberti grew up elsewhere and worked mostly outside Florence. His usual taste tended almost to ape the architectural forms of ancient Rome, but in Florence he completed the façade of Santa Maria Novella (1470) in such a harmonious manner that it has remained a symbol of the city to this day. He also built for the Rucellai family the palazzo in the via della Vigna Nuova (c1446-51), where they still live, and the lovely loggia opposite (1463). To the palazzo's façade Alberti introduced pilasters and capitals of the three classical orders that appear to support the three storeys, strongly separated with carved friezes. He completed the tribune started by Michelozzo at **Santissima Annunziata** (*see p93*) in an ornate style more compatible with Rome than Florence.

LATER RENAISSANCE

Other architects, especially Il Cronaca (Simone del Pollaiolo) and Giuliano da Sangallo, the preferred architect of Lorenzo il Magnifico, carried Brunelleschian and Albertian ideals to the end of the 15th and even into the 16th century. These were then developed in both Florence and Rome, principally by Michelangelo, whose work spanned the tense years in Florence before, during and after its subjugation by Habsburg emperor Charles V in 1530, which marked the beginning of the end for Florence's Renaissance spirit. Michelangelo left for Rome in 1534 never to return. He was followed in Florence by three main Medici court architects who all worked for Cosimo I (the first Duke of Tuscany after the siege and conquest of Florence). They were Vasari, Ammanati and Buontalenti.

Il Cronaca built the Santo Spirito vestibule and sacristy (1489-94), structures that carry the Renaissance imitation of the Ancient World almost to a culmination. He also built the **Museo** (formerly Palazzo) **Horne** (1495-1502; *see p96*), returning to an earlier, less rustic Florentine style. Sangallo could be a builder of great delicacy, as demonstrated by his cloister in **Santa Maria Maddalena dei Pazzi** (1492) in borgo Pinti. He also built two grand structures outside Florence: the beautiful **Medici villa** at Poggio a Caiano (begun 1480), and the tiny Renaissance church of **Santa Maria delle Carceri** in Prato (1484-95).

Michelangelo was certainly the greatest of these architects. He took the bold, classicising style that da Sangallo and Il Cronaca had inherited from Alberti and instilled it with a sense of uncertainty, but also of great energy and rhythm. Instead of the exterior reflecting ancient Rome, the very soul of his creations was pagan, oriented toward man's emotional state, rather than his Christianity. In this sense Michelangelo's architecture moved beyond the Renaissance. In neither of the projects he undertook in Florence, both in the church of San Lorenzo (*see p89*), the so-called **New Sacristy** (begun c1520) – a mausoleum for the Medici, as well as for Florence as a republic – and the **Laurentian Library** (begun 1524), is there even the slightest reference to Christianity. In the former, the use of levels that have nothing to do with floor structure, non-load-bearing columns and arches, and windows that don't give light instills a sense of the unreal. The overall effect is enhanced by large areas of cold, white wall. With its cupola so reminiscent of the Pantheon, the structure draws the curtain on that part of the Renaissance that posited that resurrecting the Antique would provide a new truth sufficient to supplant God. The Laurentian Library, with its inspiring vestibule calculated to raise the spirits of readers before they entered the reading room, is similarly a structure so modern as to be mysterious.

Many fine things were built in Florence during the 16th and 17th centuries – churches, private *palazzi*, gardens, *loggie*, villas – but certainly nothing that continued the essence of Brunelleschi and Michelangelo. The tenure of the age is expressed on the one hand by the two fortresses built during the 16th century: the **Fortezza da Basso** (1534; *see p103*), which, symbolically, has its strongest side facing the city, and the **Forte di Belvedere** (1590; *see p99*), which dominates from just above the Ponte Vecchio. These, together with the vast **Palazzo Pitti** (1457; *see p99*), where the Medici moved in the mid 16th century, express the total dominance the Medici had attained over their fellow Florentines at this time. Also from this period date many marvellous formal gardens laid out by wealthy patrons employing Niccolo Pericoli, known as Il Tribolo (1500-58), and his pupils and followers.

Vasari built the **Uffizi** (1560; *see p80*) for Cosimo I and, with Buontalenti's help, filled it with offices and workshops for the city's administration. On the top floor was located the Gallery, which remains there still for the ever-expanding Medici collections. Vasari also built the raised corridor that runs from their office building across the Ponte Vecchio to their home at the Palazzo Pitti, so that the family could travel without the dangers of the streets of Florence. Ammanati built the lovely **Ponte Santa Trinità** over the Arno to replace an earlier bridge that had collapsed in 1557. It was he who began the 300-year expansion of the Palazzo Pitti. Buontalenti, besides extending the Palazzo Vecchio to its present eastern limits and designing the Forte di Belvedere, built for the Medici the lovely villas at Petraia (1587) and (later demolished) Pratolino (1568).

THE LONG DECLINE

Not much happened in Florence, architecturally, between 1600 and 1860, at least not compared with the previous three centuries. The period from 1600 to the death of the last Medici ruler in 1737 was a long decline, and even after the Grand Duchy of Tuscany became property of the Habsburgs, with their capable reforms, the city remained a provincial appendage of the Austrian Empire. Napoleon, who destroyed so much, did little to damage Florence. Perhaps he felt at home? His family had been minor Florentine nobles from the 14th century onwards, until their move to Corsica – when it was still part of Italy.

As time passed, gardens and *palazzi* were enlarged, grottos were fitted into hillsides, *piazze* were decorated with fountains and statues, the vast and questionable **Cappella dei Principi** in San Lorenzo (c1604; *see p87*) was built. A few fine but unspectacular churches, necessarily in a Roman baroque style, were built: San Gaetano (1604), in via dei Tornabuoni, San Frediano in Cestello (1680-9), on the lungarno Soderini, San Giorgio alla Costa (1705-8), just up the hill from the Ponte Vecchio, and San Filippo Neri (1640-1715), in piazza San Firenze. Eventually, in the 19th century, the railway arrived in Florence and two stations were built: Leopolda (1847) and Maria Antonia near Santa Maria Novella (1848). Only the Leopolda still stands, just outside Porta al Prato, now a spectacular performance space.

DEVELOPMENT AND DESTRUCTION

Beginning with the period just before the unification of Italy in 1860, the city of Florence underwent a series of enormous architectural changes. First, much of the as yet undeveloped land inside the city walls was used for housing. Then, on the north side of the Arno, the walls themselves were pulled down (1865-9), leaving only some of the gates, standing isolated as they still do today. Where there had been walls, *viali* (avenues) were built for the carriages of the new householders, and two large open spaces were left as breaks in the *viali*: piazza C Beccaria, by Giuseppe Poggi, and piazza della Libertà. Both were meant to be elegant openings in neo-classical and neo-Renaissance style, but today, like so much of Florence, and the *viali*, they are submerged in traffic.

The new avenues were continued on the south side of the river, from what is now piazza Ferrucci, up another tree-and-villa-lined *viale* to **piazzale Michelangelo** (1875), a large open space for carriages, where a magnificent panorama of Florence and its valley awaited the visitor. They continued along the side of the hills facing Florence and the Forte di Belvedere, and then came back down again to Porta Romana. This wonderful drive of approximately six kilometres (3.5 miles), one of the prettiest in Italy, is also due in great part to Poggi.

In these same years, parts of the old city were pulled down to make space for three covered, cast-iron market buildings. This was followed, from 1890 onwards, by the most thoughtless devastation of all. The area that had been the centre of the Roman and medieval city, piazza della Repubblica, and all the streets near it, was pulled down so that the city centre could be redeveloped. Then, soon after World War I, the central government at Rome, with much the same speculative mentality, pulled down yet more large sections of the city, particularly around the new station of Santa Maria Novella, and near Santa Croce.

'These projects have attracted heavyweight names in architecture from Italy and abroad.'

Only 50 years after the centre of Florence had been gutted, yet another large area of destruction took place, once again removing scores of beautiful and irreplaceable ancient buildings. The Germans, partly out of fury with their former allies, and partly in a hopeless attempt to stem the Anglo-American advance, blew up all the bridges over the Arno except the Ponte Vecchio (1944), along with all the buildings to the immediate north and immediate south of the Ponte Vecchio. Ponte Santa Trinità was rebuilt in the 1950s to the original plans; the other three – Ponte alle Grazie, Ponte alla Carraia and Ponte alla Vittoria – were all replaced in modern style.

This means that, whereas just over 100 years ago most of the old centre of Florence was still intact, made up of buildings going back to the early Middle Ages, on foundations that went back at least to ancient Rome, today you can walk all the way from the Duomo, down via Roma, across piazza della Repubblica, through via Calimala and via por Santa Maria, right down to the Ponte Vecchio without passing more than two or three buildings that are not late 19th- or 20th-century structures. What's more, the buildings that you pass, which were erected to replace those destroyed, are banal at the very best.

FUTURE FORMS

Until relatively recently, there have been few modern buildings of note in the city. Exceptions include: the exemplary **railway station** near Santa Maria Novella, built in 1936 by Giovanni Michelucci; the **Stadio Artemio Franchi**, another fine functional structure from between the wars (finished in 1932) and recently considerably restructured; the church of **San Giovanni Battista** at the crossing of the Autostrade del Sole and del Mare (1960), also by Michelucci, has vision and sensitivity. The inter-war Fascist period produced a few other fine if typically grandiose structures: a reception building for the Italian royal family, attached to Santa Maria train station, called the Palazzina Reale; the Istituto Aeronautica Militare building in the Cascine park; and the Cinema Puccini, in piazza Puccini. Then there are Guido Spadolini's 1970s Palazzo degli Affari (part of the Palazzo dei Congressi complex) and the new buildings at Amerigo Vespucci Airport.

However, this seems set to change over the next few years: a major renovation process is under way in the city, in which architecture is to play a significant role. Having remained static for years (with the exceptions listed above), Florence is the focus of a number of initiatives designed to improve and rehabilitate increasingly large areas of the city, in the form of both public and private developments. These projects have attracted heavyweight names in architecture from both Italy and abroad, such as Norman Foster (for the high-speed train station), Arata Isozaki (the new exit of the Uffizi) and Santiago Calatrava (the extension of the Museo dell'Opera del Duomo). These are all high-profile projects, but a host of other changes are taking place behind the scenes. Important parts of the city are being reclaimed for the building of new homes, businesses, parks, public spaces and public buildings. Many of these will utilise defunct industrial areas and factories rather than eating into precious agricultural land. The biggest and most advanced of these projects is the satellite town of Firenze Nova on the ex-Fiat property in Novoli near Peretola Airport, which is now well on its way. The new university buildings are mostly up and running, the enormous law courts building is now visible in its skeletal form. Hopefully, the mistakes of the past (mostly the results of financial and political self-interest) will not be repeated and these projects will reach fruition with the hoped-for results.

Food in Tuscany

Abandon diets all ye who enter here.

BASICS

The holy trinity of the Tuscan diet is bread, olive oil and wine. Wines are famously substantial (*see pp40-4*) and the olive oil distinctively peppery, but bread is deliberately bland. Made without salt it is a neutral canvas for accompanying food. A worthy intention, but an acquired taste.

Tuscany claims to have Italy's best olive oil – just don't tell that to growers in Puglia or Umbria. And within Tuscany each region claims superiority, though the consensus is that the finest oil comes from the slightly inland groves away from the varying temperatures and high moisture levels of the coast. Judge for yourself. Many producers offer public tours of their groves and tastings of their product.

L'ANTIPASTO

Meals generally start with the *antipasto*, literally, 'before the meal'. In Tuscany, the most common *antipasto* is *crostini*, chicken liver pâté on bread or toast. Cured meats are a regional speciality – usually pork and wild boar, which are butchered or hunted during the cold winter months. *Prosciutto crudo* comes from a pig haunch buried under salt for three weeks, then swabbed with spicy vinegar, covered with black pepper and hung to dry for a further five months. *Capocollo* is a neck cut cured the same way for three days, covered with pepper and fennel seed, rolled round in yellow butcher's paper and then tied up with string so that it looks sausage-shaped. It's ready for eating a few months later. The most typical Tuscan salami is *finocchiona* (pork, flavoured with fennel seeds and peppercorns). *Salamini di cinghiale*, or small wild boar salamis, include chilli pepper and a little fatty pork to keep them from going too hard (wild boar is a very lean meat). Look out for *milza*, a delicious pungent pâté, made from spleen, herbs, spices and wine.

IL PRIMO

The *primo* (first course) is carbohydrate-based. In most parts of Italy this is pasta or rice. In Tuscany it's as likely to be a bread-based salad or soup. Old bread is never thrown away, but is mixed with what could be called the disciples of Tuscan staples: tomatoes, garlic, cabbage and *fagioli* (white beans).

These form dishes like *panzanella* (stale bread soaked in water, squeezed out, mixed with raw onion, fresh tomato and basil and dressed with oil, salt and pepper), *ribollita* (rich bean and cabbage soup with bread, made using the local *cavolo nero* or black cabbage), *acqua cotta* (toasted bread rubbed with garlic and covered with crinkly dark green cabbage, then topped with olive oil, sometimes with an egg broken into it), *pappa al pomodoro* (an exquisite porridge-like soup with onion, garlic, tomatoes, basil and chilli pepper). The ultimate winter ritual is *bruschetta* or *fettunta* (toasted bread rubbed with garlic and soaked in freshly pressed olive oil).

Fresh pasta in Tuscany usually takes the form of *tagliatelle* (flat egg-based ribbons), *pappardelle* (wide flat ribbons), *ravioli* (envelopes containing ricotta and spinach) and *tordelli* (from around Lucca, stuffed with chard, meat and ricotta). South you'll find *pici* (flour and water extruded into fattish strings) and in the Mugello *tortelli* (stuffed with potato and bacon). Ravioli are best eaten with *burro e salvia* (butter and sage) or a sprinkling of parmesan or pecorino. Flat ribbon-like pastas go well with gamey sauces like *lepre* (hare) and *cinghiale* (wild boar), and also *anatra* (duck), as well as *ragù* (made with tomato and minced beef or, occasionally, lamb) and *salsa di pomodoro* (spicy tomato sauce).

IL SECONDO

Cacciagione (game), *salsicce* (sausages) and *bistecca* (beef steak) are the main regional meats, though there is good lamb about (look out for *agnellino nostrali*, meaning young, locally raised lamb). Also common are *coniglio* (rabbit, usually roasted, sometimes with pine nuts, sometimes rolled around a filling such as egg and bacon) and *pollo* (chicken; go for *ruspante*, free-range). During the winter you'll find plenty of slowly stewed and highly spiced *cinghiale*. This species was cross-bred with the domestic pig about 20 years ago, producing a largely herbivorous creature so prolific that it has to be culled. Other common game includes *lepre* and *fagiano* (pheasant). The famous *bistecca fiorentina* is a vast T-bone steak, usually served very rare and quite enough for two or even three people. Though a *fiorentina*, grilled over a herby wood fire, might seem synonymous with Tuscany, the habit of eating huge beef steaks was, in fact, introduced in the 19th century by English aristocrats homesick for roast beef. Have no qualms, the Chianina breed of cattle found locally are a salubrious lot.

IL CONTORNO

To accompany your meat course you're normally offered a side plate of vegetables or a salad. *Bietole* (Swiss chard) is available almost throughout the year. It's scalded in salted water and tossed in the pan with olive oil, garlic and chilli pepper. *Fagiolini* (green beans) are likely to be boiled and dressed with oil and lemon or vinegar. The sublime white Tuscan *fagioli* are served lukewarm with olive oil and a sprinkle of black pepper. *Patatine fritte* (French fries) are available almost everywhere, though boiled potatoes dressed with oil, pepper and capers are often much tastier. *Pomodori* (tomatoes) and *cipolle* (onions) sliced, spiced and baked *al forno* (in the oven) are recommended. To those accustomed to watery lettuce, *radicchio* salads may seem bitter at first. Cultivate a taste for them and you'll go on to appreciate the many wild salad varieties. In early summer, artichokes are often eaten raw, stripped of their tough outer leaves and dipped into olive oil and salt.

IL FORMAGGIO

The one true Tuscan cheese is pecorino, made with ewe's milk. The sheep grazing on the hillsides are more often than not there for their milk rather than mutton, lamb or wool.

Thirty years ago each small farm would have raised enough sheep to provide the household with sufficient rounds of pecorino, which can be eaten *fresco* (up to a month old), *semi-stagionato* after about a month of ripening, or up to six months later when the cheese is fully *stagionato*, and thus drier, sharper and tastier. Nowadays sheep farming and cheese-making are mostly done by Sardinians, who came over to work the land abandoned by the Tuscans drawn to towns and factory employment.

Fresh ricotta, which is made from whey and is thus not strictly speaking a cheese, is soft, mild and wet and should be eaten with black pepper and a few drops of olive oil on top.

LA FRUTTA

Cherries, then apricots and peaches, are readily available in the summer, grapes in the late summer, and apples and pears in the early autumn. Although citrus fruits imported from the south now take pride of place in the winter months, the indigenous fruits are quinces (*mele cotogne*, excellent baked, stewed or jellied) and persimmons (*cachi*). However, for visitors to Tuscany, fruit is perhaps most interesting in sweet/savoury combinations: *il cacio con le pere* (cheese with pears), *i fichi con il salame* (figs with salami), *melone*, or *popone*, *con prosciutto* (melon and cured ham).

IL DOLCE

Although the Tuscans are not great purveyors of desserts, they do like to conclude festive meals with a glass of a dry raisin wine called *Vin Santo* into which they dunk *cantucci*, little dry biscuits packed with almonds. *Vin Santo* is made with a special white grape variety that's dried out in bunches for a month and then crushed to obtain a sweet juice, which is aged for at least five years. This is highly uneconomical – you could get five bottles of wine out of the grapes you need for one bottle of *Vin Santo*. So to offer a glass of *Vin Santo* is to honour a guest with the essence of hospitality.

The out of towners

No foodie should confine their eating experiences to Florence and the other major Tuscan towns. Some of the best nosh is found in remote country restaurants or in the many less well-known towns and villages. The restaurants below are unique, either for the quality of their food or for their special setting. The prices quoted are for a meal for one consisting of *antipasto* or *primo*, *secondo*, *contorno* and *dolce*. Drinks and cover charge aren't included.

Costachiara

Via Santa Maria 129, Località Badiola, Terranuova Bracciolini, Arezzo (055 944 318/www.costachiara.it). **Average** €25. **Open** 12.30-2.30pm Mon; 12.30-2.30pm, 7.30-10pm Wed-Sun. **Credit** AmEx, MC, V.

Costachiara is, in many ways, a typical Tuscan farmhouse restaurant, with the nicest tables in two rooms on the left as you enter. *Antipasti* is a help yourself affair. Choose between grilled marinated vegetables, marinated olives, salads, *crostini*, or a side of roast ham and a fabulous red onion marmalade. Among the *primi*, the *pici al fattore* is a must (fat, hand-rolled spaghetti with a rich pigeon and guinea fowl sauce). The *secondi* are all very traditional like *arrosto girato* (mixed meats spit-roasted over an open fire). Home-made desserts are great. Accommodation is available.

Da Delfina

Via della Chiesa 1, Artimino, Florence (055 871 8074/www.dadelfina.it). **Average** €31. **Open** 12.30-2.30pm, 7.45-10.30pm Tue-Sat; 12.30-2.30pm Sun. **No credit cards**.

Da Delfina's outdoor terrace is one of the loveliest spots in Tuscany to enjoy a good meal. The restaurant occupies a restored *casa colonica* and the food is rustic Tuscan at its best. In early summer, starters include a flavoursome galantine of rabbit and a delicate bright green *sformato* of nettles served with a lick of bean purée. *Ribollita* is given an unusual, but authentic, treatment pan fried in olive oil. In mushroom season, big chunks of *porcini* are deep fried in a light batter. Other *secondi* include guinea fowl roasted with *Vin Santo* and roast kid. Local sheep's cheeses are served with *cotognata* (quince jam). The wine list is comprehensive. But do try an excellent local wine, like one of the full-bodied *riservas*.

Da Giorgione

Via Belvedere 23, Località Sagginale, Borgo San Lorenzo, Florence (055 849 0130). **Average** €16. **Open** 12.30-2pm Mon-Wed; 12.30-2pm, 7.30-9.30pm Fri-Sun. **Credit** MC, V.

Officially called Trattoria Sagginale, but known locally as Da Giorgione after Big Giorgio, the affable *padrone*, this modest little restaurant is frequented by local families and passers-by. The kitchen makes a superb rendition of the Mugello's most famous dish, *tortelli di patate*: pillows of light egg pasta are filled with mashed potato, parmesan, minced garlic, parsley and nutmeg. The best sauces are the rich meaty ones. *Secondi* include grilled meats, *coniglio arrosto* and a delicious *coniglio ripieno* – rolled, boned rabbit stuffed with spinach *frittata* and *prosciutto* and roasted in the oven. For pudding, try the *zuppa inglese* or *tiramisù*. Giorgione's house wine is plentiful and cheap.

Gambero Rosso

Piazza della Vittoria 13, San Vincenzo, Livorno (0565 701 021). **Average** €85. **Open** 12.30-2.30pm, 7.30-10pm Wed-Sun. **Credit** AmEx, DC, MC, V.

Gambero Rosso, overlooking the sea at San Vincenzo, is extraordinary. There are eight or so well-spaced tables in the light, airy room whose centrepiece is a huge antique chandelier. Fulvio Pierangelini's food is sublime and he's very much present in the kitchen. Go for the five-course set menu of Gambero Rosso 'classics' (excellent value at €85) or eat à la carte where dishes are more creative. Try the signature dish of *passatina di ceci e gamberi*, a silky cream of chickpeas with sweet shrimp tails, or white and black ravioli stuffed with fish and served with a rose-coloured seafood sauce. Main-course catch of the day is served lightly sautéed on a bed of creamy mash topped with artichoke hearts. Puddings are divine and the wine list covers the best of Italy and beyond.

I Pescatori

Via Leopardi 9, Orbetello, Grosseto (0564 860 611). **Average** €17. **Open** *Mid June-mid Sept* 7.30-10.30pm daily. *Mid Sept-May* 7.30-10.30pm Fri-Sun. **Credit** AmEx, MC, V.

Orbetello nestles on the mainland end of the middle of three narrow spits of land joining Monte Argentario to Tuscany. The local fisherman's co-op has added another dimension to its activities by opening this simple yet delightful restaurant. Once inside, make your selection from the menu, pay at the cash desk and then take your seat. The menu features fish fresh from the lagoon; *spigola* (sea bass), *orata* (John Dory), *cefalo* (mullet) and *anguilla* (eel), with some seasonal variations. The mixed *antipasto* includes smoked mullet and *orata* and bean salad. For *secondo*, choose between a simple grilled fish or, for example, marinated grilled eel. There's no dessert, so freshen the palate with *granita al limone*. Local wines are dirt cheap, while ice-cold *vino bianco frizzante* goes down a treat. In summer, there are tables on a piazza behind the restaurant (next to the moorings).

Silene

Località Pescina 9, Seggiano, Grosseto (0564 950 805). **Average** €35. **Open** 12.45-2.30pm, 7.45-9.30pm Tue-Sun. **Credit** AmEx, MC, V.

On the northern slopes of Monte Amiata lies the hamlet of Pescina. The *albergo-ristorante* Silene has been serving guests since 1830. The carefully presented food is sophisticated rustic, using abundant indigenous ingredients. It's also excellent value. There are two set tasting menus, one featuring typical Tuscan fare, while the other involves seasonal ingredients specific to the area (€35 and €40). The menu changes every two weeks or so, but a typical selection might include creamy *taglierini* with wild asparagus, *gnocchetti* with fresh truffles, ravioli stuffed with pigeon or rich *cinghiale* stew flavoured with juniper. Try the seriously good hot chocolate soufflé for dessert. The wine list is excellent value – there are also pleasant rooms, should you need to crash.

La Tana degli Orsi

Via Roma 1, Pratovecchio, Arezzo, (0575 583377). **Average** €25. **Open** 7.45-10pm Mon, Wed-Sun. **Credit** AmEx, DC, MC, V.

La Tana degli Orsi (the Bear's Den) doesn't look that inspiring from the road, but once inside, the atmosphere is cosy and relaxed with lots of wood, warm lighting and mellow music. The chefs serve sophisticated versions of traditional dishes and have also built up a remarkable cellar. Meals typically start with a local goat's cheese salad with pine nuts and warm courgette and tomato *focaccia. Antipasti* include *tortino di funghi porcini* (a kind of quiche) with salty local *prosciutto* and a hot pecorino soufflé. For summer *primi*, expect *caramelle* (a sweet-shaped pasta parcel) stuffed with ricotta and borage, while in winter, there's risotto with local black truffles. Puddings are sumptuous too. The wine list features over 600 keenly priced labels.

Taverna del Guerrino

Via Montefioralle 39, Montefioralle (055 853 106). **Average** €22. **Open** 7.30-9.30pm Wed; 12.30-2.30pm, 7.30-9.30pm Thur-Sun. **No credit cards**.

Montefioralle is a timeless Tuscan walled village just outside Greve in Chianti. At the Taverna del Guerrino (lovely at lunchtime) the feeling is that nothing much has changed for the past fifty years. The best table sits in the long window of the first room and has restful views of the hills. The menu features Tuscan staples and never varies; liver-topped *crostini* and *fettunta* (the Tuscan word for *bruschetta*), excellent *prosciutto*, salami and fennel-flavoured *finnocchiona* from Greve. *Secondi* are based on grilled meats; the *rosticciana* (spare ribs) are superbly juicy and full of flavour. Sadly, puddings are no longer home-made. Instead, go for *biscotti* and *Vin Santo*. The local *vino della casa* suits the food and costs next to nothing.

Il Tufo Allegro

Vicolo della Costituzione 2, Pitigliano, Grosseto (0564 616 192). **Average** €34. **Open** 12.30-2pm, 7.30-9.30pm Mon, Thur-Sun; 7.30-9.30pm Wed. **Credit** AmEx, MC, V.

This informal trattoria is half carved into the mass of tufa rock on which the ancient town of Pitigliano is built. The two tiny downstairs rooms are atmospheric, but claustrophobics should stay above ground. The menu is based on traditional Tuscan recipes, with an original slant. Begin with a plate of local *salumi di cinghiale* or a rich game terrine. Go on to the excellent *gnudi* (soft ricotta and spinach balls) with truffle sauce (in season) and *acquacotta*, a vegetable soup with bread and eggs, and follow with a rack of lamb stuffed with sweetbreads. There's also a fabulous selection of cheeses, as well as some delicious desserts. The wine cellar has interesting labels, but mark-ups are high.

Understanding the menu

Techniques/descriptions

Affumicato smoked; **al forno** cooked in an oven; **arrosto** roast; **brasato** braised; **fatto in casa** home-made; **griglia** grilled; **fritto** fried; **nostrali** locally grown/raised; **ripieno** stuffed; **ruspante** free-range; **vapore** steamed.

Basics

Aceto vinegar; **burro** butter; **bottiglia** bottle; **focaccia** flat bread made with olive oil; **ghiaccio** ice; **miele** honey; **olio** oil; **pane** bread; **panino** sandwich; **panna** cream; **pepe** pepper; **sale** salt; **salsa** sauce; **senape** mustard; **uovo** egg.

Antipasti

Antipasti misto mixed hors d'œuvres; **bruschetta** bread toasted and rubbed with garlic, sometimes drizzled with olive oil and often comes with tomatoes or White Tuscan Beans; **crostini** small slices of toasted bread; **crostini toscani** are smeared with chicken liver pâté; **crostone** big crostini; **fettunta** the Tuscan name for *bruschetta*; **prosciutto crudo** cured ham, either *dolce* (sweet, similar to Parma ham) or *salato* (salty).

Primi

Acquacotta cabbage soup usually served with a *bruschetta*, sometimes with an egg broken into it; **agnolotti** stuffed triangular pasta; **brodo** broth; **cacciucco** thick, chilli-spiked fish soup (Livorno's main contribution to Tuscan cuisine); **cecina** flat, crispy bread made of chickpea flour; **fettuccine** long, narrow ribbons of egg pasta; **frittata** type of substantial omelette; **gnocchi** small potato and flour dumplings; **minestra** soup, usually vegetable; **pappa al pomodoro** bread and tomato soup; **pappardelle** broad ribbons of egg pasta, usually served with *lepre* (hare); **panzanella** Tuscan bread and tomato salad; **passato** puréed soup; **pasta e fagioli** pasta and bean soup; **ribollita** literally, a twice-cooked soup of bean, bread, cabbage and vegetable; **taglierini** thin ribbons of pasta; **tordelli/tortelli** stuffed pasta; **zuppa** soup; **zuppa frantoiana** literally, olive press soup – another bean and cabbage soup, distinguished as it's served with the very best young olive oil.

Fish & seafood

Acciughe/alici anchovies; **anguilla** eel; **aragosta** lobster; **aringa** herring; **baccalà** salt cod; **bianchetti** little fish, like whitebait; **bonito** small tuna; **branzino** sea bass; **calamari** squid; **capesante** scallops; **coda di rospo** monkfish tails; **cozze** mussels; **fritto misto** mixed fried fish; **gamberetti** shrimps; **gefalo** grey mullet; **gamberi** prawns; **granchio** crab; **insalata di mare** seafood salad; **merluzzo** cod; **nasello** hake; **ostriche** oyster; **pesce** fish; **pesce spada** swordfish; **polpo** octopus; **ricci** sea urchins; **rombo** turbot; **san Pietro** John Dory; **sarde** sardines; **scampi** langoustines; **scoglio** shell- and rockfish; **sgombro** mackerel; **seppia** cuttlefish or squid; **sogliola** sole; **spigola** sea bass; **stoccafisso** stockfish; **tonno** tuna; **triglia** red mullet; **trota** trout; **trota salmonata** salmon trout; **vongole** clams.

Meat, poultry & game

Agnellino young lamb; **agnello** lamb; **anatra** duck; **animelle** sweetbreads; **arrosto misto** mixed roast meats; **beccacce** woodcock; **bistecca** beef steak; **bresaola** cured, dried beef, served in thin slices; **caccia** general term for game; **carpaccio** raw beef, served in thin slices; **capretto** kid; **cervo** venison; **cinghiale** wild boar; **coniglio** rabbit; **cotoletta/costoletta** chop; **fagiano** pheasant; **fegato** liver; **lepre** hare; **lardo** pork fat; **maiale** pork; **manzo** beef; **ocio/ oca** goose; **ossobucco** veal shank stew; **pancetta** like bacon; **piccione** pigeon; **pollo** chicken; **porchetta** roast pork; **rognone** kidney; **salsicce** sausages; **tacchino** turkey; **trippa** tripe; **vitello** veal.

Herbs, pulses & vegetables

Aglio garlic; **asparagi** asparagus; **basilico** basil; **bietola** Swiss chard; **capperi** capers; **carciofi** artichokes; **carote** carrots; **castagne** chestnuts; **cavolfiore** cauliflower; **cavolo nero** red cabbage; **ceci** chickpeas; **cetriolo** cucumber; **cipolla** onion; **dragoncello** tarragon; **erbe** herbs; **fagioli** White Tuscan Beans; **fagiolini** green, string or French beans; **farro** spelt (a hard wheat), a popular soup ingredient around Lucca and the Garfagnana; **fave** or **baccelli** broad beans (although *fava* in Tuscany also means the male 'organ', so use *baccelli*); **finocchio** fennel; **fiori di zucca** courgette flowers; **funghi** mushrooms; **funghi porcini** ceps; **funghi selvatici** wild mushrooms; **lattuga** lettuce; **lenticchie** lentils; **mandorle** almonds; **melanzane** aubergine; **menta** mint; **patate** potatoes; **peperoncino** chilli pepper; **peperoni** peppers; **pinoli** pine nuts; **pinzimonio** selection of raw vegetables to be dipped in olive oil; **piselli** peas; **pomodoro** tomato; **porri** leeks; **prezzemolo** parsley; **radice/ravanelli** radish; **ramerino/rosmarino** rosemary; **rapa** turnip; **rucola/rughetta** rocket (UK), rugola (US); **salvia** sage; **sedano** celery; **spinaci** spinach; **tartufo** truffles; **tartufato** cut thin like a truffle; **zucchini** courgette.

Fruit

Albicocche apricots; **ananas** pineapple; **arance** oranges; **banane** bananas; **ciliege** cherries; **cocomero** watermelon; **datteri** dates; **fichi** figs; **fragole** strawberries; **lamponi** raspberries; **limone** lemon; **macedonia di frutta** fruit salad; **mele** apples; **melone** melon; **more** blackberries; **pera** pear; **pesca** peach; **pompelmo** grapefruit; **uva** grapes.

Desserts & cheese

Cantuccini almond biscuits; **castagnaccio** chestnut flour cake, made around Lucca; **cavallucci** spiced biscuits from Siena; **gelato** ice-cream; **granita** flavoured ice; **mandorlata** almond brittle; **panforte** cake of dried fruit; **pecorino** sheep's milk cheese; **ricciarelli** almond biscuits from Siena; **torrone** nougat; **torta** tart, cake; **zabaglione** egg custard mixed with Marsala; **zuppa Inglese** trifle.

Drinks

Acqua water, *gassata* (fizzy) or *senza gas* (still); **birra** beer; **caffè** coffee; **cioccolata** hot chocolate; **latte** milk; **succo di frutta** fruit juice; **tè** tea; **vino rosso/bianco/rosato** red/white/rosé wine; **Vin Santo** dessert wine.

General

May I see the menu? **Posso vedere il menù?** May I have the bill, please? **Mi fa il conto, per favore?**

Tuscan Wine

Designer labels, art and culture of a different kind.

Tuscany doesn't produce as much wine as Sicily or the Veneto, but the overall value of its wines far outstrips that of other regions. At the top end, they are almost exclusively reds, and can command very high prices. The most widespread red grape variety is Sangiovese, which is what goes into **Chianti**, **Vino Nobile di Montepulciano** and **Brunello di Montalcino**. The region does produce a few whites, but practically nothing of real repute.

During the past 15 years, wine production in Tuscany has evolved to such a degree that the change is as evident in the landscape as in the glass. Take note wherever you see an orchard of fruit trees interspersed with a few rows of tall, exuberant vines, their tendrils embracing sturdy trees for support. This is viticultural archaeology, destined to disappear entirely before long. With the demise of this sort of vine dressing went much of the quaffing wine in large bottles. Quality has become the byword, and there's not a traditional winemaker left who feels he can do without the services of an oenologist, the wine technician whose expertise is essential when it comes to balance, structure, bouquet and consistency.

The emphasis is now on densely planted vineyards. Vibrant green geometries have replaced the softer contours and mixed hues of the sparsely planted orchards tended by yesteryear's sharecrop farmers. Vines need to be 'stressed' by competition. That way they'll concentrate on survival, focusing energy on seed production and so on sturdy, healthy fruit.

Bunches of grapes grown on vines that are radically pruned in winter and again in the spring will often be thinned out to improve quality and ensure ripening proceeds evenly. The goal is to obtain relatively low yields with high concentrations of sugars and aromas.

SETTING THE STANDARD

For growers, choosing the right vine-stock and clone for a particular soil and exposure has become an art, indeed a science, often pursued in collaboration with the Departments of Agronomy from the universities of Florence and Pisa. Such territorial specificity ensures what is known as *tipicità*: a distinct character pertaining to a given place. In other words, individuality versus bland sameness.

Tipicità is, to an extent, defined by the various **DOC**s (Denominazione di Origine Controllata, which regulate wines from a specific, controlled area), the ultra-select category of **DOCG**s (Denominazione di Origine Controllata e Garantita) and **IGT**s (Indicazione Geografica Tipica, table wines from a well-defined area). These certified names are the equivalent of the French *appellation*. Each sets out production rules and regulations to which producers must adhere. Tuscany has 39 such appellations, more than any other region in the country.

The most famous of these are Chianti Classico, Brunello di Montalcino and Vino Nobile di Montepulciano. Their renown tends to overshadow some promising younger siblings: for instance, Bolgheri Rosso DOC, made in the coastal area north of Grosseto, Montescudaio DOC a little further south, and below this the Morellino di Scansano DOC. A little further inland is the recently defined Montecucco DOC, also producing promising, well-structured reds. Two other new southern Tuscan DOCs are Capalbio on the coast and Sovana, between the southern slopes of Mount Amiata and the coast. Due east and slightly north of here is the fairly extensive and variegated area devoted to the production of Orcia DOC, whose flagship in the early years is likely to be Donatella Cinelli Colombini at the Fattoria del Colle near Trequanda. While the denomination itself is more a guarantee of *tipicità* than of excellence, there's no doubt that some of the new DOCs are very promising, and still relatively reasonably priced.

'Producers have had to improve their act. Mere quaffing wines are no longer good enough.'

The well-established Tuscan whites are the Vernaccia di San Gimignano DOC and the Bianco di Pitigliano DOC. However, a number of the new DOCs also embrace white wines and it will be interesting to see whether these will be able to stand up to comparisons with the few Tuscan whites of excellence: Batàr **Pinot Bianco** made by Agricola Querciabella at Greve in Chianti and the **Cabreo La Pietra Chardonnay** made by Ruffino at Pontassieve.

WAY OF THE WINEMAKER

To match the changes in vineyards, much more attention is now also paid to the cellar. The peasant winemaker of a few years ago now either sells his grapes to larger wineries or has embarked on a programme of investment in new vineyards and appropriate winemaking facilities: spotless new cellars, temperature-controlled steel fermentation tanks, expensive pumps that shift the deep red liquid from one container to another without bruising it, small French oak barrels (called *barriques*) for oxygenating and ageing the wine, immaculate bottling equipment and, as often as not, a tasting room as well.

A number of small growers instead sell their grapes to the remaining co-operative wineries. Since these producers are placing their wines in an increasingly competitive market, in the past few years they've had to improve their act considerably or go under. Mere quaffing wines are no longer good enough. With the help of agronomists, who advise the co-operative growers, and the oenologists, who work miracles in the cellar, the better co-operative winemakers are producing perfectly acceptable wines whose good price-to-quality ratio helps smooth over what might otherwise be perceived as a lack of individuality. Cases in point include **Agricoltori del Chianti Geografico**, which produces an excellent Chianti Classico (especially the 1998); the **Cantina di Montalcino**, whose Brunello '95 meets with considerable acclaim (the Montalcino co-operative growers are paid for their grapes in relation to quality, and prices may vary by as much as 20 per cent, a policy that is certainly paying off in the end product); the **Cantina Cooperativa del Morellino**, which has a good Morellino di Scansano; Redi, the flagship for the **Vecchia Cantina** co-operative winery at Montepulciano; and **Le Chiantigiane**, producing the white Vernaccia di San Gimignano. Such products are widely distributed, both at supermarket level in Italy and in wine stores and chains abroad.

Right at the other end of the spectrum are the great aristocratic wine dynasties. These include names such as **Antinori**, **Ricasoli**, **Frescobaldi**, **Mazzei** and **Folonari** (the owners of Ruffino). With their many generations of experience, they've gradually expanded from the area south of Florence, where they principally produce Chianti Classico, to other parts of Tuscany, and indeed Umbria. They have the clout, financially and socially, to espouse quality and shape palates in anticipation of market trends.

A case in point was the development of **Galestro** back in the late 1970s. In a region that was largely identified with reds, these producers saw that the time was ripe for a white wine in which the emphasis was more on freshness and lightness than aroma and body. Made up largely of the Trebbiano Toscano grape variety, with small amounts of Malvasia del Chianti, Vernaccia di San Gimignano, Chardonnay, Pinot Blanc and Rhine-Riesling, it involved pioneering vinification techniques. In 20 years, it has grown in structure to become, perhaps not a connoisseur's choice, but an acceptable aperitif or accompaniment to lighter summer cuisine.

RISING STARS

Still more impressive and influential has been the development from the mid 1980s of what go by the name of Super Tuscans, also pioneered by the great wine estates. The idea

The shiny new face of Tuscan wine-making.

was to open up the way for wines that could satisfy changing tastes, particularly on the international market. At the time, the quality of Tuscan table wines was perceived as poor, and the production of DOC wines stultified by excessive strictures and regulations. So the farsighted few felt there was room for wines that did not conform to the established Tuscan models. They began experimenting with the grape varieties that had contributed to the renown of French viticulture: the Cabernets, the Merlot, the Chardonnay and the Sauvignon.

'These winemakers have transcended their parents' horizons, but with touching respect for what their fathers have taught them.'

Alongside these enterprising producers there was a new generation of highly trained wine technicians who could hardly wait to get involved in the creation of innovative wines. The fruits of their labours were beautifully made, commanded relatively high prices, and for consumers abroad were initially somewhat perplexing. Why should an 'ordinary' wine cost more than certain DOCs? Was there anything beyond the thick glass of the bottle and the refined label? The British and American wine press decreed that reds such as the **Tignanello** (Sangiovese and Cabernet Sauvignon) and **Solaia** (Cabernet plus a small percentage of Sangiovese) made by the Marchesi Antinori in Chianti deserved the epithet Super Tuscans, and the name stuck. Similar enthusiasm greeted Nicolò Incisa della Rocchetta's **Sassicaia** (90 per cent Cabernet Sauvignon, 10 per cent Cabernet Franc) and Lodovico Antinori's **Ornellaia** (90 per cent Cabernet Sauvignon, 10 per cent Merlot), both made at Bolgheri, near the northern Maremma coast, an area hitherto devoted entirely to Sangiovese and Trebbiano.

The new wines soon spread in range, reaching areas as distant from the original Chianti region as the western foothills of Mount Amiata and Montalcino. A number of the Super Tuscans have joined the Indicazione Geografica Tipica (IGT) category, some have continued to call themselves *vini da tavola*, and others still have achieved a more specific geographical identity of their own by associating with the newly created DOCs. Moreover, even the traditional native Sangiovese grape variety has proved to have plenty to say for itself, both on its own and in discerning combination with varieties from further afield.

REFINING THE FUTURE

Tuscan wines are currently more varied and interesting than ever before. This is partly thanks to a generation of younger winemakers who are opening up new vistas by fine-tuning a particular feature within a given DOC. Many of them are the offspring of the sharecrop farmers whose own winemaking methods were pretty much those of their medieval forebears. Better educated and travelled than their fathers, these youngsters have been keen to experiment with new clones, grape varieties, vinification methods and ageing techniques. At Bolgheri, Eugenio Campolmi's winery (**Le Macchiole**) has made quite a name for itself with Paleo, Messorio and Scrio, all excellent reds. Not far distant at Suvereto is Rita Tua's winery (called **Tua Rita**) that produces Redigaffi and Giusto di Notri, which practically have cult followings. Around Montalcino the number of *contadini* (peasant farmers, but the term has no negative connotations in Italian) who have become prestigious producers of Brunello is even greater: Giancarlo Pacenti at the winery that still bears his father's name (Pelagrilli di

Pacenti Siro); Paolo Bartolommei at the Caprili winery; Vincenzo Abbruzzese at Val di Cava; Giacomo Neri at Casanova di Neri, the Fattoi family and winery. All of these winemakers have enormously transcended their parents' horizons, but with touching respect for what their fathers have taught them.

Another interesting feature of Tuscan winemaking during the past few years has been the contribution of foreign winemakers who have settled in the region, learnt all they could from the local people and then added their own passion, expertise, individuality and insight to the business. Foremost among them is British born Sèan O'Callaghan at the **Riecine** winery outside Gaiole in Chianti. But well worth tracking down are also the young German lawyer-turned-winemaker Martin Frölich at the **Castagnoli** winery near Castellina in Chianti and the Frenchman Lionel Cousin, one time filmmaker, who in 2003 bottled his first Brunello at **Cupano**, his small organic winery near Montalcino. All three have an independence of spirit that finds its way into the bottle.

RICH PLOTS

The wine map of Tuscany is thus far more varied than a visit to a wine shop in the UK or US would ever lead you to believe. So rich, in fact, that Tuscany is at the forefront of *il turismo enogastronomico* (devoting part of your holiday to visiting wineries and sampling local foods) – over 90 per cent of Italy's wine and food tourism focuses on Tuscany. Such tourism is seen as eminently sustainable, as good for the visitor as it is for the local economy and a delightful way of getting to know the countryside as well as its products. To lure discerning palates to the lesser-known reaches of Tuscan viticulture the Movimento del Turismo del Vino (www.wineday.org) has helped set up and co-ordinate a number of specialised offices in most of the wine-producing areas. They are called **Strade del Vino** and organise guided tasting tours, visits to cellars, meals revolving around local produce and so on. Another event to look out for is Cantine Aperte, held on the last weekend of May, when wineries all over the region, and indeed the country, open their doors (and bottles) to visitors.

Visiting wineries entirely under your own steam can be both interesting and frustrating. While most welcome visitors if they are given due warning by phone, not all of them have a proper tasting facility, or staff who speak English, nor do they have the time to devote to this sort of PR. For our picks of wineries open to the public, *see pp232-3* **Visiting wineries**. Well-run local *enoteche* will be in a position to advise, both by providing a tasting experience on their own premises and by phoning their contacts in particular wineries. These wine shops are usually run by *appassionati* who will happily provide you with a number of glasses for a 'vertical' tasting of different vintages of the same wine, or a 'horizontal' tasting (no reference to your final posture) of wines of the same variety and/or year made by different producers. The *enoteche* also sell wine, by the case or as individual bottles. Prices may be higher than at the wineries, but then you may well find that the smaller wineries have no product left to sell, or are so far away that it's not worth the time and petrol slogging over there.

DRINKING OUT

The Strade del Vino di Toscana organisation is gradually working on restaurateurs to improve the level of wine expertise of their staff. In an expensive gourmet restaurant you're bound to find a waiter who really knows about the listed wines, but in simpler eateries this is not generally the case. Where suggestions are not readily to hand, you have three choices. You could arm yourself pre-emptively with the annually updated English edition of the generally reliable *Italian Wines Guide* published by Slow Food and Gambero Rosso and pick something from the wine list. You could choose a bottle made by one of the old established wine estates. Or you might discover what the local DOC is and opt for a medium-priced bottle, an approach that could lead to some gratifying discoveries. Clearly, if you are staying in a place for a number of days, it would be worth doing some agreeable groundwork in the local *enoteca*.

The finished product, ready for the shelves.

Accommodation

Accommodation 46

Features

A breath of fresh air 58

Accommodation

Here to stay.

In spite of a temporary let-up in overall hotel prices following the terrorist attacks of 11 September 2001, accommodation in Florence is still a very expensive business.

That said, there are some wonderful places to stay in the city and a refreshing absence of international chains. At the top end of the market are the new, sleek and oh-so-chic additions to the hip hotel scene and at the bottom are some fabulous, crumbling *palazzi* complete with bits of faded frescoes, wonky chandeliers and lumbering, rickety old furniture. In between are plenty of traditional, comfortable four- and five-star establishments, small boutique hotels, cheap-and-cheerful one- and two-star places and, another recent trend, a host of what call themselves B&Bs, but are in fact *affittacamere* (*see below*). Nevertheless, beware the bog-standard, over-priced establishments, of which there are still far too many.

Hotels in Italy are given a star rating from one to five, but this is an indication of the facilities on offer and nothing to do with standards. This means that there can be enormous disparity within any given category and so it really pays to shop around. The hotels in this guide have all been chosen for their value for money within their category or, simply, because they're great places to stay.

FACILITIES

Most hotels have their best and worst rooms. The best may be considered that way for various reasons ranging from size and shape, view, balcony/terrace or lack of it, natural light and furnishing style to size and type of bathroom. Usually there is a price difference. If you don't like the room you have been given, it is your right to refuse it and ask to see another one. Don't be put off by grumpy owners. By law hotels are required to display their official maximum room rates in each room. Check it out and if you feel you've been taken for a ride, there's an office for complaints (*see p294*).

If you're staying in the centre of the city during the summer months, look for a room with a private terrace or balcony (it will probably cost a bit more) or some kind of communal outside space. This can make a huge difference to be able to chill out alfresco with a Campari after a long hot day of sightseeing. Alternatively, head for the hills (*see p58* **A breath of fresh air**).

Very few hotels in the centre of town have their own parking facilities. However, there's nearly always a privately owned and probably very expensive garage nearby with which most hotels have some kind of an arrangement. Similarly, few have no-smoking rooms – although we have noticed a gradual improvement in this situation. Other improvements are being made in the way of facilities for the disabled and a law requires hotels of three stars upwards to have rooms with disabled access. But the law doesn't extend to all facilities. This results in the absurd situation where many rooms for the disabled are only accessible by a lift that's too narrow to take a wheelchair.

All rooms in the hotels in the luxury and expensive categories have their own TVs, phones and private bathrooms, but for rooms in moderate and budget categories, we list whether or not the rooms have them.

OTHER OPTIONS

If you prefer to self-cater, you could try a 'residence'. These offer apartments of varying sizes, usually in the same building, with some kind of concierge service. You can take them by the night or by the week and they're advertised in the free accommodation booklet produced by the APT tourist office, *Guida all' Ospitalità*. Otherwise there is the option of renting an apartment independently through an agency in Florence – some are listed below – or through websites or via ads in the UK press. In these cases the minimum stay, especially in high season, is usually a week.

Affittacamere (rooms for rent) often call themselves B&Bs and there has been a huge increase in the number of these since the last edition of this guide. They remain outside the official star classification as they have six rooms or fewer, which means that it's very difficult to judge on paper what the place is like. They vary from being a private house that rents a couple of rooms to something that is, to all intents and purposes, a hotel. Some are cheap and cheerful while others are quite upmarket. Their prices reflect the high-class standards. The best, a selection of which have been included below, offer a more personal, homely option than many hotels. Although they still remain a long way from the good old friendly British B&B.

ADVANCE BOOKINGS

Florence is busy most of the year, but there's particular demand for rooms from mid March to the end of June (Easter is the busiest weekend of the year) and in September. Christmas and New Year also pull in the crowds. Book well in advance at these times, but if you arrive with nowhere to stay, head for the **ITA** office in the station, which provides a booking service, or to one of the tourist offices that provide hotel lists though no booking service (*see p294*).

RATE RELATED

Many hotels slash their prices by as much as 50 per cent off season. Even outside these times it's worth haggling a bit over price as rates may be lowered if occupancy is down. This is especially true if you call to book last minute.

Prices given here (which are, of course, subject to change) are for rooms with en suite bathroom, unless otherwise stated, and include breakfast. We give the minimum to maximum rates throughout the year for each type of room. Most hotels will put at least one extra bed in a double room for a fee and many provide cots for which you may or may not have to pay extra.

The **APT** booklet *Guida all'Ospitalità* (*see p46*) lists hotels, *affittacamere*, residences, campsites and hostels in Florence and its province. It also gives a list of religious institutions called *case per ferie* that provide beds. These normally fairly cheap options are often single sex and have a curfew.

Duomo & Around

Luxury

Gallery Art Hotel

Vicolo dell'Oro 2 (055 27263/fax 055 268 557/www.lungarnohotels.com). **Rates** €226-€310 single; €264-€429 double; €473-€1,000 suite. **Credit** AmEx, MC, V. **Map** p314 C3.

Its East-meets-West design aesthetic was the talk of the town when it opened back in 1999, but Florence's original hip hotel is no longer the only trendy kid on the block. Located in a tiny piazza right near the Ponte Vecchio, the Gallery has a cosy library with squashy sofas and lots of arty books to browse and a stylish fusion bar that serves *aperitivi*, brunch, light lunch and dinner and has regular live music. The ground-floor public rooms often double as a showspace for contemporary artists and photographers. Bedrooms are businesslike but super-comfy, and the bathrooms are a dream. The penthouse suite has two terraces with stunning views.

Hotel services *Babysitting. Bar. Car park (nearby garage, extra charge). Fax. Laundry. Lift. No-smoking rooms. Restaurant.* **Room services** *Air-conditioning. Dataport. Hairdryer. Minibar. Room service. Safe. TV (satellite).*

Helvetia & Bristol

Via dei Pescioni 2 (055 287 814/fax 055 288 353/www.charminghotels.it). **Rates** €266 single; €312-€420 double; €430-€1,150 suite; €26 breakfast. **Credit** AmEx, DC, MC, V. **Map** p314 B3.

With Stravinsky, Gabriele d'Annunzio, Pirandello and Bertrand Russell among past guests, the Helvetia & Bristol has a distinguished history and has long been considered one of Florence's best hotels. Despite its 70-odd rooms and suites, it has the feel of a small-ish establishment and manages to be exclusive without being stuffy. The salon has a fireplace and velvet sofas and armchairs. In this age of minimalist design, the sumptuous decor in the bedrooms may be too much for some with swathes of ornate fabrics everywhere, but there are some gorgeous antiques and it's truly a luxury experience. The elegant restaurant serves above-average food at above-average prices; breakfast and lunch are served in the delightful Winter Garden.

Hotel services *Bar. Car park (nearby garage, extra charge). Fax. Laundry. Lift. No-smoking rooms. Restaurant.* **Room services** *Air-conditioning. Hairdryer. Jacuzzi (some rooms). Minibar. Radio. Room service (24hr). Safe. TV (satellite). Video.*

Hotel Continentale

Vicolo dell'Oro 6r (055 27262/www.lungarnohotels.com). **Rates** €185-€227 single; €265-€409 double; €730-€909 suite. **Credit** AmEx, DC, MC, V. **Map** p314 C3.

The latest of the Ferragamo family's hotel projects opened in January 2003. Situated across a little piazzetta from its sister, the Gallery (*see above*), the 'superior' bedrooms have full-on views of the river and the Ponte Vecchio. The architect and designer is the same Michele Bonan who worked on the Gallery. However, this place has a very different feel to it. While the common denominator is contemporary style, the Continentale is more feminine. Its decor is blond wood, off-white upholstery, filmy white curtains, huge glass vases, candles, pools of light and no fuss. Bedrooms feature four-posters and the bathrooms are extraordinary. One of the best places to chill out is the designated Relax Room on the first floor where light filters through slatted blinds and day beds allow a horizontal view of the crowds milling across the bridge. The penthouse suite at the top is, needless to say, spectacular and there's a fabulous roof terrace.

Hotel services *Babysitting. Bar. Car park (nearby garage, extra charge). Fax. Fitness centre. Laundry. Lift. No-smoking rooms.* **Room services** *Air-conditioning. Dataport. Hairdryer. Minibar. Radio/CD player. Room service. Safe. TV (satellite).*

The Savoy

Piazza della Repubblica 7 (055 283 313/fax 055 284 840/www.hotelsavoy.com). **Rates** €315-€500 double; €900-€1,375 suite. **Credit** AmEx, DC, JCB, MC, V. **Map** p314 B3.

Now owned by the Rocco Forte group, which was responsible for the multi-million-pound refurbishment carried out at the end of the '90s, the

Savoy is one of Florence's grand, historic hotels. Rocco Forte's sister, Olga Polizzi, is responsible for the cool, modern elegance of the decor. Some might find this a little soulless, but it's popular with the hotel's business clientele and many well-heeled tourists. The bar/bistro with tables out in the piazza is great for people-watching.
Hotel services *Babysitting. Bar. Car park (nearby garage, extra charge). Conference facilities. Fax. Laundry. Lifts. Restaurant.* **Room services** *Air-conditioning. Dataport. Hairdryer. Minibar. Radio. Room service (24hr). Safe. TV (satellite).*

Expensive

B&B Piazza Signoria

Via dei Magazzini 2 (39 055 239 9546/www.inpiazza dellasignoria.it). **Rates** €190-€240 double; €260-€350 suite; €1,200 per wk for an apartment. **Credit** AmEx, DC, MC, V. **Map** p315 C4.
This upmarket B&B just on the edge of Florence's most famous square opened in mid 2001. The nine comfortable bedrooms and three self-catering apartments are arranged on three floors and most have a view, albeit oblique, of the piazza. B&B Piazza Signoria is tastefully furnished in a fairly traditional style without being too fussy: canopied beds (including two wrought iron four-posters), oriental rugs, elegant fabrics and pastel-coloured walls. Smart bathrooms are done in travertine tiles and one has a jacuzzi. Breakfast is served at a big oval table or in the rooms.
Hotel services *Air-conditioning. Free bar service. Laundry. Lift. No-smoking rooms.* **Room services** *Air-conditioning. Car park (nearby garage, extra charge). Dataport. Hairdryer. Safe. Telephone. TV (satellite).*

Beacci Tornabuoni

Via Tornabuoni 3 (055 212 645/fax 055 283 594/www.bthotel.it). **Rates** €125-€155 single; €185-€240 double; €320-€350 suite. **Credit** AmEx, DC, JCB, MC, V. **Map** p314 B2/3.
Although this hotel is situated in the midst of Florence's designer shopping heaven and has a thoroughly modern entrance hall and lift, it has a real Edwardian feel inside. The Beacci Tornabuoni occupies the top two floors of the 15th-century Palazzo Minerbetti Strozzi. There's a wonderful flower-filled roof garden, which is used for meals in summer, while inside the old parquet floors creak and groan amid the kind of furniture you would normally expect to find at your grandma's. One of the nicest areas is the lovely, old-fashioned reading room, which smells of a mix of floor wax and wood smoke – there's a huge old *pietra serena* fireplace. It's beautifully maintained and very comfortable with loads of character.
Hotel services *Babysitting. Bar. Car park (nearby garage, extra charge). Conference facilities. Dataport. Fax. Laundry. Lifts. Restaurant. Roof garden.* **Room services** *Air-conditioning. Hairdryer. Minibar. Room service (24hr). Safe. TV (satellite).*

Dali

Via dell'Oriuolo 17 (tel/fax 055 234 0706/www.hoteldali.com). **Rates** €40 single; €60-€75 double; €80-€95 triple. **Credit** MC, V. **Map** p315 B4.
A mere pigeon's glide from the great apse of the Duomo, this little hotel is a real gem. Run with genuine care by an enthusiastic young couple, it offers spotless, bright and homely rooms at budget prices and – a miracle in central Florence – free car parking in the internal courtyard below. Four of the ten rooms have private bathrooms, but all are thoughtfully decorated and furnished with hand stencilling, pretty bedcovers and old bedheads. Rooms at the back, overlooking the courtyard, are sunny and quiet, while from the front rooms you can see Brunelleschi's cupola if you lean out. Breakfast is not provided.
Hotel services *Car parking (free). Laundry. Lift.* **Room services** *Fans. Fridges.*

Guelfo Bianco

Via C Cavour 29 (055 288 330/fax 055 295 203/www.ilguelfobianco.it). **Rates** €100-€135 single; €150-€235 double; €180-€265 triple; €200-€258 family; €350-€420 apartment. **Credit** AmEx, MC, V. **Map** p315 A5.
The owner of this pleasant and efficiently run hotel has recently developed a passion for modern art and his notable collection now adorns the walls of the two adjacent 15th-century houses, which make up this hotel and contain the 43 comfortable bedrooms. Some of the rooms are really big, allowing for an extra two beds. Those on via Cavour are soundproofed, but the ones at the back are quieter. There's also a two-bedroom self-catering apartment and two attractive courtyards offer respite from city noise.
Hotel services *Babysitting. Bar. Bicycle hire. Car park (nearby garage, extra charge). Dataport. Fax. Laundry. Lift. No-smoking rooms.* **Room services** *Air-conditioning. Dataport (some rooms). Hairdryer. Minibar. Radio. Room service. Safe. TV (satellite).*

Hermitage

Vicolo Marzio 1, Piazza del Pesce (055 287 216/fax 055 212 208/www.hermitagehotel.com). **Rates** €154-€221 single; €171-€245 double; €192-€275 triple. **Credit** MC, V. **Map** p314 C3.
One of the classic choices in the boutique category, this delightful little hotel, with its superb location practically on top of the Ponte Vecchio, warm welcome and superior facilities, is always popular. In summer, breakfast on the plant-filled roof garden is a must. The reception and public rooms are on the top floors with the comfortable bedrooms (some rather small) on the lower four floors. Jacuzzi baths and showers have recently been installed in all the rooms and the decor has been jazzed up a bit. The rooms at the front have the view, but can be noisy. Prices are a little above average for three stars. Probably worth it, though.
Hotel services *Babysitting. Bar. Car park (nearby garage, extra charge). Fax. Laundry. Lift. No-smoking rooms. Roof garden.* **Room services** *Air-conditioning. Hairdryer. Jacuzzi (8 rooms). Room service. Safe. TV (satellite).*

Relais degli Uffizi

Chiasso de' Baroncelli/Chiasso del Buco 16 (055 267 6239/fax 055 265 7909/www.relaisuffizi.it). **Rates** €120-€160 single; €140-€180 double; €180-€220 suite. **Credit** AmEx, DC, MC, V. **Map** p315 C4.

It's easy to get lost among the warren of passageways that leads off the south side of piazza della Signoria, and there is no helpful sign to guide you to this small hotel. Once inside, however, make a beeline for the comfortable sitting room, which has a fabulous view over the piazza. The ten bedrooms are situated on two floors and vary in terms of shape and size, but all are tastefully decorated and furnished; pastel colours on the walls, a mix of antique and traditional Florentine painted pieces and original features such as boxed ceilings and creaky parquet floors.

Hotel services *Air-conditioning. Car park (nearby garage, extra charge). Dataport. Fax. Laundry. Lift.* **Room services** *Air-conditioning. Hairdryer. Phone. Minibar. Room service. Safe. TV.*

Torre Guelfa

Borgo SS Apostoli 8 (055 239 6338/fax 055 239 8577/www.hoteltorreguelfa.com). **Rates** €110 single; €140-€210 double. **Credit** AmEx, JCB, MC, V. **Map** p314 C3.

This very pleasant hotel inhabits an ancient palazzo and boasts the tallest privately owned tower in the city, from which the 360-degree views are stunning. Bedrooms are decorated in pastel colours with wrought iron beds (there are several four-posters), white cotton curtains and hand-painted furniture; and one has its own roof garden. The six rooms on the first floor are cheaper, simpler, don't have TV and are a bit dark. It's popular with the fashion-show crowd.

Hotel services *Bar. Car park (nearby garage, extra charge). Fax. Laundry. Lift. No-smoking rooms. Dataport. Terrace.* **Room services** *Air-conditioning. Hairdryer. Minibar. Room service. TV (satellite).*

Moderate

Alessandra

Borgo SS Apostoli 17 (055 283 438/282 156/fax 055 210 619/www.hotelalessandra.com). **Rates** €67-€108 single; €108-€145 double; €160-€260 suite. **Credit** AmEx, MC, V. **Map** p314 C3.

Under the enthusiastic eye of the owner's son Andrea, improvements are continually made to this modest hotel on the second and third floors of an old palazzo that is well located on a quiet backstreet between Santa Trinità and the Ponte Vecchio. A couple of quite snazzy 'suites' have been added, one of which is a two-bedroom apartment with a terrace and view of the river. The best of the rest of the rooms (15 of which are no-smoking) are quite spacious, with antiques and polished parquet floors. All but eight have bathrooms.

Hotel services *Babysitting. Currency exchange. Dataport. Fax. Laundry. Lift.* **Room services** *Air-conditioning (all but 4 rooms). Dataport. Hairdryer. Phone. Room service. Safe (some rooms). TV (satellite).*

Casci

Via C Cavour 13 (055 211 686/fax 055 239 6461/www.hotelcasci.com). **Rates** €60-€100 single; €90-€140 double; €120-€180 triple; €150-€220 quad; €170-€260 family room. Closed 3wks Jan. **Credit** AmEx, DC, JCB, MC, V. **Map** p315 A4.

You're assured of a friendly welcome by the delightful Lombardi family in this cheerful *pensione* housed in a 15th-century palazzo. There are 25 bedrooms, all with new bathrooms. Those at the back look on to a beautiful garden. Two big family rooms sleep up to five. The breakfast room and bar have frescoed ceilings and shelves stocked with guidebooks.

Hotel services *Babysitting. Bar. Car park (nearby garage, extra charge). Currency exchange. Dataport. Fax. Laundry. Lift.* **Room services** *Air-conditioning. Dataport. Fridge. Hairdryer. Radio. Room service. Safe. Telephone. TV (satellite).*

Dei Mori

Via D Alighieri 12 (tel/fax 055 211 438/www.bnb.it/deimori). **Rates** €80-€100 single; €90-€110 double; reduced rates for longer stays. **Credit** AmEx, MC, V. **Map** p315 B4.

Florence is now snowed under with B&Bs, but this welcoming 15th-century townhouse was one of the first. Bedrooms on the second floor have been smartened and have gained private bathrooms, rooms on the first floor are more traditional. The owners welcome guests into their hotel as they might friends into their home – think fresh flowers, bright rugs, cheerful paintings and a comfy sitting room with TV, stereo and lots of books and magazines. Nice touches (unusual at this price) include feather duvets and dressing gowns on request. There's also a terrace from which you can just see the top of the Duomo.

Hotel services *Air-conditioning. Fax. No-smoking hotel. Terrace.* **Room services** *Air-conditioning. Dataport. Hairdryer (on request). Phone. Safe (some rooms). Room service.*

Hotel Maxim

Via dei Medici 4 (055 217 474/fax 055 283 729/www.hotelmaximfirenze.it). **Rates** €60-€78 single; €83-€103 double; €103-€125 triple; €125-€148 quad. **Credit** AmEx, MC, V. **Map** p314 B4.

This little hotel situated on one of the city's main shopping drags has taken a step up from its rather shabby origins and now offers comfortable accommodation at a good price. The modern two- and three-bed rooms are well furnished with cherrywood pieces and have private baths – one even has a jacuzzi. There's also a welcoming reception area.

Hotel services *Car park (nearby garage, extra charge). Dataport. Fax. Lift.* **Room services** *Air-conditioning. Hairdryer (some rooms). Phone.*

Budget

Scoti

Via dei Tornabuoni 7 (tel/fax 055 292 128/www.hotelscoti.com). **Rates** €60 single; €85 double; €105 triple; €125 quad. **Credit** AmEx, DC, JCB, MC, V. **Map** p314 B2/C2.

The elegant **Loggiato dei Serviti**. *See p54*.

Book well ahead for a room in the wonderful Scoti. Extensive building work has added simple but stylish touches to this characterful building and, what's more, prices remain low given its prime location. Situated on the second floor of a 15th-century palazzo, the lofty, airy rooms (now all with bathrooms) are painted a pale buttermilk and the sun filters through tall windows with diaphanous curtains. Bedheads are in cast iron and there are some nice pieces of old furniture dotted around. Thankfully, the frescoed salon hasn't changed and the same goes for the helpful owners. Breakfast served on request.
Hotel services *Lift. Safe.*

Santa Maria Novella

Luxury

Excelsior

Piazza Ognissanti 3 (055 264 201/fax 055 210 278/www.westin.com/excelsiorflorence). **Rates** €373-€497 single; €515-€745 double; €1,209-€3,691 suite; €94 supplement for river view; €45 breakfast. **Credit** AmEx, DC, JCB, MC, V. **Map** p314 B1.
More old world in style than the Grand (*see below*) across the square, the Excelsior offers luxury without pomp. A green-liveried doorman will guide you inside through a lovely old revolving door to the grand public rooms with their polished marble floors, neo-classical columns, painted wooden ceilings and stained glass. A '50s-style bar makes a cosy spot for an evening drink. The 168 rooms and suites are sumptuously appointed; some boast terraces with views over the river to the rooftops of Oltrarno. Popular with upmarket tour groups.
Hotel services *Babysitting. Bar. Car park (nearby garage, extra charge). Conference facilities (up to 180). Dataport. Fax. Laundry. Lifts. No-smoking rooms. Restaurant.* **Room services** *Air-conditioning. Dataport. Hairdryer. Minibar. Radio. Room service (24hr). Safe. TV (satellite).*

Grand Hotel

Piazza Ognissanti 1 (055 288 781/fax 055 217 400/www.luxurycollection.com/grandflorence).
Rates €376-€506 single; €519-€759 double; €1,231-€2,785 suite; €94 supplement for river view; €47 breakfast. **Credit** AmEx, DC, JCB, MC, V. **Map** p314 B1.
Smaller than its sister hotel, the Excelsior across the piazza, the Grand is equal in grandeur but different in character. Renovated in the mid '90s, this place is unashamedly luxurious. The vast hall, with its stained-glass ceiling, marble floor, *pietra serena* columns, brocades, statues and palms, contains a restaurant, bar, salon and piano bar. Less oppressive is the new restaurant off the lobby, InCanto, which serves a modern take on Tuscan food in a contemporary setting. About half of the 107 bedrooms and suites are done up in Renaissance Florentine style complete with frescoes, painted ceilings and gorgeous traditional fabrics.
Hotel services *Babysitting. Bar. Car park (nearby garage, extra charge). Conference facilities (up to 250). Fax. Laundry. Lifts. No-smoking rooms. Restaurant.* **Room services** *Air-conditioning. Dataport. Hairdryer. Minibar. Radio. Room service (24hr). Safe. TV (satellite).*

Expensive

Aprile

Via della Scala 6 (055 216 237/289 147/fax 055 280 947/www.hotelaprile.it). **Rates** €80-€120 single; €130-€180 double; €166-€230 triple; €215 suite. **Credit** AmEx, JCB, MC, V. **Map** p314 A1/B2.
The bust of Cosimo I above the entrance of the Aprile is a reminder that this building was once a Medici palace. Conveniently placed for the station, it has a comfortable, old-fashioned feel to it in spite of recent renovation work. The bedrooms vary hugely – some feature frescoes or scraps of 15th-century graffiti while others have superb

views over the convent of Santa Maria Novella. New coats of paint, in some cases in sunny yellow or seaside blue, have cheered the whole place up a bit. Rooms in the adjacent palazzo have an altogether more modern feel. The bar and breakfast room have frescoed ceilings, and there's a pretty, jasmine-scented courtyard garden. Aprile lays on a few thoughtful extras including free lectures on Florentine art and history in English.
Hotel services *Babysitting. Bar. Car park (nearby garage, extra charge). Dataport. Fax. Laundry. Lift. Safe.* **Room services** *Air-conditioning. Hairdryer (most rooms). Minibar. Room service. TV (satellite).*

Grand Hotel Minerva

Piazza Santa Maria Novella 16 (055 27230/fax 055 26828/www.grandhotelminerva.com). **Rates** €212-€250 single; €276-€350 double; €340-€700 suite. **Credit** AmEx, DC, JCB, MC, V. **Map** p314 B2.
The Minerva is probably the nicest hotel in its category and is very close to the train station. Overlooking the mess of piazza di Santa Maria Novella and the glories of its church's façade, the hotel is more upbeat than most traditional four-star places. Once an annexe hosting guests to the adjacent convent, it has been a hotel since around 1850, but the interior was revamped in the mid '90s in bright, modern colours and today it's staffed by a young, dynamic team. Many of the comfortable rooms have sunny views over the square, while unusual extras include electric kettles in rooms, special goodies for women travelling alone, and an in-house shiatsu masseuse. The roof terrace enjoys a 360-degree view of the city and there's a small pool up there too. So make the most of it and cool off after a hard day's sightseeing.
Hotel services *Air-conditioning. Babysitting. Bar. Car park (nearby, extra charge). Fax. Laundry. Lift. Restaurant.* **Room services** *Air-conditioning. Dataport. Hairdryer. Minibar. Safe. TV (satellite).*

J K Place

Piazza di Santa Maria Novella 7 (39 055 264 5181/www.jkplace.com). **Rates** €350-€470 double; €610-€740 suite. **Credit** AmEx, DC, EC, MC, V. **Map** p314 B2.
This latest in a recent wave of design hotels in Florence occupies an attractive old townhouse on piazza Santa Maria Novella. The architect is Michele Bonan (of Continentale and Gallery fame – for both, *see p47*), but this is a little different from the other hotels. The style is a contemporary take on a neo-classical mixed with Empire look. Muted colours beautifully offset some gorgeous antiques, old prints, black and white photos, artful flower and plant arrangements. Bedrooms are quite sober (some are a bit pokey) but lack nothing in the way of comfort or facilities. The penthouse suite on the top floor has a bathroom with a spectacular view over the whole of the city.
Hotel services *Air-conditioning. Laundry. Library. Lift.* **Room services** *Air-conditioning. CD/DVD player. Dataport. Fax. Hairdryer. Minibar. Safe. TV (satellite).*

Budget

Abaco

Via dei Banchi 1 (055 238 1919/fax 055 282 289/www.abaco-hotel.it). **Rates** €65-€90 double; €5 breakfast. **Credit** AmEx, MC, V. **Map** p314 B2.
There's a bit of a climb up to the second floor of this 1450 building where you will find a modest hotel in a grandiose shell. The friendly, helpful owner has painstakingly decorated his little hotel in grand style. The bedrooms, which are each named after a Renaissance artist, are done out in sumptuous fabrics with reproductions of works by the relevant artist on the walls. Gilding adorns picture and mirror frames and most of the beds are crowned with a *baldacchino*. The tiniest room (a twin room) has an enormous, beautifully carved *pietra serena* fireplace. Three rooms have their own full bathrooms, while others just have a shower. Breakfast's free if you pay your bill in cash.
Hotel services *Car park (nearby extra charge). Dataport. Laundry.* **Room services** *Air-conditioning (extra charge). Phone. TV.*

Locanda degli Artisti

Via Faenza 56 (055 213 806). **Rates** €39-€50 single; €65-€90 double; €110 suite. **Credit** AmEx, MC, V. **Map** p314 A2/3.
Effectively two separate hotels housed in the same rambling palazzo near the station, Locanda degli Artisti's ground and first floors are given over to an interesting, comfortable little hotel with very reasonable prices. It has an alternative feel to it (natural colours and materials, organic produce on the breakfast tray), plus there's a sauna, a lovely sunny terrace and, at the time of writing, talk of hosting art shows and live music. On the top floor, what was once the one-star Paola has remained just that with simple but clean rooms – the best of which have great views towards Fiesole. None of the rooms has a private bathroom and the lower prices quoted above apply to the Paola.
Hotel services *Car park (nearby garage, extra charge). Safe.*

San Lorenzo

Expensive

Palazzo Castiglioni

Via del Giglio 8 (055 214 886/fax 055 274 0521/www.florenceby/palazzocastiglioni). **Rates** €155 double; €196.50 suite. **No credit cards**. **Map** p314 A3.
This little guesthouse, located near San Lorenzo market and on the second floor of a 16th-century palazzo is under the same management as the Torre Guelfa (*see p50*). In fact, Palazzo Castiglione feels more like an elegant private apartment than a hotel with its reception area doubling as a breakfast and sitting room, and six individually

Le Stanze di Santa Croce. *See p55.*

decorated and comfortable bedrooms, half of which have elaborate frescoes. One is painted entirely as a *trompe-l'œil* of a fortified castle courtyard.
Hotel services *Babysitter. Bar. Car park (nearby garage, extra charge). Laundry. Lift. No-smoking rooms.* **Room services** *Air-conditioning. Dataport. Hairdryer. Minibar. TV.*

Moderate

Bellettini

Via dei Conti 7 (055 213 561/282 980/fax 055 283 551/www.hotelbellettini.com). **Rates** €95-€110 single; €130-€160 double. **Credit** AmEx, DC, MC, V. **Map** p314 A3/B3.
This bustling hotel near the Medici chapels and San Lorenzo is still good value for money. Dating from the 15th century, it holds one of the oldest hotel licences in the city. The warm owner is eager to please, offering amusements for bored children, a theatre-booking service and travel arrangements. The 27 rooms are quite smart. Although they are a little more expensive, the rooms in the annexe round the corner with their elegant fabrics, striking colours and soft lighting are still a bargain.
Hotel services *Babysitting. Bar. Car park (nearby garage, extra charge). Currency exchange. Fax. Laundry. Lift (to 1st floor). No-smoking rooms.* **Room services** *Air-conditioning. Minibar. Room service. Safe.Telephone. TV (satellite).*

San Marco

Expensive

Loggiato dei Serviti

Piazza SS Annunziata 3 (055 289 592/fax 055 289 595/www.loggiatodeiservitihotel.it). **Rates** €100-€140 single; €140-€205 double; €470 suite. **Credit** AmEx, DC, JCB, MC, V. **Map** p314 A5.
This is certainly one of the nicest three-star hotels in Florence. Looking across lovely piazza Santissima Annunziata to Brunelleschi's famous portico, it occupies an old 16th-century convent. Its interior tastefully combines original architectural features and wonderful antique furniture with the comforts of an upmarket hotel. The 29 bedrooms vary in size and style and the four suites are ideal for families. Breakfast is served in a bright, elegant room with vaulted ceilings. There's an additional cosy bar area.
Hotel services *Babysitting. Bar. Car park (nearby garage, extra charge). Fax. Laundry. Lift.* **Room services** *Air-conditioning. Dataport. Hairdryer. Minibar. Radio. Room service (24hr). Safe. TV (satellite).*

Moderate

B&B Borgo Pinti

Borgo Pinti 31, San Marco/Santa Croce (055 248 0056/fax 055 238 1260/www.bnb.it/beb). **Rates** €42-€47 single; €75-€83 double. **Credit** MC, V. **Map** p315 A6/B5.
Florence's tiny women-only, no-smoking guest house is a simple but stylish retreat from the city heat and dust. The four rooms, decorated in cool white and blue, on the top floor of a palazzo are airy and quiet with views over an internal garden and surrounding rooftops. The two communal bathrooms are spotless. Breakfast is help-yourself.

Hotel delle Arti

Via dei Servi 38A (055 267 8553/fax 055 290 140/www.hoteldellearti.it). **Rates** €113-€139 single; €144-€185 double. **Credit** AmEx, DC, MC, V. **Map** p315 A4.
Since summer 2002 this hotel has been under the same ownership as the Loggiato dei Serviti, but while it has been decorated with taste and style, it's a simpler place and the look's much more rustic. The nine bedrooms are painted in restful shades of green and cream with wood floors. They are furnished with pine pieces, including a couple of four-poster beds, while checked fabrics complete the unfussy country look. The three corner rooms are particularly spacious and light. There's a pretty breakfast room with a wraparound terrace.
Hotel services *Air-conditioning. Babysitting. Car park (nearby, extra charge). Dataport. Fax. Laundry. Lift. No-smoking rooms.* **Room services** *Air-conditioning. Dataport. Hairdryer. Minibar. TV (satellite). Room service. Safe.*

Morandi alla Crocetta

Via Laura 50 (055 234 4747/fax 055 248 0954/ www.hotelmorandi.it). **Rates** €90-€110 single; €140-€170 double; €180-€220 triple; €11 breakfast. **Credit** AmEx, DC, MC, V. **Map** p315 A5/6.
Book well in advance for a bed in this quiet ten-room hotel housed in a former 16th-century convent in the university area. Morandi alla Crocetta offers comfortable accommodation at reasonable prices. The owners have introduced a touch of variety, with each room different from the next. One has bits of fresco, while two others have private terraces. You've got to book years ahead if you want one of these though. The place is filled with antiques, oriental rugs and interesting pictures. Friendly and helpful staff.
Hotel services *Babysitting. Bar. Car park (nearby garage, extra charge). Fax. Laundry.* **Room services** *Air-conditioning. Dataport. Minibar. Radio. Room service. Safe. TV (satellite).*

Residenza Johlea Uno & Johlea Due

Via San Gallo 76 & 80 (055 463 3292/fax 055 463 4552/www.johanna.it). **Rates** €70 single; €90-€100 double. **No credit cards**. **Map** p315 A4.
There are now four hotels in this mini-chain of *residenza* run by a team who strive to offer value for money. They achieve this in Johlea Uno and Johlea Due, which share the same telephone numbers, booking desk and are only two doors apart on the same street. Only ten minutes' walk from the Duomo, they occupy what were elegant private apartments. Standards of comfort and service are those of a three-star hotel – rooms are decorated in soft pastel colours, furnished partly with antiques and have excellent bathrooms. Breakfast arrives on elegant lacquered trays. Johlea Uno has a cosy little upstairs sitting room with an 'honesty fridge' and a roof terrace with a 360-degree city view.
Hotel services *Lift. Roof terrace.* **Room services** *Air-conditioning. Hairdryer. Kettle. Safe. TV.*

Santa Croce

Luxury

J & J

Via di Mezzo 20 (055 234 5005/fax 055 240 282/ www.jandjhotel.com). **Rates** €268-€300 double; €352-€435 suite. **Credit** AmEx, DC, MC, V. **Map** p315 B6.
The simple façade of this former convent gives little clue as to the luxurious accommodation that lies within. Many original architectural features are visible in the bedrooms and public areas, and in the cool arched cloister where breakfast is served in summer. Opened in the early '90s ,this was one of the very first boutique hotels in Florence and the decor, while still tasteful and in good nick, is beginning to look a bit dated. No two bedrooms are alike – some are huge, with split levels and seating areas – but all feature antiques, rich fabrics and immaculate bathrooms. Slight doubts about the style aside, J & J is supremely comfortable and discreet. Its only serious defect is that it has lots of steep stairs and no lift.
Hotel services *Babysitting. Bar. Car park (nearby garage, extra charge). Fax. Laundry. No-smoking rooms.* **Room services** *Air-conditioning. Dataport. Hairdryer. Minibar. Room service. Safe. TV (satellite).*

Expensive

Le Stanze di Santa Croce

Via delle Pinzochere 6 (055 200 1366/www. viapinzochere6.it). **Rates** €130 single; €160 double. **Credit** MC, V. **Map** p315 C5.
The trend towards upmarket B&Bs is gaining ground in Florence and the Stanze di Santa Croce is an example of how it should be done properly. For a start, the location of this sweet little three-floor townhouse couldn't be better and, once there, you'll find it a really welcoming place to stay. The four comfortable double bedrooms are individually furnished with pretty fabrics, lively colours and a mix of old and new furniture; one has a romantic wrought iron four-poster. There's delightful a flower-filled terrace where breakfast is served plus dinner on request. Guests can hang out here all day and help themselves from a well-stocked 'honesty fridge'.
Hotel services *Air-conditioning. Terrace.* **Room services** *Air-conditioning. Dataport. Hairdryer. Safe.*

Moderate

Liana

Via Alfieri 18 (055 245 303/fax 055 234 4596/ www.hotelliana.com). **Rates** €50-€130 single; €70-€170 double; €90-€220 triple; €110-€280 quad. **Credit** AmEx, DC, MC, V.
Once the British Embassy, this 19th-century house is worth considering if you're travelling by car and would like to be within reach of the sights, but not in the centre. A great job has been done of redecorating and generally raising standards to transform the Liana from a crumbling two-star to a very pleasant three-star hotel. Faded frescoes have been restored and the place is filled with antiques, fresh flowers and stylish fabrics. Rooms, some of which have balconies overlooking the garden, are now comfortable and elegant, especially in the case of the spacious, so-called Consul's Room. Classical music is played in the first-floor breakfast room. Look out for the special offers.
Hotel services *Babysitting. Bar. Car park (extra charge). Fax. Garden. Hairdryer. Laundry. Safe.* **Room services** *Air-conditioning. Hairdryer (on request). Minibar (in some rooms). Room service. TV (satellite).*

Budget

Bavaria

Borgo degli Albizi 26 (tel/fax 055 234 0313/ www.welcomehotels.info). **Rates** €50 single; €72-€98 double. **No credit cards. Map** p315 B4/5.

Another one-star hotel that was pretty mediocre until new management recently breathed fresh life into it. Housed on the second floor of grand 16th-century Ramirez Montalvo (built by Ammannati and with a decorated façade attributed to Vasari), the fabulous box wood ceilings have all been sandblasted, the scruffy and dated wallpaper has been replaced with sand-coloured paint, floor tiles have been laid where there was nasty cheap carpeting and the lumbering old furniture has been tarted up. It's still a modest hotel (only three of the rooms have private baths) but it now has some style.

Hotel services *Bar. Dataport. Fax. Hairdryer. Safe.*

Hotel Orchidea

Borgo degli Albizi 11 (tel/fax 055 248 0346). **Rates** €40-€50 single; €60-€70 double; €80-€100 triple. **No credit cards. Map** p314 B4/5.

Dante's wife Beatrice was born in the 12th-century palazzo that houses the simple, cosy Orchidea with its seven bright, clean rooms, the best of which overlook a wonderful overgrown garden. The whole place has been given a facelift recently and the rooms are now all done out in dusty pink and white. Only one room has a shower, but all have wash basins, while the rest share two communal bathrooms. Friendly Anglo-Italian owners.

Hotel services *Hairdryer. Lift. Phone. Safe.*
Room services *Fan.*

Oltrarno

Luxury

Lungarno

Borgo San Jacopo 14 (055 27261/fax 055 268 437/www.lungarnohotels.com). **Rates** €213 single; €350-€440 double; €681-€909 suite. **Credit** AmEx, DC, JCB, MC, V. **Map** p314 C2/3.

The most coveted rooms in this recently refurbished hotel in the smart part of the Oltrarno have terraces overlooking the Arno. Much more classic in feel than the other Ferragamo-owned hotels (the Gallery and the Continentale), this 1960s building incorporates a medieval tower. The lounge-bar has huge windows taking advantage of the waterside setting, as does the elegant ground-floor restaurant. There's a little outside seating area right on the river too. The colour scheme throughout is cream with navy blue trimmings, but some lovely mahogany and cherry antique furniture plus a collection of fine pictures and prints on the walls lend a reassuringly traditional touch. Bedrooms are stylish and comfy but, with the exception of a couple of spacious suites, not that big.

Hotel services *Bar. Babysitting. Car park (nearby garage, extra charge). Fax. Laundry. Lifts. No-smoking rooms. Restaurant.* **Room services** *Air-conditioning. Dataport (some rooms). Hairdryer. Minibar. Radio. Room service. Safe. TV (satellite).*

Palazzo Magnani Feroni

Borgo San Frediano 5 (055 239 9544/fax 055 608 908/www.florencepalace.it). **Rates** €210-€750 suite. **Credit** AmEx, DC, MC, V. **Map** p314 C1.

As small, upmarket hotels go this elegant suite-only palazzo just south of the river is about as good as they come: expect top-class facilities and service combined with the atmosphere of a Renaissance palace. The ten suites all have separate sitting rooms furnished with squashy sofas, armchairs and antiques. There's also a romantic junior suite with floor-to-ceiling frescoes and a little private garden. Bathrooms are super-smart and superbly equipped with slippers, robes and heated towel rails – you can even choose the smell of your soap. The fabulous roof terrace offers views of the whole city.

Hotel services *Air-conditioning. Bar. Billiard Room. Garage. Gym. Laundry. Lift. Terrace.*
Room services *Air-conditioning. Dataport. Hairdryer. Minibar. Room service (24 hrs). Safe. TV (satellite).*

Moderate

Annalena

Via Romana 34 (055 222 439/fax 055 222 403/ www.hotelannalena.it). **Rates** €90-€114 single; €126-€166 double; €162-€212 triple. **Credit** AmEx, DC, MC, V. **Map** p314 D1.

The 15th-century building that houses this hotel has an interesting history. Annalena, a young Florentine noblewoman, inherited the house from the Medici, but tragic circumstances obliged her to donate it to nuns to use as a refuge for young widows. During the Mussolini years refugees from the Fascist police were lodged here. The atmosphere remains pleasingly old-fashioned (the comfortable rooms are mostly furnished with antiques and some are very spacious) despite recent upgrading of facilities by the new management. The best rooms have balconies overlooking the gorgeous Annalena gardens.

Hotel services *Bar. Fax. Laundry. Safe.*
Room services *Air-conditioning (some). Hairdryer. Minibar. Room service. TV (satellite).*

Hotel Boboli

Via Romana 63 (055 229 8645/fax 055 233 7169/ www.hotelboboli.com). **Rates** €93 single; €130 double. **Credit** MC, V. **Map** p314 D1.

This perfectly adequate little hotel near the Boboli Gardens changed management in 2001 and is being spruced up. The cramped public space on the ground floor is due to be expanded during winter 2003 and a year after that a much-needed lift will be put in. Until then, there's a steep climb up to the sunniest of the pleasant rooms on the fourth floor.

Comfortable opulence at **Palazzo Magnani Feroni**. *See p56.*

About half the rooms overlook an interior courtyard and are very quiet; others overlook the Boboli Gardens. The bathrooms, some of which are only big enough to swing a small mouse in, are also due for an update.

Hotel services *Bar. Car park (nearby garage, extra charge). Fax.* **Room services** *Dataport. Hairdryer (on request). Phone. TV.*

La Scaletta

Via de' Guicciardini 13 (055 283 028/055 214 255/fax 055 289 562/www.lascaletta.com). **Rates** €80-€95 single; €100-€135 double; €150-€160 triple; €160-€175 quad; €15 dinner. **Credit** MC, JCB, V. **Map** p314 D2/3.

The 15th-century building that houses this 16-room, two-star hotel is near the Boboli Gardens (over which the back rooms have wonderful views) and it has a delightful roof garden. It's a simple, friendly place with a lived-in feel. Recent improvements have resulted in bathrooms in all but one double and brighter colours and air-conditioning in most rooms – but you'll only want one of the dismal rooms in the newly opened *affittacamere* annexe if you're really desperate. Rooms on the noisy via de' Guicciardini have double-glazing. A good, cheap evening meal is available on request.

Hotel services *Babysitting. Bar. Car park (garage nearby, extra charge). Currency exchange. Fax. Lift. Restaurant. Roof garden. Safe.* **Room services** *Air-conditioning. Hairdryer. Phone. Room service.*

Sorelle Bandini

Piazza Santo Spirito 9 (055 215 308/fax 055 282 761/pensionebandini@tiscali.it). **Rates** €108-€130 double; €148-€178 triple. **No credit cards**. **Map** p314 D1/2.

The eccentric Sorelle Bandini occupies the top floor of Renaissance palazzo Guardagni, which stands on lovely, lively piazza Santo Spirito. Its charm lies in its setting and a sense that little has changed since the Bandini sisters opened it in the early 20th century. The loggia that runs along two sides of the building (room four has direct access) makes up for the dilapidated interior with its faded mirrors, dusty chandeliers and lumbering old furniture. The owners stick doggedly to the one-star formula but make the odd improvement such as new bathrooms and fresh paintwork. They are gradually restoring some of the furniture too. Prices are high for the category.

Hotel services *Currency exchange. Fax. Lift. Safe. Terrace.* **Room services** *Hairdryer. Phone. Fan. Room service (breakfast).*

A breath of fresh air

There's a flip side to every coin; the very physical characteristic that locks in the exhaust fumes and makes Florence so unbearably hot and humid in the summer – its immediate surrounding hills – means that there is fresh air and surprisingly rural surroundings to be had within a very short hop of the city centre. So if you are visiting in the summer months and want to stay in a place where you can breathe something other than traffic smog, escape the hordes and look out of your bedroom window on to a background of cypresses with a soundtrack of twittering birds thrown in, you really don't have to go very far. All of the hotels featured below have gardens and/or terraces, views of either the city or surrounding countryside, most have swimming pools and even the occasional tennis court. Some are on a local bus route while others provide transport for their guests into town. Of course, such luxuries come with a price tag and most of the below are in the higher prices categories.

Bencistà

Via Benedetto di Maiano 4, Fiesole (tel/ fax 055 59163). Bus 7. **Rates** (per room, obligatory half-board) 95 single; 176 double; 10 full board extra per person. **No credit cards.**

This former convent, run as a *pensione* by the Simoni family since 1925, has an unparalleled setting on a hillside just below Fiesole and bags of atmosphere. Of the three salons furnished with antiques, one has a fireplace and shelves stuffed with some early editions of English books. The 47 bedrooms are arranged off a warren of passages and stone stairways; no two are alike, but all now have a private bathroom. Those at the front of the building enjoy fabulous city views. Room prices include either lunch or dinner in the restaurant overlooking Florence but the food is pretty average.

Hotel services *Bar service. Car park. Fax. Garden. Laundry. Lift. Restaurant. Safe. TV.* **Room services** *Hairdryer. Room service (breakfast only).*

Relais Marignolle

Via di San Quirichino a Marignolle 16, Outside the City Gates (055 228 6910/fax 055 204 7396). **Rates** 130- 215 single; 130- 255 double. **Credit** AmEx, MC, V.

The Bulleri family opened the converted outbuildings of their farmhouse to guests in 2000; the property (which includes a good pool) is set in rambling grounds on a south-facing hillside at Marignolle, about 4km (2.5 miles) south of Porta Romana. Sun pours into the large, bright living/breakfast room where comfortable armchairs and sofas, an open fire and an ''honesty bar' encourage you to linger. Bedrooms, while varying in shape and size, are all decorated along the same tasteful lines; stylish country fabrics, padded bed heads, pristine white paintwork and dark parquet floors. Signora Bulleri will serve a light lunch on request.

Hotel services *Garden. Pool. Car Park.* **Room services** *Air-conditioning. Dataport. Hairdryer. Minibar. Safe. TV (satellite).*

Budget

Istituto Gould

Via dei Serragli 49 (055 212 576/fax 055 280 274). **Open** *Office* 9am-1pm, 3-7pm Mon-Fri; 9am-1pm Sat. **Rates** €32-€38 single; €46-€50 double; €57-€66 triple; €76-€84 quad. **No credit cards. Map** p314 C1/D1.

Excellent budget accommodation in a well-kept 17th-century palazzo with a serene courtyard, stone staircases, terracotta floors, a tantalisingly lovely garden (unfortunately not accessible to guests) and lots of atmosphere. It's run by the Valdese Church and is popular so book well ahead. Recent improvements mean there are more rooms now, most of which are doubles, although there are still some three-, four- and multi-bedded rooms. All but seven have private bathrooms. If you want to avoid noisy via dei Serragli, ask for a room at the back where some have access to a terrace. You have to check in during office hours, but once that's done you get your own key.

Hotel services *No-smoking hotel. Safe (at reception).* **Room services** *Phone.*

Pensionato Pio X

Via dei Serragli 106 (055 225 044). **Rates** €18 single; €16 per person double, triple, quad & quin. **No credit cards. Map** p314 C1/D1.

Overseen by a venerable lady who seems rather stern but is actually charming, this Church-owned *pensione* in a 13th-century former convent is a quiet, pleasant alternative to a youth hostel. The two singles offer amazing value, but most of the rooms are three- and four-bed. There's a cheerful sitting room and a dining room where guests can picnic. Only two rooms have private bathrooms (and they

cost a little extra), but the communal showers are new and are spotless. There's a midnight curfew, but unlike most hostels the place is open all day. The minimum stay is two nights, the maximum five.
Hotel services *Hairdryer. No-smoking hotel. Safe. Vending machines.*

Outside the City Gates

Luxury

See also p58 **A breath of fresh air**.

Villa La Massa

Via della Massa 24 (055 62611/fax 055 633 102/ www.villalamassa.com). Complimentary shuttle from Ponte Vecchio. **Rates** €300-€410 single; €420-€550 double; €740-€1,100 suite. **Credit** AmEx, DC, MC, V.

This luxurious hotel enjoys an incomparable setting on the south bank of the Arno to the east of Florence. Occupying a mellow Renaissance villa, the place had slipped into decline before new management and a complete revamp recently brought it up to scratch again. It's elegant and discreet and much favoured by the celebrity circuit (David Bowie married Iman here and Madonna has stayed several times). The style is upmarket Tuscan. There are four-poster beds, antiques, frescoes, opulent fabrics and splendid bathrooms. The elegant restaurant serves appropriately high-class food to diners on a terrace overlooking the river in warm weather.
Hotel services *Air-conditioning. Bar. Conference facilities. Pool. Restaurant. Shuttle bus to Florence.*
Room services *Air-conditioning. Hairdryer. Minibar. Room service (24hrs). Safe. Telephone. TV.*

A breath of fresh air (continued)

Villa Belvedere

Via Benedetto Castelli 3, Outside the City Gates (055 222 501/222 502/fax 055 223 163/www.villa-belvedere.com). Bus 11, then 10min walk. **Rates** 130 single; 175- 207double; 260 suite. **Credit** AmEx, DC, MC, V.

Though located in an uninspiring '20s building and generally rather dated in style, the Belvedere is set in an attractive garden (gnomes and all) with a swimming pool on a quiet residential street above Porta Romana. A family-run hotel, it has 26 comfy, spacious rooms with parquet floors and wood furnishings. All have brand new bathrooms and some have terraces and wonderful city views. Prices are very reasonable for a four-star place, rooms are spotless and staff are extremely courteous. Closed winter.

Hotel services *Babysitting. Bar. Car park. Fax. Garden. Laundry. Lift. No-smoking rooms. Pool. Restaurant (light meals). Tennis court.* **Room services** *Air-conditioning. Dataport. Hairdryer. Room service. Safe. TV (satellite).*

Villa Poggio San Felice

Via San Matteo in Arcetri 24 , Outside the City Gates (055 220 016/fax 055 233 5388/www.villapoggiosanfelice.com). Free shuttle to city centre. **Rates** 200 double; 250 suite. **Credit** AmEx, DC, MC, V.

This mellow 15th-century villa in beautiful gardens in the hills behind Porta Romana was once the summer home of a Swiss hotel magnate; his descendants rescued the house from decay and now run it as a laid-back but classy B&B. The public rooms and bedrooms, decorated with taste and imagination, are full of family antiques and pictures. One bedroom has a big terrace. The cool, peaceful garden has city views and, with the recent addition of a small pool, why bother to move?

Hotel services *Babysitting. Bar. Car park. Garden. Fax. Laundry. Pool.* **Room services** *Air-conditioning. Dataport. Hairdryer (on request). Room service.*

Villa San Michele

Via Doccia 4, Outside the City Gates (055 59 451/fax 055 598 734/ www.orient/expresshotels.com). **Rates** 588 single; 766 double; 1,819-1,964 suite. 10% VAT on all room prices. **Credit** AmEx, DC, JCB, MC, V.

The rooms in this fabulous yet understated hotel, much beloved by the celeb circuit, are among the most expensive in Italy. Housed in a building dating from the 15th century that was originally a monastery, it enjoys a superb position nestled in a beautiful terraced garden on the hillside just below Fiesole. Luxurious, yes; ostentatious, never. Understated elegance and good taste combined with a subtle aura of the past inform the style throughout. The rooms are filled with gorgeous antiques that sit on well-worn tiled floors; the service is immaculate. Views down to the city, needless to say, are splendid; dinner under the loggia at sunset is an unforgettable experience, as is the bill. The hotel is closed from late November to mid March.

Hotel services *Bar. Car park. Garden. Gym. Pool. Restaurant.* **Room services** *Air-conditioning. Minibar. TV.*

Moderate

Cimabue

Via B Lupi 7 (055 471 989/fax 055 475 601/ www.hotelcimabue.it). Bus 11, 36, 37 to Piazza San Marco. **Rates** €70-€96 single; €80-€134 double; €110-€168 triple; €138-€194 quad. **Credit** AmEx, DC, MC, V.

The two-star Cimabue is at the upper end of its category thanks to the efforts of the welcoming Rossis. The 16 rooms (five with frescoes) have their own well-equipped bathrooms. Breakfast buffet is generous.

Hotel services *Babysitting. Bar. Car park (nearby garage, extra charge). Currency exchange. Fax.* **Room services** *Hairdryer. Phone. Room service. Safe. TV.*

Classic Hotel

Viale N Machiavelli 25 (055 229 351/fax 055 229 353/www.classichotel.it). Bus 11, 36, 37 to Porta Romana. **Rates** €108-€118 single; €156-€166 double; €216 suite. **Credit** AmEx, MC, V.

In a lush garden five minutes' walk south-west of the old city walls at Porta Romana, this attractive villa has been tastefully refurbished with pristine results. Breakfast is either served in a basement room or, more pleasantly, in a conservatory leading to a garden full of mature trees and shrubs. For romantics, an annexe suite with its own terrace is tucked away in a corner of the garden.

Hotel services *Babysitting. Bar. Car park. Fax. Garden. Laundry. Lift.* **Room services** *Air-conditioning. Dataport. Room service. Safe. TV.*

Budget

Residence Johanna

Via B Lupi 14 (055 481 896/fax 055 482 721/ www.johanna.it). Bus 1, 17 to Via Micheli, then 10min walk. **Rates** €48 single; €75 double. **No credit cards.**

The owners of this discreet home from home in the north of the city centre must be again congratulated for having kept prices down. They offer comfortable, stylish rooms at near rock-bottom rates. Breakfast is provided on a tray and there's a good supply of books and magazines. Neither single has a bathroom.

Hotel services *Car park (nearby garage, extra charge). Fax. Lift. Mobile phones for hire. Safe.* **Room services** *Kettle.*

Residence Johanna Cinque Giornate

Via delle Cinque Giornate 12 (055 473 377/ www.johanna.it). Bus 4, 28 to Via dello Statuto. **Rates** €80. **No credit cards.**

Under the same management as Residence Johanna (*see above*) and offering the same set-up, this small villa in a residential area north-west of the city centre has its own garden. Considering the low prices, which, like those at the owners' other hotel, have hardly gone up in the past couple of years, the six bedrooms are elegantly furnished and each has its own bathroom.

Hotel services *Car park. Fridge. Laundry (external).* **Room services** *Air-conditioning (some rooms). Hairdryer (on request). Kettle. TV.*

Hostels

Hostel Archi Rossi

Via Faenza 94r, Santa Maria Novella (055 290 804/fax 055 230 2601/www.hostelarchirossi.com). **Open** 6.30-11am, 2.30pm-2am daily. **Rates** €18-€23.50 per person; €23.50 dorm; from €8 dinner. **No credit cards**. **Map** p314 A2/3.

Hostel Archi Rossi is a mere ten minutes' walk from the station. The reception of this hostel is covered with garish modern renditions of famous frescoes, all of which have been done by guests. The hostel's rooms are spacious and light with a maximum of nine beds per room. Many of the rooms are smaller and some have bathrooms. Facilities for the disabled are unusually good and there's a lovely garden. The management allow mixed-sex rooms as long as everyone knows each other.

Services *Bar. Dataport. Hairdryer (on request). Laundry. Lift. No-smoking hostel. Restaurant. Terrace. Vending machines.*

Ostello per la Giovent (YHA)

Viale A Righi 2-4, Outside the City Gates (055 601 451/fax 055 610 300/www.iyhf.org). Bus 17A or 17B. **Rates** €16 per person in dorm; from €40 family rooms; €10 extra meals. **No credit cards.**

Not as central as other hostels but more pleasant in the heat, Ostello per la Giovent (YHA) lies just below Fiesole in an impressive setting with a loggia and ranks of lemon trees in its extensive grounds. Most beds are in dorms, but there are smaller rooms for families. There are also camping facilities at the YHA along with five bungalows that sleep up to two people. It's worth the 20-minute bus ride and the ensuing trek up the hill from the stop from the city centre if you want some peace. If you're a party-goer, bear in mind that the hostel has a midnight curfew.

Services *Bar. Disabled: toilet. Restaurant. TV.*

Santa Monaca

Via Santa Monaca 6, Oltrarno (055 268 338/fax 055 280 185/www.ostello.it). **Rates** €16 per person. **Credit** AmEx, DC, JCB, MC, V. **Map** p314 C1.

This 15th-century convent building is convenient for those wanting to stay south of the river. But it is a bit gloomy. In spite of some effort to make the rooms (sleeping from four to 22) a bit less crowded, too many of them still have too little light. Dispensers provide basic drinks, snacks and hot meals and there's a 1am curfew.

Services *Currency exchange. Dataport. Kitchen. Laundry. No-smoking hostel. Safe. TV.*

Campsites

Camping Michelangelo

Viale Michelangelo 80, Outside the City Gates (055 681 1977). Bus 12, 13. **Open** *Office* 7am-midnight daily. **Rates** €8 per person; €4.60 5-12s; free under-4s; €5 per tent; €10.70 per camper van; incl electricity. **No credit cards**.

Though noisy in summer (there's a disco till 1am) Camping Michelangelo has room for 240 tents/caravans and 960 people. The campsite has fabulous city views, a bar, restaurant and supermarket. It's situated just below piazzale Michelangelo and is within easy walking distance of the city centre. An ideal budget option.

Camping Panoramico

Via Peramondo 1, Outside the City Gates (055 599 069/fax 055 59186/www.florencecamping.com). Bus 7. **Open** *Office* 8am-10pm daily. **Rates** €9 per person; €14.50 per tent; €14.50 per camper van. **Credit** AmEx, MC, V (for payments above €52).

With some 120 pitches, this is probably the most picturesque site within easy reach of Florence – it's about 8km (five miles) north of the city centre. Camping Panoramico's facilities include a bar, restaurant, supermarket and pool. There are also 21 self-catering bungalows that sleep up to four as well as some caravans to rent. This popular place gets packed in summer.

Villa Camerata

Viale A Righi 2-4, Outside the City Gates (055 601 451/fax 055 610 300/www.iyhf.org). **Open** *Office* 7am-midnight daily. **Rates** €6 per person; €5/€11tent depending on size; €11 camper van; incl electricity. **No credit cards**.

Villa Camerata is located in the grounds of the YHA's Ostello per la Giovent (*see above*).

Long-term accommodation

Renting a flat through an agency inevitably involves commission charges. If you want to avoid this, your best bet is to look in the local press or in the UK newspapers' holiday sections and phone around to compare prices.

Florence & Abroad

Via San Zanobi 58, San Lorenzo (055 487 004/fax 055 490 143/www.florenceandabroad.com). **Open** 10am-5pm Mon-Fri. **No credit cards**.

If you're looking for a one-bedroom flat expect to pay €1,100-€2,600 for a month's holiday let. Otherwise prices start from about €600 (for a small *monolocale* or studio flat) to €1,000 and upwards for longer rentals in the city centre. This agency has English-speaking staff.

Milligan & Milligan Rentals

Via degli Alfani 68, San Marco (055 268 256/fax 055 268 260/www.italy-rentals.com). **Open** 9am-noon, 1-4pm Mon-Fri. **No credit cards**. **Map** p315 A4/5.

Staffed by English-speakers and specialising in student-type accommodation.

YAIF (Your Agency in Florence)

Piazza Santo Spirito 2r, Oltrarno (055 282 899/fax 055 267 9611/www.yaif.it). **Open** 11am-5pm Mon-Fri. **Credit** AmEx, DC, JCB, MC, V. **Map** p314 D1/2.

Finds modestly priced accommodation in the city.

Sightseeing

Introduction	**64**
Duomo & Around	**67**
Santa Maria Novella	**84**
San Lorenzo	**87**
San Marco	**90**
Santa Croce	**94**
Oltrarno	**98**
Outside the City Gates	**103**

Features

Holes in the wall	64
The best Sights	66
Holes in the wall	72
Walk 1 The beaten track	81
Holes in the wall	85
Holes in the wall	88
Holes in the wall	96
Walk 2 The green scene	100
Walk 3 On the up and up	104

Introduction

See the sights, steer clear of the culture vultures.

To set foot in Florence is to enter a time warp. There's no getting away from it; the city is living off its past as if it were Cairo or Pompeii. Despite the fervent protestations of the Florentines that theirs is a city for the new millennium, there's no fooling the millions of visitors who come here for one thing – the Renaissance art. Close your eyes and ears to the buzzing Vespas, the souvenir stands, the tour groups and the odd neon advertising sign, and you could easily be walking the same streets 500 years ago, devouring the same visual feast. Home to the Duomo, piazza della Signoria, the Uffizi and myriad masterpieces in conspicuous and hidden churches, major and minor museums and galleries, chapels and cloisters, grand *palazzi* and architectural gems in anonymous alleyways, the historic centre of Florence contains statistically more art treasures per square metre than any other city in the world.

ORIENTATION

The city centre is compact and manageable, and it's practically impossible to get lost, with the ever-visible dome of the Duomo and the River Arno and its four central bridges acting as reference points. The majority of the main sights and museums are clustered north of the two central bridges in the area around the Duomo, and most other important sites circling this rectangle in the Santa Maria Novella, San Lorenzo, San Marco, Santa Croce and Oltrarno zones. We've organised our sightseeing chapters (along with the divisions of many of our other chapters) into these areas, though be aware that in Florence nothing is very far from anything else. The main central area sits in the river valley, so is practically flat, while the surrounding hills rise steeply on both sides, creating challenging walks and rewarding views, easily accessible by foot or bus.

MUSEUMS AND GALLERIES

During the summer, around Easter and on public holidays, Florence spills over with visitors, so the sights are crowded and huge queues can form at the main museums. The best times to sightsee in relative ease are the in-between seasons, from January to March (avoiding Easter), and from mid September

Holes in the wall

The Italian tradition of creating shrines on street corners to the Madonna, Jesus or the saints, at which to leave flowers or light a candle, is particularly strong in Florence. Not that the city has ever been home to a higher than average proportion of devotees. Actually, this high concentration of conventicles is partly due to the early 14th-century episodes of armed conflict between the orthodox followers of the Church (epitomised by the Dominicans of Santa Maria Novella) and the so-called Patarine heretics, a Ghibelline-supported reform movement advocating action against corruption in the clergy and named after the street in Milan from where their most active members hailed.

To prove their devotion (and avoid the very nasty potential repercussions of being branded heretics), many individuals, trades, guilds and confraternities built tabernacles in conspicuous positions, most often on the corner of their home or centre. The tabernacle was usually built as an *edicola*, a frame for the icon itself, almost always made of stone and often with a protruding 'roof' to protect the artwork inside from the elements, and with a mantle on which to place offerings. The icon itself could be a fresco, painting, panel, relief, sculpture or tile, and sometimes famous artists were hired to create the venerable image and to boost the cachet of the sponsor in the eyes of the Church. The result is an art heritage of sometimes astonishing value, but so accessible as to risk appearing insignificant, leading to real masterpieces being left to decay (until, that is, a recent splurge of restorations organised by the Friends of the Florentine Museums).

Throughout the Sightseeing chapters, we have highlighted some of the more interesting tabernacles in a series of boxes: **Holes in the wall**.

Amid the churches and museums, the rus in urbe of the **Boboli Gardens**. *See p99.*

to mid December. If you're intending to visit all of the main museums, it could be worth aiming for the week when state museums give free entrance (*see p152*).

Many of Florence's unrivalled museum collections have private collections at their core, whether that of a mega-family such as the Medici (**Uffizi** and **Palazzo Pitti**) or of a lone connoisseur (Bardini, Horne and Stibbert museums), while other major museums were founded to preserve treasures too precious to expose to the elements (the **Accademia**, the **Bargello** and **Museo dell'Opera del Duomo**). Administratively, they fall into three categories: private, state or municipal. The main municipal museums are **Cappella Brancacci**, **Cenacolo di Santo Spirito**, **Museo di Firenze di com'era**, **Palazzo Vecchio**, **Collezione della Ragione** (now installed in a new home; *see p77*) and **Museo Bardini** (currently closed for restoration – call 055 276 8553 for updates).

For one week of the year ('Settimana dei Beni Culturali'), which varies but is generally in the spring, entrance to all the state museums is free. For general information on the state museums and for booking, call **Firenze Musei** on 055 294 883. The state museums are the Pitti museums (for which there is a three-day pass costing €10.50), the Uffizi, the Accademia, the Bargello, Museo di San Marco, Opificio delle Pietre Dure, Cappelle Medicee and Museo Archeologico.

Firenze Musei strongly recommends booking (call 055 294 883) for the Uffizi and the Accademia, and, at busy times of year, for the Pitti museums; this could save you a two-hour wait. Booking costs €3 and tickets are collected from a window beside the normal ticket office, or, in the case of the Palazzo Pitti, from an office in the right-hand wing before you reach the main entrance. Pay when you pick up the tickets. Don't expect to be able to book tickets there directly; you will be told to phone the central number. Last issuing times for tickets vary (and we have given the closing time in our listings, not last admission). Try to get to the ticket office an hour before the museum closes. The closing time for at least half of the city's

The best Sights

...for avoiding the crowds

Cenacolo di Sant' Apollonia (*see p89*).
Districts of **Santo Spirito** and **San Frediano** (for both, *see pp98-102*).
Giardino dei Semplici (*see p90*).
Santa Maria Maddalena de' Pazzi (*see p97*).
The village of **Settignano** near Fiesole (*see p106*).

...for bizarre and eccentric artefacts

Museo Stibbert (*see p104*).
La Specola (*see p102*).

...for frescoes

Brancacci Chapel (*see p102*).
Chapels of the Palazzo Vecchio (see *p79*).
Santa Croce (*see p97*).
Santa Maria Novella (*see p86*).

...for overall city views

Top of the **Campanile** (*see p69*).
Any of the vantage points in the charming hilltop town of **Fiesole** (*see p105*).
Piazzale Michelangelo (*see p98*).
San Miniato al Monte (*see p106*).

...for river views

Corridorio Vasariano at the point where it crosses the Ponte Vecchio (*see p77*).
Ponte Santa Trinità (*see p82*).
Ponte Vecchio (*see p75*).

museums is 1.50pm. Art lovers should also be aware that works of art are often lent to other museums or to exhibitions, and restoration can be carried out with little or no notice, so it's always a wise idea to call first if you want to view a specific piece. Otherwise, it is usually poosible to pick up a leaflet at the museum ticket office with a list of exhibits that are not currently on show.

Temporary exhibitions are regularly held at a few locations in Florence (which may mean an increase in the entry charge), among them Palazzo Vecchio, Palazzo Medici Riccardi and Palazzo Strozzi; see the magazine *Firenze Spettacolo* or the local newspapers for details.

MONDAY BLUES

For residents of larger cities it can be a shock – and a spanner in the planning works – to find that some of Florence's major museums close on Monday. These include the Uffizi, the Accademia and the Galleria del Palatina in the Palazzo Pitti. If you're lucky and it's the first, third or fifth Monday of the month, you could go to the Galleria dell'Arte Moderna, the Bargello or the Museo di San Marco, or if it's the second or fourth, the Capelle Medicee and the minor museums of the Palazzo Pitti. Or factor in a visit to a smaller, less intense museum or church: not a bad idea, anyway, given how easy it is to overload.

TOURIST INFORMATION

Finding out about the sights you're looking at, or how to get to them, has just got easier. Apart from the tourist offices (*see p294*), the city police have set up permanent info points in piazza della Repubblica, on via Calzaiuoli and at the southern end of the Ponte Vecchio, from where they give directions and basic information about the main sights in various languages. Another recent development is that many of the minor sights – churches, *palazzi* and monuments – now have signs posted beside them detailing their history and distinguishing features, making a DIY tour that bit easier. Also, big plaques with useful maps have been mounted in many squares and other strategic positions.

GUIDED TOURS

There's not a great deal to choose between Florence's various tour companies, all of which offer fairly standard itineraries with English-language options covering the main monuments and museums by foot or by bus. The highly reputable **Association of Tourist Guides** (055 210 641/www.florencetouristguides.com), the **Association of Florentine Tourist Guides** (055 422 0901/www.florenceguides.it) and the **Cultural Association of Guides** (055 787 7744/www.firenze-guide.com) all offer a vast selection of standard tours. Two firms that provide a little more variety are **Walking Tours of Florence** (055 264 5033/www.artviva.com), which offers a morning jaunt into Tuscany and a 'views tour', and **CAF** (055 283 2000/www.caftours.com), which runs a Florence by night tour. Prices obviously vary depending on the type of tour you choose, but you should expect to pay approximately €25 for a three-hour walk and €37 for a tour of a major museum, including admission.

If you prefer to do it yourself when it comes to sightseeing, the best ways in which to see the city are to hire a bike or moped, or to take a ride on the electric buses that cover the central areas of the city or to hire an electric golf cart (*see p282*).

Duomo & Around

Intoxicating or simply overwhelming? Join the crowds and see for yourself.

Florence's historic and religious heart stretches from the north side of the Duomo down to the riverbank, bordered by the exclusive designer shops of via dei Tornabuoni and the heavy, fortified *palazzi* and Gothic pride of via del Proconsolo.

Around piazza del Duomo

Standing majestically at the geographical centre of the *centro storico* of Florence is the splendid piazza del Duomo. The city's cathedral, the **Duomo**, its exterior inlaid with intricately patterned marble, soars above the surrounding buildings; it's so huge that there's no point nearby from which you can see the whole church, though a walk through the surrounding streets will be peppered with tantalising glimpses of its magnificent red-tiled dome. The square itself is thronged with visitors in awe of the cathedral's magnitude. The areas outside the entrance and around the south of the Duomo are pedestrianised, while mopeds and buses roar around the north and east sides.

Directly west of the Duomo, piazza San Giovanni, named after John the Baptist, skirts his **Baptistery**; it also houses the tiny **Museo di Bigallo** (for both, *see p71*). West of the Baptistery is the busy shopping street and main traffic thoroughfare via dei Cerretani with its 11th-century parish church Santa Maria Maggiore. Following the curve of the piazza on the north side of the Duomo, the **Museo dell'Opera del Duomo** (*see p71*), which houses the treasures of the Duomo, is on the north-east of the piazza. Leading south from the façade of the Duomo is via dei Calzaiuoli, a heaving pedestrian shopping street flanked by self-service restaurants, shops and *gelaterie*. Running down from the south-west corner of the **Baptistery** is the more upmarket via Roma, which opens into the pompous **piazza della Repubblica**.

This rather ungainly piazza was built in 1882 when the ancient heart of Florence, the so-called Mercato Vecchio ('old market', and part of the Jewish ghetto), was demolished and replaced in a massive urban clean-up following a cholera outbreak. Now the only remnant from before that time is the Colonna dell'Abbondanza, which used to mark the spot where two principal Roman roads crossed – it was reinstated to its original position after World War II. Vasari's delightful Loggia del Pesce, with its ceramic marine creature *Tondi*, was once the central meeting place of the square. Later it was moved to piazza dei Ciompi where it overlooks the flea market. In the medieval period the area covered by the piazza was given over to a huge market where you could change money, buy a hawk or falcon, pay over the odds for a quack remedy, or pick up a prostitute (distinguished by the bells on their hats and gloves). Further back, the ancient Roman Forum once occupied a quarter of the piazza and the Campidoglio and Temple of Jupiter covered the rest. This suntrap piazza is now flanked by pavement cafés, and dominated at night by street artists and strollers.

Duomo

Ufficio del Duomo (055 230 2885). **Open** 10am-5pm Mon, Wed, Fri; 10am-3.30pm Thur; 10am-4.45pm Sat; 1.30-4.45pm Sun. *Also* 10am-3.30pm 1st Sat of mth. **Admission** free. **Map** p315 B4.

In the 13th century a hugely successful and expanding wool industry gave the Florentine population such a boost that several new churches had to be built, among them Santa Croce and Santa Maria Novella, but most important of all Santa Maria del Fiore, or the Duomo, which replaced the small church of Santa Reparata (*see p68*). The construction was commissioned by the Florentine Republic, who saw the project as an opportunity to show Florence as indisputably the most important Tuscan city. A competition held to find an architect was won by Arnolfo di Cambio, a sculptor from Pisa who had trained with Nicola Pisano. The first stones were laid on 8 September 1296 around the exterior of Santa Reparata. Building continued for the next 170 years with the guidance and revision of three further architects, though the church was consecrated 30 years before its completion in 1436. The rich exterior, in white Carrara, green Prato and red Maremma marbles, clearly shows the huge variation over the time of the building, in the styles of its inlaid patterns. The visionary Francesco Talenti had sufficient confidence to enlarge the cathedral and prepare the building for Brunelleschi's inspired dome. The last significant change came in the 19th century when Emilio de Fabris designed a neo-Gothic façade to replace the bland temporary façade. When Luigi del Moro took over the project after the death of de Fabris, the problem arose of how to crown the façade.

Some wanted the fussy cuspidal spires of the Siena Duomo, others a flat balustraded balcony. Each solution was built *in situ* to show Florentines how it would look, and a referendum was held to decide the outcome. Happily, the balconies outvoted the spires.

After the splendour of the exterior, the interior looks somewhat dull, though decorating the world's fourth largest cathedral was never going to be easy. It's actually full of fascinating peculiarities, notably the clock on the Paolo Uccello inner façade, which marks 24 hours, operates anti-clockwise and starts its days at sunset (it's between four and six hours fast). The clock is surrounded by the so-called *Heads of the Prophets* peering out from four roundels and showing the distinct influences of Ghiberti and Donatello in their perspective. Also by Uccello is a monument to English mercenary Sir John Hawkwood, painted in 1436 as a tribute to the soldier leading Florentine troops to victory in the Battle of Cascina of 1364. The fresco has given rise to many a debate about whether his perspective and the movement of the horse's right legs are simply wrong, or the result of Uccello's original treatment of the rules of perspective construction, learnt from Masaccio and considered by some to be visionary and even a forerunner to Cubism. Andrea del Castagno's echo monument to Niccolù da Tolentino, painted in 1456 and illustrating the heroic characteristics of a Renaissance man, forsakes perspective play for line. Beyond is Domenico di Michelino's *Dante Explaining the Divine Comedy*, featuring the poet in pink and the new Duomo vying for prominence with the Mountain of Purgatory.

A couple of strides forward and across put you directly underneath the dome, the size of which is possibly even more breathtaking inside than out. The lantern in the centre is 90m (295ft) above you and the diameter of the inner dome is 43m (141ft) across, housing within it one of the largest frescoed surfaces in the world. Brunelleschi had intended that the inner cupola be mosaic, so it would mirror the Baptistery ceiling, but interior work only began some 125 years after his death in 1572 when Cosimo de' Medici commissioned Giorgio Vasari to carry out the work, and together with Don Vincenzo Borghini, who was responsible for choosing the iconographic subjects, they decided instead to fresco the surface. The concentric rows of images were started by Vasari, whose subtle treatment of colour and form drew inspiration from Michelangelo's Sistine Chapel, but he died two years later and was succeeded by Federico Zuccari who worked for a further five years until its completion. Zuccari had a much more flamboyant, and crude, dry-painting style, believing that the distance from which the visitor would view the cupola wasted the delicacy of Vasari's wet fresco technique, especially as his own repertoire of faces included some of the best-known personalities of the time and he wanted to make them as visible as possible to reap the rewards of their gratitude. Zuccari's most important contribution to the cycle is the rendering of Dante's vision of Hell clearly inspired by Signorelli's frescoes in Orvieto Cathedral.

Crypt of Santa Reparata

Duomo (055 230 2885). **Open** 10am-5pm Mon-Fri; 10am-4.45pm Sat. *Also* 10am-4pm 1st Sat of mth. **Admission** €3. **No credit cards**. **Map** p315 B4.

The crypt and some ruins of the medieval structure of the original fifth-century church of Santa Reparata can still be seen – the entrance is inside the Duomo itself. The intricate original mosaic floor of the church was built only 30cm (11.8in) above the Roman remains of houses and shops, some of which are on display in the crypt. Also here is the tomb of Brunelleschi, although no trace of those of Arnolfo di Cambio and Giotto, supposedly buried here too, has ever been found. Local legend has it that some of the land needed for the building of the much bigger Duomo was occupied by the Florentine Bischeri family, who, when they continued to refuse the ever bigger sums of money they were offered to relocate, were unceremoniously kicked out of their palazzo with no compensation. This lead to the widely used derogatory Florentine expression *bischero* (a gullible fool).

Cupola/Dome

Open 8.30am-7pm Mon-Fri; 8.30am-5.40pm Sat. *Also* 8.30am-4pm 1st Sat of mth. **Admission** €6. **No credit cards**. **Map** p315 B4.

The Duomo's most celebrated feature needs distance to be able to fully appreciate the way in which it towers above the city – it is, as Alberti put it, 'large enough to cover every Tuscan with its shadow'. But the dome is not just visually stunning, it's also an incredible feat of engineering, thanks to Brunelleschi. He dreamed of completing the cupola since childhood and studied architecture in Rome with just that in mind. Brunelleschi won his dream commission with the more experienced Lorenzo Ghiberti, who was riding on the back of his success with the Baptistery doors, but soon found that while he was doing the important work Ghiberti was taking all the glory. He pulled a sickie, bringing work to a halt, and got the recognition he deserved.

At first Brunelleschi considered designing the classic semi-spherical dome used in existing churches around Italy, but the sheer size of the structure precluded the traditional method of laying tree-trunks across the diameter to build around. The idea was toyed with of filling the space up with earth and building up around it, then sprinkling the earth with gold florins in order to encourage locals to take it away, a tactic that was successfully used for the outside ramps. In the end a revolutionary design for an elongated dome was followed. Brunelleschi made the dome support itself by building two shells, one on top of the other, and more importantly, by laying the bricks in herringbone-pattern rings to integrate successive layers that could consequently support themselves. The design was so efficient that it risked becoming a victim of its own success; the ribs around the dome were in danger of 'springing' open at the top, so a much heavier lantern than normal was

The Duomo's **Baptistery**. *See p71*.

designed, to hold the ribs in place. As innovative as the design were the tools used and the organisation of the work: Brunelleschi designed pulley systems to winch materials, and workers, up to the dome. Between the two shells of the dome he installed a canteen so the workforce wouldn't waste time going to ground level to eat, bringing construction time down to a mere 16 years (1420-36). A separate side entrance gives access to the top of the dome (463 steps, about 20 minutes up and down) with fantastic city views.

Campanile
Open 8.30am-7.30pm daily. **Admission** €6.
No credit cards. **Map** p315 B4.

The Campanile – the cathedral's bell tower – was designed by Giotto in 1334, though his plans weren't followed faithfully (the original drawing, held in the Museo dell'Opera Metropolitana in Siena, can be seen on request). Andrea Pisano, who continued the work three years after Giotto's death, took the precaution of doubling the thickness of the walls, while Francesco Talenti, who saw the building to completion in 1359, inserted the large windows high up the tower. Inlaid, like the Duomo, with pretty pink, white and green marble, the Campanile is decorated with 16 sculptures of prophets, patriarchs and pagans (if you want to see the originals, they're in the Museo dell'Opera del Duomo, *see p71*), bas-reliefs designed by Giotto and artfully executed by Pisano recounting the *Creation* and *Fall of Man* and his *Redemption Through Industry*; look carefully and you'll make out Eve emerging from Adam's side and a drunken Noah. On three floors with 413 steps, the Campanile offers great views of the Duomo and the city from its terrace at the top.

Baptistery
Open noon-7pm Mon-Sat; 8.30am-2pm Sun. **Admission** 3. **No credit cards. Map** p315 B4.
For centuries, Florentines (including such well-educated characters as Brunelleschi and Alberti) believed the Baptistery was converted from an ancient Roman temple dedicated to Mars. This is counterpoised by the belief of many other scholars that the Roman site on which the octagonal church was undoubtedly built was the Praetorium, while others believe its ancient origins were as a simple bakery. The Baptistery of St John the Baptist was built to an octagonal design between 1059 and 1128 as a remodelling of a sixth- or seventh-century version, in between which times it functioned for a period as the cathedral for Florence, then Florentia, in the place of Santa Repararta, the church on which the Duomo now stands. The octagon reappears most obviously in the shape of the cathedral dome, but also on the buttresses of the Campanile, which constitute its corners. Today, the striped octagon is best known for its gilded bronze doors, though the interior is worth visiting for the vibrant *Last Judgement* mosaic lining the vault ceiling with the 8m (26ft) high mosaic figure of *Christ in Judgement* dominating the apse. The mosaics depicting Hell are reputed to have inspired Dante's own version. In the 1330s Andrea Pisano completed the south doors, with 28 Gothic quatrefoil-framed panels depicting stories from the life of St John the Baptist and the eight theological and cardinal virtues.

In the winter of 1400, the Calimala cloth-importers' guild held a competition to find an artist to create a pair of bronze doors for the north entrance and, having seen pieces by Brunelleschi, Ghiberti and five others, gave the commission to Ghiberti, then just 20 years old. Brunelleschi and Ghiberti's long-running colleague rivalry would later see the former draw the score with his superior work on the cupola. Relief panels on the doors displaying a masterful use of perspective retell the story of Christ from the Annunciation to the Crucifixion, while the eight lower panels show the four evangelists and four doctors. Many art buffs consider these north doors to contain the very first signs of Renaissance art with deep pictorial space and an emphasis on figures. No sooner had the north doors been installed than the Calimala commissioned Ghiberti to make another pair, the even more remarkable east doors, known (since Michelangelo coined the phrase) as the *Gates of Paradise* in deference to the innovation and brilliance of their execution. The doors you see here are copies (the originals are in the Museo dell'Opera del Duomo, *see below*) but the casts are fine enough to appreciate Ghiberti's stunning work.

Museo dell'Opera del Duomo

Piazza Duomo 9 (055 230 2885/ www.operaduomo.firenze.it). **Open** 9am-7.30pm Mon-Sat; 9am-1.40pm Sun. **Admission** 6. **No credit cards. Map** p315 B4.
One of the most interesting (and underrated) museums in the city, the Museum of the Cathedral Works contains tools and machinery used to build the Duomo, the original wood models of the cupola, and sculptures and artwork from the Duomo complex deemed too precious and vulnerable to be left to the mercy of the elements.

On the ground floor under the glass roof of the courtyard are eight of the ten original east Baptistery bronze door panels, the so-called *Porta del Paradiso* (*Gates of Paradise*) sculpted by Lorenzo Ghiberti over the 27 years between 1425 and 1452 and considered by some to be the work of art that initiated the Renaissance. When the two remaining panels have been restored, the doors will be recomposed and displayed in their original splendour. In the first rooms leading to the courtyard are Gothic sculptures from the exteriors of the Baptistery and the original but never-finished Duomo façade including a classical-style *Madonna* with unsettling glass eyes by Arnolfo di Cambio. There are also pieces from Santa Reparata, the earlier church on the site of the Duomo.

Halfway up the stairs is the *Pietà Bandini*, a heart-rending late work by Michelangelo showing Christ slithering from the grasp of Nicodemus. The sculpture was intended as Michelangelo's tombstone, and he sculpted his own features on the face of Nicodemus, showing how his lifelong obsession with the story of the pietà had become too much for him to bear. In true tortured-artist style, frustrated and dissatisfied with the piece, he smashed Christ's left arm, and it was supposedly left to his servant to pick up the fragments and save the masterpiece.

Upstairs in a newly built corridor are the brick stamps and forms, the pulleys and ropes by which building materials (and workers) were winched up to the dome. In the room on the right is Donatello's emotive wood sculpture of a distraught Mary Magdalene, dishevelled and ugly, with coarse, dirty hair so realistic you can almost smell it. The originals of his Prophets from the exterior of the Campanile are also here, notably *Habbakuk* (bald, emancipated, caught in vision), another work of such realism that Donatello himself is said to have gripped it and screamed, 'Speak, speak, speak!'

After the emotion of the Michelangelo and Donatellos it's almost a relief to turn to the light, joyful *cantorie* (choir lofts). One is by Donatello, with cavorting *putti* (small, angelic boys); the other, by Luca della Robbia, is full of angel musicians. Beyond are bas-reliefs carved by Giotto for the Campanile.

Museo di Bigallo

Piazza San Giovanni 1 (055 230 2885). **Open** 8am-noon Mon; 4-6pm Thur. **Admission** 3. **No credit cards. Map** p314 B3.
The city's tiniest museum is in a beautiful Gothic loggia built in 1358 for the Misericordia, which was a charitable organisation that cared for unwanted children and plague victims. The loggia was later

Holes in the wall

Via Arte della Lana corner Via di Orsanmichele

A stunning Gothic example with its spiral columns, pointed arch and family crest decorations, and a long and complex history, the Madonna of the Trumpet tabernacle started life in the 13th century on the corner of the Old Market and Calimala, housing the supposedly miracle-working Madonna painting, later destroyed by fire. The panel that replaced it in 1335, *Enthroned Madonna and Child, Saints John the Baptist and John the Evangelist* and angels by Lacopo di Casentino, and the *Coronation of the Virgin and Saints* by Niccolò di Pietro Gerini (added in 1380) both had colourful pasts, passing through the Uffizi or the Museo di San Marco and back, each time the church or corner home of the tabernacle was destroyed and it was dismantled or reassembled. In 1905 it was finally installed on the corner of the Palazzo dell'Arte della Lana.

renovated for another fraternity, the Bigallo, and the Misericordia moved to piazza del Duomo (No.19), from where it still works as a voluntary ambulance and medical service. The main room has frescoes depicting the work of the two fraternities, though the two scenes on the left wall as you enter were badly damaged while being transferred from the façade in the 18th century. The *Madonna della Misericordia*, a fresco of 1342 from the workshop of Bernardo Daddi, a pupil of Giotto, has the Virgin suspended above the earliest known depiction of Florence, showing the Baptistery, the original Arnolfo façade to the domeless Duomo over the original church of Santa Reparata with its two bell towers, and an incomplete Campanile.

Around piazza della Signoria

Florence's civic showpiece piazza is dominated by the crenellated and corbelled **Palazzo Vecchio** (formerly Palazzo della Signoria, *see p79*), built at the end of the 13th century as the seat of the Signoria, the top tier of the city's government. The piazza della Signoria itself started life in 1268, when the Guelphs regained control from the Ghibellines, and demolished their rivals' 36 houses in the area, leaving neighbouring houses intact, hence the unusual asymmetrical shape of the piazza. Over the next few centuries the square remained the focus of civic, though not necessarily civilised, activity; life in medieval Florence was beset with political and personal vendettas. And it didn't take much to ignite a crowd: on one occasion in the 14th century a scrap in the piazza led to a man being eaten by the mob.

It was in this piazza that the religious and political reformer Girolamo Savonarola lit his Bonfire of the Vanities in 1497, throwing on to it all the trappings of culture and wealth that he and his followers could muster, many donated by such luminaries as Botticelli and Fra Bartolomeo. Savonarola ended up burned at the stake on 23 May 1498, on the exact spot of his prophetic bonfire a year earlier (marked by a plaque in front of the *Neptune* fountain); the fickle people of the city who had cheered on the book-burning frenzy had soon tired of the puritan behaviour expected of them and bayed for the blood of the monk. When Botticelli wrote to one of Savonarola's justiciaries asking for an explanation, the reply was simply, 'The people wanted blood – it was us or him.'

However, the piazza was also the seat of civic defence. Whenever Florence was threatened by an external enemy, the bell of the Palazzo della Signoria (known as the *Vacca*, or cow, after its moo-ing tone) was tolled to summon the citizens' militia. Part of the militia's training

A copy of Michelangelo's *David* dominates **Piazza della Signoria**.

included playing *calcio* on the piazza – a quasi-homicidal version of rugby still played in piazza Santa Croce every June.

In the mid 1980s it was decided that the piazza's ancient paving stones should be taken up and restored. The state-run Sovrintendenza dei Beni Archeologici, which oversees the city's archaeological works, took the opportunity to carry out excavations on the area. In the course of the work the ruins of 12th-century Florence were discovered beneath the piazza, built over the thermal baths of Roman Florentia and parts of the Etruscans' outpost. The powers that be ordered further excavation of the ruins and there was talk of the site becoming an underground museum. But local government objected, fearing the showpiece piazza would become a building site and so lose valuable tourist income. The result was a shambles. The company taken on to restore the ancient slabs apparently catalogued the position of the stones using nothing more permanent (or, indeed, weatherproof) than chalk, which was washed away on the first rainy day. It also managed to 'lose' some of the slabs, now rumoured to grace the courtyards of various Tuscan villas. Given that most of Florence lies over the ruins of the Roman city, the decision to replace the paving with artificially aged stones and reseal the Roman site was predictable.

Dominating the piazza are a copy of Michelangelo's *David* and an equestrian bronze of Cosimo I by Giambologna, notable mainly for the horse that was cast as a single piece in a purpose-built foundry. Giambologna also created sexy nymphs and satyrs for Ammanati's *Neptune* fountain, a Mannerist monstrosity of which Michelangelo is reputed to have said, 'Ammanato, Ammanato, che bel marmo ha rovinato' or 'Ammanati, what beautiful marble you have ruined.' Even Ammanati eventually admitted the piece was a failure, in part because the block of marble used for *Neptune* lacked width, forcing him to give the god narrow shoulders and keep his right arm close to his body. Beyond are copies of Donatello's *Marzocco* (the original of the city's heraldic lion, one of Florence's oldest emblems, is in the Bargello) and his *Judith and Holofernes* (the original is in the Palazzo Vecchio). Judith, like David, was a symbol of the power of the people over tyrannical rulers: a Jewish widow who inveigled her way into the camp of Holofernes, Israel's enemy, she got the man drunk and then sliced off his head.

Beyond *David* is *Hercules and Cacus* by Bandinelli, much ridiculed by the exacting Florentines and described by rival sculptor Benvenuto Cellini as a 'sack of melons'. The marble block it's carved from fell into the river in transit to Bandinelli's workshop, hence the joke that it had tried to commit suicide. On one of the cornerstones at the edge of the Palazzo Vecchio nearest the Loggia is the etched graffiti of a hawk-nosed man said to be a tongue-in-cheek self-portrait by Leonardo, keen to leave his mark.

Cellini himself is represented by another monster-killer, a fabulous *Perseus* holding the snaky head of Medusa, standing victorious in the adjacent **Loggia dei Lanzi**. The recently restored bronze is testament to the artist's pig-headed determination. It was considered

Residenza dei Pucci
Via dei Pucci 9 (055 281886 fax 055 264314)
http://residenzapucci.interfree.it

Rates Single € 70,00 - 130,00 Double € 80,00 -145,00 Suite € 120,00 - 233,00 **Credit** AmEx, Visa, MC

Residenza dei Pucci is located in the heart of Florence, only a few steps far from the Duomo, Accademia, the central food market and all the most important museums and munuments of the city.

In an elegant 19th century building, 12 luxurious rooms, that have just been renovated , await our Guests. Every room is furnished in a different manner in soothing earth tones, with taste and great care given to details. We also have a spacious suite, with a breathtaking view on the Duomo, that can accomodate up to four people.

Hotel services *Car park (nearby garage with pick-up service, extra charge), iron, fax (on request), laundry service (nearby, extra charge)*
Room services *private bathroom with shower or bath-tub (on request), air-conditioning, TV, hairdryer.*

impossible to cast the head of the Medusa in Perseus' hands, but after several failed attempts, Cellini finally succeeded in making the cast by burning his family furniture to fan the furnace. The Loggia, whose name derives from the *lanzichenecchi*, a private army of Cosimo I, was built in the late 14th century to shelter civic bigwigs during ceremonies. By the mid 15th century it had become a favourite spot for old men to gossip and shelter from the sun, which, the architect Alberti noted with approval, had a restraining influence on the young men engaging in the 'mischievousness and folly natural to their age'. Also in the Loggia is Giambologna's spiralling marble *Rape of the Sabine Women* (1582), a virtuoso attempt to outdo Cellini and the first sculpture to have what John Pope Hennessy described as 'no dominant viewpoint'.

Leading down to the river from piazza della Signoria, the piazzale degli Uffizi is home to the greatest museum of Renaissance art in the world (*see p80*), the **Uffizi**. Also here is the separate entrance to the **Corridoio Vasariano** (*see p77*), the Vasari Corridor. Halfway down the piazzale on the right in via Lambertesca is the entrance to the **Collezione Contini-Bonacossi** (*see p76*) and the Georgofili library, where a Mafia bomb exploded in 1993.

Turning left from the riverbank leads you to the **Museo di Storia della Scienza** (*see p77*). Via Castellani heads north from the museum to piazza San Firenze with the imposing law courts and the entrance to the **Badia Fiorentina** (*see below*), which lies along via Proconsolo. This is home on its eastside to the National Museum, the sculpture-laden **Bargello** (*see p94*). We are now in Danteland. Just behind the Badia is the **Museo Casa di Dante** (Dante aficionados only, *see p*77). And opposite is the Chiesa di Dante, the delightful little church where Dante's beloved Beatrice was buried.

Back at the river end of the Uffizi and on the right is the landmark **Ponte Vecchio**. There has been a bridge spanning this point of the Arno (its narrowest within the city) since Roman times, though the first bridge was slightly upstream, where canoe club members now bask on their riverside sanctuary. The current structure was completed in 1345 to replace a bridge swept away by a flood in 1333. By the 13th century there were wooden shops on the bridge. These frequently caught fire, so when the bridge was reconstructed, the shops were built of stone. The bridge was originally occupied by butchers and tanners, whose trade involved soaking the hides in the Arno for eight months, then curing them in horse urine. But in 1593 Grand Duke Ferdinando I, fed up with retching every time he walked along the Vasari Corridor on his way to or from the Pitti Palace, banned all 'vile trades' and allowed only jewellers and goldsmiths to trade on the bridge. In the centre of the bridge is a newly restored bust by Raffaello Romanelli of Benvenuto Cellini, who is considered by many to have been the most talented goldsmith of all time.

Directly north of Ponte Vecchio is the predominantly modern architecture of via Por Santa Maria, much of which had to be rebuilt after the German bombing of the area at the end of World War II. At the top of this busy shopping street is the **Mercato Nuovo** ('new market', but often called the 'straw market'), a fine stone loggia erected between 1547 and 1551 on a site where there had been a market since the 11th century (the Mercato Vecchio occupied the area now covered by piazza della Repubblica). It now houses stalls selling leather and straw goods and cheap souvenirs, but in the 16th century it was full of silk and gold merchants and moneychangers. The market is popularly known as the Porcellino, or piglet, named after the bronze statue of a boar, a copy of a bronze by Pietro Tacca, which in turn was a copy of an ancient marble now in the Uffizi. It's considered good luck to rub the boar's nose and put a coin in its mouth – proceeds go to a children's charity, and the legend goes that the donor is assured a return trip to the city.

A block up via Calimala on the right, named after the Greek words for 'beautiful fleece', is the portico-and-ramparts grandeur of the **Palazzo dell'Arte della Lana**, the Renaissance home to the filthy-rich guild of clothmakers. This fairytale castle is connected by an arched overpass to **Orsanmichele** church (*see p79*), the main entrance to which is on via Calzaiuoli, the pedestrian thoroughfare between piazza della Signoria and the Duomo.

Badia Fiorentina

Via del Proconsolo (055 264402). **Open** *Cloister* 3-6pm Mon. *Church* 6.30am-6pm Tue-Sat; 3-6pm Mon. **Admission** donation to Eucharist. **Map** p315 C4.

The Badia Florentia, a Benedictine abbey founded in the tenth century by Willa, mother of Ugo, Margrave of Tuscany, was the richest religious institution of medieval Florence. Willa had been deeply influenced by Romuald, a monk who travelled around Tuscany denouncing the wickedness of the clergy, flagellating himself, and urging the rich to build monasteries. Eventually, Romuald persuaded Willa to found the Badia in 978. Ugo's trials started early. As a small child, his long-exiled father returned to Florence and invented a novel paternity test by expecting the boy to recognise the father he'd never seen in a crowded room of men. Happily for his mother, Ugo succeeded. The people decided that he had divine guidance and he thereafter was considered as a visionary leader. Like Willa, her son also lavished money and land on the Badia Florentia, and was eventually buried there in a Roman sarcophagus, later replaced by a tomb (made by Renaissance sculptor Mino da Fiesole) that is still housed in the abbey. It was here in 1274, just across the street from Dante's probable birthplace, that the eight-year-old poet fell instantly in love with Beatrice Portinari. He was devastated when her family arranged her marriage, at the tender age of 17, to Simone de Bardi. Sadly, Beatrice died seven years later. Poor old Dante attempted to forget his pain and anguish by throwing himself into war. The Badia has been rebuilt many times since Dante's day, but still retains a graceful Romanesque campanile. The Chiostro degli Aranci dates from 1430 and is frescoed with scenes from the life of St Bernardo. Inside the church Bernardo is celebrated once again, in a painting by Filippino Lippi.

Collezione Contini-Bonacossi

Uffizi, entrance via Lambertesca (055 294 883).
Open guided group visits by appointment only.
Map p314 C3.

An impressive collection donated to the state by the Contini-Bonacossi family in 1974. There are *Madonna and Child*s by Duccio, Cimabue and Andrea del Castagno and a room of artistic VIPs, containing works by Bernini, Veronese and Tintoretto. Among the foreigners prestigious enough to find their way into the collection are El Greco, Velázquez and Goya.

Piazza della Signoria. *See p72.*

Collezione della Ragione

Information 055 276 8325.

The modern art collection of Alberto della Ragione, which includes works by Marino Marini and Giorgio de Chirico, is about to be taken to its new permanent home: Complesso delle Oblate, via Sant'Egidio (055 283 078). It'll feature in regular temporary exhibitions.

Corridoio Vasariano

Loggiato degli Uffizi 6 (055 265 4321/ 294 883). **Open** by appointment only June-Dec. Closed Aug. **No credit cards**. **Map** p314 C3.

Aside from special openings (call for details), the only way to visit this fascinating kilometre-long corridor running the length of the Uffizi, over the Ponte Vecchio and down to the Palazzo Pitti and the Boboli Gardens is to book a place on the expensive *Percorso del Principe* (the Route of the Prince) guided tour, which starts in the Palazzo Vecchio and ends in Boboli. (Sadly, it's erratic, only operational for six months a year and is pricey at €26.50.) The corridor was built by Vasari in a lightning-quick five months so Grand Duke Cosimo I could walk from his home, the Palazzo Pitti, to work in the Palazzo Vecchio. Lined with the self-portraits of illustrious artists like Delacroix, Titian, Bernini, Andrea del Sarto, Raphael and Rembrandt, it has novel views, including an overhead view into the church of Santa Felicità. It's said that the corridor was used during Word War II to hide precious works of art from the Nazis.

Museo Casa di Dante

Via Santa Margherita 1 (055 219 416). **Open** call for post-renovation opening times. **Admission** €3. **No credit cards**. **Map** p315 B4.

Located where Dante is thought to live, this museum dedicated to the father of the Italian language is closed for renovation.

Museo dei Ragazzi

Palazzo Vecchio, Piazza della Signoria (055 276 8224/www.museoragazzi.it). **Open** varies depending on the activity. **Admission** €1.50-€6.70; €15.50 family ticket. **No credit cards**. **Map** p315 C4.

This is the perfect place to bring kids who've reached traditional museum and gallery saturation point. For ages three to seven there's a playroom with a dressing-up corner, a puppet theatre and building blocks, all with a Renaissance theme, and for older children (target audience eight to 88) there's a novel series of workshops, talks by experts dressed as Galileo or Vasari, meetings with historical characters such as Eleonora di Toledo and Cosimo I, visits on 'secret routes' and multimedia activities, all based in the Palazzo Vecchio, the Museo di Storia della Scienza (*see below*) and the Museo Stibbert (*see p104*).

Museo Diocesano di Santo Stefano al Ponte

Piazza Santo Stefano 5 (055 271 0732). **Open** *Summer* 4-7pm Fri. *Winter* 3.30-6.30pm Fri. *Also* 10am-1pm 2nd Sun of mth. **Admission** free. **Map** p314 C3.

Perseus under **Loggia dei Lanzi**. *See p73.*

This tiny, little-known museum is hidden in a square just north of the Ponte Vecchio. Among the religious icons and church relics are a few big surprises: a *Maestà* by Giotto, *San Giuliano* by Masolino and the *Quarate Predella* by Paolo Uccello.

Museo di Storia della Scienza

Piazza dei Giudici 1 (055 239 8876/www.imss.fi.it). **Open** *Summer* 9.30am-5pm Mon, Wed-Fri; 9.30am-1pm Tue, Sat. *Winter* 9.30am-5pm Mon, Wed-Sat; 9.30am-1pm Tue. **Admission** €6.50. **No credit cards**. **Map** p315 C4.

One of the most fascinating museums in Florence. Visitors are offered a view of the Renaissance and beyond, which for once is not limited to stone and pigment. Two of the most curious rooms are those devoted to Galileo; they include a really rather morbid reliquary of his middle right finger and one of his telescopes bound in leather.

In the next rooms are a collection of prisms and optical games. Art continues to mingle with science in Room 7, which is devoted to armillary spheres and dominated by a gold-leaf-decorated model commissioned by Federico II in 1593. Most of them have the earth emphatically placed at the centre of the universe, surrounded by seven spheres of the planets. Also look out for the stunning collection of spiralling 18th-century thermometers.

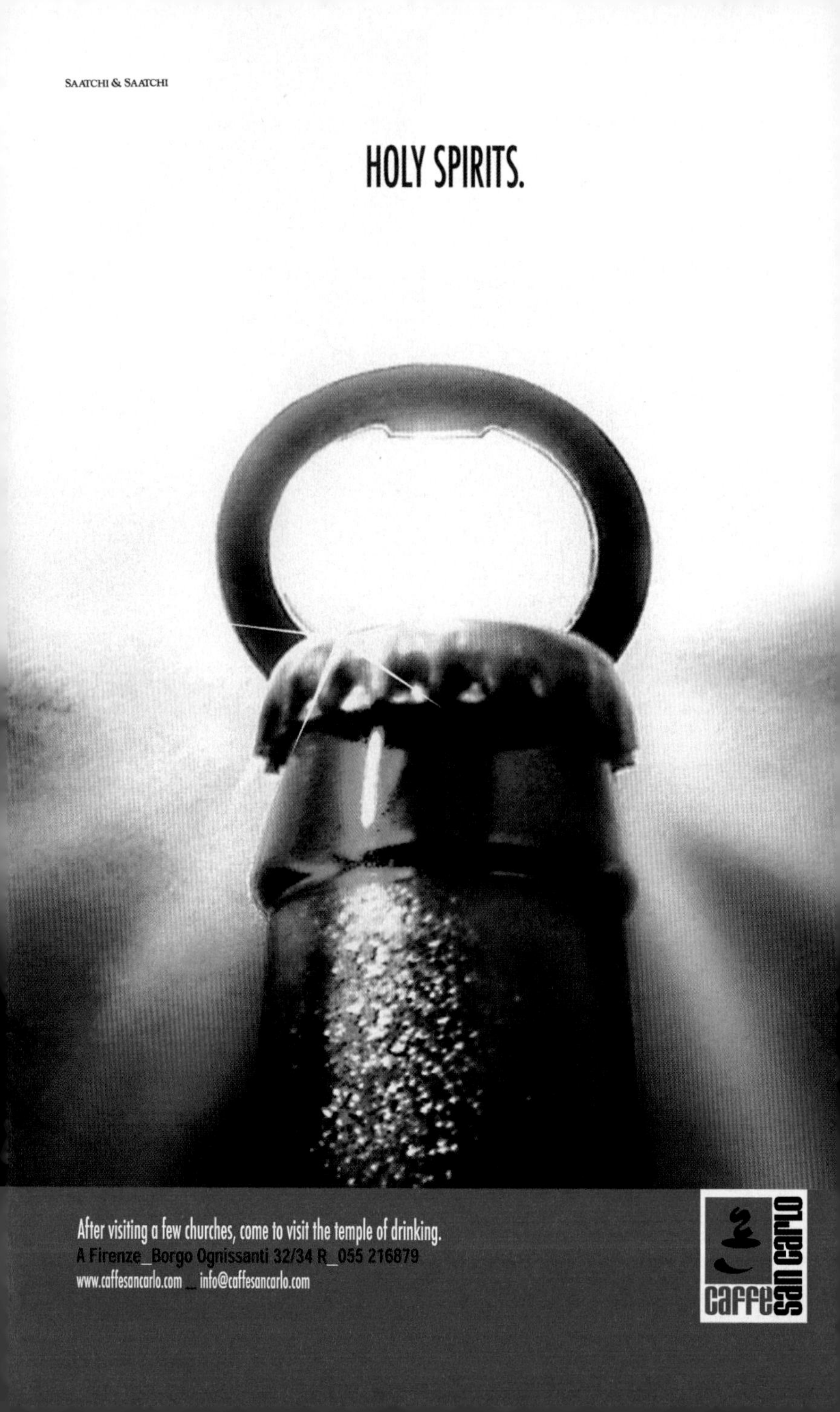

SAATCHI & SAATCHI

HOLY SPIRITS.

After visiting a few churches, come to visit the temple of drinking.
A Firenze_Borgo Ognissanti 32/34 R_055 216879
www.caffesancarlo.com _ info@caffesancarlo.com

The second floor has an eclectic mix of machines, mechanisms and models, including a 19th-century clock (*pianola*) that writes a sentence with a mechanical hand, and a selection of electromagnetic and electrostatic instruments (Room 14). Also interesting are the pneumatic pumps decorated with inlaid wood by Nollet (famous for his globe machine) and the carefully constructed illustration of the mechanical paradox of two spheres ascending a plane. The display of amputation implements and models of foetuses adorning the walls are grisly.

Orsanmichele & the Museo di Orsanmichele

Via dell'Arte della Lana (055 284 944/ 715). **Open** *Church* 9am-noon, 4-6pm daily. *Museum tours* 9am, 10am, 11am daily. Closed 1st & last Mon of mth. **Admission** free. **Map** p314 C3.

The relationship between art, religion and commerce is seldom closer than in the church of Orsanmichele. In 1290 a loggia intended as a grain store was built to a design by Arnolfo di Cambio, the original architect of the Duomo, in the garden (*orto*) of the Monastery of San Michele. Hence the name Orsanmichele. The loggia burned down in 1304 along with a painting of the Madonna said to have been invoked to put out a previous fire. The painting was held in the marvellously elaborate glass and marble tabernacle of Andrea Orcagna, and was replaced by Bernardo Daddi's *Coronation of the Madonna* with eight angels in 1347, still in place in the tabernacle.

The place was rebuilt in the mid 1300s by Talenti and Fioravante and used as grain market. Two upper floors were added so that monks could use it for religious services. From the outset the council intended Orsanmichele to be a magnificent advertisement for the wealth of the city's guilds and in 1339 each guild was instructed to fill one of the loggia's niches with a statue of its patron saint. Only the wool guild obliged with a stone statue of St Stephen. So in 1406 the council presented the guilds with a ten-year deadline. In 1412 the Calimala cloth-importers (the wealthiest guild) commissioned Ghiberti to create a life-sized bronze of John the Baptist. It was the largest statue ever cast in Florence. The other major guilds then fell over themselves to produce the finest statue. The guild of armourers was represented by a tense *St George* by Donatello (now in the Bargello), one of the first psychologically realistic sculptures of the Renaissance. The Parte Guelfa had Donatello gild their bronze, a St Louis of Toulouse – later removed by the Medici to Santa Croce in their drive to expunge all memory of the Guelphs from the public face of the city.

After the recent restoration of the church and museum, the statues in the external niches have all been replaced with copies, while the originals are on the first floor of the museum, displayed on a platform in the same order in which they appeared around the church. On the second floor is a collection of statues of 14th-century saints and prophets in *arenaria* stone. These were on the external façade of the church until the 1950s when they were saved from the elements and moved to the Opificio delle Pietre Dure (*see p93*) where they underwent a marathon restoration, from which they have only recently emerged.

Palazzo Vecchio Quartieri Monumentali

Piazza Signoria (055 276 8465). **Open** 9am-7pm Mon-Wed, Sat, Sun; 9am-2pm Thur. **Admission** €5.70. **No credit cards**. **Map** p315 C4.

The modern-day home of Florence's town hall, the Palazzo Vecchio has had a see-saw history. It was originally built to Arnolfo da Cambio's late 13th-century plans as seat to the Signoria (the city's ruling body as priors of the main guilds of the Medici). The Medici's nine-year stay (1540-49) may have been brief, but they nonetheless instigated a massive Mannerist makeover of the palace's interior, under Giorgio Vasari, court architect from 1555 to 1574. However, Arnolfo's Tower, the highest tower in the city at 94m (308ft), and the rustic stone exterior of the building, remained largely intact. The unusual projecting arches flanking the coats of arms of the main families of Florence were actually built to drop boiling oil on to any potential marauding army. The tower, set slightly off-centre to incorporate a previous tower and to fit in with the irregularity of the square, and topped by two of the main symbols of Florence (a lion holding a lily), saw the imprisonment of Savonarola and of Cosimo the Elder in a room euphemistically called the *Albergaccio* ('bad hotel'). From 1565 the Palazzo Vecchio lost some of its administrative exclusivity to the Pitti Palace and the Uffizi, but later became the seat of the Italian Government's House of Deputies from 1865 to 1871 when Florence was the capital of the Kingdom of Italy. It then returned to its original and current function as town hall.

Though a working administrative centre, much of the Palazzo Vecchio can be visited. The Salone dei Cinquecento (Hall of the Five Hundred), where members of the Great Council met, should have been decorated with battle scenes by Michelangelo and Leonardo, not the zestless scenes of victory over Siena and Pisa by Vasari that cover the walls. Leonardo, frustrated by attempts to develop new mural techniques, abandoned the project. Michelangelo had only finished the cartoon for the *Battle of Cascine* when he was summoned to Rome by Pope Julius II. One of Michelangelo's commissions did end up here: the *Genius of Victory*, a statue thought to have been carved, along with the better-known *Dying Slaves*, for the Pope's never-finished tomb.

Off the Salone is the Studiolo di Francesco I, the office where Francesco hid away to practice alchemy. Also decorated by Vasari, it includes a scene from the alchemist's laboratory and illustrations of the four elements. From the vaulted ceiling, Bronzino's portraits of Francesco's parents, Cosimo I and Eleonora di Toledo, look down. Upstairs, the Quartiere degli Elementi contains Vasari's allegories of the elements. The *Quartiere di Eleonora* (Wife of Cosimo I) has two entirely frescoed chapels; the first was partly decorated by Bronzino, who uses intense pastel hues to depict a surreal *Crossing the Red Sea*, while the Cappella dei Priori is decorated with fake mosaics and an idealised *Annunciation*.

Beyond is the garish Sala d'Udienza with a carved ceiling dripping in gold; more subtle is the Sala dei Gigli, so named because of the gilded lilies that cover the walls. Decorated in the 15th century, it has a ceiling by Guiliano and Benedetto da Maiano, and it has some sublime frescoes of Roman statesmen by Ghirlandaio opposite the door. Donatello's original *Judith and Holofernes*, which is rich in political significance, is also here.

Sightseeing

The Uffizi

Piazzale degli Uffizi 6 (055 23885/www.uffizi.firenze.it). **Open** 8.15am-6.50pm Tue-Sun. **Admission** €8.50. **No credit cards**. **Map** p315 C4.

The Uffizi building was designed by Vasari in the mid 16th century as a public administration centre for Cosimo I (hence the name 'Uffizi', meaning 'offices'). To make way for the *pietra serena* and white plaster building, inspired by Michelangelo's Laurentian Library in San Lorenzo, most of the 11th-century church of San Piero Scheraggio was demolished (the remains can still be seen beyond the main entrance hall), and the Old Mint, the Palazzo della Zecca, was incorporated into the design.

By 1581 Francesco I had already begun turning the top floor into a new home for his art collection, and the habit caught on. A succession of Medici added to the collection, culminating in the bequest of most of the family's artworks by the last of the family, Anna Maria, on her death in 1743. When the specialist art museums of the city were opened in the 18th and 19th centuries, the silver, sculptures and scientific exhibits were transferred from the Uffizi, leaving the gallery we see today.

If you're at all fond of Renaissance art, prepare to step into heaven, albeit a crowded one. Off the corridors lined with magnificent ancient Greek and Roman wrestlers, flawless Apollos and eminent-looking busts, the chronological collection begins gloriously, with three *Maestàs* by Giotto, Cimabue and Duccio in **Room 2**, painted in the 13th and early 14th centuries, all three still part of the Byzantine tradition. Stepping into **Room 3** is to enter the world of 14th-century Siena, most exquisitely evoked by Simone Martini's lavish gilt altarpiece *Annunciation*. Such delight in detail reached its zenith in the international Gothic movement (**Rooms 5** and **6**), in particular the work of Gentile da Fabriano (1370-1427), whose *Adoration of the Magi* (also known as the Strozzi altarpiece) seems a wonderful excuse to paint sumptuous brocades and intricate gold jewellery.

Walk 1
The beaten track

Begin by skirting the Duomo clockwise to the pedestrianised piazza del Duomo. Strain your neck for a look up at Giotto's bell-tower, then, queues permitting, step into the fourth-largest church in the world to experience Brunelleschi's masterpiece inside out. Back outside, stop to admire the copies of Ghiberti's *Gates of Paradise* straight ahead of you on the oldest monument on the site, the Baptistery, then take a left down via Calzaiuoli as far as the well-disguised, ornate church of Orsanmichele. Circle the building to wonder at its tabernacles and overpass, then take via Calimala down to the loggia of the Mercato Nuovo. Walk on down via Por Santa Maria, then take a left into via Vacchereccia for a double-take view of the clock-tower of the Palazzo Vecchio. In the piazza della Signoria, take time to give *Perseus and The Rape of the Sabines* in the Loggia dei Lanzi the once-over, then make your way down the daunting piazzale degli Uffizi. At the river, take in the view of San Miniato on the hill to the left, then turn right, following the arches of the Vasari Corridor to the tiny jewellery shops of the Ponte Vecchio. Cross the bridge into Oltrarno and keep going till the road widens into the piazza Pitti and its impossibly big palazzo. Past this ex-Medici playground, take the main road on the right, via Mazzetta, and end your walk in the pretty piazza Santo Spirito, where you can rest your eyes on the exquisite simplicity of the church's cream façade.

It is something of a surprise, then, to turn to a strikingly contemporary *Virgin and Child with Saint Anne* by Masolino and Masaccio (1401-28) in **Room 7**. Though Masolino was not averse to a little Gothic frivolity (note some of the costumes he dreamed up for the Brancacci Chapel), he's entirely restrained here. Masaccio painted the Virgin, whose severe expression and statuesque pose make her an indubitable descendant of Giotto's *Maestà*. In the same room is the *Santa Lucia dei Magnoli* altarpiece by Domenico Veneziano (1400-61), a Venetian artist who died a pauper in Florence and who had a remarkable skill for rendering the way light affects colour. His influence on his pupil Piero della Francesca's work is clear in the younger artist's

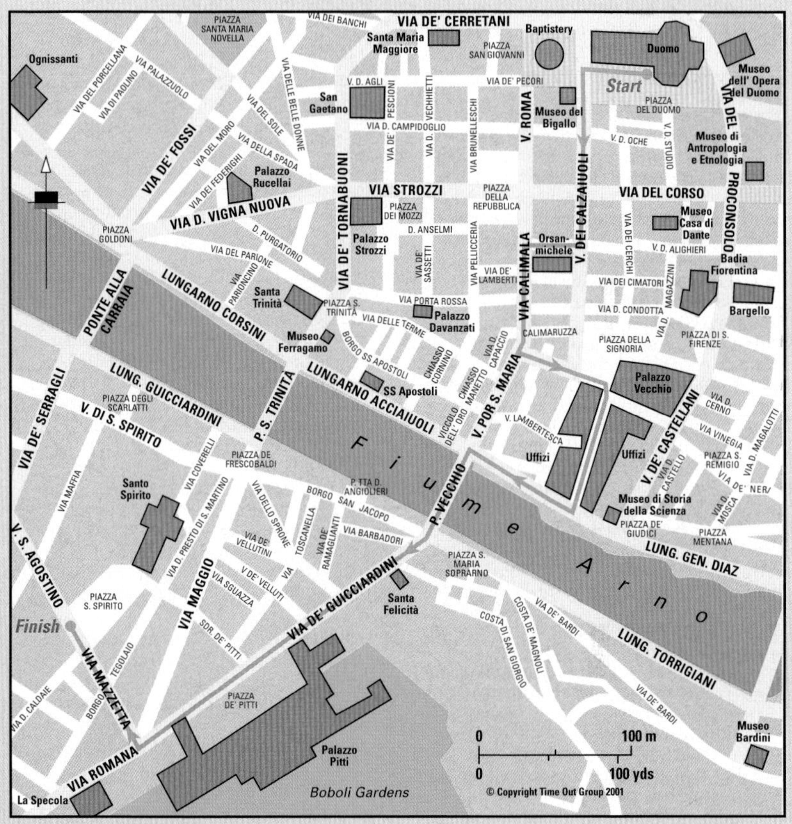

portraits of the Duke and Duchess of Urbino. Still in **Room 7**, Paolo Uccello (1396-1475) is represented by the *Battle of San Romano*, part of a triptych whose other thirds are in London's National Gallery and Paris's Louvre. A work of tremendous energy and power, it reinforces the chaos of battle with its intense, distorted perspective.

Rooms 8 and 9 are dominated by Filippo Lippi and the Pollaiuolo brothers. The Madonna in Lippi's *Madonna with Child and Angels* is a portrait of the astonishingly beautiful Lucrezia Buti, a nun whom he abducted and married once he had given up the Carmelite vows, painted with their son Filippino, who was also to become a famous painter. The more talented of the Pollaiuolos, Antonio, was one of the first artists to dissect bodies in order to study anatomy. His small panels of the *Labours of Hercules* demonstrate his familiarity with the skeletal form and musculature.

The two most famous paintings in the Uffizi and in Italy are in **Room 10**. Botticelli's *Birth of Venus*, the epitome of Renaissance romance, depicts the birth of the goddess from a sea impregnated by the castration of Uranus. This is an allegory of the birth of beauty from the mingling of the physical world (the sea) and the spiritual (Uranus). Scholars have been squabbling about the true meaning of the other, Botticelli's *Allegory of Spring,* since it was painted in 1478. Many now agree that it was intended to represent the onset of spring (reading from right to left) and to signify the triumph of Venus (centre) as true love, with the Three Graces representing her beauty and Zephyr, on the right, as lust, pursuing the nymph Chloris, who is transformed into Flora, Venus' fecundity. The painting is believed to have been a wedding present from Lorenzo il Magnifico to his cousin Lorenzo di Pierfrancesco dei Medici, and many of the 190 different flowers under Flora's feet symbolise marriage.

In **Room 15** are several paintings by Leonardo da Vinci, including a collaboration with his teacher Verrocchio, *The Baptism of Christ* (Verrocchio never painted again, reputedly because his work couldn't match up to Leonardo's). The octagonal **Room 18**, with its mother-of-pearl ceiling, is dominated by portraits by Bronzino, most strikingly that of Eleonora di Toledo, assured, beautiful and very Spanish in an opulent gold and black brocade gown.

The oval **Room 24**, originally a treasure chamber, is home to the world's biggest collection of miniatures including the ebony-framed Medici collection.

In **Room 25** the gallery makes its transition to Mannerism, championed by Michelangelo's *Holy Family* (*Tondo Doni*), which shows the sculptural bodies, virtuoso composition and luscious palette that characterised the new wave. Next you come to the Pontormo and Rosso Fiorentino **Room 27**, which once again shows Michelangelo's legacy, most notably in *Moses Defends the Daughters of Jethro* by Rosso Fiorentino. Also by Rosso Fiorentino is the *Portrait of a Young Woman*, with the ubiquitous musical angel detail. **Room 28** has works by Titian including his masterpiece *Venus of Urbino*, whose questionably chaste gaze has disarmed viewers for centuries. For more Venetian works skip to **Rooms 31-5**, but don't miss the visually challenging *Madonna with the Long Neck* by Parmigianino en route in **Room 29**. For an Old Masters cherry on the Renaissance cake, visit **Room 41**, with its classic row of portraits and self-portraits by Rubens, Van Dyck and Velázquez, and **Room 43** is home to a particularly grisly rendering of *Judith and Holofernes* by the 17th-century Caravaggio-esque woman artist Artemisia Gentileschi. Caravaggio himself is represented in this room by his famous but more shocked-looking than horror-inspiring *Medusa*, and a *Sacrifice of Isaac* that perfectly demonstrates his masterly treatment of light.

As any previous visitor to Florence will already know, the Uffizi is almost always hellishly crowded, especially in summer and during holidays, ; if you've booked your ticket, one of the best times to go is lunchtime, when the tour groups are unlikely to be around. Otherwise, aim for opening time, when the queues at the ticket office are shorter and you can jump to the rooms you're most interested in. To see the whole collection would either take several hours or, better still, a return visit – you should allow at least three hours to take in the unmissables. Several organisations provide guided tours. There are also audio tours in seven languages for €11.60 from the ticket office.

Around via dei Tornabuoni

Tracing the line of the ancient Roman city wall is the elegant shopping mecca of via dei Tornabuoni. This main street sweeps down from piazza Antinori to piazza Santa Trinità and the Santa Trinità bridge. It's crowned by Palazzo Antinori, an austere mid 15th-century palace of neat stone blocks, inhabited by the Antinori winemaking family since 1506. The rather garish church opposite is the baroque San Gaetano.

Halfway down the road stands stately **Palazzo Strozzi** (*see p83*), its mammoth fortification stones set with horse-tethering rings and embellished with the three crescent-moon motif of the family crest. Heading south towards the river and passing Gucci, Prada and other designer names, you come to piazza Santa Trinità. Just before it is via Porta Rossa, home to the Renaissance house museum **Palazzo Davanzati**. At the far end of via Porta Rossa, on the right, the road widens into a square. The ramparts and Gothic leaded windows of the Palagio di Parte Guelfa date back to the 13th century, and have been modified by, among others, Brunelleschi and Vasari. The imposing building was the headquarters of the Guelphs and is now used as a library and meeting rooms. Running parallel to via Porta Rossa is borgo Santissimi Apostoli, a narrow street in the middle of which is piazza del Limbo, so-called because it occupies the site of a graveyard for unbaptised babies. The tiny church to the left is **Santissimi Apostoli**.

Piazza Santa Trinità itself is little more than a bulge in via Tornabuoni, dominated by the extraordinary curved ramparts of Palazzo Spini Ferroni, home to Ferragamo and the **Museo Ferragamo** (*see p83*), and by an ancient column taken from the Baths of Caracalla in Rome, a gift to Cosimo I from Pope Pius I in 1560. The statue of Justice on top was designed by Francesco del Tadda. The first palazzo after via Tornabuoni is Palazzo Bartolini-Salimbeni by Baccio d'Agnolo, with its unique stone inner window frames. The architect was savaged by 16th-century critics for creating a design 'more suited to a church than a palazzo'. Opposite Palazzo Spini-Feroni on the west side of via dei Tornabuoni is the church of **Santa Trinità**, built in the 13th century over 11th-century churches and home to the Ghirlandaio frescoes in the Sassetti Chapel.

The Ponte Santa Trinità, an elegant bridge with an elliptical arch, links piazza Santa Trinità with the Oltrarno. It was first built in 1252 on the initiative of the Frescobaldi family, but was swept away by floodwaters in 1333. Rebuilt in 1346, it was carried away by the river again in 1557 and was made in its present form by Ammanati in 1567, possibly to a design by Michelangelo, and is considered by many to be the most beautiful bridge in the world. The statues at either end, which represent the four seasons, were placed there in 1608 to celebrate Cosimo II's marriage to Maria of Austria. Having been bombed on the night of 3 August 1944 by retreating Germans, the bridge was rebuilt in 1955 in the same position and to the same design. The head of the most famous, *Spring* by Pietro Francavilla, which graces the north-east side of the bridge, remained lost until 1961 when a council employee dredged it up during a routine clean-up and claimed the reward offered for its return years before by a US newspaper.

Museo Ferragamo

Via Tornabuoni 2 (055 336 0456). **Open** by appointment 9am-1pm, 2-6pm Mon-Fri. Closed Aug & 2wks Christmas. **Admission** free. **Map** p314 C2.

This small museum above Ferragamo's shop in the Palazzo Spini-Feroni displays a fraction of the company's 10,000 archive shoes, but still affords an opportunity for shoe fetishists to drool over some of the world's most beautiful footwear. Ferragamo, born in a small village outside Naples in 1898, opened his first shop at the age of 14, emigrated to the US at 16, and was soon designing shoes for movie stars. Commissions for Cecil B DeMille's *Cleopatra* gave him the opportunity to experiment. In 1927 he moved to Florence to start a factory producing handmade shoes and he bought the palazzo in via Tornabuoni, where he had been renting a studio, from the Feroni family in 1938. Since then the family business, still based in the same palazzo and with its production and admin facilities on the outskirts of the city, has continued to flourish.

Palazzo Davanzati & the Museo dell'Antica Casa Fiorentina

Palazzo Davanzati, Via Porta Rossa 13 (055 238 8610). **Open** call for post-restoration times. **Admission** free. **Map** p314 C3.

This museum decked out as a mid-Renaissance family home is still closed for restoration.

Palazzo Strozzi

Piazza Strozzi (055 288 342). **Open** varies according to exhibitions. *Library* 9am-1pm, 3-6pm Mon-Fri; 9am-1pm Sat. **Admission** free to ground-floor courtyard; exhibitions vary. **Map** p314 B3.

Mercantile Florence was at its zenith in the 1400s, a century during which more than 100 palaces were built. The most magnificent was Palazzo Strozzi. Work began on the palace in 1489 on the orders of Filippo Strozzi. The family had been exiled from Florence in 1434 for opposing the Medici but made good use of the time, moving south and becoming bankers to the King of Naples. By the time they returned to Florence in 1466 they had amassed a fortune. In 1474 Filippo began buying up property in the centre of Florence, until he had acquired enough to build the biggest palace in the city. In a marathon demolition job, 15 buildings were pulled down to make room for it, playing havoc with traffic and covering the city in dust. An astrologer was then asked to choose an auspicious day to lay the foundation stone and came up with 6 August 1489, tying in nicely with the law Lorenzo de' Medici had passed a few months earlier, tax-exempting anyone who built a house on an empty site.

Three architects were involved in the design of the palazzo: Giuliano da Sangallo, Benedetto da Maiano and Simone del Pollaiolo. When Filippo died in 1491 he left his heirs to complete the project. This eventually bankrupted them. The palace now houses institutions and stages prestigious exhibitions.

Santa Trinità

Piazza Santa Trinità (055 216 912). **Open** 8am-noon, 4-6pm Mon-Sat; 4-6pm Sun. **Admission** free. **Map** p314 C2.

This plain church was built in the 13th century over the ruins of two earlier churches belonging to the Vallombrosans. The order was founded by San Giovanni Gualberto Visdomini in 1038, following a miraculous incident 20 years earlier in the church of San Miniato al Monte: while kneeling in front of a crucifix, he saw the head of Christ nod in approval of his prayer, starting his conversion from nobleman to monk. He then spent a great deal of time attempting to persuade pious aristocrats to surrender their wealth and live a life of austerity. The said crucifix was supposedly that held in San Miniato's Ficozzi Chapel and moved to Santa Trinità in 1671. The order became extremely wealthy and powerful, reaching a peak in the 16th and 17th centuries when its huge fortress abbey at Vallombrosa, in the Casentino countryside north of Arezzo, was built. The church is well worth a visit for the Sassetti Chapel, luminously frescoed by Ghirlandaio with scenes from the life of St Francis, including one set in the piazza della Signoria featuring Lorenzo il Magnifico and his children.

Santissimi Apostoli

Piazza del Limbo 1 (055 290 642). **Open** 10am-noon, 3.30-7pm Mon-Sat; 10am-1pm, 4-6pm Sun. **Admission** free. **Map** p314 C3.

The design of Santissimi Apostoli, like that of the early Christian churches of Rome, is based on that of a Roman basilica and retains much of its 11th-century façade. The third chapel on the right holds an *Immaculate Conception* by Vasari, and in the left aisle is an odd glazed terracotta tabernacle by Giovanni della Robbia. The church holds pieces of flint reputed to have come from Jerusalem's Holy Sepulchre, which were awarded to Pazzino de'Pazzi for his bravery during the Crusades – he was the first to scale the walls of Jerusalem, although his name, 'Little Mad Man of the Mad Men', suggests his actions may have been more foolhardy than brave. These flints were used on Easter Day to light the 'dove' that sets off the fireworks display at the Scoppio del Carro (*see p152*). Note that the church has a tendency to close in the afternoon without prior notice.

Santa Maria Novella

Sleazy pleasures, holy treasures.

A mishmash of upmarket shops and grand residential areas, and the classic big city station-area degradation, this zone stretches from the striking modernist main railway station (designed by Michelucci in 1935) through the antiques emporia of via dei Fossi and the designer clothes shops of via della Vigna Nuova to elegant lungarno Corsini and the statue-topped Palazzo Corsini in the east. To the west, fine white mansion blocks around the Teatro Comunale and a dark maze of ancient streets where ageing prostitutes wait for trade on plastic garden chairs. At its centre is lively piazza Santa Maria Novella and the church of Ognissanti.

Round the train station and adjacent bus terminus, sleaze is prevalent: amid the chestnut sellers, business travellers and backpackers picking their way through the choked traffic system is a chaos of tramps, beggars, pick-pockets and men on the pull. The hellish shopping mall underpass, supposedly a safe alternative to the road, can sometimes be a case of out of the frying pan into the fire.

Across from the station, Alberti's precision-built façade for the church of **Santa Maria Novella** (*see p86*) looks out on a grassy piazza with two marble obelisks resting on turtles, by Giambologna. Opposite the church on the southern side of the square is the Loggia di San Paolo, a late 15th-century arcade built to the model of Brunelleschi's Loggiata degli Innocenti and set with the characteristic glazed terracotta medallions of the della Robbias. The square has been the subject of long-running disputes between local residents and hotel-owners and the city police, whose opinions over the degree of safety and civic care are at odds to say the least. Things came to a head recently when a group of travellers emptied a box of detergent into the fountain and proceeded to do their washing in it, to the delight of the watching children (who played in the mountains of bubbles), to the amazement of passing tourists and to the disgust of the long-suffering locals, whose solution has been to hire private security guards to patrol the square.

The triangle formed by via dei Fossi, via della Spada and via della Vigna Nuova brings you the more civilised pleasures of the fine **Palazzo Rucellai**, the **Capella Rucellai** and the adjacent modern art museum, the **Museo Marino Marini** (for all three, *see p85*).

Alberti had already designed the **Palazzo Rucellai** in via della Vigna Nuova, then the most refined in the city, for the Rucellai family when he created the façade of Santa Maria Novella. The palazzo's subtle façade was inspired by Rome's Colosseum: the pilasters that section the bottom storey have Doric capitals, those on the middle storey Ionic capitals, and those on the top storey are based on the Corinthian style. There's no rustication; Alberti considered it pompous and fit only for tyrants. The Rucellai were wool merchants

Masaccio's restored **Trinità**. *See p86.*

who had grown rich by importing from Majorca a red dye derived from lichen, known as *oricello*, from which their surname derives and which they then grew in the Orti Oricellari garden at the far end of via della Scala.

Up past piazza Goldoni, lungarno Vespucci and shopping street borgo Ognissanti open out into piazza Ognissanti, flanked by prestigious hotels and topped by the church of **Ognissanti** (*see below*). Further up, elegant residential roads lead out on to the main avenues, Porta al Prato and the mammoth park (the city's largest, in fact), **Le Cascine** (*see p159*).

Cappella Rucellai

Via della Spada (055 216 912). **Open** 10am-noon Mon-Sat. **Admission** free. **Map** p314 B2.

This tiny chapel was part of the church of San Pancrazio, now the Museo Marino Marini, and contains the tombs of many of the family of 15th-century wool magnate Giovanni Rucellai, including that of his wife Iacopa Strozzi. It's worth a visit to see Alberti's Temple of the Santo Sepolcro, commissioned in 1467 by Giovanni in an attempt to ensure his own salvation and built to the same proportions as the Holy Sepulchre of Jerusalem.

Museo Marino Marini

Piazza San Pancrazio (055 219 432). **Open** *Summer* 10am-5pm Mon, Wed-Fri. *Winter* 10am-5pm Mon, Wed-Sat. Closed Aug. **Admission** €4. **No credit cards**. **Map** p314 B2.

The original Albertian church of this site, San Pancrazio, was redesigned to accommodate the works of prolific sculptor and painter Marino Marini (1901-80), and the equine rigidity and monumentality of the pieces are reflected in its design and spaciousness. Many of the first-floor sculptures are a variation on the theme of horse and rider, championed by the central exhibit, the 6m (20ft) *Composizione Equestre*. The second floor has a series of other sculptural subjects, including the hypnotic *Nuotatore* (Swimmers) and some fabulous paintings of dancers and jugglers.

Ognissanti

Via Borgognissanti 42 (055 239 8700). **Open** 9am-12.30pm, 3.30-6.30pm daily. *Last Supper* 9am-noon Mon, Tue, Sat. **Admission** free. **Map** p314 B1.

The church of Ognissanti (All Saints) was founded in the 13th century by the Umiliati, a group of monks from Lombardy. They introduced the wool trade to Florence, and as the city's subsequent wealth was built on wool, it could be argued that without them there would have been no Florentine Renaissance. By the 14th century the Umiliati were so rich they commissioned Giotto to paint the *Maestà* (now in the Uffizi; *see p80*) for their high altar. Fifty years later they commissioned Giovanni da Milano to create a flashier altarpiece with more gold (now also in the Uffizi). Ognissanti was also the parish church of the Vespucci, a family of merchants from Peretola (near the airport) who dealt in silk, wine, wool, banking and goods from the Far East. They included 15th-century navigator Amerigo – the man who sailed to the Venezuelan coast in 1499 and had two continents named after him. The church has been rebuilt numerous times and is now visited mainly for paintings by Ghirlandaio. In fact, Amerigo himself appears in the *Madonna della Misericordia* (he is the young boy dressed in pink). Other frescoes worth seeing are a *St Augustine* by Botticelli and a *St Jerome* by Ghirlandaio. Off the cloister on a refectory wall is

Holes in the wall

Via della Spada

A decorative double-image version, this tabernacle is housed in a niche under a distinctive hexagonal parapet by the ex-monastery of San Pancrazio, now home to the Marino Marini museum. The *pietra serena edicola* frames a softly hued terracotta 16th-century *Madonna and Child* in Maiano style that, until the monastery was dissolved and the church secularised, was kept in its Federighi Chapel. The *Ecce Homo* mural in the oval frame is by the late 19th-century artist Giuseppe Iacovino and is a perfect example of the crossover period between realism and expressionism.

Sightseeing

Ghirlandaio's most famous *Last Supper* (1480). As in his work in San Marco, he uses religious iconography to load it with deeper meaning. Here, however, his Apostles' expressions are more realistic. There's also a museum of Franciscan bits and pieces, and in the church is the tomb of Botticelli, marked with his family name, Filipepi.

Santa Maria Novella

Piazza Santa Maria Novella (055 215 918/cloisters & museum 055 282 187). **Open** *Church* 9.30am-5pm Mon-Thur, Sat; 1-5pm Fri, Sun. *Cloisters & museum* 9am-2pm Mon-Thur, Sat, Sun. **Admission** *Cloisters & museum* €2.60. **No credit cards. Map** p314 B2.

This was the Florentine seat of the Dominicans, a fanatically inquisitorial order fond of leading street brawls against suspected heretics and encouraging the faithful to strip and whip themselves before the altar. The piazza outside, one of Florence's biggest, was enlarged in 1244-5 to accommodate the crowds who came to hear St Peter the Martyr, one of the viler members of the saintly canon. St Peter made his name persecuting so-called heretics in northern Italy and ended up with one of their axes in his head.

The pièce de résistance of the church is its Alberti façade. In 1465, at the request of the Rucellai family, Alberti incorporated the Romanesque lower storey into a refined Renaissance scheme, adding the triangular tympanum and the scrolls that mask the side nave exteriors in an exercise of consummate classical harmony.

The church interior, however, was designed by the order's monks and is therefore fittingly severe, with striped vaults and a peculiar architectural ruse of lowering the height of the arches as they near the altar and adding steps to create a strong horizontal perspective. Until Vasari had them whitewashed in the mid 16th century the church walls were covered with frescoes. Fortunately, Vasari left Masaccio's recently restored *Trinità* of 1427 in the third span on the left nave. Here we can see the first application of Brunelleschi's mathematical rules of perspective to a painting. The result is a triumph of *trompe l'œil* with God, Christ and two saints appearing to stand in a niche watched by the patrons Lorenzo Lenzi and his wife. The slightly sinister inscription above the skeleton on the sarcophagus reads: 'I was what you are and what I am you shall be.'

Over the next few decades the Dominicans appear to have loosened up. In 1485 they let Ghirlandaio cover the walls of the Cappella Tornabuoni with scenes from the life of John the Baptist featuring lavish contemporary Florentine interiors and a supporting cast from the Tornabuoni family. Ghirlandaio also found the time to train a young man by the name of Michelangelo while working on the chapel. At about the same time Filippino Lippi was at work next door in the Cappella di Filippo Strozzi painting scenes from the life of St Philip.

The church is also home to the *Crocifisso* by Giotto, a simple, worldly wooden crucifix. It was finally returned to the church in 2001 after a 12-year restoration and a massive political row over whether the crucifix was being used as a pawn in a general election campaign. Now it can be found in the centre of the basilica where the Dominicans had originally placed it on its arrival in 1290.

To compare Masaccio's easeful use of perspective with the contorted struggles of Paolo Uccello, pop outside to the Chiostro Verde (green cloister) left of the church – so-called because of the green base pigment the artist used, which gave the flood-damaged frescoes a chill, deathly hue. Uccello's lunettes can either be considered visionary experiments of modern art before its time or a complete perspective mess depending on your tolerance of artistic licence. Beyond the Chiostro you'll find the Cappella degli Spagnoli, whose name is in fact derived from the wife of Cosimo I, Eleonora di Toledo (she liked to use it for her various Spanish cronies). The Capella is decorated with vibrant scenes celebrating the triumph of Dominicans and the Catholic Church by Andrea di Bonaiuto. Look out for the strange-looking cupola on the Duomo fresco – the artist's own design submitted for the dome but rejected in favour of Brunelleschi's plan. On the left of the church is the Romanesque-Gothic bell tower built in 1330 and, to the right, is a cemetery surrounded by the grave niches of Florence's wealthy families. There is also the small Museo di Santa Maria Novella just off the Chiostro Verde, which was designed by Talenti and houses 35 frescoed heads by the Orcagnas.

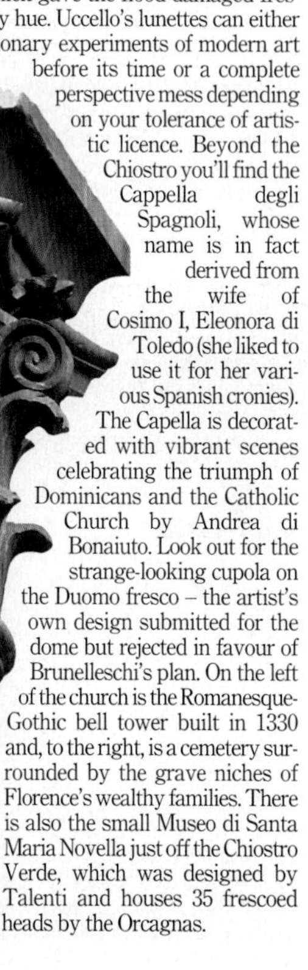

San Lorenzo

From Medici rules to market stalls.

The central market of San Lorenzo is the hub of this vibrant neighbourhood. It spreads its tentacles over a wide area of *piazze*, snaking north from the church of **San Lorenzo** (*see p89*), where the street stalls sell cheap clothes, mediocre leather goods and tacky souvenirs, and encompassing the huge covered market in the piazza del Mercato Centrale, which is chock-a-block with fresh fruit and vegetables, fish, cheese and meat stalls. The overpowering smells all around are joined by those of bakeries, delis, cafés and doughnut stands in neighbouring streets, along with piles of refuse.

Roads lead off the *piazze* around San Lorenzo in a star-shape: north-east up via dei Ginori alongside the gardens behind the **Palazzo Medici Riccardi** (*see p89*); past craft and gift shops, which lead up to the corner of via San Gallo, with the Benedictine refectory of **Cenacolo di Sant'Apollonia** (*see p89*) on the right and the **Chiostro dello Scalzo** (*see p89*) on the left, right up to the old city gate Porta a San Gallo; south alongside busy shoe and clothes shops in borgo San Lorenzo to the Duomo; south-west via tiny food stores towards the station through via Faenza; north-west past the **Cappelle Medicee** (*see below*) up via dell'Ariento with its one-star hotels and via Faenza with its **Cenacolo del Conservatorio di Fuligno** (*see p88*) to dingy via Nazionale; and north, to the main market square.

Further up via Nazionale the roads widen into piazza dell'Indipendenza, and the smell of boiled cabbage disappears. The double square, with a main road running through the middle, a few stone seats scattered round the edges, bald grass and a couple of trees, is a bad excuse for a park. But it does take you a step closer to the duck pond and flowerbeds of the gardens of the otherwise unspectacular – albeit massive – **Fortezza da Basso** (*see p103*) on the other side of the rat-run main avenue.

Cappelle Medicee

Piazza Madonna degli Aldbrandini (055 238 8602). **Open** 8.15am-5pm Tue-Sat, 1st, 3rd, 5th Sun & 2nd, 4th Mon of mth. **Admission** €6. **No credit cards**. **Map** p314 A3.

The most important Medici were laid to rest in these private chapels. Designed by Michelangelo (from 1519) as the Medici mausoleum, the floor plan of the

Never finished but forever imposing, **San Lorenzo** church. *See p89.*

Holes in the wall

Via degli Alfani, corner Borgo Pinti

The 15th-century stone *edicola* of the Tabernacle of Monteloro was built by the Company of Monteloro, who were based in the convent of Candeli near Florence and whose crest with six boundary stones can be seen on the capitals of the columns. The 14th-century fresco, *Enthroned Madonna and Child with Saints John the Baptist and Peter*, has been attributed to Pucci di Simone, Bernardo Daddi and even the illustrious Andrea Orcagni. It's full of iconographic symbolism; the baby Jesus is holding a bird (representing the spirit), John the Baptist a cross (symbolising faith), and Peter his keys to the gates of Heaven.

Via Tornabuoni, corner Via della Vigna Nuova

Eye-catchingly positioned on the junction of two of the main central shopping streets, this rather gaudy Mannerist stone tabernacle, by unknown 15th- and 16th-century Florentine sculptors, is an oddity in two respects. Firstly, the architectural and sculptural features of its surround are of more artistic importance than the early 15th-century painted stucco *Madonna and Child* it frames. And secondly, in the way it blends in perfectly with the building it adorns. The tympanum and shell (associated with the Madonna in iconography) is an exact reflection of the same features on the palazzo, which was built in 1579 by the Rucellai.

Cappella dei Principi was based on that of Florence's Baptistery and possibly of the Holy Sepulchre in Jerusalem. Inlaid with brilliant pietra dura, which kept the workers of the Opificio delle Pietre Dure busy for centuries, the chapel is constructed from huge hunks of porphyry and ancient Roman marbles hauled into the city by Turkish slaves. It was hoped that the tombs would be joined by that of Christ, but unfortunately for the Medici the authorities in Jerusalem refused to sell it. This chapel also houses the six sarcophagi of the Medici Grand Dukes buried in the crypt.

The adjoining Sagrestia Nuova is dominated by the tombs of Lorenzo il Magnifico's far from magnificent cousins, Giuliano, Duke of Nemours, and Lorenzo, Duke of Urbino, designed by Michelangelo with the allegorical figures of Night and Day, plus Dawn and Dusk reclining atop. Also here is the incomplete tomb of Lorenzo il Magnifico and his brother Giuliano, who are buried beneath it. The coffered dome of the chapel, an architectural masterpiece that was built directly on to a square base, was designed to contribute to Michelangelo's allegory within the tomb of the inevitability of death, symbolising the 'sun' of salvation.

Cenacolo del Conservatorio di Fuligno

Via Faenza 42 (055 286 982). **Open** 9am-noon & by appointment Mon, Tue, Sat. **Admission** free. **Map** p314 A2/3.

The harmonious fresco on the refectory wall of the ex-convent of St Onofrio was discovered in 1845, and at first thought to be the work of Raphael. In fact, it is one of the best of Perugino's works – a *Last*

Supper from about 1490. In the background is a representation of the Oration of the Garden in the characteristically Umbrian landscape, a dead give-away of the painter's roots, when that was in doubt. Perugino was a nickname as he hailed from Perugia.

Cenacolo di Sant'Apollonia

Via XXVII Aprile 1 (055 23885). **Open** 8.15am-1.50pm Tue-Sat, 2nd, 4th Sun & 1st, 3rd, 5th Mon of month. **Admission** free.

The works in this Benedictine refectory, like the frescoes of the *Passion of Christ*, were covered over during the baroque period and only came to light during restoration work. The most important is Andrea del Castagno's *Last Supper* (1445-50) in which the painter reverts to a 14th-century seating plan, with Judas alienated on our side of the table. The vibrant colours and enclosed space intensify the scene. There are also other works by del Castagno, including a *Pietà*.

Chiostro dello Scalzo

Via Cavour 69 (055 238 8604). **Open** 8.15am-1.50pm Mon, Thur, Sat. **Admission** free. **Map** p315 A4.

The 'Cloister of the Barefoot' (so-called because the monk holding the cross in the re-enactments of the Passion of Christ traditionally went barefoot) is frescoed with Andrea del Sarto's monochrome chiaroscuro episodes from the life of St John the Baptist and built to a design by Sangallo around a double courtyard with spindly Corinthian columns. A must-see epitome of delicacy and understatement.

Palazzo Medici-Riccardi

Via Cavour 1 (055 276 0340). **Open** 9am-7pm Mon, Tue, Thur-Sun. **Admission** €4. **No credit cards. Map** p315 B4.

A demonstration of both Medici muscle and subtlety, Palazzo Medici-Riccardi was home to the Medici until they moved into the Palazzo Vecchio in 1540. Not wishing to appear too ostentatious, Cosimo il Vecchio rejected a design by Brunelleschi as too extravagant. He plumped instead for one by Michelozzo, who had just proved his worth as a heavyweight architect in the rebuilding of the San Marco convent complex. Michelozzo designed a façade with a heavily rusticated lower storey in the style of many military buildings, but a smoother, more refined first storey, and a yet more restrained second storey crowned by an overhanging cornice. It was massively expanded and revamped in the 17th century by its new owners the Riccardi, but retains Michelozzo's charming chapel. Almost entirely covered with frescoes by Benozzo Gozzoli, a student of Fra' Angelico, the chapel features a vivid *Journey of the Magi* – actually a portrait of 15th-century Medici. In another room, off the Gallery, is Fra' Filippo Lippi's winsome newly restored *Madonna and Child*. From 2003 to 2005 there will be a series of year-long special exhibitions, starting in 2003 with *Secret Rooms – Long-Lost Rooms*, a route through rooms previously closed to the public. In 2004 there will be a reconstruction itinerary of rooms furnished with the original Medici garb and in 2005 a tribute to the Baroque artists who worked on the palace.

San Lorenzo

Piazza San Lorenzo (055 216 634). **Open** 10am-5pm Mon-Sat. **Admission** €2.50. **Map** p314 A3.

San Lorenzo was the parish church of the Medici family, who largely financed its construction, and for centuries the ruling family continued to lavish money on the place. It was built between 1419 and 1469 to a design by Brunelleschi, sprawling heavy and imposing between piazza di San Lorenzo and piazza di Madonna degli Aldobrandini, with a dome almost as prominent as that of the Duomo.

Despite the fortune spent on the place, the façade was never finished, hence the digestive biscuit bricks. In 1518 the Medici pope Leo X commissioned Michelangelo to design a façade (the models for it can be seen in the Casa Buonarroti; *see p95*). He ordained that the marble should be mined at Pietrasanta, which was part of Florence's domain, but Michelangelo disagreed, preferring high quality Carrara marble. In the end it didn't matter since the scheme was cancelled in 1520.

San Lorenzo was the first church to which Brunelleschi applied his theory of rational proportion. Like Santo Spirito, stroll around and savour it. There are a couple of artworks that merit a closer look. The first is Donatello's bronze pulpits, from which Savonarola snarled his tales of sin and doom. The reliefs are powerful too. You can almost hear the crowds scream in the *Deposition*. On the north wall is a *Martyrdom of St Lawrence* by Mannerist painter par excellence Bronzino. The painting is a decadent affair in which the burning of the saint is attended by muscle-bound men and hefty women with red-gold hair, dressed in pink, green, yellow and lilac. In the second chapel on the right is another Mannerist work, a *Marriage of the Virgin* by Rosso Fiorentino. And in the north transept there is an *Annunciation* by Filippo Lippi, which displays a clarity of line and a depth of perspective that make it perfect for this interior.

Opening off the north transept is the Sagrestia Vecchia (old sacristy). This is another Brunelleschi design with a dome segmented like a tangerine and proportions based on cubes and spheres, along with a fabulous painted *tondi* by Donatello. The doors, also by Donatello, feature martyrs, apostles and Church fathers, while to the left of the entrance there is an elaborate tomb made out of serpentine, porphyry, marble and bronze containing the remains of Lorenzo il Magnifico's father and uncle, by Verrocchio.

Reached via the door to the left of the façade, Michelangelo's architectural classic the Biblioteca Mediceo-Laurenziana was built to house the Medici's large library. It still contains priceless volumes, papyri, codices and documents, though not all of them are on permanent display. In the vestibule is one of Europe's most elegant stairwells, a slick and highly original three-sweep Mannerist design in *pietra serena*, leading into the library reading room.

San Marco

Museum city and home to *David*.

At the heart of this buzzing student quarter is the beautiful porticoed piazza of **Santissima Annunziata**. One of the most aesthetically pleasing squares in the city, it's surrounded on three sides by delicate arcades, while the centre contains a powerful equestrian statue of Grand Duke Ferdinando I by Giambologna. On its eastern side the **Spedale degli Innocenti** (*see p92*), opened in 1445 and the first foundling hospital in Europe, was commissioned by the guild of silk weavers and designed by guild member Brunelleschi. The building is one of the most significant examples of early Renaissance design in the city, and marks the advent of Renaissance town-planning. The powder-blue medallions in the spandrels, each showing a swaddled baby, are by Andrea della Robbia. Unwanted babies, often those of domestic servants, were left in a small revolving door set in the wall on the left to be collected by the nuns. Brunelleschi had envisioned a perfectly symmetrical piazza – to be modern Europe's first – but he died before realising his dream. In the 17th century the porticos were continued around two other sides of the square giving the piazza a human scale and unity absent elsewhere in the city.

Passing under the northernmost arch of the Spedale is via della Colonna with the **Museo Archeologico** (*see p92*). On the west side of the piazza is upmarket hotel **Loggiato dei Serviti** (*see p54*) and, on the north, the church of **Santissima Annunziata** (*see p93*). The street between the two, via Battisti, leads west directly into piazza San Marco, which is best known as a bus hub and as the site of the church of **San Marco** on its north egde. Beside San Marco is the unmissable **Museo di San Marco** (*see p93*), which was once home to Fra' Angelico and Savonarola. On the via Ricasoli corner of piazza San Marco a never-ending queue denotes the **Accademia** (*see below*) – the city's second most-visited museum after, of course, the Uffizi.

North of the piazza are the delightfully eclectic geology and mineral museums of **Museo di Geologia e Paleontologia** (*see p92*) and **Museo di Mineralogia e Lithologia** (*see p92*). Just around the corner is the perfect resting place after a hard morning of sightseeing, the exotic **Giardino dei Semplici** (*see below*).

Galleria dell'Accademia

Via Ricasoli 58-60 (055 238 8609). **Open** 8.15am-6.50pm Tue-Sun. **Admission** €6.50. **No credit cards**. **Map** p314 A4.

Home to Michelangelo's monumental *David* (1504), the Accademia attracts millions of visitors a year. *David* started life as a serious political icon portraying strength and resolve and designed to encourage Florentines to support their fledgling constitution. However, Michelangelo also undoubtedly considered it a monument to his genius since he managed to carve a figure from an exceptionally narrow, 5m (16ft) high slab of marble. The sculpture is top heavy because Michelangelo intended it to be placed on a high column and shaped it so that it would look its best from the beholder's viewpoint. When it was moved from piazza della Signoria in 1873 it was decided to keep the plinth low so visitors could witness his curves close-up. As befits the most famous sculpture in the world, the cleaning of the marble in preparation for *David*'s 500th birthday in 2004 (the first in modern times) was not without its dramas. The inevitable row that arose over what would be the best method to use led to the eventual resignation of the expert restorer.

But the museum is not all about *David*. Lining the walls of the salon where it is kept are Michelangelo's so-called slaves – masterly but unfinished sculptures struggling to escape from their marble prisons. They were intended for Pope Julius II's tomb, a project that Michelangelo was forced to abandon (much to his irritation) in order to paint the Sistine Chapel ceiling in Rome. On the right of *David* is the *Pietà Palestrina*, also attributed to Michelangelo. The stilted lines of the figures surrounding Jesus have led many to believe that it was taken over halfway through by a student of the master.

The gallery also houses a mixed bag of late Gothic and Renaissance paintings in the ground-floor rooms including two of Botticelli's *Madonnas* and bible scenes by Perugino, Fra' Bartolomeo and Filippino Lippi. On the first floor, housing late 14th- and early 15th-century Florentine paintings, is a moving *Pietà* (1365) by Giovanni da Milano. There's also a fabulous collection of musical instruments from the Conservatory of Luigi Cherubini.

Giardino dei Semplici

Via Micheli 3 (055 275 7402). **Open** 9am-1pm Mon-Fri. **Admission** €3. **No credit cards**.

Set up to cultivate exotic plants and research their uses, the Giardino dei Semplici (literally translated, the 'garden of samples') was planted in 1545, on the orders of Cosimo I, on lands seized from an order of

The three-headed Chimera at the **Museo Archeologico**.

Dominican nuns. Essential oils were extracted, perfumes distilled and cures and antidotes sought for various ailments and poisons. It's still a sweet-smelling haven.

Museo Archeologico

Via della Colonna 38 (055 235 75/www.comune.fi.it/soggetti/sat). **Open** 2-7pm Mon; 8.30am-7pm Tue, Thur; 8.30am-2pm Wed, Fri, Sun. **Admission** €4. **No credit cards**. **Map** p314 A5.

Take a break from the Renaissance in one of the most important museums for Etruscan art. Housed in the cross-shaped Palazzo della Crocetta, its Etruscan treasures comprise jewellery, funerary sculpture, urns and bronzes dating from the fifth century BC. Note the important Chimera, a part lion, part goat and part snake mythical beast, and the *Orator and Minerva*. The Egyptian rooms exude a pyramidal mysticism and on the second floor is an extensive collection of Greek ceramics.

Museo dello Spedale degli Innocenti

Piazza SS Annunziata (055 249 1708). **Open** 8.30am-2pm Mon, Tue, Thur-Sun. **Admission** €2.60. **No credit cards**. **Map** p314 A5.

This collection, housed in the former recreation room of Brunelleschi's foundlings hospital, received a substantial blow in 1853 when several important works were auctioned off (for a relative pittance) to raise money for the hospital. What remains constitutes a harmonious collection, with an unsurprising concentration of *Madonna and Bambino* pieces, including a Botticelli and a vivid Luca della Robbia. The highlight is Ghirlandaio's *Adoration of the Magi*, commissioned for the high altar of the hospital's church.

Museo di Geologia e Paleontologia

Via la Pira 4 (055 275 7536/www.unifi.it/unifi/msn). **Open** *Oct-May* 9am-1pm Tue-Sat. *June-Sept* 9am-1pm Wed, Fri. **Admission** €4. **No credit cards**.

An old-fashioned museum with one of the best fossil collections in Italy. In Room 4 the remains of an elephant-like creature found in the Valdarno towers above visitors.

Museo di Mineralogia e Lithologia

Via la Pira 4 (055 275 7537). **Open** *Oct-May* 9am-1pm Tue-Sat. *June-Sept* 9am-1pm Wed, Fri. **Admission** free. **No credit cards**.

Not just for boffins, this simply arranged and clearly explained collection makes gem lovers drool. It's packed full of strange and lovely stones, including 12 huge Brazilian quartzes opposite the entrance. Agates, chalcedony, tourmaline, opals and iridescent limonite sparkle from the cabinets. There are also glass models of famous stones like the Koh-i-noor diamond and treasures from Cosimo III's collection.

Museo di San Marco

Piazza San Marco 1 (055 238 8608). **Open** 8.15am-1.50pm Tue-Fri; 8.15am-6.50pm Sat; 8.15am-1. 50pm 1st, 3rd & 5th Mon of mth; 8.15am-7pm 2nd & 4th Sun of mth. **Admission** €4. **No credit cards**.

Housed in the monastery where Fra' Angelico (known to Florentines as Beato Angelico) and later Fra' Girolamo Savonarola lived with their fellow monks, this museum is largely dedicated to the ethereal paintings of Angelico, arguably the most spiritual artist of the 15th century. You're greeted on the first floor by one of the most famous images in Christendom – an otherworldly *Annunciation*. The same is true of the other images Fra Angelico and his assistants frescoed on the walls of the monks' white vaulted cells. Most of the cells on the outer wall of the left corridor are by Fra' Angelico himself. Particularly outstanding is the lyrical *Noli Me Tangere*, which shows Christ appearing to Mary Magdalene in a field of flowers, and the surreal *Mocking of Christ*, in which Christ's torturers are represented simply by relevant fragments of their anatomy (a hand holding a whip, another holding a sponge, a face spitting). The cell that was occupied by Savonarola is adorned with portraits of the rabid reformer by Fra' Bartolomeo. The bell under the portico of the main cloister was rung in alarm when Savonarola was arrested, and is nicknamed *la piagnona* (the whiner), which is in turn a nickname for the followers of the puritan Savonarola who were said to whine about the depravation and permissiveness of the times.

On the ground floor are more works by Fra' Angelico in the Ospizio dei Pellegrini (pilgrims' hospice). His first commission from 1433 for the Guild of Linen Makers is here: the *Tabernacle of the Madonna dei Linaiuoli*. Painted on wood carved by Ghiberti it contains some of his best-known images, the many-coloured musical angels. Also here is a superb *Deposition* and a *Last Judgement* in which the blessed dance among the flowers and trees of paradise while the damned are boiled in cauldrons and pursued by monsters.

To the right, the refectory is dominated by a Ghirlandaio *Last Supper*, where the disciples, by turn bored, praying, crying or haughty, pick at a frugal repast of bread, wine and cherries against a background of orange trees, a peacock, a Burmese cat and flying ducks – the oranges are the fruits of paradise, the peacock symbolises the Resurrection, the cat as a symbol of evil is near Judas, and the ducks represent the heavens.

Opificio delle Pietre Dure

Via degli Alfani 78 (055 265 111/287 123). **Open** 8.15am-2pm Mon-Wed, Fri,Sat; 8.15am-7pm Thur. **Admission** €2. **No credit cards**. **Map** p314 A4.

The 'workshop of hard stones' was founded in 1588 by Grand Duke Ferdinando I. *Pietra dura* is the craft of inlaying gems or semi-precious stones in intricate mosaics. The Opificio is now an important restoration centre, but also provides a fascinating insight into this typically Florentine art with the mezzanine display of tools and stones and of the methods used for the cutting and polishing of the stones through to the inlay and mosaic techniques.

San Marco

Piazza San Marco (055 287 628). **Open** 8.30am-noon, 4-6pm Mon-Sat; 4-6pm Sun. **Admission** free. **Map** p314 A4.

The Medici lavished even more money on the church and convent of San Marco than on San Lorenzo. In 1434 Cosimo il Vecchio returned from exile and organised the handing over of the monastery of San Marco to the Dominicans. He then funded the renovation of the decaying church and convent by Michelozzo; whether he did so to ease his conscience (banking was still officially forbidden by the Church) or to cash in on the increasing popularity of the Dominicans is uncertain. He also founded a public library full of Greek and Latin works, which had a great influence on Florentine humanists; meetings of the Florentine Humanist Academy were held in the church gardens. Ironically, later in the 15th century San Marco became the base of religious fundamentalist Savonarola who burnt countless humanist treasures in his famous Bonfire of the Vanities. The library now houses the monks' tomes with their exquisite illuminations.

It's worth noting that, at the time of going to press, the church was undergoing what was scheduled to be a sustained period of restoration (the forecasted completion date was set to be somewhere between 2006-7), so don't be surprised to find the interior lined with scaffolding.

Santissima Annunziata

Piazza SS Annunziata (055 266 181). **Open** 7.30am-12.30pm, 4-6.30pm daily. **Admission** free. **Map** p314 A4.

Despite Brunelleschi's perfectionist ambitions for the square it crowns, Santissima Annunziata, the church of the Servite order, is a place of popular worship rather than perfect proportion. There's a frescoed baroque ceiling and an opulent shrine built around a miraculous *Madonna*, purportedly painted by a monk called Bartolomeo in 1252 and, as the story goes, finished overnight by angels – it's from this legend that the church derives its name. Surrounding the icon are flowers, silver lamps and pewter body parts, ex-votos left in the hope that the Madonna will cure the dicky heart or gammy leg of loved ones. Despite its somewhat misleading baroque appearance, the church was actually built by Michelozzo in the 15th century, as can be seen in the light, arcaded atrium. The atrium was frescoed early the following century by Pontormo, Rosso Fiorentino, and most strikingly, Andrea del Sarto, whose *Birth of the Virgin* is set within the walls of a Renaissance palazzo with cherubs perched on a mantelpiece and a festooned bed canopy. There's another del Sarto fresco in the Chiostro dei Morti (cloister of the dead), but you need permission from the sacristan to see it.

Santa Croce

Time to get medieval.

The huge area of Santa Croce proudly covers a significant proportion of central Florence, carrying with it a heady air of history. Its boundaries stretch east from the main avenues leading out from the **Palazzo Vecchio** (*see p79*) in the south, the **Duomo** (*see p67*) in the centre, and the **Museo Archeologico** (*see p92*) in the north. On Santa Croce's western edge is piazza San Firenze with the imposing **Bargello** (*see below*), while via Proconsolo heads north to the **Museo di Antropologia e Etnologia** (*see p95*). In via dell'Oriuolo, off via Proconsolo, you'll find the **Museo di Firenze com'era** (*see p95*) stuffed with the city archives, and in borgo Pinti watch out for the blink-and-you-miss-it entrance to the church of **Santa Maria Maddalena dei Pazzi** (*see p97*).

Between this western border and piazza Santa Croce, with the matchless Gothic church of **Santa Croce** (*see p97*) and its mediocre mock Gothic façade, lie myriad winding streets mostly given over to leather factories and tiny souvenir shops, with the exception of borgo degli Albizi where shops are housed on the ground floors of the dour *palazzi* that line it. The piazza itself is a pedestrian playground of shops and alfresco restaurant tables. On its south side is the frescoed sepia façade of Palazzo d'Antella – decorated in 1620, it now houses smart rental apartments. Outside the church is Enrico Pazzi's 1865 statue of Dante. The sui-homicidal football game *calcio storico* is played here every June (*see p153*).

At the head of piazza Santa Croce, via dei Benci is dotted with crafts shops and bohemian restaurants running down towards the Arno, past the eclectic **Museo Horne** (*see p96*) to Ponte alle Grazie (on whose piers there used to be several oratories and chapels and a few workshops, before they were demolished in the 19th century). One of these chapels, devoted to Santa Maria delle Grazie, was much visited by distraught lovers seeking solace, giving the bridge its name. The original stone bridge, built in 1227, was the only one in Florence to survive a flood in 1333. But it was later destroyed during World War II, to be replaced by the present structure in 1957.

Continuing east on lungarno delle Grazie or corso dei Tintori (named after the dyers who lived here in medieval times) you'll come across a main parking square dominated by the **Biblioteca Nazionale**. Built to house the three million books and two million documents that were held in the Uffizi until 1935, the national library has two towers with statues of Dante and Galileo. In mock disrespect Florentines nicknamed the twin towers 'the asses' ears'.

Behind Santa Croce past the **Casa Buonarroti** (*see p95*) in via Ghibellina, it's a different scene. A young, alternative element manifests itself in ads for tattooists, graffiti and flyers for gigs and benefits at the student centres. At the heart of this district is the fruit and vegetable market of **Santí Ambrogio** (*see p140* **Trading places**) along with piazza dei Ciompi, and the shops, bars, *pizzerie* and restaurants of borgo La Croce where you'll find piazza Ghiberti, home of the renowned **Cibrèo** (*see p115*). Borgo La Croce extends as far as piazza Beccaria and rests at the east city gate, Porta alla Croce.

Named after the dyers' and wool workers' revolt of 1378, piazza dei Ciompi is taken over by an interesting junk and antiques market during the week and a huge day-long flea market on the last Sunday of the month. Dominated by the **Loggia del Pesce**, it was built by Vasari in 1568 for the Mercato Vecchio, which occupied the site of piazza della Repubblica. Taken apart in the 19th century and re-erected here, it now shelters a book stand.

Bargello

Via del Proconsolo 4 (055 238 8606/www.sbas.firenze.it/bargello). **Open** 8.15am-1.50pm Tue-Sat, 2nd, 4th Sun & 1st, 3rd, 5th Mon of mth. **Admission** €4. **No credit cards**. **Map** p315 C4.

The fortified building of the Bargello started life as Palazzo del Popolo in 1250 and soon became the mainstay of the chief magistrate, or *podestà*. In the 14th century bodies of executed criminals were displayed in the courtyard and in the 15th century law courts, prisons and torture chambers were set up inside. Its present name is derived from the 16th century when the Medici made it the seat of the chief of police, the Bargello. In 1865 it opened as a museum.

These days, the museum holds one of the city's most eclectic and prestigious collections, ranging from prime sculptures by the likes of Michelangelo, Donatello, Cellini and Giambologna to Scandinavian chess sets and Egyptian ivories. The most famous pieces are Michelangelo's *Bacchus Drunk*, Giambologna's fleet-of-foot *Mercury* and the *Davids* of Donatello. The first-floor loggia in the courtyard

The Gothic splendour of **Santa Croce**. *See p97*.

has Giambologna's virtuoso aviary of bronze birds, including a madly exaggerated turkey. This leads to the Salone Donatello with his two triumphant *Davids* and tense *St George*, the original sculpture that once adorned one of the tabernacles on the outside of Orsanmichele. Also fascinating are the two bronze panels of the *Sacrifice of Isaac* sculpted by Brunelleschi and Lorenzo Ghiberti for a competition to design the north doors of the Duomo Baptistery.

Casa Buonarroti

Via Ghibellina 70 (055 241 752/www.casabuonarroti.it). **Open** 9.30am-2pm Mon, Wed-Sun. **Admission** €6.50. **No credit cards**. **Map** p315 C5.

Michelangelo owned but never actually lived in this house. Casa Buonarroti's collection of memorabilia (put together by the artist's great-nephew Filippo) is a little contrived. Nevertheless there are some interesting reproductions of scenes from the painter's life painted on the walls of La Galleria, and two original works, a bas-relief *Madonna of the Stairs* breastfeeding at the foot of a flight of stairs and an unfinished *Battle of the Centaurs*, both of which are from Michelangelo's adolescence.

Museo di Antropologia e Etnologia

Via del Proconsolo 12 (055 239 6449). **Open** 9am-1pm Mon-Wed, Fri, Sat. **Admission** €4. **No credit cards**. **Map** p315 B4.

A newly arranged mixed bag of goodies from all over the world, including a collection of Peruvian mummies, an Ostyak harp in the shape of a swan from Lapland, an engraved trumpet made from an elephant tusk from the former Belgian Congo, Ecuadorian shrunken heads complete with a specially designed skull-beating club and a Marini-meets-Picasso equestrian monument.

Museo Fiorentino di Preistoria

Via Sant'Egidio 21 (055 295 159/www.museofiorentinopreistoria.it). **Open** 9.30am-12.30pm Mon-Sat; guided tours by appointment. **Admission** €3. **No credit cards**. **Map** p315 B4.

Museo Fiorentino di Preistoria traces humanity's development from the Paleolithic to the Bronze Age. The first floor follows hominid physical changes, and also examines Italy's prehistoric artistic legacy. Unfortunately, the evidence is mostly found in caves, so the museum has to content itself with various displays of photographs and illustrations. The second floor covers the rest of the world and includes a collection of stone implements found by Frenchman Boucher de Perthes, who ascertained that rocks previously believed to have been shaped by weathering and glacial movement were actually the work of prehistoric humans.

Museo di Firenze com'era

Via dell'Oriuolo 24 (055 261 6545). **Open** 9am-2pm Mon-Wed, Fri-Sun. **Admission** €2.70. **No credit cards**. **Map** p315 B5.

This charmingly named museum of 'Florence as it was' traces the city's development through collections of maps, paintings and archeological discoveries. There are rooms devoted to: Giuseppe Poggi's plans from the 1860s to modernise Florence by creating Parisian-style boulevards; the famous lunettes of the Medici villas painted in 1599 by Flemish artist Giusto Utens; and the history of the region from 200 million years ago to Roman times. New exhibits include a model of 'Florentia', showing how the city must have been in Roman times with the Forum right underneath present-day piazza della Repubblica and a Roman theatre buried under the Palazzo Vecchio. Also interesting is the huge reproduction of the famous *Pianta della Catena*, a 19th-century copy of

Holes in the wall

Piazza dell'Unità corner Via Sant'Antonino

Built for the 25th wedding anniversary of Cassandra Cerretani and Alessandro Capponi, this 18th-century tabernacle in *pietra serena* holds a ceramic roundel of a tender milky-white *Madonna and Child* by Andrea della Robbia, he of the swaddled baby medallions of piazza Santissima Annunziata. His work was so well considered it gave its name to a style of ceramic art – *robbiano*. Under the blue-glazed terracotta medallion are the family crests of the Capponi and the Cerretani, who owned the flashiest palazzo in the tabernacle's square, then called piazza Vecchia di Santa Maria Novella.

Via Ricasoli corner Via dei Pucci

One of the best-known in the city, this unique double-niche tabernacle is nicknamed 'the Five Lanterns'. The fresco on the left is a *Madonna and Child with Saints Stephen and Catherine of Alexandria* by an unknown 14th-century Florentine painter, while in the niche on the right is the *Enthroned Madonna and Child with Two Angels and the Saints John the Baptist and Saint Zanobi* (the two most important saints of Florence), a 15th-century fresco by Cosimo Rosselli, who worked on the Sistine Chapel with Michelangelo. The slot in the marble plaque was originally intended for donations to cover the cost of the lamp oil.

a 1470 engraving (the original of which is now in Berlin) showing the first topological plan of Florence. It's possible to pick out the monuments and other features that are still there today.

Museo Horne

Via dei Benci 6 (055 244 661). **Open** 9am-1pm Mon-Sat. **Admission** €5. **No credit cards. Map** p315 C4.

The 15th-century Palazzo Corsi-Alberti was bought by English architect and art historian Herbert Percy Horne in the late 19th century and he spent years restoring it to its original Renaissance splendour. When he died he left the palazzo and his vast and fabulous, magpie-like collection to the state. In 1922 it opened as a museum. Objects on the ground floor range from ceramics and Florentine coins to a coffee grinder and a pair of spectacles. Upstairs is a damaged wooden panel from a triptych attributed to Masaccio. Also here is an *Exorcism* by the Maestro di San Severino and the pride of the Horne collection, a gold-black *Santo Stefano* by Giotto. Other famous works include a limbless statue of an athlete by Giambologna and a painted wedding chest by Filippino Lippi.

Museo dell'Opera di Santa Croce & Cappella dei Pazzi

Piazza Santa Croce 16 (055 246 6105/www.operadisantacroce.it). **Open** 9.30am-5.30pm Mon-Sat; 1-5.30pm Sun. **Admission** €4 (incl Santa Croce church). **No credit cards. Map** p315 C5.

Access to this museum and to Brunelleschi's geometric tour de force, the Cappella dei Pazzi, is now through Santa Croce church (*see p97*). Planned in the 1430s and completed 40 years late, the chapel is based on a central square topped by a cupola flanked by two barrel-vaulted bays with decorative arches on the white walls echoing the structural arches. The pure lines of the interior are decorated with Luca della Robbia's painted ceramic roundels of the 12 apostles and the four evangelists. Across the courtyard is the small museum of church treasures, including Donatello's pious bronze *St Louis of Toulouse* from Orsanmichele. The backbone of the collection here is in the former refectory with Taddeo Gaddi's *Last Supper* – the impact of which is reduced due to its bad condition and the imposing yet poetic *Tree of Life* above. In equally poor condition is Cimabue's *Crucifixion*, which hung in the basilica until the flood of 1966. There's also a small permanent exhibition of the woodcuts and engravings of the modern artist Pietro Parigi, whose reawakening of Tuscan realism in religious illustrations earned him fame.

Santa Croce

Piazza Santa Croce (055 244 619). **Open** 9.30am-5.30pm Mon-Sat; 1-5.30pm Sun. **Admission** €4 (incl museum & chapel). **Map** p315 C5.

Santa Croce remains the richest medieval church in the city, with frescoes by Giotto, a chapel by Brunelleschi, the Cappella dei Pazzi (*see p96*), and the tombs of many of the city's illustrious, which lead to its local nickname 'the Pantheon'. At first sight the interior seems big and gloomy, with overbearing marble tombs clogging the walls. Not all the tombs contain bodies: Dante's (right aisle) is simply a memorial to the writer, who is buried in Ravenna. In the niche alongside is the tomb of Michelangelo by Vasari (he actually died in Rome, but his body was brought back to Florence, according to his wishes). Further into the church are the tombs of Leonardo Bruni by Bernardo Rossellino, Vittorio Alfieri and Count Ugolino della Gherardesca. Back at the top of the left aisle is Galileo's tomb, a polychrome marble confection that was created by Foggini more than a century after the astronomer's death when the Church finally permitted him a Christian burial, having previously branded him a heretic.

It is something of a paradox that the church is filled with the tombs of the great and the grand, given that it belonged to the Franciscans, the most unworldly of the religious orders. They founded it in 1228, ten years after arriving in the city. A recently established order, they were supposed to make their living by manual work, preaching and begging. At the time, Santa Croce was a slum, home to the city's dyers and wool workers. Franciscan preaching, with its message that all men were equal, had a huge impact on the poor people of the quarter, and it was in part due to the confidence given them by the Franciscans that, in 1378, the dyers and wool workers revolted against the guilds. As for the Franciscans, their vow of poverty slowly eroded. By the late 13th century, the old church was felt to be inadequate and a new church was planned – intended to be one of the largest in Christendom, and designed by Arnolfo di Cambio, architect of the Duomo and the Palazzo Vecchio, who himself laid the first stone on 3 May 1294. It was financed partly by property confiscated from Ghibellines who had been convicted of heresy.

The church underwent various stages of restoration and modification with one of Vasari's infamous remodernisation's robbing it of the frescoes of the school of Giotto in three naves in favour of heavy classical altars. Fortunately, he left the main chapels intact, though subsequent makeovers completely destroyed the decorations of the Cappella Tosinghi-Spinelli. Among the remaining gems, however, are the fabulous stained-glass windows at the east end (behind the high altar) by Agnolo Gaddi, the beautifully carved marble tomb of Leonardo Bruni and the Cavalcanti tabernacle (both of which are to be found flanking the side door on the south wall).

The Bardi and Peruzzi chapels, which were completely frescoed by Giotto, are masterpieces, although the condition of the frescoes is not brilliant – a result of Giotto painting on dry instead of wet plaster (a technique that's known as *secco*) and of them being daubed with whitewash – the frescoes were only rediscovered in the mid 18th century. The most striking of the two chapels is the Bardi, with scenes from the life of St Francis in haunting, virtual monotone, the figures just stylised enough to make them otherworldly yet individual enough to make them human. On the far side of the high altar is the Cappella Bardi di Vernio, frescoed by one of Giotto's most interesting followers, Maso di Banco, in fresh, vibrant colours.

Santa Maria Maddalena dei Pazzi

Borgo Pinti 58 (055 247 8420). **Open** 9am-noon daily. **Admission** €1. **Map** p315 B5.

Tucked away behind an anonymous un-numbered door is the church and monastery of Santa Maria Maddalena dei Pazzi. And it's worth all the counting of street numbers to ensure that you get here, if only for a glimpse of Perugino's luminous fresco, *Crucifixion and Saints* of 1493, which covers an entire wall in the Sala Capitolare (named after the Ionic capitals of its columns).

Synagogue & Museo di Arte e Storia Ebraica

Via Farini 4 (055 234 6654). **Open** *Apr-May, Sept-Oct* 10am-5pm Mon-Thur, Sun; 10am-2pm Fri. *June-Aug* 10am-6pm Mon-Thur, Sun; 10am-2pm Fri. *Nov-Mar* 10am-3pm Mon-Thur, Sun; 10am-2pm Fri. **Admission** €4. **No credit cards. Map** p315 B5.

Built in 1870 following the demolition of the ghetto, this synagogue is an extraordinarily ornate mix of Moorish, Byzantine and Eastern influences with its walls and ceilings covered in polychrome arabesques. Housed on the first floor, under the copper dome of the main temple, the Museum of Jewish Art and History holds a collection tracing the history of Jews in Florence from their supposed arrival as Roman slaves to their official introduction into the city as money-lenders on the invitation of the Florentine Republic in 1430. Exhibits include documented stories, jewellery, ceremonial objects and furniture, photos and drawings (many of which depict the ghetto that occupied the area just north of piazza della Repubblica).

Oltrarno

Low-key, local and loveable.

Spanning the width of the city centre south of the river, the Oltrarno (literally 'beyond the Arno'), tapers south-west to Porta Romana, through the parishes of Santo Spirito and San Frediano, and to the south-east encompasses steep picturesque country lanes that lead via the San Niccolò area to the grand main avenues and the famed tourist pilgrimage destination **piazzale Michelangelo** (*see below*).

Borgo San Jacopo, which backs on to the river, is an odd mix of medieval towers and *palazzi*, shops and '60s council-block-style monstrosities built to replace the houses bombed in the war. The street is sandwiched between the splendid *palazzi* of the antique-shop-lined via Maggio and via dei Guicciardini with its expensive paper, crafts and jewellery shops and the grandeur of the Medici's gargantuan **Palazzo Pitti** (*see p99*). The palazzo's rusticated façade bears down on its sloping forecourt, dwarfing tourists visiting its museums or to wander around the **Boboli Gardens** (*see p99*) behind it.

South-east of the Ponte Vecchio, snaking steeply uphill towards **Forte di Belvedere** (*see p99*), the Medici's summer retreat, are the *costas*, pretty narrow lanes with a country feel. Behind lungarno Serristori and its **Museo di Casa Siviero** (*see p99*) is San Niccolò, a sleepy village district – until the evening, when the wine bars and Tuscan *osterie* fill up and the bars on via dei Renai overflow on to the pavements of the riverside piazza Demidoff. The edge of San Niccolò is signalled by Porta di San Niccolò in piazza Poggi, but turn right before then into via San Miniato and cross Porta San Miniato to via del Monte alle Croci to a long trail of lichen-covered steps that take you up into the piazzale Michelangelo.

West of the Ponte Vecchio are the bohemian areas of Santo Spirito and San Frediano. Piazza Santo Spirito is a lively but low-key space that still very much belongs to the locals. Furniture restorers have workshops just off the square, nearby *trattorie* serve good, cheap food, there's a daily morning market, and an organic food market (third Sunday of the month) and a flea market (second Sunday of the month) spill across the piazza on Sundays. The bars and alfresco restaurants are meeting places for a pre-club, arty set, and in summer, crowds sit on the steps of the remarkable church of Santo Spirito (*see p102*), drinking beer and playing guitars.

South of the piazza, via Romana is a narrow main road lined with unusual craft and antiques shops and home to **La Specola** (*see p102*), the zoology museum. On the far side of via dei Serragli, in San Frediano, things are even more villagey. Local artisans bustle around with picture frames or weird pieces of furniture under their arms; by night piazza del Carmine, home to **Santa Maria del Carmine** church and the **Brancacci Chapel** (for both, *see p102*), sees the smart lot congregating outside the Dolce Vita bar (*see p131*). For a genuine taste of the locals' Florence, walk west into borgo San Frediano with its 18th-century baroque church, small *trattorie* and a few recently opened modern restaurants.

Fontana dell'Isola in the **Giardini di Boboli**. *See p99.*

Cenacolo di Santo Spirito

Piazza Santo Spirito 29 (055 287 043). **Open** 9am-1.30pm Tue-Sun. **Admission** €2.20. **No credit cards. Map** p314 D1.

The Last Supper by Andrea Orcagna isn't the foremost reason for visiting this former Augustinian refectory. The fresco was butchered by an 18th-century architect commissioned to build some doors into it so it could be used as a carriage depot. Today, only the fringes remain, although there's a more complete but heavily restored *Crucifixion* above. Otherwise, the museum houses an eclectic collection of sculptures given to the state in 1946 on the death of sailor Salvatore Romano, who considered his body in its sarcophagus a worthy partner to sculptures by Tino di Camaino and reliefs by Donatello.

Forte di Belvedere

Via San Leonardo (055 27681). **Open** Call for details. **Admission** free. **Map** p314 D3.

Also known as the Forte di San Giorgio and recently re-opened (after a major restoration job), this star-shaped fortress was built by Bernardo Buontalenti in 1590. Originally intended to protect the city from insurgents, it soon became a refuge for the Medici Grand Dukes and a strongroom for their treasures. Apart from giving a good bird's eye view of the city, the fort is used for temporary art exhibitions and, in summer, it runs an evening cultural programme and an open-air cinema (*see p161*).

Museo Bardini

Piazza dei Mozzi 1 (055 234 2427). Closed for restoration until at least 2005. **Map** p315 D4.

Art dealer Stefano Bardini, who built this palazzo in 1881 on the site of a 13th-century church using salvaged palatial fittings, bequeathed his huge collection to the city on his death in 1922.

Museo di Casa Siviero

Lungarno Serristori 1-3 (055 234 5219/guided tours 055 293 007). **Open** 9.30am-12.30pm Mon; 3.30-6.30pm Sat. **Admission** free. **Map** p314 D4.

This was previously the house of Rodolfo Siviero, dubbed 'the James Bond of art' for his relentless efforts to prevent the Nazis plundering Italian masters and for his success in retrieving many that were taken. Many artists exhibited were personal friends of Siviero (a government minister) and the collection includes works by De Chirico, Annigoni and Messina. Visits are supervised by friendly guides.

Palazzo Pitti

Piazza Pitti, Via Romana. **Map** p314 D1.

The Pitti Palace was built in 1457 for Luca Pitti, a Medici rival, probably to a design by Brunelleschi that had been rejected by Cosimo il Vecchio as too grandiose. It was also too grandiose for the Pitti, and less than a century later they were forced to sell to the doubtless gleeful Medici. The palace was more luxurious than the draughty Palazzo Vecchio and in 1549 Cosimo I and his wife Eleonora di Toledo moved in. Huge as it was, it wasn't big enough for the Medici, and Ammanati was charged with remodelling the façade and creating the courtyard. The façade was extended in the 17th century and two further wings added in the 18th century. It now holds the vast, opulent Medici collection.

One of Oltrarno's many artisans. *See p98.*

Giardini di Boboli

055 265 1816/1838. **Open** *June-Aug* 8.15am-7.30pm daily. *Nov-Feb* 8.15am-4.30pm daily. *Mar* 8.15am-5.30pm daily. *Apr, May, Sept & Oct* 8.15am-6.30pm daily. Closed 1st & last Mon of mth. **Admission** €4 (incl Museo delle Porcellane & Museo degli Argenti). **No credit cards. Map** p314 D1-3.

The Boboli Gardens, the only park in central Florence, was laid out for Eleonora di Toledo and Cosimo I. By the entrance is the repulsive fountain showing Cosimo I's obese dwarf as a nude *Bacchus*, but the gardens are a joy from there on in. A highlight is Buontalenti's famous grotto (currently being restored) with statues of *Ceres* and *Apollo* by Bandinelli, casts of Michelangelo's *Dying Slaves* and a second grotto adorned with frescoes of classic Greek and Roman myths and encrusted with shells. Directly behind the centre of the Pitti Palace with one of the best views of the city is the octagonal 'artichoke' fountain by del Tadda. Climbing the ramps takes you to the authentically classical amphitheatre, the venue where Jacopo Peri's and Giulio Caccini's *Euridice* (widely acknowledged to be the first ever opera) was staged for the Medici in 1600. Further up the hill still is the Museo delle Porcellane (*see p102*), which is entered through the Giardino dei Cavalieri. The Viottolone, a cyprus-lined avenue, leads past the rococo Kaffeehaus (1776) to L'Isolotto, a miniature island with a copy of Giambologna's *Oceanus*. The gardens, which run up to the Forte di Belvedere (no access) and down to Porta Romana, are beautifully kept. In summer Boboli now hosts prestigious ballets, plays and fashion shows. For a guided walk of the Boboli, *see pp110-11.*

Sightseeing

Walk 2 The green scene

Most visitors enter the gardens from the main Pitti courtyard. So, to avoid the queues, use the Annalena entrance in via Romana (opposite the Pensione Annalena). Immediately ahead of you is a small grotto decorated in a nautical theme and sheltering statues of Adam and Eve. Turn left, walk up the hill a few yards and take the first lane on the right. Turn immediately left again and at the top of the hill turn right. About halfway along this covered path is the entrance to the Botanical Gardens also known as the *Giardino degli Ananas* after the pineapples once grown here. Continue along the same path to the magnificent viale dei Cipressi (also known as 'il Viottolone'), a wide, steeply sloping avenue lined with glorious statues and age-old cypress trees.

At the bottom of the viale dei Cipressi lies the gorgeous Isolotto, a small island sitting in a circular moat laid out in 1612. In the middle is the *Fountain of Oceanus* designed by Tribolo for Cosimo II with its central figure of Neptune, a copy of a statue by Giambologna. The island is filled with orange and lemon trees in huge terracotta pots (200 of them). The moat is filled with murky green water evocative of the River Styx. You can rest on one of the stone benches let into the hedge.

Beyond the Isolotto is the semi-circular Prato delle Collonne. From here, turn right and join viale della Meridiana, which follows via Romana back towards the upper gardens. At the top, you emerge with the Meridiana wing of Palazzo Pitti on your left and a colossal Roman *vasca* (basin) on your right. Take one of the steep paths that climbs the hill and get splendid views of Florence. Follow the path on the left side of the tree-lined lawn at the top, past a monumental bronze sculpture by Igor Mitoraj. This comes out at the top of the viale dei Cipressi. From here follow the path that passes a row of old houses and leads to an elegant double stairway that sweeps up to the walled Giardino del Cavalieri, the highest point in the gardens. From here the views are purely rural; villas and the odd crenellated tower, olive groves, cypress trees and no sign of the modern city.

Back at the bottom of the steps, the path immediately to your right brings you to an enormous statue of *Abundance* clutching a sheaf of golden corn. Instead of going with the flow down the steps, walk past *Abundance* and along the path that follows the walls of Forte di Belvedere. At the back gate of the fort, follow any one of the little paths leading back down to the crowds and to the huge amphitheatre. Here you'll find the superb baroque fountain, *Fontana del Carciofo* (named after the bronze artichoke that once topped it). Head round to the right and a gravel path (once a carriageway) leads to a small rose garden dominated by a statue of *Jupiter* by Baccio Bandinelli. The little path to the right passes a peony- and rose-filled garden and ends at the small Grotticina di Madama, dominated by bizarre statues of goats and the first of the several grottoes for which the garden was to become famous.

Back at *Jupiter*, follow the railings round to the right along a circuitous route to the huge Grotta Grande or the Grotta di Buontalenti, which has been closed for restoration for ages. You can, however, see inside. It was

Galleria d'Arte Moderna

055 238 8616. **Open** 8.15am-1.50pm Tue-Sat (last entry 1.15pm), 2nd, 4th Mon of mth & 1st, 3rd, 5th Sun of mth. **Admission** €5 (incl Museo del Costume). **No credit cards**.

The 30 top floor rooms of the Pitti that constitute Florence's modern art museum were royal apartments until 1920. The varied collection covers neoclassical to early 20th-century art ('modern' being a relative term in Florence). Highlights are Giovanni Dupré's bronze sculptures of *Cain and Abel* (room five) and Ottone Rosai's simple *Piazza del Carmine* in room 30. There are also disaster areas: rooms 11, 12, 18 and 19 house Italian Impressionist work of the Macchiaioli school, who used dots (*macchie*) to paint.

Museo del Costume

055 238 8713. **Open** 8.15am-1.50pm Tue-Sat (last entry 1.15pm), 2nd, 4th Mon of mth & 1st, 3rd, 5th Sun of mth. **Admission** €5 (incl Galleria d'Arte Moderna). **No credit cards**.

The costume museum is next to the Palazzina della Meridiana, which periodically served as residence to the Lorraine family and the House of Savoy and also houses a permanent exhibition of works by Romantic artists no longer in the Galleria d'Arte Moderna. Archives include 15th-century costumes, 18th-century robes *à la française* and fin de siècle attire by Rosa Genoni. A large part of the collection are Cosimo I and Eleonora di Toledo's clothes, including her sumptuous velvet creation from Bronzino's portrait.

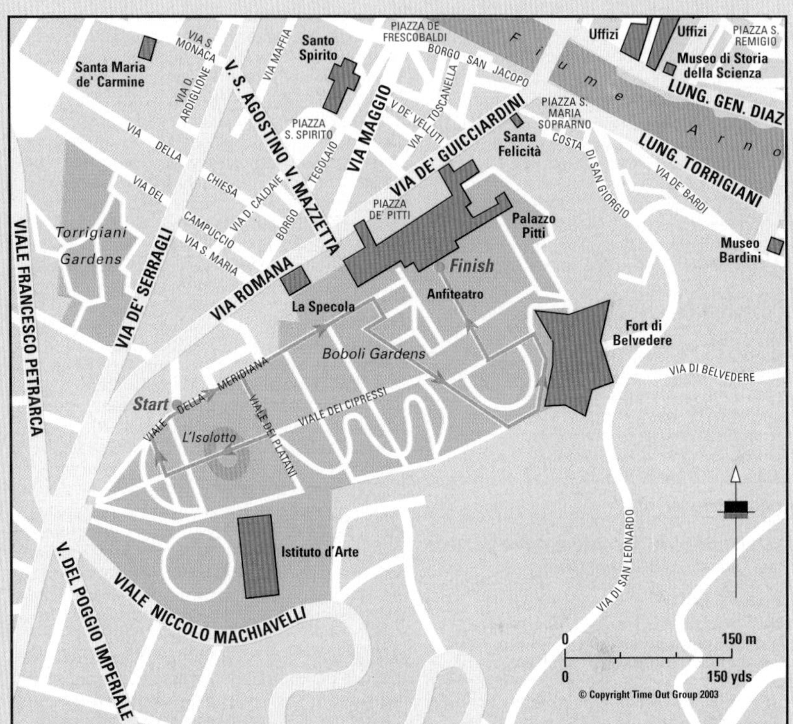

built between 1557 and 1593 by heavyweights Vasari, Ammannati and Buontalenti and contains casts of Michelangelo's unfinished *Slaves*, an erotic statue of *Paris Abducting Helen* and, at the back, a luscious *Venus* emerging from her bath by Giambologna. On the main path, the last curiosity before the exit is a famous statue of *Pietro Barbino*, Cosimo I's pot-bellied dwarf riding a turtle.

Galleria del Palatina & Appartamenti Reali
055 238 8614. **Open** 8.15am-6.50pm Tue-Sun. **Admission** €6.50. **No credit cards**.

The Galleria has paintings hung four or five high on its damask walls. Included in the collection are a beautiful Filippo Lippi, *Madonna and Child*, which shows his sophisticated understanding of line, colour and form, and several works by Raphael. For example, the innovative *Holy Family*, which was his last painting and shows his susceptibility to the influences of Michelangelo. In addition, there are some inspired works by Titian.

There are 28 rooms in all. Linger longest over the Planet Rooms: five rooms named after Venus, Mercury (Apollo), Mars, Jupiter and Saturn, supposedly in honour of Galileo Galilei. The Venus Room, Sala di Venere, is dominated by a statue of Venus by Canova. Crowned by a gilded stucco ceiling it also contains Titian's regal *La Bella*. The Sala di Apollo, overdecorated like the other planet rooms by Pietro da Cortona, houses the nine Muses and is crowded with works by Rosso Fiorentino and Andrea del Sarto. Mars, the Sala di Marte, houses Rubens's *Consequences of War* and his *Four Philosophers*, which contains a suitably detached self-portrait (the standing figure on the left). The best place to look in the Jupiter Room, the Sala di Giove, is up, in order to admire the depiction of Jupiter with his eagle and his lightning, surrounded by the Virtues, Hercules and Chance.

Also look out for Raphael's lover, the 'baker girl' Margherita Luti, in his *La Velata*. Lastly, the Sala di Saturno contains some of Raphael's best-known works, including the *Madonna of the Grand Duke*, showing a distinct Leonardo influence. The other rooms of the Palatine also follow a classical style with names like Allegory, Prometheus, Hercules, Ulysses and Iliad.

Museo degli Argenti

055 238 8709. **Open** 8.30am-6.30pm Tue-Sat, 2nd & 4th Mon of mth. **Admission** €4 (incl Museo delle Porcellane & Boboli Gardens). **No credit cards**.

Not just silver, but a two-tier museum of treasures amassed by the Medici, from beautiful vases and ornate crystal cups to a breathtakingly banal collection of miniature animals. The ornate rooms also hold Medici tapestries, furniture and carpets.

Museo delle Porcellane

055 238 8709. **Open** same as Boboli Gardens. **Admission** €4 (incl Boboli Gardens & Museo degli Argenti). **No credit cards**.

At the top of the Boboli Gardens, this former reception room for artists, built by Leopoldo de' Medici, offers inspiring views over the Tuscan hills. The museum displays china used by the various occupants of Palazzo Pitti and includes the largest selection of Viennese china outside Vienna.

Museo delle Carrozze

055 238 8614. Closed for restoration.

A collection of carriages that once belonged to the Medici, Lorraine and Savoy houses.

Santa Felicità

Piazza Santa Felicità (055 213 018). **Open** 9am-noon, 3-6pm Mon-Sat; 9am-1pm Sun (except 9am & noon services). **Admission** free. **Map** p314 D2.

This little church occupies the site of the first church in Florence, founded in the second century by Syrian Greek tradesmen who settled in the area. There are no traces of its ancient beginnings as the interior is largely 18th century. Vasari built the portico in 1564 to support the Corridoio Vasariano (*see p77*). The main reason to visit is Pontormo's *Deposition* altarpiece in the Barbadori-Capponi Chapel.

Santa Maria del Carmine & the Brancacci Chapel

Piazza del Carmine (055 238 2195). **Open** Chapel 10am-5pm Mon, Wed-Sat; 1-5pm Sun. **Admission** €4. **No credit cards**. **Map** p314 C1.

Santa Maria del Carmine is a blowsy baroque church dominated by a huge single nave adorned with pilasters and pious sculptures overlooked by a ceiling fresco of *The Ascension*. It was built in 1782 to replace a medieval church belonging to the Carmelite order, most of which burned down in 1771. Miraculously, the Brancacci Chapel, matchlessly frescoed in the 15th century by Masaccio and Masolino, escaped damage.

The artists were an odd pair with little in common other than that they were both born in the Val d'Arno; Masolino was a court painter, his graceful style in tune with the decorative international Gothic traditions of artists, while Masaccio was a revelation to the art world with his realistic and emotive style. When Masaccio died aged just 27 he'd changed the direction of art forever, kick-starting the Renaissance and reaching his peak with his cycle of frescoes here. Compare Masolino's elegant Adam and Eve in *The Temptation* with Masaccio's masterpiece, the grief-stricken *Expulsion from Paradise*, or Masolino's dandified Florentines in their silks and brocades with Masaccio's simple saints. There are two themes to the paintings: the redemption of sinners, and scenes from the life of St Peter. Work on the frescoes stopped for 60 years after Masaccio's death and was then taken up again by Filippino Lippi, whose most striking contribution was *The Release of St Peter*. Restored in the 1980s, there are now strict rules about how many people can visit the fresco (visits limited to 15 mins).

Santo Spirito

Piazza Santo Spirito (055 210 030). **Open** 8.30am-noon, 4-6pm Mon, Tue, Thur-Sun; 8.30am-noon Wed. **Admission** free. **Map** p314 D2/3.

One of Brunelleschi's most extraordinary works, though the consummately plain cream 18th-century façade gives little clue as to the incomparable achievements on its other side. Inside is a world of perfect proportions, a Latin-cross church lined with a continuous colonnade of dove grey *pietra serena* pilasters sheltering 38 chapels. There was an Augustinian church on the site from 1250, but in 1397 the monks decided to replace it, cutting one meal a day to finance the project. They eventually commissioned Brunelleschi to design it. Work started in 1444, two years before Brunelleschi died, and the façade and exterior walls were never finished. Vasari reckoned that had the church been completed as planned it would have been 'the most perfect temple of Christianity'. It's hard to disagree, especially since its just-completed major restoration, which has left it looking pristine. Left of the church is the Cenacolo di Santo Spirito museum (*see p99*).

La Specola

Via Romana 17 (055 228 8251). **Open** 9am-1pm Mon, Tue, Thur-Sun. **Admission** €5. **No credit cards**. **Map** p314 D1.

Known as La Specola (observatory) because of the telescope on the roof, this is actually Florence's zoology museum. The first 23 rooms are crammed with stuffed and pickled animals. Room nine has a repulsive collection of hunting trophies donated by the Count of Turin, including an elephant-skin sofa. From room 24 onwards, the exhibits become still more grotesque. In a Frankenstein-esque laboratory, wax corpses lie on satin beds, each a little more dissected than the last, and walls are covered with dismembered and perfectly realistic body parts crafted as teaching aids between 1771 and the late 1800s by artist Clemente Susini and physiologist Felice Fontana. Also look out for the gory tableaux devoted to Florence during the plague, made by Sicilian wax sculptor Giulio Gaetano Zumbo.

Outside the City Gates

Escape the steamy city and head for the hills.

Although most of what attracts visitors to Florence lies within the boundaries once created by the now mostly defunct medieval city walls, anyone who is prepared to venture a little further afield will be richly rewarded. Eight of the 16 original gates into the city are still standing and are now more or less linked by the ring road or *viali*. These outlying areas are well served by the ATAF bus network and almost all the places listed below are on a city bus route or within a very short walk of a bus stop. For ticket details, *see p279*.

To the north, south and east, Florence is hemmed in by hills. This fact is largely responsible for the damp climate, but also means there's a natural barrier against urban sprawl and allows you to quickly get up into what feels like the countryside. This is particularly true south of the river, where hills practically rise from the banks of the Arno. To the north, genteel suburbia extends further before being thwarted by the hills that lead up to Fiesole and Settignano. To the east, development follows the Arno for some kilometres. This isn't to say that Florence is devoid of suburban ugliness. West and north-west of the centre, unimaginative housing and industrial development have claimed swathes of land, creating *quartieri* like Brozzi, Campi Bisenzio, Scandicci and Sesto Fiorentino. Building work at Firenze Nova, the new satellite city and administrative centre, is now well underway on reclaimed land to the west. These areas have some elegant villas built in the countryside, even if they are flanked by uninspiring blocks of flats.

The **Cimitero degli Inglesi**. *See p105.*

North of the river

Any round-up of attractions beyond the city walls has to begin with the **Parco delle Cascine** in the west. A green oasis just beyond Porta al Prato and outside the carbon-monoxide hell of the *viale*, this 3.5-kilometre (2.25-mile) long public park stretches along the north bank of the Arno and is backed by woods that were once full of deer. Its name comes from *cascina*, meaning dairy farm, which is what the Medici originally used the area as. Later it became a hunting park and, simultaneously, a space for theatre and public spectacles. Shelley wrote his 'Ode to the West Wind' here in 1819, and in 1870 the body of the Maharaja of Kolhapur (who died in Florence) was burned on a funeral pyre at the far end of the park marked by an equestrian statue. Today, the park is full of children on bikes, rollerbladers, joggers and Florentines out for a stroll. It hosts a huge market on Tuesday mornings (*see p134* **Trading places**) and contains a riding school, swimming pool, horse race track and tennis courts. At night, transvestites and prostitutes strut along the parallel *viale*.

North-east of the Cascine along viale Rosselli is the restored but monstrous **Fortezza da Basso**, Florence's main exhibition centre. Commissioned from Antonio da Sangallo by Alessandro de'Medici (who met his death within its ugly walls) in 1534, it's a prototype of 16th-century military architecture.

Five minutes' walk beyond the Fortezza, among elegant residential *palazzi*, are the five polychrome onion domes of Florence's exquisite

Walk 3 On the up and up

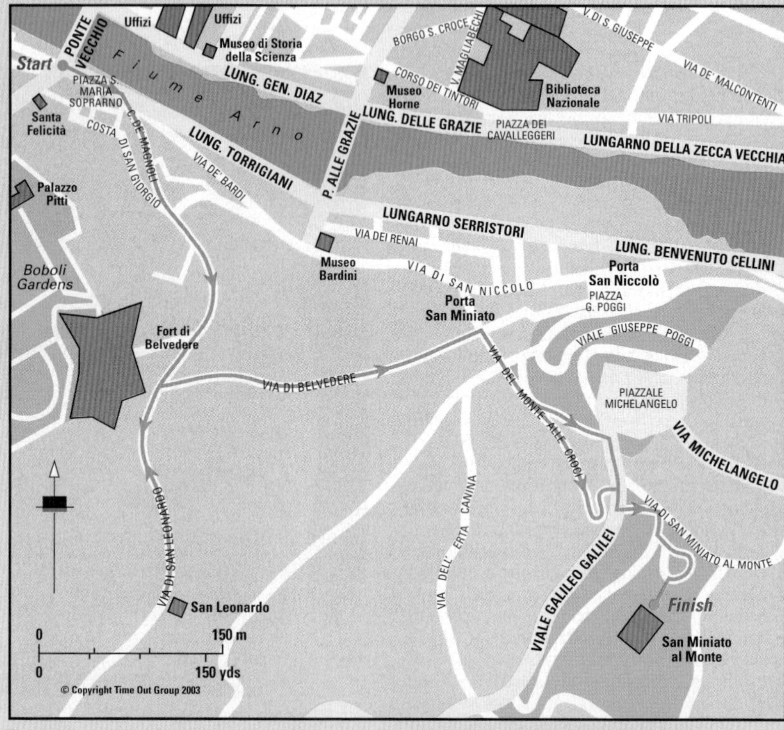

From the southern end of the Ponte Vecchio, with your back to the river, turn right up via dei Bardi and, almost immediately, turn right again (just before piazza Santa Maria Soprarno) to meet the narow beginning of costa di San Giorgio. This is an enchanting little street. But, right from the start, the ascent is steep. Stop for a breather at the

Russian Orthodox church (via Leone X). Designed by Russian architects and completed in 1904, it's a reminder that the city was once popular with wealthy Russians (Dostoevsky, Tchaikovsky, Maxim Gorky) as a retreat from harsh winters back home. The only access to the interior is during the monthly (third Sunday) Russian-language service.

Directly north of here is the eccentric **Museo Stibbert** (via Stibbert 26, 055 475 520, closed Thur, €5), whose bizarre collection, covering everything from paintings to snuff boxes, once belonged to Fredrick Stibbert (1838-1906), a brother-in-arms with Garibaldi. Stibbert was born of an English father and Italian mother, who left him her 14th-century house. He then bought the neighbouring mansion and had the two joined together to house his collection. Among the 50,000 items crammed into 64 rooms are a hand-painted harpsichord, a collection of shoe buckles, chalices and crucifixes and even an attributed Botticelli. The rambling garden is a delightfully cool escape in summer.

Piazza della Libertà, the focal point of northern access to the city, is home to the massive and rather graceless triumphal arch built to mark the arrival in Florence of the eighth Grand Duke of Tuscany in 1744. A couple of kilometres north-west of piazza della Libertà is **Villa della Petraia** (via della Petraia 40, 055 452 691, closed 2nd & 3rd Mon of mth, €2), acquired by the Medici family in intersection with costa de' Magnoli (opposite San Giorgio church), where a fabulous view of the Florence skyline suddenly appears to your left in a gap between the buildings. Press on, admiring the tall shuttered buildings and their oversailing rooftops as you go. Within five minutes' walk from the city centre, you'll hear the first twitters of bird song.

At the top of costa di San Giorgio, pass through the city gates (Porta San Giorgio), where there's the opportunity for a short detour along via di San Leonardo (the road that forks to your right). Should you decide to take it, you'll be quickly rewarded by the appearance of Chiesa di San Leonardo in Arcetri to your right. This fabulous medieval *pieve* is guarded by two towering cypress trees and contains, among other things, canvases by Francesco Conti.

Back at the Porta, bear left down via di Belvedere and begin your descent. Hugging the city walls, you'll soon come to the bottom of the hill opposite the Porta San Miniato. From here, head up the via delle Monte alle Croci, perhaps stopping for a slurp at the picturesque **Fuori Porta** wine bar (*see p125*). After a short walk, you reach the pretty, tree-lined steps of San Salvatore al Monte. Either take this, the express route to the top, or else follow the road on its tortuous journey past olive groves, finally arriving at the busy main road of viale Galileo Galilei. Directly opposite you is the splendid spectacle of **San Miniato al Monte** (*see p106*) and the end of your journey. Now all that's left to do is admire the view.

1530. Sitting on a little hill, the villa and grounds provide relief from the surrounding industrial mess. Just down the hill from La Petraia is **Villa di Castello** (via del Castello 40, 055 454 791, closed 2nd & 3rd Mon of the month, €2), another piece of Medici real estate. It's primarily famous for its gardens, which were laid out by Tribolo and which contain Ammanati's famous dripping statue *L'Appennino*, as well as the rather bizarre Grotta degli Animali – filled with animal and bird statues.

Back down in town and east of piazza della Libertà is Pier Luigi Nervi's huge football stadium, the Stadio Comunale near Campo di Marte. Built in 1932 and used for football matches plus the odd rock concert, it has a capacity of 66,000 and is one of the few modern buildings in Florence with architectural merit.

Not far south-east is the **Museo del Cenacolo di Andrea del Sarto** (via San Salvi 16, 055 238 8603, closed Mon, free). Another refectory-cum-museum, this was part of the monastery of San Salvi, used by the Vallombrosan order. The highlight is the *Last Supper* (1526-7) by Andrea del Sarto, a godfather of Mannerism. The monastery buildings are now a psychiatric hospital.

Back on the *viale* is the **Cimitero degli Inglesi** or 'English cemetery' (piazzale Donatello 38, 055 232 1477 morning/055 582 608 afternoon, closed Mon pm, Tue-Fri am, Sat, Sun, admission by donation). Opened in 1827, the cemetery's lichen-covered gravestones and tombs are fun to explore. All sorts of Anglo-Florentines are buried here, among them Elizabeth Barrett Browning.

Fiesole & around

Without Fiesole there would have been no Florence. This stubborn Etruscan hill-town proved so difficult for the Romans to subdue that they set up camp in the river valley below. When they eventually took Fiesole it became one of the most important towns in Etruria, remaining independent until the 12th century when Florence finally vanquished it in battle.

Fiesole soon found a new role as a refined suburb where aristocrats could escape the heat and hoi polloi of Florence; you can admire some of their beautiful villas and gardens on the way up. Some 14,000 people live in Fiesole today. The main square, piazza Mino, named after the artist Mino da Fiesole, is lined with cafés and restaurants and dominated by the immense honey-stone campanile of the 11th-century **Duomo**. Inside the Duomo, columns are topped with capitals dating from Fiesole's period under Roman occupation. **Museo Bandini** (via Dupré 1, 055 59477, closed Tue in winter, €6.20 incl Teatro Romano and Museo Archeologico) contains a collection of 13th- to 15th-century Florentine paintings, while down the hill are more relics of Roman Fiesole – a 3,000-seat theatre, the **Teatro Romano** (via Portigiani 1, 055 59477, closed Tue in winter, admission incl in Museo Bandini ticket). This was built in 1 BC and is still used for concerts and plays in summer and has a complex with the remains of two temples, partially restored Roman baths and a stretch of Etruscan walls. The **Museo Archeologico** (same details as Teatro Romano; admission incl in Museo Bandini ticket) houses finds from Bronze Age, Etruscan and Roman Fiesole and the Constantini collection of Greek vases.

There are some lovely walks around Fiesole, the best of which is down steep, twisting via Vecchia Fiesolana to the hamlet of **San Domenico**. On the way you pass the **Villa Medici** (to the left), which was built by Michelozzo for Cosimo il Vecchio and was the childhood home of Anglo-American writer Iris Origo. At the bottom of the hill is the 15th-century church and convent where painter Fra Angelico was a monk, which retains a delicate *Madonna and Angels* (1420) by him. In the chapter house of the adjacent monastery is a fresco by him (ring the bell at No.4 for entry). Opposite the church is a lane leading down to the **Badia Fiesolana** (via Roccettini 9, 055 59155, closed Sat pm & Sun, free), Fiesole's cathedral until 1028, when it was enlarged. The façade incorporates the original front of the older church, with its elegant green and white marble inlay. Enter via the cloister if the church doors are closed.

The village of **Settignano** lies on the hill to the east of Fiesole. There's no public transport from Fiesole (bus 10 goes from Florence station to Settignano); however, the longish walk or drive between the two through woods and cypresses is very pleasant. There's nothing special to see, but Settignano makes for an almost tourist-free trip out of town and has a history littered with eminent names – sculptors Desiderio da Settignano and the Rossellino brothers were born here and Michelangelo spent part of his childhood at Villa Buonarotti. It's just a pity no one left any art.

South of the river

The hilly area south of the Arno, a short walk from the city centre, is characterised by olive groves, cypresses, the odd farmhouse and a maze of steep lanes lined with high walls and impenetrable gates protecting beautiful villas.

The most famous viewpoint in Florence is probably **piazzale Michelangelo**, which is located up the hill directly above piazza Poggi. Il Piazzale has always been considered the city's balcony: a large, open square with vistas over the entire city to the hills beyond. Its stone balustrade is usually crowded with tourists having their photo taken against the spectacular backdrop. Laid out in 1869 by Giuseppe Poggi, it's dominated by a bronze replica of Michelangelo's *David* and crammed all day with coaches. Buses 12 and 13 come here, but the best way up is to walk along via San Niccolò to Porta San Miniato, then climb via del Monte alle Croci, winding between gardens and villas. Alternatively, walk up the rococo staircase that Poggi designed to link piazzale Michelangelo with his piazza below.

From the piazzale it's a short walk to the church of **San Miniato al Monte** (via delle Porte Sante 34, 055 234 2731, closed Sun in winter, free), whose façade is delicately inlaid with white Carrara and green Verde di Prato marble and looks down on the city. Its glittering mosaic dates from the 13th century. There's been a chapel on the site since at least the fourth century and this is the spot where, legend has it, San Miniato picked up his dismembered head and walked from the banks of the Arno up the hill, where he finally expired. The chapel was replaced with a Benedictine monastery in the early 11th century, built on the orders of reforming Bishop Hildebrand.

The church's interior is one of Tuscany's loveliest. Its walls are patchworked with faded frescoes and its choir is raised above a serene 11th-century crypt. Occasionally, a door from the crypt is open leading to an even earlier chapel. One of the church's most remarkable features is the marble pavement of the nave, inlaid with signs of the zodiac and stylised lions and lambs. It's worth timing your trip to coincide with the Gregorian chant sung by the monks (4.30pm daily in winter, 5.30pm in summer).

On a nearby hill just above Porta Romana lies the hamlet of **Bellosguardo** ('beautiful view'). It's a 20-minute slog by foot, but you can catch your breath at a viewpoint just before the piazza that affords a glimpse of every important church façade in central Florence. At the top there's a collection of old houses and grand villas grouped round a shady square.

The only sign of modern life (apart from the inevitable cars) is a postbox on a wall. The most impressive of the villas is the **Villa Bellosguardo**, down a little turning to the left. It was built in 1780 for the Marchese Orazio Pucci (ancestor of fashion designer Emilio Pucci) and bought, more than a century later, by the great tenor Enrico Caruso, who lived there for just three years before his death in 1921.

About five kilometres (three miles) south-west of Porta Romana and accessible by bus 36 or 37, the **Certosa del Galuzzo** (via Buca di Certosa 2, Galluzzo, 055 204 9226, admission by donation) looms like a fortress above the busy Siena road. The imposing complex was founded in 1342 as a *certosa* (Carthusian monastery) by Renaissance big-wig Niccolò Acciaiuoli and is the third of six built in Tuscany in the 14th century. Inhabited since 1958 by a small group of Cistercian monks, it's full of artistic interest. The main entrance leads into a large courtyard and the church of **San Lorenzo**, which is said to be by Brunelleschi. In the crypt are some imposing tombs. Around the *chiostro grande* (main cloister) are the 12 monks' cells, each with a well, vegetable garden and study.

Eat, Drink, Shop

Restaurants	**108**
Wine Bars	**123**
Cafés, Bars & *Gelaterie*	**126**
Shops & Services	**132**

Features

The best Restaurants	108
Alternative eats	120
Bar bites	128
The best Shops	133
Trading places	134
Skin cheap	139
The paper trail	148

Restaurants

Get stuffed.

Florentine eating habits have changed significantly over the past ten years. It's no longer de rigueur to sit down to a four-course meal at lunch and/or dinner time. Gone are the days of three-hour lunch breaks and, in their stead, there's now an increasing awareness of healthy eating issues. Unlike in some of the city's more traditional *trattorie*, a new generation of chefs is giving fresh life to conventional recipes and many eateries are a hybrid of restaurant, wine bar and pizzeria, offering all sorts of possibilities from a light snack to full meals. Also, there has been an increase in the number of restaurants serving non-Italian food. Although food has improved generally in Florence over the past few years, standards are not necessarily consistently high.

On a negative note, the introduction of the euro has boosted prices, particularly on wine lists, and eating out in Florence (and in Tuscany generally) is not the bargain it once was. For more on Tuscan restaurants, *see pp34-9*.

THE RESTAURANT

In your search for the perfect eaterie, rule number one is to go with this guide. Elsewhere, gauge the standard by looking for a sticker by one of the respected Italian restaurant guides, especially Gambero Rosso's *Ristoranti d'Italia*; *Veronelli*; *L'Espresso*; or Slow Food's *Osterie d'Italia*. And try to pick places where there are plenty of locals – in a tourist mecca like Florence, there are still too many sub-standard restaurants, in which no Italian would be seen, dead or alive. These restaurants prey on the unwary foreigner by offering expensive, practically inedible food. As a general guide, then, it's usually best to avoid places that advertise a fixed-price *menu turistico* written in several languages.

Eating out is a very social affair in Florence, especially in the evenings, and restaurants tend to be refreshingly informal and lively. You can wear casual dress in all but the most upmarket establishments and children are almost always

The best Restaurants

...for alfresco dining
Bibe (*see p121*), **Cavolo Nero** (*see p116*), **Omero** (*see p122*), **Osteria Santo Spirito** (*see p119*), **Trattoria 4 Leoni** (*see p119*).

...for a table with a view
Omero (*see p122*).

...for being taken by a rich aunt
Enoteca Pinchiorri (*see p115*), **Simon Boccanegra** (*see p116*).

...for being taken by your broke mate
Cibreino (*see p115*), **Da Mario** (*see p112*), **Nerbone** (*see p112*), **Pane e Vino** (*see p119*), **Sabatino** (*see p119*), **Salumeria, Vini, Trattoria** (*see p116*).

...for colourful amosphere
Finisterrae (*see p115*), **Garga** (*see p111*).

...for fish
L'Arte Gaia (*see p120*), **Fuor d'Acqua** (*see p122*).

...for Florentine atmosphere
Da Mario (*see p112*), **Da Ruggero** (*see p122*), **Da Sergio** (*see p112*), **Nerbone** (*see p112*), **Salumeria, Vini, Trattoria** (*see p116*).

...for pizza
Funiculì (*see p111*), **Il Pizzaiuolo** (*see p115*), **Santa Lucia** (*see p122*).

...for something ethnic
Nin Hao (*see p111*), **Ruth's** (*see p116*), **Salaam Bombay** (*see p122*).

...for vegetarians
Bibe (*see p121*), **Targa** (*see p122*), **Il Vegetariano** (*see p 112*), **Zibibbo** (*see p122*).

...for weird recipes
Cibrèo (*see p115*).

...for wine buffs
Beccofino (*see p116*), **Enoteca Pinchiorri** (*see p115*), **Il Guscio** (*see p117*), **Pane e Vino** (*see p119*), **Targa** (*see p122*).

Cibrèo's friendly *osteria* **Cibreino**. *See p115.*

welcome. Most restaurants are perfectly happy to produce a plate of *pasta al pomodoro* to satisfy unadventurous taste buds and you can also ask for a half portion – *una mezza porzione*. Quite a few restaurants carry high chairs (*una seggiolona*).

Booking is advisable, especially at weekends or if you want an outdoor table in the summer.

THE MENU

Apart from the ubiquitous *menu turistico*, few restaurants here offer fixed menus. The exception is the *menu degustazione* or tasting menu on offer at some of the more upmarket establishments. These are often multi-coursed and allow you to sample the house specialities without going through the agony of choice; they usually represent good value. For dish explanations and translations, *see pp34-9.*

THE WINE LIST

The price of your meal will be heavily influenced by the wine you choose. An increasing number of restaurants now have more than just a basic list, a reflection of a general upsurge in interest in wines and, although the *lista dei vini* in Tuscany is very much dominated by *vini Toscani*, other regional wines are being given more cellar space by restaurants these days. For guidelines on choosing wines, *see pp40-4*. Most budget and moderately priced restaurants offer *vino della casa* (house wine) in quarter, half or litre flasks, which is usually cheaper than buying by the bottle; this can be anything from some ghastly gut-rot to a quaffable country wine. If you find a wine undrinkable, ask to see the wine list and choose something better.

VEGETARIANS

There are few strictly vegetarian restaurants in Florence but non-meat-eaters (particularly those whose sympathies do not extend to fish) are better off here than, say, in an average restaurant in France. Many waiters still look aghast when they hear the words *sono vegetariano* ('I'm vegetarian') and don't really understand the concept at all. A classic situation is for a vegetarian to be offered *prosciutto crudo* as it is somehow thought that cured meat miraculously loses its carnal properties. However, most restaurants do offer vegetable-based pasta and rice dishes and plenty of salads and vegetable side dishes (*contorni*) and an increasing number of more upmarket places now feature a specific vegetarian option on their menus too.

THE BILL

We've given the average price per person for a meal. It covers *antipasto* or *primo*, *secondo*, *contorno* and *dolce,* but not drinks or extras – the price in a pizzeria covers an average pizza plus a *birra media*. Bills usually include a cover charge (*pane e coperto*) per person of anything from €1.50 to an outrageous €5; the average is

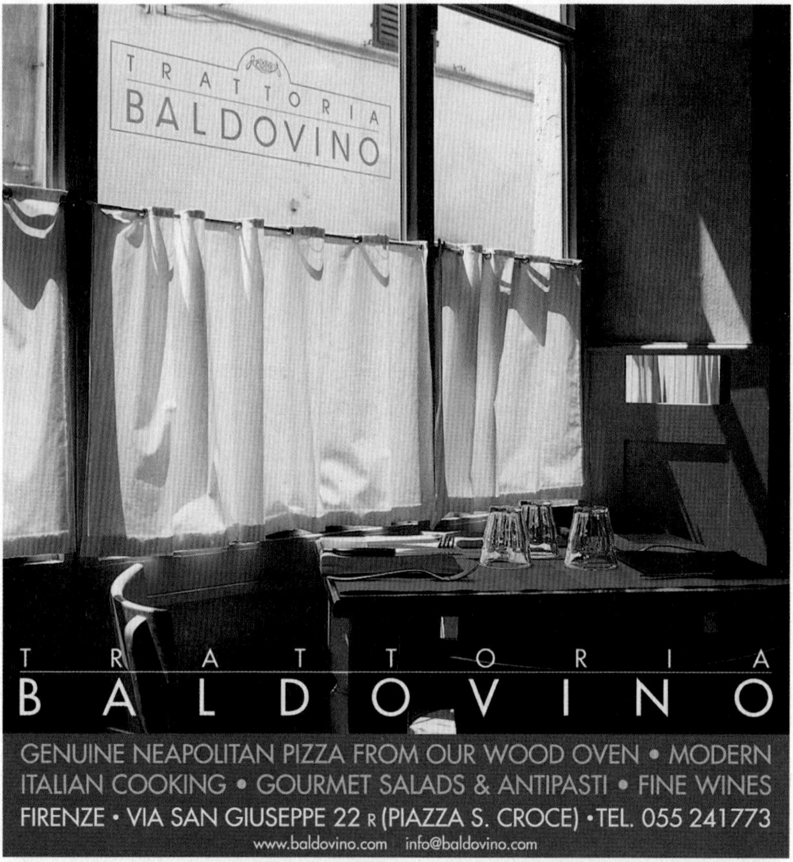

TRATTORIA
BALDOVINO
TRATTORIA
BALDOVINO
GENUINE NEAPOLITAN PIZZA FROM OUR WOOD OVEN • MODERN ITALIAN COOKING • GOURMET SALADS & ANTIPASTI • FINE WINES
FIRENZE • VIA SAN GIUSEPPE 22 R (PIAZZA S. CROCE) • TEL. 055 241773
www.baldovino.com info@baldovino.com

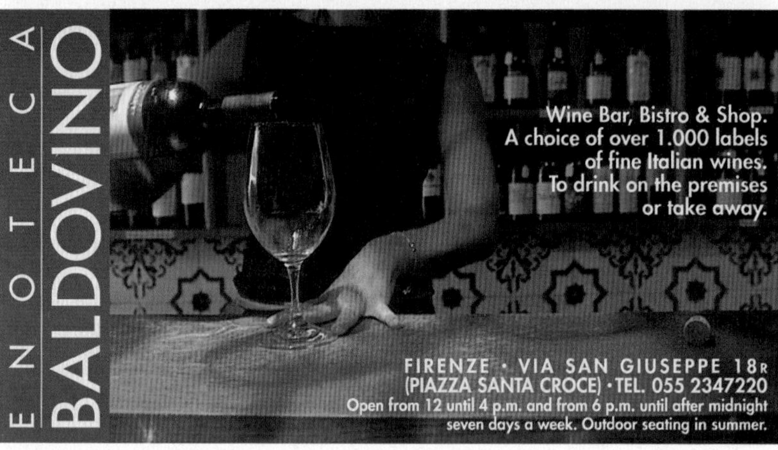

ENOTECA
BALDOVINO
Wine Bar, Bistro & Shop.
A choice of over 1.000 labels of fine Italian wines.
To drink on the premises or take away.
FIRENZE • VIA SAN GIUSEPPE 18R
(PIAZZA SANTA CROCE) • TEL. 055 2347220
Open from 12 until 4 p.m. and from 6 p.m. until after midnight seven days a week. Outdoor seating in summer.

about €2.50. This covers bread, and should also reflect the standard of service and table settings. There's also a service charge, which is included in the bill by law, though sometimes it's listed separately. Some places now include cover and service in the price of the meal. One consolation is that you're not expected to leave a hefty tip. You can leave ten per cent if you're truly happy with your service, or, in a modest place, perhaps round the bill up by a euro or so. Legally, you must be given a *ricevuta fiscale* (receipt) and keep it when you leave.

The restaurants here have been chosen either for their value for money or simply because the food is good. Even the most expensive restaurants listed cost little more than what you'd pay for a pizza and a bottle of wine in London or New York. So you can certainly allow yourself the odd treat.

Duomo & Around

Oliviero

Via delle Terme 51r (055 212 421). **Open** 7.30pm-midnight Mon-Sat. Closed Aug. **Average** €40. **Credit** AmEx, DC, MC, V. **Map** p314 C3.

Oliviero was a classic Florentine hangout in the '60s frequented by the likes of Fred and Ginger, Sophia Loren, Bogart and Maria Callas. Even today it has a curious *Dolce Vita* atmosphere with its silent grand piano, red velvet banquette seats, pink candles and a lady to check your coats. And the food is great. Generous portions of inventive Tuscan and southern Italian dishes are executed with real skill and accompanied by formal service. You get a glass of complimentary Prosecco with the menu, which changes every two months and features creative versions of familiar dishes. Try asparagus flan with a pecorino sauce, tuna steak marinated in ginger served with a marjoram-flavoured aubergine purée and a fine *bistecca alla Fiorentina*. There is also an excellent choice of cheeses and a good wine list, to boot. The obnoxious *pane e coperto* cover charge is included in the price.

Santa Maria Novella

Funiculì

Via Il Prato 81r (055 264 6553). **Open** noon-3pm, 7pm-1am Mon-Fri; 7pm-1am Sat, Sun. **Average** €13. **Credit** AmEx, MC, V.

If you're after a lively pizzeria, look no further. Since opening in 2002, Funiculì has proved hugely popular with Florentines of all ages who pour in for its excellent Neapolitan pizzas and various other southern dishes. There's seating for 300, but the modern, no-frills space is divided into a single, vast room with several smaller – but not much quieter – spaces leading off. Four Neapolitan *pizzaiuoli* turn out the puffy-crusted pizzas made using flour, buffalo mozzarella and tomatoes from Naples. They range from a simple *regina margherita* (tomato, mozzarella and basil) to combinations like *pulcinell'* (mozzarella with asparagus, tomato and porcini mushrooms).

Garga

Via del Moro 48r (055 239 8898). **Open** 7.30-10.30pm Tue-Sun. **Average** €50. **Credit** AmEx, DC, MC, V. **Map** p314 B2.

Popular with Florence's bright young things, this is definitely a fun place to eat. But while many of the dishes are unusual, don't expect a gourmet experience (but do expect high prices). Owner and chef Giuliano is a well-known Florentine character and his extrovert presence dominates the restaurant. The walls are covered with garish frescoes, cosy rooms are filled with a wonderfully eccentric clutter of objects, kitchen noise emanates from the open hatch and the staff bring their own good-humoured style. Some dishes have been on the menu for years. *Primi* are the best option headed by the delicious *taglierini del Magnifico* (pasta served in a sensual sauce of cream, parmesan, orange and lemon zest and fresh mint with a splash of cognac – not for the weight-conscious). *Secondi* include an unusual veal escalope with avocado (another Garga classic) and fish dishes such as fresh tuna steak and steamed octopus. For dessert, tuck into the excellent light cheesecake della Sharon by Giuliano's Canadian wife (who also runs cooking courses).

I Latini

Via dei Palchetti 6r (055 210 916). **Open** 12.30-2.30pm, 7.30-10.30pm Tue-Sun. **Average** €30. **Credit** AmEx, DC, MC, V. **Map** p314 B2.

Florentines and tourists alike clamour to the Latini family's legendary trattoria. If you have to wait on the pavement outside, Torello (the boss) will slosh you a glass of house wine for sustenance, sometimes accompanied by a chunk of cheese or salami. Though the typically Tuscan menu is largely unexceptional, the experience is something else. You'll probably be sat at a communal table in one of several crowded rooms hung with hams and salamis. You may or may not get a menu, but among the gargantuan dishes, soups (*ribollita*, *pappa al pomodoro*, *zuppa di farro*) are good, pastas are very mediocre, and the meat-oriented *secondi* are excellent on the whole. Avid carnivores should try the *gran pezzo*, a giant steak hacked from a rib roast. The Latini are prolific producers of a fine, sludgy green olive oil, and some good wines – the house red is very drinkable. No bookings taken after 8pm.

Nin Hao

Borgo Ognissanti 159r (055 210 770). **Open** 6.30-11pm Mon; 11am-3pm, 6.30-11pm Tue-Sun. **Average** €18. **Credit** AmEx, DC, MC, V. **Map** p314 B1.

As one of the better of the many Chinese restaurants in the city Nin Hao is often full. The good-value, yards-long menu includes tasty dim sum, *gamberoni* (giant prawns) cooked in various ways, duck and fish. Chicken or meat prepared *alla piastra* is brought sizzling to the table on a hot plate.

San Lorenzo

Da Mario

Via Rosina 2r (055 218 550). **Open** noon-3.30pm Mon-Sat. Closed 3wks Aug. **Average** €13. **No credit cards. Map** 314 A3.

Four generations of the Colsi family have been serving up Florentine home cooking for 50 years at Da Mario. It's difficult to find food like this these days and prices are remarkably low. You'll probably have to queue for a seat in the narrow room at the back of the central market where fellow lunchers are as likely to be stall-holders as suited businessmen or smartly dressed tourists. This place is famous. The menu is typically Florentine: hearty *pasta e fagioli*, an exceptionally good *bollito misto* (mixed boiled meats) served with a biting garlic *salsa verde* and excellent *bistecca* to will up the bill. Don't dare ask for your steak well done as the chef will have none of it. The rough *vino della casa* costs a mere €6 per litre, but there's also a surprisingly interesting wine list if you want something a bit more palatable.

Da Sergio

Piazza San Lorenzo 8r (055 281 941). **Open** noon-3pm Mon-Sat. Closed Aug. **Average** €20. **Credit** MC, V. **Map** p314 A3.

Tables of varying sizes fill two big, airy rooms at this quintessentially Florentine trattoria. The plain menu varies little. Expect *minestrone di verdura*, *ribollita* and *minestra di farro* followed by roast beef, roast pork or *bistecca alla Fiorentina*. There's tripe on Mondays and Thursdays and fresh fish on Tuesdays and Fridays. The *seppie in inzimino* (a rich stew of sweet, tender squid and Swiss chard) is superb. The sole dessert is *cantucci e vin Santo* and the house wine may be rough and ready but is perfectly acceptable all the same.

Nerbone

Mercato Centrale (055 219 949). **Open** 7am-2pm Mon-Sat. Closed Aug. **Average** €10. **No credit cards. Map** p314 A3.

Looking for local colour? Well, this combination of food stall and trattoria, dating from 1872 and located on the ground floor of the covered central market, is a good place to find it. From breakfast onwards it's packed with market workers. Even at the godforsaken hour of 7am they can be found munching on *lampredotto* (yummy cow's intestine) sarnies and knocking back a glass of rough red plonk for about €5.50. The more faint-hearted can opt for a plate of simple pasta or a soup. On Fridays you sample *inzimino di baccalà* (a stew of salt cod and Swiss chard) or squid stew with peas.

San Marco

Il Vegetariano

Via delle Ruote 30r (055 475 030). **Open** 12.30-2.30pm, 7.30-10.30pm Tue-Fri; 7.30-10.30pm Sat, Sun. Closed 3wks Aug. **Average** €15. **No credit cards.**

Reminiscent of British vegetarian restaurants in the '70s – both in terms of its rustic decor and the earnest, wholesome food – this is a rare breed in Florence. Ordering is a complicated process: take your pick from the long list on the blackboard, pay at the desk and get a written receipt, then collect from the counter. Don't make the mistake of ordering too much as portions are generous. The ever-changing menu has plenty of choice, including a variety of ethnic dishes. There's also a fabulous salad bar and the wines are all organic.

Santa Croce

Alle Murate

Via Ghibellina 52r (055 240 618). **Open** 7.45-11pm Tue-Sun. Closed 15-28 Dec. **Average** €63. **Credit** AmEx, DC, MC, V. **Map** p314 C6.

Alle Murate continues to win praise for its creative cooking and important wine cellar, and its prices aren't as high as you might expect. The atmosphere is elegant, intimate and discreet and the service is highly professional. You can either eat à la carte or choose one of the two set *menu degustazione* (although it's probably worth saving the Tuscan classics, on the *menu Toscana*, for a more traditional trattoria where you'll pay half as much). Instead sample the *menu creativo*, which always has something interesting to offer, such as *tortelli* stuffed with ricotta and a sauce of sweet peppers and *clamaretti* (baby squid) or roast saddle of rabbit served with crispy artichoke hearts. The wine list features labels from all over Italy and further afield – prices start at around €13 and finish somewhere in outer space. Alternatively, there's a less formal *vineria* where you can choose from a much shorter menu and pay less than half the price – booking's essential. In January and February menus are devoted to fish.

Baldovino

Via San Giuseppe 22r (055 241 773). **Open** *Apr-Oct* 11.30am-2.30pm, 7-11.30pm daily. *Nov-Mar* 11.30am-2.30pm, 7-11.30pm Tue-Sun. **Average** €27/pizza €12. **Credit** MC, V. **Map** p314 C5.

When it opened in 1996, David Gardner's first restaurant was ground-breaking in its way. The modern decor and different approach to food, which offered the choice of anything from a full meal to pizza or a salad, was a departure from the standard Florentine formula. These days, the food is decent rather than outstanding and prices are restrained. Depending on the season, you may find fresh broad bean soup, *garganelli alla Siciliana* (with sardines, Sicilian-style), tagliatelle with artichokes and pancetta, rabbit with green pepper and olives, or swordfish kebabs. Good pizzas (Napoli-style, with thick, puffy crusts), excellent *bistecca* (from Chianina beef) and main-course salads are permanent features. The English/American-style puddings are excellent and the wine list is full and varied. In season, early evenings are often packed with tour groups, but they've usually left by 8pm.

Four is the magic number at **Trattoria 4 Leoni**. *See p119*.

FINISTERRAE
RISTORANTE E BAR MEDITERRANEO
INFO@FINISTERRAEFIRENZE.COM

Cibreino

Via dei Macci 122r (055 234 1100). **Open** 12.50-2.30pm, 7-11.15pm Tue-Sat. Closed Aug. **Average** €25. **No credit cards**. **Map** p315 C6.

If you like the look of the menu at Cibrèo (*see below*) but your wallet takes offence at the prices, nip round the corner to the trattoria version of the same place, known locally as Cibreino. You can't book, the atmosphere is rustic and often overcrowded, there are no complimentary extras and the menu has less choice. But the food is the same and the bill will be about a third of what you pay in the parent restaurant. Be prepared to queue.

Cibrèo

Via Andrea del Verrocchio 8r (055 234 1100). **Open** 12.50-2.30pm, 7-11.15pm Tue-Sat. Closed Aug. **Average** €55. **Credit** AmEx, DC, JCB, MC, V. **Map** p315 C6.

Cibrèo is one of Florence's most famous restaurants and, with a branch in Tokyo, its reputation has expanded internationally. The menu is a refreshingly unpretentious combination of traditional Tuscan and creative cuisines, based on the use of prime ingredients. Flavours are intense with fresh herbs and spices. Cibrèo is really two restaurants: a rustic walk-in *osteria* (*see above*) and an elegant, understated panelled restaurant that costs three times as much (and is always full of tourists). There isn't a menu. Instead, a chummy waiter sits at your table and takes you through the options. The extraordinary *antipasti* are included in the price and arrive automatically with a glass of wine. There's no pasta, so start with smooth polenta swimming in melted butter and fresh herbs, or one of the fantastic soups. *Secondi* are divided between meat and fish. Look out for *inzimino*, a superbly rich and spicy stew of squid, spinach and chard, and the famous *collo di pollo ripieno*, a stuffed chicken neck that arrives at the table looking at you accusingly. Desserts are fabulous too, and the wine list is everything you might expect.

Enoteca Pinchiorri

Via Ghibellina 87 (055 242 777/ www.enotecapinchiorri.com). **Open** 7.30-10pm Tue; 12.30-2pm, 7.30-10pm Wed-Sat. Closed Aug. **Average** €180. **Credit** AmEx, MC, V. **Map** p315 C5.

At the time of writing, Enoteca Pinchiorri was due to reopen after a period of renovation. Famous throughout Italy, and one of only a handful of restaurants in the country with two Michelin stars, Enoteca Pinchiorri is in a class of its own. The setting is truly captivating: a palazzo near Santa Croce with an inner courtyard scented with jasmine and roses and several elegant rooms laid with the finest linens, porcelain and crystal. Although this is hovering waiters and silver domes territory, it's still more charming than intimidating. Food is exquisite and portions, in true nouvelle style, are tiny – the running local joke is that you need to book a table at a pizzeria after a meal here. There are several set menus, each involving at least eight or nine superbly executed and beautifully presented courses. The Enoteca is as famous for its wine cellar as its food. Giorgio Pinchiorri has amassed a collection that is second to none.

Finisterrae

Via de' Pepi 3-5r (055 2638675). **Open** noon-3pm, 7.30-11.30pm Mon-Fri; noon-3pm, 7.30pm-midnight Sat, Sun. **Average** €27/pizza €13. **Credit** AmEx, DC, MC, V. **Map** p315 C5.

David Gardner (of Beccofino and Baldovino fame) opened this, his latest restaurant, in early 2003. Occupying an elegant Renaissance palazzo on piazza Santa Croce, it's a gorgeous space – as we go to press, there are also plans to put a terrace out front. The food is broadly Mediterranean and features dishes from southern Spain, Provence, Greece, North Africa, southern Italy and Lebanon, and the decor is similarly eclectic. The furnishings of each room reflect a different country. In the centre is a Moroccan-style bar where you can sip a cocktail and nibble on a selection of meze. For a full meal the menu offers an extensive choice, including *soupe au pistou*, falafel, harira, pastas (such as *linguine trinacria* with sardines, raisins, pine nuts, saffron and fennel seeds) and bouillabaisse. Some dishes are more convincing than others, but even if it's not top nosh, it's fun and it's different.

Osteria dei Benci

Via de'Benci 13r (055 234 4923). **Open** 1-2.45pm, 7.45-10.45pm Mon-Sat. **Average** €23. **Credit** AmEx, DC, JCB, MC, V. **Map** p314 C4.

This lively trattoria, housed in brick-vaulted rooms and run by a young team, is slightly shabby around the edges. Still, prices are very reasonable, the food is good and portions are more than generous. The imaginative menu changes with the seasons, but some dishes are perennial, such as the famous *spaghetti dell'Ubriacone* (pasta cooked in olive oil, garlic and red wine). Steak is another constant. Try the more expensive and highly regarded *chianina* variety from cattle bred in the Valdichiana. It's vast, is cooked over an open fire and is served *al sangue*. Soups are major players in the winter, while in summer the emphasis is on light, fresh ingredients. Desserts include exquisite tarts.

Il Pizzaiuolo

Via de'Macci 113r (055 241 171). **Open** 12.30-3pm, 7.30pm-1am Mon-Sat. Closed Aug. **Average** €13. **No credit cards**. **Map** p315 C6.

This small pizzeria/trattoria is fun, noisy and extremely popular so you really need to book, especially in the evenings. Bare wooden tables are crowded into a big white-tiled room; you may find yourself sharing. Pizzas here are Neapolitan-style (light, puffy edges and a thin, slightly soggy middle) and really very good. There are about 20 pizza varieties costing from €4.50 – make sure you specify *mozzarella di bufala* (buffalo mozzarella). Delicious Neapolitan alternatives to pizza include *spaghetti gaeta* with tomato, olives and capers or *tubettoni* with mussels and fresh tomato.

Ruth's

Via Farini 2A (055 248 0888). **Open** 12.30-2.30pm, 8-10.30pm Mon-Thur; 12.30-2.30pm Fri. **Average** €18. **No credit cards. Map** p315 B6.

Located beside the city's synagogue, this restaurant serves great-value kosher vegetarian food (which, in this case, includes fish). The dining area is a pleasant, modern and bright room with a full view of the kitchen. The cooking has palpable Middle Eastern and North African influences, resulting in dishes like falafel and other typical meze, fish or vegetable couscous or fish kofta served with a Tunisian salad, along with pastas and salads. The generous *piatto* Ruth's (€8; various dips with a salad and rice) is enough for lunch on its own. Puddings include vanilla soufflé with hot chocolate sauce.

Salumeria, Vini, Trattoria

Via Ghibellina 27r (055 679 390). **Open** noon-3.30pm Mon-Fri. Closed Aug. **Average** €9. **No credit cards. Map** p315 C4.

This wonderfully old-fashioned cross between a grocer's shop, wine bar and trattoria is one of the best bargains in town. There is no official name above the door but it has been run by the Bisazzi family since the mid '50s. Walk through the long, wood panelled shop to the food counter and open fire and choose what takes your fancy. You can either take it away or eat your meal at one of the simple wooden tables in the back. *Primi* (€3) on offer might be lasagne made with pesto and courgette, *ribollita* or *pasta e fagioli*, while *secondi* (€2.50-€5) include meats and chicken roasted over the open fire, stews or the odd vegetarian dish such as *melanzane alla parmigiana*. Make sure you try Simona's superbly creamy tiramisù to finish. The house wine is also a snip at €2.20 for a half litre.

Simon Boccanegra

Via Ghibellina 124r (055 200 1098). **Open** 8pm-midnight Mon-Sat. **Average** €46. **Credit** AmEx, DC, MC, V. **Map** p315 C4.

A relatively new arrival in town, Simon Boccanegra (named after the hero in Verdi's opera of the same name) is definitely a grown-up restaurant. The atmosphere is elegantly rustic, prices are on the high side and the food is excellent. The well-presented dishes draw on traditional Tuscan recipes, such as a sublime *budino* of baby onions with a pecorino sauce, cold saddle of rabbit with sweet pepper-flavoured mayonnaise and pigeon with a velvety, reduced Morellino di Scansano wine sauce. Leave room for one of the delectable desserts.

Oltrarno

Alla Vecchia Bettola

Viale Ariosto 32-4r (055 224 158). **Open** noon-2.30pm, 7.30-10.30pm Tue-Sat. Closed 3wks Aug. **Average** €25. **No credit cards.**

Alla Vecchia Bettola's setting on the busy ring road that encircles the Oltrarno isn't particularly picturesque, but this popular place is always full of locals. The noise level in the room rises as the evening progresses, and as more wine is slurped from flasks. The super-traditional menu includes daily specials alongside regulars such as *penne alla Bettola* (with tomato, chilli pepper, vodka and a dash of cream), *topini al pomodoro* (gnocchi, literally 'little mice', with tomatoes) and a superb beef carpaccio topped with artichoke hearts and shaved parmesan. For dessert, try the ice-cream.

Beccofino

Piazza degli Scarlatti (055 290 076). **Open** *Wine bar* 7pm-midnight Mon-Sat; 12.30-3.30pm, 7pm-midnight Sun. *Restaurant* 7-11.30pm Mon-Sat; 12.30-3pm, 7-11.30pm Sun. **Average** €38. **Credit** MC, V. **Map** p314 C2

When it opened in 1999, Beccofino's combination of stylish, contemporary decor, innovative cooking (by Francesco Berardinelli, one of Tuscany's most talented chefs) and serious wines was unique in Florence. And although there have been blips along the way with the service, the food continues to win high praise. The menus tend to change regularly as Berardinelli employs seasonal ingredients for Tuscan-based dishes with a twist. Try the steak tartar with chives, celery and topped with parmesan shavings or local kid with rosemary and served with a thyme-spiked aubergine flan. Delicious puddings include *cannoli* (a kind of brandy snap) stuffed with a light, almond-flavoured ricotta cream. On Tuesday evenings all wines (from an excellent list) are half price. Be warned, though – at Beccofino busy means noisy.

La Casalinga

Via del Michelozzo 9r (055 218 624). **Open** noon-2.30pm, 7-9.45pm Mon-Sat. Closed 3wks Aug. **Average** €20. **Credit** AmEx, DC, MC, V. **Map** p314 D2.

This bustling, family-run trattoria has been an essential part of the Oltrarno scene for decades. Thankfully, it has managed to withstand the effects of the increasing numbers of tourists who have graced its tables over the years, allowing the atmosphere to remain authentic and prices to stay relatively low. This is reliably wholesome home cooking. Some dishes, such as the *minestrone di riso e cavolo* (thick, warming soup with black cabbage and rice) or *lesso rifatte con le cipolle* (a rich stew made with boiled beef and lots of onions) are proper local recipes, while others like *spaghetti alla carbonara* and *braciola alla Milanese* are more ubiquitous. Roasts (*arista*, roast beef or guinea fowl) are always good, as are the home-made desserts.

Cavolo Nero

Via dell' Ardiglione 22 (055 294 744). **Open** 8-10.30pm Mon-Sat. **Average** €30. **Credit** AmEx, MC, V. **Map** p314 C1.

This smart little restaurant continues to attract praise from the local designer set and foreigners who frequent it. However, we weren't entirely convinced by the food on our latest visit. The ambience

Finisterrae is the place to be. *See p115.*

is pleasing – with glowing yellow walls (on which big black and white framed photos sit well), white napery and spare, elegant table settings. The menu is certainly creative, though some dishes sound better than they taste – a two-tiered *sformato* of broccoli and cauliflower with a dull parmesan sauce being a case in point. Succulent and perfectly cooked fillet of Argentinian beef was much better. There's a short but reasonably priced wine list – the wines by the glass are unusually generous.

Il Guscio

Via dell'Orto 49 (055 224 421). **Open** 8-11pm Tue-Sat. Closed Aug. **Average** €27. **Credit** DC, MC, V.

This friendly, much-loved local restaurant continues to serve above-average food and offer good value for money. The atmosphere of the place is relaxed and unpretentious, the menu is interesting and the wine list is long and varied, with labels from all over Italy and beyond (starting admirably low at €9.50). The menu features familiar Tuscan standards, along with some more unusual dishes such as *robiola* (a soft, white cheese) baked in a filo crust with herbs and balsamic vinegar or an indulgent fillet of roast beef topped with a slice of melting chicken liver pâté. Desserts are an unmissable treat – we particularly recommend the warm chocolate tart with a vin santo-infused pear.

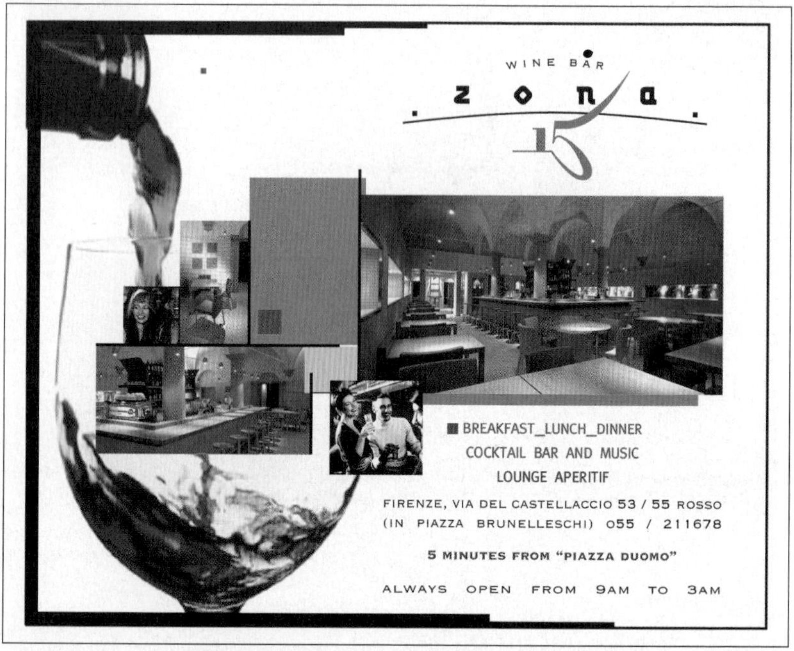
WINE BAR
zona 15
BREAKFAST_LUNCH_DINNER
COCKTAIL BAR AND MUSIC
LOUNGE APERITIF
FIRENZE, VIA DEL CASTELLACCIO 53 / 55 ROSSO
(IN PIAZZA BRUNELLESCHI) 055 / 211678
5 MINUTES FROM "PIAZZA DUOMO"
ALWAYS OPEN FROM 9AM TO 3AM

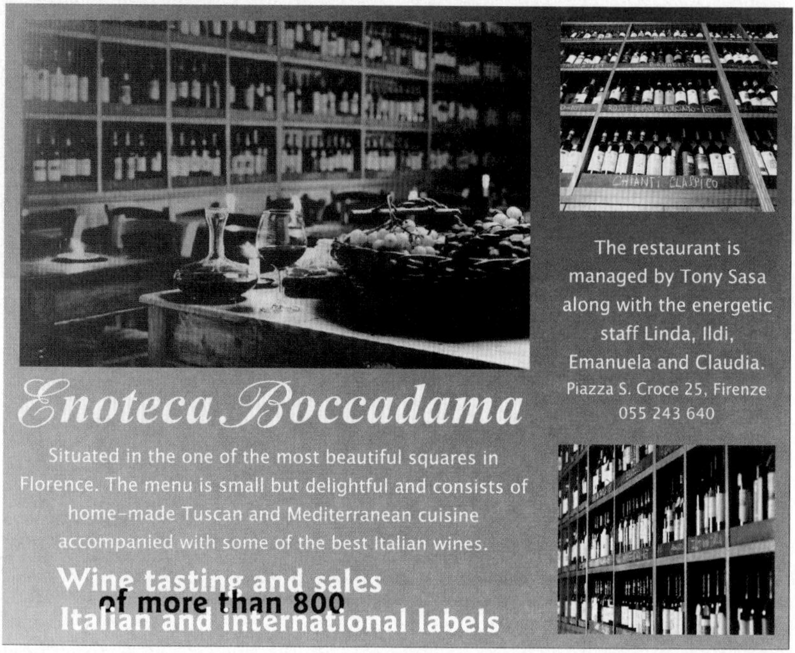
CHIANTI CLASSICO
The restaurant is managed by Tony Sasa along with the energetic staff Linda, Ildi, Emanuela and Claudia.
Piazza S. Croce 25, Firenze
055 243 640
Enoteca Boccadama
Situated in the one of the most beautiful squares in Florence. The menu is small but delightful and consists of home-made Tuscan and Mediterranean cuisine accompanied with some of the best Italian wines.
Wine tasting and sales
of more than 800
Italian and international labels

Osteria Santo Spirito

Piazza Santo Spirito 16r (055 238 2383). **Open** 12.45-11.30pm daily. **Average** €26. **Credit** AmEx, MC, V. **Map** p314 D1.

This popular *osteria* with flame-red walls, dark blue paintwork and contemporary lighting was one of the first Florentine eateries to abandon the white walls and tablecloths of the traditional trattoria. If you don't want a full meal, order a *tagliere* (wooden board) of mixed cheeses or salami and *prosciutto* or one of the generous salads – gorgonzola, walnuts and celery is good. More substantial hot and cold dishes, featuring both meat and fish, are also on offer. Some are better than others while portions are huge. When the weather allows, there are outside tables in the wonderful piazza, where life drifts past you at a commendably unhurried pace.

Pane e Vino

Via di San Niccolò 70r (055 247 6956). **Open** 7.30pm-midnight Mon-Sat. Closed 2wks Aug. **Average** €33. **Credit** AmEx, DC, JCB, MC, V. **Map** p314 D5.

Pane e Vino is a calm, informal restaurant that offers some of the best-value food in town. The menu always has something interesting on offer and recent highlights include a delicate, pastry-less parmesan flan in a pear sauce, a velvety, broad bean soup with a twist of bitter chicory purée (very pretty in shades of green) or juicy pan-fried lamb cutlets with celeriac purée. Vegetarians get a good look-in too. If you're willing to put yourself in the hands of the chef (a particularly good idea for those who want a one-stop overview of Tuscan cuisine), the day's multi-course set *menu degustazione* is still very reasonable at €31 (and you can choose wines by the glass to match each course). Good cheeses too, with loads of tasty wines to wash them down.

Sabatino

Via Pisana 2r (055 225 955). **Open** noon-2.30pm, 7.30-10pm Mon-Fri. Closed Aug. **Average** €12. **No credit cards**.

Located for decades on borgo San Frediano, Sabatino moved up the road to this new location (just outside the ancient gate to the west of the city) a few years ago. Even so, the Buccioni family managed to maintain the unique atmosphere of this trattoria: the pre-war fridge, flood-damaged chairs, '50s tiles and, most importantly, their customers. The honest, no-frills home cooking is as good as it always was and still remarkable value.

Il Santo Bevitore

Via di Santo Spirito 64/66r (055 211 264/ www.santobevitore.com). **Open** 12.30-3pm, 7.30-11.30pm Mon-Sat. **Average** €22. **Credit** AmEx, MC, V. **Map** p314 C2.

This new restaurant, occupying a huge room with vaulted ceiling and wood panelling and run by a young team of real enthusiasts, has quickly become very popular. The shortish menu features interesting dishes such as chicken liver pâté flavoured with Marsala, delicious *mezze penne* with sweet cherry tomatoes, red onions and courgette, and squid stewed with artichokes. There's also an excellent selection of well-sourced cheeses and cured meats – try the delicious marinated vegetables as an accompaniment. The initially meagre wine list now has plenty of good-value choices by the glass and bottle. The only problem is the acoustics – it can get very noisy. No smoking.

I Tarocchi

Via dei Renai 12-14 (055 234 3912/ www.pizzeriaitarocchi.it). **Open** noon-2.30pm, 7pm-1am Tue-Fri; 7pm-1am Sat, Sun. **Average** €12. **Credit** MC, V. **Map** p315 D4.

This lively, perennially popular pizzeria is a great place for a good, cheap, late-night pizza (eat-in or take-away) or a plate of pasta washed down with beer. Pizzas are Florentine-style with crisp, thin, slightly charred crusts and cost from €4 for a simple *marinara* (tomato, garlic and oregano, no mozzarella) to €7 for a filling *tarocchi* (tomato, mozzarella, capers, *salsiccia*). Karlsbrau beer on tap (*alla spina*) costs €4 for a medium. There are also *primi* such as gnocchi with gorgonzola, rocket salads, plus the odd meat or fish *secondo*.

Trattoria del Carmine

Piazza del Carmine 18r (055 218 601). **Open** noon-2.30pm, 7.15-10.30pm Mon-Sat. Closed 3wks Aug. **Average** €18. **Credit** AmEx, DC, MC, V. **Map** p314 C1.

Trattoria del Carmine still offers excellent value for money and the kind of comfortably traditional atmosphere and food that draw a nicely mixed crowd of locals and tourists. Sadly, piazza del Carmine is a car park, but the few tables squeezed on the terrace are still pleasant enough for a meal. There's a long, fixed menu as well as a seasonal *menu del giorno*. Try home-made *porcini ravioli* with a meaty *ragu*, *carpaccio* (wafer-thin slices of beef) with *porcini* and *vitella tonnata*, a curious but delicious summer dish with slices of roast veal smothered in rich tuna mayonnaise. Finish with the delicious *torta della nonna*.

Trattoria 4 Leoni

Via dei Vellutini 1r (055 218 562/www.4leoni.com). **Open** noon-2.30pm, 7-11pm daily. **Average** €25. **Credit** AmEx, DC, MC, V. **Map** p314 C2.

Once a simple, spit-on-the-floor local trattoria, the 4 Leoni is now a trendy version of its old self. This has translated into much higher prices, red and white checked tablecloths, flasks, rustic tables and chairs, and a vaguely intrusive level of background music. Set in the delightful little piazza della Passera just south of the river (lovely terrace in summer), the place buzzes with a mixed crowd who turn up for the friendly atmosphere and acceptable Tuscan-based food. There's gnocchi with rocket pesto, grilled meats, *polpo lesso con patate* (boiled octopus with potatoes – tastier than it sounds) or swordfish. It's best to book in advance.

Alternative eats

If eating out in restaurants is to remain a treat, sometimes you need to take a break – even on holiday. Luckily, there are plenty of alternatives in Florence.

The most obvious solution to restaurant overload is the good old picnic. While many of the city's *gastronomie* or delicatessens (*see pp132-150*) are a goldmine, the obvious one-stop-shop for loading up on edible goodies are the two big food markets – **Mercato Centrale** in San Lorenzo and **Mercato di Santí Ambrogio** near piazza Santa Croce (for both, *see p134* **Trading places**). Fill your hamper from stalls selling cheeses of every description, cured meats, olives, sun-dried tomatoes, breads, toppings for *crostini*, salad leaves, fruit and wines.

Armed with your booty, take it back to the terrace of your hotel room or find a quiet and picturesque spot to enjoy an alfresco feast. Don't go for obvious places like piazza delle Signoria. Instead, you should seek out one of the following: a stone bench in the lovely piazza Santa Spirito; the steps leading down to piazza del Limbo and the church of SS Annunziata; the newly restored Forte Belvedere; the grassy riverbank in the Parco delle Cascine; or a bench in the tree-filled Piazza d'Azeglio. For something more rural, catch bus 7 to Fiesole or bus 10 to Settignano and walk a little way to find fields where you can dig in for a few hours of beautiful scenery and fresh air.

If you want something a little more substantial that doesn't require the effort of making up a sandwich, *rosticcerie* are great sources of inspiration. These takeaway food bars can supply you with the wherewithal for a complete hot or cold meal, starting with *antipasto* and finishing with *dolce*. In between are *primi* (pastas and risotti), *secondi* (all kinds of roast meats – the spit-roasted chickens are usually delicious and very cheap) and *contorni*. You can also buy drinks (alcoholic and otherwise), bread, plastic plates, cups and cutlery. For a selection of the best *rosticcerie, see pp132-150*. There are also a few ethnic takeaway joints; the **Ramraj** (via Ghibellina 61r, 055 240 999, closed Mondays) serves respectable Indian dishes, **Ying Yang** (via Ghibellina 48r, 055 247 8343, open daily) and **La Gustosa** (Borgo Ognissanti 82r, 055 212 821, closed Saturdays) serve Chinese specialities. Many pizzerias also do pizzas to take away.

Another alternative is to order food in. Although most hotels will not take kindly to the idea of you having a meal delivered to your room, this is a good option if you are renting a room or apartment. The most obvious choice is pizza; these usually take about 30 minutes from the time of your phone call and arrive on a motorbike with a 'hot box' on the back (try **Pizza Okey**, 055 288 888). The following firms also deliver basic *primi*, salads, drinks and ice-cream: **Runner Pizza** (055 333 333/www.tipicopizza.it) and **Pizza Taxi** (055 434 343/www.pizzataxi.it). Some Chinese restaurants like **Ying Yang** (*see above*) also deliver. **Room Service** (055 680 0460/www.roomservice.it) collects your order from local restaurants rather than preparing food on the premises, and brings it to your door piping hot. Its menu covers anything from Chinese and Indian to full Tuscan meals including fish dishes and wood-oven baked pizza. Its prices are a little higher than the other delivery companies listed here, but this is justified by the superior food, and you still end up paying less than you would in a restaurant. Deliveries over 20 are free. Otherwise, you should expect to pay anything between 1 and 3.

Outside the City Gates

L'Arte Gaia

Via Faentina 1 (055 597 8498). Bus 1A. **Open** noon-2.30pm; 8-10.30pm Tue-Sun. Closed 2wks Aug. **Average** €45. **Credit** AmEx, MC, V.

L'Arte Gaia is a delightful new fish restaurant on the bridge crossing the Mugnone – a scruffy tributary of the Arno. The interior is modern and welcoming (warm wood floors, white walls broken by a couple of big splashy paintings) and there's also a closed-in veranda and a tiny terrace. The chef used to have a restaurant in El Salvador and his cooking is suitably colourful and punchy. The menu comes with a complimentary glass of Prosecco and a fishy nibble. Enjoy these while you wait for the interesting *antipasti* – home-made *stracetti* (wide pasta ribbons) with meaty chunks of swordfish, black olives and sun-dried tomatoes, perhaps. The *tegame di mare* (a kind of garlic shellfish stew) arrives in a big sautée pan and octopus is marinated before it's grilled. Desserts are sinfully good and the wine list is decent (the crisp Greco di Tufo from Campania is an excellent accompaniment to fish).

Bibe

Via delle Bagnese 1r (055 204 9085). Bus 36, 37, then taxi. **Open** 12.15-1.30pm, 7.30-9.45pm Mon, Tue, Fri-Sun; 7.30-9.45pm Thur. Closed last wk Jan-1st wk Feb, 1st 2wks Nov. **Average** €22. **Credit** AmEx, V.

Ever-popular Bibe occupies an old farmhouse 3km (two miles) out of Porta Romana. It is run by the fifth generation of the Scarselli family, who have been making things a little more sophisticated over the years, while being careful not to sacrifice the rustic atmosphere or push prices up too much. You're better off inside here – although there's a lovely, flower-filled terrace, the combination of traffic and mosquitoes means that this can be an uncomfortable experience. The menu features interesting variations on traditional dishes such as stuffed, deep-fried courgette flowers or an excellent, earthy *zuppa di porcini e ceci* (*porcini* mushroom soup with chick-peas). *Secondi* are classic Tuscan: excellent steak or veal done over an olive-wood grill, roast pigeon or guinea fowl, and deep-fried chicken, rabbit and brains (a speciality). The puddings – try *tortino di cioccolato* or the *semifreddo di caffè* – and the wine list are both a few notches above average.

Da Ruggero

Via Senese 89r (055 220 542). Bus 11, 36, 37 to Porta Romana, then 5min walk south. **Open** noon-2.30pm, 7.30-10.30pm Mon, Thur-Sun. Closed mid July-mid Aug. **Average** €25. **No credit cards.**

Don't risk the trek to Porta Romana without booking at the tiny and popular Da Ruggero. One of the few genuine family-friendly *trattorie* left in Florence, it's always packed. The food is local and home-cooked, and prices are reasonable. Traditional soups are a permanent fixture. The *ribollita* is particularly good, as is the excellent spicy *spaghetti alla carattiera*. Meat dishes always include a superb *arista al forno* (full of rosemary and garlic flavours) and an exemplary *bollito misto* (mixed boiled meats) served with tasty, parsley-fresh *salsa verde*. Puddings are home-made, of course.

Fuor d'Acqua

Via Pisana 37r (055 222 299). **Open** 8-11.30pm Mon-Sat. Closed 3wks Aug. **Average** €60. **Credit** AmEx, DC, MC, V.

Since it opened a couple of years ago, Fuor d'Aqua has provoked extreme reactions. While some believe it to be the best fish restaurant in town, others complain that prices are excessive. There's a whopping €5 cover charge, fish is served with minimum preparation and service can be very sloppy. Discreetly hidden behind smoked glass doors, the restaurant's decor is a weird combination of elegant rustic and plain tasteless. There's no menu. The chef cooks what's considered as the best of the day's catch when the trawler arrives in Viareggio at about 6pm. So if there's a delay on the *autostrada* into Florence, you just have to wait. But once it arrives, fish will be jumping fresh and prepared with olive oil, lemon juice and seasoning to complement. Mixed *antipasto* is a mini-meal in itself. Very simple and, some say, very good. See for yourself.

Omero

Via Pian de' Giuliari 11r (055 220 053). Bus 13, 38. **Open** noon-2.30pm, 7.30-10.30pm Mon, Wed-Sun. **Average** €30. **Credit** MC, V.

Omero should be visited at lunchtime for maximum appreciation of its fantastic position in the quiet, exclusive hamlet of Pian dei Giuliari. The entrance is on a narrow cobbled street, but walk through the back of the grocer's that fronts Omero and you emerge into a sunny room with great views of the rural surroundings. (Downstairs is not so nice.) The menu features traditional Florentine food, which is reliably cooked if not particularly exciting. Never mind, you're here for the old-fashioned atmosphere, the respectful service and the wonderful position.

Salaam Bombay

Viale Rosselli 45r (055 357 900). **Open** 7.30-11.30pm daily. **Average** €15. **Credit** AmEx, DC, MC, V.

One of several Indian restaurants in Florence, Salaam Bombay serves the sort of decently cooked standards found on the menus of most Indian restaurants in Italy. It's often full of Italians, for whom ethnic cooking is still something of an adventure. Though not wildly exciting, it does make a pleasant change from *ribollita* and *rosticciana*. The north Indian food includes tandoori dishes and a number of vegetarian options. Staff are very friendly.

Santa Lucia

Via Ponte alle Mosse 102r (055 353 255). Bus 30, 35. **Open** 7.30pm-1am Mon, Tue, Thur-Sun. Closed Aug. **Average** €13. **No credit cards.**

Many Florentines reckon that the pizza at Santa Lucia (ten minutes' walk north-west of Porta al Prato) is the best in town. So book in advance. Service is notoriously slow, but if you dare complain you risk being relegated to the bottom of the list – as locals well know. Like the atmosphere, the pizza is authentically Neapolitan topped with the sweetest tomatoes and milkiest mozzarella. Alternatively, there are excellent fish *primi* such as *spaghetti allo scoglio* (with mixed seafood). There are no outside tables, but air-con makes summer eating bearable (in spite of the heat from the pizza oven).

Targa

Lungarno C Colombo 7 (055 677 377). Bus 31, 32. **Open** 12.30-2.30pm, 7.30-11pm Mon-Sat. Closed 1st 3wks Aug. **Average** €35. **Credit** AmEx, DC, MC, V.

Out with the expensive, dated Caffè Concerto and in with a revamped Targa. Gabriele Tarchiani's delightful and refreshingly not-too-ultra-hip space on the river has been transformed from an upmarket eaterie into an informal bistro without compromising the quality of the food. The menu is shorter and simpler and features *crema di fave con cicoria alla pancetta* (broad bean soup with crispy pancetta), *carrè di agnello con fave e asparagi* (rack of lamb with broad beans and asparagus) and *filetto di tonno al pepe rosa e porri brasati* (tuna fillet with pink peppercorns and braised leeks). Desserts include a superb hot chocolate soufflé. There's a limited selection of reasonably priced wines with the daily menu, but if you're feeling adventurous, ask for the formidable full list, which also includes 127 whiskies (Scotch is a passion here).

Zibibbo

Via di Terzollina 3r (055 433 383). Bus 14. **Open** 1-3pm, 8-11pm Mon-Sat. Closed Aug. **Average** €40. **Credit** AmEx, DC, MC, V.

Benedetta Vitali moved on from Cibrèo (*see p115*), where she was co-founder and chef, to open this delightful restaurant. The simple but stylish decor with pink-varnished floorboards, open kitchen and big windows looking into the trees is refreshingly modern. The superb, unfussy food, on the other hand, derives from classic Florentine and Italian traditions. The menu features *tortelli di pere e pecorino* (pears and pecorino is a marriage made in heaven), spaghetti with swordfish, spaghetti with kidneys, *involtini* with artichoke hearts, *salmon al cartoccio* (wrapped in a parcel) with raspberries and a classic *trippa alla parmigiana*. The wine list features an interesting selection from all over Italy. Lunchtimes are more casual and the bill is about 25% less.

Wine Bars

Grape expectations.

Florence has been breeding *enoteche* like rabbits; wine – and the drinking of it – is becoming increasingly popular, particularly among young people. The problem is that many of these are run by opportunists keen to jump on the bandwagon. Often, they know little or nothing about wine, stock a random selection of very standard bottles with a huge mark-up and sell mediocre food to go with the drink. So beware, all that glitters is definitely not gold, but we can vouch for the selection listed here.

Wine has played an important part in Florentine life for centuries and wine bars are often full at lunch and *aperitivo* time. Although far fewer than there used to be, there are various types of wine bar in Florence. First, there are the tiny street booths (*fiaschetteria*, *vineria* or *mescita*) with virtually no seating, serving basic Tuscan wines and rustic snacks. These sit alongside comfortable, traditional drinking holes and the new, upmarket *enoteche* that offer a huge range of labels from all over Italy and beyond.

All the wine bars listed have a selection of wines by the glass and eats of some description, ranging from basic *panini* and *crostini* to sophisticated snacks and meals. Traditional places tend to stay open all day, closing around dinner time, while many of the newer ones stay open until late, particularly when they serve meals. The difference in price between a bottle consumed on the premises and one taken away is about 20-30 per cent in most places.

Duomo & Around

Cantinetta dei Verrazzano

Via dei Tavolini 18-20r (055 268 590/ www.verrazzano.com). **Open** *Sept-June* 8am-9pm Mon-Sat. *July, Aug* 8am-4pm Mon-Sat. **Credit** AmEx, DC, MC, V. **Map** p315 B4.

Cantinetta del Verrazzano belongs to one of Chianti's major vineyards, the Castello da Verrazzano estate. The panelled rooms are continually crowded with smartly dressed Florentines and tourists; on one side is the bakery and coffeeshop, while on the other is the wine bar serving exclusively estate-produced wines. Excellent value, both by the glass and by the bottle; the latter start at €13 for a Rosso Toscano and go up to €57 for a Riserva '90. Snacks include *focaccia* straight from the wood oven filled with sautéed funghi *porcini* or a slice of delicious *cecina*, a kind of flat crêpe made with chickpea flour.

I Fratellini

Via dei Cimatori 38r (no phone). **Open** 8am-8pm Mon-Sat. **No credit cards**. **Map** p315 C4.

I Fratellini (the little brothers) is one of a very few hole-in-the-wall *vinaii* left today. Founded in 1875, it is squirrelled away in a block north of piazza della Signoria. Cheerful service charms customers who stand in the road or squat on the pavement for a glass of the red house plonk (80c for a small glass) or something a bit more special (about €2). To eat, perhaps liver-topped *crostino* or a great slab of *porchetta* (rosemary roast pork) on a hunk of bread.

Frescobaldi Wine Bar

Vicolo dei Gondi, off Via della Condotta (055 284 724). **Open** 7pm-midnight Mon; noon-midnight Tue-Sat. **Credit** AmEx, MC, V. **Map** p315 C4.

The Frescobaldis are one of Tuscany's foremost wine-growing families and this is their second venture into the catering business – a wine bar annexe to a smart restaurant where, at a price, you can dine extremely well in elegant surroundings. Brightly lit with deep terracotta-coloured walls, the bar is relaxed and usually not too crowded. Wines come from the family's estates in Tuscany and elsewhere in Italy, or from the Mondavi estates in California and Chile – the Frescobaldis and the Mondavis have been making wine together for years. Mark-ups are very reasonable. Reds range from a basic, but perfectly acceptable, Remole 2001 at €9 per bottle/€2 per glass, the ever-popular Nipozzano 1999 Riserva (€19/€4.50) to such sophisticated wines as the superb Castelgiocondo Brunello di Montalcino Riserva 1997 (around €160) and various Super Tuscans. White-drinkers could try an excellent, good-value Pomino Bianco 2002 (€14/€3.50) or one of the delicious Friulian wines from the Attems estate. Snacks include excellent Italian cheeses and cured meats.

San Lorenzo

Casa del Vino

Via dell' Ariento 16r, San Lorenzo (055 215 609/ www.casadelvino.it). **Open** 8am-2.30pm, 5-8pm Mon-Fri; 9am-2.30pm Sat. Closed Aug. **Credit** AmEx, MC, V. **Map** p314 A3.

There's virtually nowhere to sit in this cramped, authentic wine bar hidden away behind the stalls in the San Lorenzo market. But that doesn't stop punters piling in for a glass of good wine and some delicious *panini* and *crostini*. The room is lined with carved shelves stacked with wines for all budgets. There's a huge choice of Super Tuscans and wines from all over Italy, plus labels from further afield.

Zanobini

Via Sant'Antonino 47r (055 239 6850). **Open** 8am-2pm, 3-8pm Mon-Sat. **Credit** (over €25) AmEx, MC, V. **Map** p314 A3.

Just off the San Lorenzo market's main drag, this no-frills, stand-up wine bar is full of surly types heavily into their glasses, many of whom may well have been there since opening time. It's good for a quick slurp and a snack before you repair to the back room with shelves full of interesting bottles to buy; prices are very reasonable. Wine is the main game here, but there's lots more besides, including a fine selection of *digestivi* that will help ease the stomach after a heavy Tuscan meal.

Santa Croce

All'Antico Vinaio

Via dei Neri 65r (no phone). **Open** 8am-8pm Tue-Sat; 8am-1pm Sun. Closed Aug. **Credit** AmEx, MC, V. **Map** p315 C4.

Situated in a street with a real neighbourhood feel to it, All'Antico Vinaio has been selling wine for a century or so. The new, friendly management has (thankfully) succeeded in modernising the interior without forsaking the old-fashioned character that gives the place its charm. Locals perch on the high stools to while away time drinking and exchanging the news; tourists eat and run. Wines are mostly Tuscan; a *gottino* (a stubby glass) of house plonk is only €1.10 while serious reds like Vino Nobile and Brunello cost from €4 to €9. Food includes delicious *crostini* (topped with truffle pâté or artichoke paste), excellent *panini* and pastas.

Boccadama

Piazza Santa Croce 25-6r (055 243 640/ www.boccadama.it). **Open** *Summer* 8.30am-6pm Mon; 8.30am-midnight Tue-Sun. *Winter* 8.30am-midnight Tue-Sun. **Credit** AmEx, DC, MC, V. **Map** p315 C5.

Enjoying a superb position on piazza Santa Croce with tables outside in summer, Boccadama is popular with tourists at lunchtimes during the season. But don't let the crowds put you off: this is a delightful place where serious wine lovers are given a run (and value) for their money. The wine list comprises over 1,000 labels, 90% of which are Italian and 40% of those are Tuscan. Meanwhile, the southern Italian section continues to grow. There's plenty of choice by the glass (starting from €2.90). Adjacent to the bar are several rooms with a more relaxed vibe. The menu features well-sourced cheeses, salami and *prosciutto*, as well as more substantial fare; *cacciucco* (Livornese fish soup), *tortelli di pere e pecorino* (pears and pecorino cheese – a marriage made in heaven – stuffed into pasta) or *spigola* (sea bass) stuffed with cabbage.

Enoteca Baldovino

Via San Giuseppe 18r (055 234 7220/ www.baldovino.com). **Open** noon-4pm, 6pm-midnight daily. **Credit** MC, V. **Map** p315 C5/6.

Annexe to the popular Baldovino trattoria (*see p112*), Enoteca Baldovino is a modern wine bar. A marble-topped counter is backed by shelves laden with jars while salamis and hams hang from butcher's hooks. House wines are cheap and cheerful, quality wines by the glass are on the expensive side but bottles drunk on the premises have only a small mark-up. The full wine list features about 500 labels, including a huge section of Piedmont reds. The menu relies on quantity rather than quality with an endless list of *crostini*, *carpacci* and *panini*.

Enoteca de' Giraldi

Via dei Giraldi 4r (055 216 518/www.vinaio.com). **Open** 11am-3.30pm, 6.30pm-1am Mon-Sat. Closed 2wks Aug. **Credit** AmEx, MC, V. **Map** p315 C4.

This *enoteca* seems to have lost its way a bit. On a recent visit, the place was virtually empty – a pity as the space is pleasant, the wine list (featuring both familiar and lesser-known wines mostly from Tuscany) interesting and the food is better than average, although prices are quite high. Occupying a lofty vault that once housed the stables of Palazzo Borghese, Enoteca de' Giradi serves wines to a background of mellow sounds. Wines by the glass (some 25) start at €3 while *spuntini* (snacks) cost from €1.05. Heartier fare includes rustic wooden boards generously filled with, say, grilled vegetables, cheeses, anchovies, swordfish and marinated fish. Wine courses and gastro-trips are organised.

Oltrarno

Pitti Gola e Cantina

Piazza Pitti 16 (055 212 704). **Open** *Summer* 10am-midnight Tue-Sun. *Winter* 10am-9.30pm Tue-Sun. **Credit** AmEx, MC, V. **Map** p314 D2.

Dark green paintwork and marble-topped tables give this little wine bar a classy, classic feel. Bang opposite Palazzo Pitti (the little terrace gets the full view), it's inevitably full of tourists and prices are on the high side, but the atmosphere is very pleasant and there's a good choice of wines, heavily weighted towards Tuscany. By the glass, expect to pay from €4 for a Vernaccia di San Gimignano or a Chianti Classico to €9.50 for a distinguished Brunello, Barolo or Amarone. Complimentary olives and *focaccia* are served, but there's a good choice of snacks too, including Dario Cecchini's famous *tonno di chianti* – not tuna fish at all but pork marinated in white wine and herbs.

Le Volpi e L'Uva

Piazza dei Rossi 1r (055 239 8132). **Open** 10am-8pm Mon-Sat. **Credit** AmEx, JCB, MC, V. **Map** p314 C4.

This chilled-out little wine bar, tucked away behind the south side of the Ponte Vecchio, has a faithful following of local wine aficionados who drop in after work. There's not a lot of space in the narrow room where the walls are lined with wine and cases are stacked on the floor. In summer the terrace eases the crush a bit. Wine is taken seriously here, and enthusiastically expert staff are ready with advice about

Frescobaldi Wine Bar. *See p123.*

Casa del Vino. *See p123.*

what to drink with what food and explanations of their stock, most of which will be unfamiliar to all but the most clued-up oenophiles. It's house policy to search out small, little-known producers that give the best value for money. About 35 wines are available by the glass at any one time. The day's selection might include a crisp, complex Tuscan Viogner 2002 from I Campetti at €2.60 per glass (€10.30 per bottle) or the dark, Sicilian Benuara (€2.60/€9.30). By the bottle, there are interesting wines from all over Italy, along with an increasing number of French labels. Then there are the dessert wines, the brandies and armagnacs, and the grappas. Limited but delicious nibbles include a great selection of cheeses, *panini tartufati* (stuffed with truffle cream), smoked duck and rich pâtés.

Outside the City Gates

Enotria

Via delle Porte Nuove 50 (055 354 350/www.enotriawine.it). Short walk from Porta al Prato. **Open** 8am-3.30pm Mon; 8am-3.30pm, 7pm-midnight Tue-Fri; 8pm-midnight Sat. Closed 2wks Aug. **Credit** AmEx, MC, V.

You're unlikely to stumble upon this bright, new-ish *enoteca* given its location on a busy arterial road leading west from Porta al Prato. However, it's well worth a visit for its convivial atmosphere, serious selection of wines and excellent food. The wine list features familiar and lesser-known labels, with an admirable choice for less than €15. Enotria is particularly interested in the robust wines of southern Italy and Sicily; try a red Ranitello from Molise at €11 or the aptly named Magnifico (made from a blend of Cabernet Sauvignon, Merlot and Nero d'Avola grapes) at €25. Lunch is an informal affair but in the evening a creative menu combines tempting dishes from all over Italy with wine suggestions.

Fuori Porta

Via Monte alle Croci 10r (055 234 2483/www.fuoriporta.it). Bus D. **Open** 12.30-3pm, 7pm-12.30am Mon-Sat. Closed 2wks Aug. **Credit** AmEx, MC, V.

Just outside one of the old city gates in San Niccolò, this is probably the most famous wine bar in Florence, and it's understandably popular. At any one time there's between 500 and 650 labels on the wine list and about 50 available by the glass and carafe (rotating roughly every week). Glasses start at €2 for a simple white Trebbiano or €3 for a crisp Prosecco di Valdobbiadene; a good Chianti Classico costs about €3.40 while a hefty, sun-packed Tancredi red from Sicily costs €5.40. Tuscan and Piedmontese reds dominate the list, but other Italian regions are also well represented (there are some fabulous whites from the Alto Adige and Friuli, for example) and there is a formidable choice of grappas and Scotch. The daily menu has a choice of pastas, *carpacci* and salads from €6.50. Although recently expanded, the terrace space is still quite small and much in demand in warm weather.

Cafés, Bars & *Gelaterie*

The drinking scene, frozen cream and plenty in-between.

The concentration of cafés and bars in Florence has long been testament to the locals' love affair with caffeine, while the spate of openings of upmarket hybrids, with any combination of café, wine bar, restaurant or brasserie, indicates a growing thirst for something new. And for the most part, that newness manifests itself in flexibility, with an increase in buffet lunches and *aperitivi* (*see p128* **Bar bites**), longer opening hours and more imaginative food on offer. But for all these changes it's the myriad local bars and cafés that continue to form the real backbone of Florentine life. This is a fact that quickly becomes apparent when strolling languorously through the backstreets of Oltrarno in search of bitter or sweet delights.

The etiquette of coffee, however, remains rigidly unchanged. Begin with a cappuccino at breakfast, moving on to the concentrated shot of espresso at a bar two or three times a day, with a strong hit of sweet black coffee after an evening meal. If you want more than a knock-it- back dribble that barely covers the bottom of the cup, ask for a *lungo* (the water is allowed to run through the coffee grounds for longer) or *caffè americano* (espresso with added hot water). And if you want milk in your espresso, ask for a *caffè macchiato caldo* or *freddo* (with a spoon of hot froth or a dash of cold milk). Caffeine diehards could order a *ristretto*, an even more concentrated espresso. To perk it up order your espresso *corretto*, 'corrected' with a shot of your spirit of choice. One final word of advice: many bars serve their cappuccinos disappointingly tepid, so if you want to ensure yours is good and hot, ask for *ben caldo*.

Classic bars come in several guises depending on their licence. In café-bars you can usually sit down for a full lunch; in bar-*tabacchi* you can also buy cigarettes, bus tickets and stamps; in *latterie*, milk and dairy products; and in *drogherie*, groceries. In many other shops, especially *pasticcerie*, there's also a bar. In bigger bars and cafés you pay for coffee at the till before you order it from the barman with your receipt, unless you want to sit down. Location is everything when it comes to the bill. It usually costs far less if you stand at the bar rather than sit at a table, and you often pay more to sit outside.

Duomo & Around

Astor Caffè

Piazza Duomo 20r (055 239 9000). **Open** 10am-3am Mon-Sat; 5pm-3am Sun. **Credit** MC, V. **Map** p315 B4.

A vast, contemporary chrome and glass bar with light flooding in from a central skylight. Perch on a padded bar stool for an aperitif or a freshly made vegetable or fruit juice, or linger for a lunch of smoked trout salad or steaming olive and cherry tomato pasta. Some evenings there's jazz in the downstairs bar, while upstairs you can sip cocktails, eat a full Tuscan dinner or check your emails at the bar's internet point.

Bar Perseo

Piazza della Signoria 16r (055 239 8316). **Open** 7am-midnight Mon-Sat. Closed 3wks Nov. **Credit** MC, V. **Map** p315 C4.

Though the centrepiece of this bar is its sculptural art deco chandelier, most eyes are drawn to the mountains of home-made ice-cream topped with cherries, berries and chocolate curls. Stand at the bar for an aperitif, or sit outside and admire the bar's namesake, *Perseus*, which is in the Loggia dei Lanzi (*see p73*). Cappuccinos €1.30 at the bar, €5 outside.

Caffè Concerto Paszkowski

Piazza della Repubblica 31-5r (055 210 236/ www.paszkowski.it). **Open** 7am-1.30am Tue-Sun. **Credit** AmEx, DC, JCB, MC, V. **Map** p314 B3.

Founded in 1846 as a beer hall and later as a meeting point for artists, Concerto was declared a national monument in 1991. It now distinguishes itself from the other bars lining the square by its dodgy summer evening concerts, its chocolate and semolina tarts and as one of the few places still open after the late-night cinema for a nicotine or caffeine fix.

Caffè Italiano

Via della Condotta 56r (055 291 082). **Open** 8am-8pm Mon-Sat (lunch 1-3pm); 11am-8pm Sun. Closed 3wks Aug. **Credit** MC, V. **Map** p315 C4.

A hidden treasure with old world charm: mahogany cabinets filled with silver teapots, gourmet chocolates and famous own-brand coffee. Downstairs is the bar, while at the top of the spiral staircase red velvet benches line the salon where lunches and home-made cakes are served. *Caffè-choc* (espresso laced with bitter chocolate powder) is a must. Hot drinks come with a plate of melt-in-the-mouth biscuits.

Caffè Rivoire

Piazza della Signoria 5r (055 214 412). **Open** 8am-midnight Tue-Sun. Closed last 2wks Jan. **Credit** AmEx, DC, JCB, MC, V. **Map** p315 C4.

Old world charm and melt-in-the-mouth biscuits at **Caffè Italiano**. *See p126.*

The grande dame of Florentine cafés, Rivoire was founded in 1872 as a steamed chocolate factory and is still famous for its chocs – the best in town. Its displays of chocolate sculptures are as breathtaking as the view of the Palazzo Vecchio from the outside tables. Cappuccinos €1.20 at the bar, €5 seated.

Chiaroscuro

Via del Corso 36r (055 214 247). **Open** 7.45am-8.30pm Tue-Fri; 8.45am-9.30pm Sat, Sun. **Credit** MC,V. **Map** p315 B4.

The window of espresso machines, collector's coffee cups and coffee-bean resin trays (all for sale) shows Chiaroscuro is serious about its coffee. At the tables beyond the narrow bar you can have lunch or a slice of cake. Cappuccinos €1 at the bar, €2.50 seated.

Colle Bereto

Piazza Strozzi 5r (055 283 156). **Open** *Winter* 8am-9pm Mon-Sat. *Summer* 8am-midnight Mon-Sat (food from noon). **Credit** AmEx, MC, V. **Map** p314 B3.

Owned by the Tuscan wine producer of the same name, Colle Bereto is a newly opened bar with a prime position. The bar has a menu as carefully chosen as its sleek decor, with a daily choice of hot *primi*, a fixed menu of perfect salads and snacks, and, best of all, tiny fruit tarts with whipped yoghurt fillings.

Coquinarius

Via delle Oche 15r (055 230 2153). **Open** 9am-11pm Mon-Thur; 9am-11.30pm Fri, Sat (food from noon). Closed 2wks Aug. **Credit** MC, V. **Map** p314 B3.

A vaulted bar with a friendly, homely atmosphere, Coquinarius also has an extensive wine list. And on its food menu, the unmissable sheep's cheese and pear pasta parcels, imaginative salads and smoked fish platters. At tea-time try the exotic range of chais and speciality hot chocolate with fudge or meringues.

The Fusion Bar Shozan, Gallery Art Hotel

Vicolo dell'Oro 3 (055 272 66987). **Open** noon-midnight daily. **Credit** DC, MC, V. **Map** p314 C3.

A minimalist's delight and a magnet for the bright young things of the city, the Fusion Bar is run in collaboration with the famous Shozan restaurant of Paris and Tokyo. This can mean that the menu, a fusion of French, Japanese and Italian foodie clichés, sometimes misses. Part of the Gallery Art complex (*see p47*), the bar's decor echoes the hotel's masculine feel with square leather sofas and dark wood coffee tables.

Gilli

Piazza della Repubblica 36-9r (055 213 896). **Open** 8am-midnight Mon, Wed-Sun. **Credit** AmEx, DC, JCB, MC, V. **Map** p314 B3.

Gilli's belle époque interior is original, its seasonally themed window displays of sweets, chocolates and pastries wickedly tempting and its staff delightful. Not to be missed are its rich hot chocolates – *gianduia* (hazelnut), almond, mint, orange and coffee – and an irresistible spread of snacks on the bar at *aperitivo* time. There's outside seating year round.

Giubbe Rosse

Piazza della Repubblica 13-14r (055 212 280/ www.giubberosse.it). **Open** 7.30am-2am daily. **Credit** AmEx, DC, JCB, MC, V. **Map** p314 B3.

Dating from the end of the 19th century and an intellectuals' haunt since 1909, when the Futurist manifesto was launched from here, this café is still popular with the Florentine literati. Keeping its name alive the waiters still wear the red jackets that spawned the title. There's outside seating for people-watching in the piazza.

Bar bites

Stopping off for an early evening aperitif has taken on a whole new meaning in many bars in Florence. A far cry from the ubiquitous bowls of olives and nuts, *aperitivo* has now come to mean something altogether more sophisticated. Arrive between 7pm and 9pm, buy yourself a drink and you can expect to stock up for free on a buffet of often delicious, usually freshly cooked food from the bar's own kitchens.

Angels (via del Proconsolo 29-31r, 055 239 8762) serves classic Tuscan dishes of *pappa al pomodoro* and *ribollita*, alongside delicate *crostini*, rich pâtés and hot salads. Non-alcoholic drinks €6, alcoholic €6.50. **Capocaccia** (*see p129*) offers a mega-buffet in a frescoed salon with salads, hot pastas, risottos, and sweet dishes of tiramisù, cakes and fresh fruit. All drinks are €7 and there's a sushi buffet on Tuesdays. Wander into **Dolce Vita** (*see p130*), a horseshoe bar loaded with crudités with tiny individual bowls of olive oil dip, Tuscan *crostini* and sushi. All drinks €6. The trendy **Fusion Bar** (*see p127*), with drinks from €6-€10, takes an oriental slant with snacks of sushi and tempura, beautifully presented on lacquered black plates. **Negroni** (*see p180*) serves Mediterranean dishes of couscous, grilled peppers and cold pastas to wash down with its namesake cocktail, all drinks are €6.

For huge trays of cold meats, cheeses and hot chocolate fondue with fresh fruit served on a mosaic bar visit **Rex** (*see p180*) where drinks are €4.50 from 6.30pm to 8.30pm. Traditional cold *aperitivo* snacks are piled high on the bar at **Ricchi** (*see p131*). Expect filled *focaccia* squares, canapés, dips, cocktail stick classics, mini pizzas and more with drinks between €3 and €7. At **Slowly** (*see p180*) you'll find a different full-blown meal each day from the bar's own kitchens, served (on a central pedestal) in courses that just keep on coming, and a platter of crudités brought to your table. All drinks €8.

Gold

Piazza Pesce 3/5r (055 2396 810). **Open** *Summer* 11am-1am daily. *Winter* 11am-8pm Mon, Tues, Thur-Sun. Closed Jan. **No credit cards.** **Map** p315 C4.

This home-made ice-cream shop just by the Ponte Vecchio attracts crowds to its tiny serving hatch and is known for its exotic fruit flavours.

L'Incontro, Savoy Hotel

Piazza della Repubblica 7 (055 273 5891). **Open** 9am-9pm Mon-Sat; 10.30am-8pm Sun. **Credit** AmEx, DC, JCB, MC, V. **Map** p314 B3.

An elegant brasserie-style bar in the recently restored Savoy hotel, with clean lines, pale wood and leather furnishings. The formal appearance of the bar belies the friendly informality of the staff, which makes it a pleasant place for lunch or drinks, especially if you clinch a table under the outside canopy.

Perche' No!

Via dei Tavolini 19r (055 239 8969). **Open** *Summer* 11am-midnight daily. *Winter* midday-7.30pm Mon, Wed-Sun. **No credit cards. Map** p315 B4.

A local institution trading since 1939, this *gelateria*'s pistachio and chocolate flavours are legendary.

Sugar e Spice

Via dei Servi 43r (055 290 263). **Open** 10am-2.30pm, 3.30-7.30pm Tue-Sat. **No credit cards.** **Map** p315 A4.

Home-made American-style treats at this sweet café include carrot cake, muffins, brownies, apple pie and speciality cheesecakes.

La Terrazza, Rinascente

Piazza della Repubblica 1 (055 219 113). **Open** 9am-9pm Mon-Sat; 10.30am-8pm Sun. **Credit** AmEx, DC, JCB, MC, V. **Map** p314 B3.

The rooftop terrace of this department store café affords one of the most stunning views of the city, the splendour of Brunelleschi's cupola at such close range more than making up for the inexplicably mediocre menu and the odds-on risk of churlish service. Still, it's well worth a visit – especially at sundown when you can experience the delight of the city at 360 degrees and bathed in pink light.

Santa Maria Novella

Amerini

Via della Vigna Nuova 63r (055 284 941). **Open** 8.30am-8.30pm Mon-Sat. Closed 2wks Aug. **No credit cards. Map** p314 B2.

Smart but cosy with a gravity-defying display of the finest Tuscan wines, this is a lunchtime favourite for local designer-emporium shop assistants. Choose from sandwiches such as marinated artichoke or grilled vegetables with brie, or order a bowl of fresh pasta. Breakfast time is mercifully relaxing and in the afternoon you can sample the luscious lemon tart relatively undisturbed. A cappuccino costs €1 at the bar, €3 seated.

Bar Curtatone

Borgo Ognissanti 167r (055 210 772). **Open** 7am-1am Mon, Wed-Fri, Sun; 7am-2am Sat. Closed 3wks Aug. **No credit cards. Map** p314 B1.

A vast, bustling but stylish café serving a decadent selection of pastries, cakes and savouries. Have a three-course meal (12.30pm to 2.30pm) or sip on a selection of liqueurs and aperitifs.

Caffè Megara

Via della Spada 15-17r (055 211 837). **Open** 8am-2am daily (lunch 11.30am-3pm). **No credit cards.** **Map** p314 B2.

Crowds flock to this laid-back, airy bar for the pasta lunch dishes, the smooth jazz sounds, and most of all for its football coverage. But don't worry, there are two screens so no one will miss out. Conversation is accordingly muted, and generally limited to groans or cheers at missed penalties. Still, the atmosphere is convivial enough. Cappuccinos at the bar are €1 or €2.50 seated.

Capocaccia

Lungarno Corsini 12-14r (055 210 751). **Open** noon-2am Tue-Sun. **Credit** MC, V. **Map** p314 C2.

With a frescoed (non-smoking) salon and doors opening from a tiled central bar room on to the riverbank seating area, Capocaccia is undoubtedly one of Florence's most desirable café-bars. Sunday brunch is legendary, with a choice of food platters including eggs benedict or smoked salmon bagels as well as a buffet of salads, cold meats and cheeses. On other days you can also choose from the *primi* of the day. There are also *panini*, champagne by the glass and an extensive collection of aged whisky. Cappuccino and espresso come with a handmade chocolate ice-cream.

Giacosa Roberto Cavalli

Via della Spada 10r (055 277 6328). **Open** 7.30am-8.30pm Mon-Sat. Closed 2wks Aug. **Credit** AmEx, MC, V. **Map** p314 B2.

Out with the genteel atmosphere of the original Bar Giacosa, in with the leopard-skin poufs and full wall-screen catwalk shows of flamboyant Florentine designer, Cavalli, who has transformed the site into a clothing shop and café. Even Giacosa's renowned chocolate is piped into animal print patterns. The outside tables are often frequented by the man himself, so beware about making derogatory comments over cocktails about the price-to-value ratio of the scraps of chiffon in the window displays. Such asides are probably best kept to a whisper.

Latteria Moggi

Via del Parione 44r (no phone). **Open** 7.30am-8pm Mon-Sat. **No credit cards. Map** p314 C2.

A small, relaxed no-smoking café with bleached wood tables and benches, this 'dairy' is a popular spot for a salad or a *piadina Romagnola* (toasted flatbread with grilled vegetables and cheese or ham) or for the milk-based puddings and rich ice-cream.

Rose's

Via del Parione 26r (055 287 090/www.roses.it). **Open** 8am-1.30am Mon-Sat; 5pm-1.30am Sun (brunch 12.30-3.30pm Sat). Closed 2wks Aug. **Credit** MC, V. **Map** p314 C2.

This spacious, restaurant-bar with its modern but cosseting decor and a non-smoking salon is invariably packed with a young crowd from local shops and offices. Breakfast is muffins and brownies. At lunch choose from hamburgers, vegetarian Mexican tacos or classic pastas, risottos and salads. In the evening it's one of the hippest sushi bars in town. Cappuccinos €1.10 at the bar, €3 seated.

San Lorenzo

BZF – Bizzeffe Vallecchi

Via Panicale 61r (055 274 1009/www.bzf.it). **Open** noon-midnight Tue-Sun. **Credit** MC, V. Map p314 A3.

Stunningly renovated 13th-century convent, now home to this hybrid of bar, bookshop, internet point, live jazz venue and art space. Go for the divine pumpkin soup, flame-charred tuna *carpaccio*, or cheeseboards served with wine chutney or honey. Or concentrate on American-style sweets and the choice of coffees and teas from around the world. Sunday brunch buffet is more Sunday lunch, with pastas, roast meats and veg, and unlimited drinks (€18).

Nabucco

Via XVII Aprile 28r (055 475 087). **Open** 6.30am-10pm Mon-Sat. **Credit** MC, V.

Despite a near-constant influx of students from the nearby university faculties, you can always get a seat at one of the many tables or bar stools lining the huge windows of this spacious, pleasant café-wine bar. Regular wine tastings are organised by Tuscan producers and the lunch and snack menus tend to be arranged around the wine list.

Nannini Coffee Shop

Via Borgo 7r (055 212 680). **Open** 7.30am-8pm Mon-Thur; 7.30am-9pm Fri-Sun. **Credit** MC, V. **Map** p314 B3.

Perennially bustling, Nannini is perfect for coffee and *panforte* (a sticky Sienese cake) after a visit to the nearby central market. It's owned by ex-racing driver Alessandro Nannini, who has a confectionery factory in Siena, so you can also buy *cantuccini* (almond biscuits), *ricciarelli* (choc-covered marzipan petits fours) and hexagonal *panfortes* of all sizes.

Porfirio Rubirosa

Viale Strozzi 38r (055 490 965). **Open** 11am-2am Tue-Sun. Closed 2wks Aug. **Credit** MC, V. **Map** p314 B3.

Across from the Fortezza da Basso and overlooking the park with its duck pond and fountains, this chic bar was named after a Brazilian playboy and is a monument to hedonism. Lunch on truffle mozzarella or smoked tuna salad, lounge on the balcony mezzanine with a slice of passion fruit cheesecake at teatime, or come back in the evening to make a night of it.

San Marco

Caffellatte

Via degli Alfani 39r (055 247 8878). **Open** 8am-midnight Mon-Sat; 10am-6pm Sun. **No credit cards. Map** p315 A4.

Licensed in 1920 to sell 'coffee and milk beverages', Caffellatte continues to supply the neighbourhood's milk. In 1984 an organic bakery was added and the current café – one tiny room kitted out with rustic wooden tables and chairs – was born. The *caffellattes*, served piping hot in giant bowls, are the best in Florence.

Robiglio

Via dei Servi 112r (055 214 501). **Open** 7.30am-7.30pm Mon-Sat. Closed 3wks Aug. **No credit cards. Map** p315 A4.

This is the place for superb old-fashioned *pasticceria*. The thick *cioccolato caldo* is also worth a try. Outside tables in summer.

Branch: Via Tosinghi 11r, Duomo & Around (055 215 013).

Zona 15

Via del Castellaccio 53-5r, Piazza Brunelleschi (055 211 678/www.zona15wine.it). **Open** 11am-3am Mon-Sat; 6pm-3am Sun. **Credit** AmEx, DC, MC, V. **Map** p315 A4.

Like a futuristic American diner, this hip new café-cum-wine bar's leather and chrome bar stools hug a huge central spotlit bar area. Tables filled with thoroughbred Florentines neatly line the grey mosaic-tiled walls, crowned by dramatic vaulted ceilings. Splash out on oysters and champagne or choose from the Mediterranean-inclined menu and over 200 wines.

Santa Croce

Caffè dei Macci

Via dei Macci 92r (055 241 226). **Open** 6am-1am Mon-Sat; 5-8pm Sun. **Credit** AmEx, MC, V. **Map** p315 C6.

A small café oozing rustic charm. The menu, hand-written on rough recycled paper, is refreshingly cheap, with cappuccinos at €1, *crostini*, cold meats and speciality hot dishes between €3 and €7 and apple pie for a mere €1.50. Great range of wines by the glass.

Caffè Cibreo

Via Andrea del Verrocchio 5r (055 234 5853). **Open** 8am-1am Tue-Sat; lunch served 1-2.30pm. Closed 2wks Aug. **No credit cards.**

This is a delightful café with exquisite carved wood ceilings, antique furniture, candlelit mosaic outside tables, along with a knack for making everything it presents as beautiful as the bar itself. You'll find that the savoury dishes are inventive and refined. But this is as you would expect from an outpost of Cibrèo restaurant (*see p115*). Desserts are also phenomenal, notably the dense chocolate torte and the cheesecake served with *arancia amara* (bitter orange) sauce. If you want to prolong the experience, you can call a day in advance and order a whole cake to take home.

Caffetteria Piansa

Borgo Pinti 18r, nr Piazza G Salvemini (055 234 2362). **Open** 8am-1am Mon-Sat; lunch served noon-3pm. Closed 2wks Aug. **No credit cards. Map** p315 B5.

In a quiet street, Piansa (the best-known Florentine coffee brand) is a self-service café popular with local students and business folk. It has a rustic canteen style with wooden benches and shared tables, and is big enough to ensure that finding a seat is rarely a problem outside the busy lunch period. Cappuccino costs €1 at the bar and seated until 4.30pm.

Gelateria dei Neri

Via dei Neri 22r (055 210 034). **Open** *Summer* 11.30am-11.30pm daily. *Winter* 11.30am-11.30pm Mon, Tue, Thur-Sun. **No credit cards. Map** p314 C4

One of the few parlours to serve soya ice-cream alongside the classic creamy concoctions, so even those with a dairy intolerance can indulge.

La Loggia degli Albizi

Borgo degli Albizi 39r (055 247 9574). **Open** 7am-8pm Mon-Sat. Closed Aug. **No credit cards. Map** p315 B4/5.

With some of the best pastries and cakes in town, La Loggia degli Albizi is the perfect stopoff after some hard shopping; try the *torta della nonna* (crumbly pastry filled with baked pâtisserie cream).

Vivoli

Via Isola delle Stinche 7r (055 292 334). **Open** *Summer* 7.30am-1am Tue-Sun. *Winter* 7.30am-midnight Tue-Sun. **No credit cards. Map** p315 C5.

Vivoli is reputed to have the best ice-cream in Florence and is revered for its *semi-freddi*, creamier and softer than ice-cream, and for its divine *riso* (rice pudding) flavour.

Oltrarno

Caffè degli Artigiani

Via dello Sprone 16r (055 291 882). **Open** *May-Sept* 8.30am-midnight Mon-Sat. *Oct-Apr* 8.30am-10.30pm Mon-Sat. **Credit** AmEx, DC, JCB, MC, V. **Map** p314 C2.

This charming, laid-back gem of a café is well worth seeking out for its rustic-chic atmosphere (think low ceilings and fraying, beautifully carved antique chairs). Cappuccino is €1 at the bar, €1.50 seated. Friendly multilingual staff.

Caffè Ricchi

Piazza Santo Spirito 9r (055 215 864). **Open** *Summer* 7am-1am Mon-Sat. *Winter* 7am-8pm Mon-Sat. Closed 1st 2wks Jan. **Credit** MC, V. **Map** p314 D2.

Weather permitting, one of the most pleasant settings for alfresco drinking in Florence, Ricchi is set on the traffic-free piazza of the sublime Santo Spirito church. The lunch menu of sandwiches, pasta dishes and speciality *sformati* (hot vegetable terrines) changes daily, and a quiet side room plastered with artists' versions of the church façade is a great place to chill out with coffee and cakes on a rainy day.

Dolce Vita

Piazza del Carmine (055 284 595). **Open** *Apr-Oct* 10am-2am daily. *Nov-Mar* 6pm-2am Tue-Sun. **Credit** AmEx, JCB, MC, V. **Map** p314 C1.

Though Dolce Vita is known mainly as the supreme pre-club hangout (*see p178*), a lunchtime or evening aperitif sipped outside in the square, shaded from the sun at the canopied tables, is a hallowed Florentine institution. Typically, this is done while wearing designer shades and talking business into the hands-free of your last-model Nokia. Pretentious? You bet. But it definitely makes compulsive viewing.

Hemingway

Piazza Piattellina 9r (055 284 781). **Open** 4.30pm-1am Tue-Thur; 4.30pm-2am Fri, Sat; 11.30am-8pm Sun (brunch noon-2.15pm). Closed mid June-mid Sept. **Credit** AmEx, DC, JCB, MC, V. **Map** p314 C1.

This charming non-smoking café has a huge selection of teas, at least 20 types of coffee and unusual tea cocktails, but is best known for its chocolate delectables. This is no surprise given that proprietor Monica Meschini is the secretary of the Chocolate Appreciation Society – its *sette veli* chocolate cake once won the World Cake Championship. Hemingway high tea (6-7.30pm) tempts with ten different morsels of sweet delights. There's also a Sunday brunch (booking advisable).

Il Rifrullo

Via San Niccolò 53-7 (055 234 2621). **Open** 8am-2am daily. Closed 2wks Aug. **Credit** MC, V. **Map** p315 D5.

Set in peaceful San Niccolò, this bar is a laid-back place to linger over your morning cappuccino. Things liven up later, when music comes on, the back rooms and summer roof garden open, and the cocktail barman starts to perform some tricks. Meanwhile, it's €1 for a cappuccino at the bar, €3 at a table.

Outside the City Gates

Chalet Fontana

Via San Leonardo 8r (055 221 187). Bus 12, 13. **Open** 7am-2am Tue-Sun. **No credit cards.**

Enjoy the view of cypress trees on distant hills from this charming wooden chalet (on the bus route to piazzale Michelangelo from the station or 15 minutes on foot uphill from the Forte di Belvedere). Light lunches are served, and the succulent pear and chocolate cake is unmissable. The place also opens late as a piano bar.

Shops & Services

Join the counter culture.

Licking good: satisfied customers of **Vestri**. *See p143*.

Despite an apparent shift on some of the main shopping streets of Florence away from the old-fashioned family-owned gems towards the ubiquitous upmarket international stores, any shopper worth their salt need only step off the major thoroughfares to find themselves in a paradise of original and individual goods.

Wander through the backstreets of the Oltrarno where you can watch the artisans carrying out their centuries-old skills of marquetry, jewel inlay, gilding, carving, book-binding and paper-making. See the masterpieces of their ancestors in the wonderful antiques shops lining via Maggio and via dei Fossi. Or marvel at the tiny 16th-century jewellery shops on the Ponte Vecchio, which proudly display the past and present work of the Arezzo goldsmiths (for more on this, *see p259* **City of gold**).

Whether you're looking for an original gift for someone else or a new wardrobe for yourself, the central pedestrian zone is no less tempting to those with itchy wallet fingers. The lively, bustling markets and delicious-smelling food stores punctuate the central causeway of clothes, shoes and gift shops, all displaying with characteristic Florentine peacock flair their various window-dressings. It's all too easy to be enticed in.

All you designer devotees should concentrate your efforts on the area around via Tornabuoni, while bargain-hunters should head for the spokes leading off the Duomo wheel-hub (particularly to the north, up towards the San Lorenzo market, *see p134*). But the best way to shop in Florence is to let your feet do the walking and keep your eyes peeled for that special find.

Some shops have a baffling *entrata libera* (free entrance) sign in the window, which means you're free to browse with no obligation to buy. Although this may seem obvious, there are still a few places – mainly older, family-run shops – where you're expected to tell the assistant what you're looking for as soon as you enter. (And you'd better provide a good excuse if you don't like what they offer.)

Non-EU visitors are entitled to a VAT rebate on purchases of goods over €154.94 and some shops keep the requisite forms. Look for the 'Tax-free' signs in the shop window (*see p290*).

OPENING HOURS

While supermarkets and larger stores in the city centre now stay open through the day (*orario continuato*), most shops still operate standard hours, closing at lunchtime and, food shops excepted, on Monday mornings. Standard opening times are 3.30pm to 7.30pm on Monday, and 9am to 1pm then 3.30pm to 7.30pm Tuesday to Saturday, with clothes shops sometimes opening around 10am. Food shops open earlier in the morning and later in the afternoon and they close on Wednesday afternoons. Many of the central stores now stay open for at least part of Sunday and several more open on the last Sunday of the month.

Hours do alter slightly in mid June until the end of August when most shops close on Saturday afternoons. Small shops tend to shut completely at some point during July or August for anything from a week to a month for their summer break.

The times listed apply most of the year, but they can vary and some shops, especially small ones, may open or close more randomly.

Books

Many bookshops stock books in English, but prices are 15 to 40 per cent higher than in the UK. For children's books, *see p158*.

Alinari

Largo Alinari 15, Santa Maria Novella (055 23 951/www.alinari.com). **Open** 9am-1pm, 2.30-6.30pm Mon-Fri; 9am-1pm, 3-7pm Sat. Closed 3wks Aug. **Credit** AmEx, DC, MC, V. **Map** p314 A2.

The world's first photographic firm, established in 1852, stocks photography books and exhibition catalogues, and will order prints of virtually anything in the Alinari archives.

City Lights

Via San Niccolù 23, Oltrarno (055 234 7882). **Open** 5.30-10.30pm Mon-Fri but erratic (call beforehand). **No credit cards. Map** p315 D5.

Modelled on the San Francisco bookstore of the same name, City Lights stocks Beat literature, much of it in English, and organises literary events.

Edison

Piazza della Repubblica 27r, Duomo & Around (055 213 110/www.libreriaedison.it). **Open** 9am-midnight Mon-Sat; 10am-midnight Sun. **Credit** AmEx, DC, MC, V. **Map** p314 B3.

This comprehensive book superstore, with its video screens showing the latest news, internet points, café and lecture area, also sells maps, magazines, calendars and CDs. The travel section at Edison has lots of guides in English to inspire further adventures.

Feltrinelli International

Via Cavour 12-20r, San Marco (055 219 524/ www.feltrinelli.it). **Open** 9am-7.30pm Mon-Sat. **Credit** AmEx, DC, MC, V. **Map** p315 A4.

Feltrinelli International is a modern and well organised book shop with strong art, photography and comic book sections. There's also a huge selection of titles in English, language-teaching books, original-language videos and a gift section.

Franco Maria Ricci

Via delle Belle Donne 41r, Santa Maria Novella (055 283 312). **Open** 3.30-7.30pm Mon; 10am-1pm, 3.30-7.30pm Tue-Sat. **Credit** AmEx, DC, MC, V. **Map** p314 B2.

A delightful art bookshop and arts and crafts gallery, stocking mostly limited editions, numbered prints and handmade stationery.

The best Shops

...for design

For unique design gifts you won't find anywhere else, try **Borgo degli Albizi 48 Rosso** (*see p147*), **Frammenti** (*see p147*), **N'Uovo** (*see p148*) and **Rosa Regale** (*see p148*).

...for the essence of Florence

For an alchemist's heaven visit **Bizzarri** (*see p145*) or pop down to **Officina Profumo-Farmaceutica di Santa Maria Novella** (*see p146*) for its world-renowned soap. Smell your way to the frescoed **Spezieria Erboriseria Palazzo Vecchio** (*see p146*) for handmade perfumes.

...for food gifts

Bottega della Frutta (*see p143*) for wine, balsamic vinegar, grappa and biscuits.
La Bottega dell'Olio (*see p143*) for extra virgin olive oils and oil-preserved delicacies.
Dolceforte (*see p143*) for chocolate Duomos, Davids and Leaning Towers.
Procacci (*see p143*) for truffles, truffle oils and pâtés.

Libreria delle Donne

Via Fiesolana 2B, Santa Croce (055 240 384). **Open** 3.30-7.30pm Mon; 9.30am-1pm, 3.30-7.30pm Tue-Fri. Closed Aug. **Credit** MC, V. **Map** p315 B5.

This women's bookshop is a good reference point for women visiting the city. The feminist literature is mostly Italian, but there's a useful noticeboard with info about local activities.

Paperback Exchange

Via Fiesolana 31r, Santa Croce (055 247 8154/ www.papex.it). **Open** 9am-7.30pm Mon-Fri; 10am-1pm, 3.30-7.30pm Sat. Closed 2wks Aug. **Credit** AmEx, DC, MC, V. **Map** p315 B5.

The Paperback Exchange has a good choice of new English-language fiction and non-fiction, particularly art, art history and Italian culture. The shop's noticeboard has info about literary events, courses, accommodation and language lessons. Second-hand books can be traded.

Communications

Centro AZ

Via degli Alfani 20r, San Marco (055 247 7855). **Open** 9am-1pm, 3-7pm Mon-Fri; 9am-12.30pm Sat. **No credit cards. Map** p315 A4.

If you're in need of somewhere to do your admin, Centro AZ is a good bet. Faxes carry a charge of €1 plus the cost of the call. Copies cost 5c.

Department stores

COIN

Via dei Calzaiuoli 56r, Duomo & Around (055 280 531/www.coin.it). **Open** *Jan-Mar* 10am-7.30pm Mon-Sat; 11am-7.30pm Sun. *Apr-Dec* 10am-8pm Mon-Sat; 11am-8pm Sun. **Credit** AmEx, DC, MC, V. **Map** p314 B3.

Furnishings are the strong point of this mid-range store, which sells heavy tapestry throws and bright contemporary homeware. Coin also sells crisp modern fashions, shoes, accessories and gifts.

Principe

Via del Sole 2, Santa Maria Novella (055 292 764/ www.principedifirenze.com). **Open** *Summer* 3.30-7.30pm Mon; 9.30am-7.30pm Tue-Sat. *Winter* 10.30am-7.30pm Mon; 9.30am-7.30pm Tue-Sat. **Credit** AmEx, DC, MC, V. **Map** p314 B2.

Stuffy staff, but this should be your first port of call for the twee English country look: linens, bath accessories and toiletries. Men's suits made to measure.

La Rinascente

Piazza della Repubblica 1, Duomo & Around (055 219 113). **Open** 9am-9pm Mon-Sat; 10.30am-8pm Sun. **Credit** AmEx, DC, MC, V. **Map** p134 B3.

La Rinascente is a classic store, which sells decent menswear, perfume counters and Versace bedding along with a vast lingerie section. There's also a recently opened café on the fifth floor (*see p129*).

Trading places

One of the first things visitors to Florence will notice is the abundance of market stalls that seem to appear in even the tiniest of piazzas, selling all manner of goodies and tat. Know when and where to look, however, and bargain-hunting habitués are in for a treat.

The main market of **San Lorenzo** (8.30am-7pm Mon-Sat) covers a cobweb of streets around San Lorenzo church, with stalls of leather goods, clothes and souvenirs, while at its centre the 19th-century covered market in the **piazza del Mercato Centrale** (with entrances on the piazza itself and on via del Arientois) is dedicated to fruit, vegetables, meats, fish and cheeses (open 7am-2pm Mon-Sat). Foodies can also head to the **Sant'Ambrogio** market in piazza Ghiberti just north of Santa Croce (open 7am-2pm Mon-Sat) for the freshest and cheapest farmers' produce. Leave time to stop off on the way back into the centre of town at the flea market, the **Mercato delle Pulci**, round the corner in piazza dei Ciompi (open 9am-7pm Mon-Sat) to browse through the bric-a-brac for that elusive antique find. You may not find anything of value at the **Mercato Nuovo** in the covered Loggia del Mercato Nuovo just off via Calimala (open 9am-7pm Mon-Sat) – also known as the Mercato del Porcellino in honour of the bronze boar statue whose nose it is *de rigueur* to rub if you want a return visit to Florence – but the alabaster chess sets, cheap tapestries and lace, stationery, leather and scarves make good souvenirs and gifts.

Of the weekly and monthly markets, the biggest is at the **Cascine**, the gardens just west of the city centre (open 8am-1pm Tue), where more than 300 stalls line the main avenue viale Lincoln, and you can buy anything from live chickens to popcorn to shoes and clothing. **Piazza Santo Spirito** is home to a small daily weekday morning market, but is better known for the monthly antique and flea market (open 8am-6pm 2nd Sun) with the odd treasure to be found among the old photos, furniture, frames and jewellery, and for the **Fierucola**, a delightful market (open 8am-6pm 3rd Sun) with stalls selling organic foods and wines, handmade clothing, cosmetics and natural medicines.

Splurge with elegance at **Ermanno Scervino**.

Fashion

For sports clothes and equipment, *see pp181-4*; for kids' clothes, *see pp157-9*; for gloves and handbags, *see p139* **Skin cheap**.

Designer

Most of Florence's designer shops are strung along via Tornabuoni and via Vigna Nuova in Santa Maria Novella (map p314 B2/C2).

Armani

Via Tornabuoni 48r, Santa Maria Novella (055 219 041/www.giorgioarmani.com). **Open** 3-7pm Mon; 10am-7pm Tue-Fri; 10.30am-7.30pm Sat. Closed Sat pm Aug. **Credit** AmEx, DC, JCB, MC, V.
Understated, elegant – just don't look at the price tags.

Bulgari

Via Tornabuoni 61-3r, Santa Maria Novella (055 239 6786/www.bulgari.com). **Open** 3-7.30pm Mon; 10am-7pm Tue-Sat. **Credit** AmEx, DC, JCB, MC, V.
The ultimate status-symbol designer jewellery.

Emporio Armani

Piazza Strozzi 16r, Duomo & Around (055 284 315/www.emporioarmani.com). **Open** 3-7pm Mon; 10am-7pm Tue-Fri; 10.30am-7.30pm Sat. Closed Sat pm Aug. **Credit** AmEx, DC, JCB, MC, V. **Map** p314 B3.
Emporio Aramani is still understated, but younger and hipper than the Armani lines.

Dolce & Gabbana

Via della Vigna Nuova 27, Santa Maria Novella (055 281 003/www.dolcegabbana.it). **Open** 3-7pm Mon; 10am-7pm Tue-Sat. Closed Sat pm Aug. **Credit** AmEx, DC, JCB, MC, V.
Black bustiers and tight trousers by the Sicilian duo.

Ermanno Scervino

Piazza Antinori 10r, Santa Maria Novella (055 260 8714/www.ermannoscervino.it). **Open** 3-7.30pm Mon; 10am-7.30pm Tue-Sat. **Credit** AmEx, DC, JCB, MC, V. **Map** p314 B3.
The essence of femininity is embodied in Ermanno Scervino's chiffon mermaid dresses in pinks and translucent whites. Men's lines feature crisp linens and crumpled silk shirts.

Ferragamo

Via Tornabuoni 14r, Santa Maria Novella (055 292 123/www.salvatoreferragamo.it). **Open** 3.30-7.30pm Mon; 9.30am-7.30pm Tue-Sat. **Credit** AmEx, DC, JCB, MC, V.
Fabulous footwear from the king of the shoemakers. The megastore on the ground floor of the Palazzo Spini Ferroni also has mens- and womenswear and leather goods.

Gai Mattiolo

Piazza Santa Trinità 1r, Santa Maria Novella (055 265 4451). **Open** 3.30-7.30pm Mon; 9am-1.30pm, 3-7.30pm Tue-Sat. Closed 2wks Aug. **Credit** AmEx, DC, JCB, MC, V. **Map** p314 C2.
Whimsical frocks for It-girls.

Gianni Versace

Via Tornabuoni 13-15r, Santa Maria Novella (055 282 638/www.gianniversace.com). **Open** 3-7pm Mon; 10am-7pm Tue-Sat. **Credit** AmEx, DC, JCB, MC, V.
Sparkle and flair by Gianni's sister Donatella.

Gucci

Via Tornabuoni 73r, Santa Maria Novella (055 264 011/www.gucci.it). **Open** 3-7pm Mon; 10am-7pm Tue-Sat. **Credit** AmEx, DC, JCB, MC, V.
Gucci is ever expanding to accommodate the growing numbers of pilgrims. The avant-garde feel is reflected in the art gallery-style displays. Italians buy from the factory outlet (via Aretina 63, Leccio, Reggello, 055 865 7775).

Luisa

Via Roma 19-21r, Duomo & Around (055 217 826/ www.luisaviaroma.com). **Open** 10am-7.30pm Mon-Sat; 11am-7pm Sun. **Credit** AmEx, DC, MC, V. **Map** p314 B3.
Designer collections from Issey Miyake, Roberto Cavalli, Alessandro dell'Acqua and others.

La Perla

Via della Vigna Nuova 17-19r, Santa Maria Novella (055 217 070). **Open** 3-7.30pm Mon; 9.30am-7.30pm Tue-Sat. **Credit** AmEx, DC, MC, V.
Luxury lingerie, swimwear and boudoir apparel in pastel silks, dévoré and handmade lace. Shop online at www.laperla.com.

Prada

Via Tornabuoni 51-53r, 67r, Santa Maria Novella (055 283 439/www.prada.it). **Open** 3-7pm Mon; 10am-7pm Tue-Sat. **Credit** AmEx, DC, JCB, MC, V.
Chic minimalist clothing and the famous bags. The factory outlet has discounts of 30-60 % (località SS Levanella, Montevarchi, 055 919 6528).

Pucci

Via Tornabuoni 20-22r, Santa Maria Novella (055 265 8082/www.emiliopucci.com). **Open** 10am-7.30pm Mon-Sat; 10am-1.30pm, 2.30-7pm last Sun of mth Sept-June. **Credit** AmEx, DC, JCB, MC, V.
Psychedelic printed shirts and leggings, little has changed since the '50s designs by Emilio Pucci.

Raspini

Via Roma 25-9r, Duomo & Around (055 213 077/ www.raspini.com). **Open** 3.30-7.30pm Mon; 9.30am-7.30pm Tue-Sat. **Credit** AmEx, DC, JCB, MC, V. **Map** p314 B3.
One-stop shops for Romeo Gigli, Armani, Prada, Miu Miu, Anna Molinari, D&G and many others.
Branches: Via Por Santa Maria 72r, Duomo & Around (055 213 901); Via Martelli 3-7, Outside the City Gates (055 239 8336).

Roberto Cavalli

Via Tornabuoni 83r, Santa Maria Novella (055 239 6266). **Open** 3.30-7.30pm Mon; 9.30am-7.30pm Tue-Sat. **Credit** AmEx, DC, JCB, MC, V.
Colourful creations for men and women, including trademark animal prints.

Womenswear

BP Studio

Via della Vigna Nuova 15r, Santa Maria Novella (055 213 243). **Open** 3-7.30pm Mon; 10am-7.30pm Tue-Sat. **Credit** AmEx, DC, MC, V. **Map** p314 B2.
Delicate knitwear, rosebud-edged chiffon skirts and mohair stoles from young designers in an upmarket but youthful store.

Elio Ferraro

Via del Parione 47r, Santa Maria Novella (055 290 425/www.elioferraro.com). **Open** 10am-8pm Mon-Sat. **Credit** AmEx, DC, MC, V. **Map** p341 B2/C2.
Vintage designer clothes with heart-stopping prices, amid an eccentric selection of original '50s and '60s furniture and accessories.

Emilio Cavallini

Via della Vigna Nuova 24r, Santa Maria Novella (055 238 2789/www.emiliocavallini.com). **Open** 3.30-7.30pm Mon; 10am-2pm, 2.30-7.30pm Tue-Sat. Closed 2wks Aug. **Credit** AmEx, DC, MC, V. **Map** p314 B2.
The famous wacky tights with a line of printed lycra and lurex tops and lingerie.

Expensive!

Via Calzaiuoli 78r, Duomo & Around (055 265 4608). **Open** 10am-8pm Mon-Thur; 10am-8.30pm Fri, Sat; 11am-8.30pm Sun. **Credit** AmEx, DC, MC, V. **Map** p314 B3.
Great colour-coded collections include simple dresses, jackets and accessories. Accessible prices.

Il Guardaroba

Via Verdi 28r, Santa Croce (055 247 8250). **Open** 9.30am-7.30pm Mon-Sat. **Credit** AmEx, DC, MC, V. **Map** p315 B5/C5.
Designer end-of-lines and past seasons' stock.
Branches: Throughout the city.

Intimissimi

Via Calzaiuoli 99r, Duomo & Around (055 230 2609/www.intimissimi.it). **Open** 10am-8pm Mon; 9.30am-8pm Tue-Sat; noon-8pm Sun. **Credit** AmEx, MC, V. **Map** p314 B3.
Simple cotton lingerie plus jersey vests and trousers, silk satin pyjamas and boa-trimmed tops.
Branch: Via Cerretani 15-17, Duomo & Around (055 260 8806).

Liu Jo

Via Calimala 14r, Duomo & Around (055 216 164/ www.liujo.it). **Open** 3.30-7.30pm Mon; 10am-7.30pm Tue-Sat; 3-7pm last Sun of mth. **Credit** AmEx, MC, V. **Map** p314 B3/C3.
Net dresses, pretty vest tops, dressy combat gear and high wooden mules from this hip young designer.

Melo e Grano

Via del Giglio 27r, San Lorenzo (055 265 4383/ www.meloegrano.it). **Open** 9.30am-1.30pm, 3.30-7.30pm Mon-Sat. Closed 2wks Aug. **Credit** AmEx, DC, MC, V. **Map** p314 A3.
Pay a pittance here for staple wardrobe pieces.

Miss Trench

Via Porta Rossa 16r, Duomo & Around (055 287 601). **Open** 3.30-7.30pm Mon; 10am-7.30pm Tue-Sat. **Credit** AmEx, DC, MC, V. **Map** p314 C3.
Rock chick chic. Stocks Miss Sixty accessories such as daisy bags and sequinned low-slung hip belts.

Zini

Borgo San Lorenzo 26r, San Lorenzo (055 289 850). **Open** 11am-7.30pm Mon; 10am-7.30pm Tue-Sat; 2-7.30pm Sun. Closed Sun July & Aug. **Credit** AmEx, DC, MC, V. **Map** p314 B3.
Wearable styles from selected young designers. Well-cut bell-sleeved jackets, little black dresses, fine knits and printed crêpe.

Menswear

AteSeta

Via Calzaiuoli 1r, Duomo & Around (055 214 959). **Open** 9.30am-7.30pm daily. **Credit** AmEx, DC, MC, V. **Map** p314 B3/C3.
Row on row of mix 'n' match shirts and ties.

Eredi Chiarini

Via Roma 16r, Duomo & Around (055 284 478). **Open** 3.30-7.30pm Mon; 9.30am-7.30pm Tue-Sat. **Credit** AmEx, DC, MC, V. **Map** p314 B3.
A favourite with Florentines for effortlessly stylish polos, softly tailored jackets and cool wool suits. Eredi Chiarini for women is at via Porta Rossa 39r.

Gerard Loft

Via dei Pecori 36r, Duomo & Around (055 282 491/www.gerardloft.com). **Open** 2.30-7.30pm Mon; 10am-7.30pm Tue-Sat. **Credit** AmEx, DC, MC, V. **Map** p314 B3.
Achingly hip clothing and assistants. Gerard Loft stocks men's and women's lines from Marc Jacobs, Chloé and Helmut Lang.

Massimo Rebecchi

Via della Vigna Nuova 18-20r, Santa Maria Novella (055 212 559). **Open** 3.30-7.30pm Mon; 10am-7.30pm Tue-Sat; 2.30-7.30pm last Sun of mth. **Credit** AmEx, DC, MC, V. **Map** p314 B2.
Quality cotton and wool jumpers and casual suits. Womenswear two doors down.

Matucci

Via del Corso 71r, Duomo & Around (055 239 6420). **Open** 3.30-8pm Mon; 10am-8pm Tue-Sat. **Credit** AmEx, DC, MC, V. **Map** p315 B4.
Collections by Armani, Diesel, Hugo Boss and Versace. Womenswear is at 46r.

Replay

Via dei Pecori 7-9r Duomo & Around (055 293 041). **Open** 3-7.30pm Mon; 10am-7.30pm Tue-Sat. **Credit** AmEx, DC, MC, V. **Map** p314 B3.
Purveyor of casual wear par excellence, Replay also has women's sections both at this branch and the at the branch on via Pos Santa Maria.
Branch: Via Por Santa Maria 27r, Duomo & Around (055 287 950).

Dry-cleaners & laundrettes

Dry-cleaners (*tintorie*) also do washing.

Lucy & Rita

Via dei Serragli 71r, Oltrarno (055 224 536). **Open** 7am-1pm, 2.30-7.30pm Mon-Fri. Closed 2wks Aug. **Credit** AmEx, MC, V. **Map** p314 D1.
Reliable dry-cleaning at €2.70 a shirt, €9.50 a suit. Laundry done by hand.

Tintoria Serena

Via della Scala 30-32r, Santa Maria Novella (055 218 183). **Open** 8.30am-8pm Mon-Fri; 9am-8pm Sat. Closed 2wks Aug. **No credit cards**. **Map** p314 A1/B2.
Dry-cleaning in one hour (€2.60 a shirt, €8.85 a suit). Self-service washing at €7.75 for wash and dry.

Wash & Dry

Via Nazionale 129r, San Lorenzo (055 580 480). **Open** 8am-10pm daily. **No credit cards**. **Map** p314 A3.
A self-service wash and dry here takes 50 minutes. It's €3.50 for 8kg, €3.50 for a dry.
Branches: Via della Scala 52-54r, Santa Maria Novella; Via dei Servi 105r, San Marco; Via dei Serragli 87r, Oltrarno; Via Ghibellina 143r, Santa Croce.

Jewellery

For traditional gold- and silversmiths, visit via Por Santa Maria and the Ponte Vecchio (see map p314 C3).

Alisi

Via Porta Rossa 60r, Duomo & Around (055 218 231/www.alisigioielli.com). **Open** 10am-1pm, 3-7pm Tue-Sat. **Credit** AmEx, MC, V. **Map** p314 C3.
Designer Susanna Alisi gives a modern twist to Renaissance-inspired shapes for her beautifully crafted and innovatively displayed lattice-work creations in precious metals.

Antico Orologeria Nuti

Via della Scala, Santa Maria Novella (055 294 594). **Open** 4-7.30pm Mon; 9am-12.30pm, 4-7.30pm Tue-Sat. Closed Aug. **Credit** AmEx, MC, V. **Map** p314 A1/B2.
Fabulous antique or reproduction art deco and art nouveau jewellery and watches, and an eclectic collection of lantern, longcase, bracket and mantle clocks. Antico Orologeria Nuti also carries out jewellery and timepiece repairs.

Aprosio e Luthi

Via dello Sprone 1r, Oltrarno (055 290 534). **Open** 9am-1pm, 3-7pm Mon-Sat. **Credit** AmEx, MC, V. **Map** p314 C2.
Aprosio e Luthi sells intricate necklaces, bracelets, brooches, earrings, evening bags and belts made from tiny glass beads, plus their its animal brooches and earrings.

Skin cheap

Florence is famous for its leather goods but, with a leather shop on virtually every corner and a market stall in every square, the sheer volume of outlets and the wide range of quality on offer can make buying a jacket, a bag or even a wallet a daunting experience.

The first port of call for anyone looking for mid-range locally made bags or leather clothing should be the **Santa Croce** area. Call into the **Scuola del Cuoio** (the leather school, inside the cloisters of Santa Croce, piazza Santa Croce 16, or via San Giuseppe 5r on Sunday mornings, 055 244 533) to watch the experts at work, pay a visit to the sprawling **Peruzzi** (borgo dei Greci 8-22r, 055 289 039) where you can find shoes, bags and accessories by famous designers and local artisans all under one roof, or stop off to haggle in one of the many smaller leather workshops and stores.

For a smart, contemporary look, seasonally changing collections, decent workmanship and durable leather with a smooth finish go to **Coccinelle** (via Por Santa Maria 49r, Duomo & Around, 055 239 8782), **Leoncini** (via della Vigna Nuova 44r, Santa Maria Novella, 055 267 0173) or **Furla** (via Calzaiuoli 47r, Duomo & Around, 055 238 2883), where wallets cost around €70, and bags start at about €130. **Nannini** (via Porta Rossa 64r, Duomo & Around, 055 213 888) leather is of a similar quality and it also does a great line in shoes.

If you're looking for a classic style bag to last a lifetime and are prepared to pay upwards of €200, the renowned **Il Bisonte** (via del Parione 31r, Santa Maria Novella, 055 215 722), **Cellerini** (via del Sole 37r, Santa Maria Novella, 055 282 533) and **Bojola** (via Rondinella 25r, Duomo & Around, 055 211 155) outclass most other leather shops. Their hides are of the very best quality with slight natural imperfections that only serve to underline their superiority, and their craftsmanship, passed down through generations, gives them the edge.

Saja (via Vacchereccia 22r, Duomo & Around, 055 288 731) is a stunning new leather clothing, bags and shoe shop concentrating on customer service, a concept often sadly lacking in shops in the city. If the jacket you want is not available in your size, SAJA will have it made within 24 hours for a moderate extra charge. It also stocks all seasons' jackets and shoes, so you can still buy your winter boots or coat even if it's summer when you visit.

For gloves you can't beat **Madova** (via Guicciardini 1r, Oltrarno, 055 239 6526), which makes every imaginable style and colour in the factory behind its tiny shop (€25-€180).

However, the most popular places to buy *that* jacket or bag are the markets (*see p134*); there are real bargains to be had, but remember to check the seams and to think bazaar – you can almost always knock 10-20 per cent off the first asking price.

Classy glass at **Borgo degli Albizi 48 Rosso**. *See p147.*

Parenti

Via Tornabuoni 93r, Duomo & Around (055 214 438/www.parentifirenze.it). **Open** 3.30-7.30pm Mon; 9am-1pm, 3.30-7.30pm Tue-Sat. Closed Aug. **Credit** AmEx, DC, MC, V. **Map** p314 B2.
Baccarat rings, art deco and '50s Tiffany jewellery.

Pianegonda

Via dei Calzaiuoli 96r, Duomo & Around (055 214 941/www.pianegonda.com). **Open** 3.30-7.30pm Mon; 10am-7.30pm Tue-Sat. **Credit** AmEx, DC, MC, V. **Map** p314 B3.
Highly desirable set topaz gems and amethysts.

Luggage

See also p139.

Mandarina Duck

Via Por Santa Maria 23-25r, Duomo & Around (055 210 380/www.mandarinaduck.com). **Open** 9.30am-7.30pm Tue-Sat; 11am-2pm, 3-7pm Sun. **Credit** AmEx, DC, JCB, MC, V. **Map** p314 D1.
At Mandarina Duck each new season's desirable collection of rubber, canvas and leather bags and cases has a distinguishing feature easily recognisable to initiates. Utility chic.

Segue

Via degli Speziali 6r, Duomo & Around (055 288 949/www.segue.it). **Open** 10am-7.30pm Mon-Sat; 1-7.30pm Sun. **Credit** AmEx, DC, JCB, MC, V. **Map** p314 B3.
Segue sells the full range of Benetton's smart bags and luggage.

Repairs

Il Ciabattino

Via del Moro 88, Santa Maria Novella (no phone). **Open** 8am-1pm, 2-7pm Mon-Fri; 8am-12.30pm Sat. Closed 2wks Aug. **No credit cards**. **Map** p314 B2.
If you don't find the shoemaker in his workshop during opening hours, he'll be on call in the bar on the corner opposite. Ask for *il ciabattino*!

Presto Service

Via Faenza 77, San Lorenzo (no phone). **Open** 3.30-7pm Mon; 9am-12.30pm, 3.30-7pm Tue-Sat. Closed 2wks Aug. **No credit cards. Map** p314 A3.
While-you-wait heel bar and key-cutting service.

Silvana e Ombretta Riparazioni

Borgo San Frediano 38r, Oltrarno (368 7571 418). **Open** 9am-12.30pm, 4-6.30pm Mon-Fri. **No credit cards. Map** p314 C1.
Repairs and alterations to clothes.

Walter's Silver & Gold

Borgo dei Greci 11Cr, Santa Croce (055 239 6678/www.walterssilverandgold.com). **Open** 9am-6pm daily. Closed Nov. **Credit** AmEx, DC, MC, V. **Map** p315 C4.
English-speaking Walter does all jewellery repairs.

Shoes

Bologna

Piazza Duomo 55r, Duomo & Around (055 212 890). **Open** 9am-7.30pm Mon-Sat. **Credit** AmEx, DC, MC, V. **Map** p315 B4.
Weird and wonderful styles to be found in the Florentines' favourite shoe store.

Calvani

Via degli Speziali 7r, Duomo & Around (055 265 4043). **Open** 10am-7.30pm Mon-Sat; 3-7pm Sun. **Credit** AmEx, DC, MC, V. **Map** p314 B3.
Men's and women's shoes in hip styles and colours from young designers such as Roberto del Carlo, along with the sports casual line by Camper.

Divarese

Piazza Duomo 55r, Duomo & Around (055 212 890). **Open** 9am-7.30pm Mon-Sat. **Credit** AmEx, DC, MC, V. **Map** p315 B4.
Head to Divarese for a great range of well-made, reasonably priced shoes in the latest styles for both men and women.

Dominici

Via Calimala 23r, Duomo & Around (055 210 251). **Open** 3.30-7.30pm Mon; 9.30am-7.30pm Tue-Sat. **Credit** AmEx, DC, MC, V. **Map** p314 B3/C3.
Dominici sells mid-priced high-quality strictly seasonal collections and a small range of clothing and leather accessories.

JP Tod's

Via Tornabuoni 103r, Duomo & Around (055 219 423/www.tods.com). **Open** 10am-7pm Mon-Sat. **Credit** AmEx, DC, JCB, MC, V. **Map** p314 B2.
JP Tod's trademark unisex bobbly soles win first prize for comfort on Florence's cobbles. Essential sightseeing footwear.

Marco Candido

Piazza Duomo 5r, Duomo & Around (055 215 342). **Open** 10am-7.30pm Mon-Sat; 11am-2pm, 3-7.30pm Sun. Closed Sun Feb, July & Aug. **Credit** AmEx, DC, MC, V. **Map** p315 B4.
Marco Candido is a purveyor of sexy but stylish modern women's shoes and boots, and classic but modern shoes, some handmade, for men.

Peppe Peluso

Via del Corso 5-6r, Duomo & Around (055 268 283). **Open** 4-7.30pm Mon; 10am-7.30pm Tue-Sat; 11am-1pm, 2-7pm Sun. **Credit** AmEx, DC, MC, V. **Map** p315 B4.
A pair of shoes or boots from the vast men's and women's selections here may or may not last the season. But at these prices, who cares?

Paola del Lungo

Via Cerretani 72r, Duomo & Around (055 280 642/ www.genius2000.it). **Open** 9am-7.30pm daily. **Credit** AmEx, DC, JCB, MC, V. **Map** p314 B3.
Paola del Lungo's utterly feminine boots and shoes are sold alongside a tempting range of matching bags and accessories.

Roberto Ugolini

Via Michelozzi 17r, Oltrarno (055 216 246). **Open** 9am-1.30pm, 3.30-7.30pm daily. Closed Mon am, Sat pm in summer, 3wks Aug. **Credit** MC, V. **Map** p314 D2.
Beautiful handmade shoes at more affordable prices, starting at around €450.

Stefano Bemer

Borgo San Frediano 143r, Oltrarno (055 211 356/ www.stefanobemer.it). **Open** 9am-1pm, 3.30-7.30pm Mon-Sat. Closed Aug. **Credit** AmEx, DC, JCB, MC, V. **Map** p314 C1.
Well-heeled Florentine men head here for luxury shoes handmade by a young craftsman.

Florists

Al Portico

Piazza San Firenze 2, Duomo & Around (055 213 716/www.semialportico.it). **Open** 8.30am-7.30pm Mon-Sat; 10am-1pm Sun. **Credit** AmEx, DC, MC, V. **Map** p315 C5.
An extraordinary shop in the courtyard of a magnificent palazzo. The owner is delighted to show customers round, even if they don't want to buy.

Calvanelli

Via della Vigna Nuova 81r, Santa Maria Novella (055 213 742). **Open** 8am-1pm, 3.30-7.30pm Mon, Tue, Thur-Sat; 7am-1pm Wed. **No credit cards. Map** p314 B2.
A delightful shop tucked away off the main street, with flowers wrapped in lovely crêpe paper posies. Delivery is free within the city centre.

La Rosa Canina

Via dell'Erta Canina 1r, Outside the City Gates (055 234 2449/www.larosacaninafioristi.it). **Open** 9.30am-1.30pm, 4.30-11pm Tue-Sat; 9.30am-1.30pm Sun. **No credit cards.**
On a stroll up to piazzale Michelangiolo, take time to stop off at this shop to admire its wonderful displays of plants and flowers.

Food & drink

For food markets, *see p134*.

Bottega della Frutta
Via dei Federighi 31r, Santa Maria Novella (055 239 8590). **Open** 8am-7.30pm Mon, Tue, Thur-Sat; 8am-1.30pm Wed. Closed Aug. **Credit** MC, V. **Map** p314 B2.
Not just fruit and vegetables in this charming, friendly shop, but well-chosen wines, vintage balsamic vinegar, truffle-scented oils, speciality sweets and flavoured grappas. Be prepared to queue.

La Bottega dell'Olio
Piazza del Limbo 2r, Duomo & Around (055 267 0468). **Open** 10am-2pm, 3-7pm Mon-Sat. Closed 2wks Jan. **Credit** DC, MC, V. **Map** p314 C3.
All things olive oil, from soaps and delicacies preserved in the green gold to olive-wood breadboards and pestle and mortars.

Dolceforte
Via della Scala 21, Santa Maria Novella (055 219 116). **Open** 10am-1pm, 3.30-8pm Mon-Sat. **Credit** AmEx, DC, MC, V. **Map** p314 B2.
The best range of connoisseur chocolates in town includes chocolate Duomos and Ponte Vecchios. In hot months the melting stock is replaced with speciality jams, sugared almond flowers and jars of *gianduja*, a chocolate hazelnut spread from Turin.

Friggitoria
Via San *Antonino 50r, San Lorenzo (055 211 630).* **Open** *Jan-July* 10am-10pm daily. *Sept-Dec* 10am-10pm Tue-Sun. Closed Aug. **No credit cards**. **Map** p314 A3.
Kiosk selling freshly made doughnuts, rice or apple fritters and *coccoli* (deep-fried dough balls).

Mariano Alimentari
Via del Parione 19r, Santa Maria Novella (055 214 067). **Open** 8am-3pm, 5-7.30pm Mon-Fri; 8am-3pm Sat. Closed 3wks Aug. **Credit** AmEx, MC, V. **Map** p314 C2.
Tiny, rustic food shop-cum-sandwich bar with focaccia filled with artichokes, marinated aubergines and oil-preserved pecorino cheeses, and an array of delicacies on display. You can drink a coffee at the bar or in the vaulted wine cellar.

Pane & Co
Piazza San Firenze 5r, Duomo & Around (055 265 4272). **Open** 8am-7pm Mon-Sat. Closed 2wks Aug. **Credit** MC, V. **Map** p315 D4.
Enjoy a glass of wine or a pasta lunch after shopping in this deli. Regular wine and cheese tastings.

Pegna
Via dello Studio 8, Duomo & Around (055 282 701/www.pegna.it). **Open** 9am-1pm, 3.30-7.30pm Mon, Tue, Thur-Sat; 9am-1pm Wed. **Credit** AmEx, MC, V. **Map** p315 B4.
Upmarket grocery store and deli with pâtés, coffee, cheeses, ethnic specialities and general provisions.

Peter's Tea House
Piazza di San Pancrazio 2r, Santa Maria Novella (055 267 0620). **Open** 3.30-7pm Mon; 10am-1pm, 3.30-7pm Tue-Sat. **Credit** AmEx, MC, V.
Hundreds of teas from around the world, biscuits to dunk and tea-themed gifts.

Procacci
Via Tornabuoni 64r, Duomo & Around (055 211 656). **Open** 10.30am-8pm Mon-Sat. Closed Aug. **Credit** AmEx, MC, V. **Map** p314 B2/C2.
This is the place to buy truffles; in season (Oct-Dec) they come in daily to Procacci at around 10am. The panelled bar is good for a glass of Prosecco and a truffle-filled brioche.

I Sapori del Chianti
Via dei Servi 10, San Marco (055 238 2071/ www.isaporidelchianti.it). **Open** 10.30am-8pm daily. **Credit** AmEx, V. **Map** p314 B2.
The 'flavours of Chianti' sold here come in the form of wines, grappas, olive oils, salami, and jars of pesto, condiments and vegetables in extra virgin olive oil.

Sugar Blues
Via dei Serragli 57r, Oltrarno (055 268 378). **Open** 9am-1.30pm, 4.30-8pm Mon-Sat. Closed Sat pm July & Aug. **Credit** AmEx, DC, MC, V. **Map** p314 D1.
Sugar Blues is filled with organic healthfoods and fresh produce, eco-friendly detergents and ethical beauty products.
Branch: Via XXVII Aprile 46-48r, San Lorenzo (055 483 666).

Vestri
Borgo degli Albizi 11r, Santa Croce (055 234 0374/ www.cioccolateriavestri.com). **Open** 10am-7.30pm Mon-Sat. Closed 3wks Aug. **Credit** AmEx, MC, V. **Map** p315 B4/5.
Handmade chocolates with chilli pepper, nutmeg, cinnamon or more prosaic champagne varieties. Flavoured hot chocolates are served from huge urns in winter. Rich ice-creams in summer.

Bakeries

Il Forno di Stefano Galli
Via Sant'Agostino 8r, Oltrarno (055 219 703). **Open** 7.30am-7.30pm daily. **Credit** MC, V. **Map** p314 A3.
Delicious biscuits, cakes, hot focaccia and pizzas come out of the oven of this great little bakery.

Forno Top
Via della Spada 23r, Santa Maria Novella (055 212 461). **Open** 7.30am-1.30pm, 5-7.30pm Mon, Tue, Thur-Sat; 7.30am-1.30pm Wed. **No credit cards**. **Map** p314 B2.
Tasty sandwiches, batches of hot focaccia every day, fabulous carrot or chocolate and pear cakes, plus seasonal specialities.
Branch: Via Orsanmichele 8r, Duomo & Around (055 216 564).

Sartoni

Via dei Cerchi 34r, Duomo & Around (055 212 570). **Open** 8am-8pm Mon-Sat. **Credit** AmEx, JCB, MC, V. **Map** p315 B4.

Central pit-stop for slices of delicious hot pizza, filled focaccia and apple pies.

Deliveries

See also p120 **Alternative eats**.

Ciao

Via Masaccio 101A, Outside the City Gates (055 574 485). **Open** 10.30am-2.30pm, 5.30-10.30pm daily. **Credit** V.

Ciao is a good Chinese takeaway that also delivers (minimum order €15).

Ramraj

Via Ghibellina 61r, Santa Croce (055 240 999/ www.ramraj.org). **Open** 11.30am-3.30pm, 6-11pm Tue-Sun. Closed Aug. **Credit** MC,V. **Map** p315 C4/5/6.

Indian takeaway with tandoori and Moghul specialities. Free delivery with orders over €7.

Runner Pizza

055 333 333/www.runnerpizza.it. **Open** noon-2.30pm, 6.30-11pm daily . **Credit** MC.

Pizzas cost €5-€7, including a drink or ice-cream. Delivery is €1 if you order one pizza, free if you order more.

Ethnic

Asia Masala

Piazza Santa Maria Novella 22r, Santa Maria Novella (055 281 800/www.ramraj.org). **Open** 4-8pm Mon; 10am-1.30pm, 3.30-9pm Tue, Wed, Fri; 10am-9.30pm Thur, Sat, Sun. **Credit** MC, JCB, V. **Map** p314 B2.

Asia Masala stocks a wonderful source of foods and spices from Asia.

Vivimarket

Via del Gigio 20r, San Lorenzo (055 294 911). **Open** 9am-2pm, 3-7.30pm Mon-Sat. **Credit** MC, V. **Map** p314 A3.

The shelves at Vivimarket groan with food from all across Asia. There's Indian, Chinese, Japanese, Thai, Mexican and North African specialities, including tofu and lemongrass. It stocks good-quality kitchen equipment as well.

Pasta

Bianchi

Via del Albero 1r, Santa Maria Novella (055 282 246). **Open** 9am-1pm, 4.30-7.30pm Mon, Tue, Thur-Sat; 9am-1pm Wed. Closed mid July-end Aug. **No credit cards**. **Map** p314 A1.

Spinach and ricotta ravioli and potato gnocchi are among the delights on offer in this modest shop.

La Bolognese

Via dei Serragli 24, Oltrarno (055 282 318). **Open** 7am-1pm, 4.30-7.30pm Mon-Fri; 7am-1pm Sat. **No credit cards**. **Map** p314 C1.

Pasta parcels filled with pumpkin, potato, ricotta, herbs, even truffles. Call in advance for the fabulous smoked salmon tortelloni.

Pasticcerie

Most serve breakfast coffee and snacks, and takeaway cakes and savouries (*da portare via*).

Dolci e Dolcezze

Piazza Cesare Beccaria 8r, Santa Croce (055 234 5458). **Open** 8.30am-8pm Tue-Sat; 9am-1pm, 4.30-7pm Sun. Closed Sun when football match in Florence (open next day). Closed 2wks Aug. **No credit cards**.

The finest *pasticceria* in town, with its storybook window displays, is famous for its delectable, flourless chocolate cake, but you may be tempted by the strawberry meringue too. Savouries, including roquefort and mustard croissants, are as good.

I Dolci di Patrizio Cosi

Borgo degli Albizi 11r, Santa Croce (055 248 0367). **Open** 7am-8pm Mon-Sat. Closed Aug. **No credit cards**. **Map** p315 B5.

Famed for its huge range of sweet treats, including hot doughnuts (*bomboloni caldi*) served at 5pm.

Sugar e Spice

Via dei Servi 43r, Duomo & Around (055 290 263). **Open** 10am-2.30pm, 3.30-7.30pm Tue-Sat. **No credit cards**. **Map** p315 A4

Home-made American-style sweets and cakes, like carrot cake, muffins and its speciality cheesecakes.

Rosticcerie

Rosticcerie offer everything you need for a full meal, ready-cooked. Pack a hamper with plenty of *crostini*, roast meat and potatoes, vegetables and desserts, plus basic wines.

Rosticceria Alisio

Via dei Serragli 75r, Oltrarno (055 225 192). **Open** 8am-2pm, 5-9pm Tue-Sun. **No credit cards**. **Map** p314 D1.

Free delivery on orders over €7 in central Florence.

Rosticceria Giuliano

Via dei Neri 174r, Santa Croce (055 238 2723). **Open** 8am-3pm, 5-9pm Tue-Sat; 8am-3pm Sun. Closed Aug. **Credit** AmEx, MC, V. **Map** p315 C4.

Huge choice of roast meats and savoury dishes.

Rosticceria La Spada

Via della Spada, Santa Maria Novella (055 218 757). **Open** noon-3pm, 7-10.30pm daily. **No credit cards**. **Map** p314 B2.

Usual *rosticceria* fare, but here pasta dishes are cooked for you while you wait. Charming staff.

Il Forno di Stefano Galli.
See p143.

Supermarkets

Esselunga

Via Pisana 130-132, Outside the City Gates (055 706 556). Bus 6, 12, 13. **Open** 8am-9pm Mon-Fri; 7.30am-8.30pm Sat. **Credit** AmEx, DC, MC, V.

A wide choice of general groceries, including an excellent deli counter, fresh fish and reasonably priced wines and spirits, plus some CDs, flowers and newspapers. Good organic range. Free parking. Shop online at www.esselunga.it.

Margherita Conad

Via L Alamanni 2-10r, Santa Maria Novella (055 211 544). **Open** 8am-7.30pm Mon, Tue, Thur-Sat; 8am-1pm Wed. **Credit** MC, V. **Map** p314 A1.

This is a small, well-stocked, supermarket right beside the station.

Natura Si'

Viale Corsica 19-23, Outside the City Gates (055 366 024/www.naturasi.com). Bus 23. **Open** 3.30-8pm Mon; 9am-7.30pm Tue-Sat. **Credit** MC, V.

Healthfoods supermarket with mostly organic fresh produce. Order online at www.naturanetwork.it.

Branch: Via Masaccio 88-90, Outside the City Gates (055 200 1068).

Wine

See also pp123-5.

Alessi

Via delle Oche 27r, Duomo & Around (055 214 966). **Open** 9am-1pm, 4-6pm Mon-Sat. Closed Aug. **Credit** AmEx, DC, MC, V. **Map** p315 B4.

A fabulously stocked *enoteca* with a difference – half of it is piled with cakes, biscuits and chocolates, and coffee is ground on the spot.

Millesimi

Borgo Tegolaio 33r, Oltrarno (055 265 4675/ www.millesimi.it). **Open** 3-8pm Mon-Fri; 10am-10pm Sat; 10am-8pm 2nd Sun of mth. Closed 2wks Aug. **Credit** AmEx, DC, MC, V. **Map** p314 D2.

Home to one of the biggest selections in town, Millesimi has an especially good range of Tuscan wines, plus plenty of bottles from around Italy. French wines include an emphasis on Burgundy. Tastings by appointment. Door-to-door shipments.

Health & beauty

Bizzarri

Via Condotta 32r, Duomo & Around (055 211 580). **Open** 9.30am-1pm, 4-7.30pm Mon-Fri; 9.30am-1pm Sat. Closed Aug. **Credit** AmEx, DC, JCB, MC, V. **Map** p314 C4.

Like a cross between an apothecary and an alchemist's workshop, Bizzarri sells gold, frankincense and myrrh, tinctures, food essences and spices, along with traditional herbal concoctions.

Erboristeria Inglese

Via Tornabuoni 19, Duomo & Around (055 210 628/www.officinadeitornabuoni.com). **Open** 3.30-8pm Mon; 10am-8pm Tue-Sat. Closed 2wks Aug. **Credit** AmEx, DC, JCB, MC, V. **Map** p314 B2.

The gifts, perfumes, remedies and skincare in this lovely shop with its frescoed ceilings include Diptych fragrances and Dr Hauschka skincare.

Ismail

Via dello Studio 25r, Duomo & Around (055 210 394). **Open** 10am-7pm Mon-Sat. **Credit** MC, V. **Map** p315 B4.

Ismail (once called Experimenta) is a charming little shop with original gifts, including cappuccino or brioche-scented bubble bath.

There's nothing like a real fire. **Rosticceria La Spada**. *See p144.*

Officina Profumo-Farmaceutica di Santa Maria Novella

Via della Scala 16, Santa Maria Novella (055 216 276/www.smnovella.it). **Open** 9.30am-7.30pm Mon-Sat; 10.30am-6.30pm Sun. Closed Sun Feb & Nov, 2wks Aug. **Credit** AmEx, DC, MC, V. **Map** p314 A1/B2.
Ancient herbal pharmacy in a wonderful palazzo with a 13th-century frescoed chapel. Lotions and potions include Acqua di Santa Maria Novella, known for its calming properties. The soap is reputed to be the best in the world.

Spezieria Erboristeria Palazzo Vecchio

Via Vaccherccia 9r, Duomo & Around (055 239 6055/www.erbitalia.com). **Open** 9.30am-7.30pm Mon-Sat; open 1st & last Sun of mth. **Credit** AmEx, DC, MC, V. **Map** p314 C3.
Old-fashioned frescoed apothecary specialising in handmade perfumes and floral eaux de toilette, such as Acqua di Caterina di Medici and Iris di Firenze.

Hairdressers & barbers

Hairdressers in Florence close on Mondays.

Bacci

Via delle Oche 26r, Duomo & Around (055 214 026). **Open** 8.30am-12.30pm; 3.30-7pm Tue-Sat. **No credit cards. Map** p315 B4.
Very central old-fashioned barber.

Gabrio Staff

Via Tornabuoni 5, Duomo & Around (055 214 668). **Open** 9am-7pm Tue-Sat. Closed 2wks Aug. **Credit** MC, V. **Map** p314 C2.
This unisex hair and beauty centre is set in an amazing atelier. If your appointment falls in the middle of the day, don't worry about getting hungry as staff serve buffet snacks to clients at lunchtime. A wash and cut here is €60.

Jean Louis David

Lungarno Corsini 52r, Santa Maria Novella (055 216 760). **Open** 9am-7pm Tue-Sat. Closed 2wks Aug. **Credit** MC, V. **Map** p314 C2.
A women's wash and cut at Jean Louis David is €35; men are also welcome. There's a student discount of 20%. Otherwise you could ring for a free haircut in the salon's school. The branch in via Ghibellina 202-204 (055 265 4461) offers an express service.

Health/beauty treatments

Hito Estetica

Via de' Ginori 21, San Lorenzo (055 284 424). **Open** 9am-7.30pm Mon-Fri; 9am-7pm Sat. **Credit** AmEx, MC, V. **Map** p315 A4.
Hito Estetica offers a range of natural treatments and pampering for men and women, including Ayurvedic techniques. Prices start at around €35 for a facial.

International Studio

Via Porta Rossa 82r, Duomo & Around (055 293393). **Open** 10am-8pm Tue-Sat. **Credit** MC, V. **Map** p314 C3.

Solarium, hair and beauty treatment, box office and showcase for objets d'art, all rolled into one.

Freni

Via Calimala, Duomo & Around (055 239 6647). **Open** 9am-6.30pm Mon-Fri; 9am-12.30pm Sat. **Credit** AmEx, MC, V. **Map** p314 A3.

If your feet give out after tramping around all those museums, come here for a pedicure. Staff also do facials, manicures and massages.

Opticians

Camera and optical lenses go hand in hand in Italy: photography shops sell glasses and opticians sell basic photo equipment. *See p149.*

Pisacchi

Via Condotta 22-24r, Duomo & Around (055 214 542). **Open** 3.30-7.30pm Mon; 9am-1pm, 3.30-7.30pm Tue-Sat. **Credit** AmEx, DC, MC, V. Closed 2wks Aug. **Map** p315 C4.

This contact lens specialist carries out eye tests and also sells a good range of prescription glasses and sunglasses.

Sbisa

Piazza Signoria 10r, Duomo & Around (055 211 339). **Open** 3.30-7.30pm Mon; 9am-7.30pm Tue-Sat. **Credit** AmEx, DC, MC, V. **Map** p315 C4.

Designer frames include Armani, Gucci, Ralph Lauren, Valentino and Versace, plus a good range of optical and photo equipment.

Homeware

Ceramics & glass

La Bottega dei Cristalli

Via dei Benci 51r, Santa Croce (055 234 4891). **Open** 10am-7.30pm daily. Closed mid Jan-late Feb. **Credit** AmEx, DC, MC, V. **Map** p315 C5.

Murano and Tuscan-made plates, lamps and chandeliers, and tiny glass sweets and bottles.

La Botteghina del Ceramista

Via Guelfa 5r, San Lorenzo (055 287 367/ www.labotteghina.com). **Open** 10am-1.30pm, 3.30-7.30pm Mon-Fri; 10am-1.30pm Sat. Closed 2wks Aug. **Credit** AmEx, DC, JCB, MC, V. **Map** p315 A4.

Superb hand-painted ceramics in intricate designs and vivid colours. Prices from €15 to €400.

Sbigoli Terrecotte

Via Sant' Egidio 4r, Santa Croce (055 247 9713). **Open** 9am-1pm, 3.30-7.30pm Mon-Sat. **Credit** AmEx, DC, MC, V. **Map** p315 B5.

Handmade Tuscan ceramics and terracotta in traditional designs.

Home accessories & gifts

Arredamenti Castorina

Via di Santo Spirito 13-15r, Oltrarno (055 212 885/www.castorina.net). **Open** 9am-1pm, 3.30-7.30pm Mon-Fri; 9am-1pm Sat. Closed Aug. **Credit** AmEx, DC, MC, V. **Map** p314 C1.

Arredamneti Castorina is an extraordinary old shop with all things baroque: gilded mouldings, frames, cherubs, *trompe l'œil* tables and fake malachite and tortoiseshell obelisks.

Atmosfere

Via della Vigna Nuova 69r, Santa Maria Novella (055 264 5274). **Open** 3.30-7.30pm Mon; 10am-1pm, 3-7.30pm Tue-Sat; 3.30-7.30pm last Sun of mth. **Credit** DC, MC, V. **Map** p314 B2.

An ethereal shop with voluminous blown-glass vases and long-stemmed cups and goblets filled with rose petals or orchids set in transparent gel candlewax. Also exquisite leaf-embossed candles and globes.

Bartolini

Via dei Servi 30r, San Marco (055 211 895/ www.dinobartolini.it). **Open** 3.30-7.30pm Mon; 9am-1pm, 3.30-7.30pm Tue-Sat. Closed 2wks Aug. **Credit** AmEx, DC, MC, V. **Map** p315 A4.

Huge kitchen emporium with everything from Alessi mincers to Le Creuset woks to kitchen sinks.

Borgo degli Albizi 48 Rosso

Borgo degli Albizi 48r, Santa Croce (055 234 7598/www.borgoalbizi.com). **Open** 3.30-7.30pm Mon; 10am-1pm, 3.30-7.30pm Tue-Sat. **Credit** AmEx, DC, MC, V. **Map** p31 B4/5.

Opulent chandeliers and glass pear-drop lamps made with antique or new crystals. You can order ones to your own design.

Carte Etc

Via dei Cerchi 13r, Duomo & Around (055 268 302). **Open** 9.30am-7.30pm daily. **Credit** MC, V. **Map** p315 B4/C4.

A delightful little shop chock-a-block with exquisite glass and stationery, unusual black and white postcards of Florence and handmade greetings cards, and tiny intricate models of itself.

Frammenti

Via Ghibellina 148r, Santa Croce (055 243 596/ www.frammentimasaici.it). **Open** 9.30am-7.30pm Mon-Sat. **Credit** AmEx, DC, MC, V. **Map** p315 C4/5/6.

Gifts and reproductions of artwork made of mosaics and tiny drops of coloured Murano glass. Commissions made to order.

Giraffa

Via Ginori 20r, San Lorenzo (055 283 652). **Open** 3.30-7.30pm Mon; 10am-1pm, 3.30-7.30pm Tue-Sat. Closed 3wks Aug. **Credit** AmEx, DC, MC, V. **Map** p315 A4.

Silk lamps, Italian and Moroccan ceramics, Japanese tableware, candles, candelabra and small fun gifts.

G Veneziano

Via dei Fossi 53r, Santa Maria Novella (055 287 925). **Open** 3-7pm Mon; 9am-12.30pm, 3-7pm Tue-Sat. Closed Aug. **Credit** AmEx, DC, MC, V. **Map** p314 B2.

G Veneziano is an upmarket gift shop selling tiny flower-embroidered cushions and tablecloths, lanterns, glass tableware and jewellery, and unusual gifts for the home.

N'Uovo

Via dei Fossi 21r, Santa Maria Novella (055 238 2290/www.nuovoitaly.com). **Open** 3.30-7pm Mon-Sat; am by appointment. Closed Aug. **Credit** AmEx, DC, MC, V. **Map** p314 B2.

Ultra-modern objets d'art and furniture – conical silver or gold lamps with mesh shades, olive-green velvet settees and footstools inlaid with baguette jewels and waist-high geometric-shaped candleholders.

Passamaneria Toscana

Piazza San Lorenzo 12r, San Lorenzo (055 214 670). **Open** 9am-7.30pm Mon-Sat; 10am-7.30pm Sun. **Credit** AmEx, DC, MC, V. **Map** p314 A3.

Come to Passamaneria Toscana for brocade cushions, embroidered Florentine crests, tapestries and wall hangings, table runners, fringes and tassels. An interiors renaissance.

Branch: Via Federighi 1r, Santa Maria Novella (055 239 8047).

La Porcellana Bianca

Via dei Bardi 49, Oltrarno (055 211 893/www.laporcellanabianca.it). **Open** 9.30am-7.30pm Mon-Sat; 11am-1pm, 3.30-7.30pm Sun. **Credit** AmEx, DC, MC, V. **Map** p314/5 D3/4.

Kitchen accessories for all occasions, as long as they're white porcelain (although other colours are creeping in).

Progetto Verde

Piazza Torquato Tasso 11, Oltrarno (055 229 8029). **Open** 3.30-7.30pm Mon; 9am-1pm, 3.30-7.30pm Tue-Sat. Closed Aug. **Credit** AmEx, DC, MC, V.

A mecca for the eco-minded, selling everything from non-toxic paints to recycled paper and essential oils.

Rosa Regale

Volta Mazzucconi 3r, Duomo & Around (055 267 0613/www.rosaregale.it). **Open** 3.30-7.30pm Mon; 10am-1pm, 2.30-7.30pm Tue-Sat. **Credit** AmEx, DC, MC, V. Closed 2wks Aug. **Map** p314 B3.

Hidden at the top of a rosebush-lined vaulted passageway, Rosa Regale's ceiling is covered in Florentine crests. This dazzling shop sells everything from velvet sculpted flower chairs to 3D rose-shaped cushions to a line of flower-themed clothing and accessories.

Signum

Borgo dei Greci 40r, Santa Croce (055 280 621/www.signumfirenze.it). **Open** 10am-7.30pm daily. **Credit** MC, V. **Map** p315 C4.

Mini models of shop windows and bookcases, tiny tarot cards, Murano glass inkwells and more.

Branches: Lungarno Archibusieri 14r, Duomo & Around (055 289 393); Via dei Benci 29r, Santa Croce (055 244 590).

Via Toscana

Piazza N Sauro 16r, Oltrarno (055 219 948). **Open** 3.30-7.30pm Mon; 10am-1pm, 3.30-7.30pm Tue-Sat. Closed Aug. **Credit** MC, V. **Map** p314 C1.

Ceramics, unbleached cotton clothes and bathrobes, velvet slippers and other Tuscan handicrafts.

Picture framers

Leonardo Romanelli

Via di Santo Spirito 16r, Oltrarno (055 284 794). **Open** 9am-1pm, 3-7.30pm Mon-Fri; 9am-1pm Sat. Closed Aug. **No credit cards**. **Map** p314 C2.

Handmade gilded frames from about €20.

The paper trail

For many centuries the ancient art of producing brightly coloured marbled paper has been a part of Florentine tradition. A gelatine solution made of water and marine algae is poured into a shallow tray. Coloured inks are dropped in, which float on the gelatine solution, and patterns are made by drawing metal combs through the liquid. A sheet of paper is placed on the surface, absorbing the inks and is then hung up to dry. Each sheet takes about ten minutes to make.

Giulio Giannini e Figlio (piazza Pitti 37r, Oltrarno, 055 212 621), a book-binding and paper-making company, was founded in 1856 by the Gianninis, the family who still run it from the workshop upstairs on the first floor, and stocks marbled books, leather desk accessories and unusual greetings cards. **Il Papiro** (via Cavour 55r, San Marco, 055 215 262; piazza del Duomo 24r, Duomo & Around, 055 281 628; piazza Rucellai 8r, Santa Maria Novella, 055 211 652) is a chain of old-fashioned shops with an amazing array of marbled paper products. At **Il Torchio** (via dei Bardi 17, Oltrarno, 055 234 2862) you can watch bookbinding in action, and stock up on handmade paper boxes, stationery and albums. **A Cozzi** (via del Parione 35r, Santa Maria Novella, 055 294 968) is a bookbinder's workshop and showroom with a wonderful selection of books with swirled-coloured paper covers, and some bound in leather.

La Botteghina del Ceramista's hand-painted ceramics. *See p147.*

Photography

Bongi

Via Por Santa Maria 82-84r, Duomo & Around (055 239 8811/www.otticabongi.com). **Open** 3.30-7.30pm Mon; 9.30am-7.30pm Tue-Sat; 11am-7pm Sun. **Credit** AmEx, DC, MC, V. **Map** p314 C3.
One of the best-stocked photographic shops in the city centre, with a wide range of new and good condition second-hand equipment.

Foto Ottica Fontani

Viale Strozzi 18-20A, San Lorenzo (055 470 981). **Open** 2-7.30pm Mon; 8.30am-1pm, 2.30-7.30pm Tue-Sat. **No credit cards**. **Map** p314 B3.
A mecca for photography enthusiasts, this shop's prices for processing and developing are the lowest in town: €5 for 24 exposures (overnight service). Also glasses by Armani, Byblos and Ralph Lauren.

Records & CDs

Whether you're after chart-topping hits or an operatic soundtrack to your visit, Florence has music shops for all tastes. For more record shops, *see p172* **Plastic people**.

Data Records

Via dei Neri 15r, Santa Croce (055 287 592/www.superecord.com). **Open** 3.30-7.30pm Mon; 10am-1pm, 3.30-7.30pm Tue-Sat. Closed 2wks Aug. **Credit** MC, V. **Map** p315 C4.
Home to more than 80,000 titles, new and second-hand, with an emphasis on psychedelia, blues, R&B, jazz and soundtracks, Data also specialises in finding the unfindable.

Ricordi

Via Brunelleschi 8r, Duomo & Around (055 214 104). **Open** 3.30-7.30pm Mon; 9am-7.30pm Tue-Sat; 10am-1pm, 3-7.30pm last Sun of mth. **Credit** AmEx, DC, MC, V. **Map** p314 B3.
Probably the best selection of CDs in town, with classical, jazz, rock and dance sections and helpful English-speaking staff. Also sells instruments, sheet music and scores.

Setticlavio

Via Guelfa 19r, San Lorenzo (055 287 017). **Open** 3.30-7.30pm Mon; 9am-1pm, 3.30-7.30pm Tue-Sat. **Credit** DC, MC, V. **Map** p315 A4.
A well-stocked classical record shop with over 30,000 titles, Setticlavio is something of a specialist in unearthing hard-to-find opera recordings.

Shipping

Fracassi

Via di Santo Spirito 11, Oltrarno (055 283 597). **Open** 8.30am-12.30pm, 2.30-6.30pm Mon-Fri. **No credit cards**. **Map** p314 C1/2.

Fracassi is not the cheapest place in town for shipping. However, they have the virtue of being very central and will move anything, anywhere.

Stationery & art supplies

Cartoleria Ecologica La Tartaruga

Borgo Albizi 60r, Santa Croce (055 234 0845). **Open** 1.30-7.30pm Mon; 9.30am-7.30pm Tue-Sat. **Credit** DC, MC, V. **Map** p315 B5.

Unusual stationery and gifts made of recycled paper can be found at Cartoleria Ecologica La Tartaruga.

Le Dune

Piazza Ottaviani 9r, Santa Maria Novella (055 214 377). **Open** 9am-7pm Mon-Fri; 9am-1pm Sat. Closed 2wks Aug. **Credit** AmEx, DC, JCB, MC, V. **Map** p314 B2.

This is a small, friendly gift and stationery shop, which has a good choice of greetings cards. Le Dune also offers photocopying, photo developing and faxing services.

Mandragora

Piazza Duomo 50r, Duomo & Around (055 292 559/ www.mandragora.it). **Open** 10am-7.30pm Mon-Sat; 10.30am-6.30pm Sun. **Credit** DC, MC, V. **Map** p315 B4.

Stunning reproductions by local artists of famous Florentine works of art on furnishings, scarves, bags and ornaments, plus great books, cards and prints.

Pineider

Piazza Signoria 13r, Duomo & Around (055 284 655/www.pineider.com). **Open** 3-7pm Mon; 10am-7pm Tue-Sat. *Apr-Oct* noon-6pm Sun. **Credit** AmEx, DC, JCB, MC, V. **Map** p315 C4.

Famous for its high-quality writing paper and accessories and top of the range office leather goods. **Branch**: Via Tornabuoni 76r, Duomo & Around (055 211 605).

Romeo

Via Condotta 43r, Duomo & Around (055 210 350). **Open** 9.30am-7.30pm Mon-Sat. **Credit** AmEx, DC, JCB, MC, V. **Map** p314 C4.

Spalding's full range, Aurora pens and Giorgio Fedon's smart coloured leather bags and cases fill this great stationer's literally to the ceiling.

Zecchi

Via dello Studio 19r, Duomo & Around (055 211 470/www.zecchi.com). **Open** 8.30am-12.30pm, 3.30-7.30pm Mon-Fri; 8.30am-12.30pm Sat. Closed 3wks Aug. **Credit** AmEx, DC, MC, V. **Map** p315 B4.

The centre for art supplies, with everything from pencils to gold leaf.

Ticket agencies

In order to avoid any confusion or disappointment, when booking tickets for events by phone ensure that all the arrangements for collection or delivery are clearly specified.

Box Office

Via Alamanni 39, Santa Maria Novella (055 210 804/www.boxol.it). **Open** 3.30-7.30pm Mon; 10am-7.30pm Tue-Sat. **Credit** MC, V. **Map** p314 A1.

Box office sells tickets for concerts, plays and exhibitions in Italy, as well as abroad. It's best to go in person as phone lines here seem to be constantly engaged.

Branch: Chiasso de Soldanieri 8r, Duomo & Around (055 293 393/055 219 402).

Travel agents

See also p279 for details of getting around Florence and Tuscany by rail, bus and car. You'll also find information on the region's major airports.

CTS (Student Travel Centre)

Via dei Ginori 25r, San Lorenzo (055 289 570/ www.cts.it). **Open** 9.30am-1.30pm, 2.30-6pm Mon-Fri; 9.30am-12.30pm Sat. **Credit** MC, V. **Map** p314 A3.

The official student travel service offering discounted (some student-only) air, coach and train tickets. Obligatory membership is €26 for non-students, €10.50 for students.

Intertravel

Via Lamberti 39r, Duomo & Around (055 217 936). **Open** 9am-6.30pm Mon-Fri; 9.30am-1.30pm Sat. **Credit** AmEx, MC, V. **Map** p314 C3.

Intertravel is a busy and efficient place, which has a full range of services, a currency exchange and a DHL service.

Video rental

Blockbuster

Viale Belfiore 6A, Outside the City Gates (055 330 542). **Open** 11am-11pm Mon-Thur, Sun; 11am-midnight Fri, Sat. **Credit** V.

You'll find a good number of mainstream films in English, plus cinema-style trimmings of popcorn and ice-cream. Registration is €5.50 and films cost €3.50-€4.50 for 48 hours.

Branch: Via di Novoli 9-11, Outside the City Gates (055 333 533).

Punto Video

Via San Antonino 7r, San Lorenzo (055 284 813). **Open** 9am-8pm Mon-Sat. **Credit** AmEx, DC, MC, V. **Map** p314 A2.

Has over 500 titles in English. Membership is free and videos cost €3.10 per night.

Arts & Entertainment

Festivals & Events	**152**
Children	**157**
Film	**160**
Galleries	**162**
Gay & Lesbian	**164**
Music: Classical & Opera	**167**
Music: Rock, Roots & Jazz	**170**
Nightlife	**174**
Sport & Fitness	**181**
Theatre & Dance	**185**

Features

Street party	154
Queer Versilia	166
The hills are alive…	168
Plastic people	172
Cocktail classics	177
In the heat of the night	179

Festivals & Events

Music, food and fun in the sun.

What Tuscany may lack in cutting-edge arts it more than makes up for with its traditional festivals and outdoor summer events. Throughout the year, visitors will be able to find an event involving food, drink, music and dancing. Some are elaborate affairs with medieval re-enactments that attract thousands of spectators, such as the famous **Palio** in Siena, the **Giostra del Saracino** in Arezzo or the **Scoppio del Carro** in Florence. Others are simple country *sagre* (rites) where locals celebrate anything from the humble cannellini bean to the glories of the new season's wine. Music ranges from full-blown operatic productions to solo recitals in tiny cloisters or from mainstream jazz or rock gigs to ethnic combos in remote village squares.

Contact local tourist boards and keep an eye open for posters as events are rarely well publicised (especially from one province to the next), and phone numbers listed may only be operational during festivals.

Spring

Festa della Donna

Date 8 Mar.

Italy makes quite a meal of International Women's Day. Traditionally, women are given bunches of yellow mimosa, while in the evening, restaurants and clubs (many of which put on male strippers) are full of girly gangs out on the town.

Holy Week

Date week before Easter.

Many small Tuscan towns celebrate Holy Week with religious processions, often in Renaissance costume. More important ones include Buonconvento (near Siena), Castiglion Fiorentino (near Arezzo) and Bagno a Ripoli (just outside Florence). In Grassina and San Gimignano, re-enactments of episodes from the life of Christ are staged on Good Friday.

Scoppio del Carro

Piazzale del Porta al Prato to Piazza del Duomo, Florence. **Date** Easter Sun.

Dating back to the 12th century, *lo scoppio del carro* features a long parade of trumpeters, drummers, costumed dignitaries and flag-throwers who escort the *carro* (a tall, heavy wooden cart) pulled by four white oxen adorned with garlands of flowers, from the west of Florence to piazza del Duomo. At 11am, during mass, a priest lights a mechanical dove, which then flies along a wire from the high altar to the *carro* outside and ignites an explosion of fireworks (*lo scoppio*). If all goes smoothly, things look good for harvest-time. Piazza del Duomo is invariably heaving with spectators – to get a clear view of the procession stand in front of the tall wooden doors to the left of Hotel Villa Medici (via il Prato 2) at 9.30am.

Settimana dei Beni Culturali

Florence & throughout Tuscany. **Information** 055 290 832. **Date** 1wk early spring.

State museums, including the Uffizi, Accademia and Palatina galleries, open their doors free for a week.

Mostra Mercato di Piante e Fiori

Giardino di Orticoltura, Via Vittorio Emmanuele 4, Outside the City Gates, Florence. Bus 4. **Information** 055 290 832. **Date** around 25 Apr-1 May, 6 & 7 Oct.

This is a spectacular plant and flower show, which is centred around a grand, 19th-centuryglasshouse. The event attracts growers from miles around.

Maggio Musicale Fiorentino

Teatro Comunale, Santa Maria Novella, Florence. **Information** 055 211 158/www.maggiofiorentino.com. **Date** late Apr-late June.

Maggio Musicale Fiorentino is a two-month-long festival with opera, concerts and ballet featuring international artists. It closes with two free jamborees (a ballet and a concert) in piazza della Signoria.

Palio, Magliano in Toscana

Magliano in Toscana. **Information** 0564 59341. **Date** during 1st wk May.

Though the *palio* (horse race) no longer takes place, this little town in the Maremma still holds an intimate version of the torchlit procession that used to be part of the ritual blessing of the horses on the night before the race.

Mille Miglia

Florence. **Information** 030 280 036/ www.millemiglia.it. **Date** Sat in May (depends when Easter is).

The 1,000 miles (1,600km) refers to a race undertaken each year by no less than 350 vintage cars. The race starts and finishes in Brescia, northern Italy. You can catch the Florence leg of the race on the Saturday afternoon.

Artigianato e Palazzo

Florence. **Information** 055 265 4589/www.artigianatoepalazzo.it. **Date** weekend in mid May.

An upmarket craft show-cum-market held in the gorgeous gardens of the Palazzo Corsini. Artisans from all over Italy exhibit and sell their wares.

Festa del Grillo

Parco delle Cascine, Outside the City Gates, Florence. **Date** Sun late May/early June.

This ancient symbolic event has become an excuse for a big general market. The crickets that were once sold in hand-painted cages (intended to woo sweethearts and cheer them up during separations) have now been replaced by mechanical versions due to pressure from animal rights activists. Fun for kids.

Cantine Aperte, Toscana

Information 0577 738 312/www.movimentoturismovino.it (guide available at tourist offices). **Date** last Sun May.

Wine-producing estates, many of which aren't normally open to the public, hold tastings.

Summer

Throughout Tuscany open-air venues emerge around the end of May, while restaurants and bars put up their outside tables. In Florence open-air cinemas show two films a night (*see p161*), open-air bars double as live music venues (*see* pp174-80) and clubs relocate dancefloors outside, while cloisters and squares host classical concerts. Meanwhile, locals fill the piazzas and gardens.

Giostra del Saracino

Piazza Grande, Arezzo. **Tickets** standing €5; sitting €25-€35. **Information** 0575 377 678/ tickets 0575 377 262. **Date** June, Sept.

This reconstruction of an ancient jousting tournament between the four *quartieri* of Arezzo is held in piazza Grande on the penultimate weekend of June and the first Sunday of September. The Giostra del Saracino originated in the 13th century and musicians and acrobatic flag-throwers dress in period costumes in their team's colours. The first parade starts at about 10am, another starts at 2.30pm, and at 5pm the procession of horses, knights and their escort arrives in the piazza, and the tournament begins.

Calcio in Costume

Piazza Santa Croce, Florence.
Information 055 290 832. **Date** June.

Also known as *calcio storico*, this violent variation on football is played in medieval costume in piazza Santa Croce and is one of the most colourful events in the Florentine calendar. Three matches are played in June with the final on 24 June. Four teams of bare-chested lads represent the city's ancient quarters (Santa Croce, Santa Maria Novella, Santo Spirito and San Giovanni) and parade through the streets accompanied by costumed dignitaries before settling old rivalries in a one-hour no-holds-barred match played by two teams of 27. Blood is spilled.

Estate Fiesolana

Teatro Romano, Fiesole. **Information** 055 597 8308/ www.estatefiesolana.it. **Date** mid June-mid Aug.

This is a festival of music, dance and theatre set in an atmospheric Roman amphitheatre. There's the odd worthwhile event, but bear in mind that standards aren't always the highest.

Wild and controversial: Siena's annual horse race, the **Palio**. *See p155.*

Street party

Il Carnevale di Viareggio is Italy's oldest carnival. It all started in 1873 with a group of young aristocrats, regular drinkers at the Caffè I Casino, who decided that *Martedi Grasso* should be celebrated in style. They donned costumes and masks, filled their carriages with flowers and paraded through the town. So began a tradition that went on to become very popular with rich and poor alike, growing more elaborate with the years.

Towards the end of the century the first floats appeared, modelled by sculptors and

Luminaria di San Ranieri

Pisa. **Information** 050 560 464. **Date** 16 June.
Thousands of candles are lit along the Arno. On 17 June, 6.30pm, boat race between the town's *quartieri*.

Festa di San Giovanni

Florence. **Date** 24 June.
Public holiday in honour of Florence's patron saint. Huge fireworks display near piazzale Michelangelo.

Il Gioco del Ponte

Pisa. **Tickets** €11. **Information & tickets** 050 910 393. **Date** last Sun June.
13th-century 'push-of-war' fought on the Ponte di Mezzo. Processions start 4.30pm; competition 6.30pm.

Festa Internazionale della Ceramica

Montelupo. **Information** 0571 518 993.
Date 8 days late June.
Celebration of Tuscan ceramics with Renaissance music and costume, and demos of various techniques.

Florence Dance Festival

Teatro Romano, Fiesole. **Information** 055 289 276.
Date 2wks July.
An excellent dance festival with international performers (*see p187*).

Estate Musicale Chigiana

Accademia Musicale Chigiana, Siena. **Information** 0577 22091/www.chigiana.it. **Date** July-Aug.
Siena's summer concert season with performances in the city and the nearby abbeys of San Galgano, Sant'Antimo and Monte Oliveto Maggiore. The highlight is the Settimana Musicale Senese (usually mid July): a week of concerts in Siena's churches.

Giostra dell'Orso

Pistoia. **Information** 0573 21622. **Date** 25 July.
Pistoia's annual bun fight culminates on 25 July in its main square after a month of concerts, markets and pageantry. The Joust of the Bear dates from the 14th century: 12 knights are pitted against a bear (two wooden dummies) dressed in a checked cloak.

built in wood, *scagliola* and jute by the blacksmiths and carpenters of the town's large shipyards. In 1921 the floats were launched along the double avenue that runs parallel to the sea, the route still used today. In 1923 the traditional figure of Pierot appeared with moving head and eyes and in 1925 papier mâché was used as a much less weighty alternative to the original materials. Consequently, builders could construct enormous yet incredibly light creations that seemed to hover over the floats. This unique feature of the Viareggio carnival has given it an international reputation.

Apart from during the two World Wars there's never been a break in the festivities, not even when the huge hangar where the floats were constructed was destroyed by fire in 1960.

In 2003 the carnival celebrated its 130th birthday and, like they are every year, the floats were enormous and elaborately designed. Decorated by giant puppets, floats may carry up to 200 people, ten or so of whom are actually inside the puppets so they can manoeuvre the weights and counterweights that create movement, and stop the things toppling over.

Floats take the best part of a year to assemble in a series of enormous hangars in the new **Cittadella del Carnevale** (*see below*) with a prize awarded to the best float after the last parade. Satire is the most important element of Carnevale. The floats mercilessly lampoon politicos, sports and entertainment celebs and the social and political hot issues of the day. No subject, sacred or profane, is safe. Victims in 2003 included George W Bush, the Pope and Silvio Berlusconi.

Five parades take place around Mardi Gras, on the three Sundays before and the Sunday after. You can buy a seat in one of the spectator stands flanking the *lungomare*. However, it's much more fun to be in with the enormous crowds – be prepared to dodge kids wielding cans of squirty shaving foam. There are plenty of peripheral festivities too, including masked balls, street parties, treasure hunts, fireworks displays, sporting and cultural events.

The Cittadella del Carnevale, on the north side of town near the *autostrada* exit, is open to the public. Book a guided tour or just turn up to look around. There are hangars of old carnival floats, a performance and exhibition space, a museum and papier mâché and mask-making schools.

Fondazione Carnevale Viareggio

Piazza Mazzini 22 (0584 962568).

Cittadella del Carnevale

Via Santa Maria Goretti (0584 51176/ www.viareggio.ilcarnevale.com). **Open** 9am-6pm daily. **Admission** 3.50 for 3hrs. **No credit cards**.

Incontri in Terra di Siena

La Foce, Chianciano Terme. **Information** 0578 69101. **Date** 10 days late July.

These top-notch chamber music concerts are performed by internationally renowned musicians in dramatic settings such as La Foce (the family estate of writer Iris Origo), Pienza, Cetona and Radicofani.

Batignano Opera Festival

Batignano, nr Grosseto. **Information** 0564 462 611 (Grosseto tourist office). **Date** July-Aug.

Little-known opera productions with well-known musicians in an idyllic hilltop town. A bit precious.

Puccini Opera Festival

Torre del Lago. **Information** 0584 359 322/ www.puccinifestival.it. **Date** July-Aug.

Standards of performance aren't always high. Nevertheless, Puccini's lakeside villa is certainly a magnificent setting for his operas. The stage is built over the lake while the audience sits on the shore. Be sure to take mosquito repellent.

Palio, Siena

Piazza del Campo, Siena. **Information** 0577 280 551. **Date** 2 July & 16 Aug.

This controversial, often violent horse race around Siena's piazza del Campo is Tuscan pageantry at its best. Trial races run on three days leading to the two main dates. The last is at 9am on the big days. In the early afternoon qualifying horses and jockeys are blessed in their team's church. At about 4.30pm the procession enters the piazza del Campo and, after acrobatic flag-throwing, the race runs at about 7pm. It's free to stand in the square, but get there early and take a sun hat. Tickets for balconies overlooking the piazza are sold in bars and cafés on the piazza. However, they're hard to come by and expensive.

Effetto Venezia

Livorno. **Information** 0586 204611. **Date** 10 days late July-Aug.

Evening shows and concerts in Livorno's 'Venetian quarter's – so-called because of its canals. Restaurants stay open late serving local delicacies.

Medieval Festival

Monteriggione. **Information** 0577 304 810. **Date** mid July.

Re-enactment of Monteriggione medieval town life with food, drink and craft stalls, music and dancing, shops and performances. Action focuses on the third weekend of July, but there are events during the ten days before. Torches are lit after dark. Visitors must change their cash into medieval currency.

On The Road Festival

Pelago. **Information** 055 832 6236. **Tickets** €7. **Date** 1 weekend (Thur-Sun) mid-late July, from 6pm.

A festival of street performers in a pretty village.

Autumn

Settembre Musica

Teatro della Pergola & various venues, Florence. **Information** 055 608 420 c/o Amici della Musica. **Date** Sept.

Month of early-music concerts, by young or relatively obscure ensembles with the odd bigger name.

Rassegna Internazionale Musica dei Popoli

Auditorium Flog, Outside the City Gates, Florence. Bus 4, 8, 14, 20, 28. **Information** 055 422 0300. **Date** Oct-Nov.

An innovative world music festival.

Winter

Italians love Nativity scenes and many churches set up cribs, some *viventi* (with live animals). The main ones in Florence are at San Lorenzo, Santa Croce, Chiesa di Dante and Santa Maria de' Ricci. Winter's also a season when *sagre* in country towns and villages celebrate truffles, olive oil and chestnuts.

Florence Marathon

Florence. **Information** tel/fax 055 600 664/ www.firenzemarathon.it. **Date** late Nov/early Dec.

A full and half marathon.

Florence Dance Festival Winter Edition

Teatro Goldoni, Florence. **Information** 055 289 276. **Map** p314 D1. **Date** late Nov/early Dec.

Winter session of the innovative festival organised by the Florence Dance Cultural Centre (*see p187*).

Christmas Concert

Teatro Verdi, Florence. **Information** 055 263 8777/ tickets 055 212 320. **Map** p314 C5. **Date** 24 Dec.

Given by the Orchestra Regionale Toscana.

Christmas

Mainly marked in Florence by late shopping, town decorations and *comune* events. Midnight mass is held in the Duomo. Some restaurants open on Christmas Day, but you'll find more choice on Boxing Day.

New Year's Eve

Many Florentines see the New Year in at home with copious amounts of food and drink. However, lots of restaurants do put on a special *Cena dell' Ultimo dell'Anno* menus involving endless courses and including, traditionally, stuffed pigs' trotters and lentils, for which you'll pay through the nose. Alternatively, take to the streets: in the past few years, street parties, both official and impromptu, have begun to pop up all over town.

Sfilata dei Canottieri

Florence. **Date** 1 Jan.

A traditional parade of boats on the Arno.

New Year Concert

Teatro Comunale, Florence. **Information** 055 597 851 (for free tickets). **Date** 1 Jan.

Put on by the Scuola di Musica di Fiesole.

La Befana (Epiphany)

Date 6 Jan.

This is an Italian holiday. Still it's really one for the kids, who open their stockings on La Befana. As legend has it, the *Befana* (a ragged old woman riding a broomstick) brings presents to well-behaved children. Naughty ones aren't so lucky – they get a sock full of dirty coal. Many of the small towns around the region hold street parties in celebration.

Carnevale

Date 10 days up to Shrove Tuesday, Feb/Mar.

Many Tuscan towns have *carnevale* celebrations, most of which feature parades of elaborate floats, fancy dress parties and excessive eating and drinking. In Florence children dress up and parade with their parents in the piazzas and along lungarno Amerigo Vespucci, scattering confetti and squirting anything that moves with foam. Elsewhere in Tuscany, head for Borgo San Lorenzo for kids' events and street performances, Calenzano for medieval revellers or to San Gimignano for general festivities.

Viareggio Carnevale

Viareggio. **Transport** LAZZI bus from Piazza Adua, Florence (055 351 061) to Viareggio; train from Florence SMN (8488 88088) to Viareggio via Pisa. **Tickets** for all days €11; €22 in stands. **Information** 0584 962 568/www.viareggio.ilcarnevale.com. **Date** 4 consecutive Suns Feb/early Mar.

These are the biggest *carnevale* celebrations in Italy outside Venice. Viareggio Carnevale is a wild delight for all ages. The first three parades of the carnival begin at about 2.30pm. The last begins at 5pm and finishes around 9.30pm. The latter, an over-the-top procession of gigantic floats, often lampooning political and public figures, is rounded off with a fireworks display and a prize ceremony for the best float. You can buy tickets at booths in the town from 8am on the day, or otherwise by phone in advance. For a full round up of events, *see also p154* **Street party**.

Children

How to satisfy your *bimbo.*

Every child's introduction to Florence should begin with a bird's eye view of the city. Climb to the top of the Duomo or hike up the magnificent stairway between Porta San Miniato and piazzale Michelangiolo (there's a *gelateria* at the top of the stairs for added incentive) from where little explorers can survey the domain.

As for the museums, some have specific children's programmes for which you must book ahead. The **Museo dei Ragazzi** within the Palazzo Vecchio (*see p77*) has storytelling, costumed theatrical re-enactments and a behind the scenes tour of the palace's secret passages. The **Stibbert Museum** (*see p104*) holds a massive collection of armour, swords and shields in an old villa north of the city, while the **Museo di Storia della Scienza** (*see p77*) is home to intriguing objects such as Galileo's telescope and (rather more morbidly) his middle finger.

Elsewhere, there's still plenty to capture the imagination. The Palazzo Pitti's **Museo del Costume** (*see p*100) has a beautiful collection of costumes and just behind it you'll find the massive Boboli Gardens. The **Museo di Geologia e Paleontologia** (*see p92*) has a strange fossilised elephant, **La Specola** (*see p102*) has life-size anatomical models of humans (some quite gory) and the **Museo Archeologico** (*see p92*) houses Egyptian tombs and mummies.

The food markets can also be fascinating for children. Go early to San Lorenzo market (*see p134* **Trading places**), which is one of the central arteries of daily Florentine life and is great for picnic supplies. If children can summon the courage to try out a few Italian words with the vendors, they might be surprised by the extras that get tossed into the grocery bag.

In addition to city gardens, parks and swimming pools, the countryside is within easy reach – olive groves are a good place for walks. A day by the sea or the promise of eggy-smelling hot springs tend to make kids more tolerant of visits to monasteries and Etruscan tombs. But should they dig their heels in, English-speaking childcare at Canadian Island (*see p159*) is always handy.

I scream, you scream, we all scream for...

Book & toy shops

BM American British Bookstore

Borgo Ognissanti 4r, Santa Maria Novella (055 294 575). **Open** 9.30am-7.30pm Mon-Sat; 10.30am-7pm Sun. **Credit** AmEx, DC, MC, V. **Map** p314 B1.

This is a tiny shop packed with one of the best collections of English books you'll find in Florence with a wide range of kids' books on the Renaissance and related topics.

Città del Sole

Via dei Cimatori 21r, Duomo & Around (055 219 345/www.cittadelsole.com). **Open** 3.30-7.30pm Mon; 10am-2pm, 3-7.30pm Tue-Sat. Closed 2wks Aug. **Credit** AmEx, MC, V. **Map** p315 C4.

Well-made children's toys as well as a selection of board games and puzzles. There's now a branch of Natura e... (*see below*) upstairs.

Dreoni Giacattoli

Via Cavour 31-3r, San Marco (055 216 611). **Open** 3.30-7.30pm Mon; 9am-1pm, 3.30-7.30pm Tue-Sat. **Credit** AmEx, DC, MC, V. **Map** p315 A4.

It's not hard to get lost in the maze of themed rooms that stretch all the way from via Cavour to via San Gallo. The craft toy room at the back also has costumes for *Carnevale* and Halloween (an American import celebrated more and more each year).

Feltrinelli International

Via Cavour 12r, San Marco (055 219 524/ www.feltrinelli.it). **Open** 9am-7.30pm Mon-Sat. **Credit** AmEx, DC, MC, V. **Map** p315 A4.

A large selection of videos, games and books.

Menicucci

Via de' Guicciardini 51r, Oltrarno (055 294 934). **Open** 9.30am-8pm daily. **Credit** AmEx, MC, V. **Map** p314 D2/3.

A good all-round toyshop known for its window display of soft toys and wooden Pinocchios. Wander through to the stationery store where you'll find leather-bound books, feather quills, personalised seals and sealing wax.

Natura e...

Via dello Studio 30r, Duomo & Around (055 265 7624/www.natura-e.com). **Open** *Summer* 10am-2pm, 3-7.30pm Mon-Fri; 10am-2pm Sat. *Winter* 3-7.30pm Mon; 10am-2pm, 3-7.30pm Tue-Sat. **Credit** MC, V. **Map** p315 B4.

A shop for nature-lovers selling everything from scientific toys, experiments and optical illusions to outdoor trekking gear. It also has pamphlets on WWF activities and parks in Tuscany.

Branch: Città del Sole, Via dei Cimatori 21r, Duomo & Around (055 219 345).

St James's American Church

Via Bernardo Rucellai 9, Santa Maria Novella (Kathy Procissi 055 577 527). **Open** 10-11.30am, 3.30-5.30pm Wed; 10-11am, noon-1pm Sun. **Membership** *Books & videos* €15. **No credit cards. Map** p314 A1.

A friendly place with an extensive selection of English-language books, videos and games. Often on Saturdays before festivals, children make decorations and masks. Ring the doorbell to enter.

Festivals

During February's *Carnevale*, especially on Sundays, look for children in fancy dress in the *piazze* and on lungarno Amerigo Vespucci. Children wanting to join in the fun can get kitted out in the costume department at Dreoni Giacattoli (*see above*).

La Befana

In the past it was at **La Befana** (Epiphany; *see p156*), not Christmas, when children in Italy got their presents as that's when the Magi brought theirs. The story goes that on the eve of 6 January a poor, tattered old woman (*la befana*) riding a donkey (or a broom) and carrying a sack full of toys, filled children's stockings with toys and sweets (or coal, if they'd been naughty). On the eve of La Befana children leave biscuits and milk for the old lady, and hay for her donkey, next to where they hang their stockings. Christmas is more celebrated now, but there's still a lingering affection for La Befana. So much so that there was an uproar when this public holiday was cancelled a few years ago; it was rapidly restored.

La Rificolona

La Rificolona is a day in September when Florentine children make or buy paper candle lanterns. They then gather in the evening either in piazza Santissima Annunziata in San Marco or along the river (look for posters that give details of the gatherings). After dark, with their lanterns bobbing on the end of long bamboo poles, children parade about the place singing. Traditionally, boys use peashooters to blow paper darts into little girls' lanterns to set them on fire.

Food

The best meals are usually found by keeping a keen eye out for a bustling family trattoria with an appealing menu and atmosphere. Meanwhile, try the places listed below, which are accustomed to children with less adventurous palates.

For snacks, tear off a hunk of *schiacciatta all' olio* (pizza bread with salt and olive oil). Mothers give this to babies to chew on and the taste clearly stays with children, who buy big squares of it before school. It's delicious plain or stuffed with a little ham or *mortadella.*

Il Cucciolo

Via del Corso 25r, Duomo & Around (055 287 727). **Open** 7.30am-8.30pm Mon-Sat. Closed 2wks Aug. **No credit cards. Map** p315 B4.

This bar is known to Florentine children because the *bomboloni* (pastries, plain or filled with cream, chocolate or jam) are made on the floor above and are then dropped down a tube to the bar below and served hot. Go in the morning to catch the action.

Mr Jimmy's American Bakery

Via San Niccolò 47, Oltrarno (055 248 0999/ www.mr-jimmy.com). **Open** 11am-7pm Mon-Sat; 11am-2pm Sun. Closed July, Aug. **Credit** AmEx, DC, MC, V. **Map** p315 D5.
American-style apple pie, chocolate cake, cheesecake, muffins, brownies and bagels.

Pit Stop

Via F Corridoni 30r, Outside the City Gates (055 422 1437). Bus 14, 28. **Open** 12.30-2.30pm, 7pm-1am Mon, Wed-Fri; 7pm-1am Sat, Sun. Closed 3wks Aug. **Average** €15. **Credit** MC, V.
There are several Pit Stops around the city. They offer an amazing 128 different *primi* (starters) and 100 different kinds of pizzas.
Branches: Throughout the city.

I Tarocchi

Via dei Renai 12-14r, Oltrarno (055 234 3912/ www.pizzeriaitarocchi.it). **Open** 12.30-2.30pm, 7pm-1am Tue-Fri; 7pm-1am Sat, Sun. **Average** €12. **Credit** MC, V. **Map** p315 D4/5.
Child-sized pizzas and pastas served in a friendly, casual atmosphere. The room with long tables and benches is perfect for boisterous families.

Gardens & parks

Boboli Gardens

For listings, *see p99.*
Labyrinths, grottoes, fountains, statues and hiding places make the Boboli a great diversion for children with magnificent views of the city.

Le Cascine

Entrance near Ponte della Vittoria, Outside the City Gates.
Florence's largest park (west of the city along the river) is the site of regular fairs and markets and is most animated on Sundays with football and picnics. Racehorses are often exercised in the Ippodroma in the early mornings. There's also a public swimming pool (via della Catena 2, 055 362 233, closed mid Sept-May, €7). Playgrounds dot the park with snacks and balloons for sale at vending trucks.

Parco Carraia

Entrance off via dell'Erta Caninna, Outside the City Gates.
This little-known park surrounded by countryside, has swings, picnic benches and plenty of green space for a good game of football. It's a lovely stroll up from Porta San Miniato, with strangely placed but fun climbing structures along the side of the road. The friendly Carraia Tennis Club is just up the street from the park and offers a variety of activities for children including tennis and *calcetto* (football).

Play centres

Canadian Island

Via Gioberti 15, Outside the City Gates (055 677 567/www.canadianisland.com). Bus 3, 6, 14. **Open** *June, July, Sept* 8am-5pm Mon-Fri. *Oct-May* 8am-5pm Mon-Fri; 9am-1pm Sat. Closed Aug. **Admission** €30 per afternoon. **No credit cards**.
Childcare for ages three to 12 by responsible, English- and Italian-speaking adults. They also organise summer camps on farms and day camps at the Ugolino in Chianti.

Mondobimbo Inflatables

Parterre, Piazza della Libertà, San Lorenzo (055 553 2946). **Open** 10am-midnight daily. Closed *June-Aug* noon-4.30pm. **Admission** €5 day ticket . **No credit cards**.
Under-tens can let off steam here on huge inflatable castles, whales, dogs and snakes. It's wise to bring spare socks (or you can buy some at the entrance).

Sketching Florence

Sharon Okun (055 655 7438/ inquiry@sharonokun.com).
A group of artists offer one-hour workshops in historical *piazze*. Costs €25 including materials.

Out of town

Escape the hustle and bustle of the city and take the kids off for a day trip by car, bus or train. Alternatively, go on a one-day bike ride, organised by **I Bike Italy** (055 234 2371; open all year; no credit cards). Guides will pick you up from the centre of the city.

Giardino Zoologico

Via Pieve a Celle 160, Pistoia (0573 911 219/ www.zoodipistoia.it). **Open** *Summer* 9am-7pm daily. *Winter* 9am-5pm daily. **Admission** €9; €7 3-9s; free under-3s. **No credit cards**.
Giraffes, rhinos, crocodiles, jaguars and a growing gang of Malagasy lemurs in a large park with palm and banana trees. No entrance after 6pm.

Parco Giochi Cavallino Matto

Via Po 1, Marina di Castagneto Donoratico, Livorno (0565 745 720/www.cavallinomatto.it). **Open** *Mar & Oct* 10am-7pm Sun. *Apr* 10am-7pm Sat, Sun. *May & June* 10am-7pm daily. *July* 10am-9pm daily. *Aug* 10am-midnight daily. *1st 2wks Sept* 10am-7pm daily. *Last 2wks Sept* 10am-7pm Sat, Sun & hols. **Admission** €10-€13. **Credit** AmEx, DC, MC,V.
The largest funfair of the coastal region.

Parco Preistorico

Peccioli Via Cappuccini 20, Pisa (0587 636 030/ 635 430/www.parcsmania.it). **Open** 9am-sunset daily. **Admission** €4; €3 children; free tours in Italian (English info sheet). **No credit cards**.
About 50 km (32 miles) from Pisa, this park has impressive life-size models of 18 dinosaurs, a play area, bar and picnic facilities. Tours last one hour.

Film

See the reel Florence.

If a walk around Florence seems strangely familiar even on a first visit, it's probably because you've seen it all before in one of the hundreds of celluloid homages paid by generations of filmmakers. Remember the balcony of the Palazzo Vecchio or the gilded lilies of its Sala dei Gigli? *Hannibal*'s gutted police inspector Giancarlo Giannini should jog the memory. The Giotto frescoes in the Bardi Chapel or Uccello's *Battle of San Romano* will ring a bell if you've seen *A Room with a View* or *Asia Argento*. Recognition of the Duomo's interior, Santa Maria Novella or piazza Santissima Annunziata are brought forth by John Malkovich's seduction of Nicole Kidman in *Portrait of a Lady* and the grandes dames of English cinema taking a small boy on a tour of the sights in Zeffirelli's autobiographical *Tea with Mussolini*.

Tuscany too has played its part – the honey colours of the Creti Senesi where the Gladiator made his gruesome find or the convent in Sant'Anna near Pienza where Juliet Binoche tended her English patient – as well as producing such golden movie talent as the irrepressible Roberto Benigni (pictured) who was born in Misericordia near Arezzo. But despite its obvious advantages for filmmakers, Florence's film-going scene is less accessible for non-Italian-speakers. Italians are generally loath to sit through a subtitled film and Italy has one of the biggest dubbing industries in the world. Nonetheless, several cinemas do now show international films in their original language (*versione originale*) one or more nights a week. More varied programmes are shown at cineclubs, often with subtitles.

If you speak Italian, check out the cheaper matinées at many main cinemas on weekdays before 6.30pm or all day Wednesday at €5, instead of the standard €7.20. This reduction doesn't apply to original-language screenings.

Expect long queues on Friday and Saturday nights for new releases and for blockbusters in original language. When the *posto in piedi* light is on tickets sold are standing room only. For screening times check listings in daily newspapers. Most bars display 'La Maschera' – an info sheet listing what's on at cinemas and theatres. For festivals and other special events not listed here, pick up a copy of the monthly listings magazine *Firenze Spettacolo*.

Cinemas

British Institute Cultural Programme

Lungarno Guicciardini 9, Oltrarno (055 2677 8270). **Open** lectures start 6pm, film screenings 8.30pm. **Tickets** €7; €5 with library membership. **No credit cards**. **Map** p314 C2.

On Wednesdays the film shown is sandwiched between an introduction and a debate, all in English. On Fridays there's a film appreciation course with retrospectives of famous directors or seasons of films by British auteurs followed by a discussion.

Fulgor

Via Maso Finiguerra 22r, Santa Maria Novella (055 238 1881/www.staseraalcinema/cinemafulgor.it). **Open** box office times vary according to film. **Tickets** €7. Closed 3wks Aug. **No credit cards**. **Map** p314 B1.

Mainstream English-language films on Thursdays in this multi-screen. A ticket valid for ten entrances costing €50 can be used the same evening (for Italian and English-language films).

Odeon Original Sound

Via Sassetti 1, Duomo & Around (055 214 068/ www.cinehall.it). **Open** box office times vary according to film. Closed Aug. **Tickets** €7.20. **No credit cards**. **Map** p314 B3.

On Mondays, Tuesdays and Thursdays this art nouveau cinema shows films on current release in English, sometimes with English or Italian subtitles. There's a discount of up to 40% with a club card for six films out of a programme of 13 (€27) or cut the voucher from the previous Sunday's *La Repubblica* newspaper for a 30% discount.

Officina Move Bar

Via il Prato 58r, Santa Maria Novella (055 210 399/www.officinamovebar.com). **Open** 8am-2am Mon-Fri; 3pm-2am Sat, Sun. Closed Aug. **Credit** MC, V.

Every Monday Officina shows a film at 7.30pm in Italian with English subtitles. It screens the same film at 10pm in the original language with Italian subtitles. There's also a range of art and design activities and exhibitions in the bar.

Film clubs

Part of the attraction of Florence's film clubs is that they are cheap to join, especially for students. Also, the main cinemas sometimes offer discounts for members.

CineCittà

Via Baccio da Montelupo 35, Outside the City Gates (055 732 4510). **Shows** 8.30pm Wed-Sun. **Tickets** €4-€5, plus €6 membership. **No credit cards.**
Hollywood action pictures and festivals of obscure Italian films. Some screenings are shown in their original language or with subtitles.

Cineteca di Firenze

Via R Giuliani 374, Outside the City Gates (055 450 749/www.cinetecadifirenze.it). Bus 2, 20, 28. **Shows** times vary. **Tickets** €4.50, plus €3 membership. **No credit cards.**
Shows cycles of films showcasing various actors, some in original language.

Stensen Cineforum

Viale Don Minzoni 25C, Outside the City Gates (055 576 551/www.stensen.org). Bus 1, 7, 12. **Shows** 9.15pm Thur-Sat but days can vary. **Tickets** prices vary. **No credit cards.** **Map** p314 B2.
Italian and foreign films screened for season ticket holders only (price depends on number of films shown). Also organises lectures and debates.

Seasonal cinema

There are two major international festivals, one in Florence and one in Fiesole (where films are usually screened in their original language). The **Festival dei Popoli** (055 244 778) of narrative and documentary films includes shows in clubs and cinemas throughout Florence. The festival's theme changes each year but always centres around a social issue.

The **Premio Fiesole ai Maestri del Cinema**, held in July in Fiesole's open-air Roman theatre, pays homage to the works of one great film director.

The **France Cinema** festival (055 214 053; www.francecinema.it), usually held in November at the French Institute (piazza Ognissanti 2; 055 239 8902) and at the Teatro della Compagnia (via Cavour 50r; 055 217 428), has also grown in importance.

Many cinemas are air-conditioned and some stay open throughout summer. But a pleasant alternative for Italian-speakers (though some international films may be shown in original language) or those wanting to sample local life are open-air cinemas, which screen recent films from June to September. Some have bars and restaurants and a couple have double screenings – the second films finish at around 1.30am. Shows usually start around 9pm to 9.30pm.

Arena di Marte

Palazzetto dello Sport di Firenze, Viale Paoli, Outside the City Gates (055 293 169/www.ateliergroup.it). Bus 10, 20, 34. **Dates** late June-late Aug. **Open** 8pm (shows 9.30pm & 10pm) daily. **Tickets** €5. **No credit cards.**

Talented Tuscan **Roberto Benigni**. *See p160.*

Two screens. One shows cult and less mainstream films, some in original language with Italian subtitles, while the larger shows the previous year's major blockbuster movies. Good restaurant too.

Chiardiluna

Via Monte Oliveto 1, Outside the City Gates (055 233 7042/218 682). Bus 12, 13. **Dates** June-Sept. **Open** 8pm (shows 9.30pm) daily. **Tickets** €5. **No credit cards.**
Surrounded by woodland, Chiardiluna is cooler than the other cinemas – but take mosquito repellent. Recent commercial releases, some double screenings.

Forte di Belvedere

Via San Leonardo, Oltrarno (055 239 169/www.ateliergroup.it). **Dates** late June-late Aug. **Open** 8pm (shows 9.30pm Mon-Wed, Fri-Sun). **Tickets** €5. **No credit cards.**
The long-awaited reopening of this cinema has now come with showings of cult films and recent releases. Set on the breezy terrace of the star-shaped fortress.

Raggio Verde

Palacongressi Firenze, Via Valfondo, San Lorenzo (055 239169/www.ateliergroup.it). **Dates** July-late Aug. **Open** 8pm (shows 9.30pm) daily. **Tickets** €5. **No credit cards.**
Nightly double screenings at a stunning amphitheatre-style cinema overlooking a 16th-century villa. Unlike other open-air venues, it's five minutes' walk from the main railway station. There's also simple restaurant in the gardens.

Galleries

Innovation, not restoration.

For years constant equivocation about plans for a public contemporary arts centre for Florence created a climate of inertia. That is until now. Spurred on by the promise of European funding, and the blessing of both the established galleries and the clutch of major new art spaces – all of whom are convinced that the city can become the hub for the Italian contemporary art scene – a proposal has finally been stamped and sealed. The chosen venue is the ex-Meccanotessile factory, a sprawling site on the outskirts of the centre. When it will open is anyone's guess, but at least the ball's rolling.

Meanwhile, the impressive collection at the Centro per L'Arte Contemporanea Luigi Pecci, on the outskirts of Prato, remains as the public sector's sole contribution. In the private sector an honourable mention should go to Pitti Imagine, best known for its organisation of the twice-yearly men's, children's, textiles and home fashion collections. With its recent move into contemporary art and with shows at the Alcatraz space of the disused railway station Stazione Leopolda, it's keeping the scene buzzing. In a high-profile publicity coup Pitti brought Björk's artist boyfriend Matthew Barney to Florence – starting as it means to go on with shows of big international names.

Gallery spaces

Base

Via San Niccolo 18r, Oltrarno (055 2207 281/ 679 378 www.baseitaly.org). **Open** 5-8pm Mon-Sat. **Map** p315 D4.

A centre of excellence for installation and digital art.

La Corte Arte Contemporanea

Via de'Coverelli 27r, Oltrarno (055 284 435/ www.lacortearte.it). **Open** 4-7pm Tue-Sat. Closed 20 July-10 Sept. **No credit cards**. **Map** p314 C2.

The fantastical qualities of *Alice in Wonderland* spring to mind when Rosanna Tempestini organises shows of *gigantografia* (mammoth celluloid artworks) in this tiny gallery. The gallery showcases a diverse range of local artists with particular emphasis on the experimental scene.

Galleria Alessandro Bagnai

Via Maggio 58r, Oltrarno (055 212 131/ www.galleriabagnai.it). **Open** 10.30am-1pm, 4-7.30pm Tue-Sat. **Credit** AmEx, DC, JCB, MC, V. **Map** p314 C2/D2.

Irony plays its part in this sleek gallery: Tuscan sculptor Roberto Barni's bronze men sit nonchalantly with their coffee cups in the middle of the stately art space while Dormice's bimbos gaze provocatively from canvases.

Galleria Biagiotti Arte Contemporanea

Via delle Belle Donne 39r, Santa Maria Novella (055 214 757/www.artbiagiotti.com). **Open** 2-7pm Tue-Sat. Closed Aug. **Credit** AmEx, MC, V. **Map** p314 B2.

Carole Biagiotti runs this stunning 15th-century converted atrium gallery like a fairy godmother. The result is a stream of innovative exhibitions of the best works by mostly young artists whose pieces often sell to collectors unviewed.

Galleria Festina Lente

Via Condotta 18r, Duomo & Around (055 292 612). **Open** 10am-1pm, 4-8pm Mon-Sat. Closed Aug. **Credit** AmEx, DC, JCB, MC, V. **Map** p315 C4.

Rita Pedulla's loose, sultry nudes and tantric Indians engaged in Kama Sutra contortions are the showstoppers in this consummately consumerist gallery-shop.

Galleria Pananti

Via Maggio 15, Oltrarno (055 274 1011/ www.pananti.com). **Open** 9.30am-1.30pm, 3-7pm Mon-Fri. Closed Aug. **Credit** AmEx, DC, JCB, MC, V. **Map** p315 C5.

One of the most important galleries in town as well as a respected art auction house, Pananti hosts major contemporary shows and retrospectives of internationally renowned modern artists, with the emphasis on the Tuscan tradition of figurative photography and painting.

Galleria Il Ponte

Via di Mezzo 42/B, Santa Maria Novella (055 240617). **Open** *Sept-June* 4-7.30pm Tue-Sat. *July* 4-7.30pm Mon-Fri. Closed Aug. **Credit** AmEx, DC, JCB, MC, V. **Map** p315 B6.

A well-respected gallery and art publishing house featuring predominantly modern and contemporary abstract painters.

Galleria Santo Ficara

Via Ghibellina 164r, Santa Croce (055 234 0239/www.santoficara.it). **Open** 9.30am-12.30pm, 3.30-7.30pm Mon-Sat. Closed Aug. **Credit** AmEx, DC, JCB, MC, V. **Map** p315 C5.

Mostly well-established artists with an international market, including the 1950s abstract Gruppo Forma member Carla Accardi.

Galleria Sergio Tossi

Via Pindemonte 63, Outside the City Gates (055 228 6163/www.tossiarte.com). **Open** 3-7pm Tue-Fri; 11am-1pm Sat. Closed Aug. **No credit cards**.

This loft-style gallery space is a hothouse for young contemporary neo-figurative artists specialising in painting and digital photography. Among them is Matteo Basilé, best known for his music video work.

Galleria Tornabuoni

Via Tornabuoni 74r, Duomo & Around (055 284 720/www.galleriatournabuoni.it). **Open** 3.30-7.30pm Mon; 9.30am-1pm, 3.30-7.30pm Tue-Sat. **Credit** AmEx, DC, JCB, MC, V. **Map** p314 B2.

The prestigious permanent home to some of the best-known artists sold in the city, including Francesco Musante whose whimsical work sells as postcards beside Botticellis and Duomo views. The gallery also sells Tomaino's fabulous rocking horses.

Isabella Brancolini

Lungarno Acciaiuoli 4, Duomo & Around (055 281 549/www.isabellabrancolini.it). **Open** 10am-1pm, 3-7pm Mon-Sat. Closed Aug. **No credit cards**. **Map** p314 C2/3.

A sparkling new gallery that's part of the Gallery Art Hotel and Lungarno Suites complex (*see p47*). At its prime riverbank location a pool of dozen young, emerging artists from all over the world are chosen for their originality and outlandish styles.

Ken's Art Gallery

Via Lambertesca 15-17r, Duomo & Around (055 239 6587/www.kensartgallery.com). **Open** 10am-1pm, 3-8pm Mon-Sat. **Credit** AmEx, DC, JCB, MC, V. **Map** p314 C3.

Walter Bellini's exciting gallery has several artists in residence and an exhibition programme with a rapid turnover. Contemporary works, all by Florentine residents, include Paolo Staccioli's Etruscan-inspired decorated urns and warrior busts.

Poggiali e Forconi

Via della Scala 35A, Santa Maria Novella (055 287 748/www.poggialieforconi.it). **Open** *Oct-May* 9.30am-1.30pm, 2.30-7.30pm Mon-Sat. *June-July, Sept* 9.30am-1.30pm, 2.30-7.30pm Mon-Fri; 9.30am-1.30pm Sat. Closed Aug. **Credit** AmEx, DC, JCB, MC, V. **Map** p314 A1/B2.

Huge vaulted-ceilinged walls hung with the figurative paintings of young Italian artists of international renown. Notable recent exhibitions have showcased Luca Pignatelli and Enzo Cucchi.

Consumer art

One of the most important contributions to contemporary art in Florence comes from the many bars, restaurants and hotels that showcase the work of local artists, often commission-free. Potential customers are normally put in direct contact with the artist.

Figure it out at **Galleria Pananti**. See *p162*.

Astor Caffè

Piazza Duomo 20r, Duomo & Around (055 239 9000). **Open** 10am-3am Mon-Sat; 5pm-3am Sun. **Map** p315 B4.

Astor's huge central skylight helps create the perfect environment for its regular exhibitions of local photographers and bas-relief sculptors.

Dolce Vita

Piazza del Carmine, Oltrarno (055 284 595). **Open** *Summer* 10am-2am daily. *Winter* 6pm-2am Tue-Sun. **Map** p314 C1.

As well as displaying some of the most inventive and beautiful lamps you'll ever see, Dolce Vita also puts on week-long shows of new and established artists.

Gallery Art Hotel

Vicolo Oro 5, Duomo & Around (055 27263). **Open** for viewing 24hrs daily. **Map** p314 C3.

Isabella Brancolini (*see above*) also takes in hand the innovative two-monthly art cycles at this avant-garde hotel (*see p47*). Shows have become increasingly prestigious, including the vivid celluloid images of lens legend David La Chapelle.

Negroni

Via dei Renai 17r, Oltrarno (055 243 647). **Open** 7.30am-2am Mon-Sat; 6pm-2am Sun. **Map** p314 D4/5.

The finishing touches to the slick decor of the hippest new bar in town are provided by regular shows of mainly black and white photography from artists such as Ileana Peris and Alessandro Botticelli.

Rex Art Bar

Via Fiesolana 25r, Santa Croce (055 248 0331). **Open** 6pm-3.30am daily. **Map** p315 B5.

Rex Bar's omnipresent mosaics vie for attention with the Red Room exhibitions of paintings, including Andrea Orani's colourful abstracts and Marina Lainati's plaintive portraits.

Gay & Lesbian

Cruising and carousing.

For a long time, gay and lesbian travellers, artists and writers have been drawn to Florence, but it wasn't until 1970 that the city got its first gay disco, **Tabasco** (*see p165*), in the heart of the historic centre. The venue was soon packed every weekend as Italians from every part of the boot came to kick up their heels. At around the same time, the Fronte Unitario Omosessuale Rivoluzionario Italiano or FUORI (Italian for 'out'), Tuscany's first gay and lesbian organisation, was set up by members of the Radical party. Other landmarks included the opening of the queer cultural space Banana Moon in borgo degli Albizi in 1977 and the founding of **ARCI Gay/Lesbica**, the leading organisation for gay political initiatives in Tuscany, in the '80s. In the mid '90s the latter split into two groups: **Ireos** is a social, cultural and information centre, while **Azione Gay e Lesbica** focuses on political issues. For both, *see p286*.

As far as gay etiquette is concerned, there should be no problem with holding hands in the streets, but anything much more overt than this in public places is less acceptable. For gay men, there are lots of cruising areas, though some can be quite dangerous. The **Parco delle Cascine**, for instance, is active from sunset till late at night, but local cognoscenti warn against it. Another popular area is the **Campo di Marte** (in eastern Florence) where most of the cruising takes place in cars. The park at **viale Malta** is active too, but subject to frequent incursions from police checking IDs.

The age of consent in Italy is 18 and clubs and bars are very strict about age checks, so it's definitely a good idea to bring some form of ID along with you.

The bold and the...

Florence

Bars

Crisco

Via Sant' Egidio 43r, Santa Croce (055 248 0580/ www.crisco.it). **Open** 10.30pm-3.30am Mon, Wed, Thur, Sun; 10.30pm-6am Fri, Sat. **Membership** free. **Credit** MC, V. **Map** p315 B5.

Bar with (mostly X-rated) videos, special events, parties and performances. The exclusively male crowd is mixed but leathermen and bears prevail.

Cruising Z

Via dell'Oriuolo 19-21r, Santa Croce (055 246 6387/www.crisco.it). **Open** 4pm-midnight Tue-Sun. **Membership** free. **Credit** MC, V. **Map** p315 B4/5.

Affiliated with Crisco (*see above*), this is a men's bar for afternoon encounters. It features internet access, video rooms and a labyrinth.

Il Piccolo Caffè

Borgo Santa Croce 23, Santa Croce (055 200 1057/www.piccolofirenze.com). **Open** 5pm-2am daily. **Admission** free. **Credit** AmEx, MC, V. **Map** p314 C5.

Attracting a very mixed crowd, Il Piccolo tends to get especially crowded on Saturdays. In the week there are contemporary art exhibitions along with frequent live shows.

Silver Stud

Via della Fornace 9, Oltrarno (055 688 466/ www.silverstud.it). **Open** 9pm-4am Mon-Sat. **Membership** free. **Credit** AmEx, MC, V.

New, recently opened and pleasant cruising bar. Videos, lounge bar, labyrinth, darkroom, music, male strip shows. Men only.

...well, the rest, at **Tenax**.

YAG B@R

Via de'Macci 8r, Santa Croce (055 246 9022/ www.yagbar.com). **Open** 9pm-3am Mon-Sat; 5pm-3am Sun. **Admission** free. **Credit** AmEx, DC, MC, V. **Map** p314 C6.

This spacious, futurist dance-bar draws a young crowd of both genders. There's a full bar, internet access and video games. It plays the latest music and is a popular first stop on the club-hopping route.

Bed & breakfast

Gay-friendly accommodation, in the form of low-key bed and breakfasts, are proving popular with visitors in the know.

Casa Visconti

Via Santa Maria 3, Oltrarno (055 229 019/www. viscontirooms.it). **Rates** €46 single; €77 double. **Credit** MC, V. **Map** p314 D1.

Located in the Santo Spirito area, this small, comfortable B&B offers the experience of life in one of the city's traditional neighbourhoods.

Dei Mori

Via D Alighieri 12, Duomo & Around (055 211 438/ www.bnb.it/deimori). **Rates** €80 single; €110 double. **Credit** AmEx, DC, MC, V. **Map** p315 B4.

Friendly B&B right in the city centre.

Martindago

Via de'Macci 84, Santa Croce (055 234 1415/ www.martindago.com). **Rates** €85 single; €120 double. **Credit** AmEx, DC, MC, V. **Map** p315 C6.

Situated in the Santa Croce area, this is one of the city's most recently opened B&Bs.

Clubs

Azione Gay e Lesbica at Auditorium Flog

Via M Mercati 24B, Outside the City Gates (055 240 397). Bus 4, 8, 14, 20, 28. **Open** 10pm-3am 1 Fri per mth. **Admission** €10. **No credit cards**.

Once a month (on a Friday, call for details), a megafest of DJs, cabaret acts and bands draws a huge and diverse crowd out to this Poggetto venue in support of the Associazione Azione Gay e Lesbica. It's also a great place to get literature and information on all the latest goings-on in the local queer community.

Tabasco

Piazza Santa Cecilia 3r, Duomo & Around (055 213 000/www.tabascogay.it). **Open** 10pm-late Tue-Sun. **Admission** €13. **Credit** AmEx, MC, V. **Map** p315 C5.

As Florence's first gay club, Tabasco has stood the test of time and remains popular among both tourists and young locals of both sexes. The music is mostly techno, with some '70s-style disco thrown in here and there.

Tenax

Via Pratese 46, Outside the City Gates (055 308 160/www.tenax.org). Bus 29, 30. **Open** 10pm-4am Sat. **Closed** mid May-Sept. **Admission** €25. **Credit** AmEx, V.

Saturday nights at this trendy Peretola club go by the name of Nobody's Perfect. But, hey, that doesn't stop an international fashion crowd going all out to look absolutely flawless. Just make sure you look the part.

Queer Versilia

Along the coastal strip known as Versilia, **Viareggio** and **Torre del Lago** have long been popular with gay and lesbian tourists. They're at their busiest in the summer, when there are all kinds of events, concerts and happenings, one of which is the week-long **Friendly Versilia Mardi Gras**, held on the seafront at Torre del Lago in mid August. A real crowd-puller, it includes evening concerts, book presentations and meetings with film and theatre directors, followed by DJ music until dawn. It's organised by **Gay.it** (http://it.gay.com), the largest and most-visited gay internet site in Italy providing useful information, a calendar of daily and weekly events and a guide to the gay and lesbian scene. Below, we have listed some of the area's more popular and interesting venues.

Bar Notturno

Via Aurelia 220 (piazza del Popolo), Torre del Lago (0584 341 359). **Open** 7am-3am Wed-Fri, Mon; 7am-6am Sat, Sun. **No credit cards.**
Coffee and breakfast after all-night dancing.

Bed & Breakfast Libano

Via Tabarro 23, Torre del Lago (0584 340 631/www.bed&breakfastlibano.it). Closed Nov-Jan. **Rates** €50 single; €100 double. **No credit cards.**
Relaxed B&B situated on Puccini's lake. Booking essential in the summer. It also organises parties on the premises.

Boca Chica

Viale Europa 30, Torre del Lago (0584 350 976). **Open** 1pm-2am Tue-Sun. **Closed** 2wks Nov & Feb. **Admission** free. **Credit** MC, V.
A seafront bar with music. The garden quickly fills up with a trendy young crowd.

Freedom House

Via Fabio Filzi 53, Viareggio (0584 387 084, 333 257 8805/www.freedomhouse.interfree.it). **Rates** €55 single; €110 double. **No credit cards.**
A comfortable and welcoming B&B near the Lecciona beach.

Mamma Mia

Viale Europa 5, Torre del Lago (0584 351 111/389 626 2642/www.gay.it/mammamia). **Open** *May-Oct* 3pm-5am daily. **Admission** free. **Credit** AmEx, MC, V.
DJs play to a big and varied crowd at nightly themed parties. There's a lounge bar as well as a terrace overlooking the sea.

Voice Music Bar

Viale Margherita 61, Viareggio (0584 45814/www.galleriadeldisco.com). **Open** *Summer* 10am-2am daily. *Winter* 9.30am-2am Tue-Sun. **Admission** free. **No credit cards.**
A friendly seafront bar with an eclectic music selection – to match the very mixed crowd that frequent it.

Sauna

Florence Baths

Via Guelfa 93r, San Lorenzo (055 216 050). **Open** *Winter* 2pm-1am daily. *Summer* 3pm-1am daily. **Admission** €14. **Membership** €6 per yr. **Credit** AmEx, MC, V. **Map** p315 A4.
Italian saunas hot up late afternoon to early evening. Florence Baths offers dry sauna and steam, jacuzzi (always cold), bar, TV and private rooms. There's a very friendly mixed crowd here and the steam room is one of the best anywhere.

Tuscany

The Versilia Riviera (*see above*) is becoming something of a gay mecca, with lots of clubs and bars, but gay beaches are also numerous along the rest of the Tuscan coast. Pisa is home to many gay clubs and organisations. Other groups and bars are scattered throughout Tuscany.

Pistoia

Montecatini Terme

Corso Matteotti 121 (0572 81652/www.thermas.org). **Open** 4pm-2am Thur-Tue. **Admission** €16; ARCI membership required. **Credit** MC, V.
New, elegant sauna on two floors. Recommended.

Pisa

Absolut

Via Mossoti 10 (050 220 1262/www.absolut.gay.it). **Open** 8pm-late Tue-Sun. **No credit cards.**
Mixed high-tech DJ bar. ARCI membership required.

Sauna Siesta Club 77

Via di Porta a Mare 25-7 (050 220 0146). **Open** *Sept-May* 3pm-1am daily. *June* 6pm-1am. *July-Aug* 8.30pm-1am. **Admission** €13. **No credit cards.**
Bathhouse with sauna, steam jacuzzi, video and private rooms. ARCI membership required.

Music: Classical & Opera

Know the score.

Florence is a city with a rich musical past. In its heyday in the early 17th century and under the rule of the last Medicis it was one of the most interesting musical centres in Europe. But even before then a musical form was evolving in the city that was to have a huge impact on European music right through to the present day. In the mid 1500s the group of Florentine intellectuals known as the Florentine Camerata began experimenting with the setting of words to music, and as a result, opera was truly invented in Florence. Peri and Caccini's *Euridice*, performed in the city in 1600, is generally considered to be the first opera.

While Tuscany can hardly be called a hotbed of new music today and most of what you hear will be fairly mainstream, there's plenty going on. They like to play it straight – conservative Florentines don't take kindly to the avant-garde, especially when it comes to interpretations of their favourite operas – but Florence still has a lively classical music scene. So, if you do get a chance to go to the opera here, take it. Opera is the stuff of many an Italian soul. A performance of a Puccini or Verdi opera by a good Italian orchestra and chorus is almost always a worthwhile experience.

Although programmes suffer from the same conservatism, there's lots in the way of symphonic and chamber concerts too.

Smaller events are promoted on fly-posters and in local papers and listings magazines. From June to October there are concerts in churches, and outdoor concerts at villas, gardens and museums, some free. They're not always well advertised, but tourist offices do usually have information. For events outside Florence, *see p168*.

TICKETS

For main ticket agencies, *see p150*. Many hotels and travel agents also book tickets for the biggest venues.

Tickets for the **Teatro Comunale** can be hard to come by as many seats are taken by season ticket holders. Advance bookings for the whole year for single events open around mid September. You can book online (www.maggiofiorentino.com) up to a week before the performance. Phone bookings and credit cards are accepted. If you can't get a seat in advance, turn up on the night for the chance of a return or one of the restricted-vision seats that go on sale an hour before the start.

For chamber music concerts and Orchestra Regionale Toscana concerts, tickets are usually available on the door half an hour beforehand, but the safest plan is to go to the box office in good time with cash. Unless otherwise stated, box offices don't accept credit cards.

Benjamin Britten's *Peter Grimes* at the **Teatro del Maggio**. *See p169*.

The hills are alive...

If you are looking for classical music and opera, don't just limit your search to Florence. Particularly in the summer months, seasons of music events spring up all over the place.

Those worth looking out for include the **Estate Musicale Chigiana** series of courses and concerts in Siena and at such gorgeous venues as the abbeys of San Galgano and Sant'Antimo (July-Aug; 0577 22091); the **Tavernelle Val di Pesa** concerts at the Badia in Passignano monastery (late May; tourist office 055 807 7832); the **Barga Opera Festival** with productions of little-known operas (July-mid Aug; 0583 723 250); the **Batignano** opera festival, which promotes yet more unknown operas in a beautiful hilltop town in the Maremma (July-Aug; 0564 462 611); the **Incontri in Terra di Siena** chamber music festival based at La Foce in the Val d'Orcia (information 0578 69101/www.lafoce.com); the **Puccini Opera Festival** where several of the Lucca-born composer's favourite operas are performed on the lakeside near his villa in Torre del Lago (0584 359 322); and the **International Choral Festival** in Impruneta (June; tourist office 055 231 3729).

Local tourist offices can supply further information about these and other events. *See also p294.*

TICKET PRICES

At the Teatro Comunale, tickets for the opening night of an opera cost from €32 in the upper circle to €87 for a box or stalls seat. Repeat performances cost a little less. Symphonic concerts cost from €18 to €29 and ballets from €11 to €25. Restricted-view seats are €11.

Tickets for the Orchestra Regionale Toscana concerts at **Teatro Verdi** cost €12-€15, while the Amici della Musica series at the **Teatro della Pergola** costs €11-€20/€16-€29 Saturday/Sunday per seat. One-off concerts usually cost around €15 or less, and some outdoor events or concerts in churches are free.

Venues

Accademia Bartolomeo Cristofori

Via di Camaldoli 7r, Oltrarno (055 221 646, 4.30-7pm Mon, Wed, Thur).

Accademia Bartolomeo Cristofori is a fine private collection of early keyboard instruments, and a workshop for restoration and repair. Chamber concerts and seminars, which often feature well-known early keyboard players, are held in a beautiful little hall next door.

Chiesa Luterana

Lungarno Torrigiani 11, Oltrarno (tourist office 055 290 832). **Map** p315 D4.

Organ recitals and other chamber music, often involving early repertoire, all year. Usually free.

Scuola Musica di Fiesole

Villa la Torraccia, San Domenico, Fiesole (055 597 851). Bus 7, then 10min walk. **Open** 8.30am-8.30pm Mon-Sat. **Tickets** €3; concessions for students, OAPs.

One of Italy's most famous music schools occupies a 16th-century villa in large grounds. The annual Festa della Musica, an open house with concerts and workshops by pupils, is held on 24 June while the 'Concerti per gli Amici' series takes place in the 200-seat auditorium from September to June.

Teatro del Maggio Musicale Fiorentino

Corso Italia 16, Santa Maria Novella (055 213 535/bookings 199 109910/www.maggiofiorentino.com). **Open** *Phone bookings* 9am-9.30pm Mon-Fri; 9am-3.30pm Sat. *Box office* 10am-4.30pm Tue-Fri; 10am-1pm Sat; & 1hr before performance. **Tickets** *see above.* **Credit** AmEx, DC, MC, V.

After a period of stability and a rise in the number of young orchestra and chorus members, Florence's municipal opera house is on good form. Although there has been a shake-up in the administration recently with the arrival of the highly experienced Giorgio Von Stratten as administrator, Zubin Mehta continues in his post as principal conductor while under the direction of the enigmatic Spaniard José-Luis Basso, the chorus has hugely improved in recent years and is now among the best in Italy. When on form, the Teatro del Maggio's resident orchestra and chorus is on a level with La Scala in Milan. However, lack of funds means that big-name conductors and soloists are often padded out with mediocre unknowns who just don't get the same results. It also means that risks can't be taken in terms of repertoire. One exception to this was the outstanding production of Benjamin Britten's *Peter Grimes* in November 2002, directed by David Kneuss and conducted by Seiji Ozawa. But, still, audience numbers were disappointing.

The line-up of principal singers at the Teatro del Maggio isn't usually star-studded, but emerging talents often get breaks here. And there's the odd diva. A word of warning: check your programme to make sure you won't be watching the potentially mediocre B-listers, which in some productions are alternated with the A-list of big names. The theatre's performing year is divided roughly into three parts: January to March is the concert season, with a new programme weekly; October to December is the opera and ballet season, with about four operatic productions, a couple of ballets and the odd concert; and the Maggio Musicale Fiorentino festival (founded in 1933 and one of the oldest in Europe; *see p152*) runs for two months from late April/early May. The latter offers a mix of opera, ballet, concerts and recital programmes, generally with a theme, and culminates in two free open-air jamborees held in piazza della Signoria.

The building itself, constructed in 1882 and renovated in 1957, is architecturally unexciting. Of the 2,000 seats, the best acoustics are to be had in the second gallery (they are also the cheapest), but if you want to mix with the designer-clad clothes horses of *Firenze per bene*, you need to fork out for an opening night in the stalls or one of the *palchi* (boxes).

Teatro della Pergola

Via della Pergola 12-32, San Marco (055 226 4316). **Open** *Box office* 9.30am-1pm, 3.30-6.45pm Tue-Sat; 10am-12.15pm Sun. **Season** Oct-Apr. **Credit** AmEx, DC, MC, V. **Map** p315 A5/B5.

Set up in 1656, the exquisite and intimate Pergola is one of Italy's oldest theatres. Richly decorated in red and gold and with three layers of boxes, it's ideal for chamber music and small-scale operas. Most of the Amici della Musica chamber concerts (*see below*) are held here, while the Teatro Comunale also uses it for opera during the Maggio festival *(see p186*).

Teatro Goldoni

Via Santa Maria 15, Oltrarno (055 210 804/ Teatro Comunale 055 211 158). **Open** *Box office* 1hr before performance. **Map** p314 D1.

This divine little theatre in the heart of the Oltrarno dates from the early 18th century and seats only 400 people. A long-drawn-out restoration was finally finished in the late 1990s and it is now under the direction of the Teatro del Maggio. It's used – though not regularly enough – for chamber music, small-scale opera and ballet.

Teatro Verdi

Via Ghibellina 99, Santa Croce (055 212 320/ www.teatroverdifirenze.it). **Open** *Box office* 10am-1pm, 3-7pm Mon-Fri. **Season** Sept-June. **Map** p315 C4/5/6.

A large theatre and Florence's regular venue for the Orchestra della Toscana.

Tempo Reale

La Limonaia di Villa Strozzi, Via Pisana 77, Outside the City Gates (055 717 270/www.centrotempo reale.it). Bus 6, 12, 13, 26, 27, 80.

This centre for contemporary music in Monte Uliveto places an emphasis on music technology. Concerts, workshops and seminars are held.

Performance groups/ promoters

Amici della Musica

055 608 420/607 440/www.amicimusica.fi.it.

An organisation promoting world-class chamber music concerts, most presented at the Teatro della Pergola, from September through to late April/early May. The year's programme will include some of the world's great string quartets and recitalists; early music groups appear regularly too. Concerts are usually on Saturday and Sunday at 4pm or 9pm.

L'Homme Arm

Tel/fax 055 695 000.

A small, semi-professional chamber choir whose repertoire ranges from medieval to baroque. It gives about ten concerts a year in Florence and regularly runs excellent courses on aspects of early music.

Orchestra da Camera Fiorentina

055 783 374/www.orcafi.it.

This young chamber orchestra under the direction of violinist Giuseppe Lanzetta plays a season of mostly baroque and classical concerts from February to September, with a break in August. Standards are mixed.

Orchestra della Toscana

055 281 792/www.orchestradellatoscana.it.

This 40-strong chamber orchestra was founded in 1980 with the brief of taking classical music into Tuscany. During the season (November/December-May) it gives two or three concerts a month in Florence at the Teatro Verdi, and 35 to 40 in other Tuscan towns. The management, artistic director and musicians are all relatively young. This is reflected in the creative programming, which covers everything from baroque to modern, though the emphasis is on 19th-century works. International names frequently appear as soloists and conductors.

Music: Rock, Roots & Jazz

From roots and blues to the ones and the twos.

Florence has enjoyed a musical explosion in the last decade and a number of producers have sprung up in the area and are contributing to what is now a thriving local, and global, scene. Cult and mainstream bands have also cottoned on to locals' desire for bigger and better live music programming, with the result that the city has become a regular on the tour itinerary of many big names and has even featured as one of the only stopoffs for some – a compliment normally only paid to Rome or Milan. The local music scene can also be a vehicle to greater things. A number of Florentines have made the jump from DJ to producer, including local legend Stefano Noferini (he still often plays sets in the city) along with Francesco Farfa and Alex Neri, who are both from the new breed of DJs in the area. While pioneering their own production style for record labels including the Tuscany-based Stella Recordings, they also DJ regularly in Tenax, the best-known dance club in the city (*see p173*). Live jazz too, in all its incarnations, is having its heyday in the city with new bars springing up and offering weekly or even nightly sessions.

The city perks up still further from June to September with open-air stages playing to crowds sipping cocktails as the sun goes down. Especially noteworthy are the Jazz&Co nightly live jazz sounds in piazza Santissima Annunziata and the Rime Rampanti series at piazza Poggi, with its mix of sounds and views over the Arno (for both, *see p179* **In the heat of the night**).

To book tickets for concerts, either call the venue direct or contact the box office.

Astor Caffè

Piazza del Duomo 20r, Duomo & Around (055 239 9000). **Open** 10am-3am Mon-Sat; 5pm-3am Sun. **Admission** free. **Credit** MC, V. **Map** p315 B4.

The downstairs to this sparkling red and chrome bar hosts live music nights with variations through the jazzy spectrum, from Latin and laid-back to bossanova to blues.

Auditorium Flog

Via M Mercati 24B, Outside the City Gates (055 487 145/www.flog.it). Bus 4, 8, 14, 20, 28. **Open** 10pm-late Tue-Sat (call for details). Closed June-Aug. **Admission** €8-€13. **No credit cards.**

Flog hosts concerts every Thursday, Friday and Saturday night, with Friday often dedicated to reggae and ska. On a good night, the place (though not always great acoustically) can definitely be fun. Flog serves up a medley of genres from hard rock and funk/R&B to Tex Mex. Enthused crowds keep on dancing after the concerts wind down, when a DJ usually takes over the helm. Keep an eye out early in the week for themed dance parties and other theatrical showcases as Flog expands its repertoire. It also hosts the excellent world music festival, the Rassegna Internazionale Musica dei Popoli, in November (*see p156*).

Be Bop

Via dei Servi, San Marco (no phone). **Open** times vary, usually 6pm-1am daily. **Admission** free. **No credit cards. Map** p315 A4.

Like many clubs in the city centre, Be Bop is a sweaty, windowless underground cave. It attracts a brat pack of foreign students plus a handful of brooding arty types. The varied music is rarely original. You might encounter a band doing Beatles covers or old blues standards, or else a motley crew of Italian wannabe Rastafarians muddling their way through a set of reggae classics. Drinks are expensive, but on Mondays, when many other clubs are closed, there's a free shot with every beer.

BZF (Bizzeffe)

Via Panicale 61r, San Lorenzo (055 274 1009/ www.bzf.it). **Open** noon-midnight Tue-Sun. **Admission** free; minimum drinks €9. **Credit** MC, V. **Map** p315 A3.

Every Tuesday and many Fridays there's live jazz at this stunning new mix 'n' match venue of bar, restaurant, internet point, art space and bookshop in the converted convent of San Barnaba. Thanks to the vaulted ceilings, the acoustics are spot-on. There's also a world food buffet on hand, which appeals to the thirtysomething clientele.

Caffè la Torre

Lungarno Cellini 65r, Oltrarno (055 680 643/ www.caffelatorre.it). **Open** 10.30am-3am daily. **Admission** free. **Credit** AmEx, DC, MC, V. **Map** p315 D6.

A well-known local hangout for an aperitif and late-night snack, this small riverside café has nightly live music ranging from polka to spicy Brazilian beats. *See also p177.*

Always crowded, rarely original: **Be Bop**. *See p170.*

Eskimo

Via dei Canacci 12, Santa Maria Novella (no phone). **Open** 6pm-4am daily. **Admission** €6 annual membership. **No credit cards. Map** p314 A1/B1.

Communal wooden tables burst with Italian university students at this tiny joint with its amateur art and open mike. Its back-alley entrance and cheap beer conjure up images of an old speakeasy and it's a gem if you're looking for a taste of the student music scene. It's hard to resist swaying with the exuberant crowd as local groups jam to the accompaniment of jolly, Santa Claus-like owner Lalo on the piano. There's live music at about 11pm every night, from jazz, blues and Neapolitan to staple rock cover bands. Happy hour is 6-9pm.

Girasol

Via del Romito 1, Outside the City Gates (055 474 948). Bus 14. **Open** 8pm-2.30am Tue-Sun. **Admission** free. **No credit cards.**

Trying its best to be a Little Havana, complete with fake palm trees, Girasol is the place for live Latin sounds. Dim lighting and flamboyantly fruity cocktails transport you far from the incessant buzz of Florentine scooters. However, while the Cuban, Brazilian, rumba, flamenco, Caribbean and Latin jazz rhythms tempt you to your feet, there's scant space for you to get your swerve on. Drink prices are a bit steep but include admission. Crowds start arriving around 11pm, so aim for 10pm to be sure of a table.

Jazz Club

Via Nuova de' Caccini 3, Santa Croce (055 247 9700). **Open** 9pm-2am Mon-Fri; 9pm-2.30am Sat. Closed Aug. **Admission** €3 visitor membership; €7 annual membership. **No credit cards. Map** p315 B5.

One of the few places in Florence where you can hear live jazz regularly, this sophisticated basement venue is popular with large groups of thirtysomethings and beatniks, though there are a few smaller tables for more intimate conversations. Live performers range from traditional bands to smoky fusion and contemporary experimental groups, with other evenings dedicated to musical styles such as blues, Latin, folk and flamenco. Further novelties are a big band on Thursdays and the Jazz Club Gospel choir two Sundays a month. On Tuesday nights there's an open, and free, jamming session. Cocktails average €6.20, beer €4.50.

Loonees

Via Porta Rossa 15r, Duomo & Around (055 212 249). **Open** 8pm-3am Tue-Sun. Closed Aug. **Admission** free. **No credit cards. Map** p314 C3.

Loonees brims with a mixed crowd of tipsy foreign students, random punters and locals out on the pull. Crowds are usually elbow to elbow by 11pm, to sounds ranging from reggae and funk to rock covers and Italian pop. Two easily accessible bars offer free shots with every beer, which may help to assuage those with a more critical ear. The vaulted ceiling captures the sound nicely, although it does make conversation virtually impossible. Depending on the night, you may find room to dance in front of the stage. On Saturdays you can catch bluesman Jeff Jones, whose smooth tunes have earned him a following. Beer is €4, a spirit with mixer about €6, and there's a two-for-one happy hour every night (8-10pm).

Palasport

Viale Paoli, Outside the City Gates (055 678 841). Bus 3. **Open** *Box office* 8am-8pm Mon-Fri; 8am-2pm Sat. **Tickets** prices vary. **No credit cards.**

The big international names make tour stops at this expansive arena, and international headliners sell out fast despite a decent seating capacity of about 7,000. The majority of concerts at Palasport

Plastic people

One of the best ways to find out the latest news of happenings and events in the local rock, roots, jazz, indie and dance music scenes is to drop into one of Florence's record shops. This is where you will find the beating heart of the city's dance music scene (many shops are owned by big-name local DJs), along with flyers promoting various upcoming gigs, festivals and events.

For all flavours of house, techno and drum 'n' bass, head to **Frequenze** (viale Guidoni 85C, 055 412 841) or to **Disco Smile** (viale Don Minzoni 44, 055 587 500), purveyors of quality jungle, garage and trip hop. **Black Out** (via Maccari 133-5, 055 733 0056) is another port of call for those in search of cutting-edge house sounds, drum 'n' bass and hip hop. In the centre of town **Disco Mastelloni** (piazza del Mercato Centrale 21r, 055 215 365) specialises in techno and trance. **Galleria del Disco** (piazza Stazione 14, in the underpass, 055 211 319) is a hothouse for hip hop, R&B, rap and house, and also sells tickets for gigs at Tenax (*see p173*), while **Fish** (via Allori 42, 055 410 447) peddles deep house and specialist drum 'n' bass.

For the really obscure, **Data Records** (via dei Neri 15r, 055 287 592) has 80,000 titles, mainly soundtracks, psychedelia and R&B, and specialises in finding the unfindable. Jazz lovers should make for **Dischi Fenice** (via Santa Reparata 8, 055 238 1880) or the new specialist jazz music centre **Twisted** (borgo San Frediano 21r, 055 282 011). Otherwise, **Alberti Dischi** (borgo San Lorenzo 45r, 055 294 271), the oldest record shop in Florence, has a vast repertoire of pop, dance, jazz and indie recordings, and promotes regular nights at Negroni (*see p180*).

Groove Armada rock **Stazione Leopolda**.

showcase Italian commercial pop stars such as Alex Britti and Eros Ramozzotti, but Bruce Springsteen, Elton John and Peter Gabriel have all played here. Try to avoid the area left of the stage if possible, since it has a limited view of the action.

Pinocchio Jazz

Viale Giannotti 13, Outside the City Gates (055 680 362/683 388/www.pinocchiojazz.it). Bus 23 to Piazza Gavinana. **Open** Sat only 9.30pm-2am. Closed May-Oct. **Tickets** €7.50. **No credit cards**.

Situated in the south-east corner of the city, this venue books recognisable international names as well as Italian artists, covering a variety of musical styles, including big band, traditional Tuscan folk, blues, Latin, experimental and classical jazz. As a venue, it lacks cosiness and atmosphere but the quality acts and friendly staff make up for this. A mellow, older set tends to fill up the small, amphitheatre-like stage area at around 9.30pm. Call for concert information or check the well-circulated flyers.

Saschall-Teatro di Firenze

Lungarno A Moro 3, Outside the City Gates (055 650 4112/www.saschall.it). Bus 14. **Tickets** prices vary. **No credit cards**.

The first-choice venue for many major mainstream bands and recently packed to the gills by Morcheeba, David Gray and the darling of Italian teeny-boppers, Cesare Cremonini. The upper balconies have seating, but the acoustics are decidedly better in the downstairs hall.

Sala Vanni

Piazza del Carmine 14, Oltrarno (055 287 347/ www.musicusconcentus.com). **Open** times vary. **Admission** €12. **No credit cards**. **Map** p314 C1.

This large warehouse-like auditorium is by far the best place in town to hear good progressive jazz, showcasing an excellent series of concerts organised by Musicus Concentus throughout the year.

Stazione Leopolda

Fratelli Rosselli 5, Outside the City Gates (055 263 8480/248 0515). Bus 17, 22. **Tickets** prices vary. **Credit** MC, V.

This huge disused railway station beloved of street-chic designers for their catwalk shows is also one of the top venues in town for big dance-scene bands. Massive Attack played their New Year's Eve 2002 set here and Groove Armada followed with a sell-out gig in 2003. The Fabbrica Europa contemporary performing arts festival is held here every year.

Tenax

Via Pratese 46, Outside the City Gates (055 308 160/www.tenax.org). Bus 29, 30. **Open** 10.30pm-4am Thur-Sat. Closed mid May-Sept. **Admission** varies. **Credit** AmEx, MC, V.

The hip and happening Tenax offers a healthy stew of acts, from international artists as varied as Tori Amos and Radiohead to Italian rock favourites such as Ligabue and Hooverphonic. Bands touring Italy, but who are not big enough to fill the arenas, often stop off here and the organisers sometimes pull off real coups in bringing tour-shy bands to the club – Thievery Corporation being one of the latest. The spacious club boasts an enormous raised dancefloor and antechambers stuffed with computers, pool tables and bars. Upstairs are more bars, sofas and café-style seating areas with balconies to watch the action below. *See also p176.*

Universale

Via Pisana 77r, Outside the City Gates (055 221 122/www.universalefirenze.it). Bus 6. **Open** 7pm-3am daily. Closed June-Sept. **Admission** €7-€18 incl 1st drink. **Credit** AmEx, MC, V.

Live music sets often warm up the crowd in this stunning converted cinema. The tone can swing from progressive piano jazz, to urban funk bands, depending on the night's DJ set. *See also p176.*

Nightlife

Dress up and get down.

Florence's eagerness to protect its reputation as an aesthete's paradise even extends obligingly to its nightlife. There are clubs in Renaissance *palazzi* and lush bars on riverbanks, in gardens by medieval towers or overlooking world-famous monuments. Even the underground venues have been treated to the designer touch, with state-of-the-art lighting and decor, and an ultra style-conscious clientele to boot. Favourite evening pastimes are as faddy as the must-wear fashions of the punters. The hip nightlife routes of the moment are the *aperitivo* crawl (*see p128* **Bar bites**) followed by cocktail hour (*see p177* **Cocktail classics**) and, for big nights out, a stagger on to the club scene.

Most clubs have replaced entrance fees with a card system. You're given a card that's stamped whenever you buy drinks or use the cloakroom. You then hand the card in at the till and pay before leaving (usually there's a minimum cost that includes the first drink).

Opening times and closing days of bars and clubs are notoriously vague and erratic, and phones that are answered are the exception. So be prepared to take a chance. Musical genres often vary with the day of the week – check fliers or *Firenze Spettacolo* for information.

Clubs

Central Park

Via Fosso Macinante 2, Outside the City Gates (055 353 505). Bus 1, 9, 26. **Open** *Summer* 11pm-4am Tue-Sat. *Winter* 11pm-4am Fri, Sat. **Admission** €20 (incl 1st drink). **Credit** AmEx, DC, MC, V.

Central Park comes into its own in summer, when it becomes L'Isola che C'e, a desert island complete with bamboo, palm trees and love-starved Man Fridays. Desert Island Discs consist of deep house classics, techno, mediocre live acts or commercial hits depending on which of the four music zones you wash up on. Thursdays (featuring some of the best drum 'n' bass in Italy) and Fridays are usually good bets, but Saturdays cater to the influx of out-of-towners when the hip crowd heads to the beach. It can be worth the trek in winter if you're up for a big night out. The card system can be excruciating when you leave (the queue for the till is huge). Drinks cost €8.

Dolce Zucchero

Via Pandolfini 26r, Santa Croce (055 243 356). **Open** 11pm-4am Tue-Sun. Closed June-Sept. **Admission** free before midnight. **Credit** AmEx, MC, V. **Map** p315 C5.

Even the hippest Florentines sometimes throw caution to the wind and head for this, the most central pure-breed disco in town and a monument to cheesy fun. You may get '70s, '80s, or even '90s Italian sounds, just don't expect to hear anything progressive. Fine for a good old-fashioned boogie, though.

ExMud

Corso dei Tintori 4, Santa Croce (055 263 8583/ www.exmud.it). **Open** 11.30pm-4am Tue-Sun. **Admission** €9-€12 (incl first drink). **Credit** AmEx, MC, V. **Map** p315 C5.

In the labyrinthine basement of the much-loved defunct nightspot the Mood, ExMud tries to emulate the success of its predecessor with mixed results. On a good night (Saturday can hit the right note) the place is rocking, with international DJs spinning house and garage, drum 'n' bass or liquid funk, and the floor-lit corridor to the sweaty dancefloor packed with a young cosmopolitan crowd. Hit less lucky and you get hard-core electronica *all'Italiana*.

Full-Up

Via della Vigna Vecchia 25r, Santa Croce (055 293 006). **Open** 11pm-4am Tue-Sat. Closed June-Sept. **Admission** free; €10 after midnight (incl 1st drink). **Credit** AmEx, MC, V. **Map** p315 C4.

A long-running temple to kitsch and a smoothie's paradise, Full-Up is generally full of sugar daddies sitting round the roulette and miniskirted models looking for a Mercedes ride home. Wednesdays have always been the exception to the steer-clear rule, though, with cool if flash Florentines enjoying funky house. Avoid Thursdays and Fridays at all costs when it's the very iffy American Sound and Lolly Pop Party. Drinks cost €7 on average.

H2O2

Via Pandolfini 26r, Santa Croce (055 243 356). **Open** 11pm-4am Tue-Sun. Closed June-Sept. **Admission** free before midnight. **Credit** AmEx, MC, V. **Map** p315 C5.

Currently experiencing a purple patch in its long history, H2O2 is now packed most nights with a local and international student crowd. Midweek music is mostly dub and breakbeat, weekends techno house, and Sundays see live acts in the cramped dancefloor area, but anytime it all gets too much you can head upstairs to the cinema screen of the video chill-out lounge.

Maracana Casa di Samba

Via Faenza 4, San Lorenzo (055 210 298). **Open** *Club* midnight-4am Tue-Sun. *Restaurant* 8.30-11.30pm Tue-Sun. Closed June-Aug. **Admission** €10-€20. **Credit** (restaurant only) AmEx, DC, JCB, MC, V. **Map** p314 A3.

Crowd control at **Yab**. *See p176.*

Give this place a wide berth if you can't stomach middle-aged suits dribbling lecherously over wiggling Brazilian booties – after the restaurant stops serving South American fare to mop up the long drinks, all decorum is shed. The central dancefloor is surrounded by poseur platforms and the balconies assure views of cleavages and bald patches. Exhibitionists will love the video cameras freeze-framing shots of themselves on the huge screen. Bottled beers and spirits cost €7, draught beer is €6.

Maramao

Via dei Macci 79r, Santa Croce (055 244 341). **Open** 11pm-3am Tue-Sat. Closed May-Sept. **Admission** €15-€20 (incl 1st drink). **Credit** AmEx, DC, MC, V. **Map** p315 C6.

Maramao's famously tight door policy can make the wait to get in on busy nights seem quite a lot less than worthwhile. However, on a good night it still can't be beaten, with a heady mix of (refreshingly unleery) camaraderie and fine tunes that touch all points of the spectrum from house anthems and hip hop to St Germain-style jazzy beats. But, whatever you do, don't turn up on one of the lacklustre hard house nights. On average, drinks cost €6.

Rio Grande

Viale degli Olmi 1, Outside the City Gates (055 331 371/www.rio-grande.it). Bus 1, 9, 16, 26, 27. **Open** *Summer* 11.30pm-4am Tue-Sat. *Winter* 11.30pm-4am Mon-Sat. **Admission** €8-€20 (incl 1st drink). **Credit** AmEx, DC, MC, V.

Rio Grande caters to the masses, who come out in force to play in its theme-park atmosphere. It's easy to play hide-and-seek in the labyrinthine tangle of bars and dancefloors, especially when the garden opens in summer, adding a fourth bar and dance area. Music is mostly Latin, commercial party and trashy pop, but there's often a sprinkling of hip hop and funky house. Drinks cost €6-€8.

Tenax

Via Pratese 46, Outside the City Gates (055 308 160/www.tenax.org). Bus 29, 30. **Open** 10.30pm-4am Thur-Sat & for gigs. Closed mid May-Sept. **Admission** €10-€15. **Credit** AmEx, MC, V.

The most warehousey of the Florentine clubs, Tenax has long held the record for best-known local nightspot, especially as a live venue for hip international bands and for its DJ exchanges with big-name London clubs – Pacha is the latest. Nobody's Perfect on Saturday is the hottest night in the city by a long way, heaving with house, big beat, progressive or drum 'n' bass, depending on the one-nighter DJ. Notable recent visits have been from spin-meisters Roger Sanchez and Bob Sinclair.

Universale

Via Pisana 77r, Outside the City Gates (055 221 122/www.universalefirenze.it). Bus 6. **Open** 7.30pm-3am. *Restaurant* 7.30pm-midnight Wed-Sun. Closed June-Sept. **Admission** €7-€18 (incl first drink). **Credit** AmEx, MC, V.

A visually stunning club, fittingly converted from a 1950s cinema, Universale is pure heaven for those who've grown tired of traipsing from one Florentine hotspot to another. It's an all-round emporium of entertainment with restaurant, bar, video screen and club areas with regular live jazzy music sessions handing over to DJs as the night wears on. Restaurant-goers can peer over the balustrade of the magnificent double curved *Gone with the Wind* staircases towards a flash central oval bar.

XO Disco

Via Verdi 57r, Santa Croce (055 234 1529). **Open** 10pm-3am Mon-Sat. Closed June-Sept. **Admission** €10-€15 (incl 1st drink). **No credit cards. Map** p315 C5.

This sprawling bar and club, the latest incarnation of a long-running venue, opens out on to the main street, its red hues casting a warm glow over the fresh-faced twentysomethings who lounge at the chrome tables in full view of passing traffic. Inside, a friendly mixed crowd hits the dance floor to a selection of mainstream, predominantly housey sounds (Saturday sets can be a little more adventurous). If you do not have fond memories of school discos, be sure not to venture in here on a Wednesday night. Drinks cost between €6 and €8.

Yab

Via Sassetti 5r, Duomo & Around (055 215 160). **Open** 9pm-4am Mon, Tue, Thur-Sat. Closed June-Sept. **Admission** free (€15 drinks minimum Fri, Sat). **Credit** AmEx, DC, V. **Map** p314 B3.

Mondays at Yab are an institution among certain older Florentines – the average age of the punters goes up each year. Yab's freshest novelty is the buffet dinner (€15), while the powerful sound system still has the mammoth dancefloor shimmying with fortysomething dancers, while wall-to-wall bar areas on raised platforms cater to those with tired feet. Thursdays play deep house, with a younger crowd letting it all hang out. The door policy can be heavy-handed if you're not a regular. Drinks average €7.

Pubs & bars

Apollo

Via dell'Ariento 41r, San Lorenzo (055 215 672). **Open** 10am-3pm, 6.30pm-3am Tue-Thur; noon-3pm, 6.30pm-3am Fri; noon-3pm, 4.30pm-3am Sat; noon-3pm, 9pm-3am Sun. Closed 2wks Aug. **Credit** AmEx, DC, MC, V. **Map** p314 A3.

A pulsating, late-opening bar, brimming with see-and-be-seen Italians. On Fridays and Saturdays by 11.30pm the bar is bursting at the seams, all conversation drowned out by the thumping bassy tunes of DJ Marco, whose decks appear as if by magic, when the banquet of aperitif snacks has disappeared. Midweek is marginally calmer.

Art Bar

Via del Moro 4r, Santa Maria Novella (055 287 661). **Open** 7pm-1am Mon-Sat. Closed 3wks Aug. **No credit cards. Map** p314 B2.

Battered French horns hanging from the ceiling and sepia photographs of blues and jazz musicians lend a beatnik air to this perennially popular bar. The ambience is cosy but animated, with student types holed up in the brick cellar sipping their potent Pina Coladas. Drinks cost €4 at happy hour (7-9pm), then beer is €5 and cocktails start at €7.

Astor Caffè

Piazza Duomo 20r, Duomo & Around (055 239 9000). **Open** 7.30am-1am Mon-Sat; 5pm-3am Sun. **Credit** MC, V. **Map** p315 B4.

This huge, lively jazz bar with soft red lighting, a flash chrome bar and regular art exhibitions is pepping up central Florence nights with live and DJ-piped dance-jazz played to an enthusiastic young crowd. Internet points provide distraction from the busy socialising under the skylight of the main bar. Happy hour is 6-10pm.

Cabiria

Piazza Santo Spirito 4r, Oltrarno (055 215 732). **Open** 8am-1am Mon, Wed-Thur; 8am-1.30am Fri-Sun. **No credit cards. Map** p314 D2.

The grungiest of the pre-club bars with a crowd that often overflows past the outside seating into the square and sometimes ends up in drunken heaps on the steps of nearby Santo Spirito. Inside, the principal congregating area is in the micro corridor alongside the bar, which leads into a back room where DJs start up at around 9pm and blast out anything from reggae to jazz. Beers cost €4, a gin and tonic is €5.

Cocktail classics

In the fickle world of Florentine nightlife and feeding habits the goalposts have been shifted by the huge success of the *aperitivo* phenomenon (*see p128* **Bar bites**). Going for a blow-out meal after the freebie so-called snacks (some are more *Babette's Feast* than bowl of olives and filberts) is just not an option. Many of the new breed of restaurant have cottoned on to this and now cover all the options by turning themselves into hybrid restaurant-bars with some setting aside an area for after-dinner drinks and lazy cocktails,while others stay open for drinks long after the kitchens close.

Moorish meets metropolitan slick in the Moroccan bar of the Mediterranean restaurant **Finisterrae** (*see p115*), where the barman will mix you up a surprise cocktail concoction. Ask for the dangerously refreshing house special with absinthe and fresh mint. Twinkling lanterns and dark wood give an authentic taste of modern Marrakesh mixed with Parisian chic, to the background sounds of Buddha Bar-style beats, in the newly opened **Sèsame** (via delle Conce 20r, 055 200 1381), where a row of long low tables leads to the delightful garden and roof terrace with a view of the city.

Minimalism has suddenly landed in the Renaissance capital, and there's nowhere better to see it than in the white temple of the bar at hip-chic **Angels** (via del Proconsolo 29-31r, 055 239 8762), which arguably serves the best cocktails in town, alongside refined Tuscan cuisine in its colonnaded dining room. It does a mean Cosmopolitan. Mixing minimalism with neo-classical cool, the people-watching paradise **Zona 15** (*see p130*) has a list of 80 cocktails to work your way through, while the fashionistas' favourite haunt, the Ferragamo-owned **Fusion Bar Shozan** (*see p127*), is also a strong contender for the best cocktail crown. Don't miss the Sakèpirina (saké, gin, lime juice and fruit). For something more laid-back, head to **Rose's** (*see 130*), where bar staff will shake you up a Caipirina or Caipiroska in the mellow surroundings of the bar beside the sushi restaurant. Incurable romantics should cross the river to **Il Caffè** (piazza Pitti 9r, 055 239 9863), the restaurant shrine to the aphrodisiac truffle, where you can sip demurely on a Between the Sheets at a candlelit table overlooking the imposing edifice of the Pitti Palace.

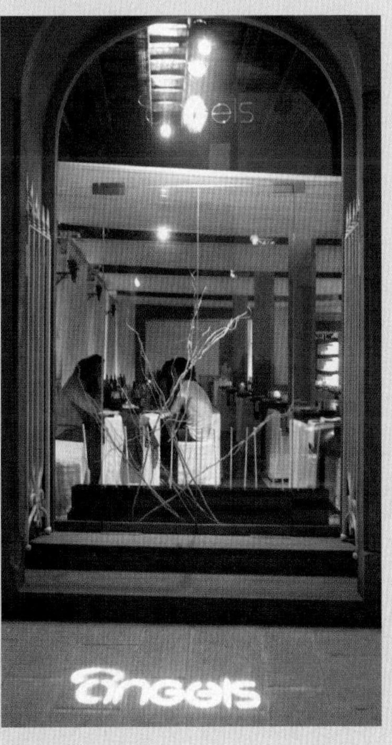

Caffè la Torre

Lungarno Cellini 65r, Oltrarno (055 680 643/ www.caffelatorre.it). **Open** 10.30am-3am daily. **Credit** AmEx, DC, MC, V. **Map** p315 D6.

Follow the river to this nice 'n' easy bar. The post-clubbing music is mercifully mellow, but if you make it here earlier you can sway in a dignified and gentle manner to the foot-tapping tunes of the various (almost) nightly live acts. Beer is €3.50 before 6.30pm, €4.50 thereafter; tapas and *tortellini* are served to late munchers.

Capocaccia

Lungarno Corsini 12-14r, Santa Maria Novella (055 210 751). **Open** noon-2am Tue-Sun. **Credit** MC, V. **Map** p314 C2.

Busy most nights of the year, but heaving in summer when you can join half the population of cool Florence outside blocking the traffic, Capocaccia is the most delightfully atmospheric of Florence's evening bars. It also fits the bill for all moods. Sit in the packed bar room people-watching and nursing a cocktail, or dig the clubby atmosphere with the DJ set pumping out Latin jazz and big beats in the central bar room. Otherwise, you can just chill out in the amazing frescoed salon. *See also p129.*

Dolce Vita

Piazza del Carmine, Oltrarno (055 284 595/ www.dolcevitafirenze.it). **Open** *Summer* 10am-2am daily. *Winter* 6pm-2am Tue-Sun. *Restaurant* 12.30-3pm, 7.30-11.30pm Mon-Sat. **Credit** AmEx, DC, JCB, MC, V. **Map** p314 C2.

Dolce Vita has stood the test of time to remain Florence's number one wannabe bar. The interior, with its sofas and beautiful crystal lamps, is much less popular than the outside meeting area – to the point that neighbours have invested in soundproof windows. If you ever make it as far as the impossibly busy bar, a beer is €2.50 (€4 seated), while a gin and tonic costs €6 (€7 seated). *See also p131.*

Fiddler's Elbow

Piazza Santa Maria Novella 7r, Santa Maria Novella (055 215 056/www.thefiddlerselbow.com). **Open** noon-1am Mon-Thur; noon-2am Fri; 2pm-2am Sat; 2pm-1am Sun. **No credit cards**. **Map** p314 B2.

Come here for the draught beers, the satellite TV showing sports on request or the international company. But most of all come here for the rare (in

Slowly does it. *See p180.*

In the heat of the night

The torrid summer months mean Florentine nightlife shifts from the crowded, overheated underground clubs to outdoor venues in piazzas, gardens and villas, all giving free admission and staying open until well into the small hours.

Vie di Fuga at Le Murate (via dell'Agnolo, 0338 506 0253), the coolest of the summer bars in the kooky setting of a former prison, has a dancefloor, pizzeria and even a cinema three nights a week. It also hosts concerts, theatre and dance events. The two main summer venues are **Parterre** (piazza della Libertà, no phone), a huge indoor and outdoor bar, club and gig venue, and the **Anfiteatro Parco delle Cascine**, which is something of a small festival site with concerts most evenings, followed by a dance-till-dawn disco. But permission from the council for both sites is a recurring problem so check local press, or *Firenze Spettacolo* for the annual decision.

For riverside seats, head for **Teatro sull'Acqua** (lungarno Pecori Giraldi, 055 234 3460) or **Lido** (*see below*), sprawling bar-cum-clubs right on the riverbank. Street bars are also a hot summer phenomenon. **Le Rime Rampanti** (open 7pm-1am Tue-Sat) overlooks the river on the terraces above piazza Poggi and has live bands and a bar, while **piazza Santo Spirito** comes alive with nightly live music, dance and theatre. For free jazz, **Jazz&Co** (www.firenzejazz. it) has live acts and a bar against the charming backdrop of piazza Santissima Annunziata.

Florence) pub commodity of pleasant outdoor seating, which is certainly worth foregoing a happy hour for on hot nights. Beer is €4, gin and tonic €4.

James Joyce

Lungarno B Cellini 1r, Oltrarno (055 658 0856). **Open** 6pm-2am Mon-Thur; 6pm-3am Fri-Sun. **No credit cards.**

The best of Florence's pubs in spring and summer, thanks to its large enclosed garden with long wooden tables, JJ has a high-spirited vibe. Happy hour, when drinks (beer €4.50, G&T €5) come with free snacks, lasts till 9.30pm. There's a small bookshop selling paperbacks, some in English. Closes early on Sunday in winter.

JJ Cathedral Pub

Piazza San Giovanni 44r, Duomo & Around (055 280 260). **Open** 10am-2.30am daily. **Credit** AmEx, DC, MC, V. **Map** p314 B3.

When this authentic Irish pub opens there's always a frantic scrabble to get to the most coveted drinking table in the city on the tiny Juliet balcony overlooking the 11th-century Baptistery. If you're thwarted in your aim, drown your sorrows with a Guinness at one of the nearby tables, to the occasional sound of fiddled jigs, or settle on a downstairs bar stool with a Beamish (€4.50 a pint) and expose yourself to an earful of the Corrs.

Lido

Lungarno Pecori Giraldi 1r, Santa Croce (055 234 2726). Bus 12, 13, 14, 71. **Open** 12.30pm-2am Tue-Sat; 1pm-2am Sun. Lunch served 1-3pm daily. Closed Jan & Feb. **Admission** free. **No credit cards.**

Large glass doors open from this bar to a garden that extends down to the riverbank, making it a good bet for hot summer nights, when queues inevitably form. The music is a thumping collection of drum 'n' bass, R&B and the like, though the dancefloor is entirely taken up by the queue for the bar. Fridays are stomping deep house. Come early if you want to hire a boat for a quick punt (€8 an hour). Beer is €4, long drinks €6.

Loonees

Via Porta Rossa 15r, Duomo & Around (055 212 249). **Open** 8pm-3am Tue-Sun. Closed Aug. **Admission** free. **No credit cards. Map** p314 C3.

Hugely popular with US students, who queue en masse to get in, this mainly live music bar has a relaxed atmosphere that's partly due to the loud music, which leaves punters with little to do but sway and take advantage of the free shot with every pint. A beer costs €4.50, a gin and tonic is €6.

Mayday Lounge Café

Via Dante Alighieri 16r, Duomo & Around (055 238 1290). **Open** 8pm-2am Mon-Sat. Closed 2wks Aug. **Admission** free, but membership required. **No credit cards. Map** p315 B4.

The wackiest joint in town, Mayday is dark and smoky, dotted with odd art installations and hung with hundreds of old Marconi radios. The owners gleefully admit they make up the next evening's events as they go along, the only constant being a jazzy edge to the sounds. So a visit could coincide with anything from a 'Japanese porn' night (complete with kinky-shaped sushi), a nu-jazz karaoke night or a jamming session from a visiting band.

Montecarla

Via dei Bardi 2, Oltrarno (055 234 0259). **Open** 10pm-5am daily. **Admission** free. **No credit cards. Map** p315 D4.

Montecarla's reputation is built on Chinese whispers; the chief rumour is that it was once a brothel (it wasn't, but its low-slung leopard-skin couches, hidden recesses and oriental drapery encourage the fantasy). Soft background music plays, a pile of board games is on hand and service is conspiratorial and intimate. The drinks, which are mainly cocktails, come in monster measures; the house special is Montecarla (gin, rum, Cointreau and orange). Non-alcoholic drinks cost €6, others are €7.

Negroni

Via dei Renai 17r, Oltrarno (055 243 647/ www.negronibar.com). **Open** 8am-2.30am Mon-Sat; 6pm-2am Sun. Closed 2wks Aug. **Credit** MC, V. **Map** p315 D5.

Risen from the ashes of the famous bar Amici Miei, which inspired a '70s cult film, and named after Mr Negroni himself, who sat at a bar here and invented the Negroni (gin, red vermouth, Campari), this is the hippest and coolest of the rash of newly opened bars. The streamlined ultra-designed interior is a backdrop for art and photography exhibitions, while outside seating in the garden square is mobbed on summer nights. The music works around CD promotion nights run in conjunction with Alberti Dischi (*see p172* **Plastic people**) record shop and showcases the latest releases from St Germain, Thievery Corporation and other progressive lo-fi bands.

Officina Move Bar

Via il Prato 58r, Santa Maria Novella (055 210 399/www.officinamovebar.com). **Open** 8am-2am Mon-Fri; 3pm-2am Sat, Sun. Closed Aug. **Credit** MC, V. **Map** p315 B5.

Eclectic, original and varying wildly, a night in the Officina can bring anything from reggae to hip hop to techno to nu-jazz, with art installation performances, modern dance shows, interactive multimedia arts sessions, impromptu live music sets or film screenings. All in the low-slung seating, low-lit bar setting. Expect the unexpected. *See also p160.*

Porfirio Rubirosa

Viale Strozzi 38r, San Lorenzo (055 490 965). **Open** 11am-2am Tue-Sun. Closed 2wks Aug. **Credit** MC, V.

Though not the buzzing hub for the smart set it once was (local roadworks have eaten up the unofficial car park for the cabrio Mercs, Ferraris and Audi TTs that were the bar's trademark), those that do find a parking spot for their flash motors can still be found inside this hedonist's haven propping up the long marble bar and trying to live up to its namesake – Porfirio, the famously womanising Brazilian playboy. Cocktails are about €7.

Rex Caffè

Via Fiesolana 25r, Santa Croce (055 248 0331). **Open** 6pm-3.30am daily. Closed June-Aug. **Credit** MC, V. **Map** p315 B5.

With more of a club than a bar atmosphere, Rex is the king of the east, filling up with loyal subjects who bow, scrape and sashay to the sounds of the session DJs playing bassy beats and jungle rhythms. Gaudí-esque mosaics decorate the central bar and columns, wrought iron lamps shed a soft light and a luscious red antechamber creates seclusion for more intimate gatherings. Tapas is served during the *aperitivo* happy hour (5-9.30pm), and Rex prides itself on its cocktails (from €7; wine starts at €3).

La Rotonda

Via Il Prato 10-16r, Santa Maria Novella (055 265 4644/www.larotonda.it). **Open** 7pm-2am daily. Closed 2wks Aug. **Credit** AmEx, DC, MC, V.

A saloon-style pub-cum-pizzeria decked out in tacky wood panelling and inexplicably watched over from the upper-floor balcony by wooden models of jazz musicians. The DJ session music wavers from hip hop to mainstream, while upstairs live bands drive you to drink from Thursdays to Sundays. The beer selection (€3) is the bar's saving grace, with Chimays and bottled Guinness. And the crowd is friendly, despite the rowdy stag nights and birthday parties held on the premises.

Slowly

Via Porta Rossa 63r, Duomo & Around (055 264 5354). **Open** 7pm-2am Mon-Sat. **Credit** MC, V. **Map** p314 C3.

The ultimate chill-out bohemian-chic bar, Slowly offers soft lighting from blue and red mosaic lanterns, big squashy seating in alcoves, laid-back staff and mellow Café del Mar-style sounds when the DJ gets stuck in. Even the inevitable crowds of pretty young things and hip thirtysomethings milling round the snacks aperitif-time or spilling on to the pavements on busy nights can't break the nice 'n' easy spell. The restaurant up the spiral staircase on a balcony overlooking the bar serves imaginative global cuisine. *See also p128* **Bar bites**.

The William Pub

Via Magliabechi 7-11r, Santa Croce (055 263 8357). **Open** 12.30pm-1.30am Sun-Thur; 12.30pm-2am Fri-Sat. **Credit** AmEx, DC, JCB, MC, V. **Map** p315 C5.

British pub culture, complete with photos of English sporting heroes and quaint village scenes, has been transplanted into this most frescoed and Florentine of buildings. The identity crisis extends to the clientele, which runs from butch bikers to caressing couples. The downstairs bar is generally packed, the upstairs bar and the back room have space to sit with a Newcastle Brown and a late-night ploughman's. Stick to bottled beers rather than draught. Beer costs €4.50, a gin and tonic is €6.50.

Zoe

Via dei Renai 13r, Oltrarno (055 243 111). **Open** 8am-1.30am Mon-Thur; 8am-2am Fri, Sat; 6pm-1am Sun. **Credit** AmEx, MC, V. **Map** p315 D4.

Siren Zoe's red neon signs have lured many a parched modern-day Odysseus into her clutches, where she plies them with lethal cocktails (try the Crimson Zoe – vodka, gin and Cointreau blended with fresh strawberries, sugar and crushed ice) and salty snacks. Most passing travellers are an easy catch and by midnight the crowd sprawls into the garden square on hot summer nights. Beer is €4, a gin and tonic €6. Happy hour is from 5pm to 10pm.

Sport & Fitness

Something for every body.

From *canottaggio* (crew rowing) and cycling to running and skiing, Florence is a surprisingly athletic city. Clubs and gyms of all kinds, are happy to welcome newcomers and visitors, and there are also three pools dotted around town.

Spectator sports

Car & motorbike racing

Autodromo del Mugello

Nr Scarperia (055 849 9111/www.mugellocircuit.it). **Open** Mar-Nov. Closed Dec-Feb. **Rates** Formula 1 trials. **No credit cards.**

Top-notch racing, including Formula 3 and motorcycle world championship competitions. If you have your own motorbike, you can take it for a spin on the test track at €50 for 20 minutes. Call in advance for reservations.

Football

Stadio Artemio Franchi

Campo di Marte, Outside the City Gates (055 262 5537). Bus 11, 17. **Tickets** about €10-€113; call for current prices. **No credit cards.**

In 2002 this football team, once called the Fiorentina, went bankrupt amid a storm of scandal, and was re-founded as Florentia. Falling from the top 'A' rank of the Italian football teams, they were forced to start all over again beginning at the lowest 'C2' rank. Now under new ownership, the team has regained its original name, Fiorentina, and has already managed to pull itself up into the 'C1' rank. The season runs from August to May, with matches generally every other Sunday at 3pm. Purchase tickets at the 45,000-capacity stadium two to three hours prior to a match or pre-book at the Chiosco degli Sportivi outlet (via Anselmi, near piazza della Repubblica, 055 292 363) or at the Box Office ticket agency (via Alamanni 39, 055 210 804/www.boxoffice.com).

Horse racing

Ippodromi e Città

Viale del Pegaso 1, Outside the City Gates (055 422 6076). Bus 17C. **Open** June-July. **Admission** €4. **No credit cards.**

Florence's racecourse for *il trotto* (trotting), where the driver sits in a carriage behind the horse. The Premio Duomo in June is among Tuscany's biggest racing events. Look out for Enrico Bellei, one of Italy's top *trotto* drivers.

Ippodromo il Visarno

Via delle Cascine, Outside the City Gates (055 353 394/422 6076). Bus 17. Closed Aug. **Admission** €4. **No credit cards.**

Florence's *galoppo* (flat-racing) course. The season lasts from spring to summer, and you might spot leading Tuscan jockeys such as Muzzi and Colombi.

Active sports & fitness

Climbing & trekking

Cave di Maiano

Via Cave di Maiano, Fiesole.

If you are into free-climbing, this is the place to go. The caves, which are actually old mines, make an ideal rock wall. Until the beginning of the 20th century the stone from the mines was used for many of the most important buildings in Florence, including the Palazzo Vecchio and the Palazzo Medici Ricciardi. You'll be on your own there, without guides or instructors, so bring your own equipment.

Galleria dello Sport

Via Venezia 18-20, San Marco (055 580 611/ www.galleriadellosport.com). **Open** 3.30-7.30pm Mon; 9am-7.30pm Tue-Sat. Closed last 3wks Aug. **Credit** AmEx, MC, V.

Primarily a sporting goods shop, Galleria dello Sport houses a rare treasure in Florence: an 8m (26ft) climbing wall. With proper gear and a friend to spot you, you can flex your skills free of charge.

Gruppo Escursionistico CAI (Club Alpino Italiano)

Via del Mezzetta 2, Outside the City Gates (055 612 0467/www.caifirenze.it). Bus 3, 6, 20. **Open** 3.30-7.30pm Mon-Fri. Closed Aug. **Rates** about €20, depending on group size. **No credit cards.**

Guided Sunday treks in Tuscany, mostly on trails through gentle countryside, rated easy to moderate. Prices include transport to and from the city centre, but don't cover lunch. In May the Prato section of CAI organises an 84km (52-mile) two-day walk, including overnight arrangements, called 'Piazza to Piazza'. For information, contact the Associazione Sportiva Sci CAI Prato, Via Altopascio, Prato (0574 29267).

Guide Alpine

These Alpine guides are mountaineering experts who organise courses throughout the summer. Courses run for three weekends in a row at a cost of €250. For reservations and information, call 338 931 3444 or 349 793 3893 (www.ufficioguide.it).

Libreria Stella Alpina

Via Corridoni 14, Outside the City Gates (055 411 688). Bus 14, 28. **Open** 4-7pm Mon; 9am-1pm, 4-7pm Tue-Sat. **No credit cards.**

A good source of further information on trekking and mountaineering in Florence and Tuscany.

Cycling

Florence by Bike

Via San Zanobi 91R-120, San Lorenzo (055 488 992/www.florencebybike.it). **Open** 9am-7.30pm daily. **Credit** AmEx, DC, MC, V.

Bike rental and organised bike tours – especially good for a one-day tour through Chianti (30km/ 17 miles). The Chianti tour costs €70 per person and included in the price is bike rental, a water bottle, a helmet, an English-speaking guide and lunch in a restaurant. Be sure to book in advance, as the groups are made up of ten to 12 people maximum.

Golf

Circolo Golf Ugolino

Via Chiantigiana 3, Grassina (055 230 1009/ www.golfugolino.it). Bus 31. **Open** 8.30am-6.30pm daily. Closed Jan. **Rates** €60 for 18 holes Mon-Fri; €80 Sat, Sun. **Credit** AmEx, DC, JCB, MC, V.

This is the nearest course to the city (about 20 minutes south by bus), but it's not open during the frequent weekend tournaments. It's best to phone or send an email (info@golfugolino.it) for reservations at least a week in advance.

Gyms

Bodyworks

Via Passavanti 35, Outside the City Gates (055 587 399/www.bodyworkssrl.it). **Open** 9am-10pm Mon-Sat. **Membership** €10 per day; €70 per mth. **No credit cards.**

A small high-quality gym with numerous fitness courses. A complete resistance machine area is also available for use, which you can use with or without the help of an instructor.

Palestra Porta Romana

Via G Silvani 5, Outside the City Gates (055 232 1799). Bus 11, 12, 36, 37. **Open** 10am-10pm Mon-Fri; 10am-12.30pm Sat. **Membership** €10 per day; €60 per mth. **No credit cards.**

Expect to find a weights room, plus aerobics, step, boxing and spinning classes. There are also some martial arts classes.

Palestra Ricciardi

Borgo Pinti 75, Santa Croce (055 247 8462/ www.palestraricciardi.com). **Open** *Sept-July* 9am-10pm Mon-Fri; 9.30am-6pm Sat; 10am-2pm Sun. *Aug* 5-10pm Mon-Sat. **Membership** €10 per day; €77 per mth. **Credit** MC, V.

One of the largest and most modern of Florence's gyms. But, also one of the most expensive.

TROPOS

Via Orcagna 20A, Outside the City Gates (055 678 381/www.troposclub.it). **Open** 8am-10pm Mon-Sat. **Membership** €25 trial visit, then various options. **Credit** AmEx, MC, V.

Oars play on the River Arno. *See p184.*

Working it out at **Bodyworks**. *See p182*.

The most exclusive and most expensive gym in Florence, Tropos offers just about every possibility to exercise, relax and pamper imaginable. The setting is luxurious, whether you're splashing about in the aerobics pool, clocking up laps in the main pool or steaming in one of the saunas.

Zero Uno/Indoor Club

Via dei Caboto 30-32, Outside the City Gates (055 430 275/703/www.zerounoilpolicentro.it). Bus 29, 30. **Open** 7am-11pm Mon-Fri; 9am-7pm Sat; 10am-2.30pm Sun. **Membership** €25 per day; €55-€95 per mth. **No credit cards**.
Sauna, indoor pool, weights and classes are among the options at Zero Uno.

Horse riding

Centro Ippico I Loti

Via di Picile 108, Localita' Antella, Bagno a Ripoli (055 656 9002/333 363 8855). **Rates** €15 per hr. **No credit cards**.
Guided tours on horseback just north of Florence. Also half-day or full day trips. Book in advance.

Maneggio Marinella

Via di Macia 21, Travalli Calenzano (055 887 8066/ www.lamarinellasupereva.it). Bus 28. **Open** 9am-1pm, 3-7pm daily. **Rates** €13 per hr. **No credit cards**.
Phone during the week to book one of the daily rides. Lessons and special or group trips are also organised on request.

Rendola Riding

Montevarchi (055 970 7045/www.rendolariding.freeweb.org). **Open** 9am-1pm, 3-6pm Tue-Sun. **Rates** €15 per hr. **No credit cards**.
This stable, 30 minutes' drive south of Florence on the border with Chianti, offers one- to five-hour rides through the countryside. Lessons are available as well as a package that includes two hours of riding, lunch and transport to and from the nearest train station. Book a day in advance at the latest. Also organises two- to three-day trips, with lodging provided at a neighbouring *agriturismo*.

Ice skating

Florence sets up a temporary ice skating rink every winter from December to January. The venue tends to change every year so contact the APT (055 597 8373) for the latest information. You pay by the session (there are three or four daily); the last ends at about 11pm.

In-line skating

Le Pavoniere

Via della Catena 2, Parco delle Cascine, Outside the City Gates (335 571 8547). Bus 17C. **Open** 3-8pm Tue-Thur; 10am-8pm Sat, Sun. Closed when raining. **Rates** €5 per hr. **No credit cards**.
Hire in-line skates from this kiosk in the Parco delle Cascine and take advantage of miles of traffic-free paths along the Arno river. On Tuesday mornings, there's an enormous outdoor market along the riverside paths, so unless you're an expert zig-zagger, you may want to avoid it.

Pool

Gambrinus

Via dei Vecchietti 16r, Duomo & Around (no phone). **Open** 1.30pm-1am daily. **Rates** tables €8 per hr. **No credit cards**. **Map** p314 B3.
The only pool hall in central Florence, Gambrinus offers nine pool tables and eight tables without pockets, where you can try your hand at *boccette* or *cinque birilli*. The clientele here is predominantly serious, though non-hostile, men.

Rowing

Società Canottieri Firenze

Lungarno Luisa dei Medici 8, Duomo & Around (055 282 130/www.canottierifirenze.it). **Open** 8am-8.30pm Mon, Sat; 8am-9.30pm Tue-Fri; 8am-1pm Sun. **Visitor membership** €70 per mth. **No credit cards. Map** p314 C3.

Hidden away in the underground caverns of the Uffizi Museum (you enter the club through a tiny green door on the lungarno), this is a fairly exclusive club that pushes its boats out on the Arno. There's also a gym, indoor rowing tank, sauna and showers.

Running

Most joggers hit the Parco delle Cascine, but you can also head for the hills, towards Fiesole, Settignano and piazzale Michelangiolo. Along the small winding streets of Florence, you'll meet many of your kind working off all that pasta and pizza. Of course, be careful of the normal hazards of cars and air pollution.

Associazione Atletica Leggera

Viale Matteotti 15, Outside the City Gates (055 576 616/571 401). Bus 8, 80. **Open** 1-6pm Mon, Wed; 9am-1pm Tue, Thur-Sat.

This is a good source of information on running clubs and races. Foreigners can only participate in races for amateur runners.

Florence Marathon

Organizzazione Firenze Marathon, Casella postale 597-50100, Firenze (055 600 664/612 3933/ www.firenzemarathon.it).

Every November Florence organises a marathon and each year it's becoming more and more popular, attracting many foreign runners.

Skiing

See pp197-9 for the Abetone ski area.

Squash

Centro Squash Firenze

Via Empoli 16, Outside the City Gates (055 732 3055). Bus 1. **Open** 9.30am-11pm Mon-Fri; 9.30am-6pm Sat. Closed Sat June, July & Aug. **Rates** €8 per person for 45mins court time. **No credit cards.**

If you're dying to get some squash in while you're in Florence, this is the place to go. It also has a complete gym, aerobics and step courses, spinning, and sauna. Equipment rental available.

Swimming

Many pools are only open in the summer. During winter some pools require at least a month's membership and may limit access to a few times a week.

Costoli

Viale Paoli, Outside the City Gates (055 623 6027). Bus 10, 17, 20. **Open** *June-Aug* 2-6pm Mon; 10am-6pm Tue-Sun. **Admission** €6.50; €4.50 under-12s; free under-7s. **No credit cards.**

A swimmer's dream with an Olympic-size pool, a diving pool and a children's pool, surrounded by a lovely green park. The pool is also open in the winter (phone for details).

Hotel Villa Le Rondini

Via Vecchia Bolognese 224, Outside the City Gates (055 400 081/www.villalerondini.com). **Open** *May-Sept* 10am-7pm daily. Closed Oct-Apr. **Admission** €16 Mon-Fri; €19 Sat, Sun.

A small pool in the park of a chic, hillside hotel surrounded by a lovely lawn and shady trees.

FLOG

Via Mercati 24B, Poggetto, Outside the City Gates (055 484 465/www.flog.it). **Open** *June & July* 10am-6.30pm Sat, Sun. *Aug* 10am-6.30pm daily. Closed Sept-May. **Admission** €5. **No credit cards.**

This small pool is a great place to hang out on a hot day. Part of an 'afterwork club' of a metal working factory, it has a sun terrace and a refreshments stand.

NUOTO+

Giovanni Franceschi (0571 944 701/335 617 2453/ www.giovannifranceschi.it).

Through this organisation you can book week-long swim camps in locations across Italy. They run during the summer and are open to children, adults and entire families. Instruction at all levels combined with a relaxing holiday.

Piscina Bellariva (indoor/outdoor)

Lungarno Aldo Moro 6, Outside the City Gates (055 677 521). Bus 14. **Open** *Summer* 10am-6pm daily. *Winter* 8.30am-11pm Tue, Thur; 10am-1pm Sat; 9.30am-12.30pm Sun. **Admission** €6.50; €4.50 children. **No credit cards.**

A lovely Olympic-size pool in a beautiful green park with refreshments stand, and a separate pool for small children. Open in winter too (phone for details).

Tennis

Unione Sportivo Affrico

Viale Fanti Manfredo 20, Outside the City Gates (055 600 845). Bus 17, 20. **Open** 9am-10.30pm Mon-Fri; 9am-7pm Sat; 9am-1pm Sun. Closed 2wks Aug. **Rates** €11.50 1hr court rental. **No credit cards.**

Down-to-earth club with eight courts. Non-members can reserve a court at most three days in advance (pay on reservation). You must go to the club to book.

Zodiac Sport

Via A Grandi 2, Outside the City Gates (055 202 2847). **Open** 9am-11pm Mon-Sat; 9am-1pm Sun. **Rates** €12.90 1hr court rental. **No credit cards.**

A bit posh, but has the benefit of a swimming pool. Make reservations on the above number.

Theatre & Dance

Dance is skipping ahead but theatre is still lagging behind.

Theatre in Italy as a whole has enjoyed a long and distinguished history. There are around 300 of local theatres scattered across Tuscany, some of which date back to the 15th and 16th centuries. Many were allowed to slip into total dereliction, but there seems to be a move towards revival. Town councils are putting up the money for restoration and these lovely old theatres are once again part of civil life. Some of the most interesting buildings are in Montalcino, San Casciano, Massa, Pescia, Pistoia, Prato, Montecarlo di Lucca, Lucca and Pisa. Florence has two historic theatres: **Teatro della Pergola** (*see p186*) and **Teatro Goldoni** (*see below*). The former hosts a full season of plays, the latter is used principally for dance events and chamber music concerts. The city's Teatro Verdi is not as picturesque, but hosts a varied programme of productions. Still, many new productions bypass the region's capital in favour of the renowned Teatro Metastasio in Prato or the Teatro Manzoni in Pistoia. Others skip Tuscany altogether.

The main problem with theatre in Tuscany is the reluctance of funding bodies and producers to stage risky experimental or fringe events combined with a general lack of public curiosity. Middle-of-the road productions guarantee the fullest houses, so these shows are favoured by sponsors.

Most theatre productions in both Florence and Tuscany are in Italian, but there's a fair amount of non-verbal theatre too. In general musicals have seen a huge revival in Italy, now a European leader in terms of the level of production. Many of the biggest hits have come through Tuscany in recent years. Otherwise, you can see anything from Pirandello, Goldoni and foreign classics (in Italian) to mainstream contemporary productions and radical fringe shows. The Tuscan theatre season is short, running from (roughly) September to April.

In contrast to theatre, there have been significant progressions in the dance scene. Tuscany is very lucky as its cultural office is keen to promote dance; it currently finances ten different companies and is forging ahead with its dance programmes. Florence, too, is developing its own dance public for the first time. Full-length classical and contemporary productions by the **MaggioDanza** are performed at the **Teatro del Maggio Musicale Fiorentino** (the former Teatro Comunale; *see p186*); while modern work comes from the likes of the **Virgilio Sieni Dance Company**, the **Florence Dance Company** and other experimental companies, who perform all year. Elsewhere in Tuscany, look out for groups such as Motus (Siena), Aldes (Lucca), Sosta Palmizi (Cortona), Micha Van Hoeke (Castiglioncello), Compagnia Xe (San Casciano) and Giardino Chiuso (San Gimignano). These companies perform in festivals like La Versiliana in Marina di Pietrasanta or the Armunia Festival della Riviera, Castiglioncello.

Organisations promoting dance in Tuscany include ADAC and Fondazione Toscana dello Spettacolo. The latter now has an official mandate from the Regione to promote dance in Tuscany. For upcoming events, see the monthly magazine Firenze Spettacolo or local press.

Venues

Teatro Cantiere Florida

Via Pisana 111, Outside the City Gates (055 713 1783/www.elsinor.net). Bus 6, 26, 27. **Open** Telephone bookings only 9am-1pm, 3-6pm Mon-Fri. **Season** end Oct-Apr. **No credit cards**.

Inaugurated in December 2002, this 288-seater theatre occupies an ex-cinema. It is a great space with a big stage, rough brick walls and huge copper-painted air vents. One of the theatre's main objectives is to promote young actors, directors and playwrights, aiming to target a young public. Productions range from reworks of classics to Tom Stoppard to contemporary works. There are also lots of shows for children.

Teatro Goldoni

Via Santa Maria 15, Oltrarno. **Open** For tickets, contact relevant organising body (*see below*) or buy on door 1hr before show. **Map** p314 D1. **No credit cards**.

The tiny Teatro Goldoni has been used mainly for classical music until recently (*see p169*) but a new project instigated in 2001 and now taking full shape means that, these days, dance events play a major role in the programming. The scheme, run by the city of Florence and the Maggio Musicale Fiorentino (*see p186*), hands over the theatre to four dance bodies for certain periods of the year: the Florence Dance Cultural Centre, MaggioDanza, Compagnia Virgilio Sieni and Versilia Danza (*see pp186-7*). A nearby building is being restored and will be opened as the Cantiere Goldonetta, an exciting new space to be used for the promotion of contemporary performing arts with dance as the major player. The programme of events will include workshops, choreography competitions, stages and promotional dance platforms.

Teatro della Limonaia

Via Gramsci 426, Sesto Fiorentino, Outside the City Gates (055 440 852/www.teatro-limonaia.fi.it). Bus 28A, 28B. **Open** Telephone bookings only 10am-6.30pm Mon-Fri. **No credit cards.**

A small, delightful space that could be in New York. Shows are mainly alternative. Look out for the Intercity Festival in June (*see p187*).

Teatro del Maggio Musicale Fiorentino

Corso Italia 16, Santa Maria Novella (055 213 535/ticket sales 199 109 910/www.maggio fiorentino.com). **Open** *Box office* 10am-4.30pm Tue-Fri; 10am-1pm Sat; & 1hr before performance. *Phone sales* 9am-9.30pm Mon-Fri; 9am-3.30pm Sat. **Credit** AmEx, DC, MC, V.

Home to Maggio Danza (*see p187*), this theatre includes mainstream dance in its year-round programme of events. The Maggio Musicale Fiorentino festival always includes a free-for-all dance jamboree in its closing days, which is usually held in piazza della Signoria.

Teatro della Pergola

Via della Pergola 12-32, San Marco (055 226 4316). **Open** *Box office* 9.30am-1pm, 3.30-6.45pm Tue-Sat; 10am-12.15pm Sun. **Season** Oct-Apr. **Credit** AmEx, DC, MC, V. **Map** p315 B5.

A state-controlled theatre, the Pergola presents a full programme of productions from visiting companies. Catch anything from Shakespeare to Noel Coward to Ibsen. *See also p169.*

Teatro Puccini

Piazza Puccini, Outside the City Gates (055 362 067/ www.teatropuccini.it). Bus 17, 22, 30, 35. **Open** *Box office* 3.30-7.30pm Mon-Fri. **Season** Oct-Apr. **No credit cards.**

Light opera, musicals and one-man variety shows fill the bill at this large Fascist-style building.

Teatro di Rifredi

Via Vittorio Emanuele 303, Outside the City Gates. (055 422 0361/www.toscanateatro.it). Bus 4, 14, 28. **Open** *Box office* 4-7pm Mon-Sat; also 30mins before performance. **Season** Sept-May. **No credit cards.**

Resident company Pupi e Fresedde offers a varied programme featuring mainly contemporary and fringe shows, many of them concerned with the social and political issues of the day with a particular emphasis on young and up-and-coming playwrights and directors. There is also the odd classic production and regular appearances by guest companies.

Teatro Studio di Scandicci

Via Donizetti 58, Outside the City Gates (055 757 348/www.scandiccicultura.org). Bus 16. **Season** Oct-June. **No credit cards.**

This small theatre in the suburbs is a good place to see alternative theatre on a regular basis. Though the principal resident Compania di Krypton (*see below*) is now well established and no longer avant-garde, there are several new companies that have an on-going relationship with the theatre. Kinkalerierli continues to make big waves with its shows involving dance, physical theatre and multimedia. The work of young, local company Gogmagog often examines the human psyche, while Piccoli Principi writes and performs for children.

Fringe theatre companies

Compania di Krypton

Piazza Santa Croce 19, Santa Croce (055 234 5443/ kryptonteatro@inwind.it). **Closed** 2wks Aug.

Founded by Giancarlo and Fulvio Cauteruccio in 1982 and the resident company at the Teatro Studio di Scandicci (*see above*), Krypton is well established and widely respected. Lighting, stage and sound techniques were avant-garde when it started out, and it still experiments with video, projections, lasers, microphones and other effects. The 2002/2003 season included *Ico no clast*, a tribute to the Sex Pistols, and a highly experimental interpretation of Samuel Beckett's play *Krapp's Last Tape* at the Fabbricone in Prato.

Elsinor, Teatro Stabile d'Innovazione

Via Pisana 111, Outside the City Gates (055 713 1783/www.elsinor.net). Bus 6, 26, 27.

Resident at the new Teatro Cantiere Florida (*see p185*), this company produces, performs and promotes a diverse repertoire of shows principally for children and young people.

Pupi e Fresedde

A young company that does a lot of work with schools and has an eclectic repertoire. Contact via Teatro de Rifredi (*see above*).

Teatro delle Donne

Piazza Santa Croce 19, Santa Croce (055 234 7572). **Open** 10am-4pm Mon-Fri. **Season** Oct-May. **Map** p315 C5.

Now resident at the Teatro Manzoni in Calenzano (a suburb of Florence), this all-female company promotes and performs plays by women.

Dance companies

Compagnia Virgilio Sieni Danza

Via San Romano 13, Outside the City Gates (055 655 7435).

Dancer and choreographer Virgilio Sieni directs one of the few local avant-garde dance companies to have achieved international fame. Performances are often creative collaborations with instrumentalists, composers and designers. The company is one of the residents at the Teatro Goldoni (*see p185*).

Face to face at **Teatro Cantiere Florida**. *See p185.*

Florence Dance Cultural Centre

Borgo della Stella 23r, Oltrarno (055 289 276). **Closed** Aug. **Map** p314 C1.

Directed by Marga Nativo and American choreographer Keith Ferrone, this eclectic centre offers a range of dance classes, from children's activities to advanced ballet at professional level, and organises the Florence Dance Festival (*see below*). There are daily open classes, so you can attend even on a short-term basis. Since its inauguration in 2001, the Florence Dance Company has collaborated with the likes of Karole Armitage and Igal Perry and will be making its New York debut in October 2003.

MaggioDanza

Teatro Comunale, Corso Italia 16, Santa Maria Novella (055 213 535/www.maggiofiorentino.com).

The resident company at the Teatro del Maggio Musicale Fiorentino (*see p186*), MaggioDanza presents a range of ballet from such classics as *Giselle* and *The Nutcracker* to contemporary works by visiting choreographers. In summer, performances are held in the Boboli Gardens. Standards are not always what they should be; apart from its major financial problems, the director (at present Florence Clerc) has changed so many times in recent years that the company has never really found its feet, which is a pity as there are a fair number of young, talented dancers there now.

Festivals

Estate Fiesolana

Teatro Romano, Fiesole (055 597 8308/ www.estatefiesolana.it). **Date** mid June-mid Aug.

A major change to the way this inconsistent arts festival is organised means that it will host the Florence Dance Festival summer run – a three-week long programme of dance events from the resident Florence Dance Company. Guests that included the fantastic Eifman Ballet Theatre from St Petersburg in 2003. There are also theatre events in Italian.

Fabbrica Europa

Borgo degli Albizi 15, Santa Croce (055 248 0515/www.fabbricaeuropa.net). **Date** May/June. **Map** p315 B5.

The former Stazione Leopolda forms a big, versatile space for this innovative festival of the contemporary performing arts in which theatre, but more particularly dance, both play a major part.

Florence Dance Festival

Borgo della Stella 23r, Oltrarno (055 289 276/www.florencedance.org). **Date** July & Dec. **Map** p314 C1.

The only festival dedicated solely to dance in Tuscany and now in its 14th year, this summer event can be relied upon to bring some of the great names of contemporary, traditional and classical dance to Florence. The brainchild of Marga Nativo, Keith Ferrone and the Florence Dance Cultural Centre, it puts on three weeks of performances by acclaimed companies in Fiesole's Teatro Romano and dedicates several evenings to up-and-coming choreographers. Also features choreography contests, seminars and art exhibitions. The shorter, winter edition is held in the Teatro Goldoni (*see p185*).

Intercity Festival

Teatro della Limonaia, Via Gramsci 426, Sesto Fiorentino, Outside the City Gates (055 440 852/ www.teatro-limonaia.fi.it). **Date** June.

A rare opportunity (in Florence, that is) to see contemporary theatre performed in its mother tongue. Each year a European city is chosen as a guest. Playwrights, actors and theatre companies from the country concerned are invited to participate. Athens was the featured city in 2002 and 2003.

Tuscany

Introduction 190
Florence & Prato Provinces 193
Pistoia Province 197
Pisa 200
Pisa & Livorno Provinces 208
Siena 212
Siena Province 224
Lucca 238
Massa-Carrara & Lucca Provinces 248
Arezzo 254
Arezzo Province 261
Southern Tuscany 268

Features

Don't miss In Tuscany 190
That way inclined 207
Animal magnetism 222
Spa hopping 226
Visiting wineries 232
The villas 242
You looking at me? 244
City of gold 259

Introduction

Come down to earth and back to nature.

Even if you have just a few days to devote to this most beguiling of regions, you are sure to fall under its spell. Quite separate from the cerebral allure of Florence's churches and museums, yet equally steeped in complex, often turbulent history, Tuscany has a charm that is in every way unique.

Fuelled by endless infighting between its *comuni*, which climaxed between the 13th and 15th centuries, Tuscany gathered commercial strength, mustered military respectability and, most significantly, outpaced its neighbours both artistically and culturally. Eventually, it imposed its language on the rest of the country and then produced an unmatched crop of everything from poets and painters to scientists, explorers and architects. Tuscany's rulers also had the foresight to amass the greatest artistic wealth anywhere in Europe. To this day, the region has the single highest concentration of art anywhere in the country and, by extension, in the world. Italy, by most accounts, holds more than half of the planet's artistic treasures.

Tuscany's geography also went a long way towards ensuring its overall unity amid constant internal squabbling. More than 90 per cent of its territory is mountainous or hilly, which leaves only small slivers of level ground around the rivers and along the coast.

AN OVERVIEW

Tuscany's popular image is of sunset-drenched and cypress-lined rolling hills. Needless to say, there's much more. The Apuan Alps in the north-west and the Apennine peaks to the east set the region apart and provide a plethora of giddy, winding roads to explore by car, as well as ski resorts and high-altitude trekking. These self-contained, forested valleys – such as the Garfagnana and Lunigiana, which stretch north from Lucca, and the Valtiberina, which branches east from Arezzo – have always provided both the basic ingredients for Tuscany's culinary tradition and the backdrop for many of its paintings.

In the deep south is the Maremma, a large expanse of sparsely populated and previously malaria-infested swampland that was once the region's poorest part but is now a playground for Italy's rich and famous. Etruscan remains are scattered all over this southern part of Tuscany, and inland a series of small, ancient towns, including Pitigliano, cling precariously to hillsides. Towards the northern end of the coast is the modern port of Livorno, Tuscany's historical melting pot, and the Versilia, with its beach umbrellas and nightspots. But despite all its other attributes, mainland Tuscany can hardly be considered ideal for a seaside holiday: its coast is dominated by grey-brown sand, heavy industry and large crowds.

The chapters that follow don't aim to provide exhaustive information on the towns and provinces of Tuscany so much as to lead you in the direction of the area's very best elements.

A SENSE OF PLACE

The region's identity, and that of its people, is permeated by a profound sense of belonging known as *campanilismo* – visceral attachment to one's city, town, village or even, as in the case of Siena's *contrade* (*see p222* **Animal magnetism**), one's home district. Having foregone the habit of assaulting one another's walled enclaves, today's Tuscans re-enact their historical enmities mostly verbally, and often colourfully and musically. Florence is generally despised, though this is on account of its

Don't miss In Tuscany

Best of the country

The beaches of **Elba** and **Isola del Giglio**. (*see pp274-6*); the unspoilt beauty of the **Parco Naturale della Maremma** (*see p271*) or the **Mugello** (*see pp193-6*); the **Grotta del Vento** 'wind caves' (*see p252*).

Best of the town

A walk on **Lucca's ramparts** (*see p242*); the cloud-capped serenity of **Fivizzano** (*see p253*); a dip in one of the healing spas at **Montecatini Terme** (*see p198*); the hill towns of **Barga** (*see p251*) and **Pitigliano** (*see p270*); the views from the **Torre Guinigi** (*see p243*), the **Torre de la Mangia** (*see p216*) or **Pisa's campanile** (*see p204*); the feudal town of **Fosdinovo** (*see p252*); **Siena** (*see pp212-23*), particularly during the colourful chaos of its annual palio (*see p155*).

Suckers for sale in the melting pot of Livorno. *See p210.*

historical arrogance and is directed at Florentines as a group rather than individual *Fiorentini*. The capital's two main challengers for regional supremacy have historically been Pisa and Siena. While Pisans are also universally disliked, it's the Sienese, conscious of being frozen in their medieval glory, who epitomise the idea of identification with place and history.

Prato commands respect for its wealth-generating entrepreneurial spirit, while Pistoia elicits the same for its sense of age. For its part, Montecatini also recalls the past, with its turn-of-the-19th-century parks and grandiloquent bathing establishments. A bit further west, Lucca, hermetically sealed by its chunky sixth-century walls, always managed to pay off would-be conquerors and now seems to have many more friends – even in Tuscany – than enemies. Bourgeois Arezzo has also kept a high standard of living while falling under Florentine dominion, and working-class Livorno has always been open-minded with loud-mouthed inhabitants and a pioneering spirit.

WHERE, WHEN, HOW

The best overall advice, especially if you only have a week or two, is to concentrate on one or two provinces or parts of the region, allowing at least two full days for major towns such as Siena or Lucca. Unless you want to dedicate your holiday to, say, wine tourism or art and architecture, Tuscany invites you to be eclectic. In other words, mix it up while you're here. Visit and enjoy ornate churches and galleries in moderation; try not to saturate your days with perfect Tuscan hill towns or devote all your time to long drives around the countryside. Instead, spend a day walking (*see below*) and try to sit down at least once each day to a memorable Tuscan meal. If you need to recuperate from sightseeing, you could spend a few hours at one of the region's many thermal spas. Or, of course, another possibility is to build your holiday around a language, cookery or painting course (*see p192*).

Inevitably, in Easter and summer, many places get horribly busy and you have to weigh up whether they're worth fighting through the hordes for. The gorgeous hill town of San Gimignano, for instance, is like honey to the tourist bees, so go in months either side of the rush, such as May or September/October. Winter is especially good for its lack of crowds but many attractions and restaurants either close or are open for limited hours only, and the weather won't be as good. In peak season, you should book rooms in advance, and even at other times you shouldn't leave it until the last minute.

OUTDOOR PURSUITS

Tuscany offers endless possibilities for walkers. One popular area to hoof it (partly because you can pop into wineries) is to be found within the gentle hills of Chianti. There are more serious walks throughout the Apuan Alps, Monte Amiata and coastal tracks in the Maremma or on the island of Elba. Contact the local tourist offices for further information.

The news for cyclists is mixed. Major roads are a no-no but there are some lovely if hilly areas of Tuscany with backroads just ripe for exploration. These include Chianti, the Crete Senesi (south-east of Siena) and the Maremma (particularly inland). A bike is also a good way to get round towns such as Lucca, Montecatini Terme, Pisa and Arezzo.

It's worth considering booking a customised trip or joining a group (*see p192*) – having pre-booked accommodation and luggage transfer cuts out a lot of slog.

TOURIST INFORMATION
The general tourist information website for the Tuscany region is www.turismo.toscana.it

Specialist holidays

There are a number of companies that offer a variety of tours, although just a few are listed here. For Florence-based companies offering cycling, walking and hiking tours, *see below*.

Walking & cycling

The Alternative Travel Group
69-71 Banbury Road, Oxford OX2 6PJ (01865 315 678/fax 01865 315 696/www.atg-oxford.co.uk). **Dates** all year.
Escorted walking and cycling trips (from £895, excluding flights) in groups of no more than 16, plus customised unguided walking trips with rooms in family-run hotels and luggage transfer (eight days from £425 B&B, flights not included).

Ramblers Holidays
PO Box 43, Welwyn Garden City, Herts AL8 6PQ (01707 331 133/fax 01707 333 276/ www.ramblersholidays.co.uk).
Dates spring, summer & autumn.
Centre-based (Florence, Siena, Ronta or San Marcello) walking/sightseeing holidays from £406.

Art history

Prospect Art Tours
36 Manchester Street, London W1U 7LH (020 7486 5704/fax 020 7486 5868/www.prospecttours.com).
Dates spring, summer & autumn.
Music and art history holidays in Florence and Tuscany, with concert tickets, museums and specialist guides. Six-day all-inclusive tour costs £875.

Specialtours
2 Chester Row, London SW1W 9JH (020 7730 2297/www.specialtours.co.uk). **Dates** Feb & May.
One-off tours of museums and gardens, with lectures by art historians, for £1,400 a week all inclusive.

Cookery schools

La Bottega Del 30
Via Santa Caterina, 2 località Villa a Sesta, 53019 Castelnuovo Berardenga, Siena (tel/fax 0577 359 226/www.labottegadel30.it).
Popular five-day courses focusing on Chianti cookery. Classes (for up to ten) end with lunch and wine tastings. A wine cellar, library and *videoteca* are also at students' disposal.

Italian Cookery Weeks
PO Box 2482, London NW10 1HW (020 8208 0112/fax 020 7627 8467/www.italian-cookery-weeks.co.uk). **Dates** May.
Excellent food and wine with daily tuition by cook Susanna Gelmetti, accompanied by occasional trips and excursions. Prices start at £1,599 per week including flights.

Painting courses

Simply Travel
King's Place, Wood Street, Kingston-on-Thames, Surrey KT1 1SG (020 8995 9323/fax 020 8541 2280). **Dates** Apr-Oct.
Package holidays and city breaks to Florence and Tuscany. Accommodation is offered in private villas and hotels that are off the beaten track of mass tourism. A week-long holiday in a villa, including flights, transfers or car hire and accommodation starts from £500 per person.

Verrochio Art Centre
Via San Michele 16, Casole d'Elsa. Bookings through Maureen Ruck, 119 Lynton Road, Harrow, HA2 9NJ (020 8869 1035/www.verrocchio.co.uk).
Dates May-Sept.
Specialist painting and sculpture courses in a hilltop village. Prices start at £779 for a two-week course (accommodation, breakfast and dinner, excluding flights).

Language schools

See also p292.

Cooperativa 'Il Sasso'
Via del Voltaia nel Corso 74, Montepulciano (0578 758 311/fax 0578 757 547/www.ilsasso.com).
Two- and four-week language courses for all levels, plus courses in art history and mosaics. Rooms can be arranged in hotels, flats or with families. Prices start at €340 for a two-week course.

Italian Cultural Institute
39 Belgrave Square, London SW1 8NX (020 7235 1461/fax 020 7235 4618/ www.italcultur.org.uk).
The Italian Cultural Institute is a good source of info about language courses in Italy.

Farming holidays

WWOOF (Willing Workers on Organic Farms)
PO Box 2675, Lewes, East Sussex, BN7 1RB (01273 476 286/www.wwoof.org/www.wwoof.it) or contact Bridget Matthews, Via Casavecchia 109, 57022 Castagneto Carducci, LI, Italy.
Working holidays on organic farms, especially during the grape and olive harvests. Food and board are usually provided in exchange for about six hours work a day. It is wise, however, to find out as much as you can about living and working conditions before you go. For a regular newsletter and list of farms you need to become a member of WWOOF. *See also p296.*

Florence & Prato Provinces

Beyond the city limits.

Most towns around Florence have something to offer and are easily visited as day trips from the busy Tuscan capital. The textile industry in Prato and the town's shrewd business acumen have made it a place where Florentines hop to shop. Pistoia, with its immaculately preserved historic centre, has provided settings for TV and film.

To the south-west of Florence lie the medieval town of Carmignano, surrounded by vineyards, and the birthplace of Leonardo da Vinci, the town of Vinci. Also nearby are Montelupo, known for its glazed pottery, and the enchanting hilltop town of Certaldo Alto.

The area to the north and north-east of Florence is known as the Mugello. It's divided into the Val di Sieve and the Alto Mugello (the Sieve valley and the Upper Mugello). The space-loving Medici adored its gentle contours and peppered it with villas. The six balls on the Medici coat of arms are attributed to the legend that a Carolingian knight named Averardo (one of the first Medici) clashed with a giant, which he defeated not far from Scarperia. In battle, he suffered six blows, each represented by a ball.

Work on the man-made but picturesque Lake Bilancino near Barberino di Mugello was only recently finished and the lake is now being developed for fishing and windsurfing.

Prato

Prato will perhaps always suffer from little sister syndrome. Florence is so much more famous and beautiful that few give its industrial sibling, devoted to the manufacture of worsted cloths, the attention it deserves. Florentines can be pretty snotty about it too, dismissing the Pratese as a bunch of nouveau riche Rolex-wearers. But don't let their prejudice put you off. Prato has a lively and upbeat feel to it and the city is spending huge amounts on upgrading its many attractions. Several of the existing sights are undergoing restoration and there are plans to develop a large area near the train station for hotels and exhibitions. Housed in a 19th-century textile mill, the recently opened textile museum, **Museo del Tessuto** (via Santa Chiara 24, 0574 611 503, closed Tue, €4) now showcases a collection of fabrics and looms dating from the fifth century to the present day.

Like Florence, Prato was a dynamic trading centre in the Middle Ages. Accountancy was virtually invented here in the 14th century by Francesco di Marco Datini, on whose meticulous accounts and private letters Iris Origo based her 1957 novel *The Merchant of Prato*. Prato honours its chief bean-counter with a large statue in the piazza del Comune.

The **Duomo** is a striking Romanesque-Gothic building in pinkish brick with a half-finished green-and-white striped marble façade. On one corner is the 15th-century Pulpit of the Sacred Girdle (Sacro Cingolo), designed by Michelozzo and carved with reliefs of dancing children and cherubs by Donatello (now replaced by casts). Inside are frescoes by Paolo Uccello and Filippo Lippi. The latter was responsible for the *Lives of Saints John the Baptist and Stephen* in the choir and apparently used his nun-lover Lucrezia Buti as a model for Salome at *Herod's Banquet*. The Lippi frescoes are under long-term restoration, but they can be viewed by appointment ten days in advance. The city's religious icon, the Sacro Cingolo, is paraded through the Duomo during the **Ostensione della Sacra Cintola** every Easter, 1 May, 15 August, 8 September and 25 December.

The **Museo dell' Opera del Duomo** (piazza Duomo 49, 0574 293 39, closed Tue, €5 incl Museo di San Domenico & Prato castle) is in Palazzo Vescovile to the left of the Duomo. Exhibits include Donatello's bas-reliefs of dancing *putti* that once decorated the pulpit, a fresco attributed to Paolo Uccello and works by both Filippo and Filippino Lippi. The **Museo di San Domenico** (piazza San Domenico, 0574 440 501, closed Tue, for admission see Museo dell'Opera del Duomo), sometimes called Museo di Pittura Murale, also houses works by Filippino and Filippo Lippi, including the latter's *Madonna del Ceppo* (1453) with its realistic portrayal of Prato merchant Datini.

The church of Santa Maria delle Carceri, opposite the tourist office, is a masterpiece of early Renaissance architecture by Giuliano da Sangallo.

During your visit, don't forget to step outside the walls and take a wander along the banks of the picturesque Bisenzio. Also recommended, if ongoing restoration work has finished, is the **Museo d'Arte Contemporaneo Luigi Pecci** (viale della Repubblica 277, 0574 5317, closed Tue, free, exhibitions €6). Since its opening in 1988, it has established itself as Italy's leading centre of contemporary art.

Where to eat

Prato's Chinese community is among the largest in Tuscany, so the city is home to some of the region's best Chinese food. **Hua Li Du** (via Marini 4, 0574 24163, closed lunch Tue, €15), is one of the foremost Chinese restaurants in the Florence area. Of the Italian places, **Enoteca Barni** (via Ferucci 22, 0574 607 845, closed lunch Sat, all Sun, €12 lunch, €40 dinner), a family-owned spin-off from the 40-year-old deli next door, stands out. **Il Baghino** (via dell' Accademia 9, 0574 27920, closed lunch Mon, Sun, average €30) serves local specialities. In the process of changing owners as we go to press, La Cucina di Paola has changed its name to **Osteria 900** (via Banchelli 14, 0574 24353, closed Mon, average €31), but is still one of the town's best-loved restaurants. **Osteria Cibbe** (piazza Mercatale 49, 0574 607 509, closed Sun, average €20) and, a little further out of town, the atmospheric **La Fontana** (via di Canneto, 0574 27282, closed dinner Sun, all Mon, average €25) are two popular new eateries.

Where to stay

Hotel Museo (viale della Repubblica 289, 0574 5787, doubles €145-€165) is a luxury option out near the Luigi Pecci museum. More central, and cheaper, is the recently renovated **Hotel Flora** (via Cairoli 31, 0574 33521, doubles €90-€140). **Hotel Giardino** (via Magnolfi 4, 0574 26189, doubles €88-€123) is an agreeable place with good facilities just behind the Duomo. Further out, characterful **Villa Rucellai** (via di Canneto 16, 0574 460 392, doubles €80-€90) is a lovely hillside villa with a medieval tower that's been home to the Rucellai family for generations.

Carmignano

Carmignano seems untouched by the proximity of Florence's hubbub. The doors of the 13th-century church of San Michele and San Francesco on its main street remain unlocked even though one of Pontormo's most famous works, *Visitation* (1530), and paintings by Andrea di Giusto grace the interior.

This area is known for wines that marry Sangiovese, Canaiolo and Cabernet grapes. Nearby villa-farms that offer public tastings of Carmignano wines are **Capezzana** (via Capezzana 100, Seano, 055 870 6005, closed Sun, tours by appointment) and **Fattoria di Bacchereto** (Bacchereto, 055 871 7191, closed 2wks Nov or Jan, tours by appointment). The latter also has a shop-restaurant called **Cantina di Toia** (closed Mon, lunch Tue, average €35), rooms (€35-€50) and apartments (€530-€1,900 per wk).

Fattoria di Artimino (viale Papa Giovanni XXIII, 055 875 141, tours and tastings by appointment) produces DOC and DOCG wines on its beautiful land. It also makes extra-virgin olive oil and grappa.

Where to eat & drink

For a taste of the local wine, try **Il Poggiolo** (via Pistoiese 90, 055 871 1242, closed Sat afternoon & Sun) and **Castelvecchio** (via delle Mannelle 19, 055 870 5451, closed Sun and 2wks Aug), two bars that serve their own well-balanced reds. In Artimino, dine at the elegant **Da Delfina** (via della Chiesa 1, 055 871 8074, closed Mon, dinner Sun, 3wks Aug and 2wks Jan, average €45).

Vinci

As the birthplace of Leonardo da Vinci, this quaint little hill town attracts a constant stream of visitors. The **Museo Leonardiano** (being extended at the time of writing to two locations: inside Castello dei Conti Guidi and another building nearby on piazza Castello dei Conti Guidi, call 0571 56055 for information) displays models of machines and instruments devised by the Renaissance polymath.

Where to eat

The originally named **Leonardo** (via Montalbano Nord 16, 0571 567 916, closed Wed in winter and 3wks Jan, average €25) serves reasonable food to busloads of tourists. **La Torretta** (via della Torre 19, 0571 56100, closed Mon, dinner Sun, average €22) is quieter.

Montelupo

The people of **Montelupo** have been making beautiful, colourful glazed pottery since the Middle Ages. In 1973 an old public laundry in the Castello district was dismantled to

All things brick and beautiful – Prato's **Duomo** makes an impact. *See p193.*

reveal a well two metres (6.5 feet) in diameter that had been filled over the centuries with ceramic rejects and shards. Many are now in the **Museo della Ceramica** (via Sinibaldi 43-5, 0571 51352, closed Mon, admission €3).

The locals have never forsaken their vocation and hold markets on some Sundays in the town centre or in nearby towns and villages. The town also hosts a flower festival in March, an antiques market in April and October and the Festa Internazionale della Ceramica towards the end of June.

Certaldo Alto

This picturesque hill settlement's main claim to fame is that Giovanni Boccaccio (1313-75, author of the *Decameron*) was born and died here. Its historic centre monopolises a great view over the Val d'Elsa, looking over to Volterra. During the first week in August the town is bathed in candlelight for the Mercantia – a festival aimed at recreating the atmosphere of the town before the advent of electricity. The **Palazzo del Vicario** (piazzetta del Vicario, 0571 661 219, admission €3) is worth a visit for its beautiful frescoed rooms.

Where to stay & eat

Osteria del Vicario (via Rivellino 3, 0571 668 228, closed Wed, doubles €85, average €35) has rooms and a restaurant with a romantic little terrace. **Il Castello** hotel and restaurant (via G della Rena 6, 0571 668 250, closed Nov, doubles €60-€100, average €30) has a funicular that carries up to 30 passengers (€1 single, €2 return) to the terrace, where candlelit tables surround a 17th-century fountain. Antique Russian samovars and Tuscan swords sustain the medieval atmosphere inside.

Scarperia & around

North-east of Florence, the pleasant little town of Scarperia in the rolling Mugello countryside was founded in 1306 as the northernmost military outpost of the Florentine Republic. Because of its strategic location it enjoyed considerable prosperity until the 18th century, when the main road over the Apennines to Bologna opened further west.

Scarperia is most famous for producing traditional bone-handled pocket knives. **Saladini** (via Roma 25, 055 843 1010) in the town centre is one of the few workshops still making these knives by hand. The **Conaz Factory** (via G Giordani 2, 055 846 197, closed Mon morning, free tours) outside the walled nucleus of the town holds knife-making demonstrations.

In the spacious central square is the **Palazzo dei Vicari**, built in the 13th century to designs by Arnolfo di Cambio. Distinctly reminiscent of the Palazzo Vecchio in Florence, it was the residence of the Republican governors, whose coats of arms decorate the façade. Inside are frescoes dating back to the 14th and 16th centuries, including a *Madonna and Child with Saints* by the school of Ghirlandaio. Between 31 May and 15 September, there's a permanent exhibition of cutting tools in the palazzo.

Near Scarperia, in the Sieve valley and ringed by mountains, **Borgo San Lorenzo** is a busy market town with an attractive historic centre and a few decent shops.

Where to stay & eat

For Mugello cuisine in Scarperia, try **Il Torrione** (via Roma 78-80, 055 843 0263, closed Mon, average €22) or the more upmarket **Fattoria Il Palagio** (viale Dante, 055 846 376, closed Mon and 3wks Aug, average €30) just outside the town. Otherwise, try **Teatro de' Medici** (Località La Torre 14, 055 845 9876, closed Mon, average €38) in a mellow old villa on the road from Borgo to Scarperia, which offers really good Mugello cooking in an elegant setting (*tortelli di patate* with duck sauce comes highly recommended). Nearby is the wonderfully rustic **Il Paiolo** (via Cornocchio 1, Barberino di Mugello, 055 842 0733, closed Tue, Aug & late Dec to early Jan, average €35), where diners are greeted by the irresistible sight and smell of juicy slabs of meat grilling on the roaring wood-fired oven.

The most comfortable hotel in the whole area is the **Villa Campestri** (via di Campestri 19, 055 849 0107, doubles €140-€165), a lovely old villa dating from the 13th century and set in green rolling hills just above Sagginale between Borgo and Vicchio.

Resources

Tourist information

Carmignano *Inside the Wine Museum, Piazza Vittorio Emanuele II 1-2 (055 871 2468).* **Open** *Winter* 9am-noon, 3-5.30pm Tue-Fri & 1st Sun of mth; 9am-noon Sat, Sun. *Summer* 9am-12.30pm, 3.30-7pm Tue-Sun.
Certaldo Alto *Via Cavour (0571 664 935).* **Open** 9am-12.30pm, 3.30-6.30pm Mon-Thur; 9am-12.30pm, 3.30-7pm Fri-Sun.
The Mugello *A1 exit for Barberino di Mugello (055 842 0106).* **Open** 10am-7pm Mon-Tue, Fri-Sun; 10am-1.30pm, 2.30-7pm Wed, Thur.
Prato *Piazza Santa Maria delle Carceri 15 (0574 24112/www.prato.turismo.toscana.it).* **Open** *Summer* 9am-1.30pm, 2-7pm Mon-Sat; 10am-1pm, 3-7pm Sun. *Winter* 9am-1pm, 3-6pm Mon-Sat.
Vinci *Via della Torre 11 (0571 568 012).* **Open** *Summer* 10am-7pm daily. *Winter* 10am-6pm Mon-Fri; 10am-3pm Sat, Sun.

Getting there

By bus

SITA (800 373 760) runs bus services to Borgo San Lorenzo in the Mugello. Journey time is 1hr. From there, there are connections to Scarperia.

By car

Montelupo and, further west, San Miniato are both just off the main Florence-Livorno road. The quickest way to Certaldo is to turn south off this road on to the SS429 between the two towns near Empoli. To reach Vinci, turn off this main road near Empoli heading north in the direction of Pistoia.

Borgo San Lorenzo can be reached via one of two roads from Florence: the SS65 (the old road to Bologna) or the more winding SS302 (the old road to Faenza). For Scarperia, take the former and pick up the SS503 at San Piero a Sieve. It takes about 45mins to get to Borgo; Scarperia is 10mins further on.

By train

Carmignano, Montelupo and San Miniato are on the Florence/Empoli/Pisa train line. Journey times are Florence-Carmignano 25mins (irregular service), Florence-Montelupo 30mins and Florence-San Miniato 45mins. Certaldo can be reached from Florence by changing at Empoli (journey time about 1hr) or from Siena on the same line (35mins).

There's a regular service from Florence's Campo di Marte station to Borgo San Lorenzo. Journey time is 45mins. There's also a train from Santa Maria Novella via Pontassieve but it takes longer. For timetable information, call 892 021 or consult www.trenitalia.com.

Pistoia Province

Mountains, spas and sleepy retreats: this province has it all.

This varied region to the west of Florence has a great deal to offer the museum-overloaded visitor looking to whizz out of the city for a few days. Either get your skis on and hit the slopes at Abetone, a cheaper alternative to Italy's northern ski runs, or change down a gear and ease yourself into Pistoia's sleepy pace of life. Otherwise, upmarket Montecatini Terme has plenty of swish hotels and spas for those looking to put a dent in the credit card.

Pistoia

If Prato is Florence's sparky little sister, **Pistoia** is its maiden aunt. It's an old-fashioned, slow-paced town that has remained in tune with the countryside. Circled by 14th-century walls, the quiet historic centre has some fine Romanesque and Gothic buildings leading in towards its elegant colonnaded cathedral.

The Duomo has a simple Romanesque interior and a campanile with exotic tiger-striped arcades on top. Opposite is the octagonal 14th-century, green-and-white-striped Baptistery. The **Museo Civico** (0573 371 296, closed Mon, admission €3.50) behind the Duomo has fine 14th-century paintings on the ground floor and some fairly dreadful late Mannerist works two floors above. There's also a section on famous Pistoian Giovanni Michelucci (1891-1990), architect of Florence's Santa Maria Novella station. **Palazzo Tau** (corso Silvano Fedi 30, 0573 30285, closed Sun, admission €3.50) houses the Centro di Documentazione e Fondazione (0573 31332), devoted to the other Pistoian of renown, sculptor Marino Marini (1901-80). Ospedale del Ceppo is famous for its splendid della Robbia ceramic frieze (1526-9). Sant'Andrea has a magnificent stone pulpit (1298-1301) by Giovanni Pisano.

Local events include an art and craft show and market of local products in the ex-Breda coach factory (May/June); Pistoia Blues music festival (July); Giostra dell'Orso procession and jousting tournament (25 July); and Befana, a fun re-enactment of a story about an old witch's rescue from the bell tower, put on by the fire brigade (6 January).

Where to eat & drink

Regional specialities are *biroldo*, a spicy boiled sausage; *migliaccio*, a pancake made with pig's blood, pine nuts, raisins and sugar; and *confetti*, small, spiky white sweetmeats.

Lo Storno (via del Lastrone 8, 0573 26193, closed dinner Mon, all Sun and 2wks Nov, average €16) is a good traditional *osteria*. **La Bottegaia** (via del Lastrone 17, 0573 365 602, closed lunch Sun and all Mon, average €10) is Pistoia's most popular enoteca-restaurant with a cheerful, unpretentious ambience and fantastic dishes such as carpaccio of smoked fish with aromatic butter. It also has a deli and wine shop at number four on the same street.

Famous for its della Robbia frieze, the **Ospedale del Ceppo**.

San Jacopo (via Crispi 15, 0573 27786, closed Mon & Tue lunch, average €15) is renowned for its warm atmosphere and seafood.

Drinks-wise, **Vecchia Praga** (via del Sala 6, 0573 3115) is good for beer in the evenings, while trendy taverna **Lupulula** (vicolo de Bacchettoni 10, 0573 23331, closed Mon) also has a strong following. For a more genteel slurp, try **Caffè Pasticceria Valiani** (via Cavour 55, 0573 23034, closed Tue and 1st 3wks Aug), where frescoed walls were uncovered back in 1864 when its foundations were being laid. Regulars have included Verdi, Rossini, Bellini, Leoncavallo, Giordano and Puccini. It also houses a private art gallery.

Where to stay

There's a country-house atmosphere and great grub at the comfortable, slightly eccentric **Villa Vannini** (villa di Piteccio 6, Villa di Piteccio village, 0573 42031, doubles €35). More mainstream is the pleasant, central **Hotel Leon Bianco** (via Panciatichi 2, 0573 26675, doubles €50-€100). **Hotel Firenze** (via Curtatone e Montanara 42, 0573 23141, doubles €50-€80) is friendly, comfortable and good value. **Hotel Piccolo Ritz** (via A Vannucci 67, 0573 26775, doubles €42-€85) is convenient for the station. There are over 100 farm-stays around Pistoia. Call the tourist office for a brochure.

Montecatini Terme

Montecatini has a restrained elegance that's always charmed the European bourgeoisie. But the town's historic thermal spas are attracting interest from a new generation of alternative health enthusiasts and its grand parks are packed at weekends with Tuscans enjoying Montecatini's atmosphere. This can mean that the town's 200-plus hotels can't match the demand. The spas themselves are modernising to keep up with trends. There are several of them dotted around the gardens in the north side of town. On a balmy evening, a lovely diversion is to ride the funicular railway (viale Alfredo Diaz, €3 single, €5 return) up to Montecatini Alto to take in one of the area's most stunning panoramas.

Where to eat & drink

Of several restaurants with outdoor tables grouped around Alto's main piazza, **La Torre** (piazza Giusti 8, 0572 70650, closed Tue, average €22) is a good choice. Back down in Montecatini, it's tougher deciding where to eat. The smart, exclusive **Gourmet Restaurant** (via Amendola 6, 0572 771 012, closed Tue, average €50) has a long list of great seafood dishes such as gnocchi with spider crabs. More fun and down to earth, though, is **Egisto's** (piazza Cesare Battisti 13, 0572 78413, closed Tue, average €23), with its funky interior and non-traditional pastas alongside Tuscan classics. Despite the 1970s decor, **San Francisco** (corso Roma 112, 0572 79632, closed Thur, average €35) does good wood-oven pizzas and seafood pasta. If you want to sample Tuscan wines, staff at **Il Chicco d'Uva Vineria** (viale Verdi 35, 0572 910 300, closed Mon and Feb) are laid-back experts. Stand at the bar for wine by the glass or lounge in the back room.

Where to stay

Up near Montecatini Alto there are one or two accommodation options including the upmarket and tasteful **Casa Albertina** (via Baccelli, 0572 900 238, doubles €104) with glorious views over Nievole valley. In town, the **Grand Hotel Bellavista Palace** (viale Fedeli 2, 0572 78122, doubles €70-€150), with its indoor and outdoor pools and fading opulence, is the glitzy option. The **Hotel Savoia & Campana** (viale Cavallotti 10, 0572 772 670, doubles €50-€89) is in one of Montecatini's oldest buildings. **Hotel Verena** (viale Cavallotti 35, 0572 72809, doubles €26-€49) is a gem of a *pensione*. There's also **Minerva Palace** (via Cavour 14, 0572 904 406, doubles €88-€146) and, if it's full, there's a host of other budget to mid range hotels nearby.

Collodi

East of Lucca on the SS435, a puppet regime of a different kind rules over **Collodi**. It's the birthplace of the author of Italy's most cherished fairytale character, Pinocchio. This claim to fame brings the tourist dollar to what is an otherwise minor, but not unattractive, town. There's no shortage of signs directing visitors to **Pinocchio Park** (0572 429 342, admission €8.50, €6.50 under-14s). Opened in 1956, it features a walk-through maze and Pinocchio statues, including one by Emilio Greco, and a colourful mosaic-lined courtyard by Venturino Venturi.

Just across the road from the park, **Giardino Garzoni** (piazza della Vittoria 1, 0572 429 590, admission €5.20) are baroque gardens that took more than 170 years to complete after the construction of the Garzoni residence in 1633. Designed by the Marquis Romano di Alessandro Garzoni, they're a

The discreet charm of **Montecatini Terme**. *See p198.*

masterpiece of perspective and symmetry, and their current state of faded glory can make them seem either highly atmospheric or simply in need of some TLC.

Pescia

Certainly the main, and arguably the only reason to visit this long strip of a town straddling the humid Pescia river is its budding flower industry. Like nowhere else in Italy, Pescia cultivates, auctions and exports everything from chrysanthemums to bonsai olive trees. The hills surrounding the town are studded with greenhouses, and flower merchants gather for Pescia's international fairs. See and smell the results of the industry at the **Centro di Commercializzazione dei Fiori** just south of the train station (via S d'Acquisto 10-12, 0572 440 140).

Abetone

If you don't want to fork out for the northern ski resorts and are willing to try gentler slopes, head for Abetone. Just 85 kilometres (53 miles) from Florence, it's easy to get to for the weekend or even a day trip. It can get very crowded (particularly during the busy *settimana bianca* season, from January to March, when parents take kids out of school for a week on the slopes), but its wide runs are ideal for beginners and intermediate skiers. On average, ski-boot hire costs €15 per day and ski passes are €21.50 per weekday, €26.50 at the weekend.

Where to stay

The one-star **Noemi** (via Brennero 244, 0573 60168, €26-€49) has ten en suite rooms.

Resources

Tourist information

Abetone *0573 60231 tourist information, 0573 60001 ski line.*
Montecatini Terme APT *Viale Verdi 66 (0572 772 244).* **Open** 9am-12.30pm, 3-6pm Mon-Sat; 9am-noon Sun.
Pistoia APT *Piazza Duomo (0573 21622).* **Open** 9am-1pm, 3-6pm Mon-Sat.

Getting there

By bus

Lazzi (055 363 041) runs regular buses between Florence, Prato, Pistoia and Montecatini Terme. Florence-Prato and Florence-Pistoia take 45mins and Florence-Montecatini about 1hr. **Cap** (055 214 637) links Pistoia and Prato with Florence. **CLAP** (0583 587 897) buses connect Lucca with Pescia (journey time around 45mins) and less regularly with Collodi. Regular 'ski buses' run daily from Florence to Abetone in season. For timetable information, call 0573 60001.

By car

Prato, Pistoia, Montecatini and nearby Monsummano are accessible off the east–west A11 *autostrada*.

By train

Regular trains on the Florence-Lucca line service Prato (journey time from Florence 25mins), Pistoia (35mins) and Montecatini (50mins). Pescia is served by regular trains on the line from Florence (60-75mins) to Lucca (20mins).

Pisa

Lean, mean tourist machine.

As well as its world-famous tower, Pisa is known for having two New Years. When the rest of Europe opted for the Gregorian calendar (introduced in Tuscany in 1749 by ducal decree) that starts on 1 January, Pisa stuck to 25 March. As well as being the zodiacal new year, it's widely accepted as the date of the Annunciation when the angel delivered the results of Mary's unsolicited pregnancy test.

Pisa's glory days have gone, but the attitude hasn't. If you want to drive a Pisan insane, ask: 'How could Pisa have been a maritime republic if it isn't on the coast?' The answer is the rivermouth silted up and moved 15 kilometres (9.5 miles) west.

In 1998 the original harbour was discovered just 500 metres from the **Leaning Tower** and one far-fetched tale even has it that the tower was orginally planned as a lighthouse. An Italian government minister described the old harbour site as the marine equivalent of Pompeii. Now 22 of the 2,000-year-old ships have been found and several extensively excavated. Most are still on site and you can only see them by pre-arranged tour; contact the Arsenale Medicio (lungarno Simonelli, 050 21441, admission €3).

Pisa, straddling the River Arno, is enclosed within the remains of its medieval city walls. Between piazza della Stazione and the Arno the Mezzogiorno (south) part of the city contains few sights, though the riverbank views themselves are rather fine. The main focus for visitors is north of the river in Tramontana, especially around the **Campo dei Miracoli**.

Pisa has two major festivals, the **Luminaria di San Ranieri** (16 June), followed by a regatta, and the **Gioco del Ponte** (bridge pageant) on the last Sunday in June. For both, *see pp152-6*.

Sightseeing

Campo dei Miracoli

It's a miracle that the 'Field of Miracles' is still in evidence at all. Every structure on this expanse of grass and stone – reclaimed from marshes and built on between the 11th and 13th centuries – tilts in a different direction.

The layout of the Duomo, Baptistery, Leaning Tower and Camposanto is haphazard. Perhaps realising that future generations would not understand it, 13th-century court astrologer Guido Bonatti detailed its cosmological symbolism, attributing it to the theme of Aries. Arrive early morning before the crowds.

General information

050 560 547/www.duomo.pisa.it. Bus 3A from train station to piazza del Duomo. **Admission** €10.50 (all sights); €8.50 (any 4 sights, without Duomo); €6 (any 2 sights, without Duomo). **No credit cards.**

The ticket offices are in four sites (depicted by yellow triangles on maps and signposts at the Campo) with the tourist office next to the ticket office in the north-east corner. There's also a left luggage facility.

Baptistery

050 560 547/www.duomo.pisa.it. **Open** *Summer* 8am-7.40pm daily. *Spring & autumn* 9am-7.40pm daily. *Winter* 9am-4.40pm daily. **Admission** €5.

The marble Baptistery was designed by Diotisalvi (meaning 'God save you') in 1153 but not finished until 1395 when the 12-sided pyramid that first topped it was covered by a more harmonious, onion-shaped dome. Nicola Pisano's 1260 pulpit was the first of the commissions setting the style for the rest, but most of the precious artwork has been shuffled to the Museo dell'Opera del Duomo for safekeeping. Before you leave tip a guard and he'll sing. The echoes turn the soloist into an ethereal chorus of angels.

Camposanto

Open *Summer* 8am-7.40pm daily. *Spring & autumn* 9am-5.40pm daily. *Winter* 9am-4.40pm daily. **Admission** €5.

The Camposanto (Holy Field) centres on a patch of dirt supposedly carried from the Holy Land to Pisa by the Crusaders. Lining the Gothic cloisters around the edge of the field are the gravestones of VIP Pisans buried in holy soil. On the west wall hang two massive lengths of chain that were once strung across the entrance to the Pisan port to keep out enemy ships. In 1944 an Allied bomb landed on the campo destroying frescoes and sculptures, including a reportedly fabulous cycle by Benozzo Gozzoli. A few survived, though, including *Triumph of Death*, *Last Judgement* and *Hell*.

Duomo

050 560 547/www.duomo.pisa.it. **Open** *Spring-autumn* 10am-7.40pm Mon-Sat; 1-7.40pm Sun. *Winter* 10am-12.45pm Mon-Sat; 3-4.45pm Sun. **Admission** €2. **No credit cards.**

Pisa's cathedral is one of the earliest and finest examples of Pisan Romanesque architecture. Begun in 1063 by Buscheto the delicate, blindingly white marble four-tiered façade incorporates Moorish

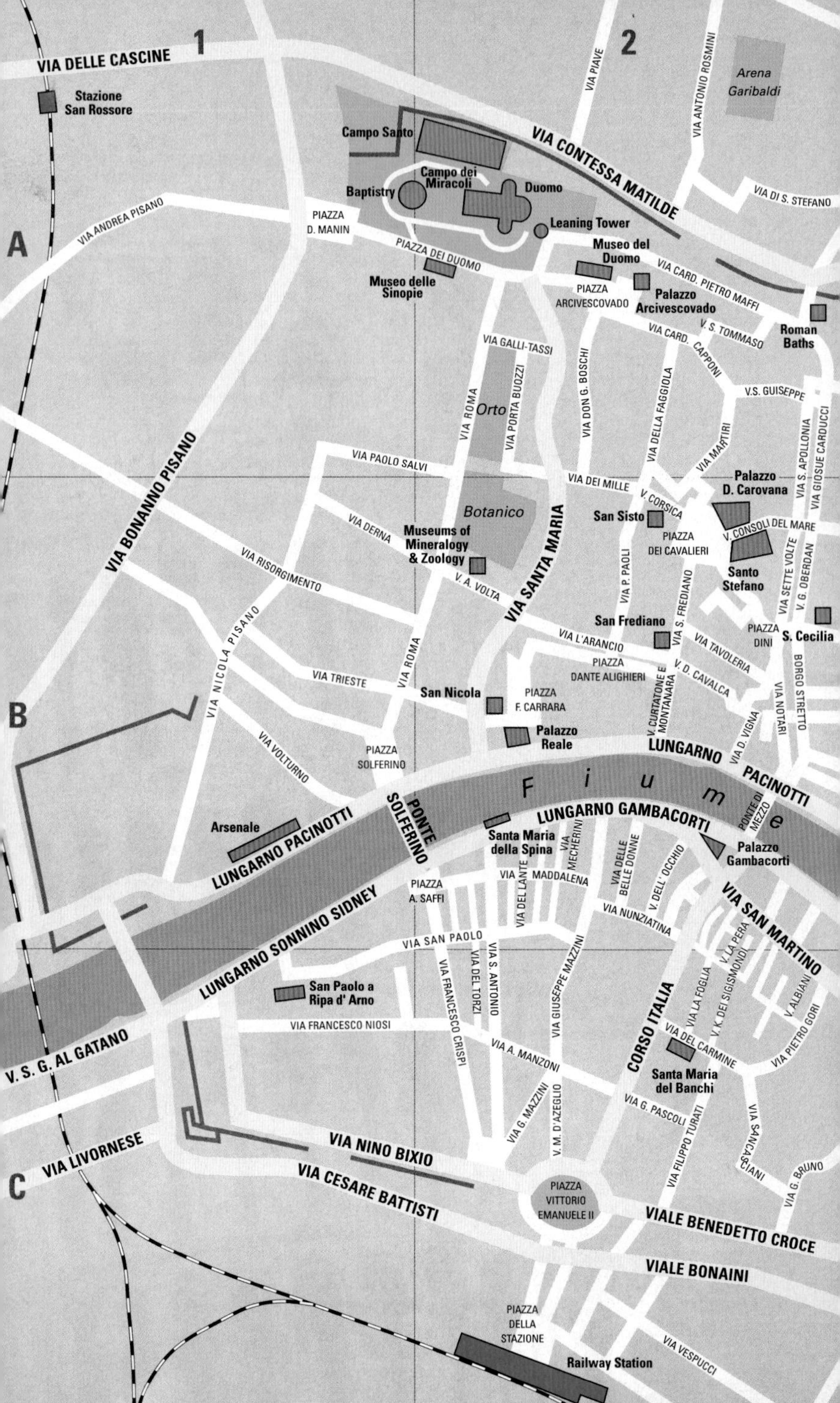
1
2
A
B
C
VIA DELLE CASCINE
Stazione San Rossore
VIA PIAVE
VIA ANTONIO ROSMINI
Arena Garibaldi
Campo Santo
VIA CONTESSA MATILDE
Campo dei Miracoli
Baptistry
Duomo
VIA DI S. STEFANO
VIA ANDREA PISANO
PIAZZA D. MANIN
Leaning Tower
PIAZZA DEI DUOMO
Museo del Duomo
Museo delle Sinopie
VIA CARD. PIETRO MAFFI
PIAZZA ARCIVESCOVADO
Palazzo Arcivescovado
Roman Baths
V. S. TOMMASO
VIA CARD. CAPPONI
VIA GALLI-TASSI
VIA DON G. BOSCHI
VIA DELLA FAGGIOLA
V.S. GUISEPPE
VIA ROMA
VIA PORTA BUOZZI
Orto
VIA MARTIRI
VIA S. APOLLONIA
VIA GIOSUE CARDUCCI
VIA PAOLO SALVI
VIA DEI MILLE
Palazzo D. Carovana
V. CORSICA
VIA BONANNO PISANO
Botanico
San Sisto
VIA DERNA
Museums of Mineralogy & Zoology
PIAZZA DEI CAVALIERI
V. CONSOLI DEL MARE
VIA SANTA MARIA
VIA RISORGIMENTO
V. A. VOLTA
VIA P. PAOLI
VIA S. FREDIANO
Santo Stefano
VIA SETTE VOLTE
V. G. OBERDAN
VIA NICOLA PISANO
San Frediano
PIAZZA DINI
S. Cecilia
VIA L'ARANCIO
VIA TAVOLERIA
PIAZZA DANTE ALIGHIERI
V. D. CAVALCA
BORGO STRETTO
VIA TRIESTE
VIA ROMA
San Nicola
PIAZZA F. CARRARA
V. CURTATONE E MONTANARA
VIA NOTARI
Palazzo Reale
VIA D. VIGNA
VIA VOLTURNO
PIAZZA SOLFERINO
LUNGARNO
PACINOTTI
Fiume
PONTE SOLFERINO
LUNGARNO GAMBACORTI
PONTE DI MEZZO
Arsenale
LUNGARNO PACINOTTI
Santa Maria della Spina
VIA MECHERINI
VIA DELLE BELLE DONNE
Palazzo Gambacorti
VIA MADDALENA
VIA DEL LANTE
V. DELL' OCCHIO
PIAZZA A. SAFFI
VIA SAN MARTINO
LUNGARNO SONNINO SIDNEY
VIA NUNZIATINA
VIA SAN PAOLO
V. LA PERA
San Paolo a Ripa d' Arno
VIA FRANCESCO CRISPI
VIA DEL TORZI
VIA S. ANTONIO
VIA GIUSEPPE MAZZINI
CORSO ITALIA
VIA LA FOGLIA
V. K. DEI SIGISMONDI
V. ALBIANI
VIA FRANCESCO NIOSI
VIA DEL CARMINE
VIA PIETRO GORI
V. S. G. AL GATANO
VIA A. MANZONI
Santa Maria del Banchi
VIA G. PASCOLI
VIA G. MAZZINI
V. M. D'AZEGLIO
VIA FILIPPO TURATI
VIA SANCASCIANI
VIA LIVORNESE
VIA NINO BIXIO
VIA CESARE BATTISTI
PIAZZA VITTORIO EMANUELE II
VIA G. BRUNO
VIALE BENEDETTO CROCE
VIALE BONAINI
PIAZZA DELLA STAZIONE
VIA VESPUCCI
Railway Station

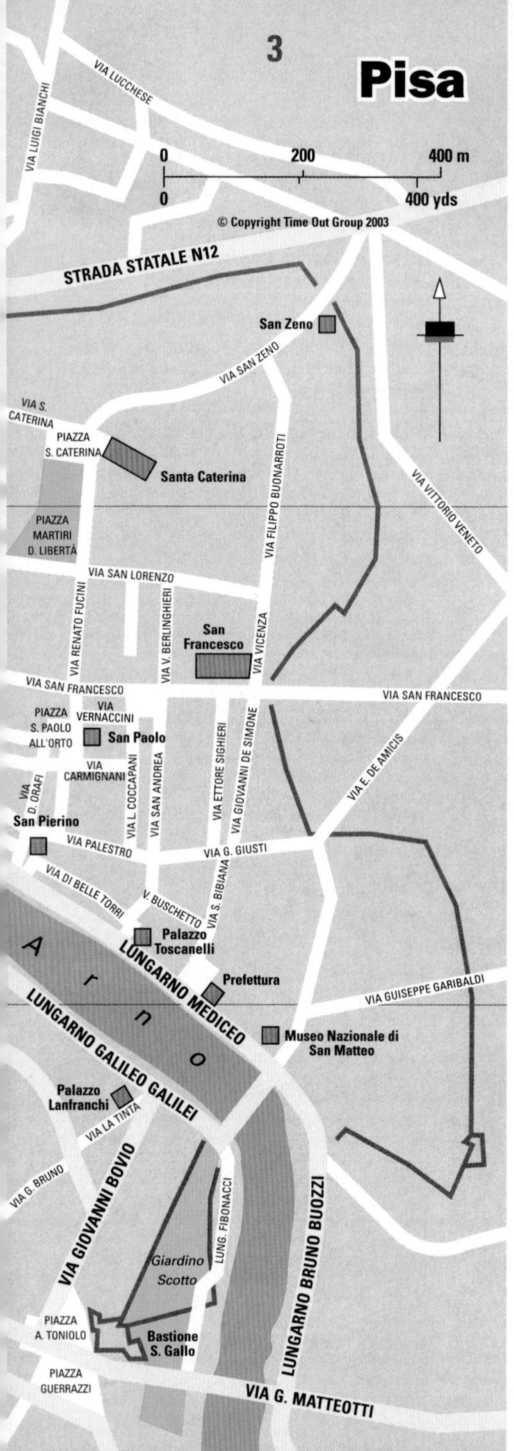

A. Volta, Via - B2
Albiani, Via - C2
Andrea Pisano, Via - A1
Antonio Rosmini, Via - A2
Belle Donne, Via Delle - B2
Benedetto Croce, Viale - C2
Berlinghieri, Via V. - B3
Bonaini, Viale - C2
Bonanno Pisano, Via - A1, B1
Borgo Stretto - B2
Buschetto, Via - B3
Card. Pietro Maffi, Via - A2
Card. Capponi, Via - A2
Carmignani, Via. - B3
Carmine, Via Del - C2
Cascine, Via Delle - A1
Cesare Battisti, Via - C1, 2
Consoli Del Mare, Via - B2
Contessa Matilde, Via - A2
Corsica, Via - B2
Corso Italia - B2, C2
Curtatone E Mont, Via - B2
D. Cavalca, Via - B2
D. Orafi, Via - B3
D. Vigna, Via - B2
De Amicis, Via E. - B3
Del Lante, Via - B2
Del Torzi, Via - C2
Dell' Occhio, Via - B2
Derna, Via - A2
Di Mezzo, Via - B2
Don G. Boschi, Via - A2
Ettore Sighieri, Via - B3
Faggiola, Via Della - A2
Filippo Buonarroti, Via - A3, B3
Filippo Turati, Via - C2
Francesco Crispi, Via - C2
Francesco Niosi, Via - C1, 2
G. Bruno, Via - C2
G. Giusti, Via - B3
G. Matteotti, Via - C3
G. Oberdan, Via - B2
G. Pascoli, Via - C2
Galli-Tassi, Via - A2
Giosue Carducci, Via - A2
Giovanni Bovio, Via - C3
Giovanni De Simone, Via - B3
Giuseppe Mazzini, Via - B2, C2
Guiseppe Garibaldi, Via -B3
K. Dei Sigismondi, Via - C3
L. Coccapani, Via - B3
La Foglia, Via - C2
La Pera, Via - B2
La Tinta, Via - C3
L'arancio, Via - B2
Livornese, Via - C1
Lucchese, Via - A3
Luigi Bianchi, Via - A3
Lung. Fibonacci - C3
Lungarno Bruno Buozzi - C3
Lungarno Galileo Galilei - C3
Lungarno Gambacorti - B2
Lungarno Mediceo - B3, C3
Lungarno Pacinotti - B1/2
Lungarno R. Simonelli - B1, 2
Lungarno Sonnino Sidney - B1, C1
Maddalena, Via - B2
Martiri, Via - A2
Mecherini, Via - B2
Mille, Via Dei - B2
Nicola Pisano, Via - B1
Nino Bixio, Via - C1,2
Notari, Via - B2
P. Paoli, Via - B2
Palestro, Via - B3
Paolo Salvi, Via - A1
Piave, Via - A2
Piazza A. Saffi - B2
Piazza A. Toniolo - C3
Piazza Arcivescovado - A2
Piazza D. Manin - A2
Piazza Dante Alighieri - B2
Piazza Dei Cavalieri - B2
Piazza Dei Duomo - A1, 2
Piazza Della Stazione - C2
Piazza Dini - B2
Piazza F. Carrara - B2
Piazza Guerrazzi - C3
Piazza Martiri D. Libertà - B3
Piazza S. Caterina - A3
Piazza S. Paolo All'orto - B3
Piazza Solferino - B1
Piazza Vittorio Emanuele Ii - C2
Pietro Gori, Via - C2
Porta Buozzi, Via - A2
Renato Fucini, Via - B3
Risorgimento, Via - B1
Roma, Via - A2
S. Antonio, Via - B2, C2
S. Apollonia, Via - A2/B2
S. Bibiana, Via - B3
S. Frediano, Via - B2
S. G. Al Gatano, Via - C1
S. Stefano, Via - A2
S. Tommaso, Via - A2
San Andrea, Via - B3
San Francesco, Via - B3
San Lorenzo, Via - B3
San Martino, Via - B2
San Paolo, Via - B2
San Zeno, Via - A3
Sancasciani, Via - C2
Santa Maria, Via - A2, B2
Sette Volte, Via - B2
Solferino, Ponte - B1/2
Strada Statale N12 - A3
Tavoleria, Via - B2
Torri, Via Di Belle -B3
Trieste, Via - B1
V. M. D'Azeglio, Via - C2
Vernaccini, Via - B3
Vespucci, Via - C2
Vicenza, Via - B3
Vittorio Veneto, Via - A3, B3
Volturno, Via - B1

mosaics and glass within the arcades (there are more examples in the Museo dell'Opera del Duomo, *see below*). Buscheto's tomb is set in the wall on the left side of the façade. The brass doors (touch the lizard for good luck) by the Giambologna school were added in 1602 to replace the originals, which were destroyed in a fire in 1595. The main entrance facing the Leaning Tower is called the Portale di San Ranieri and features bronze doors by Bonanno da Pisa (1180), which survived the fire. After the fire the Medici family came to the rescue and immediately began restorations. But at the time nothing could be done for Giovanni Pisano's superb Gothic pulpit (1302-11), which was incinerated and lay dismembered in crates until the 1920s. Legend has it that the censer suspended near the now-restored pulpit triggered Galileo's discovery of the principles of pendular motion, but it was actually cast six years later. Crane your neck to admire the Moorish dome decorated by a vibrant fresco of the *Assumption* by Orazio and Girolamo Riminaldi (1631). Behind the altar is a mosaic by Cimabue of St John (1302).

Leaning Tower

In the south-east corner of the campo, the famous tower has a seven-tiered campanile. Begun in 1173 (the commemorative plaque says 1174 because of the offbeat Pisan New Year) it started to lean almost as soon as it was erected. The top level, housing the seven bells not rung since 1993, was added in 1350. In 1989, the last year before the tower was closed to the public, more than a million visitors scrambled up its 294 steps. After years of restoration work (*see p207*) it reopened in December 2001 with visits restricted to groups of 30 paying €15 a head for a guided tour. This can only be booked on the internet at www.opapisa.it at least 15 days before, or in person at the ticket office next to the tourist information. Children under eight aren't allowed. If you don't manage to get one of the coveted tickets, the best views of the campanile are from the courtyard of the Museo dell'Opera del Duomo. But be warned: according to Pisan superstition, seeing the tower before an exam will bring disastrous results.

Museo dell'Opera del Duomo

050 560 547/www.duomo.pisa.it. **Open** *Summer* 8am-7.20pm daily. *Spring & autumn* 9am-5.20pm daily. *Winter* 9am-4.20pm daily. **Admission** €5.

This museum contains works from the monuments of the piazza del Duomo. It houses sculptures from the 12th to 14th centuries, including a clutch of notable works by Giovanni Pisano.

Museo delle Sinopie

050 560 547/www.duomo.pisa.it. **Open** *Summer* 8am-7.40pm daily. *Spring & autumn* 9am-5.40pm daily. *Winter* 9am-4.40pm daily. **Admission** €5.

The 1944 bombings and subsequent restoration work uncovered *sinopie* from beneath the frescoes in the Camposanto. These reddish-brown preliminary sketches were meant to be hidden forever after the artist covered the original *arriccio* (dry plaster on which the sketches were made) with a lime-rich plaster called *grassello*. Among the most important *sinopie* are the *Triumph of Death, The Last Judgement, Stories from the Anchorites* and *The Crucifixion* by Francesco Traini, and the *Theological Cosmography* by Piero di Puccio.

Torre di Santa Maria

Open 10am-6pm daily. **Admission** €2.
No credit cards.

Head here for a good overview of the Campo dei Miracoli and access to a small part of the city walls.

Other sights

Museo Nazionale di Palazzo Reale

Lungarno Pacinotti 46 (050 220 1384). **Open** 9am-3pm Mon-Fri; 9am-2pm Sat. **Admission** €3; €6.50 with Museo Nazionale di San Matteo.
No credit cards.

Housed in a Medici palace dating from 1583, this museum shows many works donated by private collectors of Medici pieces. Portrait paintings represent members of various European dynasties. There's also authentic Gioco del Ponte gear, the garb worn by medieval Pisans when they locked heads on the Ponte di Mezzo.

Museo Nazionale di San Matteo

Piazza San Matteo in Soarta, lungarno Mediceo (050 541 865). **Open** 8.30am-7.30pm Tue-Sat; 8.30am-1.30pm Sun. **Admission** €4; €6.50 with Museo Nazionale di Palazzo Reale. **No credit cards**.

Once a convent, this 12th- to 13th-century building now contains Pisan and Islamic medieval ceramics, works by Masaccio, Fra' Angelico, and Domenico Ghirlandaio, and a bust by Donatello.

Orto Botanico

Via L Ghini 5 (050 911 374). **Open** 8am-5pm Mon-Fri; 8am-1pm Sat. **Admission** free.

Closed for restoration until 30 April 2004, this is the oldest university garden in Europe and was originally used to study the medicinal values of plants. Founded by Luca Ghini in 1543 it was then replanted in different parts of the city until it found its permanent home here in 1595.

Piazza dei Cavalieri

Pisa's second most important piazza houses the Palazzo dei Cavalieri. The palazzo is the seat of one of Italy's most esteemed universities, the Scuola Normale Superiore, which was established by Napoleon Bonaparte in 1810. A beautiful piazza, it has long been a focal point of Pisa.

Vasari designed most of the piazza's buildings in the 16th century, including the Chiesa dei Cavalieri, Palazzo della Conventuale (opposite the church), erected as home to the Cavalieri of Santo Stefano, Palazzo del Consiglio dell'Ordine and Palazzo Gherardesca. Palazzo Gherardesca occupies the site of a medieval prison. In 1288 Count Ugolino della Gherardesca and three of his male heirs were condemned to starve to death there for covert negotiations with Florentines. It took Ugolino nine months to die. He allegedly ate his own kids. Dante, seizing the chance to get at the Pisans, depicted the count gnawing on someone's head for eternity in Hell (Canto XXXIII, *Inferno*).

You'll see the Maltese Cross everywhere in this piazza, but nowhere else in Pisa. Cosimo wanted to hammer home the parallel between his new Cavalieri of Santo Stefano and the crusading Knights of Malta. Elsewhere you're likely to spot the Pisan cross with two balls resting on each point.

San Nicola

Via Santa Maria 2 (tel/fax 050 24677).
Open 8am-noon, 5-6.30pm Mon-Sat; 9am-noon, 5.30-6.30pm Sun. **Admission** free.
Dating from 1150, the church of San Nicola is dedicated to one of Pisa's patron saints, San Nicola da Tolentino. In one chapel is a painting showing the saint protecting Pisa from the plague in around 1400. Built on unstable ground, the campanile leans.

Santa Maria della Spina

Lungarno Gambacorti (050 21441). **Open** *June-Aug* 11am-1.30pm, 2.30pm-6pm Tue-Fri; 11am-8pm Sat, Sun. *Apr-May, Sept* 10am-1.30pm, 2.30-6pm Tue-Sun. *Oct-Mar* 10am-2pm Tue-Sun. **Admission** €1.10. **No credit cards**.
This gorgeous, tiny Gothic church on the bank of the Arno is finally open again after restoration. Originally an oratory, it took its present form in 1323. It gets its name from the fact that it used to own what was claimed to be a thorn (*spina*) from Christ's crown, brought back by Crusaders.

Where to eat & drink

Restaurants

Cèe alla Pisana (eels) has been one of Pisa's culinary assets for centuries (*cèe* comes from ciechi or 'blind ones'). Sadly, the poor little creatures have been fished almost to extinction, and few venues now serve the costly winter delicacy. When they are available, the eels are fished out of the Arno and tossed in warm oil, garlic and sage, then sautéed and served seconds after they cease wriggling.

Bruno

Via Luigi Bianchi 12 (050 560 818). **Open** noon-3pm, 7-10.30pm Wed-Mon. **Average** €40. **Credit** AmEx, DC, MC, V.
Bruno concentrates on typical, good-value Tuscan cooking. Try the *ribollita*, supposedly the best this side of the Arno, or pasta with rabbit and wild boar.

Cagliostro

Via del Castelletto 26-30 (050 575 413/ cagliostro@csinfo.it). **Open** 7.45pm-1am Mon; 12.45-2.30pm, 7.45pm-1am, Wed, Thur, Sun; 12.45-2.30pm, 8pm-2am Fri, Sat. **Average** €15 lunch, €25 dinner. **Credit** AmEx, DC, MC, V.
This intriguing *enoteca* and restaurant, located off via Ulisse Dini close to piazza dei Cavalieri, is named after a Sicilian count who masqueraded as an alchemist in France and Italy in the 18th century. The extensive wine list here complements the eclectic menu, which draws on recipes from all over Italy. It's tricky to find so ask for the restaurant not the street.

Il Campano

*Via Cavalca 19 (050 580 585).***Open** 12.30-3pm; 7.30-10pm Mon, Tue, Thur-sun. **Average** €20. **Credit** AmEx, DC, MC, V.
A cool trattoria tucked away in the fruit market offering an exciting array of colours, tastes and textures. Try home-made pastas such as *maltagliati* with huge chunks of delicious fresh lobster in its shell with asparagus (the kind of dish that can put you in a good mood for the rest of the day) or the fabulous *antipasti completo*.

La Mescita

Via Cavalca 2 (050 544 294).
Open 1-2.15pm Sat, Sun; 1-2.15pm, 8-10.30pm Tue-Fri. Closed 3wks Aug. **Average** €30.
No credit cards.
Set in the heart of Vettovaglie market, La Mescita is pretty and tranquil. Try *brandade di stoccafisso* (salt cod) with tomatoes. Check the window for its calendar of *degustazione* and creative cooking nights.

Osteria dei Cavalieri

Via San Frediano 16 (050 580 858). **Open** 12.30-2pm, 7.45-10pm Mon-Fri; 7.45-10pm Sat. Closed late July-late Aug. **Average** €30. **Credit** AmEx, DC, MC, V.
One of Pisa's best eateries, especially for the money, serving typical Tuscan dishes with flair – steak with beans and mushrooms or *tagliolini* with rabbit and asparagus, perhaps. Noteworthy wine list.

Osteria del Violino

Via La Tinta 33 (050 43452).
Open noon-2pm, 8-10.30pm Mon-Sat. **Average** €20. **Credit** AmEx, MC, V.
South of the river and fancy something cheap and tasty? Head for this new backstreet eaterie. Cheerful staff serve dishes such as ravioli with ricotta in cream of leek and truffle sauce for a princely €5.50.

Re di Puglia

Via Aurelia Sud 7 (050 960 157). **Open** 8-10pm Wed-Sat; 1-3pm, 8-10pm Sun. Closed 2wks Jan. **Average** €25. **No credit cards**.
Slabs of succulent meat grilled in front of your eyes on the open fire are the focus of this rustic restaurant a few kilometres south of Pisa on the Livorno road. While the meat (especially beef, lamb and rabbit) reigns supreme, the menu also includes five types of Tuscan *antipasti*. Eat outdoors in summer.

Il Ristoro del Vecchi Macelli

Via Volturno 49 (050 20424). **Open** 12.30-3pm, 7.30-10pm Mon, Tue, Thur-Sat; 7.30-10pm Sun. Closed 2wks Aug. **Average** €40. **Credit** AmEx, DC, MC, V.

A blend of elegant atmosphere with quality ingredients and classy presentation makes this one of Pisa's best-loved restaurants. Sample sophisticated offerings such as sea bass in a delicate onion sauce with oyster gratinée or breast of duck with basil and carrot sauce. Excellent service. Booking's advised.

Il Vecchio Dado

Lungarno Pacinotti 21-22, nr Ponte di Mezzo (050 580 900). **Open** 12.30-2pm, 7.30pm-12.30am Mon, Tue, Fri-Sun; 7.30pm-12.30am Thur. **Average** €22. **Credit** AmEx, DC, MC, V.

There's been a restaurant at this riverside site for 200 years. Most recently it's become a trendy and popular pizzeria. Make sure you reserve your seat.

Cafés, bars & *gelaterie*

Bar Duomo

Via Santa Maria 114 (050 561 918). **Open** 8am-7.20pm Mon-Wed, Fri-Sun. **No credit cards.**

Sip a Prosecco right next to the Campo dei Miracoli. Naturally, you'll pay twice the price but, if you can get a seat outside or by the window, it's worth it.

Pasticceria Salza

Borgo Stretto 46 (050 580 144). **Open** 7.45am-8.30pm Tue-Sun. **No credit cards.**

Distinguished venue with café tables in the front, sweet shop inside and restaurant for well-to-do society and business types at the back.

Pizzicheria Gastronomia a Cesqui

Piazza delle Vettovaglie 38 (050 580 269). **Open** 7am-1.30pm, 4-8pm Mon, Tue, Thur-Sat; 7am-1.30pm Wed. **No credit cards.**

This is a great deli for stocking up on cheeses, pastas, wines and snacks while you banter and gossip with staff and regulars.

Nightlife

Borderline

Via Vernaccini 7 (050 580 577). **Open** 9pm-2am Mon-Sat. **Admission** free-€10.50. **No credit cards.**

Good for late drinks or the occasional live gig.

Dottorjazz

Via Vespucci 10 (339 861 9298). **Open** 9pm-2am Tue-Sun. Closed June-Sept. **Admission** €10. **No credit cards.**

This unsigned live jazz venue is at the far end of what seems like a warehouse car park. With small candlelit tables and pictures of jazz greats on the walls it attracts folk from in and out of town. Thursday night is blues night.

Teatro Verdi

Via Palestro 40 (050 941 111/542 600/ www.teatrodipisa.p.it). **Open** *Box office* 4-7pm Mon-Sat & 1hr before events. *Phone bookings* 11am-1.30pm Mon-Fri. Closed Aug. **Credit** MC, V.

An enjoyable venue for dance, drama and music.

Shopping

Most of the main shops in Pisa, especially the more expensive ones, are on corso Italia. Across from the Ponte di Mezzo is a funkier shopping zone starting at the loggia of borgo Stretto. Where the two meet you'll find the **Mercatino Antiquario** on the second weekend of every month. It also has a lot of modern arts and crafts for sale. Every morning there's the **Mercato Vettovaglie**, a fruit and vegetable market.

Where to stay

Accommodation in Pisa can be a bit hit and miss. And if you want to be sure of basic standards, don't go budget in this city. You'll find the nearest camping in **Marina di Pisa** (*see p208*).

The tourist information centre at the campo dei Miracoli (*see p207*) has a list of hotels. To ensure that you get a decent room reserve during high season, and book well in advance for major festivals.

Albergo Galileo

Via Santa Maria 12 (tel/fax 050 40621). **Rates** €45 single; €60 double. **No credit cards.**

Though it's illegal to employ Galileo Galilei's full name for commercial purposes in Pisa, this *pensione* manages to get away with using half of it. Five of Albergo Galileo's nine rooms are decorated with 17th-century frescoes.

Amalfitana

Via Roma 44 (050 29000). **Rates** €55 single; €65 double.

A favourite of visiting Italians seeking central, two- star accommodation.

Casa della Giovane

Via F Corridoni 29 (050 43061). **Rates** per person €15.50 double/triple. **No credit cards.**

This college with a women-only boarding house is close to the station and caters mostly to students and is therefore packed in term-time. Beware of the 10pm curfew at the Casa.

Centro Turistico Madonna dell'Acqua

Via Pietrasantina 13 (tel/fax 050 890 622). Bus 3. **Open** *Office* 6-11pm. **Rates** per person €21 double; €18 triple; €16 quadruple or bigger. **Credit** MC, V.

This is the only youth hostel in the Pisa area and its in a village a short distance outside the city. The hostel opens at 6pm. Don't turn up before otherwise you'll be hanging around.

Grand Hotel Duomo

Via Santa Maria 94 (050 561 894/fax 050 560 418/ www.grandhotelduomo.it). **Rates** €123 single; €178 double; €210 suite. **Credit** AmEx, DC, MC, V.

That way inclined

Pisa's emblematic campanile was an early leaner. When construction began in 1173 it rapidly became clear that architect Bonnano Pisano hadn't done his groundwork.

By the time the third storey was completed the tower was tilting northwards. In 1178 work was suspended. Nearly 100 years construction resumed. During this time the tower then begun veering south (its present direction). By late 14th century, despite all attempts to correct the impression of a curve as further tiers were added, the world's most famous leaning tower was finally completed.

If the quirky tower was ever a cause of embarrassment to Pisans, its merits as a tourist attraction made up for that. But while millions made the unnerving climb up the 294 steps, the belltower continued to tilt until in 1989, it was deemed in danger of collapse.

A complex rescue operation slowly swung into action. Of course, it was never the aim to straighten the tower entirely, but to correct its tilt by 40 centimetres (18 inches). In 1995 the scheme threatened to go wrong as the lean increased fractionally. But by December 2001, the then Minister of Public Works, Nerio Nesi, declared the 27.5 million project a triumph, with the monument now safeguarded for at least the next 250 years.

The supports are now gone and the tower is open to pre-arranged, guided groups (*see pp200-1*; eight-12 year olds must be hand-held by an adult, 12-18 year-olds must be accompanied by an adult).

Like an ageing aunt who's known better days, the Grand hints at bygone opulence that is now somewhat frayed around the edges. You can't fault its location though, nor the sweeping views it offers over the Campo dei Miracoli from its fourth-floor terrace. If you arrive by car, make sure you ask for a parking permit for via Santa Maria.

Relais dell'Orologio

Via della Fagiola 12-14 (behind Cavalieri, 050 830 361/www.hotelrelaisorologio.com). **Rates** €225-€286 single; €326-€620 double.

Managing director Maria Louisa Bignardi dreamed of turning her 13th-century house into a five-star hotel. This is the result. The 25 rooms are individually decorated. Go for the Peli di Vaglio suite with its exposed frescoes.

Royal Victoria

Lungarno Pacinotti 12 (050 940 111/fax 050 940 180/www.royalvictoria.it). **Rates** €95 single; €115 double. **Credit** AmEx, DC, MC, V.

This elegant hotel has been run by the Piegaja family since 1839. The building, some parts of which are more than 1,000 years old, has been carefully preserved. Many rooms, including those in the tower, face the Arno. Book in advance.

Resources

Hospital

Santa Chiara Via Roma 67 (050 992 111).

Police station

Questura via Mario Lalli 3 (050 583 511).

Post office

Piazza Vittorio Emanuele II 8 (050 5194).
Open 8.15am-7pm Mon-Sat.

Tourist Information

Turistica (APT) *Campo dei Miracoli 050 560 464 (for information on the whole Pisa area call 050 929 777/fax 050 929 764/www.pisa.turismo.toscana.it).* **Open** 9am-6pm Mon-Sat; 10.30am-6.30pm Sun. **Branches**: Piazza della Stazione 11 (050 42291); Galileo Galilei Airport (050 503 700).

Getting there & around

By air

Galileo Galilei Airport (050 849300) is Tuscany's major international airport (although Florence has pretty much caught up with it). The airport handles flights from all around Europe. For further information and details. There are frequent buses and regular trains into Pisa and Lucca from here. For further information, *see p278.*

By bus

Lazzi (piazza Sant Antonio, 050 46288) operates a regular service to Lucca (journey time 50mins) with onward connections to Florence (2hrs 30mins), as well as buses to Viareggio (50mins). **CPT** (piazza Sant Antonio, 050 505 511) covers the area around Pisa and runs buses to nearby areas such as Livorno and Marina di Pisa.

By taxi

Call **Radio Taxi** on 050 541 600, or there are taxi ranks at piazza Stazione and piazza del Duomo.

By train

Pisa is on a main train line to Rome (journey time 3hrs Intercity, 4hrs otherwise) and Genoa (2hrs). There are also frequent trains to Florence via Empoli (80mins), Livorno (15mins) and Lucca (25mins). Some trains also stop at Pisa Aeroporto and San Rossore. The train station is Pisa Centrale Piazza della Stazione (train info 892 021).

Pisa & Livorno Provinces

Rich pickings if you know where to look.

While the provinces of Pisa and Livorno contain many treasures, Livorno itself is unlikely to be a priority visit on many tourists' itineraries. Indeed, its low-key polyglot population is probably the most interesting thing about it. However, the stretch of coastline between Livorno and Piombino has, as well as pricey, parasol-stabbed beaches overrun with holidaymakers, a number of discreet, sandy coves surrounded by dunes and pine groves. A little further inland, between the coast and the Colline Metallifere to the east, is the northern section of the Maremma; stretching between Cecina and Follonica, this section is known as the Pisan Maremma.

San Miniato

Snaking along the crest of a lofty hill, with views over to Fiesole and to the coast, the town of San Miniato is dominated by the Pisa-Florence road and the via Francigena, which brought pilgrims from the north to Rome. In the 12th and 13th centuries the town was fortified and became one of Tuscany's foremost imperial centres, but it succumbed to Florence in the mid 1300s. Unfortunately, the interiors of both the 13th-century **Duomo** and the slightly later church of **San Domenico** were subjected to some heavy-handed baroque 'improvements'.

The spacious *loggiati* of San Domenico are used for an antiques and collectibles fair on the first Sunday of each month and an arts and crafts fair on the second. The surrounding area is rich in truffles and November weekends (part of the Festa del Tartufo, the truffle festival) are devoted to tasting them.

Where to eat

Caffè Centrale (via IV Novembre 19, 0571 43037, closed Mon, 1st 2wks Sept, average €10) serves simple pastas for lunch and has a great view. **L'Antro di Bacco** (via IV Novembre 13, 0571 43319, closed Sun, dinner Wed, average €25) serves up dishes such as roast lamb scotaditto and fillet of pork *al brunello*, while just outside town there's **Il Convio** (via San Maiano 2, 0571 408 114, closed Wed, average €30) with more Tuscan favourites plus a vegetarian menu. Even friendlier is **La Trattoria dell' Orcio Interrato** in nearby Montopoli Valdarno (piazza San Michele 2, 0571 466 878, closed Mon, dinner Sun in winter, average €35), which has a summer terrace.

Marina di Pisa

About five kilometres out of Pisa, halfway to Marina di Pisa, you'll see a signpost to the 11th-century church of San Pier in Grado. This area used to sit on Pisa's river estuary, but the Arno altered its course and left the church out on a limb. Built on the spot where St Peter is said to have first set foot off the boat from Antioch it now has a conspicuous lack of water. Vibrant 14th-century frescoes depicting the lives of Peter and Paul sit above 24 columns. An excavation to the rear of the church revealed a pillar from the first century.

Where to stay, eat & drink

Cliff (via Repubblica Pisana 4, Lungomare, Marina di Pisa, 050 36830, average €22) is one of several restaurants and cafés on the front where you can enjoy a meal or refreshments while soaking up the seaside atmosphere. **Il Pappafico** (Marina di Pisa, 050 35037, closed Mon-Wed, Sun, admission €15) on the southern road near Camping Internazionale (*see below*) is a lively bar and disco.

Camping Internazionale (via Litoranea in Marina di Pisa 7, 050 36553, closed Oct-Apr, rates €5.50-€7) is an upbeat campsite with bungalows, a private beach, beach amusements, watersports and lots more. To get there take the bus from piazza della Stazione to Marina di Pisa/Tirrenia and ask for the *campeggio*. The website at www.pisacamping.com also has a link to the site for **Camping St Michael**, 12 kilometres (nearly eight miles) from Pisa in San Rossore (*see p209*).

Tuscany

Fortezza Vecchia in Livorno. *See p210.*

Tirrenia

Still on the coast, south of Marina di Pisa and towards Livorno, Tirrenia has two public and a few private beaches along with a US military base and the flashy **Grand Hotel Continental** (largo Belvedere 26, 050 37031, doubles €86-€180), which sits directly on the beach. It boasts 200 luxury rooms, an Olympic-size pool, beach access, garage and parking. Book well in advance in summer.

San Rossore park (via Aurelia Nord 4, 050 525 500) offers guided walks and bike tours on weekends. It also organises horse treks and jaunts in horse-driven carriages.

Casciana Terme

Tucked away in the Pisan hills and less crowded than Montecatini or Saturnia, this spa town, known as Castrum ad Aquas to the Romans, was destroyed in World War II and rebuilt in the 1960s. **Terme di Casciana** (piazza Garibaldi 9, 0587 64461) has a large, luxurious modern pool and spa facilities fronted by a more traditional café. The lush hills between Casciana and the village of Terricciola resemble a uniformly rolling ocean.

A kilometre east of Calci, the **Certosa di Pisa** (050 938 430, closed Mon, Sun afternoon, admission €4) is a vast complex that was originally a monastery. From 1366 it was used on and off until it was completely abandoned by the Carthusian monks in 1969. The interior includes a 14th-century church, various cloisters and gardens. The former granaries, carpenters' workshops and cellars in the grounds now house the **Natural History Museum of the University of Pisa** (via Roma 103, 050 937 092, closed Mon, admission €5), which was founded in 1591 by Grand Duke Ferdinando I. It is considered one of the top three natural history museums in Italy.

Where to stay

Check out **La Speranza hotel** (via Cavour 44, 0587 646 215, doubles €57-€77) down the street from the thermal waters. It has an attractive little pool and gardens. **Villa Margherita** (via

Marconi 20, 0587 646 113, closed Nov-Apr, doubles €60-€80) is spacious and inviting. Two or three kilometres and a couple of hamlets further on from Terricciola is the stately new **Villa San Marco** (località San Marco 13, Terricciola, 0587 654 054, suites €200-€395), a recently restructured building dating back to the 11th century. When it's finished it will be a highly luxurious affair but only eight of the 20 suites were ready at the time of writing so check before booking. More accommodation options are available from the tourist office (via Cavour 9, 0587 646 258, closed winter).

Volterra

Volterra stands proudly on a 531-metre (1,750ft) peak between the Cecina and Era valleys in Pisa province. Traces from the Neolithic period were discovered here, but it wasn't until the fifth century BC that Etruscan culture flourished and Volterra's population grew to 25,000 – it became one of the 12 Etruscan states. Velathri (its Etruscan name) put up a hearty resistance to the expansionist Romans and was the last Etruscan city to fall to the Empire in 260 BC, when it was renamed Volaterrae.

The town as it appears today was built in the 12th and 13th centuries and virtually all traces of the Etruscans have been erased, save patches of the fortified walls that reveal its Etruscan foundations. Etruscan buffs shouldn't miss the **Museo Etrusco Guarnacci** (via Don Minzoni 15, 0588 86347, closed afternoons in winter,€7). It houses one of the world's most complete collections of artefacts discovered from this mysterious ancient population, including the celebrated 'evening shadow' statuette. The long thin statue was found by a local farmer and used as a firestoker until someone recognised its importance. The €7 ticket also gives you admission to Volterra's other two museums, the **Pinacoteca** (0588 87580, closed afternoons in winter) in the late 15th-century Palazzo Minucci Solaini – with its astounding use of colour, the fabulous Mannerist *Deposition* by Rosso Fiorentino alone is worth the visit – and the **Museo d'Arte Sacra** (0588 86290, closed afternoons in winter), which also boasts work by Rosso Fiorentino.

Since Etruscan times, Volterra's most important industry has been the production of alabaster artefacts (the area around the city contains one of Italy's largest deposits of the stone). Once used to adorn abbeys and palaces, the quality of products had declined so ruinously by the 1970s that famous designers from Milan were invited to inject new impetus into production. As a result, you can find some stylish items as well as a lot of complete kitsch.

Where to stay & eat

Trattoria del Sacco Fiorentino (piazza XX Settembre, 0588 88537, closed Wed, Jan & Feb, average €25) near the Etruscan museum is a cosy restaurant serving seasonal goodies such as gnocchi with spring vegetables or tagliatelle with courgettes and basil. There's a good choice of cheeses and an excellent wine list. Otherwise, for traditional home cooking try **Osteria il Ponte** (via Massetana-Locallità San Lorenzo, 0588 44160 closed Tue, average €15) on the road to Larderello.

Within the city **Hotel San Lino** (via San Lino 26, 0588 85250, doubles €47-€99), converted from a 15th-century convent, has its own pool and a shady cloister offering repair from the bustle. Two kilometres outside town, 15th century **Villa Rioddi** (0588 88053, €52-€88, €520-€925 weekly for a two-room apartment) also has a pool and a lovely garden.

Livorno

Livornese like to quip that they're like their local dish, *cacciucco*. Not literally a 'steamy dish of sea-beast parts cooked in wine', but rather a mix of people from different places, who together form a lively whole. A look in the local directory is telling: letters usually passed by in Italian (J, H, K and W) are more common.

The Livornese are among the most left-wing of all Italians, with an abundance of industrious fishermen and factory workers. Native flavours are strong, fresh and warming. *Il torpedine* is a short coffee with chilli and locally produced rum.

Livorno came into being when Pisa was in a pinch. The Arno silted up and the maritime republic of Pisa found itself without any sea, so Cosimo I pounced on this tiny fishing village in 1571. In 1593 a far-sighted constitution allowed foreigners to reside in the city regardless of nationality and religion, instantly endowing it with a cosmopolitan mentality.

The **Porto Mediceo**, with the red-brick bastion of the **Fortezza Vecchia** designed by Sangallo the Younger in 1521, quickly became the focus of city life. From here the canals of **Venezia Nuova** (or I Fossi) extend, tracing the pentagonal perimeter of Francesco I's late 16th-century plan for an ideal city. Look out for the concerts of the Effeto Venezia that take place in late July.

Blanket bombing during World War II did away with most of Livorno's historic monuments, and post-war reconstruction finished the job off. Buontalenti's piazza Grande was cut in two and, sadly, all that remains of the 16th-century Duomo is Inigo Jones's fine portico.

Where to stay, eat & drink

Osteria da Carlo (viale Caprera 43-45, 0586 897 050, closed Sun & 3wks Sept, average €22) does decent *cacciucco*, the famous spicy fish soup. Other good spots to try out the local fare are the renowned **La Chiave** across from Fortezza Nuova (scali delle Cantine 52, 0586 888 609, closed lunch, closed dinner Wed, average €30) and **Il Sottomarino** (via de' Terrazzini 46, 0586 887 025, closed Mon, Tue and 2wks July, average €30).

Disco-pubs are flourishing on Livorno's canals. **The Barge** (scali delle Anchore 6, 0586 888 320, closed Sun, Mon) has a piano bar, English bar and canalside tables. If you've stayed too late to make it back to Pisa, try the central **Hotel Gran Duca** (piazza Micheli 16, 0586 891 024, doubles €86-€124).

Cecina

Bypass Cecina proper and head for Marina di Cecina, a pleasant enough seaside town with a popular windsurfing beach. It has two two-star hotels that tend to fill up quickly – **Azzura** (viale della Vittoria 3, 0586 620 595, doubles €64) and **La Lampara Dipendenza** (viale della Vittoria 5, 0586 620 681, doubles €35-€65) – along with several three stars. Contact tourist information (piazza S Andrea 6, 0586 620 678) for a list.

From here you can head south to an area set aside as Italy's first World Wildlife Fund (WWF) nature reserve. Called the **Oasi di Bolgheri**, it provides a haven for rare ducks, geese and storks.

San Vincenzo

This former watchtower base is about halfway between Livorno and Grosseto on the via Aurelia. Its historic role is clear from the ruins left behind, in particular a Pisan tower from 1304 that still stands here as it has for 700 years, though it recently had an unfortunate paint job and now looks a bit like a sandcastle.

Many visitors come to San Vincenzo to eat at the charming, Michelin-starred **Gambero Rosso** (*p36* **The out of towners**). Some would call it snobby, others classy, but this restaurant's creative menu is a definite departure from the traditional norm of Tuscan cuisine.

About 20 kilometres (13 miles) north of San Vincenzo there's a left turn off via Aurelia that takes you up a magnificent tree-lined road leading to Bolgheri. This is where the Romantic poet Giosuè Carducci (1835-1907) grew up and where the medieval Gherardesca castle still stands.

Piombino & around

Not the first stop on your itinerary in its own right, Piombino is the place to catch ferries to Corsica, Elba (*see pp274-6*) and Pianosa.

The stretch of coastline north of Piombino up to the ruins of Etruscan Populonia is sandy and rocky by turns. This area has mystifying rock formations, necropolises, beaches and unspoilt waters. Follow signs to Silvoni on the far west of Piombino and keep going until you get to a trail head at Cala Moresca by the car park above the beach, where a series of tiny trails follow the coastline to the Golfo di Baratti.

Populonia, with its Etruscan necropolis, perches high above the little fishing port of Baratti. The historic remains and visitors' centre are across the road from the car park, outside the village. Within the village walls there's a small Etruscan museum and a tower to visit.

If you head south from Piombino to Grosseto, stop in at **Castiglione della Pescaia**. This busy fishing port offers a good choice of hotels, eateries and a pleasant town beach. Otherwise, go inland to Massa Marittima (*see p269*).

Resources

Tourist information

Livorno APT, *Piazza Cavour 6 (0586 204 611).* **Open** 9am-1pm, 3-5pm Mon-Fri; 9am-1pm Sat.
Piombino Ufficio Turismo, *Torre Comunale, via del Ferruccio (0565 225 639).* **Open** 9am-3pm, 5-11pm summer only.
San Miniato Ufficio di Turismo, *Piazza del Popolo (0571 42745).* **Open** *Summer* 9.30am-1pm, 3.30-7.30pm daily. *Winter* 9am-1pm, 3-6.30pm daily.
Associazione Pro Volterra *Via Giusto Turazza 2 (0588 86150/www.provolterra.it).* **Open** *Spring-Autumn* 9am-1pm, 3-7pm daily. *Winter* 9am-12.30pm, 3-6pm Mon-Sat.

Getting there

By car

Livorno is just off the coastal SS1 and a 20min drive south of Pisa along the same road. The A12 autostrada also runs past the city. The Poggibonsi exit of the Si-Fi (Siena-Florence) *autostrada* quickly gives access to Volterra.

By train & bus

Livorno's main station (on piazza Dante) is on the main Rome/Pisa train line, a 12min journey from Pisa. Trains also run to and from Florence (journey time 1hr 20mins) via Pisa and Empoli.

Driving is the easiest option, although **SITA** (800 373 760) runs buses from Florence to Volterra (1hr 50mins). **Lazzi** buses connect Livorno with Pisa, Lucca, Viareggio and Florence. Livorno is also a major port with departures to Sardinia, Corsica, Capraia and Sicily.

Siena

Discreet charm and animal magic.

Siena is a strange mixture of the sedate and the manic. Its harmonious pink buildings embrace the centrally located **piazza del Campo**, which expresses both facets of the city's soul: the quietude of prosperity well governed, epitomised by the ancient City Hall or **Palazzo Pubblico**; and the folly that is unleashed in July and August, during the two annual runs of the **Palio** horse race (*see p155*) around its perimeter.

What holds these dual realities together is a Sienese identity, a sameness in time that derives from stability. In the recent past Siena lost few citizens to emigration. Likewise, it has attracted relatively few workers from afar since its wealth is not due to industry, but to the activities of one of the world's oldest banks, the Monte dei Paschi di Siena, founded in 1472 and now a major local employer and a forefront player in national and international finance.

The historic centre of the city is actually divided into three sections: **Terzo di Città** was the original residential nucleus of Siena and comprises the Duomo; **Terzo di San Martino** grew up around the via Francigena, or pilgrim route heading south to Rome (St Martin was the patron saint of pilgrims and wayfarers); and **Terzo di Camollia**, with its churches and basilicas on the north side. Piazza del Campo is neutral, but generally connected with Terzo di San Martino. However, the Sienese sense of belonging is channelled through the organisation of the 17 *contrade*, or city districts that vie with each other for supremacy in the Palio. Each *contrada* has its own visible emblem, proudly affixed to walls and fountains to mark out its patch (*see p222* **Animal magnetism**).

SOME HISTORY

Siena's history is shrouded in mystery: who founded this ancient city and where does its name originate? Some traces of Bronze Age fortifications suggest its geographic vantage point has always been highly contested. The Etruscans settled here, creating an important trading colony with Volterra, and one theory is that the city was named after the prominent Etruscan Saina family. The city was refounded as a Roman colony, Saena Julia, by Emperor Augustus and it was another 1,000 years before it became an independent republic. What really put Siena on the map was the via Francigena, a pilgrim route that spanned the whole of Tuscany and was heavily trafficked throughout the Middle Ages. It brought trade in its wake, and this provided Siena with commercial and political clout. By 1125 the young city had amassed enough self-confidence to pick fights with its neighbours (it embarked on a plan to expand its territory, a move that didn't go unnoticed by Florence).

The hatred between Tuscany's sister cities over the following century was one of history's more malevolent rivalries. Things came to an explosive climax on 4 September 1260 when Siena won the bloody Battle of Montaperti.

A 15,000-strong Sienese army killed 10,000 Florentine soldiers and captured 15,000. The jubilant Sienese danced on the bodies of the fallen Florentines with nails in their shoes to hammer home the victory.

It was short-lived. Nine years later the two cities clashed again in Colle di Val d'Elsa and Florence came out on top. This 1269 defeat marks a profound shift in Siena's social and political identity that paradoxically forged the way for its prosperous golden age.

With their minds off expansion, the Sienese channelled their creative juices into commerce. Gradually, successful merchants and bankers gave rise to a wealthy middle class. Trade with France and England brought in cash and also nourished a flourishing wool industry. Siena's civic infrastructure developed, and in 1287 its governing body, the Council of Nine, was first established, in friendship with Florence. The city's most important public works occurred under the Council: much of the **Duomo**, the Palazzo Pubblico, the **Torre del Mangia** and piazza del Campo (divided into nine brick sections to represent the Council).

Siena's golden age came to an abrupt halt in 1348 when the Black Death struck, with brutal force. Its vicious impact slashed the population from 100,000 to 30,000 in less than a year. After that, the city never fully recovered. Internal fighting ensued, bringing down the Council of Nine in 1355, and 44 years later Siena fell under the control of Gian Galeazzo Visconti, Grand Duke of Milan, until his death in 1402. He was followed by the tyrannical, exiled nobleman, Pandolfo Petrucci.

In 1552 Spain's Charles V besieged the city but, three years later, a popular insurrection against the Spanish left Siena open to Cosimo

Where it all happens: the **piazza del Campo**.

I de' Medici. Reduced to 8,000 inhabitants, the city could not defend itself. A group of Sienese nobles tried to keep their republic alive in exile for a few years in nearby Montalcino, but the effort proved fruitless. The definitive end of the Sienese Republic came in 1559.

Following that period, once again Siena poured its energies into commerce, this time building on its earlier achievements. One of the world's oldest banks, the Monte dei Paschi di Siena, founded in 1472 as a protectionist measure against Florence's heavy taxes, matured into an economic powerhouse. But one of the most spectacular institutions to be born from the 1600s was Siena's Palio.

In 1859 Siena became the first major Tuscan city to join a united Italy. Two years later, it was plugged into Italy's budding rail system, allowing faster communication and commerce with the rest of the country. More importantly, it launched a lucrative tourist trade.

If you're planning on seeing all the sights, it's worth visiting the ticket office at the Museo Civico (0577 292 263), which offers two types of combined ticket. For €9 you can visit the **Museo Civico**, **Santa Maria della Scala Museum** complex and the **Palazzo delle Papesse** centre for contemporary art over a two-day period; for €16 you get a seven-day pass for the above three, plus the **Museo dell'Opera del Duomo**, the **Battistero**, the **Libreria Piccolomini** (off the Duomo) and the **Oratorio di San Bernardino**.

Sights

Piazza del Campo

One of Italy's most beautiful squares, built on the site of an ancient Roman forum, this shell-shaped piazza lies at the base of Siena's three hills and curves downward on the southern side to the Palazzo Pubblico and Torre del Mangia. It was paved in 1347 and its nine sections pay homage to the city's Council of Nine.

The Fonte Gaia, designed by Jacopo della Quercia (built 1408-19), sits on the north side of the piazza. In 1868 the eroded marble panels of the basin were replaced by copies; what's left of the originals can be seen in the loggia of the Palazzo Pubblico. The fountain's basin serves as a terminus for the elaborate network of underground wells and aqueducts (totalling 25 kilometres/16 miles throughout the province) developed by Siena. According to legend, before the Fonte was built, a construction team uncovered a perfectly preserved antique marble statue of Venus. When the Black Death struck, in the middle of the 14th century, the Sienese blamed the treasure, which was smashed to pieces. The fragments were buried in Florentine territory.

Palazzo Pubblico

This elegant example of Gothic architecture took more than 50 years to build, between 1288 and 1342. The brick and stone building housing the town hall and the Museo Civico (*see p217*) is a symbol of medieval Siena's mercantile wealth. Its striking façade – with its she-wolf and Medici balls – reads like a history book of the city.

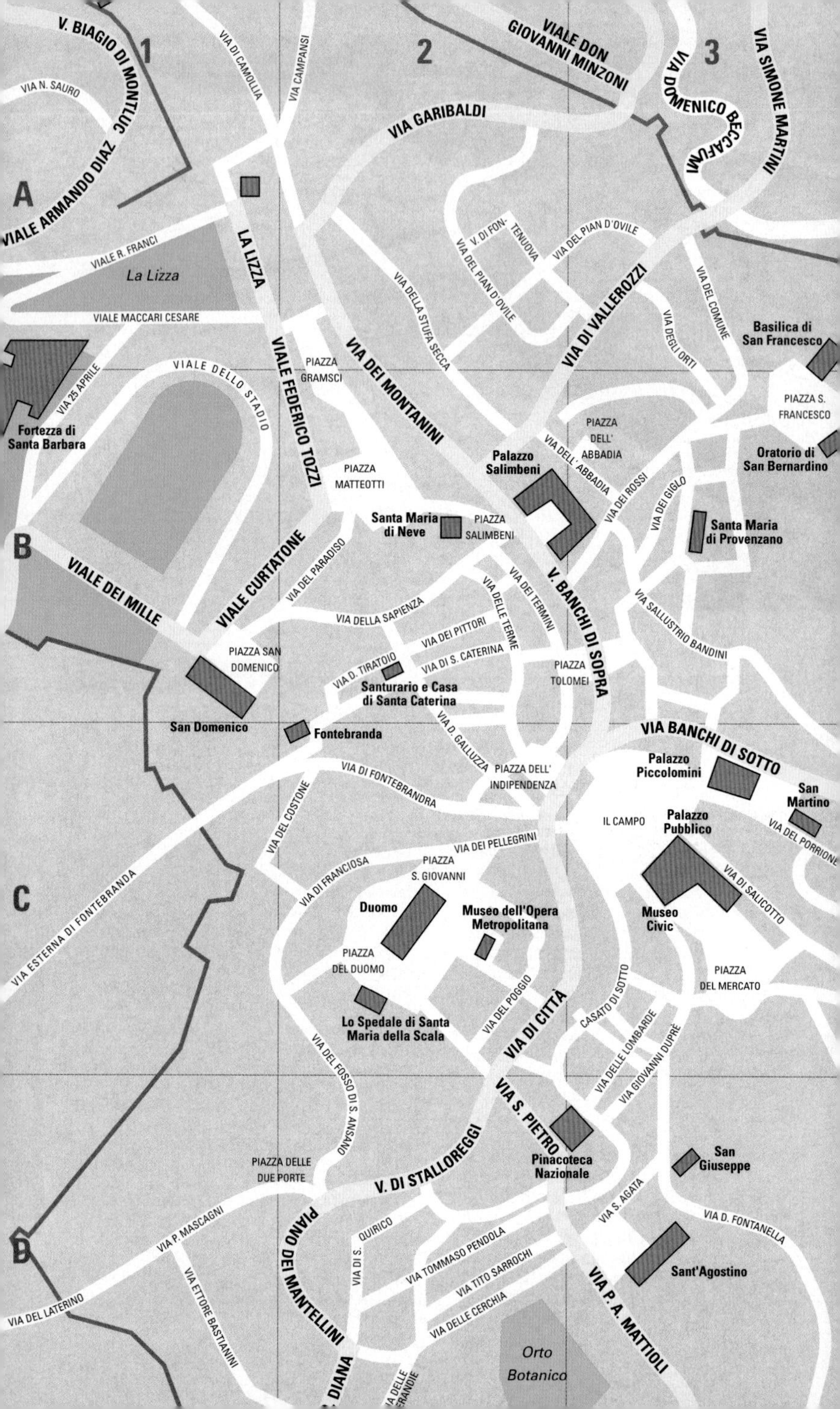

1
2
3
A
B
C
D
V. BIAGIO DI MONTLUC
VIA N. SAURO
VIALE ARMANDO DIAZ
VIA DI CAMOLLIA
VIA CAMPANSI
VIALE DON GIOVANNI MINZONI
VIA DOMENICO BECCAFUMI
VIA SIMONE MARTINI
VIA GARIBALDI
LA LIZZA
VIALE R. FRANCI
La Lizza
VIALE MACCARI CESARE
V. DI FONTENUOVA
VIA DEL PIAN D'OVILE
VIA DELLA STUFA SECCA
VIA DI VALLEROZZI
VIA DEL COMUNE
VIA DEGLI ORTI
Basilica di San Francesco
PIAZZA S. FRANCESCO
Oratorio di San Bernardino
Fortezza di Santa Barbara
VIA 25 APRILE
VIALE DELLO STADIO
VIALE FEDERICO TOZZI
PIAZZA GRAMSCI
VIA DEI MONTANINI
PIAZZA MATTEOTTI
Palazzo Salimbeni
PIAZZA DELL' ABBADIA
VIA DELL' ABBADIA
VIA DEI ROSSI
VIA DEI GIGLO
Santa Maria di Provenzano
Santa Maria di Neve
PIAZZA SALIMBENI
VIALE DEI MILLE
VIALE CURTATONE
VIA DEL PARADISO
VIA DELLA SAPIENZA
VIA DELLE TERME
VIA DEI TERMINI
V. BANCHI DI SOPRA
VIA SALLUSTRIO BANDINI
VIA DEI PITTORI
VIA DI S. CATERINA
PIAZZA SAN DOMENICO
VIA D. TIRATOIO
Santurario e Casa di Santa Caterina
PIAZZA TOLOMEI
San Domenico
Fontebranda
VIA D. GALLUZZA
VIA BANCHI DI SOTTO
Palazzo Piccolomini
San Martino
VIA DI FONTEBRANDRA
PIAZZA DELL' INDIPENDENZA
IL CAMPO
Palazzo Pubblico
VIA DEL PORRIONE
VIA DEL COSTONE
VIA DEI PELLEGRINI
VIA DI FRANCIOSA
PIAZZA S. GIOVANNI
Duomo
Museo dell'Opera Metropolitana
Museo Civic
VIA DI SALICOTTO
VIA ESTERNA DI FONTEBRANDA
PIAZZA DEL DUOMO
PIAZZA DEL MERCATO
VIA DEL POGGIO
CASATO DI SOTTO
Lo Spedale di Santa Maria della Scala
VIA DI CITTÀ
VIA DELLE LOMBARDE
VIA GIOVANNI DUPRÈ
VIA DEL FOSSO DI S. ANSANO
VIA S. PIETRO
Pinacoteca Nazionale
San Giuseppe
PIAZZA DELLE DUE PORTE
V. DI STALLOREGGI
VIA S. AGATA
VIA D. FONTANELLA
VIA P. MASCAGNI
VIA DI S. QUIRICO
VIA TOMMASO PENDOLA
PIANO DEI MANTELLINI
VIA TITO SARROCHI
Sant'Agostino
VIA DEL LATERINO
VIA ETTORE BASTIANINI
VIA DELLE CERCHIA
VIA P. A. MATTIOLI
Orto Botanico

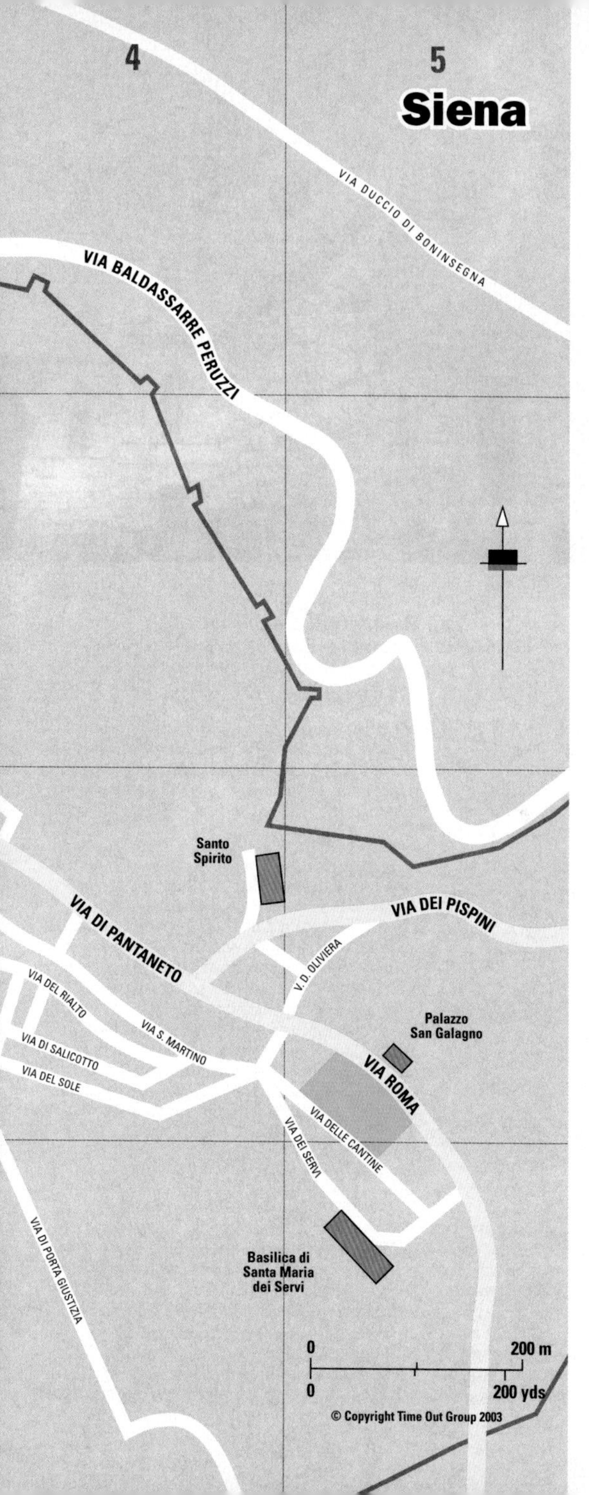

25 Aprile, Via - A1/B1
Abbadia, Piazza Dell' - B3
Abbadia, Via Dell' - B2/3
Armando Diaz, Viale - A1
Baldassarre Peruzzi, Via - A4/B4/5
Banchi Di Sopra, Via - B2/3
Banchi Di Sotto, Via - C3
Biagio Di Montluc, Via - A1
Camollia, Via Di - A1
Campansi, Via - A2
Cantine, Via Delle - C5/D5
Casato Di Sotto, - C3
Cerchia, Via Delle - D2
Città, Via Di - C2
Comune, Via Del - A3
Costone, Via Del - C2
Curtatone, Viale - B1/2
Diana, Via D. - D2
Domenico Beccafumi, Via - A3
Don Giovanni Minzoni, Viale - A2/3
Duccio Di Boninsegna, Via - A4/5
Duomo, Piazza Del - C2
Duprè, Via Giovanni - C3/D3
Esterna Di Fontebranda, Via - C1
Ettore Bastianini, Via - D1
Federico Tozzi, Viale - B2
Fontanella, Via D. - D3
Fontebrandra, Via Di - C2
Fontenuova, Via Di - A2
Fosso Di S. Ansano, Via Del - C2/D2
Franci, Viale R. - A1
Franciosa, Via Di - C2
Galluzza, Via D. - B2/C2
Garibaldi, Via - A2
Giglo, Via Dei - B3
Gramsci, Piazza - A2/B2
Il Campo - C3
Indipendenza, Piazza Dell' - C2
La Lizza - A1
Laterino, Via Del - D1
Lombarde, Via Delle - C3/D3
Maccari Cesare, Viale - A1
Mantellini, Piano Dei - D2
Mascagni, Via P. - D1
Matteotti, Piazza - B2
Mattioli, Via P. A. - D3
Mercato, Piazza Del - C3
Mille, Viale Dei - B1
Montanini, Via Dei - A2/B2
Oliviera, Via D. - C5
Orti, Via Degli - A3/B3
Pantaneto, Via Di - C4
Paradiso, Via Del - B2
Pellegrini, Via Dei - C2
Pian D'ovile, Via Del - A2/3
Pispini, Via Dei - C5
Pittori, Via Dei - B2
Poggio, Via Del - C2
Porrione, Via Del - C3
Porta Giustizia, Via Di - D4
Porte, Piazza Delle Due - D1/2
Rialto, Via Del - C4
Roma, Via - C5/D5
Rossi, Via Dei - B3
S. Agata, Via - D3
S. Caterina, Via Di - B2
S. Francesco, Piazza - B3
S. Giovanni, Piazza - C2
S. Martino, Via - C4
S. Pietro, Via - D2
S. Quirico, Via Di - D2
Salicotto, Via Di - C3/4
Salimbeni, Piazza - B2
Sallustrio Bandini, Via - B3
San Domenico, Piazza - B1
Sapienza, Via Della - B2
Sauro, Via N. - A1
Servi, Via Dei - C5/D5
Simone Martini, Via - A3
Sole, Via Del - C4
Sperandie, Via Delle - D2
Stadio, Viale Dello - B1
Stalloreggi, Via Di - D2
Stufa Secca, Via Della - A2/B2
Terme, Via Delle - B2
Termini, Via Dei - B2
Tiratoio, Via D. - B2
Tito Sarrochi, Via - D2
Tolomei, Piazza - B2/3
Tommaso Pendola, Via - D2
Vallerozzi, Via Di - A3

The inspiring spires of Siena's **Duomo**.

Torre del Mangia

0577 292 263. **Open** *Mid Mar-Oct* 10am-7pm daily. *July & Aug* 10am-11pm daily. *Nov-mid Mar* 10am-4pm daily. **Admission** €5.50 from Museo Civico ticket office.

Architects Minuccio and Francesco di Rinaldo were instructed to build their tower as tall as possible and what they completed in 1348 was, in fact, medieval Italy's tallest tower at 102m (335ft). With views over much of Siena province, Torre del Mangia is named after one of its first bell-ringers, the pot-bellied *mangiaguadagni* ('eat-profits'), who bulked up at the local trattoria, despite a daily climb up the tower's 503 steps. Only 15 visitors are allowed up at any one time, and tickets sell out quickly. At the foot of the tower is the Gothic Cappella di Piazza, finished in 1352 to commemorate the end of the plague.

Churches

Basilica di San Domenico

Piazza San Domenico (0577 280 893). **Open** *Nov-April* 9am-6pm daily. *May-Oct* 7am-6.30pm daily. **Admission** free.

This soaring brick edifice was one of the earliest Dominican monasteries in Tuscany. Begun in 1226 and completed in 1465, unfortunately it has not been treated kindly by history – fires, military occupations and earthquakes have all wreaked havoc, and what you see today is largely the result of an extensive mid 20th-century restoration. Luckily, a few things of interest have survived intact; at the end of the nave is a *Madonna Enthroned* attributed to Pietro Lorenzetti, while halfway down on the right is the restored chapel of Siena's patron saint, St Catherine. Inside, in a container, is her head – her body was chopped up by heretics after her death and various Italian cities made off with pieces, but her birthplace got the grand prize.

Basilica di San Francesco

Piazza San Francesco (0577 289 081). **Open** 7am-noon, 3-7pm daily. **Admission** free.

The Franciscans built this grand, somewhat severe church of Gothic origins in 1326. Little of its original artwork survived a big fire in 1655 – the mock Gothic façade is a 20th-century addition. One work that does remain is Pietro Lorenzetti's *Crucifixion* (1331) in the first chapel of the transept. In the third chapel are two frescoes by his brother Ambrogio.

Battistero

Piazza San Giovanni (no phone). **Open** *Summer* 9am-7.30pm daily. *Winter* 9am-1pm, 2-5pm daily. **Admission** €2.50. **No credit cards**.

Squeezed under the Duomo's apse is the unusual rectangular Baptistery (most are octagonal). Its unfinished Gothic façade includes three arches adorned with human and animal busts. On the inside, colourful frescoes by various artists, mainly Vecchietta, fill the room. The focal point is the central font (1417-34). Designed by Jacopo della Quercia and considered to be one of the masterpieces of early Renaissance Tuscany, it features a gilded bronze bas-relief by Jacopo, Donatello and Lorenzo Ghiberti.

Duomo

Piazza del Duomo (0577 280 204). **Open** *Summer* 7.30am-7.30pm Mon-Sat; 2-7.30pm Sun. *Winter* 7.30am-5pm daily. **Admission** free.

The Siena Duomo was one of Italy's first Gothic cathedrals. Construction started in 1150 on the site of an earlier church, but plans for what was to have been a massive cathedral had to be abandoned because of the Black Death of 1348 and technical problems from an unlevelled foundation. The result is Gothic in style but Romanesque in spirit. Even in its more modest state, the Duomo is an impressive achievement. The black and white marble façade was started in 1226 and 30 years later work began on the dome, one of the oldest in Italy. The lower portion of the façade and the statues in the centre of the three arches were designed by Giovanni Pisano (built 1284-96). Inside, the cathedral's polychrome floors are its most immediate attraction – if you can see them. Worked on by more than 40 artists between 1369 and 1547, the intricately decorated inlaid boxes are usually covered by protective planks (they're visible mid Aug-mid Sept). The most impressive are those beneath the dome by Domenico Beccafumi, who single-handedly created 35 of the 56 scenes (1517-47). In the apse there's a splendid carved wooden choir (14th-16th centuries); above this, after an absence of several years due to restoration, the stained-glass rose window (7m/23ft across) made by Duccio di Buoninsegna in 1288 will finally be back in place in 2004. It depicts the life of the Virgin in nine sections. The tabernacle has Bernini's *Maddalena* and *San Girolamo* statues.

Another highlight is the pulpit (1266) by Nicola Pisano, with the help of his son Giovanni and a young pupil, Arnolfo di Cambio. The Piccolomini altar includes four statues of saints by a young Michelangelo (carved 1501-4), and above that is a *Madonna* attributed to Jacopo della Quercia.

At the far end of the left aisle a door leads to the Libreria Piccolomini (admission €1.50), built in 1495 to house the library of Sienese nobleman Aeneas Silvius Piccolomini, the Renaissance humanist who became Pope Pius II. This vaulted chamber was constructed at the behest of his nephew (who became Pope Pius III for 28 days) and frescoed by Pinturicchio (1502-9, his last work), reportedly assisted by a young Raphael. The vibrant frescoes depict ten scenes from Pius II's life, including a scene in which he meets James II of Scotland.

Oratorio di San Bernardino

Piazza San Francesco (0577 283 048). **Open** *Mid Mar-Oct* 10.30am-1.30pm, 3-5.30pm daily. *Nov-mid Mar* phone for appointment. **Admission** €2.50.

To the right of San Francesco, this oratory was built in the 15th century on the site where St Bernard used to pray. On the first floor is a magnificent fresco cycle (1496-1518) by Beccafumi, Sodoma and their lesser contemporary, Girolamo del Pacchia.

Museums

Complesso Museale di Santa Maria della Scala

Piazza del Duomo 2 (0577 224 811). **Open** *16 Mar-5 Nov* 10am-6pm daily. *6 Nov-15 Mar* 10.30am-4.30pm daily. **Admission** €5.20. **No credit cards**.

This museum in progress is set in a former hospital: Siena was an important stopover for pilgrims on the via Francigena, and this hospital, founded in the ninth century and named after the Duomo's marble staircase, was considered the finest of its time. Funded by donations from local noble families, it was one of the first to ensure disinfected medical equipment and bug-free cots. It was still taking in patients until relatively recently, and author Italo Calvino died here in 1985. From 1440 to 1443, the *Pellegrinaio* (pilgrim's room), an emergency care unit, was embellished by, among others, Domenico di Bartolo, with the elaborate frescoes that depict the history of the hospital. The Museo Archeologico is also housed here and has several rooms devoted to Etruscan and Roman artefacts.

Museo Civico

Palazzo Pubblico, piazza del Campo (council cultural office 0577 292 226/ticket office 0577 292 263). **Open** *16 Feb-15 Mar* 10am-6.30pm daily. *Mid Mar-Oct* 10am-7pm daily. *1-25 Nov* 10am-6.30pm daily. *26 Nov-15 Feb* 10am-5.30pm daily. **Admission** €6.50. **No credit cards**.

Access to this museum is through the courtyard of the Palazzo Pubblico and up an iron staircase. Its first four rooms house work dating from the 16th to 19th centuries. The Sala del Risorgimento pays homage to the fact that Siena was one of the first cities of the region to embrace a united Italy. In the Sala del Concistorio are frescoed vaults (1529-35) on a judicial theme by Domenico Beccafumi and a marble portal sculpted in 1448 by Bernardo Rossellino.

In the *anticappella* you can admire Taddeo di Bartoli's (1362-1422) frescoes, which reflect his fascination with Greek and Roman antiquity and mythological heroes, plus a *Madonna and Child with Saints* by Sodoma at the altar of the Cappella del Consiglio. The Sala del Mappamondo was decorated by Ambrogio Lorenzetti around 1320-30, and its barely visible cosmological frescoes depict the universe and celestial spheres. This room also houses one of Siena's most cherished jewels: the *Maestà* fresco painted by Simone Martini in 1315, thought to be one of his earliest works. It is also considered one of the first examples of political painting, because the devotion to the Virgin Mary depicted is said to represent devotion to the Republic's princes. The faces of the main figures are repaints, as Martini got a second inspiration following a visit to Giotto's masterpiece frescoes in the Basilica di San Francesco in Assisi. The equestrian *Il Guidoriccio da Fogliano* (1328) is also attributed to Martini and celebrates a victorious battle in Montemassi.

Museo dell'Opera del Duomo

Piazza del Duomo 8 (0577 42309). **Open** *Mid Mar-Sept* 9am-7.30pm daily. *Oct* 9am-6pm daily. *Nov-Mar* 9am-1.30pm daily. **Admission** €5.50; €7.50 combined ticket Museo dell'Opera del Duomo, Libreria Piccolomini, Oratorio San Bernardino. **No credit cards**.

The museum occupies the never-completed nave of the Duomo and displays works taken from the cathedral. On the ground floor is a large hall divided in two by a stunning 15th-century wrought-iron gate. Along the walls you can enjoy a better view of Giovanni Pisano's 12 magnificent marble statues (carved 1285-97) that once adorned the façade of the Duomo. In the centre of the room is the bas-relief of

the *Madonna and Child with St Anthony* by Jacopo della Quercia, commissioned in 1437 and probably not quite completed when the artist died in 1438. On the first floor is the *Pala della Maestà* (1308-11) by Duccio di Buoninsegna, used as the high altar of the Duomo until 1506. The front has a Madonna with Saints and the back depicts 26 religious scenes; all in dazzling colours on a gold background. A climb to the *Facciatone* (the unfinished nave) affords a beautiful view of the city.

Palazzo delle Papesse

Via di Città 126 (0577 22071). **Open** noon-7pm daily. **Admission** €5. **No credit cards.**

This new centre for contemporary art operates from within an edifice built in 1460 at the behest of Caterina Piccolomini, whose brother became Pope Pius II: hence the curious name, a neologism equivalent to 'popess'.

Pinacoteca Nazionale

Palazzo Buonsignori, via San Pietro 29 (0577 281 161). **Open** 8.30am-1.30pm Mon; 8.15am-7.15pm Tue-Sat; 8.15am-1.30pm Sun. **Admission** €4. **No credit cards.**

One of Italy's foremost art collections, this lovely 15th-century palazzo holds more than 1,500 works of art. It's renowned for its Sienese *fondi d'oro* (paintings with gilded backgrounds). The second floor is devoted to Sienese masters from the 12th to 15th centuries, including Guido da Siena, Duccio di Buoninsegna, Simone Martini and the Lorenzettis. Don't miss Lorenzetti's Cubist-in-feel *A City by the Sea*, one of the first examples of landscape painting. The first floor features works by the Sienese Mannerist school of the early 1500s, including Sodoma and Beccafumi. The large room on the third floor is devoted to the Spannocchi Collection: works by northern Italian and European artists of the 16th and 17th centuries.

Monuments

Fonte Branda

Via di Fontebranda.

It's a steep walk down from via di Città to this monumental 12th-century spring. Housed in a red-brick structure with three arches, the fountain is fed by the miles of underground aqueducts that stretch across Tuscany. In its day it supplied half the city with water and powered numerous flour mills.

Fortezza Medicea

Viale C Maccari.

This huge red-brick fortress slightly outside the city is a sore reminder of Siena's troubled past. Charles V of Spain forced the Sienese to build a fortress here in 1552, but as soon as his reign ended they celebrated by demolishing it. A few years later Cosimo I de'Medici annexed the city and demanded the fortress be rebuilt. When Florentine rule finally came to an end, Siena named the square within the fortress walls piazza della Libertà. These days, with its views over Siena, it's a good place for an evening stroll or for a glass of wine at the Enoteca Italiana (*see p220*), especially during the *settimana dei vini*, a week-long showcase of regional wines held here in early June.

Piazza Salimbeni

A beautiful square flanked by three of Siena's most glorious *palazzi*: Tantucci, Spannocchi and Salimbeni. The latter serves as the headquarters of the Monte dei Paschi di Siena, founded by shrewd Sienese in 1472 to pre-empt the emergence of usury in the wake of developing trade. To this day 50 per cent of the bank's profits have by statute to be ploughed back into the community.

Shopping

The main shopping street is via di Città, which forks above the Campo: Banchi di Sotto heads down and Banchi di Sopra climbs up to piazza della Posta. Just before sunset, locals emerge for the *passeggiata* (stroll through town).

Siena's fantastic general market (8am-1pm Wednesday) stretches from piazza La Lizza to the Fortezza. Get there early. The third Sunday of the month sees an antiques market at piazza del Mercato behind the Campo.

Dolci Trame

Via del Moro 4 (0577 46168). **Open** 3.30-7.30pm Mon; 10am-1pm, 3.30-7.30pm Tue-Sat. **Credit** AmEx, DC, JCB, MC, V.

Hip women's clothing at the back of piazza Tolomei.

La Fattoria Toscana

Via di Città 51 (0577 42255). **Open** 9.30am-8pm daily. **Credit** AmEx, DC, MC, V.

Excellent selection of choice gastronomic goodies, including wines, oils, sweetmeats, local truffles and Val d'Orcia saffron.

Libreria Senese

Via di Città 62-6 (0577 280 845). **Open** 9am-8pm Mon-Sat; 11am-8pm Sun. **Credit** AmEx, DC, MC, V.

A family-run bookshop with plenty on local art and history, including publications in English.

Morbidi

Via Banchi di Sopra 73 (0577 280 268). **Open** 8.15am-1.15pm, 5-8pm Mon-Sat; 8.15am-1.15pm Sat. **Credit** V.

A long room full of savoury Tuscan treats.

Branch: Via Banchi di Sotto 27 (0577 280 541).

La Nuova Pasticceria di Iasevoli

Via Giovanni Duprè 37 (0577 40577). **Open** 8am-12.45pm, 5-7.30pm Tue-Sat; 9am-12.30pm Sun. **No credit cards.**

Choose from the fine selection of Sienese baked confectionery such as *cantuccini*, *pan dei santi* (bread with raisins and walnuts made for All Saints' Day), *cavallucci* (dry bread buns spiced with aniseed), *panforte* and *ricciarelli* (soft almond biscuits topped with powdered sugar).

The **Palazzo Pubblico**, with its symbolic she-wolf. *See p213.*

Restaurants

Many recipes commonly used in this region today have survived since medieval times, including *pici* (like thick, irregular spaghetti) and *panzanella* (dried bread soaked in water, then made into a bread salad with basil, onion and tomato). Popular Sienese desserts include *panforte* (a dense slice of nuts, candied fruits and honey) and *ricciarelli* (almond biscuits).

Al Marsili

Via del Castoro 3 (0577 47154). **Open** 12.30-2pm, 7.30-10.15pm Tue-Sun. **Average** €35. **Credit** AmEx, DC, MC, V.

The place to go if you're dressed up and in need of a splurge. The food is classic Tuscan, from *crostini* to *faraona alla Medici* (guinea fowl with pine nuts, almonds and plums). Next door, Enoteca Marsili is filled with sumptuous wines stashed in a cave carved out of stone that dates back to the Etruscans.

Cane e Gatto

Via Pagliaresi 6 (0577 287 545). **Open** 8-10.30pm Fri-Wed. Lunch bookings for small groups by appointment. **Average** €60. **Credit** AmEx, DC, MC, V.

This is a family-run restaurant with a *menu degustazione* (€57) that will teach you everything you could ever wish to know about Sienese cooking. The decadent lunch menu offers risotto and champagne.

Compagnia dei Vinattieri

Via delle Terme 79 (0577 236 568). **Open** 11am-1am daily. **Average** €40. **Credit** AmEx, DC, MC, V.

Cinzia Certosini, ex-restaurateur in Chianti, started this excellent downstairs *enoteca* two years ago, to take some of the hot air out of wine and restore approachability and enjoyment. Her admirable wine list includes products from other regions and countries as well as a rich array of respectable Tuscan labels. Appropriately fine food is also served.

La Costarella

Via di Città 33 (0577 288 076). **Open** 8.30am-midnight Mon-Wed, Fri-Sun. **No credit cards.**

If you've made it all the way up the steep hill from the Fonte Branda, La Costarella's excellent ice-cream and home-made *cornetti* (similar to sweet croissants) are a refreshingly indulgent prize.

Da Trombicche

Via delle Terme 66 (0577 288 089). **Open** 10am-3pm, 5-10pm Mon-Sat. **Average** €12. **Credit** V.

Small and cheerful venue for non-smokers. Ideal place for a light lunch or supper.

Enoteca i Terzi

Via dei Termini 7 (0577 44329). **Open** 11.30am-3.30pm, 6.30pm-1am Mon-Sat. **Credit** AmEx, DC, MC, V.

This wine cellar, run by the knowledgeable Michele, also serves light snacks.

Enoteca Italiana

Fortezza Medicea (0577 288 497). **Open** noon-8pm Mon; noon-1am Tue-Sat. **Credit** AmEx, MC, V.

A refreshing surprise for those who thought anything run by the fumbling Italian government can't amount to much, Italy's only national wine cellar is located in the massive vaults of the fortress. The *enoteca* stocks more than 1,000 wines from all over the country (400 from Tuscany). There are group tastings and occasional evening concerts.

Fiorella

Via di Città 13 (0577 271 255). **Open** 7am-7pm Mon-Sat. **No credit cards.**

Fabulous coffee, roasted on the spot.

Hosteria Il Carroccio

Via del Casato di Sotto 32 (0577 41165). **Open** noon-2.30pm, 7.30-10pm Mon, Tue, Thur-Fri. **Average** €25. **Credit** MC, V.

A small restaurant run by Renata Toppi and her children, Hosteria Il Carroccio is something of a local gem. Try the *tegamate di maiale* (pork cooked in a ceramic bowl) based on an old Sienese recipe that's virtually extinct today.

Nannini Conca d'Oro

Via Banchi di Sopra 24 (0577 236 009). **Open** 7.30am-11pm Mon-Sat; 8am-9pm Sun. **Credit** AmEx, DC, MC, V.

The original Nannini establishment, injected with new life by ex-racing driver scion Alessandro. Good for substantial snacks, coffee and pastries, *aperitivi* and *digestivi*.

Nuovo Ristorante Tullio ai Tre Cristi

Vicolo di Provenzano 1 (0577 280 608). **Open** 12.30-2.30pm, 7.30-10pm Mon, Tue, Thur-Sun. **Average** €25. **Credit** MC, V.

Founded in 1830, this is the traditional eaterie of the *giraffe contrade* – witness the banners and symbols on every available bit of wall space. In a lively neighbourhood atmosphere, chef Tullio cooks up specialities such as potato *gnocchetti* with asparagus, or warm steak marinated with spices.

L'Osteria

Via de' Rossi 79-81 (0577 287 592). **Open** 12.30-2.30pm, 7.30-10.30pm Mon-Sat. **Average** €20. **Credit** AmEx, DC, MC, V.

This informal haunt frequented by neighbouring university faculty members serves up simple, well-cooked Tuscan food at wooden tables.

Osteria Castelvecchio

Via Castelvecchio 65 (0577 49586). **Open** 12.30-2.30pm, 7.30-9.30pm daily. Closed Tue in winter. **Average** €25. **Credit** AmEx, DC, MC, V.

Just a few steps from the Pinacoteca Nazionale in former horse stables, Castelvecchio offers vegetarian dishes at least twice a week on a menu that is inventively based on seasonal fare.

Osteria Il Grattacielo

Via dei Pontani 8 (0577 289 326). **Open** 8am-3pm, 5.30-8.30pm Mon-Sat. **Average** €12. **No credit cards**.

Classic hole-in-the-wall (on the corner of via dei Termini) that's been going since 1840, Il Grattacielo sells hams, cheeses and vegetables preserved in oil. Get there early if you want a seat.

Osteria La Chiacchera

Costa di Sant'Antonio 4 (0577 280 631). **Open** noon-3.30pm, 7pm-midnight daily. **Average** €15. **Credit** AmEx, DC, MC, V.

A charming spot for traditional Sienese recipes, Osteria La Chiacchera has friendly service and, more important still, a decent house wine.

Osteria La Sosta di Violante

Via di Pantaneto 115 (0577 43774). **Open** noon-2.30pm, 7-10pm Mon-Sat. **Average** €25. **Credit** AmEx, DC, MC, V.

Newish eaterie with a useful focus on matching wines to dishes, especially meats.

Osteria Le Logge

Via del Porrione 33 (0577 48013). **Open** noon-2.45pm, 7.15-10.30pm Mon-Sat. **Average** €35. **Credit** AmEx, DC, MC, V.

This is a popular and conveniently central *osteria* (via del Porrione leads directly into the piazza del Campo) with good food and a charming setting.

La Taverna del Capitano

Via del Capitano 6-8 (0577 288 094). **Open** noon-3pm, 7-10pm Mon, Wed-Sun. **Average** €30. **Credit** AmEx, MC, V.

This place oozes Siena, from the vaulted ceilings to the dark wood furnishings. On Fridays try *baccalà* (salt cod), a Sienese speciality. Great house wine.

Where to stay

Siena doesn't have enough hotels to meet the demand, so book in advance. It's worth contacting the **Hotels Promotion Service** (0577 288 084) or checking out its user-friendly website www.hotelsiena.com.

Antica Torre

Via di Fieravecchia 7 (tel/fax 0577 222 255/www.anticatorresiena.it). **Rates** €90 double; €107 double. **Credit** AmEx, DC, JCB, MC, V.

Siena's most eclectic hotel, set in a well-restored 16th-century tower, is so sought after that it gets booked up weeks in advance (there are just two rooms per floor round a central staircase).

Centrale

Via Cecco Angiolieri 26 (0577 280 379/fax 0577 42152/www.hotelsiena.com). **Rates** €75 double. **Credit** MC, V.

Located one block north of piazza del Campo on a quiet street, this small, pleasant hotel has seven large, comfortable rooms.

Certosa di Maggiano

Strada di Certosa 82 (0577 288 180/fax 0577 288 189/www.certosadimaggiano.com). **Rates** €382-€647 double. **Credit** AmEx, MC, V.

Raised from the ruins of a 13th-century monastery, this hotel is located just south of the city and is renowned for its stunning garden and extensive amenities, including tennis courts, swimming pools and even a heliport.

Chiusarelli

Viale Curtatone 15 (0577 280 562/fax 0577 271 177/www.chiusarelli.com). **Rates** (incl breakfast) €75.50 single; €112.50 double. **Credit** AmEx, MC, V.

Recently renovated three-star hotel on the edge of the historic centre. Ask for a quiet room at the back.

Animal magnetism

Tartuca (tortoise), *Onda* (wave), *Lupa* (she-wolf), *Oca* (goose), *Nicchio* (shell), *Istrice* (porcupine), *Drago* (dragon), *Civetta* (owl), *Chiocciola* (snail), *Pantera* (panther), *Aquila* (eagle), *Bruco* (caterpillar), *Leocorn* (unicorn), *Montone* (ram), *Giraffa* (giraffe), *Selva* (forest), *Torre* (tower). These are the 17 *contrade* or districts of Siena, whose origins date back to the 12th century. Each one demarcates its territory with its own heraldic sign.

The unique stability of Siena as a city owes much to the *contrade*, which forge individual and collective social identity. The *contrade* act like social clubs that politely admit occasional guests, but are really for members only. As such, they host all the major rites of passage of their members: from baptism through marriage to funerals. For such purposes, each *contrada* has its own headquarters and museum, its own chapel, its own meeting places, its own prior (director), general council and officers (elected every two years, and no longer an exclusively male prerogative), and its own micro-economy.

The christenings that take place in the *contrada* fountains are often the fruit of careful negotiation. The fact that membership derives automatically from being born within a *contrada* is of little use to 90 per cent of the population of Siena, who now live outside the confines of the *contrade* in the new residential suburbs. Happily, membership can also be claimed through descent. If the parents belong to different *contrade*, the child's *contrada* membership will be established in relation not only to extended kinship but also to the role played by the parents within their respective *contrade*.

Once a year, between spring and late summer, each *contrade* celebrates the feast day of its patron saint. This involves a solemn reception to which the priors of allied *contrade* are invited, a religious service, a colourful open-air dinner around long trestle tables set up in the street and processions to visit neighbouring *contrade*.

The famous Palio horse race that takes place twice a year (*see p155*) in the piazza del Campo is the absolute apotheosis of *contrada* culture. The square itself is divided into sections representing each *contrada*, whose supporters stick together, proudly wearing the colours of their membership, waving their banners and singing.

The Palio starts in the late afternoon with a parade of drummers and flag carriers dressed in medieval costumes. The horses charge three times around the square, and the first over the line wins the race and earns the banner of the Virgin Mary as a trophy. The reactions of the Sienese, depending on their allegiance, range from weeping and hair-tearing to rapturous kissing and embracing. Banquets and festivities sponsored by the winning *contrada* last well into September, and animosity between the first- and second-placed teams lasts until the following year.

Duomo Hotel

Via Stalloreggi 38 (0577 289 088/fax 0577 43043/www.hotelduomo.it). **Rates** €104 single; €130 double. **Credit** AmEx, DC, MC, V.

This very central hotel has a location that simply cannot be beaten, although its sterile, sober rooms certainly could be. To avoid disappointment, make sure you ask for one of the two rooms with a small balcony that overlook the Duomo and have a view of Siena's characteristic red roofs. Service is informal and perfectly friendly.

Grand Hotel Villa Patrizia

Via Fiorentina 58 (0577 50431/fax 0577 50442/ www.villapatrizia.it). **Rates** €185 double. **Credit** AmEx, DC, MC, V.

This grand hotel on the northern side of the city has known better days, although at the time of writing new owners were planning renovations. Among the existing offerings that keep guests coming back are its outdoor pool (something of a bonus in the summer, when the heat can be oppressive), friendly service and peaceful and attractive gardens.

Grand Hotel Continental

Via Banchi di Sopra 85 (0577 56011/reservations 0577 44204/www.ghcs.it). **Rates** €300 single; €480 double; €637-€1,490 suite. **Credit** AmEx, DC, JCB, MC, V.

Recently opened in the richly frescoed interiors of what was once Palazzo Gori Pannilini, the area's only five star hotel is clearly not for all pockets. Still, this shouldn't stop you popping in to admire the magnificently ornate first-floor reception room.

Pensione Palazzo Ravizza

Pian dei Mantellini 34 (0577 280 462/fax 0577 221 597/www.palazzoravizza.it). **Rates** (incl breakfast) €160-€180 double. **Credit** AmEx, DC, JCB, MC, V.

Owned by the same family for more than 200 years, this 1800s palazzo still has its original furnishings. Many of the 38 rooms overlook a charming, well-kept garden. Others have a view of the city.

Piccolo Hotel Etruria

Via delle Donzelle 3 (0577 288 088/fax 0577 288 461). **Rates** €45 single; €75 double. **Credit** AmEx, DC, JCB, MC, V.

This is a 12-room hotel located just off Siena's commercial artery, banchi di Sotto.

Residence Paradiso

Via del Paradiso 16 (0577 222613/www.residence paradiso.siena.it). **Rates** €30 single; €67 double. **Credit** AmEx, DC, MC, V.

A welcome addition to centrally located accommodation in Siena with 12 furnished mini-apartments in a historic building, offering the use of cooking and laundry facilities. Handsome reductions are offered for longer stays and in the winter. There are ten more apartments in similarly historic surroundings in via del Porrione (rates are the same, ask at reception).

Villa Scacciapensieri

Via di Scacciapensieri 10 (0577 41441/fax 0577 270 854/www.villascacciapensieri.it). **Rates** €113-€128 single; €180-€235 double. **Credit** AmEx, DC, JCB, MC, V.

As the name ('banish your thoughts') suggests, you can leave your worries behind once you're at this family-run hotel. It's 3km (two miles) north of the city – follow the signs up a private tree-lined drive to the crest of the hill. There's an excellent restaurant, a tennis court and a swimming pool.

Camping

Colleverde

Strada Scacciapensieri 47 (0577 280 044). **Closed** Nov-Mar. **Rates** €7.75 adults; €4.13 children. **Credit** MC, V.

The closest campsite to the city (3km/two miles) and one of southern Tuscany's most attractive. Swimming pool open June to September. There's a bar, restaurant and store all to hand and reductions for longer stays.

Resources

Hospital

Viale Bracci, north of the city (0577 586 111).

Police station

Via del Castoro (0577 201 111).

Post office

Piazza Matteotti 37 (0577 214 295).

Tourist information

Centro Servizi Informazioni Turistiche Siena (APT) *Piazza del Campo 56 (0577 280 551/fax 0577 270 676/www.terresiena.it).* **Open** 8.30am-7.30pm Mon-Sat; 9am-3pm Sun.

Getting there & around

By bike & moped

For the pedal-powered variety contact **DF Bike** (via Massetana Romana 54, 0577 271 905). For mopeds try **Automotocicli Perozzi** (via del Romitorio 5, 0577 223 157).

By bus

If you're reliant on public transport, the bus is the way to go in Siena, especially if you're travelling to or from Florence. Siena's major bus terminal is at the edge of the historic centre at piazza Gramsci; the main ticket office (0577 204 246) is underground. Most buses leave from the adjacent via Frederico Tozzi or nearby piazza San Domenico. **Tra-in**, the principal bus company serving Siena and beyond (same phone as ticket office), has departures every 30mins for Florence (direct service takes 75mins) as well as services to Arezzo and to Grosseto, and most regional towns of interest. The excellent www.comune.siena.it/train gives full timetable information on all services.

By car

The SS2 links Florence and Siena (journey time around 1hr). The historic centre of Siena is mainly traffic-free so you have to park on the outskirts and walk in; there are big car parks at the Stadio Comunale and near the Fortezza Medicea, but even these can fill rapidly on weekends, public holidays or around the time of the Palio. To hire a car try **Avis** (via Simone Martini 36, 0577 270 305) or **Hertz** (viale Sardegna 37, 0577 45085).

By taxi

Call **Radio Taxi** (0577 49222) or go to one of the taxi ranks at piazza Stazione (0577 44504) or piazza Matteotti (0577 289 350).

By train

There are some direct trains to and from Florence, but more often you'll have to change at Empoli (journey time up to 2hrs). For Pisa, change at Empoli. Siena's train station is at the bottom of the hill on the east side of the city (piazza Fratelli Rosselli, tickets 0577 280 115/national timetable information 892021). From here a local bus makes the short journey up to piazza Gramsci, close to the historic centre.

Siena Province

Where life is beautiful.

It's little wonder that such great numbers of Italians and foreigners make the journey south of Florence to this beguiling part of Tuscany. Its unique magic lies in the perfect blend of elements: stunning, unspoiled countryside, excellent food and wine, and a rich cultural heritage. Far from leaving art behind as the images of Florence recede, you will discover a network of beautifully designed museums housing largely medieval and Renaissance art and Etruscan and Roman archaeology spread out among the smaller towns. They belong to the Sistema Musei Senesi and are havens of quietude where you can enjoy leisurely contact with great works.

Chianti

Chianti is the name given to the hilly area between Florence and Siena, not all of which falls directly in Siena province, yet for simplicity's sake we have included such towns as Greve and Panzano (both of which lie just inside the borders of Florence province) in this chapter.

Many of the gentle slopes are clad with vines, though olive groves also abound and there is plenty of woodland. If you are interested in art, you will know this landscape even if you have never before visited Italy. It found its way into paintings when the artists of the 15th century began to look at their surroundings as examples of good governance and a source of aesthetic pleasure. To this day we perceive it as idyllic and there's hardly a barn or farmhouse that hasn't been ennobled to cater to the widespread demand for a therapeutic taste of paradise. But popularity has its drawbacks: the heavy traffic of tourists through this region means you will never have the place entirely to yourself.

Greve in Chianti

Greve makes a pleasant base from which to explore the surrounding area. Its triangular main square, piazza Giacomo Matteoti, with an arcaded perimeter is particularly attractive. On Saturday mornings the square's wine bars and appealing food shops heave with gossiping locals. As you'll guess from the square's statue, Giovanni da Verrazzano hailed from these parts before discovering New York harbour in 1524. Another pioneer, Amerigo Vespucci, the 16th-century explorer who gave his name to America, was born in nearby **Montefioralle**.

Where to stay & eat

In Greve itself, you can find delectable meat dishes at the tiny **Mangiando Mangiando** (piazza Giacomo Mattoetti 80, 055 854 6372, closed Mon and 4wks mid Jan-mid Feb, average €25). Kitchen and dining room are all one, making it cosy in winter. If you're looking for a room, the best option is **Albergo Giovanni da Verrazzano** (055 853 189, doubles €60-€122) on the main square, which has an attractive restaurant on its geranium-lined terrace.

A tiny road of hairpin bends leads up from Greve's northern side to the ancient walled village of Montefioralle, where you can find one of Tuscany's best rustic restaurants, the family-run **La Taverna del Guerrino** (via Montefioralle 39, 055 853 106, closed Mon, Tue & lunch Wed, 2wks Dec, average €22). As a contrast, try **La Tenda Rossa** in the village of Cerbaia (piazza del Monumento 9-14, 055 826 132, closed Sun, lunch Mon, average €85), north-west of San Casciano Val di Pesa. It boasts two Michelin stars and an exceptionally broad wine list. The cuisine is rural but refined, and the atmosphere somewhat formal.

Resources

Tourist information

Ufficio Turistico *Viale G da Verrazzano 59 (055 854 6287/fax 055 854 4149).* **Open** 10am-1pm, 2.30-7pm Mon-Fri; 10am-1pm, 2.30-5pm Sat.

Panzano in Chianti

Another seven kilometres (4.5 miles) south, along the SS222 or the road from Montefioralle, is the fortified village of **Panzano**. With stunning views of the **Conca d'Oro valley**, it is probably best known today as the home of the renowned traditionalist butcher Dario Cecchini, whose shop on via XX Luglio is often ringing with the sounds of the proprietor's voice as he boldly holds forth on various themes from politics to literature.

The triangular main square at **Greve in Chianti**. *See p224.*

On an eroded dirt road about eight kilometres (five miles) north-west of town is the **Badia a Passignano**, which was once a centre of the wealthy Vallombrosan order. The 11th-century abbey is now in private hands, but you can visit the church.

A sudden bend in the SS222 to Badia brings the hilltop town of **Castellina** into postcard-perfect view. The surrounding hills marked the battlefront between the armies of Siena and Florence, hence the town's heavy fortification. Its main square, piazza del Comune, is in the shadow of the imposing Torre, while a covered walkway evokes a chilly 14th-century feel. There are plenty of places to taste and buy wine and one of Chianti's top wineries, Castello di Fonterutoli (*see p233*), is nearby.

Where to stay & eat

Right of the church in Panzano is the **Enoteca Il Vinaio** (via Santa Maria 22, 055 852 603, closed dinner Thur, all Thur Nov-Mar, average €12), which serves a hearty *pappa al pomodoro* and *ribollita* accompanied by a vast selection of local wines. Otherwise, try nearby **Il Vescovino** (via Ciampolo da Panzano 9, 055 852 464, closed Tue, average €30). It does a fine roast duck in orange and has a large terrace with a wonderful view.

On the road to Badia is a dirt road turn-off for **La Cantinetta di Rignana** (via Rignana, Greve, 055 852 601, closed Tue, average €25). Set among ancient farmhouses, this is the quintessential Tuscan restaurant. The extraordinary food and views are the stuff of fantasy. In season, meals start off with sensational steamed artichokes, followed by classic *primi* such as papardelle with rabbit sauce and ending with succulent grilled meats. La Cantinetta is one of Chianti's best-kept secrets, probably because it really is so hard to get to.

If you're staying, **Colle Etrusco Salivolpi** (via Fiorentina 89, 0577 740 484/ fax 0577 740 998, doubles €93), up a steep hill from the village, is a restored farmhouse-turned-country club with an outdoor pool.

About 200 metres (220 yards) away is **Ristorante Albergaccio** (via Fiorentina 63, 0577 741 042, closed lunch Wed-Thur, Sun, average €40), which offers two 'Taste of Tuscany' fixed menus. Just north of town on the Chiantigiana in Pietrafitta is the terraced **Bar-Ristorante Pietrafitta** (0577 741 123, closed Tue, doubles €27). It looks like a truck stop, but makes a top spot for lunch.

Radda

A short distance before Castellina, a fork in the road indicates the direction (SS429) for Radda, yet another Chianti jewel. In its early days, Radda was the capital of the medieval League of Chianti, a chain of Florentine defensive outposts against Siena that included Castellina and Gaiole.

Just out of town on the same road you'll see a sign on the right for **La Ceramica**. Drive up there to Angela Panigiani's small workshop and showroom of beautifully hand-painted glazed ceramics (0577 738466, closed Sat, Sun).

Beyond Radda, the Etruscan tomb-rich area around **Volpaia**, seven kilometres (4.5 miles) to the north, makes worthwhile exploring.

Spa hopping

Small spas abound in southern Tuscany. They owe their existence to Mount Amiata, which began life as a volcano and still harbours fiery heat in its viscera. The nicest *terme* offer panoramic pools filled with naturally steaming mineral-rich water for self-indulgent wallowing.

At Bagno Vignoni the recently revamped **Hotel Marcucci** (0577 887 112/www.hotelpostamarcucci.it) has an ample pool set in pleasant gardens. The hot cascade will deliver you of all aches and pains, spiritual as well as physical. It's open 9am to 1pm and 2.30pm to 6pm (the pool is off-limits during the lunch break, but bathers may stay poolside). From June to August, late opening hours operate on the weekends from 9pm to midnight. It costs 10 for a full day or 7 for an afternoon.

The water at **Bagni San Filippo** (0577 872 982/www.termesanfilippo.it, mid Apr-Sept 8.30am-7pm Mon, Wed-Sun, 8.30am-4.30pm Tue, opening hours shorten as winter approaches, 10), a little further south, is hotter and more sulphurous. The 42°C cascade is a real scorcher.

The **Terme di San Casciano** (0578 572 405, 0577 572 408/www.fonteverdeterme.com), looking over the valley towards Mount Amiata, offers upmarket facilities and a pool with a thundering hydro-massage that reaches parts the other cascades miss. The 9am to 7pm (6pm on Tue) opening hours lengthen in summer and diminish in winter. The spa is usually closed from mid January for a month. Entrance on weekdays is 12, 15 at weekends (Mon-Fri 8 afternoons only, not available on weekends).

At Rapolano there are two spas with warm pools. At **Le Terme di San Giovanni** (0577 724 030/www.termesangiovanni.it, 9am-7pm daily, closed mid Jan-mid Feb, 10 Mon-Fri, 12 Sat & Sun, afternoon only 8 and 9 respectively) the pool is fed by an 1,800 litre-per-minute flow of slightly sulphurous water. At the **Terme Antica Querciolaia** (0577 724 091/www.termeaq.it, 10am-6.45pm Mon-Fri, 10am-midnight Sat, 10am-8.30pm Sun, closed Jan, 11 Mon-Thur, 13 Fri-Sun) you can go and bask in some less odoriferous water, rich in calcium, magnesium and bicarbonate.

Where to stay & eat

A particularly nice place to stay and eat is **Palazzo Leopoldo** (via Roma 33, 0577 735 605, doubles €150-€290), a patrician residence only recently turned into a hotel. Non-guests can also enjoy the **Perla del Palazzo** restaurant (average €40), which has a garden dining area and focuses on local cuisine. Another impressive, albeit expensive, dining option is the elegant **Ristorante Vignale** (via XX Settembre 23, 0577 738 094, closed Thur, Dec-late Feb, average €40). Similar style is to be found at the **Relais Fattoria Vignale** (via Pianigiani 8, 0577 738 300, doubles €135-€300), the hotel owned by the same people. For a reasonably priced alternative, try the **Villa Sant' Uberto** (località Sant Uberto 33, 0577 741 088, doubles €82-€120 incl breakfast), four kilometres (2.5 miles) down the road towards Castellina, which is a pleasant country villa with its own pool.

Another enchanting option is the *agriturismo* **Podere Terreno** (via della Volpaia, 0577 738 312, €90 per person), in a stone farmhouse. The rate includes an excellent dinner with wine around a long table. Fine wine is produced here.

Resources

Tourist information

Ufficio Informazioni Turistiche *Piazza Ferucci 1 (0577 738 494/proradda@chiantinet.it).* **Open** 10am-1pm, 3-7pm Mon-Sat; 10am-1pm Sun.

Gaiole

On the steep eastern edge of Chianti, surrounded by the Monti dei Chianti, the area around Gaiole is wild yet well tramped. Gaiole itself was a bustling market in the Middle Ages but is quieter now. It makes for a pleasant stop on the way to the nearby wineries (*see pp232-3*) and castles.

The **Badia a Coltibuono**, four kilometres (2.5 miles) north of Gaiole, is a Vallombrosan abbey. Magnificently situated amid cedar forests, it makes a great starting point for anyone up for a hike.

Where to stay & eat

The **Badia a Coltibuono**'s restaurant (0577 749 031, closed Mon Mar-May, mid Dec-early Mar, average €35) specialises in game. In summer you can eat at tables in the beautiful gardens.

For somewhere to stay, go south to the hamlet of San Sano, just off SS408, where the friendly **Hotel Residenza San Sano** (0577 746 130, doubles €115-€135) has a pool set among old stone houses.

Resources

Tourist information

Ufficio Informazioni Pro Loco *Via Antonio Casbianca (0577 749 411/fax 0577 749 375/ prolocogaiole@libero.it).* **Open** *Apr-Oct* 9.30am-1pm, 3-6.30pm Mon-Sat. Closed Nov-Mar.

Castelnuovo Berardenga

An alternative to continuing along the SS408 from Gaiole towards Siena is to branch off to the east on the SS484. Before you get to the ninth-century town, you'll come to one of the region's best-known castles, **Castello di Brolio**. It's largely a 19th-century reading of what a castle should look like since the original was wrecked by Spanish troops in 1478 and completely destroyed by the Sienese 50 years later. It was rebuilt by Baron Bettino Ricasoli, who was also responsible for pushing Chianti's wine industry into the major league. The **Barone Ricasoli** winery below the castle remains one of the region's best, along with nearby **Felsina** (for both, *see pp232-3*).

Where to eat

A surprising find, given the distance from the sea, is **Da Antonio** in Castelnuovo Berardanga (via Fiorita 28-32, 0577 355 321, closed Mon and lunch in winter, set meal €55), considered by many to be Tuscany's best fish restaurant. Owner Antonio Farina makes dawn trips to the coast to bring back the freshest catches for his fixed menus. Always interesting, they feature *antipasti*, *primi* and a *secondo* of the day's catch.

West of Siena

The Poggibonsi exit of the Si-Fi (Siena-Florence) *autostrada* quickly gives access to western Siena province.

Poggibonsi

Poggibonsi is an ugly commercial centre, but nearby **Colle di Val d'Elsa** is certainly worth exploring. The birthplace of Arnolfo di Cambio (who was the architect responsible for Florence's Duomo and the Palazzo Vecchio), it has an interesting medieval core. The town is renowned for its crystal glassware, which at its best is still hand-blown and ground.

Where to eat

Another good reason for hanging out in Poggibonsi is **Da Arnolfo** (via XX Settembre, 0577 920 549, closed Tue and Wed, average €75), which carries two Michelin stars. Its typical offerings include steamed shrimp with candied tomatoes, and pigeon stuffed with chicken livers, followed by exquisite desserts.

San Gimignano

The 13 stone towers that now punctuate the skyline of San Gimignano actually numbered 72 in the 12th and 13th centuries, when the town was at its political and financial peak. Its good fortune came from its strategic position on the via Francigena pilgrim route, which passes through the perfectly preserved medieval city.

Tourism has brought it further wealth, and masses of day-trippers now congest its narrow pedestrian streets between the two main squares. The 11th-century **Collegiata** or cathedral (0577 940 316, closed Sun morning, late Jan-early Mar except services, admission €3.50) is usually pretty crowded as well, but should still be visited for the astounding frescoes by, among others, Bartolo di Fredi and Ghirlandaio. However, the best way to enjoy this jewel of a town is to buy an all-in-one ticket (€7.50) for its museums,

which are part of the Sistema Musei Senesi. Retire to a different world until the evening, when the tourist throngs beat a retreat and the locals re-emerge. You'll also be able to appreciate the works of contemporary sculpture (Jannis Kounellis, Giulio Paolini, Nick Jonk and Luciano Fabro) dotted here and there throughout the town. On a more traditional note, up in piazza del Duomo is the **Pinacoteca** (0577 990 312, average €5) in part of the building that houses the **Palazzo Comunale** (town hall) and the **Torre Grossa**. Clamber up here for a fine view of the town and surrounding area. The Pinacoteca has an important collection of 12th- to 15th-century Florentine and Sienese art, including a lovely pair of paintings by Filippino Lippi and some delightful frescoes on the subject of love by Memmo di Filippuccio. Walk down via San Matteo from the main square and you'll reach the **Museo Archeologico**, the **Spezzeria di Santa Fina** and the **Galleria d'Arte Moderna e Contemporanea Raffaele De Grada**, all of them located in what was once the Convent of Santa Fina (via Folgore 11, admission €3.50). These are gems, with just enough in them to entice without giving rise to surfeit. The archaeology is largely Etruscan, found locally but influenced by the culture of nearby Volterra in Pisa province. The glazed ceramics in the Spezzeria were made for the convent's pharmacy and the paintings on the floor above provide a surprisingly rich overview of Italian art of the early and mid 1900s. There's also an **Ornithological Museum** (via Quercecchio, 0577 941 388, admission €1.50) on the other side of town.

February's carnival procession is the best time to visit in the off-season, along with 12 March, the day of patron saint Fina, when museum entrance is free. In July the **Festival Internazionale** series of daily concerts includes piano recitals and opera.

Where to eat

For regional cooking with a twist, head to **Osteria delle Catene** (via Mainardi 18, 0577 941 966, closed Wed, average €25). One of San Gimignano's more elegant places, **Ristorante Dorandù** (vicolo dell'Oro 2, 0577 941 862, closed Mon in winter, average €45) serves food based on a variety of Etruscan, medieval and Renaissance recipes. Try the *pici* with mint pesto accompanied by a local white wine.

For a treat at any time of day, **Gelateria di Piazza** (piazza della Cisterna, 0577 942 244, closed Nov-Feb) claims to sell the best ice-cream in the world – apparently backed up by Tony Blair, if the framed photo and letter inside are anything to go by.

Where to stay

Because this isn't a particularly big town, there's not a wide selection of hotels. Luckily, however, there's a sprawling network of *affittacamere* (rooms for rent in private houses) in the city and *agriturismi* in the surrounding countryside. These vary in quality and price, so ask around before you decide. For details, contact the tourist office (*see below*).

In town, one of the classiest hotels you'll find is the **L'Antico Pozzo** (via San Matteo 87, 0577 942 014, doubles €95-€150), while a pleasant alternative is the recently renovated family-run **Hotel Bel Soggiorno** (via San Giovanni 91, 0577 940 375, doubles €80-€120 incl breakfast), whose restaurant is also tempting. There's an interesting tasting menu for two (€50) and inventive yet sensible à la carte dishes like *lasagnette* with rabbit sauce, or (in spring) lamb with thyme, new potatoes and artichokes.

Resources

Tourist information

Pro Loco Ufficio San Gimignano Informazioni Turistiche *Piazza del Duomo 1 (0577 940 008/ fax 0577 940 008/www.sangimignano.com).*
Open *Summer* 9am-1pm, 3-7pm daily. *Winter* 9am-1pm, 2-6pm daily.

Abbazia di San Galgano

This abandoned abbey is worth a detour even if you do feel like you've overdosed on Tuscan churches. Located in the **Valdimerse**, midway between Siena and Roccastrada on SS73, it's like something out of a fairytale – or a nightmare. Built between 1218 and 1288, the abbey was a Cistercian powerhouse until the 14th century. Its monks devised complex irrigation systems and sold their services as doctors, lawyers and architects. But the abbey was sacked one time too many and eventually abandoned. The ruins retain an atmosphere of eerie spirituality.

St Galgano Guidotti lived in a hut on a hilltop next to the abbey where the **Cappella di Montesiepi** now stands. A knight from a local noble family, St Galgano Guidotti renounced his warlike ways to become a Cistercian hermit. When fellow knights persuaded him to revert to his old self in 1180, he defiantly stabbed a stone and his sword slid in. The (alleged) sword in the stone is now on display in the centre of this curious circular Romanesque chapel, which has fading frescoes by Ambrogio Lorenzetti.

South-east of Siena

The landscape south of Siena opens up to reveal rolling hills of open fields interspersed with solitary cypress trees. In the spring it ripples greenly with durum wheat, and in the autumn, after ploughing, is a textured hue of brown and beige. To the east are the Sienese claylands or **Crete Senesi**, which explain the warm pink brick that is a feature of many of the towns in the area. And to the west, you will find a number of well-preserved hill towns to explore.

Buonconvento

If you're heading south by car, take the SS2 towards Cassia and stop off in **Buonconvento** to visit the **Museo d'Arte Sacra della Val d'Arbia** (0577 807 181, closed Mon, admission €3.10) in the Palazzo Ricci Socini. The beautifully displayed collection comprises a *Madonna and Child* by Duccio di Buoninsenga, two works by Pietro Lorenzetti and much more besides.

Where to eat

To refuel your energies after the museum, try **I Poggioli** (via Tassi 6, 0577 806 546, closed Mon & Tue lunch, average €25), where you can sit in the garden and enjoy well-prepared dishes based on premium ingredients.

Monte Oliveto Maggiore

A stone's throw from Buonconvento, up a winding road that leads towards the lunar landscape of the Crete Senesi, is the magnificent abbey of Monte Oliveto Maggiore. Founded in 1313 by Bernardo Tolomei, a scion of one of Siena's richest families, the monastery began as a solitary hermitage in an area so arid it was referred to as a *deserto*. But Bernardo soon drew a large following and the Olivetan order was recognised by the pope in 1344. Expanded territory brought wealth that was channelled into embellishing the buildings and creating a library (sadly closed to the public since the theft of some priceless volumes). However, the biggest project was the *Saint Benedict* fresco cycle. Ghostly white-robed monks greet you as you enter the cloister, where the technicolour kicks in again. The panels were painted by Giovanni Antonio Bazzi (better known as Il Sodoma and Luca Signorelli) and are fascinating for what you can read between the brushstrokes – Sodoma was a colourful character with a taste for exotic pets and young boys (if Vasari and his nickname are to be believed). Outside, a Benedictine gift shop sells home-brewed *amaro* drinks, honey and herbal medicines.

Montalcino

Montalcino (*see pp232-3*) produces one of Italy's premier wines, the imposing Brunello di Montalcino, whose consistent quality has earned it Italy's highest wine honour, the DOCG seal. Brunello ages in oak for at least two years and matures in the bottle for a further year before being released. Look out for the much acclaimed 1997 vintage. However, not all Brunellos are equally memorable. Though younger and less majestic, a good Rosso di Montalcino, like the one made by Siro Pacenti, can be more impressive than many a dully dutiful Brunello.

The existence of a hilltop town here can be traced to AD 814, when it was ceded to the nearby abbey of Sant'Antimo. Under Siena's rule in the 13th century, four families dominated the town's political identity and are represented today in Montalcino's four *contrade*. The Fortezza was built by the Sienese in 1362 and in 1555 became the last and short-lived stronghold of the Sienese Republic following the fall of Siena to the Florentine troops under Cosimo I de' Medici. Shortly after this glory moment, Montalcino fell on hard times and plague. Until the late 1950s it was one of Tuscany's poorest corners. But now tourism, olive oil and the mighty Brunello have turned its luck.

Rolling hills...

All roads in Montalcino lead to piazza del Popolo, the peculiar triangle that marks the heart of the town. This is where you'll find the shield-studded Palazzo Comunale (with the tall tower), modelled after Siena's Palazzo Pubblico in 1292. Around the corner, annexed to Sant'Agostino church, is another admirable example of the Sistema Musei Senesi, the **Museo Civico e Diocesano** (via Ricasoli 31, 0577 846 014, closed Mon, admission €4.50, €6 incl entrance to the Fortezza). Its magnificent, beautifully displayed collection, includes works by Simone Martini and Sano di Pietro and a fascinating section devoted to glazed pottery, which was made locally in the 13th century. The Romanesque and Gothic church of Sant'Agostino (1360) has superb frescoes by Bartolo di Fredi.

Montalcino enjoys views that extend all the way to Siena on a clear day. To appreciate them to the full brace the climb up to the **Fortezza**'s battlements (0577 849 211, admission €3.50). Following your descent you can reward yourself by sampling wines at the well-stocked *enoteca* inside the fortress walls.

Where to eat

Montalcino's restaurants aren't really up to the fame of its wine. The best in town is the **Re di Macchia** (via Saloni 21, 0577 846 116, closed Thur, tasting menu excl wine €20), which has a small, well-thought-out menu. Try the duck breast cooked in Brunello (*petto d'anatra al Brunello*). For nicely presented food and a wonderful view, head slightly out of town towards Torrenieri until on your right you come to the **Boccon di Vino** (località Colombaio Tozzi 201, 0577 848 233, closed Tue, average €40. This restaurant has two lunchtime tasting menus, which cost €30 and €35 excluding wine. If you want to while away time people-watching over a coffee or an *aperitivo*, join the others at the **Fiaschetteria Italiana** (piazza del Popolo 6, 0577 849 043, closed Thur). **Bacchus** (via G Matteotti 15, 0577 847 054, closed Tue in summer, Mon, Tue, Thur & Sat in winter) is and ideal place for light meals in the shape of good cold cuts, cheeses, vegetables preserved in oil and a good variety of wines.

As for wine tasting, there are myriad *enoteche* in Montalcino. Take time to look around. The classiest establishment is **Enoteca Osteria Osticcio** (via Matteotti 23, 0577 848 271, closed Sun, average €20), where your samplings may cost you a bit, but come with a priceless view.

Where to stay

On the southern edge of town, the three-star **Hotel Vecchia Oliviera** (Porta Cerbaia, Angolo via Landi 1, 0577 846 028, doubles €83-€235) has a pool, a terrace and lovely views over the valley. In town, the **Albergo Il Giglio** (via S Saloni 5, 0577 848 167, doubles €53-€75) is a family-run place with 12 frescoed rooms in its main building and an additional five (no bath) next door. The **Hotel Residence Montalcino** (via S Saloni 31, 0577 847 188, doubles €50-€80) has clean, comfortable apartments.

...and rich crops at **Sant'Antimo** abbey.

Visiting wineries

Tuscany boasts three of Italy's foremost quality wine appellations – the Chianti area between Siena and Florence, and further south, the vineyards producing Brunello di Montalcino and Vino Nobile di Montepulciano. The Tuscan reds outshine the whites, but the hills surrounding San Gimignano are also worth a visit for the more than acceptable white Vernaccia. In general, most wineries are happy to show visitors round, but few are equipped with staff and tasting rooms for proper guided tours. Forewarning by phone is thus highly recommended. Most wineries open their doors to the public for Cantine Aperte, held during the last weekend of May. It's an excellent occasion for getting to know some of the smaller wineries focusing on quality that might otherwise be hard to visit. Keep a look out for the Strada del Vino offices, which can arrange tasting tours relating to the particular DOC they cover.

For more on Tuscan wines, *see pp40-4*. Here we've listed our choice of the prominent wineries as a starting point.

Chianti

The heartland of Chianti Classico is best defined by the towns of **Radda**, **Castelnuovo Berardenga**, **Gaiole**, **Castellina Greve** and **Panzano**. The wineries below are given in north–south order. All times listed are for the outlets. Visits to the wineries and tastings are by appointment only.

Badia a Coltibuono

Gaiole in Chianti (0577 74481/shop 0577 749 479/www.coltibuono.com). **Open** *May-July & Sept-Oct* 2.30-4pm Mon-Fri, visits every half hour, rest of the year by request. **Credit** MC, V.

In a 700-year-old abbey (*see p227*).

Barone Ricasoli

Castello di Brolio, Gaiole in Chianti (0577 730 220/www.ricasoli.it). **Open** 8am-7pm Mon-Fri; 11am-7pm Sat, Sun. **Credit** AmEx, DC, MC, V.

An excellent winery situated below the castle, (*see p227*).

Castello di Fonterutoli

Fonterutoli, Castellina in Chianti (0577 73571/www.fonterutoli.it).
This winery is run by the handsome scions of a family that competes with the Antonori for aristocratic panache. There's a country residence to match. Unfortunately, the winery itself is never open to the public. Tasting and selling is done through the Osteria Fonterutoli (Via G Puccini 4, 0577 740 212, 10am-10pm Mon, Wed-Sat, 10am-5pm Tue, Sun).

Felsina

SS Chiantigiana 484, near Castelnuovo Berardenga (0577 355 117). **Open** 8.30am-5.30pm Mon; 8.30am-7pm Tue-Sat. **Credit** MC, V.
On Chianti Classico's southernmost border, this winery produces some of Siena's best wines, including the Super Tuscan Fontalloro.

Riecine

Gaiole in Chianti (0577 749 098/www.riecine.com). **Open** 9am-1pm, 2.30-6pm Tue-Sat. **Credit** MC, V.
Run by Sèan O'Callaghan, this smaller winery has won widespread international acclaim.

Further information

Consorzio Chianti Classico (055 82285/www.chianticlassico.com).

Chianti Rufina

This area comprises the towns of **Pontassieve** and **Rufina**. Its wineries are protected by low mountains and enjoy a dry microclimate.

Fattoria Selvapiana

Via Selvapiana 43, Rufina (055 836 9848/www.selvapiana.it). **Open** 9am-1pm, 3-7pm Mon-Fri. **Credit** AmEx, DC, MC, V.
The pick of the Rufina wineries.

Montalcino

One of Italy's top wines, **Brunello di Montalcino** (DOCG), is produced around this hilltop town 40 kilometres (25 miles) south of Siena, and standards are kept high. There are a number of *enoteche* in town (*see p231*) and 171 producers whose output reflects differences in soil and microclimate within this widespread municipality.

Fattoria dei Barbi

Podere Novi village 170, Montalcino (0577 841 111/www.fattoriadeibarbi.it).
Open 10am-1pm, 2.30-6pm Mon-Fri; 2.30-6pm Sat, Sun. **Credit** AmEx, DC, MC, V.
Fine old cellars, with a variety of wines, plus sales of oil, grappa and cheese made on the property. The winery has its own restaurant.

Fattoria del Casato

17 località Pod. Casato (0577 849 421/www.cinellicolombini.it). **Open** 9am-1pm, 3-6pm Mon-Fri; Sat & Sun by appointment. **Credit** MC, V.
Donatella Cinelli Colombini's new cellars are entirely manned, as it were, by women. The tour is fun and instructive, the wines very promising.

Further information

Consorzio del Vino Brunello di Montalcino
Costa del Municipio 1, Montalcino (0577 848 246/www.consorziobrunellodimontalcino.it).

Montepulciano

In 1685 poet Francesco Redi declared in verse that Montepulciano was 'of all wines the King'. With this head start, in 1981 the Vino Nobile di Montepulciano was among the first Italian wines to achieve the prestigious DOCG, hot on the heels of Montalcino.

Avignonesi

Via Colonica 1, Valiano di Montepulciano (0578 724 304/www.avignonesi.it). **Open** 9am-6pm Mon-Fri. **Credit** AmEx, DC, MC, V.
The main Avignonesi vineyard, Le Cappezzine, is about 23 kilometres (14 miles) outside Montepulciano and has tastings and tours on weekdays. There's also a small cellar in town (via di Gracciano nel Corso 91).

Poliziano

Via Fontago 11, Montepulciano (0578 738 171/www.carlettipolizano.it). **Open** 8.30am-12.30pm, 2.30-6pm Mon-Fri. Closed 2wks Dec & Aug. **Credit** AmEx, DC, MC, V.
Vineyards on three different sites, producing three different types of Vino Nobile, two of which are single-vineyard crus.

Further information

Consorzio del Vino Nobile di Montepulciano
Piazza Grande 7, Montepulciano (0578 757 812/www.vinonobiledimontepulciano.it).

Resources

Tourist information

Ufficio Informazioni *Costa del Municipio (0577 849 331/www.prolocomontalcino.it)*. **Open** 10am-1pm, 2-5.50pm daily. Closed Mon in winter.

Abbazia di Sant'Antimo

Sant'Antimo is reached by taking the middle of the three roads radiating south of the Fortezza. The sensational country lane snakes through ten kilometres (six miles) of unspoiled landscape. It's best appreciated if you have three hours to walk it.

Lying quietly in a vale beneath the hamlet of Castelnuovo dell'Abate, the Benedictine abbey is built of creamy travertine with translucent alabaster highlights. It stood empty for 500 years before a handful of French Premonstratensian monks (Cistercian branch) moved here in 1979. Its founding is attributed to Charlemagne in 781, and it's said to be the first of more than 20 abbeys established by the emperor. In 1118 funds were granted to construct the present church and additional monastic buildings, since fallen to rubble. This grant was so important it was literally written in stone, engraved in the steps of the altar.

Thanks to the via Francigena pilgrim route, Sant'Antimo soon grew into a true regional powerhouse, but by the 15th century financial mismanagement saw the beginning of its demise. Over the subsequent years, it fell, leaving Siena to divide up its territory.

In 1462 Pope Pio II evicted the remaining monks, citing moral degeneration. Inside, there are finely carved capitals. Don't miss *Daniel in the Lion's Den* (second column from the right of the nave) by a northern craftsman known as the Master of Cabestany.

San Quirico d'Orcia

San Quirico d'Orcia is a diamond of a town with a go-getting entrepreneurial spirit. Many of Tuscany's foremost building firms hail from here, so it's no wonder they have done such a splendid job in restoring the vast late 17th-century Palazzo Chigi. Just opposite is the 13th-century Collegiata church, whose portals are adorned with remarkably imaginative creatures carved in stone. Inside, there's a magnificent altarpiece by Sano di Pietro. Wander down the main street and you'll arrive in the square that provides dawn-to-dusk access to a lovely formal garden, the 16th-century Horti Leonini, at the back of which you'll find a delightful rose garden. Like many towns around here, San Quirico has its own traditional olive press, which becomes the focal point of the annual Festa dell'Olio held around 10 December. It's a convivial, somewhat bibulous opportunity for gorging on *bruschetta* soaked in the excellent freshly pressed olive oil.

Where to stay

Hotel Casanova (SS 146, 0577 898 177, doubles €70-€86 per person half board) is just outside San Quirico on the Pienza road, five minutes on foot from the centre of town. Its style is modern-traditional and you'll find plenty of parking space and an indoor and an outdoor pool.

Bagno Vignoni

Bagno Vignoni, just south of San Quirico d'Orcia, has to be seen to be believed. Piazza delle Sorgenti, its main square, has a large pool of thermal water in its centre flanked by a ragged collection of houses along a low Renaissance loggia. Featured in a memorable scene in Tarkovsky's *Nostalgia*, it's been off limits since 1979 after crowds grew too big, but there's a stream of thermal run-off 200 metres (220 yards) south – perfect for soaking tired feet. The thermal pool at **Hotel Posta Marcucci** (*see p226*) is open to the public.

Where to stay & eat

The family-run **Hotel Posta Marcucci** (via Ara Urcea 43, 0577 887 112, doubles €133-€174), with its thermal pool, also has a delightful open-air restaurant. The other family-run hotel is **Hotel Le Terme** (0577 887150, doubles €61-€99), right beside the antique baths in the centre. You can eat well at its restaurant (closed Wed in winter) for around €20. The **Locanda del Loggiato** (piazza del Moretto 30, 0577 888 925, doubles €130) has eight pleasant rooms and its own eaterie, which focuses on quiches, salads and lighter fare (average €20).

Pienza

Originally called Corsignano, this little town took the name Pienza after the man who remodelled it between 1458 and 1462. This was Aeneas Silvius Piccolomini, the son of a local landowner who became Pope Pius II in 1458. Much travelled, well read and singularly talented, the 'Humanist pope', as he was later called, was a close friend of Renaissance genius Leon Battista Alberti, designer, among other things, of the façade of the church of Santa Maria Novella in Florence and author of the *Treatise of Architecture* that was to influence town-planning for centuries. The executive architect entrusted with making Pienza what it is and who created a central square flanked by the cathedral, the town hall and the Pope's Palace was Bernardo Rossellino, Alberti's foremost assistant.

If you stand in **piazza Pio II** and slowly spin around, you'll notice decorative themes and variations (the tondo and the garland) that lend a sense of unity to the different types of building and the materials used. It's pretty astounding to think the whole project was accomplished in four years. In fact, this rather suggests that, with a certain optimism, designs had been drawn up before Aeneas Silvius got the top job. The body of the **Duomo** is in tuff stone and at the back is deliberately Gothic in style, as if to fit into the existing urban context. By contrast, the travertine façade is as Renaissance as it could be, for those days a bold declaration of modernity. Interestingly, the painting by Vecchietta placed beneath the most Gothic-looking window behind the altar also deliberately harks back to an earlier period in painting. The coeval painting by the same artist now kept in the museum in Pienza is much more modern, as if Vecchietta were finally able to work without constraints. **Palazzo Piccolomini** (0578 748 503, closed Mon, admission €3), the pope's residence, was modelled after Alberti's Palazzo Rucellai in Florence. There is a delightful hanging garden overlooking the Val d'Orcia that you can view from the gate – this was probably the first garden deliberately designed for aesthetic pleasure since antiquity. You need a ticket for tours of Pius II's lavish private apartments, but access to the courtyard is free.

Pienza's art collection is kept in the new **Museo Diocesano** (0578 749 905, closed Tue, admission €4.10). The sections devoted to medieval and early Renaissance art are, as you would expect, particularly striking.

Where to stay & eat

Trattoria Latte di Luna (via San Carlo 6, 0578 748 606, closed Tue, average €25) is the best bet for a meal. Otherwise, head down to the charming little town of Monticchiello, a few miles away, and eat at **La Porta** (via del Piano 1, 0578 755 163, closed Thur, average €30). Pienza has an excellent, reasonably priced wine shop with well-selected bottles from all over Tuscany and well beyond called **Enoteca di Ghino** (via delle Mura 8, 0578 748 057). Those wanting to stay the night will enjoy the comfort and calm of **Hotel Relais Il Chiostro** (corso Rossellino 26, 0578 748 400, closed early Jan-late Mar, doubles €120-€220), housed in a 15th-century convent overlooking the Val d'Orcia. It has an inviting pool and a restaurant (closed lunch Mon, average €50) that offers refined modern Tuscan cuisine. **Camere Gozzante** (Corso Rossellino, 0578 748 500, doubles €62-€70) has a handful of pleasant rooms in the main street, while the **San Gregorio Residence** (via della Madonnina, 0578 748 059, doubles €70-€100) is better for families with small children.

Bagno Vignoni. *See p234.*

Resources

Tourist information

Ufficio Informazioni *Palazzo Publico, piazza Pio II* (0578 749 071/infopienza@quipo.it). **Open** 9.30am-1pm, 3-6.30pm daily.

Montepulciano

It's hard to imagine anyone ever voluntarily pushing heavy oak wine barrels up a steep two kilometres (1.25 miles) of cobblestone in the torrid heat of August, but that's what Montepulciano's proudest menfolk do each year in the highly anticipated Bravio delle

Montepulciano's essential sight: the pilgrimmage church of **San Biagio**.

Botti. During this festival held on the last Sunday of August, eight rival *contrade* battle it out for the honour of being the first to roll their barrel to the town's highest point. The best easily complete the task in under ten minutes, while the winner is doused in the local wine, Vino Nobile di Montepulciano, and brings glory to his *contrada*.

Montepulciano is clearly a town of greater substance than others south of Siena. Its fine buildings speak for the influence of Florentine architects, which is hardly surprising since the town read the writing on the wall earlier than most and in 1511 swore allegiance to Florence to defend itself from Sienese expansion. Among the eminent architects of the time brought in to rework the town's medieval fabric were Antonio da Sangallo the Elder and Vignola.

The best way to see the town is by tackling the steep via di Gracciano del Corso, which starts near Montepulciano's northern entrance, Porta al Prato. Along the way, note the Roman and Etruscan marble plaques cemented into the base of **Palazzo Bucelli** (No. 73). These were gathered together by Pietro Bucelli, an early 18th-century collector whose interest in antiquities supplied the Museo Civico with some of its finest items. A bit further up, on piazza Michelozzo, you can't help but notice the towering **Torre di Pulcinella**, a clock tower topped by a mechanical figure typical of the Neapolitan *Commedia dell'Arte*. It was the nostalgic gift of a priest from Naples long resident in Montepulciano. Further up, your efforts will be rewarded when you reach piazza Grande, the town's highest and most beautiful point. The spacious square carpeted with chunky stones is reminiscent of Pienza's 'ideal city' layout. Don't let the rough brick front of the **Duomo** put you off. Although it was never finished with a proper façade, the interior is a treasure trove comprising a fine Gothic *Assumption* by Taddeo di Bartolo over the altar (1401) and, towards the top of the left of the nave, a *Madonna and Child* by Sano di Pietro. Look out for the *Ciborium*, a rare marble sculpture by Vecchietta, one of the artists invited by Pius II to embellish the Duomo in Pienza with a painting. The highlight of the Duomo is the delicately carved tomb of humanist Aragazzi (1428) by Michelozzo.

Also in the square are Sangallo's Palazzo Tarugi, with loggia; the 13th-century Palazzo Comunale, which deliberately echoes Palazzo Vecchio in Florence; and Palazzo Contucci across the square. Whatever else you see, the pilgrimage church of **San Biagio**, 20 minutes' walk from Porta al Prato, is a must. Designed by Sangallo and built between 1518 and 1545, this Bramante-influenced study in proportion is a jewel of the High Renaissance.

Where to stay & eat

For drinks or light midday snacks, don't miss **Antico Caffè Poliziano** (via di Voltaia nel Corso 27, 0578 758 615, average €35), an art deco institution that's a great place to sample Vino Nobile. Below in San Biagio, there's more substantial food at **La Grotta** (0578 757 607, closed Wed, average €40), a former 14th-century staging post where Sangallo ate when working on the church.

For accommodation, you could try the **Albergo Il Marzocco** (piazza Savonarola 18, 0578 757 262/fax 0578 757 530, doubles €60-€90), just inside the Porta al Prato in a 16th-century palazzo. It has spacious rooms, a few of which have terraces.

Resources

Tourist information

Ufficio Informazioni Pro Loco *Via del Corso 59A (0578 757 341/www.prolocomontepulciano.it).*
Open *Summer* 9.30am-12.30pm, 3-8pm Mon-Sat; 10am-12.30pm Sun. *Winter* 9.30am-12.30pm, 3-6pm Mon-Sat; 10am-12.30pm Sun.

Chianciano & Chiusi

From Montepulciano head along the 146 road towards Chianciano and Chiusi. Although both of these towns have a pleasant historic district, their expansion outwards is pretty hideous. However, they do both have excellent archeological museums, which are a good reason to visit. **The Museo Archeologico delle Acque** at Chianciano (0578 30471, closed Mon-Fri Nov-Mar, Mon Apr-Oct, admission €4) reveals how the healing waters of the town were exploited and embellished back in Roman times. The much larger **Museo Archeologico Nazionale** (via Porsenna 7, 0578 20177, admission €4) in Chiusi houses one of the country's most important Etruscan collections.

Sarteano

Between Chianciano and Chiusi there's a turning on the right that takes you to **Sarteano**, a delightful, well-preserved and relatively untouristy town. With its wonderful collection of Etruscan funerary urns shaped like heads, the tiny **Museo Civico Archeologico** (0578 269 261, closed Mon-Fri Oct-May, Mon June-Sept, admission €2.50) is a must.

While you're in the area, enjoy a wander round San Casciano dei Bagni. Nestled in the hillside above the Val di Paglia it looks over towards Mount Amiata. Before leaving, indulge in a long soak in the hot spring waters of the **Centro Termale Fonteverde** (0578 57241, entrance €12, €15 weekend).

Radicofacini

From Sarteano head for Celle sul Rigo and beyond until you see the turning on your left for Radicofani, the hilltop town that you can see from afar, perched on what looks like a truncated cone. This stony stronghold is built from the volcanic basalt that must have erupted from Mount Amiata in its fiery prehistoric youth. For the pilgrims of past centuries travelling south to Rome, it must have appeared foreboding, but safer than the easier valley route. To reinforce the strategic nature of this location, from the ninth century a **Città Fortificata** or fortress was built on the summit of the hill to which Radicofani clings. Recently restored, it now contains a museum (0578 55905, summer 10am-dusk Tue-Sun, winter 10am-dusk Fri-Sun, admission €3). By climbing to the top you will gain the most glorious view of the whole area – images like this never leave you.

Where to stay & eat

Just opposite the museum, you can eat well at the **Osteria da Gagliano** (via Roma 5, 0578 268 022, closed Tue, lunch in winter, average €20). It only seats 25, so in summer you it's probably a good idea to book. The **Residenza Santa Chiara** (piazza Santa Chiara 30, 0578 265 412, doubles €130), once a convent and now a charming hotel overlooking the town, also has an excellent restaurant (average €30) and an impressive *enoteca* of its own.

Getting there

By bus

If you decide against car hire, there's a regular **SITA** bus service (800 373 760) from Florence to Greve (50mins) and Panzano (70mins) and some buses continue on to Radda (90mins) and Gaiole (2hrs). SITA also runs buses from Florence to San Gimignano (via Poggibonsi, 70mins) via Colle di Val d'Elsa (1hr).

By car

Siena province is best experienced at leisure in your own transport. In Chianti, a car will allow you to explore La Chiantigiana and the SS222, which wiggles its way south of Florence to Siena through hilltop towns such as Panzano and Castellina. This section is organised along the north to south route of the SS222.

By train

Tra-in (0577 204 246) operates a regular service between Siena and Montalcino (1hr) and another regular service between Siena and Montepulciano (via Pienza, 90mins). There are also regular trains to San Gimignano (1hr) via Monteriggioni (30mins).

Lucca

Wall-to-wall loveliness.

In some ways it's as if the stout 16th- and 17th-century walls that encircle this beguiling city have allowed its character to remain wholly untainted by outside influences. The moment you walk through one of its six gates the immediate impression is of a relaxed and prosperous community untouched by the kind of culture-vulture tourism that can be an unpleasant feature of so many other Tuscan cities. That's not to say that tourists aren't welcome – they are. In fact, if you decide to join the *Lucchesi* strolling on their tree-lined ramparts, congregating in their cafés and restaurants or even just enjoying a moment's peace in a quiet square or garden, you'll be made to feel very much at home. Of course, on the down side, visitors will find fewer major art treasures to admire than they might in Florence, Siena or Arezzo. Although, by the same token, queues are shorter and prices less exorbitant.

Much of Lucca is pedestrianised and the gentlest way to discover the city is on foot, or better still, to do as the locals do and spend a day in the saddle – the *Lucchesi* prefer bikes to cars. Either way you'll be rewarded with a surprise at nearly every corner. The ornate white façades of the Romanesque churches – overplayed **San Michele in Foro** (*see p241*), the glistening mosaic of **San Frediano** (*see p240*) and the asymmetrical **Duomo di San Martino** (*see p240*) – all appear unexpectedly. The colourful piazza dell'Anfiteatro with its rather touristy bars and cafés has retained the oval shape of the ancient Roman amphitheatre and is accessed through four arches, while the tree-lined ramparts and oak-topped Torre Guinigi afford splendid views of the cityscape.

Another good starting point for an exploration of the central sights is the prettily symmetrical piazza Napoleone. Here, you'll also find a laid-back branch of the APT tourist information centre inside the Palazzo Ducale (*see p247*).

Lucca's flatness and relatively simple grid plan make everything easily accessible. A lovely way to get your bearings is to hire a bike and cycle the four kilometres (2.5 miles) along the top of the city walls (*see p242*).

SOME HISTORY

Possibly the site of a Ligurian and then an Etruscan settlement, Lucca acquired political significance as a Roman municipium in 89 BC and hosted the signing of the first triumvirate between Pompey, Julius Caesar and Crassus in 56 BC. It was crucially positioned at the crossroads of the Empire's communications with its northern reaches and controlled the Apennine passes along the Serchio valley.

Despite Rome's fall the city continued to maintain its supremacy in Tuscany first as capital of Tuscia under Lombard rule and then as the seat of the Frankish Margravate from 774. By the turn of the millennium Lucca had grown into Tuscany's largest city and consolidated itself as a commercial powerhouse thanks to the wool and silk trades and to its command of a strategic juncture of the Via Francigena. Wealth engendered commercial rivalry with its upstart neighbours. This soon turned into open military clashes with Pisa and a gradual loss of political dominance to Florence during the drawn-out Guelph-Ghibelline conflict.

The 14th century was turbulent for Lucca. A short-lived heyday as the capital of a mini-empire in western Tuscany under the helm of the *condottiere* Castruccio Castracani (1320-28) soon gave way to a series of setbacks leading to domination by Pisa from 1342. In 1369 Lucca was granted autonomy and independence by Emperor Charles IV of Bohemia; this was to last unbroken until 1799.

Having renounced claims to regional leadership, Lucca moved into relative obscurity and turned in on itself. An oligarchy of ruling families, foremost among them the Guinigi, tightly controlled all public offices and private wealth and set about enlarging the medieval urban nucleus. In 1805 Lucca passed under the direct rule of Elisa Baciocchi, Napoleon's sister, and then in 1817 to the Infanta Maria Luisa di Borbone of Spain. Both did much to recast the city architecturally and patronised a brief but intense period of artistic ferment. In 1847 Lucca was ceded to the Grand Duchy of Tuscany and then joined a united Italy in 1860.

The city's almost uninterrupted history as an opulent, free commune has left it largely unaffected by outside developments, both architecturally and psychologically. Indeed, by very literally minding their own business, the *Lucchesi* have stayed both safe and prosperous. In so far as the timing of your visit is concerned, some of the following dates may be

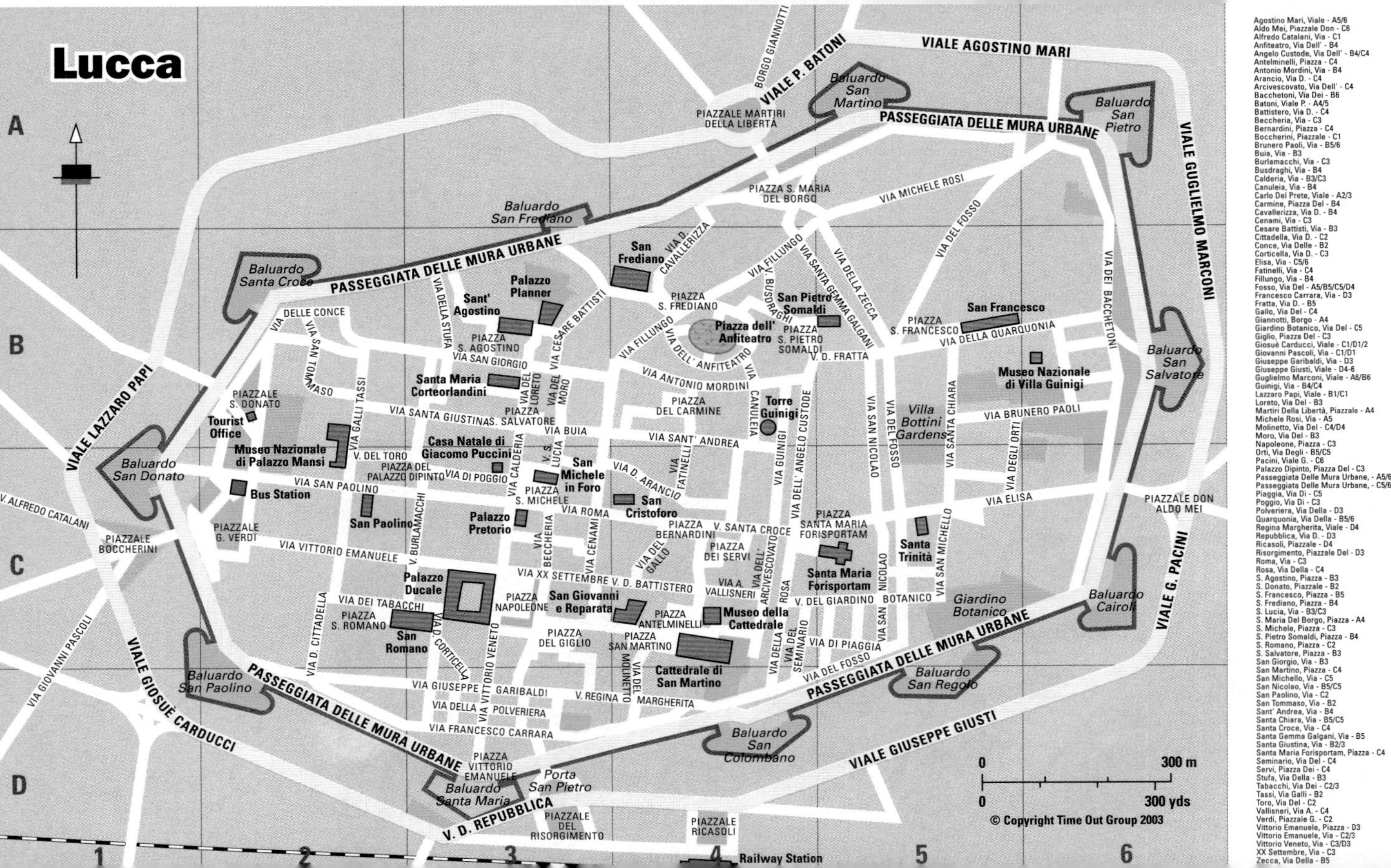
Lucca
A
B
C
D
1
2
3
4
5
6
VIALE AGOSTINO MARI
VIALE GUGLIELMO MARCONI
VIALE G. PACINI
VIALE GIUSEPPE GIUSTI
VIALE GIOSUÈ CARDUCCI
VIALE LAZZARO PAPI
VIALE P. BATONI
BORGO GIANNOTTI
V. D. REPUBBLICA
PASSEGGIATA DELLE MURA URBANE
Baluardo San Martino
Baluardo San Pietro
Baluardo San Salvatore
Baluardo Cairoli
Baluardo San Regolo
Baluardo San Colombano
Baluardo Santa Maria
Baluardo San Paolino
Baluardo San Donato
Baluardo Santa Croce
Baluardo San Frediano
PIAZZALE MARTIRI DELLA LIBERTÀ
PIAZZA S. MARIA DEL BORGO
PIAZZALE DON ALDO MEI
PIAZZALE RICASOLI
PIAZZALE DEL RISORGIMENTO
PIAZZA VITTORIO EMANUELE
Porta San Pietro
PIAZZALE BOCCHERINI
PIAZZALE G. VERDI
PIAZZALE S. DONATO
V. ALFREDO CATALANI
VIA GIOVANNI PASCOLI
San Frediano
Palazzo Pfanner
Sant' Agostino
San Pietro Somaldi
Piazza dell' Anfiteatro
San Francesco
Museo Nazionale di Villa Guinigi
Villa Bottini Gardens
Torre Guinigi
Santa Maria Corteorlandini
Casa Natale di Giacomo Puccini
San Michele in Foro
San Cristoforo
Palazzo Pretorio
San Paolino
Museo Nazionale di Palazzo Mansi
Tourist Office
Bus Station
Palazzo Ducale
San Romano
San Giovanni e Reparata
Museo della Cattedrale
Cattedrale di San Martino
Santa Maria Forisportam
Santa Trinità
Giardino Botanico
Railway Station
0
300 m
0
300 yds
© Copyright Time Out Group 2003
Agostino Mari, Viale - A5/6
Aldo Mei, Piazzale Don - C6
Alfredo Catalani, Via - C1
Anfiteatro, Via Dell' - B4
Angelo Custode, Via Dell' - B4/C4
Antelminelli, Piazza - C4
Antonio Mordini, Via - B4
Arancio, Via D. - C4
Arcivescovato, Via Dell' - C4
Bacchetoni, Via Dei - B6
Batoni, Viale P. - A4/5
Battistero, Via D. - C4
Beccheria, Via - C3
Bernardini, Piazza - C4
Boccherini, Piazzale - C1
Brunero Paoli, Via - B5/6
Buia, Via - B3
Burlamacchi, Via - C3
Busdraghi, Via - B4
Calderia, Via - B3/C3
Canuleia, Via - B4
Carlo Del Prete, Viale - A2/3
Carmine, Piazza Del - B4
Cavallerizza, Via D. - B4
Cenami, Via - C3
Cesare Battisti, Via - B3
Cittadella, Via D. - C2
Conce, Via Delle - B2
Corticella, Via D. - C3
Elisa, Via - C5/6
Fatinelli, Via - C4
Fillungo, Via - B4
Fosso, Via Del - A5/B5/C5/D4
Francesco Carrara, Via - D3
Fratta, Via D. - B5
Gallo, Via Del - C4
Giannotti, Borgo - A4
Giardino Botanico, Via Del - C5
Giglio, Piazza Del - C3
Giosuè Carducci, Viale - C1/D1/2
Giovanni Pascoli, Via - C1/D1
Giuseppe Garibaldi, Via - D3
Giuseppe Giusti, Viale - D4-6
Guglielmo Marconi, Viale - A6/B6
Guinigi, Via - B4/C4
Lazzaro Papi, Viale - B1/C1
Loreto, Via Del - B3
Martiri Della Libertà, Piazzale - A4
Michele Rosi, Via - A5
Molinetto, Via Del - C4/D4
Moro, Via Del - B3
Napoleone, Piazza - C3
Orti, Via Degli - B5/C5
Pacini, Viale G. - C6
Palazzo Dipinto, Piazza Del - C3
Passeggiata Delle Mura Urbane, - A5/6/B2/3
Passeggiata Delle Mura Urbane, - C5/6/D2/3/4
Piaggia, Via Di - C5
Poggio, Via Di - C3
Polveriera, Via Della - D3
Quarquonia, Via Della - B5/6
Regina Margherita, Viale - D4
Repubblica, Via D. - D3
Ricasoli, Piazzale - D4
Risorgimento, Piazzale Del - D3
Roma, Via - C3
Rosa, Via Della - C4
S. Agostino, Piazza - B3
S. Donato, Piazzale - B2
S. Francesco, Piazza - B5
S. Frediano, Piazza - B4
S. Lucia, Via - B3/C3
S. Maria Del Borgo, Piazza - A4
S. Michele, Piazza - C3
S. Pietro Somaldi, Piazza - B4
S. Romano, Piazza - C2
S. Salvatore, Piazza - B3
San Giorgio, Via - B3
San Martino, Piazza - C4
San Michello, Via - C5
San Nicolao, Via - B5/C5
San Paolino, Via - C2
San Tommaso, Via - B2
Sant' Andrea, Via - B4
Santa Chiara, Via - B5/C5
Santa Croce, Via - C4
Santa Gemma Galgani, Via - B5
Santa Giustina, Via - B2/3
Santa Maria Forisportam, Piazza - C4
Seminario, Via Del - C4
Servi, Piazza Dei - C4
Stufa, Via Della - B3
Tabacchi, Via Dei - C2/3
Tassi, Via Galli - B2
Toro, Via Del - C2
Vallisneri, Via A. - C4
Verdi, Piazzale G. - C2
Vittorio Emanuele, Piazza - D3
Vittorio Emanuele, Via - C2/3
Vittorio Veneto, Via - C3/D3
XX Settembre, Via - C3
Zecca, Via Della - B5

Duomo di San Martino.

worth bearing in mind: the Santa Zita flower show and market (four days at the end of April); a summer music festival in piazza Anfiteatro (July); the Luminara di San Paolino, a torchlit procession celebrating Lucca's patron saint (11 July); the Luminara de Santa Croce procession of the Volte Santo (13 September); the cultural, religious and sporting events of Settembre Lucchese (September, October); and, the Natale Anfiteatro Christmas market.

Sights

Churches

Duomo di San Martino

Piazza San Martino (0583 957 068). **Open** *Summer* 9.30am-7pm daily. *Winter* 9.30am-5pm daily. Sacristy *Summer* 9.30am-5.45pm Mon-Sat; 11.20-11.50am, 1-4.45pm Sun. *Winter* 9.30am-4.45pm Mon-Sat; 11.20-11.50am, 1-4.45pm Sun. **Admission** €2. **No credit cards.**

At first glance Lucca's Romanesque cathedral seems somewhat out of kilter and unbalanced. A closer look reveals why. The oddly asymmetrical façade has the arch and the first two series of *logge* on the right literally squeezed and flattened by the campanile. Nobody is really to blame (or commend) for this as the Lombard belltower was erected before the rest of the church in around 1100 and completed only 200 years later. It predates the Duomo, on which work only began in earnest in the 12th century. The asymmetry of the façade, designed by Guidetto da Como, only adds to the overall effect of exuberance and eccentricity provided by the carvings of beasts, dragons and wild animals in the capitals and in the multi-chrome columns.

San Martino's interior is so dimly lit that coin-operated lights are on hand to illuminate paintings like Tintoretto's *Last Supper*, while restoration work in 2003 has enhanced the quality of the frescoes in the apse. Midway up the left nave is Matteo Civitali's octagonal marble *Tempietto* (1484), home to a dolorous wooden crucifix known as the *Volto Santo* (Holy Visage), which is perpetually surrounded by candle-holding worshippers. The effigy – what we see is a copy – was supposedly begun by Nicodemus and finished by an angel, set on a pilotless ship from the Orient in the eighth century and brought into Lucca on a cart drawn by steer. This miraculous arrival quickly spawned a cult following and the relic soon became an object of pilgrimage throughout Europe. Nowadays it is draped in silk and gold garments and ornaments and marched through Lucca's streets in night-time processions on 13 September.

The Duomo's Sacristy contains the other top attraction: the tomb of Ilaria del Carretto (1408), a delicate sarcophagus sculpted by Sienese master Jacopo della Quercia. It represents the young bride of Paolo Guinigi – Lucca's strongman at the time.

San Francesco

Via della Quarquonia (no phone).

Since the Franciscans left it in November 2002 this 14th-century barn-shaped church has been closed to the public. Whether this is likely to change in the future was, as we went to press, still uncertain – contact the ATP (*see p247*) for up-to-date information.

San Frediano

Piazza San Frediano (0583 493 627). **Open** 8.30am-noon, 3-5pm daily; 10.30am-5pm public holidays. **Admission** free.

San Frediano's strikingly resplendent Byzantine-like mosaic façade is unique in Tuscany, rivalled only by that above the choir of San Miniato al Monte in Florence. A church was founded on this site by Fredian, an Irish monk who settled in Lucca in the sixth century and converted the ruling Lombards by allegedly diverting the River Serchio and saving the city from flooding. This miracle put the finishing touches on Christianity's hold on Lucca and earned Fredian a quick promotion to bishop, eventually leading to canonisation. A few centuries later in the 1100s this singular church was built for him.

Apart from its mosaic, the façade of San Frediano is in the Pisan-Romanesque style of many of Lucca's other churches and was the first to face east. The façade's mosaic is an *Ascension* in which a monumental Jesus is lifted by two angels over the heads of his jumbled apostles. Inside, immediately on the right, is a small gem: the *fonte lustrale* (or baptismal font) carved by unknown Lombard and Tuscan artists who surrounded the fountain with scenes from the Old and New Testaments. Behind it is a glazed terracotta *Ascension* by Andrea della Robbia. In the chapel next to it is another of Lucca's revered relics, the miraculously conserved though somewhat shrivelled body of St Zita, a humble servant who was canonised in the 13th century and whose mummy is brought out for a close-up view and a touch by devotees on 27 April. Ongoing restoration projects care for San Frediano's many frescoes.

San Giovanni e Reparata

Via del Duomo (0583 490 530). **Open** *mid Mar-Oct* 10am-6pm daily. *Nov-mid Mar* 10am-5pm daily. **Admission** €2.50; €5.50 with Museo della Cattedrale; excavations included in admission for basilica. **No credit cards**.

Originally Lucca's cathedral, the 12th-century basilica of San Giovanni, now part of the Duomo, is on the site of a pagan temple. Apart from its magnificently ornate ceiling the church's main draw is the architectural remains uncovered by excavations in the 1970s, ranging from a mosaic dating back to Imperial Rome to a fifth-century early Christian basilica.

Santa Maria Corteorlandini

Piazza Giovanni Leonardi (0583 467 464). **Open** 8.30am-noon, 4-6pm daily; 9am-1pm, 3-6pm public hols. **Admission** free.

This overwhelming late baroque church is Lucca's odd man out. Its *trompe l'œil* frescoed roofs – an abundance of coloured marble and the gilded and ornamented tabernacle by local artist Giovanni Vambre (1673) – provide a break from the stark and grey interiors of the city's other churches.

Santa Maria Forisportam

Piazza Santa Maria Forisportam (0583 467 769). **Open** 7.30am-noon, 3-6pm daily. **Admission** free.

Set on the square known to *Lucchesi* as piazza della Colonna Mozza (referring to the truncated column at its centre), Santa Maria takes its name from its location just outside Lucca's older set of walls. The unfinished marble façade dates mostly from the 12th and 13th centuries and is a slightly toned-down version of the Pisan-Romanesque style present throughout the city, with lively carvings in the lunettes and architraves above the portals.

San Michele in Foro

Piazza San Michele (0583 48459). **Open** 7.40am-noon, 3-6pm daily. **Admission** free.

San Michele's façade is a feast for the eyes. Set on the site of the ancient Roman forum, Lucca's consummate take on the Pisan-Romanesque style is one of the city's most memorable sights. Each element lightly plays off against the other: the knotted, twisted and carved columns with their psychedelic geometric designs, the fantastical animals and fruit and floral motifs in the capitals. The façade culminates in a winged and stiff St Michael precariously perched while vanquishing the dragon. San Michele's sombre interior contrasts sharply with its façade. On the right as you enter is a *Madonna and Child* by Matteo Civitali – a copy of the original is on the church's right-hand outside corner. Further on, you'll find Filippino Lippi's *Saints Jerome, Sebastian, Rocco and Helena*.

San Paolino

Via San Paolino (0583 53576). **Open** 8.15am-noon, 3.30-6pm daily. **Admission** free.

Giacomo Puccini received his baptism of fire here in 1881 with his first public performance of the *Mass for Four Voices*. San Paolino had, in fact, always been the Puccini family's second home with five generations of them serving as its organists. Built from 1522 to 1536 for Lucca's patron St Paulinus, who allegedly came over from Antioch in AD 65 and became the city's first bishop and whose remains are buried in a sarcophagus behind the altar, it's Lucca's only example of late Renaissance architecture.

Museums

Casa Natale di Giacomo Puccini

Corte San Lorenzo 9, off Via di Poggio (0583 584 028/fax 0583 331 838). **Open** *Mar-May & Oct-Dec* 10am-1pm, 3-6pm Tue-Sun. *June-Sept* 10am-6pm daily. Closed Jan & Feb. **Admission** €3; €2 under-14s & groups of 10 & over. **No credit cards**.

Ongoing restorations at the birthplace of Lucca's most famous son, Giacomo Puccini, mean that it's worth phoning ahead just to check that this charming museum is open (or, failing that, phoning the tourist office). If it is, you'll be in for some interesting insights into the artist's sheltered youth, turbulent private life and artistic genius. The rooms of memorabilia include the original librettos of his early operas *Mass for Four Voices* and *Symphonie Caprice*, his private letters on subjects both musical and sentimental, the piano on which he composed *Turandot* and the gem-encrusted costume used in the opera's American debut in 1926.

Museo della Cattedrale

Via Arcivescovado (0583 490 530). **Open** *May-Oct* 10am-6pm daily. *Nov-Apr* 10am-2pm Mon-Fri; 10am-5pm Sat, Sun. **Admission** €3.50; €2 incl San Giovanni. **No credit cards.**

Attractively laid out over various levels, this well-curated modern museum houses many treasures transferred from the Duomo di San Martino (*see p240*) and from nearby San Giovanni (*see p241*). Displays are arranged in strict chronological order, encompassing everything from the cathedral's furnishings, its gold and silverware to its sculptures, including Jacopo della Quercia's splendid *Apostle.*

Museo Nazionale di Palazzo Mansi

Via Galli Tassi 43 (0583 55570/312 221). **Open** 8.30am-7.30pm Tue-Sat; 8.30am-1.30pm Sun. **Admission** €4.10; free concessions; €6.50 incl Villa Giunigi. **No credit cards.**

Beyond the impressive stagecoach at the entrance to this, Lucca's most remarkable example of baroque exaggeration, is a 16th- to 17th-century palazzo housing a collection of mostly Tuscan art. While the frescoed Salone della Musica and the neo-classical Salone degli Specchi are light on the eye, the overindulgence climaxes in the Camera della Sposa, an over-the-top bridal chamber with a *baldacchino* bed. The largely uninspiring art includes pieces from the Venetian school with lesser-known works by Tintoretto and Tiziano and some Flemish tapestries. Perhaps the best draw is Pontormo's manneristic portrait of his nasty patron Alessandro De' Medici. Decorative woven goods made on the original looms are sold.

Museo Nazionale di Villa Guinigi

Via della Quarquonia (tel/fax 0583 496 033). **Open** 8.30am-7.30pm Tue-Sat; 8.30am-1.30pm Sun. **Admission** €4.10; free concessions; €6.50 incl Palazzo Manzi. **No credit cards.**

This porticoed pink-brick villa (1403-20) surrounded by tranquil gardens and medieval statues was erected at the height of the rule by Lucca's 'enlightened despot' Paolo Guinigi and now houses art from Lucca and its surrounding region. The first floor of the Museo Nazionale di Villa Guinigi has a recently expanded selection of Roman and Etruscan finds along with some 13th- and 14th-century capitals and columns by Guidetto da Como, which were taken from the façade of San Michele in Foro (*see p241*). The rooms upstairs start with a selection of 13th-century painted crucifixes and some wooden tabernacles. The highlights, though, are Matteo Civitali's *Annunciation,* some impressive altarpieces by Amico Aspertini and Fra Bartolomeo and the intarsia panels by Ambrogio and Nicolao Pucci.

Monuments

Ramparts

On a good day you'll see *Lucchesi* of all ages strolling, picnicking, cuddling and enjoying the views from *le nostre mura* as the ramparts are lovingly known. Built in the 16th- and 17th-centuries, Italy's best-preserved and most impressive city fortifications measure 12m (39ft) in height and 30m (98ft) across with a circumference of just over 4km (2.5 miles). They are punctuated by 11 sturdy bastions, which were meant to ward off the most heavily armed of invaders. A proper siege, though, has never happened and the only real use the ramparts have had was in 1812 when they enabled the city to hermetically close itself off to floodwaters. Soon after Maria Luisa di Borbone turned them into a public park and promenade dotting them with plane, holm-oak, chestnut and lime trees. Today,

The villas

The gently rolling countryside around Lucca is dotted with a number of elegant villas and gardens that were originally the country retreats of wealthy merchants from the nearby city. A handful are open to the public. Elisa Baciocchi, Napoleon's sister, once lived at the 17th-century **Villa Reale** at Marlia (0583 30108, open Mar-Nov 10am-6pm Tue-Sun, €6). Although the house is closed you can visit Orsetti's lovely garden, which is full of statues and also contains a little theatre. The garden of the 16th-century **Villa Oliva Buonvisi** at San Pancrazio (0583 406 462, open 9.30am-12.30pm, 2-6pm daily, €6) is open from March until November, as is the large English-style park and orangery of nearby **Villa Grabau** (0583 406 098, open 10am-1pm, 3-7pm Tue-Sun, €5). Otherwise, 17th-century **Villa Mansi** (0583 920 234, open Feb-Oct 10am-1pm, 3-5pm Tue-Sun, €7) at Segromigno is another fine house, with frescoes of the *Myth of Apollo* by Stefano Tofanelli in the salon – it also hosts the occasional summer concert. The statue-filled garden was laid out by the great Sicilian architect Juvarra. It's partly Italian (geometric) and partly English (not geometric) in style. The **Villa Torrigiani** (0583 928 041, open Mar-mid Nov 10am-1pm, 3-7pm Wed-Mon, €9) and its fine park at Camigliano is open to the public from March to November. Inside are some good 16th- to 18th-century paintings and a collection of porcelain.

Get a look at Lucca from the tree-topped **Torre Guinigi**.

cyclists and pedestrians are still making the most of them not to mention the families who populate the play areas found in almost every *baluardo*.

Torre Guinigi

Via Sant'Andrea 14 (0583 316 846). **Open** *Nov-Feb* 9am-5.30pm daily. *Mar-Sept* 9am-6pm daily. *Oct* 10am-6pm daily. **Admission** €3.50; €2.50 concessions. **No credit cards.**

It's worth the climb to reach the tranquil and leafy summit with its distinctive cluster of oak trees. From the top of this 14th-century, 44m (144ft) high tower, there are spectacular views over Lucca's rooftops to the countryside beyond.

Parks & gardens

Giardino Botanico

Via del Giardino Botanico 14 (0583 442 160). **Open** *Summer* 10am-1pm, 3-7pm daily. *Winter* 9.30am-12.30pm by appointment only. **Admission** €3; free-€2 concessions. **No credit cards.**

Nestling in the south-east corner of the city walls, the Giardino Botanico makes a relaxed spot for a romantic stroll or a quiet sit-down – as do the gardens of the Villa Bottini just a little further up via Santa Chiara. The greenhouse and arboretum are planted with a wide and impressive range of Tuscan flora, many of which are rare species, providing Lucca with its greenest and most exotic spot.

Palazzo Pfanner

Via degli Asili 33 (340 923 3085/fax 0583 342 525). **Open** *Mar-mid Nov* 10am-6pm daily. *Nov-Feb* by appointment. **Admission** €4; free under-8s.

The statues in this palazzo's interior courtyard are a well-known Luccan landmark, as is the open-air marble staircase. Both can also be viewed from the walls above. The 18th-century palazzo itself is the subject of continual restoration.

Shopping

Lucca's main shopping artery is via Fillungo, which has everything from designer clothing to regional cheeses. The other main hubs are via Vittorio Veneto (leading off piazza San Michele) and via Santa Croce where you'll find familiar high-street outlets.

The town's general market is held on via dei Bacchettoni by the eastern wall on Wednesdays and Saturdays, selling clothes, food, flowers and household goods. There's an antiques market in piazza San Martino and surrounding streets on the third weekend of each month and a crafts market (*arti e mestieri*) in piazza San Giusto on the last weekend of the month.

Cacioteca

Via Fillungo 242 (0583 496 346). **Open** 7am-1.30pm, 3.30-8.30pm Mon, Tue, Thur-Sat; 7am-1.30pm Wed. **Credit** MC, V.

An intense waft of seasoned cheese emanates from this inconspicuous but well-known specialist. Typical products from the Garfagnana include the *pecorino* in *barile* (in a barrel).

Cuoieria Fiorentina

Via Fillungo 155 (0583 491 139). **Open** 9.30am-8pm daily. **Credit** AmEx, MC, V.

The last word in soft Italian leather, this emporium of boots, bags, shoes, wallets, coats and trousers has everything the hide enthusiast could want.

Mercato del Carmine

Off Piazza del Carmine. **Open** 8am-noon, 4-7.30pm daily. **No credit cards.**

Between its fruit and vegetable stalls, fishmongers, butchers and delis, this superb covered market offers the best of Lucca's regional produce. There's also a café where you can rest your weary feet and refuel along with the locals.

You looking at me?

As was evident from the media attention surrounding the grisly exorcism of a teenage girl at the convent of Santa Gemma just outside Lucca's city walls (the event featured in Channel 4's 2002 documentary *Tuscany*), the devil, or at least a very real fear of his doings, is alive and well in 21st-century Italy. In fact, this became such an issue in 1999 that the Vatican actually updated its official exorcism service for the first time in more than 350 years. But there is still one form of diabolical shenanigans from which, it appears, none of us is truly safe: *malocchio*, or 'the evil eye'.

So at what point does a dirty look become a satanic stare? Well, for one thing, *jettatori* (those capable of giving the evil eye) are supposed to be easily identifiable through certain physical idiosyncrasies (bushy eyebrows, unusual scars and the like) or, failing that, you can simply nip home and take the test to discover if you really have been dished a dodgy goggle. This is a simple procedure involving (guess what?) olive oil, which is dripped into a bowl of water and olive leaves. If the oil coalesces, you're in the clear; if not, it's *malocchio* city. And the cure? It's quite simple really: you pray.

Vini Liquori Vanni

Piazza del Salvatore 7 (0583 491 902).
Open 4-8pm Mon; 9am-1pm, 4-8pm Tue-Sat.
Credit AmEx, DC, MC, V.
This *enoteca*'s seemingly endless cellar is a treasure for those seeking out Lucca's better vintages. Call ahead and book a wine lesson and *degustazione*, plus a mini-tour of this 13th-century *cantina*. Sample the Maiolina, Tenuta da Valgiano, Michi and Fattoria Colleverde.

Vissidarte

Via Calderia 20 (0583 48383/www.vissidarte.it).
Open 10am-7.30pm Mon-Sat. Closed 3wks Jan.
Credit MC, V.
Beautiful hand-painted ceramics vie for shelf space in this fabulous shop. Everything from olive dishes to tiles depicting Tuscan panoramas.

Delicatessens

There are any number of excellent delis in Lucca stocked with everything from dried mushrooms and olive oils from the surrounding countryside to a locally produced salami made with pig's blood and raisins. Three of the best are **G Giurlani** (via Fillungo 241) with its myriad own-made pastas; **Pot Pourri dell'Ingordigia** (via San Giorgio 5) with its unusual selection of preserved fruits; and **La Grotta** (via dell Anfiteatro 2) with sacks of beans, pulses and flour, and a fine selection of olive oils.

Where to eat & drink

Restaurants

The nearby Garfagnana valley contributes many prime ingredients to Lucca's cuisine, including chestnut flour, river trout, olive oil and above all *farro* (spelt grain made into soup), which pops up on every menu. The signature pudding is *buccellato* (a doughnut-shaped sweet bread flavoured with aniseed and raisins and topped with sugar syrup).

Antico Caffè delle Mura

Piazzale Vittorio Emanuele 2 (0583 467 962).
Open 1.30-2.30pm, 7.30-10.30pm Mon, Thur-Sun; 7.30-10.30pm Wed. **Average** €35. **Credit** AmEx, JCB, MC, V.
Antico Caffè delle Mura is a wonderfully preserved 19th-century restaurant, whose wood-panelled dining room is the setting for accomplished Tuscan cuisine and fine local wines. Adjacent is a superb bar of similarly faded grandeur with DJs every Friday, Saturday and Sunday nights. Great outside tables too.

La Buca di Sant'Antonio

Via della Cervia 3 (0583 55881). **Open** 12.30-3pm, 7.30-11pm Tue-Sat; 12.30-3pm Sun. **Average** €26-€31. **Credit** AmEx, DC, MC, V.
A charmingly restored 19th-century hostelry with a few outside tables amid tubs of plants and flowers, La Buca serves traditional food with the occasional innovative touch. Expect dishes like *occa ripiena al forno* (stuffed goose) and *capretto nostrale al forno* (roast goat with potatoes and artichokes).

Da Giulio in Pelleria

Via della Conce 45 (0583 55948). **Open** noon-2pm, 7-10.30pm Tue-Sat. **Average** €15.50. **Credit** AmEx, DC, MC, V.
Hard by the city walls at the top of the winding via delle Conce this vast trattoria continues to pack in the punters. The menu (available in four different languages) includes specialities like *testina di vitella* (veal cheek) or *panzanetta*.

Da Guido

Via Cesare Battisti 28 (0583 467 219). **Open** noon-2.30pm, 7.30-10pm Mon-Sat. **Average** €12. **Credit** AmEx, MC, V.

A wonderfully down-to-earth (and remarkably good-value) little trattoria, Da Guido attracts droves of loyal regulars to its humble dining room with the promise of simple food well cooked. From the daily *menu turistico*, fill up on juicy *bistecca* or a big plate of *pollo arosto*. Very friendly staff will happily help if you're stuck.

Da Leo

Via Tegrimi 1 (0583 492 236). **Open** noon-2.30pm, 7.30-10.30pm daily. **Average** €15.50. **No credit cards**.
The waiters sing and families of locals compete to be heard over the din of their children, yet despite all this noise and bustle, Da Leo is one of Lucca's most mellow restaurants. You won't be hurried through your meal, which will inevitably be made up of hearty country dishes like rabbit with *porcini* mushrooms, delicious *tortelli* with smoked cheese and bacon, and huge plates of rocket and tomatoes. Remember to bring cash, though, as in true country fashion credit cards are not accepted.

Gli Orti di Via Elisa

Via Elisa 17 (0583 491 241). **Open** 7.30pm-midnight Mon, Tue, Fri-Sun; 7.30-10.30pm Thur (pizzeria till 11.30pm). **Average** €13. **Credit** AmEx, MC, V.
An attractive little trattoria and pizzeria at the eastern end of town, Gli Orti serves up a decent selection of salads – choose your own at a salad station – as well as local delights that include *trippa alla lucchese*.

Locanda Buatino

Borgo Giannotti 508, nr piazzale Martiri della Libertà (0583 343 207). **Open** noon-2pm, 7.30-10pm Mon-Sat. Closed Aug. **Average** €13. **Credit** MC, V.
The dining room of this convivial little restaurant – mellow lighting, coloured glass door panels and shelves of wine bottles – is reason in itself to venture outside Lucca's walls. But add to that the allure of decent Tuscan food at great prices with a serious wine list to match and this becomes one of the city's most worthwhile dining experiences.

La Mora

Località Ponte a Moriano, Via Sesto di Moriano 1748, Sesto di Moriano (0583 406 402). **Open** noon-2.30pm, 7.30-10pm Mon, Tue, Thur-Sun. Closed 1st 2wks Jan & last 2wks June. **Average** €35. **Credit** AmEx, DC, MC, V.
Culinary heavyweight Sauro Brunicardi has turned this old post-house 10km (six miles) north of Lucca into a regionally renowned *osteria* where you can eat outside in refined surroundings. Look out for *cacciucco di pesce d'acqua dolce* (freshwater fish chowder), *piccione in casseruola* (pigeon casserole) and tempting desserts. La Mora also has a good list of wines from the nearby Lucchese hills.

Osteria Baralla

Via Anfiteatro 5-9 (tel/fax 0583 440 240). **Open** 12.30-2.30pm, 7.30-10.30pm Mon-Sat. **Average** €16-€20. Closed 2wks Aug. **Credit** AmEx, DC, MC, V.
With its vaulted brick ceiling and lively local clientele Osteria Baralla gets loud and lively at lunchtimes. The decent rustic dishes on offer here (*prosciutto di cinghiale*, for instance) can be washed down with any of several wines by the glass.

Ristorante Puccini

Corte San Lorenzo 1-2, off Piazza Cittadella (0583 316 116). **Open** *Summer* 12.30-2.30pm, 7.30-10.30pm Mon, Thur-Sun; 7.30-10.30pm Tue, Wed. *Winter* 12.30-2.30pm, 7.30-10.30pm Mon, Thur-Sun; 7.30-10.30pm Wed. Closed Nov-Feb. **Average** €35. **Credit** AmEx, DC, MC, V.
In a quiet courtyard with a secluded terrace, Puccini is Lucca's best bet for fish dishes. Try baked turbot with tomatoes, capers and olives.

Vineria i Santi

Via dell'Anfiteatro 29A (0583 496 124). **Open** 11am-3pm, 6pm-1.30am Thur, Fri, Sun-Tue; 11am-3pm, 6pm-2am Sat. **Average** €20. **Credit** AmEx, DC, MC, V.
A bright newcomer to the Luccan restaurant scene, this superb little *vineria* simply oozes style – from its modern rustic furniture and delicate light fittings to the discreet wine paraphernalia dotted around its walls. Enthusiastic, knowledgeable owner Leonardo will talk you through the short menu of great-value local cured meats, robust soups, salads and occasional hot dishes. The extensive wine list is its real forte, though. A class act.

Pizzerie

Tuscany isn't really known for its pizza, however Lucca's tradition of immigrants from the south has spawned a good number of *pizzerie* throughout the town. There are a couple of places worthy of a mention. **Da Felice** (via Buia 12, 0583 494 986, closed Sun), close to San Michele, it is great for a crispy, tasty slice on the run. And **La Sbragia** (via Fillungo 144-6, 0583 492 641, closed Mon), towards the top end of Lucca's main shopping artery, is popular for both sit-down and takeaway pizza.

Cafés, bars & *gelaterie*

If you're in Lucca for the nightlife, you'll be disappointed: the big nightspots are out towards the Versilia coast. The closest is **Riva Marina** (Bar Casina Rossa, via Sarzanese 1978, 4km towards Viareggio, 0583 327 732), an expansive 1960s disco with eaterie and swimming pool.

Caffè di Simo

Via Fillungo 58 (0583 496 234). **Open** *Bar* 7.30am-11pm Tue-Sun. *Restaurant* 12.30-2.30pm Mon, Tue, Thur-Sun. Summer also 7-10pm Thur-Sat. **Average** €18. **Credit** DC, MC, V.

Bottles of wine and bags of style at **Vineria i Santi**. *See p245.*

Lucca's beautifully preserved belle époque café-*pasticceria* is worth the expense. As well as some fine pastries, there's a daily menu offering regional specialities (*lardo di Colonnata*) and more chi-chi modern dishes like smoked swordfish.

Casali

Piazza San Michele 40 (0583 492 687). **Open** *Summer* 7am-11pm daily. *Winter* 7am-8.30pm Thur-Tue. **Credit** MC, V.
The perfect spot for watching the crowds, with either an ice-cream or an aperitif in hand.

Gelateria Veneta

Chiasso Barletti 23 (0583 493 727). **Open** *Winter* 11am-midnight Mon, Wed-Sun. *Summer* 11am-midnight daily. Closed early Jan-mid Feb. **No credit cards.**
Heavenly ice-creams are sold at this venerated *gelateria*, which has set the standards in Lucca for 150 years. There are some nice pavement tables for those who don't want to walk and lick.
Branch: Via Vittorio Veneto 74 (0583 467 037).

Girovita

Piazza Antelminelli 2 (0583 469 412). **Open** 8am-1am Mon-Wed. **Credit** AmEx, DC, MC, V.
Directly opposite the cathedral, the terrace of this stylish café-bar is the perfect spot for a morning coffee and pastry or, come cocktail hour, a sundowner accompanied by a great spread of free nibbles.

Li Per Li

Via Fillungo 150 (0583 496479). **Open** noon-8pm Wed-Fri, Sun; noon-9pm Sat. **No credit cards.**
This diminutive, tunnel-like café is Lucca's healthiest pit stop, offering sweet and savoury crêpes, filled focaccia, fresh fruit salad, milkshakes, fruit smoothies and vegetable juices.

Where to stay

You can count the hotels within Lucca's walls on the fingers of one hand. And there are no signs that this is going to change in a hurry. The *Lucchesi* like it this way and have no intention of turning their precious city into an appendage of the overcrowded Versilia coast.

Diana

Via del Molinetto 11 (0583 492 202/fax 0583 467 795/www.albergodiana.com). **Rates** €47 single; €67 double. **Credit** AmEx, DC, MC, V.
Characterful and clean, Diana is small but conveniently located between the cathedral of San Martino and the train station. Questions should be directed to the owners' sons, who are both extremely helpful.

Locanda Buatino

Borgo Giannotti 508 (0583 343 207/fax 0583 343 298). **Rates** €25 single; €50 double. **Credit** MC, V.
About ten minutes' walk to the north of the city walls, Locanda Buatino's five rooms are as welcoming as they come. Plus there's the bonus of a terrific restaurant downstairs (*see p245*).

Locanda L'Elisa

Via Nuova per Pisa 1952, Massa Pisana (0583 379 737/fax 0583 379 019/www.locandaelisa.com). **Rates** €215 single; €310 double; €470 suite. **Credit** AmEx, DC, MC, V.
In a league of its own, this elegant five-star hotel 4km (2.5 miles) south of Lucca is one of the region's best. The villa's current appearance dates back to 1805, when Napoleon's sister and Lucca's ruler Elisa Baciocchi had the interiors and gardens refashioned. Highlights include a restaurant modelled after an English conservatory, 18th-century furnishings, revamped gardens and a large swimming pool.

La Luna
Corte Compagni 12 (0583 493 634/fax 0583 490 021/www.hotellaluna.it). **Rates** €90 single; €105 double; €170 suite. **Credit** AmEx, DC, MC, V.
An indisputable bargain in this price range, La Luna has a great location at the upper end of busy via Fillungo. Rooms, housed in two 17th-century *palazzi* facing each other across a courtyard, are comfortable. The Pizzeria Italia just opposite is a good bet for a quick, tasty snack.

Palazzo Alexander
Via Santa Giustina 48 (0583 583 571/fax 0583 583 610/www.palazzo.alexander.it). **Rates** €115 single; €180 double. **Credit** AmEx, DC, V, MC.
Easily missed, this B&B hides some elaborately furnished – some would say kitsch – public rooms and bedrooms behind its unassuming exterior.

Piccolo Hotel Puccini
Via di Poggio 9 (0583 55421/fax 0583 53487/ www.hotelpuccini.com). **Rates** €55 single; €80 double. **Credit** AmEx, DC, MC, V.
Just a baton's throw from Puccini's boyhood home, this discreet, cosy hotel has helpful English-speaking staff, rooms with great views and, of course, Puccini memorabilia. It's best to book ahead at this hotel.

Rex
Piazza Ricasoli 19 (0583 955 443/fax 0583 954 348/www.hotelrexlucca.com). **Rates** €75 single; €100 double. **Credit** AmEx, DC, MC, V.
Conveniently placed, right next to the train station, this modern hotel has air-conditioned rooms, minibars, cable and satellite TV.

Universo
Piazza del Giglio 1 (0583 493 678/fax 0583 954 854/www.hoteluniverso.it). **Rates** €120 single; €170 double. **Credit** MC, V.
Right beside the elegant piazza Napoleone, the Universo is the faded old gent of Lucca's hotels – although new owners are promising to give the bedrooms and grand public spaces the overhaul that they have long been needing.

Resources

Hospital
Campo di Marte hospital, Via dell'Ospedale (0583 9701).

Police station
Viale Cavour 38, nr train station (0583 4551).

Post office
Via Vallisneri 2, nr Duomo (0583 43351).

Tourist information
Azienda di Promozione Turistica (APT)
Piazza Santa Maria 35 (0583 91991/ www.luccatourist.it). **Open** 9am-7pm daily.
Pick up the useful 'My Guide' audio commentary on the city. It has a suggested itinerary and costs €7 for three and a half hours. There's also plenty of other information, plus internet access, a bookshop and a bureau de change.
Branch: Palazzo Ducale, cortile Carrara (0583 919 941).

Commune di Lucca Tourist Office
Piazzale Giuseppe Verdi, nr Vecchia Porta San Donato (0583 442 944). **Open** 9am-7pm daily.
By far the best-equipped of Lucca's tourist information centres, the Comune di Lucca has all the usual resources plus some useful extras like bike hire (€2.50 per hour), translation and even babysitting services and Tuscan cookery courses.
Branches: viale Luporini (0583 583 462); Porta Elisa (0583 462 377).

Getting there & around

By air
Lucca's own small airport (0583 936 062) does not take commercial flights, so the best way of getting there by air is from Pisa airport, which has a train link (*see p278*). Also, there's a direct Lazzi bus from Florence airport to Lucca.

By bicycle
The largest concentration of bike hire shops is in piazza Santa Maria; try **Cicli Bizzarri** at No.32 (0583 496 031) or **Poli Antonio** at No.42 (0583 493 787/www.biciclettepoli.com).

By bus
The bus station is at piazzale Guiseppe Verdi. CLAP (0583 587 897) operates buses to towns in Lucca province. **LAZZI** run buses to Florence, Pisa, Bagni di Lucca, Montecatini, La Spezia and Viareggio (0583 584 876). At least one bus an hour leaves Florence for Lucca (first 5.58am, last 8.15pm) and from Lucca to Florence (first 6.10am, last 7.45pm). The journey takes around 1hr 15mins.

By car
To hire a car contact **Europcar** (via Dante Alighieri 214, 0583 464 590), **Hertz** (via Catalani 59, 0583 505 472) or **Nolo Auto Pittore** (piazza Santa Maria 34, 0583 467 960). Within the city walls parking is expensive, and free only for hotel guests, but there's a spacious free car park just outside the walls past Porta San Donato.

By taxi
There are **radio taxi** ranks at piazza Napoleone and the train station. For both call 0583 333 434.

By train
Lucca's train station is at piazza Ricasoli (0583 467 013), two minutes' walk from the southern gate, Porta San Pietro. Trains from Florence to Viareggio stop at Lucca (as well as Prato and Pistoia). The trip from Florence takes about 1hr 20mins, with trains leaving almost every hour from early morning to 10pm. For train info phone 892021 (no prefix) or have a look at www.trenitalia.com.

Massa-Carrara & Lucca Provinces

Welcome to the great outdoors.

Clinging to the heights and spreading out from the lowlands of the Apuan Alps, Massa-Carrara and Lucca provinces are both characterised by the mountainous landscape around them. But it's there that the similarity ends. While Massa-Carrara province creeps up from a coastline of sun-lotioned bodies and pulsating discos to flinty quarries and remote villages, Lucca province is an Alpine wonderland of snow-capped peaks, leafy valleys and medieval towns, where chocolate-box scenery remains largely untrampled by tourists – although, this is becoming an increasingly popular area for British and German expats to set up house.

The Versilia Riviera

Running parallel with the miles of heavy industry and huge unfinished blocks of Carrara marble that lie a few kilometres inland, this belt of sand, bathing establishments and hotels welcomes sun-worshippers and pleasure-seekers all the way from the Ligurian border in the north to **Viareggio** in the south. For Verisilia's lively gay scene, *see p166* **Queer Versilia**.

Viareggio

Viareggio's main attractions are its beach and palm-tree lined promenade flanked by art deco villas and outdoor cafés. Summer nights pulsate to the sound of techno when Florence's club scene virtually transplants itself here – party-goers crowd the mega-clubs that throng the Cancun-like strip between **Viareggio** and the swanky resort town of **Forte dei Marmi** ten kilometres (six miles) up the road. By day the *stabilimenti balneare* (bathing establishments) are full of tourists topping up their tans. One of Europe's first *stabilimenti*, the **Balena**, was founded here in 1827. Now modernised to include the B2K annexe, it offers five pools, an underground sports centre and an impressive range of classes and treatments. The 130-year-old *Carnevale*, held around February, is one of Italy's wildest (*see p154* **Street party**). Head to the north of town on via Santa Maria Goretti (take the exit marked 'Viareggio Nord') to visit La Cittadella del Carnevale.

Six kilometres (four miles) south of town is the reed-fringed **Lago di Massaciuccoli**. On its shore is the town of **Torre del Lago Puccini** where the composer spent his summers. His villa is open to visitors (0584 341 445, closed Mon, admission €5), but contains little of interest except to specialists, who may want a peek at the composer's Förster pianoforte. During July and August the town hosts an outdoor Puccini festival (*see p155*).

Nightlife

Surrounded by designer clothes stores **Il Giardino** (via IV Novembre 10, Forte dei Marmi, 0584 81462, closed Tue) is a good, though not cheap, spot for pre-club drinks. It's also popular with twentysomething *figli di papa* (rich kids who cruise around in Daddy's car), but the garden makes up for this.

Slick new club on the scene **Twiga** (viale Roma 2, 0584 21518, closed Oct-Nov, admission varies) is instantly recognisable by its distinctive giraffe logo and hordes of beautiful young things streaming through its doors. **Seven Apples** (viale Roma, Marina di Pietrasanta, 0584 20458, closed Mon-Thur, admission €15.50 incl 1st drink) continues to draw a trendy crowd to its beachside bar with tables straddling a swimming pool and two dancefloors. Otherwise **La Capannina** (viale Franceschi, Forte dei Marmi, 0584 80169, closed Mon-Thur & Sun spring & autumn, Mon-Fri & Sun winter, admission €20.50 incl 1st drink) attracts clubbers of all ages. Next to the sea (but without access to the beach) it is Versilia's oldest and club, with two dancefloors that are packed all summer. **La Canniccia** (via Unità d'Italia 1, Marina di Pietrasanta, 0584 745 685, closed Mon-Wed summer, Mon-Thur & Sun winter, admission €15.50 incl 1st drink) has a huge garden, walkways, a lake and a dancefloor under a gazebo. There are three bars and a late-night restaurant.

Viareggio's busy port.

Where to stay & eat

Although Viareggio has more than 100 hotels, rooms are hard to find in high season. Try via Vespucci, via Leonardo da Vinci and via IV Novembre, which run from the station down to the sea. Places that stand out are **Hotel Garden** (viale Ugo Foscolo 70, 0584 44025, doubles €107-€156), a glorious Liberty-style building with chandeliers in the foyer, and the swish **Hotel Plaza et de Russie** (piazza d'Azeglio 1, 0584 44449, doubles €90-€310), which offers fin-de-siècle luxury in a refurbished 19th-century building with a roof garden.

On the other side of the marina affordable fish restaurants such as **La Darsena** (via Virgilio 150, 0584 392 785, closed Sun and 23 Dec-7 Jan, average €30) attract locals to the backstreets behind the boatyards, while a little further south are the *stabilimenti* and modern bars and restaurants of viale Europa. If you only have time for one meal in Viareggio, make sure it's at **Ristorante di Giorgio** (corner via Zanardelli and via IV Novembre, 0584 44493, closed Wed, average €25). Its yellow walls are cluttered with paintings and there are displays of sea-fresh fish by the door. Be sure to try the house speciality of *spaghetti trabaccolara*.

Pietrasanta

Carrara is home to the raw material itself but Pietrasanta (literally, 'holy stone') is where artists transform the famous marble. Wandering through the backstreets of this relaxed little town you'll see modern-day Michelangelos with newspaper hats, which absorb sweat but filter fine marble dust, sculpting from marble, bronze and clay. Check out the two busy studios side by side on via Sant' Agostino (Nos.51 and 53). Small groups wanting in-depth tours of the town's various studios and foundries or the nearby marble quarries should contact Barbara Paci (339 77 80 379, barbarapaci@inwind.it).

In summer piazza del Duomo becomes an open-air exhibition space for artists to display work against the splendid backdrop of the 13th-century cathedral and the citadel up the hill, Rocca Arrighina.

Where to stay & eat

Accommodation options are fairly limited. The sumptuous 17th-century style of **Albergo Pietrasanta** (via Garibaldi 35, 0584 793 727, doubles €230-€280) caters to the town's grander visitors, leaving **Hotel Palagi** (piazza Carducci 23, 0584 70249, doubles €85-€150) and **Hotel Stipino** (via Provinciale 50, 0584 71448, doubles €68) to mop up the rest. Budget travellers may have to consider Pietrasanta as a day trip.

Of the bars and restaurants dotted among the modern art galleries and trendy clothes shops that dominate the town centre **Pizzeria Betty** (piazza del Duomo 32-3, 0584 71247, closed Mon, average €11) offers good-value food in cool surroundings.

Massa & Carrara

Locked between the sea and the Apuan Alps these twin cities are barely distinguishable from the dreary mesh of industry and traffic that congests the area. But where **Massa** is of little interest, **Carrara** is a marble mecca. Throughout the year the steep ridges of the mountains flanking the town glow brilliant white with the world's largest concentration of pure marble. The ancient Romans mined here and built most of their Imperial City with it. These days Carrara marble is exported all over the world.

Michelangelo considered Carrara's marble the purest and whitest in the world. Its greatest asset, according to artists, is that it reflects light off its thinnest outer layer giving the stone a translucent, wax-like lustre. Carrara mines less marble these days, but about 1.5 million tonnes are extracted from the nearby hills each year.

If you want to visit the quarries, take the scenic route marked *strada panoramica* towards the tiny mountain town of **Colonnata**, where every second house seems to make or sell the famous *lardo di Colonnata*. Three kilometres (two miles) out of town in the area of Stadio, opposite the football stadium, is the **Museo Civico del Marmo** (viale XX Settembre 85, 0585 845 746, closed Sun, admission €3.10) that documents marble history and production.

Carrara itself has a lived-in feel. **Piazza Alberica**, its most attractive square, is lined with pastel-coloured buildings. Off the north-east end of the piazza, via Ghibellina opens up to reveal a seductive view of the 11th-century **Duomo** with its Pisan façade and 14th-century rose window carved from a single slab of marble.

Where to eat

Overlooking piazza Alberica the retro **Caffeteria Leon d'Oro** (8 piazza Alberica, no phone, closed Sun) is a nice spot for a drink. A few streets away the cheap, informal **Pizzeria Tognozzi** (via Santa Maria 12, 0585 71750, closed Sun) is a good bet for on-the-hop snacks.

Resources

Tourist information

Agenzia per il Turismo (APT)
Viale Carducci 10, Viareggio (0584 962 233/ www.versilia.turismo.toscana.it). **Open** *Summer* 9am-1pm, 4-7pm Mon-Sat. *Winter* 9am-1pm, 3-6pm Mon-Sat (plus 4 Sun afternoons during Carnevale).

Getting there

By bus

CLAP buses (0584 30996) service Viareggio andlink the city several times a day with Pietrasanta and Lucca. **LAZZI** buses (0584 46234) also make the longer journey between Viareggio and Florence (journey time 2hrs).

By car

Both the main A12 coastal *autostrada* and via Aurelia (SS1, very busy in summer) run through the entire Versilia area. Viareggio, Pietrasanta and Carrara are all accessible via the *autostrada*. Another autostrada (A11) in turn links Versilia with Lucca (about 30mins) and other cities inland.

By train

Viareggio is linked to Florence (100-120mins) by regular trains on the Lucca (20mins) line. Trains between Pisa and Genoa also pass through the Versilia area, stopping at Viareggio (20mins from Pisa), Pietrasanta (35mins) and Carrara-Avenza (a bus ride from Carrara, 50mins from Pisa).

The Garfagnana

A walkers' paradise of snowy peaks and river valleys lined with chestnut trees and wild flowers, the **Garfagnana** is just an hour's drive from Lucca. Check at the regional tourist office (*see p253*) for information on the area's many sporting activities.

Bagni di Lucca

A mood of vanished gentility still haunts this charming little spa village deep in the bosom of the Lima valley. Its renowned saline and sulphurous thermal waters, together with the less virtuous pleasures of its once glorious casino where roulette was invented, have attracted many famous names over the decades. Bagni's visitors' book boasts everyone from the intellectual elite (Puccini, Heine, Shelley and Byron) to Elisa Bonaparte Baciocchi (the Grand Duchess of Tuscany and Napoleon's sister), who had a summer home here (now Hotel Roma; *see p251*). Today, however, the casino entrance is weed-choked and the building in need of some smartening up.

For healthier indulgences, visit the **Terme Jean Varraud** above the river (piazza San Martino 11, 0583 87221, closed Sun), which offers a range of services, including mud treatments and hydro massage. But don't go expecting 21st-century gloss: facilities here are purely functional. Admission varies according to the treatments chosen.

On the SS12 from Lucca, six kilometres (four miles) south of Bagni, is a rather striking sight: the arched spine of the **Ponte della Maddalena** spans the Serchio river. Nicknamed the Devil's Bridge, it was built in the 11th century by, according to legend, Beelzebub himself in return for the soul of the first person who crossed it. The locals decided to send a dog.

From the quarries...

...to the studio, marble is everywhere.

Where to stay & eat

Even if it's not the chi-chi resort it once was, Bagni continues to hold a good number of regular visitors in its thrall. For accommodation in the centre of town try the beguiling **Hotel Roma** (via Umberto I 110, 0583 87278, doubles €35-€45), whose cheap, elegant rooms have parquet flooring and splendid antique furniture. A little further out, at the top of a steep and snaking driveway, **Locanda Maiola** in Maiola di Sotto caters well for its guests with decent regional cooking (0583 86296, doubles €55, average €22). For good eating in town try the rather grand **Circolo dei Forestieri** (piazza Varraud 10, 0583 86038, closed Mon & Tue lunch, average €20) or **Ristorante Antico Caffè del Sonno** (viale Umberto I, 146-8, 0583 805 080, closed Thur, average €15) across the street.

Barga

With its perfectly preserved medieval streets and alleyways threading through the walled city and up to the stunning 11th-century duomo at its highest point, **Barga** is as picturesque as they come. The cathedral was built in a pale local stone called *Albarese di Barga*. Its most striking feature is its pulpit, which was carved by Como sculptor Guido Bigarelli in the 13th century and is supported by carved lions and dwarves – the latter a symbol of crushed paganism. But there's much more to this town than its history, since Barga is a lively cultural centre and a must for jazz and opera fans.

Barga Jazz, the city's annual jazz festival, runs on and off throughout the summer season culminating in a heady week of concerts and competition events towards the end of August. Each year has a different theme with the top billing of alto sax legend Lee Konitz setting the tone for 2003. Among the slew of other cultural events during the summer months, an opera festival (*see p168* **The hills are alive...**) also draws the crowds. For information on all events and festivals, check the exhaustive www.barganews.com.

Where to stay & eat

A pleasant spot for a late-afternoon aperitif is the central **Caffè Capretz** (piazza Salvo Salvi, 0583 723 001, closed Tue and 2wks Nov). It was founded in 1870 and its outdoor tables are set beneath a wood-beamed loggia that used to host the town's vegetable market. Otherwise, there's the wonderful low-key style of **Osteria Angelio** (piazza Angelio 13-14, 0583 724 547, closed Mon, average €16), which serves excellent Tuscan food, decent wines by the glass and constant, occasionally live, jazz.

Accommodation options vary but one of the best is the **Hotel Villa Libano** (via del Sasso 6, 0583 723 774, doubles €36-€52), despite its surly staff. The hotel has quaint rooms and there are mountain views from its tree-shaded forecourt.

L'Eremo di Calomini

This monastery, set on the other side of the Serchio river valley from Barga, is built into a vertical cliff and seems to hang in mid-air. To organise a visit call the parish priest (0583 767 003) or the Convent of the Capuchin Fathers (Monte Santa Quirico, via della Chiesa 87, Lucca, 0583 341 426).

At its outdoor **Antica Trattoria dell'Eremita** (0583 767 020, closed Nov-Feb, average €16) there's grilled trout fresh from the Serchio river and spaghetti with a fine trout sauce, served on a shady, sycamore-lined terrace with great views.

Between March and November there's basic accommodation in the **monastery** (doubles €20-€23 per night, ask in the trattoria) and a little shop selling herb syrups and various medicinal plant extracts.

Grotta del Vento

Seven kilometres (4.5 miles) of hairpin bends and steep ridges from **L'Eremo di Calomini** lead to the semi-abandoned town of **Fornovolasco** and to Tuscany's geological wonder the **Grotta del Vento** or 'wind cave' (0583 722 024, open all year, admission €6.50-€15), which is packed with stalactites, stalagmites and underground lakes. The cold air that blows from the cave's entrance gave it its name and a practical purpose: it was used as a refrigerator until the 17th century. It wasn't until 1898 when local bullies forced a little girl to go in and she came back out describing the wonders inside that scientists became aware of its existence. There are one-, two- and three-hour tours.

Vagli di Sotto

Another valley pass into the Apuan Alps leads to the artificial lake of **Vagli**, fed by the Edron river. When Vagli was formed, the tiny stone town of **Fabbriche di Careggine** had to be abandoned, but every ten years the lake is emptied for maintenance (the next time is 2004) and the ruins of the ghost town can be seen.

Castelnuovo di Garfagnana

Garfagnana's capital makes a decent base from which to explore the area. Encased by ancient walls and dominated by a 13th-century castle, its historic centre is a lovely place to refuel and pick up supplies.

For daytime and early-evening snacks **Il Vecchio Mulino** (via Vittorio Emanuele 12, 0583 62192, closed Mon, average €18) is a characterful wine bar with top-notch salamis, cured meats and cheeses. For rooms try **Hotel-Ristorante Ludovico Ariosto** (via Francesco Azzi 28, 0583 62369, doubles €45-€62). And just up the street is a must for wine enthusiasts, **La Bottega del Fattore** (via Francesco Azzi 1A, 0583 62179, open daily), where a huge selection of regional and national wines is sold by the glass and bottle. Or do as the locals do and get your own container filled from one of the shop's giant barrels.

Parco Orecchiella

This park (0583 619 098/058365169, open daily June-Sept, by appointment Oct-May, museum €1.50) is perhaps the loveliest part of the Apuan Alps. Abundant rain gives the area lush forests and meadows, and wildlife includes deer, boar, goats, predatory Apennine wolves and more than 130 species of bird, including the eagles that are Orecchiella's symbol. Hiking and biking paths of varying length and difficulty criss-cross the park, which is best visited in late spring or early autumn.

The Lunigiana

Named after the Luni, the area's aboriginal population, the **Lunigiana** is Tuscany's least-explored region as the **Cisa pass** (where the A15 *autostrada* runs) and the area surrounding **Pontremoli** and **Aulla** (the hub for buses and transport to the rest of the area) are way off most tourist itineraries. The people of the Lunigiana don't identify with either Tuscany or nearby Liguria or Emilia Romagna but are a curious blend of all three – a fact that's reflected in the dialect and cuisine.

Fosdinovo

Lunigiana hasn't always been Tuscany's most isolated corner. For more than ten centuries from prehistory and the Romans to the heyday of the traffic-heavy Via Francigena trade route, the region was of utmost geographic significance. And with prime location comes fortification. Lunigiana is dotted with scores of castles and towers, of which the **Castello Malaspina** in the idyllic feudal town of **Fosdinovo** is a prime example. There are three daily tours of the castle (0187 688911 for tour times, closed Tue, admission €5) or you can simply wander through the pretty sloping streets that surround it and take in some breathtaking views of mountains and sea. Fosdinovo was built by local warlords, the Malaspinas, and some of their descendants still live here 800 years later.

Fivizzano

Apart from its gorgeous views and sleepy pace of life, this isolated place is worth a visit just to spend a night in the wonderful **Hotel Il Giardinetto** (via Roma 151, 0585 92060, doubles €25-€82). Elegant rooms, dark old corridors and day rooms creaking with antiques attract a similarly old world clientele, while some seriously tasty Tuscan cooking is offered in the restaurant (closed Oct & Mon Nov-June, average €20). This is very much a family concern and you can expect to be greeted, checked in and served at table by members of all three generations.

Just around the corner is **piazza Medicea** (also called piazza V Emanuele) where the main fountain sports four marble dolphins – a gift from Cosimo III in 1683, when the town served as the Medici government's Lunigiana capital. The bell tower belonging to the church of **San Jacopo and San Antonio** and built on the site of a 13th-century church bristles with a Heath Robinson-style collection of giant cogs.

On the perimeters of the square are **Caffè Elvetico** (0585 926 657, closed Sun in winter), which has tables spilling into the square, **Ricci** café-*gelateria* just opposite, and the mediocre **Pizzeria Medicea**.

North-east of town on the SS63 **Castello della Verrucola** was also built by the Malaspinas, who controlled the area from here all the way to Carrara.

Pontremoli

Pontremoli is the Lunigiana's biggest town, though only 11,000 people live here. Its wealth grew from its position as an important station on the Via Francigena trade route and the Cisa pass. These days the route here is more likely to be clogged with packs of cyclists who pit themselves against the steep, winding roads.

Looking down over the pretty arched streets of Pontremoli's old town is the **Castello del Piagnaro**, which offers great views and houses the **Museo delle Statue Stelle** (Castello di Piagnaro, 0187 831 400, closed Mon, admission €3.50). The museum is home to 19 prehistoric statues discovered in this area (Henry Moore was apparently transfixed when he saw them).

In the town itself, the **Duomo Santa Maria del Popolo** (piazza del Duomo) was designed in 1633 by the Cremonese architect Alessandro Capra. Finished in 1687 it is interesting for its aisleless nave and short transept, but most of all for its notably high, luminous dome. Also worth a look is the 14th-century **Torre del Campanone** with its beautiful little park and picnic area by the burbling Magra river.

Where to stay & eat

There's no shortage of restaurants and trattorias in Pontremoli but two of the best are **Da Bussé** (piazza del Duomo 32, 0187 831 371, closed Fri, average €22) and the atmospheric **Osteria della Bietola** (0187 831 949, via della Bietola 4A, closed Thur, average €15). Be sure to try the local speciality of *testaroli*, a pancake-like dish smothered in pesto. If you decide to stay the night, the anonymous **Hotel Napoleon** (piazza Italia 2, 0187 830 544, doubles €46.50-€72.50) is the better of the two hotels, despite its rather nondescript residential location.

Resources

Tourist information

Tourist information for both the Garfagnana and the Lunigiana can be obtained from the **Centro di Coordinamento del Turismo Rurale** at Castelnuovo di Garfagnana (piazza delle Erbe 1, 0583 65169/garfagnana@tin.it). The English-speaking staff have plenty of information, not just on the main sights and attractions, but also on the possibilities for *agriturismo* accommodation, as well as walking routes and who to contact in order to organise various other sporting activities in the Apuan Alps.

Getting there

By bus

CLAP (0583 587 897) operates buses to Barga and Castelnuovo di Garfagnana from Lucca. **LAZZI** (0583 584 876) runs several buses a day from Lucca to Bagni di Lucca. Neither company runs services to the Lunigiana.

By car

Take the SS12 north out of Lucca; it follows the Serchio river valley and branches off toward Bagni di Lucca just beyond Borgo. At the same intersection you can take the winding hill road (SS445) toward Barga (there's a turn-off after a few kilometres) and Castelnuovo di Garfagnana. This is the main route through the Garfagnana region and smaller roads fan off from it towards highlights such as the Grotta del Vento (turn off near Barga to the south) and the Parco Orecchiella. It also leads, eventually, to the SS63 (and then the SS62), which go through the Lunigiana region to the far north. The drive through the mountains is very scenic but you should allow plenty of time (at least a day from Lucca) and perhaps aim to stop over en route.

By train

An irregular but very scenic rail service (892 021) goes through this area between Lucca and Aulla in the north, with stops at Bagni di Lucca (30mins), Castelnuovo di Garfagnana (60mins) and piazza al Serchio (75mins).

Arezzo

A wealth of history and precious metal.

Arezzo has plenty to offer, but it suffers somewhat from its proximity to Siena and Florence – the art cities par excellence. One of the world's foremost centres of gold jewellery production (*see p259* **City of gold**), Arezzo also has a flourishing textile industry. This may account for some unprepossessing outskirts but it also means that the *Aretini* have retained a greater degree of their natural shrewd candour than many of the inhabitants of Tuscany's tourist destinations. Arezzo has produced its quota of illustrious citizens, from Guido d'Arezzo (c997-1050), who gave us our do-re-mi and the musical staff, and Francesco Petrarca (1304-74), who perfected the sonnet form named after him, to Giorgio Vasari (1511-74), whose *Lives of the Artists* injects the Renaissance with colourful detail. The historic city centre is well preserved, the newly restored Piero della Francesca fresco cycle is a true wonder, and the monthly antiques and junk fair is a haven for *flâneur*s and bargain-hunters.

HISTORY

Strategically built at the intersection of four fertile valleys (the Casentino, Valdarno, Valtiberina and Valdichiana), Arezzo has seen much external conquest and only a brief period of city-state independence. In the seventh century BC the settlement of Arretium was a significant member of the Etruscan federation. It soon caught the eye of upstart Romans moving north and became a military stronghold and economic outpost. By 89 BC its people were granted honorary Roman citizenship, which brought with it an amphitheatre, baths and fortified walls.

But with the glory came decadence. Arezzo's trade routes were supplanted and it was overrun by Barbarians. The darkest days came under the Lombards in the sixth century. Yet, gradually, a feudal economic system began to pull the city from its slump, paving the way for Arezzo's golden age in the 1200s.

The turning point came in 1100 when the emerging merchant class started to question its subservience to Arezzo's clerical-feudal overlords. Secular power began to shift to the budding bourgeoisie and in 1192 the Commune was established. There was extensive building and Arezzo began to take on its current urban contours. However, another foreign power, this time Florence, set its sights on the city. The two clashed in the Battle of Campaldino in 1289, from which Arezzo never fully recovered. The city eventually succumbed to Florence in 1384.

Fortunately, political submission didn't equal artistic or cultural paralysis as Medici patronage in Florence provided wider scope for those with talent. In time, however, it meant that Arezzo's population turned in on itself, growing rural and conservative. But in recent years a parochial outlook has largely been supplanted by more forward-looking policies, no doubt fired by the establishment in Arezzo of off-shoots from the University of Siena. A younger, better educated generation of entrepreneurs and local administrators has realised the potential benefits of tourism. As a result, numerous fine buildings in the centre have been restored, the pedestrian precinct has been enlarged and the range of accommodation has at last been enriched with some more appealing options.

Sights

Churches

Duomo

Piazza Duomo (0575 23991). **Open** 7am-12.30pm, 3-7pm daily. **Admission** free.

Arezzo's Gothic Duomo was begun in 1277 but the finishing touches were made only in the early 1500s and it would be a further 300 years before its campanile was erected. The overall effect of its size and the vertical thrust of its ogival vaulted ceilings is inspiring, as are the exquisite stained-glass windows (c1515-20) by Guillaume di Marcillat. The Duomo's real attractions are along the left aisle: Piero della Francesca's *Mary Magdalene* (c1465), and the *Cappella della Madonna del Conforto*, screened off from the rest of the church.

Pieve di Santa Maria

Corso Italia (0575 22629). **Open** *Oct-Apr* 8am-noon, 3-6pm daily. *May-Sept* 8am-7pm daily. **Admission** free.

A striking example of Romanesque architecture built mostly in the 12th and 13th centuries, Santa Maria's pale stone façade is remarkably harmonious, with five arcades surmounted by three increasingly busy orders of *loggie*. The ornate columns holding them up, all 68 with an eccentric motif, reach a climax in the bell tower *delle cento buche* (of the 100 holes).

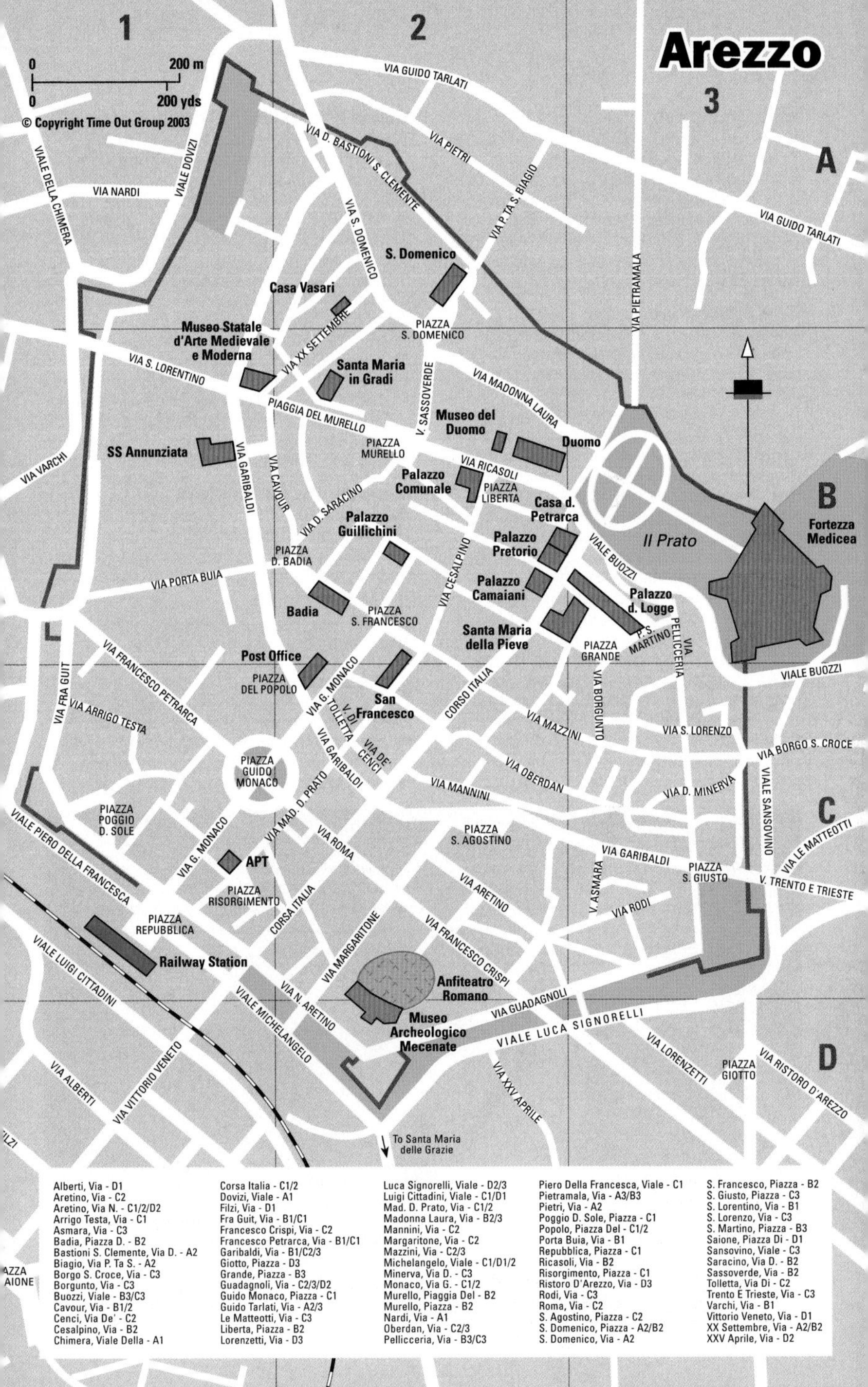

Alberti, Via - D1
Aretino, Via - C2
Aretino, Via N. - C1/2/D2
Arrigo Testa, Via - C1
Asmara, Via - C3
Badia, Piazza D. - B2
Bastioni S. Clemente, Via D. - A2
Biagio, Via P. Ta S. - A2
Borgo S. Croce, Via - C3
Borgunto, Via - C3
Buozzi, Viale - B3/C3
Cavour, Via - B1/2
Cenci, Via De' - C2
Cesalpino, Via - B2
Chimera, Viale Della - A1
Corsa Italia - C1/2
Dovizi, Viale - A1
Filzi, Via - D1
Fra Guit, Via - B1/C1
Francesco Crispi, Via - C2
Francesco Petrarca, Via - B1/C1
Garibaldi, Via - B1/C2/3
Giotto, Piazza - D3
Grande, Piazza - B3
Guadagnoli, Via - C2/3/D2
Guido Monaco, Piazza - C1
Guido Tarlati, Via - A2/3
Le Matteotti, Via - C3
Liberta, Piazza - B2
Lorenzetti, Via - D3
Luca Signorelli, Viale - D2/3
Luigi Cittadini, Viale - C1/D1
Mad. D. Prato, Via - C1/2
Madonna Laura, Via - B2/3
Mannini, Via - C2
Margaritone, Via - C2
Mazzini, Via - C2/3
Michelangelo, Viale - C1/D1/2
Minerva, Via D. - C3
Monaco, Via G. - C1/2
Murello, Piaggia Del - B2
Murello, Piazza - B2
Nardi, Via - A1
Oberdan, Via - C2/3
Pellicceria, Via - B3/C3
Piero Della Francesca, Viale - C1
Pietramala, Via - A3/B3
Pietri, Via - A2
Poggio D. Sole, Piazza - C1
Popolo, Piazza Del - C1/2
Porta Buia, Via - B1
Repubblica, Piazza - C1
Ricasoli, Via - B2
Risorgimento, Piazza - C1
Ristoro D'Arezzo, Via - D3
Rodi, Via - C3
Roma, Via - C2
S. Agostino, Piazza - C2
S. Domenico, Piazza - A2/B2
S. Domenico, Via - A2
S. Francesco, Piazza - B2
S. Giusto, Piazza - C3
S. Lorentino, Via - B1
S. Lorenzo, Via - C3
S. Martino, Piazza - B3
Saione, Piazza Di - D1
Sansovino, Viale - C3
Saracino, Via D. - B2
Sassoverde, Via - B2
Tolletta, Via Di - C2
Trento E Trieste, Via - C3
Varchi, Via - B1
Vittorio Veneto, Via - D1
XX Settembre, Via - A2/B2
XXV Aprile, Via - D2

San Domenico

Piazza San Domenico (0575 22906). **Open** 8.30am-1pm, 3.30-7pm daily. **Admission** free.

San Domenico was started by Dominicans in 1275 around the same time as their Franciscan brothers were getting under way with San Francesco (*see below*). It faces a simple, open square and has an attractive quaintness about it accentuated by its uneven Gothic campanile with two 14th-century bells.

San Francesco

Piazza San Francesco (0575 20630/24001 to reservè tickets). **Open** *Summer* 8.30am-noon, 2-7pm daily. *Winter* 8.30am-noon, 2.30-6.30pm daily. **Admission** free.

Begun by Franciscan friars in the 1200s, San Francesco's interior was adorned with frescoes, chapels and shrines throughout the 1500s thanks to Arezzo's merchant class. By the 19th century, however, it was being used as a military barracks. Yet no visit to Arezzo would be complete without seeing Piero della Francesca's magnum opus, *The Legend of the True Cross* (c1453-64). Considered to be one of the most important ever produced, the fully restored fresco cycle was begun in 1453, the year Constantinople fell to the Ottoman Turks, and portrays the fear this induced in the Christian world. Miraculously, the frescoes have survived fire, earthquake and the destruction of chapels. The ticket price of €5.03 gains you access to the chapels as well as an audio guide, but a word of advice: some of the frescoes are high up, too high to be properly appreciated by the naked eye, so it's a good idea take a pair of binoculars in with you.

Santa Maria delle Grazie

Via Santa Maria (0575 323 140/www.abd.it/santamaria). **Open** 8am-7pm daily. **Admission** free.

On the site of an ancient sacred spring, the Fonte Tecta (the religious complex built around Santa Maria delle Grazie) is known for housing the Renaissance's first porticoed courtyard. Started in 1428, the religious buildings were imposed by San Bernardino of Siena on the recalcitrant *Aretini*. In a well-publicised gesture he marched over from San Francesco brandishing a wooden cross and destroyed the spring site, replacing it with a *Madonna della Misericordia* by local artist Parri di Spinello. Fortunately, the enlightened Antonio da Maiano, one of the Renaissance's foremost architects and the man who created the loggia, reconciled the church's late Gothic, essentially medieval design with the then emergent classical style.

Santissima Annunziata

Via Garibaldi (0575 26774). **Open** 8am-12.30pm, 3.30-7pm daily. **Admission** free.

A miracle in which a statue of the Madonna wept before a passing pilgrim is reputed to have occurred on this site in 1460.

Museums

Casa Vasari

Via XX Settembre 55 (0575 409 040). **Open** 9am-7pm Wed-Mon. **Admission** €2. **No credit cards.**

Medici favourite Giorgio Vasari bought and decorated this house in extravagant style before he entered Florence's big league in 1564. Today, the

Business as usual in the **Piazza Grande**. *See p257.*

museum houses the Archivio e Museo Vasariano and proudly exhibits a number of recently restored Vasari frescoes and other late Mannerist paintings.

Fondazione Ivan Bruschi

Corso Italia 14 (0575 900 404/24001/www.fondazionebruschi.it). **Open** *Summer* 10am-1pm, 3-7pm Tue-Sun. *Winter* 10am-1pm, 2-6pm Tue-Sun. **Admission** €3. **No credit cards.**
Located opposite the Pieve, this was the home of the founder of the Arezzo antiques fair. Today, it is a Wunderkammer of antiquarian delights.

Galleria Comunale d'Arte Contemporanea

For up-to-date information, contact the APT (0575 377 678).
At the time of writing, the municipal collection of contemporary art was in the process of being allocated a home of its own in what was once the Hotel Chiavi d'Oro in piazza San Francesco. Until this is ready (possibly in 2004) keep your eyes peeled for some interesting thematic temporary exhibitions in Palazzo Chianini Vincenzi (via Cesalpino 15), the Auditorium Montetini (via dei Montetini) and Sant'Ignazio (via Carducci).

Museo Archeologico Mecenate

Via Margaritone 10 (0575 20882). **Open** 8.30am-7.30pm daily. **Admission** €4. **No credit cards.**
Located beside the Roman amphitheatre, this fine collection of Etruscan and Roman artefacts has recently benefited from considerable renovation. The Etruscan bronze votive figurines and jewellery found at the neighbouring Poggio del Sole necropolis are splendid, likewise the splendid Attic bowl decorated by Euphronios (AD 500-10) and the equally magnificent *coralline* pottery.

Museo d'Arte Medievale e Moderna

Via San Lorentino 8 (0575 409 050). **Open** 8.30am-7.30pm Tue-Sun. **Admission** €4. **No credit cards.**
Bearing in mind that *moderna* does not mean contemporary in Italian, this is an interesting, if uneven, collection of sculpture and painting that spans the period from the Middle Ages right through to the 19th century. The latter part includes works belonging to the Macchiaioli school, the Italian equivalent of the Impressionists. The baroque vestibule on the first floor is dominated by Vasari's *Wedding Feast of Ahasuerus and Esther* (1548) and just past this are rooms containing one of Italy's finest collections of 13th- to 17th-century glazed ceramics from the Della Robbia school.

Museo dell'Oro

Via Fiorentina 550 (0575 925 862/www.unoaerre.it). Bus 4, 6. **Open** 9am-5pm Mon-Fri. **Admission** free.
A few years ago Uno A Erre, one of the world's foremost producers of gold jewellery (*see p259* **City of gold**), opened a museum of its own featuring a unique collection of gold jewellery dating from the 1930s to the present day.

Landmarks

Anfiteatro Romano

Accessible from via Margaritone or via Crispi (no phone). **Open** *Apr-Oct* 7am-8pm daily. *Nov-Mar* 7.30am-6pm daily. **Admission** free.
In the second century this amphitheatre could be packed with up to 10,000 people. Its travertine and sandstone blocks were plundered by Medici grand duke Cosimo I for the Fortezza Medicea (*see below*) in 1531. You can make out its elliptical shape and stage, plus parts of what were probably the stands.

Fortezza Medicea

No phone. **Open** *Summer* 7am-8pm daily. *Winter* 7.30am-6pm daily. **Admission** free.
When the Medici finally decided to turn Arezzo into a duchy in 1531 they set about improving the city's defences and the introduction of cannons prompted them to embark on another (the eighth) stint of wall-building. The perimeter is visible in sections round the city and dominated by the architecturally revolutionary Fortezza Medicea (1538-60). Its pentagonal form was designed by Antonio da Sangallo the Elder and required the razing of towers, alleys and medieval *palazzi* in the hills of San Donato.

Piazza Grande

This sloping piazza is a visual feast of architectural irregularity resulting from its growth from peripheral food market to political heart of the city. The jumble of styles includes the arcaded, rounded back of the Romanesque Pieve di Santa Maria at the square's lowest point, the baroque Palazzo del Tribunale and next to it the Palazzo della Fraternità dei Laici, designed mostly by Bernardo Rossellino. Unsurprisingly, Vasari also had a hand in piazza Grande – his is the typically arcaded Palazzo delle Logge, which presides over the assortment of medieval homes around the rest of the square. Like Siena, Arezzo holds its own historic event in its main square, the **Giostra del Saracino** (*see p153*).

Parks & gardens

Il Prato

Arezzo's only park, between the Duomo and the Fortezza Medicea, has views over the town. On summer nights locals flock to La Casina del Prato bar (*see p258*).

Shopping

As you climb corso Italia, mainstream shops peter out to make way for a proliferation of antiques shops around piazza Grande. Stray off the corso if you're looking for something more.

On Saturdays a general market sells clothes, food, flowers and household goods. On the first Sunday of the month and the previous Saturday the city centre is taken over by a huge and important antiques fair. The APT (*see p260*) has a handy Italian-English glossary and a map with listings to get you round the maze of wares.

Al Canto De' Bacci

Corso Italia 65 (0575 355 804). **Open** 8am-2pm, 3-8pm Mon-Sat. **Credit** AmEx, DC, MC, V.
An enticing range of local gastronomy, run by the Pellegrini family, who also own a good *enoteca* and local produce store by the same name in piazza Grande 16 (0575 401 440).

Busatti

Corso Italia 48 (0575 355 295). **Open** 3.30-7.30pm Mon; 9am-1pm, 3.30-7.30pm Tue-Sat. **Credit** AmEx, DC, MC, V.
Upholstery fabrics and household linens woven on proto-industrial jacquard looms in Anghiari.

Eyes Ottica

Corso Italia 265 (0575 302 034). **Open** 4-8pm Mon; 9am-1pm, 4-8pm Tue-Sat. **Credit** AmEx, DC, MC, V.
Since Italy produces about 60% of Europe's glasses frames, it's a good place to opt for a new look. This friendly store carries some of the coolest models.

Galleria Ivan Bruschi

Piazza San Francesco 1 (0575 370 921). **Open** 9am-7pm 1st Sat & Sun of mth. **No credit cards.**
Each month, coinciding with the antiques fair, 27 select exhibitors display their precious treasures. Expensive, but ogling is definitely an option.

Macelleria-Gastronomia Aligi Barelli

Viale della Chimera 20 (0575 357 754). **Open** 8am-1pm, 4.30-8pm Mon, Tue, Thur, Fri; 8am-1pm Wed, Sat. Closed Aug. **Credit** DC, MC, V.
Justly renowned *macelleria* with mouthwatering salamis from the Casentino and a range of ready-made meat-based dishes.

Pane e Salute

Corso Italia 11 (0575 20657). **Open** 7.30am-1.30pm, 4-8pm Mon-Sat. Closed Aug. **No credit cards.**
Traditional Tuscan breads like *schiacciate* (flattened bread with rosemary), plus oven-baked sweets.

Pasticceria de'Cenci

Via de' Cenci 17 (0575 23102). **Open** 9am-1pm, 4-8pm Tue-Sat; 9am-1pm Sun. Closed Aug. **No credit cards.**
This *pasticceria* is full of elegant delights like *bigne' al limone* (lemon cream puff).

Where to eat & drink

Restaurants

Arezzo's culinary specialities draw heavily on the products of the four rich valleys that encircle it. Pasta dishes may include *funghi porcini* (ceps) or *tartufo nero* (black truffle). Local Chianina steak crops up on many a menu, and oddities such as *grifi* (stewed cheek of veal) and *zampucci* (leg of pork) occasionally feature.

Antica Osteria L'Agania

Via Mazzini 10 (0575 295 381). **Open** noon-2.30pm, 7-10.30pm Tue-Sun. **Average** €18. **Credit** AmEx, DC, MC, V.
A cosy two-level hideaway with traditional decor and no-frills service. *Primi* are more mainstream than the *secondi*, which include *grifi con polenta*.

Il Cantuccio

Via Madonna del Prato 76 (0575 26830). **Open** noon-2.30pm, 7-10.30pm Mon, Tue, Thur-Sun. **Average** €17. **Credit** AmEx, DC, MC, V.
The vaulted cellar here is the city's most rustic. Home-made pasta dishes include *tortelloni alla Casentinese* (with a potato filling).

La Curia

Via Di Pescaja 6 (0575 333 007). **Open** 7.30-11pm Thur; 12.30-2.30pm, 7.30-11pm Mon, Tue, Fri-Sun. **Average** €25. **Credit** AmEx, DC, MC, V.
Classy outfit with good, imaginative food. Try the *carabaccio* or the onion soup with almonds.

Sbarbacipolle

Via Garibaldi 120 (0575 299 154). **Open** 7.30am-8pm daily. Closed 3wks Aug. **Average** €9. **No credit cards.**
A colourful corner deli with a good choice of *panini* and cold dishes. Immensely popular with the locals.

Trattoria Il Saraceno

Via Mazzini 6A (0575 27644). **Open** 12.30-3pm, 7-11pm Mon, Tue, Thur-Sun. Closed 2wks Jan. **Average** €25. **Credit** AmEx, DC, MC, V.
Fine food, including a *porcini* soup and *pici al cinghiale* (egg pasta in wild boar sauce with pine nuts and juniper).

Bars, *enoteche* & *gelaterie*

Wines produced in Arezzo's hinterland may not reach the quality levels of their Chianti and Montalcino counterparts, but they are certainly improving. Moreover, Arezzo now has a number of wine bars in which you can taste a range of Colli Aretini vintages as well as Tuscany's more acclaimed labels.

Enoteca Al Canto De' Bacci

Piazza Grande 16 (0575 401 440). **Open** 10am-8pm daily. **Credit** AmEx, DC, MC, V.
A good selection of wines, Tuscan and otherwise, some quite unusual, plus other products of local gastronomy. Sample at leisure on an outside table.

La Casina del Prato

Via Palagi 1, Il Prato park (0575 299 757). **Open** 10am-2am Mon, Wed-Sun. Closed Dec. **No credit cards.**
An open-air summer hotspot overflowing with the hipper *Aretini* crowd. Some snacks are available.

City of gold

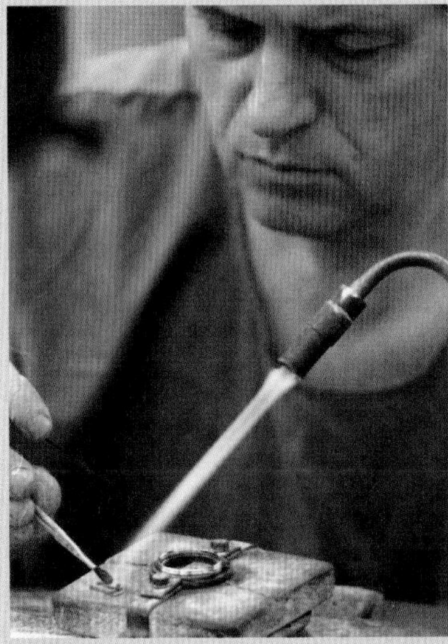

If you wear a wedding ring, chances are it was made in Arezzo. Every year the city exports around €2 billion worth of gold jewellery, with the UK following the Arab Emirates and the USA as prime markets. While gold chains of every imaginable variety are churned out by the kilometre, greater individuality of output is also obtained by inviting famous artists and designers such as Piero Dorazio, Alessandro Mendini, Ettore Sottsass and Joe Tilson to work with local firms. The **Oro d'Autore** exhibitions offer a regular showcase for their work.

The 1,600 firms currently involved in the gold jewellery business in Arezzo annually work their way through a staggering 200 tonnes of the metal. The *Aretini* like to trace this vocation back to their Etruscan forebears, who were indeed excellent goldsmiths. In fact, the local industry didn't really emerge until after World War II, with the founding of **Uno A Erre**, now the world's largest gold jewellery manufacturer. In 1998 the company opened Italy's first museum devoted to the art of the goldsmith, the Museo dell'Oro (*see p257*).

Since gold is indestructible, major firms find it worth their while to install sophisticated filtering systems to catch the gold dust that ends up in the workers' washbasins, showers and, yes, toilets. Look after the pennies, as it were... Little wonder, then, that Arezzo is said to harbour more Ferraris in its garages than any other city in Italy.

Enoteca La Torre di Gnicche

Piaggia San Martino 8 (0575 352 035). **Open** noon-3pm, 6pm-1am Mon, Tue, Thur-Sun. Closed 2wks Jan. **Credit** DC, MC, V.
A tastefully decorated bar with a superb selection of local wines, including its standard-bearers Bricco di Gnicche and Bigattiera di Val d'Ambra, and a number of Gratena reds. Hot food is served.

Fiaschetteria de'Redi

Via de' Redi 10 (0575 355 012). **Open** noon-3pm, 7-11pm Tue-Sun. **Credit** DC, MC, V.
A bustling wine bar just off corso Italia, with cosy dark wood and tan walls and a good wine selection to boot. *Osteria*-style food is served.

Il Gelato

Via dei Cenci 24 (0575 300 069). **Open** *Summer* 11am-midnight Mon, Tue, Thur-Sun. *Winter* 11am-8pm Mon, Tue, Thur-Sun. **No credit cards.**
An unassuming, busy *gelateria*. Try *pinolata* (with pine nuts) or *arancello al liquore* (liqueur orange).

Where to stay

Cavaliere Palace Hotel

Via Madonna del Prato 83 (0575 26836/fax 0575 21925/www.cavalierehotels.com). **Rates** (incl breakfast) €93 single; €135 double. **Credit** AmEx, DC, MC, V.
A recently renovated four-star hotel that is conveniently located and reasonably priced.

Corte del Re

Via Borgunto 5 (0575 401 603/348 695 9100/ www.lacortedelre.com). **Rates** €680-€1,000 weekly. **Credit** AmEx, MC, V.
Six fully equipped and furnished mini-apartments a stone's throw from piazza Grande.

La Foresteria

Via Bicchieraia 32 (tel/fax 0575 370 474). **Rates** €29-€58. **No credit cards.**
A dozen simple rooms in a 14th-century ex-Benedictine convent. Many of the rooms are frescoed and, although simple, are stylishly furnished. One of Arezzo's best bargains.

I Portici

Via Roma 18 (0575 403 132/www.hoteliportici.com). **Rates** €130-€155 single; €185-€235 double; €260-€310 suite. **Credit** AmEx, MC, V.
Once a private house, I Portico is now an upmarket small hotel run by the scions of the original owners.

Val di Colle Residenza di Campagna

Località Bagnoro (tel/fax 0575 365 167/ www.valdicolle.it). **Rates** €120-€160 single; €180 double. **Credit** AmEx, DC, MC, V.
The urge to splurge may bring you to this refined, recently refurbished 14th-century country residence 4km (2.5 miles) from the town. You shouldn't be disappointed: the rooms are delightful.

Villa Severi Youth Hostel

Via dei Cappucini, or via Redi 13 if coming by bus (tel/fax 0575 299 047). **Rates** €15 dorm; €1.60 breakfast. **No credit cards.**
Good value for money and a relaxed atmosphere with rooms that sleep up to ten people. Take bus 4 from outside the station towards Ospedale Vecchio, alighting at the Ostello della Giovent.

Resources

Hospital

San Donato Hospital *Viale Alcide de Gasperi 17 (0575 255 003).*

Internet point

The Phone Centre *Piazza Guido Monaco 8/B, (0575 371 245).* **Open** 9am-1pm, 3-8.30pm Mon-Sat. Closed 2wks Aug.

Police

Questura State Police Office *Via Poggio del Sole, (0575 318 1602).*

Tourist information

Azienda di Promozione Turistica (APT) *Piazza della Repubblica 28 (0575 377 678).* **Open** *Oct-Mar* 9am-1pm, 3-6.30pm Mon-Sat; 9am-1pm 1st Sun of mth. *Apr-Sept* 9am-1pm, 3-7pm Mon-Sat; 9am-1pm Sun.

Getting there & around

By bus

Bus services to Florence are slow and irregular, so it's better to take the train. **LFI** (La Ferrovia Italiana, 0575 39881) has direct buses to Siena (90mins) and Cortona (1hr, via Castiglion Fiorentina). **Sita** (for Sansepolcro; 0575 74361/743681) also covers the region. Buses leave from the terminal opposite the train station. For information and ticket sales for local routes call ATAM Point in the same square (0575 382 651).

By car

Arezzo is a few kilometres off the A1 (Florence-Rome) *autostrada*. Journey time from Florence is around 1hr, though the *autostrada* experiences big jams on summer weekends and public holidays. The SS73 links the city with Siena to the west (about 1hr) and Sansepolcro to the north (30mins).

Parking can be difficult and expensive in Arezzo. The tourist office (*see above*) has a list of free places to park outside the city walls. For car hire there's **Avis** (piazza della Repubblica 1, 0575 354 232) or **Hertz** (via Calamandrei 97D, 0575 27577).

By taxi

Radio taxi (0575 382 626).

By train

Regular **Intercity** and **InterRegionale** trains link Arezzo with Florence (50-60mins) and Rome (90mins). The train station is located at piazza della Repubblica (0575 20553).

Arezzo Province

Peace in the valleys.

The four valleys that make up Tuscany's eastern province branch out like spokes in a wheel along the Arno, Tiber and Chiana rivers from the hub of Arezzo city.

The **Valdarno**, a largely industrial region connecting Florence to Arezzo, is encased by the imposing Pratomagno Apennine range to the north and the gentler Chianti hills to the south. North-east of the Arno, the Setteponti ('seven bridges') route along the Pratomagno foothills crosses the Arno's tributaries amid olive and chestnut groves. It's less direct than the *autostrada* but more interesting.

To the north is the **Casentino**. Abruptly closed off by some of the Apennine's highest peaks and surrounded by forests, it's always been a peaceful area, with one bloody exception. The Battle of Campaldino in 1289, when Arezzo capitulated to Florence. Today, serenity emanates over the valley from the monastery of Camaldoli and the sanctuary of La Verna.

The **Valtiberina**, Tuscany's easternmost fringe, takes its name from the Tiber that flows down from the Apennine peaks. You'll be constantly reminded by its inhabitants that this valley marks the border between a land that has produced the likes of Michelangelo and Piero della Francesca and the less sophisticated Umbrians and Marchegiani next door.

Finally, in the south is the Etruscan heartland and modern-day agricultural flatland, the **Valdichiana**. This area has whetted the appetites of Arezzo, Siena and Florence over the centuries, with the Medici eventually appropriating or buying control of virtually all of it by the late 15th century. Its name today is synonymous with Chianina beef – large, greyish white-horned creatures. They are mostly raised organically, producing particularly flavoursome meat. The valley west of the Chiana river is dotted with self-contained outposts such as Monte San Savino and Lucignano. But it's to the east of the river that Arezzo province shows off its very best, in splendid sandstone, Cortona.

Castelfranco di Sopra & Loro Ciuffenna

There are a few worthwhile stops along the Setteponti route. The first is Castelfranco di Sopra, which was founded as a Florentine military outpost in the late 13th century. Just outside it is the **Badia di San Salvatore a Soffena**, a 12th-century abbey with a bright interior sporting an *Annunciation* and other pastel-coloured frescoes. The second is the town of **Loro Ciuffenna**, precariously set on the edge of a gorge over the roaring Ciuffenna torrent. Loro grew up around an ancient *borgo* (hamlet), and has its own Ponte Vecchio.

A couple of kilometres outside Loro on the Arezzo road, a dirt path twists off towards the stark and simple church of **San Pietro a Gropina**, a Romanesque parish church dating

Pieve di Romena near Poppi. *See p262.*

back to the ninth century. The carved detail on the capitals and knotted columns on the pulpit, with stylised human figures, grapes, knights and hunting eagles, are a proto-Christian rendition of the circle and knot of life.

The Setteponti's last attraction before reaching Arezzo is **Ponte a Buriano**, a harmonious 13th-century bridge. It's the Arno's oldest bridge and pre-dates the Ponte Vecchio in Florence by almost 100 years.

The Val d'Ambra

The Val d'Ambra is technically Chianti's easternmost reach. It's nestled against the Monti del Chianti, past the Valdarno's two main cities, San Giovanni Valdarno and Montevarchi, which are both significant manufacturing and leather centres. Hidden away are **Cennina**, where a crumbling castle is sentinel to the sprawling Valdarno below, and **Civitella in Val di Chiana**, a perfectly preserved medieval village.

Where to eat

One of the highlights of Val d'Ambra is off the road between Montevarchi and Mercatale Valdarno. At the well-signposted **Osteria di Rendola** (via di Rendola 78, 055 970 7490, tasting menu excl wine €38), Alberto Fusini has created a welcoming space with Cubist artwork and good grub. Also near Montevarchi (to the east, just off the Florence-Rome *autostrada*) is the **Hostaria Costachiara** (via Santa Maria 129, Badiola, Terranova Bracciolini, 055 944 318, closed dinner Mon, all Tue, average €30). It's one of the region's best family-run farmhouse restaurants with a groaning *antipasto* table and open-fire roasts.

Poppi & Camaldoli

A delightful small town, **Poppi** slopes down through arcaded streets from the 13th-century **Castello dei Conti Guidi** (0575 520 516, closed Mon-Wed Oct-Mar, admission €4 incl audio guide). This castle is well worth a visit, not only for its frescoed rooms, including the chapel, but also for the magnificent view of the Casentino. Dante is said to have stayed in the castle and there's a noble statue of him outside.

Head out of Poppi towards Pratovecchio and you'll see signs for the **Pieve di Romena**. This is a 12th-century baptismal church built over a much earlier place of worship. Inside there are sculpted stone capitals and some remarkable pieces of contemporary art made with recycled rural materials. This is the work of the local priest.

In the wooded hills north-east of Poppi, in the midst of the Foreste Casentinesi national park, are the monastery and hermitage of Camaldoli Romualdo, an itinerant Benedictine monk. He set up the Camaldolite congregation within the larger Benedictine order in 1012, and his followers still meditate in the splendid isolation of this holy retreat, surrounded by fir trees, their individual cells visible only through a gate. Romualdo's original cell, with its wooden panelling and cot, is open to visitors, as is the contrasting baroque church.

Three kilometres (two miles) downhill, the monastery links the Camaldolites to the outside world. Its church contains some early Vasaris, including a *Madonna and Child* and *Nativity*. The young artist took refuge here from 1537 to 1539, after the murder of his patron Alessandro de' Medici. Around the corner, a dark wood *farmacia* sells monk-made soaps and liqueurs.

If you've got time, take the road that twists across to Pratovecchio from the hermitage. The views over the Arno valley are superb.

Where to stay & eat

In the square at Poppi, a good base from which to explore the region is homely **Albergo Casentino** (piazza della Repubblica, 0575 529 090, doubles €47-€62) with its own little enclosed garden and a restaurant (closed Wed, average €16). Otherwise dally at the **Antica Cantina** (via Lapucci 2, 0575 529 844, closed Mon, average €21 excl wine), housed in a cellar dating back to the 12th century. Try the chestnut ravioli in a chestnut sauce. There's an excellent wine list, and a number of bottles are available by the glass.

La Verna

A little further south, close to the town of **Chiusi**, this is an even more important monastic complex. In 1214 St Francis's vagabondage brought him to La Verna, an isolated peak at 1,129 metres (3,670 feet), where he and some followers were inspired to build cells for themselves. Ten years later, Italy's most famous saint received the stigmata here and, ever since, this evocative spot has been a must-see on the Franciscan trail.

The basilica contains a reliquary chapel with the saint's personal effects, while, in the walkway towards the stigmata chapel, a door leads to the place St Francis used to rest – a humid cavern, the rocks of which miraculously split apart at the moment of Christ's death. The sanctuary also contains a great number of Andrea della Robbia glazed terracottas.

The quiet life at **Camaldoli** monastery. *See p261.*

This impressive religious compound of interconnected chapels, churches, corridors and cloisters attracts large numbers of visitors. But on a quiet weekday the stunning sunset over the Casentino inspires meditative silence.

Sansepolcro

The Valtiberina's largest town, **Sansepolcro**, gives meaning to the expression 'quality of life'. It is both tranquil and culturally alive, and off the beaten track yet welcoming to visitors. Although the outskirts are unprepossessing, the largely pedestrian walled centre is charming.

Sansepolcro is best known as the birthplace of the early Renaissance maestro of perspective and proportion Piero della Francesca, whose works are prominently displayed in the excellent **Museo Civico** (via Aggiunti 65, 0575 732 218, admission €6.20). Works include the important *Madonna della Misericordia* (c1445), in which della Francesca overturns the laws of proportion by depicting an all-encompassing, monumental Madonna dwarfing the faithful and protecting them with her mantle. Della Francesca can't resist placing himself among the Virgin's followers. He faces us to the Madonna's left. Another self-portrait appears in *The Resurrection* (c1460). A muscular Christ steps from his tomb. Carrying with him a renewal of life, he reawakens the somnolent soldiers at his feet. Among them, to the left of Christ, is della Francesca.

The 14th-century Romanesque **Duomo** contains on its left altar an imposing wooden crucifix known as the *Volto Santo*, probably brought to Sansepolcro from the Orient, and very similar to its better-known and more revered equivalent in Lucca's Duomo di San Martino.

Local events include a torchlit Easter procession on Good Friday and a traditional crossbow tournament, Palio della Balestra, held on the second Sunday in September.

Where to stay, eat & drink

Central **Albergo Fiorentino** (via L Pacioli 60, 0575 740 350, doubles €50-€70) on the corner of via XX Settembre offers perfectly acceptable accommodation, while the **Ristorante da Ventura** (via Aggiunti 30, 0575 742 560, closed dinner Sun, all Mon, average €30) serves the best grub.

For tipples, choose between the **Enoteca Guidi** (via L Pacioli 44, 0575 741 086, closed Sat, lunch Sun & Wed) or the **Caffè degli Appennini** (via XX Settembre 48, 0575 741 755, closed Wed), a relaxed night-time haunt.

Monterchi

This cluster of hilltop homes on the road between Arezzo and Sansepolcro is practically synonymous with Piero della Francesca's *Madonna del Parto*, the famous painting of a pregnant Madonna that once graced a little wayside church and is now the prize possession of the **Museo Madonna del Parto** (via Reglia 1, 0575 70713, admission €3.10). The rotund Madonna is circled by angels lightly drawing back a canopy. This sublime rendition of a sacred, rustic maternal figure is the only one of its kind in Renaissance art. There's also a fascinating display about the restoration of some of Piero's pieces, including his masterpiece *The Legend of the True Cross*, displayed in the church of San Francesco in Arezzo (*see p256*).

Monterchi itself began life as Mons Ercules, a centre for the cult worship of pagan Hercules.

The 15th-century **Castello di Sorci** is home to a popular rustic restaurant. *See p265.*

Where to eat

For an atmospheric meal, head up to **Ristorante Al Travato** (piazza Umberto 1, 0575 70111, closed Mon Apr-Oct, Mon-Thur & dinner Fri-Sun Nov-Mar, average €18) in part of Monterchi's fortress.

Anghiari

Perched on a hill overlooking the Valtiberina and Sansepolcro, Anghiari's dominant position and impressive walls made it a stronghold from which Florence controlled the far east of Tuscany, following victory over the Milanese Visconti family in the Battle of Anghiari in 1440. Leonardo consigned the event to posterity in his (unfinished) rendition on display in the Palazzo Vecchio in Florence. Today, with its maze of vaulted alleys and flower-strewn doorways, it's a peaceful place.

The town's also renowned for its wood craft and antique furniture restoration. It hosts the annual Valtiberina crafts market in late April and an antiques fair on the third Sunday of every other month. The **Museo Statale di Palazzo Taglieschi** (piazza Mameli 16, 0575 788 001, closed Mon, admission €2) displays numerous local artefacts, a polychrome terracotta by della Robbia and a striking wooden sculpture of the *Madonna* by Jacopo della Quercia.

Across the road is the Istituto Statale d'Arte, a training school for furniture and wooden antique restorers. Their products can be seen in the workshop of **Mastro Santi** (via Nova 8), a carving and marquetry specialist.

Anghiari's other big traditional and commercial draw is its woven and naturally dyed textiles, exemplified by the **Busatti** store-cum-factory (via Mazzini 14, 0575 788 013, closed Sun & Mon morning). Their deafening shuttle looms, some of them almost a century old, produce household linens, upholstery and curtain fabrics using only natural fibres.

Where to eat

The popular **Locanda Castello di Sorci** (0575 789 066, closed Mon, set meal €20), on the estate of a 15th-century castle just off the main Arezzo-Sansepolcro route, is guaranteed to fill you up without emptying your wallet. It serves 'a taste of natural products and fresh air', including mixed *antipasti* and plates of meats cooked *alla griglia*.

Monte San Savino

Circular and enclosed, Monte San Savino is a prominent provincial town. Its Renaissance heyday, however, was brief, coinciding with the commercial patronage and religious power exercised by the Di Monte family in the late 1400s and 1500s. The main architectural attractions, both bearing the family's imprint, face each other along the corso Sangallo.

The quintessential Renaissance Palazzo Di Monte, now Palazzo Comunale, (designed between 1515 and 1517 by Antonio Sangallo the Elder), contains an arcaded courtyard, via which you reach hanging gardens and an open-air theatre overlooking a cypress-dotted landscape. Across from it is the Loggia dei Mercanti, attributed to architect and sculptor Andrea Sansovino, Monte San Savino's most eminent son. He also retouched the nearby Piazza Di Monte and helped embellish the church of Santa Chiara with two terracottas: the *Madonna* and *Saints Lawrence, Sebastian and Rocco*.

Monte San Savino is known for engraved pottery designed in delicate floral motifs, with examples on display at the **Museo del Cassero** (piazza Gamurrini, 0575 843 098, admission €1.55). **Ceramiche Artistiche Lapucci**'s (corso Sangallo 8-10, 0575 844 375, ring bell for entry) work still reflects this tradition.

The Estate Savinese event in July puts on open-air concerts and films, the Festival Musicale in the first half of August and the Sagra della Porchetta all-you-can-eat roast suckling pig celebration is in mid September.

Where to stay & eat

For a pleasantly relaxed meal, try the *enoteca-osteria* **La Pecora Nera** (via Zanetti 4, 0575 844 647, closed Thur, average €20), near Porta San Giovanni. Six kilometres (3.5 miles) west of town, the medieval **Castello di Gargonza** (0575 847 021, average €110) has furnished mini-apartments with modern facilities.

Lucignano

Tiny Lucignano has a curious spiral layout: walk round and up and you find yourself at the steps of the church of the Collegiata di San Michele. Behind it is the 13th-century church of San Francesco, barn-like in its simplicity.

Inside the Palazzo Comunale, the **Museo Civico** (piazza del Tribunale 22, closed Mon, Wed, admission €3) exhibits Lucignano's symbol, the *Albero di San Francesco*, a late Gothic reliquary representing a plant-like cross, along with panels by Signorelli and a Bartolo di Fredi triptych.

Where to eat

The town has two good restaurants: **Il Goccino** (via G Matteotti 90, 0575 836 707, closed Mon, average €25), which has a good wine list and space for eating outside in the summer; and **La Rocca** (via G Matteotti 15-17, 0575 836 775, closed Tue, average €25), which serves an excellent *zuppa dei tarlati* (chicken soup made with wild fennel and served with croutons). Paradise on a plate here is fried eggs topped with plenty of fresh truffle shavings.

Foiano della Chiana

Foiano's buildings and steeples are distinguished by the warm, reddish tones of their *cotto* bricks. Its oval shape centres on piazza Cavour, dominated by the Palazzo delle Logge, formerly a Medici hunting lodge. Today, it houses the Fototeca Furio del Furia, an engrossing display of early 20th-century photographs of rural life in Italy.

Outside the walls is Foiano's other main draw, the neo-classical Collegiata di San Martino. It houses an Andrea della Robbia terracotta, the *Madonna of the Girdle*, and Signorelli's last work, *Coronation of the Virgin* (1523), influenced by Piero della Francesca.

Castiglion Fiorentino

Castiglion Fiorentino (formerly Castiglion Aretino and, briefly, Castiglion Perugino) is a bustling town set against the lower Apennines and overlooked by its impressive Cassero tower, situated on the town's highest point.

Its Etruscan origins were reaffirmed by recent excavation of walls and the discovery of artefacts dating to the fifth century BC, now on display in the crypt of the Chiesa di San Angelo al Cassero. Above this is the **Pinacoteca Comunale** (via del Cassero,

0575 657 466, closed Mon, admission €3), which displays paintings by Giotto's godson and follower Taddeo Gaddi and 15th-century artist Bartolomeo della Gatta.

Castiglion Fiorentino's top spot for admiring the views over the Valdichiana is the Loggiato Vasariano in the piazza del Municipio. Past the Loggiato is the **Panificio Melloni** (via San Michele 48) which piles up its alluring baked goods behind a tiny wooden door.

On the way south to Cortona, standing imperiously on top of a hill, is the Castello di Montecchio, which belonged to English mercenary and war strategist John Hawkwood.

Where to eat

For a refuel, head to the lower end of Castiglion Fiorentino, near the Porta Fiorentina, to **Da Muzzicone** (piazza San Francesco 7, 0575 658 403, closed Tue, average €25).

Cortona

Both refined Tuscan and rustic Umbrian in feel, architecture and dialect, Cortona is in a league of its own. Its jumble of irregular, angular buildings, windswept city walls, layered urban development and its strategic position dominating the Valdichiana distinguish it among central Italy's historic cities.

Probably founded as an Umbrian fortress, Cortona grew into an important Etruscan outpost around the eighth century BC and then passed under Roman rule. Following depredation by the Goths, it thrived as a free community from the 11th century. Sacked by Arezzo in 1258, it bounced back and was taken over and quickly sold by the King of Naples to Florence in 1411. Since then, it's prospered.

Today, it's a quintessential *città d'arte* that attracts almost more tourists than it can cope with. Foreign study groups set up summer courses here, and devotees of Frances Mayes's books (notably *Under the Tuscan Sun*, a sort of upmarket American soapie set among the olive groves) flock here as on pilgrimage. Cortona also provides a spectacular venue for the final days of the Umbria Jazz Festival in late July and for the sizzling Chianina beef feast, Sagra della Bistecca, in mid August.

The town is best absorbed from the steps leading up to the crenellated clock tower of the heavy-set Palazzo Comunale, overlooking uneven piazza della Repubblica. Adjacent is piazza Signorelli, containing the arcaded Teatro Signorelli. Both honour Cortona's foremost offspring, high Renaissance artist Luca Signorelli (c1445-1523).

On the piazza, in the Palazzo Casali, is the eccentric **Museo dell'Accademia Etrusca** (0575 630 415, admission €4.20), which spans history from ancient Egyptian remnants to visionary Futurist pieces by Gino Severini (1883-1966), another of Cortona's natives. It includes Etruscan findings, like a bronze lamp adorned with sirens and satyrs.

The piazza del Duomo opens on to a picture-postcard view of the valley, while opposite the bland Duomo is the **Museo Diocesano** (0575 62830, admission €5), which is home to Fra Angelico's glorious *Annunciation* and works by Signorelli and Pietro Lorenzetti.

For more of Cortona's rewarding sights, climb via Berrettini towards the Fortezza Medicea. Here is the 15th-century church of San Nicolò with its delicate courtyard and baroque-roofed interior containing a Signorelli altarpiece. Also worth the schlep is the Chiesa di Santa Margherita, which has vivid ceilings, and the fort above with views to Lake Trasimeno.

Cortona's only flat surface is lively via Nazionale, dotted with antiques and wood-crafting stores. At No.54, Giulio Lucarini's laboratory showcases traditional terracottas in typical yellow-red sunflower patterns. Sublime aromas waft from the *pasticceria* at No.64.

Where to eat

The **Osteria del Teatro** (via Maffei 5, 0575 630 556, closed Wed, average €25) serves good food in an operatic setting. **Preludio** (via Guelfa 11, 0575 630 104, closed Mon and lunch Nov-May, average €30) serves great gnocchi with chestnuts or *funghi porcini*. **Tonino** (piazza Garibaldi 1, 0575 630 500, average €35) is good for Tuscan *antipasti* and has lovely views over the valley. For the same view but cheaper, quicker nosh (*bruschette* and omelettes), try its outdoor Belvedere terrace. **Trattoria Dardano** (via Dardano 24, 0575 601 944, closed Wed, average €16) is a locals' haunt that serves home cooking.

Where to stay

The **Albergo Athens** (via Sant'Antonio 12, 0575 630 508, doubles €23-€41.50) is the only budget option within Cortona's walls, with dorm-like rooms at unbeatable prices. The newly renovated **Hotel Italia** (via Ghibellina 7, 0575 630 254, doubles €65-€98) has the best quality-to-price ratio, offering rooftop views from top-floor rooms and terrace. **Hotel San Luca** (piazza Garibaldi 1, 0575 630 460, doubles €70-€100) is generic and modern, but

Dominating the Valdichiana, Cortona is an ancient strategic stronghold.

has spectacular views over the valley. If you're looking for something central and classy, the **Hotel San Michele** (via Guelfa 15, 0575 604 348, doubles €83-€200) boasts a unique 1700s ceiling in the breakfast room. For a complete spoil-yourself option, book into the recently opened four-star **Hotel Villa Marsili** (via Cesare Battisti 13, 0575 605 252, doubles €110-€310), a beautifully restored 18th-century private residence with its own gardens. Alternatively, just outside Cortona, the **Hotel Oasi Neumann** (Località Contesse 1, 0575 630 354, doubles €86-€108) offers all creature comforts among plenty of greenery at reasonable prices.

Resources

Tourist information

Arezzo APT (*see p260*).
Cortona
APT *Via Nationale 42 (0575 630 352/ fax 0575 630 656/www.apt.arezzo.it)*.
Open *May-Sept* 9am-1pm, 3-7pm Mon-Sat; 9am-1pm Sun. *Oct-Apr* 9am-1pm, 3-6pm Mon-Sat.
Sansepolcro
Piazza Garibaldi (0575 740 536).
Open 9.30am-1pm, 3.30-6.30pm daily.

Getting there

By bus

Lazzi (055 919 9922) has regular buses linking Montevarchi, Terranuova Bracciolini and Loro Ciuffenna with Arezzo. Irregular **LFI** buses (0575 39881) serve Camaldoli and Chiusi Verna from Bibbiena station. They run more regular buses between Cortona (from piazzale Garibaldi) and Arezzo, which also stop in Castiglion Fiorentino. **SITA** (0575 74361) runs buses between Arezzo and Sansepolcro (journey time 1hr) that also stop in Anghiari (45mins) and sometimes Monterchi.

By car

There are several routes through the Valdarno, including the Florence-Rome *autostrada* (A1), the slower A69, which runs through San Giovanni and Montevarchi and on to Arezzo, or the Setteponti route through the country.

By car is the best way to see the Casentino, and there are thrilling mountain roads to explore, but progress is slow, and snow can be a problem between October and April. The region's main arteries are the SS70 and SS71.

To explore the Valtiberina, take the SS73 out of Arezzo, heading north-east toward Sansepolcro. Monterchi and, further on, Anghiari are signposted off this road, a few kilometres before Sansepolcro.

The A1 *autostrada* passes right through the Valdichiana, with exits for Monte San Savino and Valdichiana (for Cortona, off the main SS75 to Perugia). From Arezzo, Castiglion Fiorentino and Cortona are reached via the SS71.

By train

Local trains on the Florence-Arezzo line stop at Montevarchi (45mins from Florence, 25mins from Arezzo). Timetable information 892 021.

A tiny train line run by La Ferroviaria Italiana (LFI) links Pratovecchio (journey time 1hr), Poppi (40mins) and Bibbiena (30mins) to Arezzo, with departures roughly every hour during the day.

Cortona has two train stations: Camucia-Cortona, 5km (3 miles) away, and Terontola-Cortona, 11km (7 miles) from town. Castiglion Fiorentino is on the same line. Trains from Arezzo take 15mins to Castiglion, 22mins to Camucia and 27mins to Terontola. Slow trains between Florence (journey time to Terontola 90mins) and Rome (Terontola 80mins) also pass through all three stations. A regular bus service links Cortona with its two stations.

Southern Tuscany

Still the beautiful south, despite the crowds.

With its scarcity of major transport arteries, it is perhaps understandable that southern Tuscany lags behind the rate of development experienced elsewhere in the region. Even the area known as the Maremma was barely touched by the 1980s development boom that was a great boost to tourist earnings elsewhere in Italy.

That said, however, you should avoid the peak periods of Easter, July and August, when you can expect to find crowds pretty much everywhere, especially at the resorts on the **Monte Argentario** (*see p273*) and the main two island destinations of **Elba** and **Giglio** (*see pp274-6*). But if you go at any other time, you'll find much of the region idyllic: be it viewing awesome 2,500-year-old Etruscan necropolises, trekking through one of the huge WWF nature reserves sheltering wildlife that's disappearing from other parts of Tuscany, visiting the amazing hill towns around **Pitigliano**, or simply sunning yourself on one of the gorgeous islands.

Grosseto Province & the Maremma

The beaches are undoubtedly the most famous of Grosseto province's attractions and in season the Maremma, the region's most popular coastal strip, can get very crowded. The hinterland, however, remains relatively unexplored.

The Maremma (as distinct from the Pisan Maremma; *see pp208-11*) covers the coastal strip south of Piombino and the inland region between Grosseto and the Tuscan border with Lazio. Its people have seen centuries of cruel overlords and dynasties but the area's past struggles have lent it a distinct character and cuisine that have little to do with the gentle, privileged image of the rest of Tuscany.

Though they do get a stream of visitors, Maremma's amazing hilltop towns, with their sheer cliff walls and castles, have retained a unique, unspoilt character. Up here the air is clean and, on a clear day, the light has an ethereal quality that accentuates the fairytale atmosphere.

Grosseto

The largest Tuscan town south of Siena, Grosseto is the capital of the province. It traces its history back to the fifth century when it was an Etruscan settlement. During the Middle Ages it represented civilisation for inhabitants of the malaria-ridden swamplands. These days, there's little to see, although the 16th-century walls were left unscathed by the bombing that destroyed almost everything in the city centre in World War II.

If you're driving to Grosseto along the SS223 from Siena, an interesting stop is Roselle, just off the SS223 about eight kilometres (five miles) north-east of Grosseto. Here you'll find the excavated ruins of an Etruscan city, which was conquered by Rome in the third century.

Grosseto itself is hardly one of Tuscany's most attractive towns, but it's in the middle of a fantastic area and if you want to visit the stunning **Parco Naturale della Maremma** (*see p271*) you have to get a bus from here (take Nos. 15 or 16 from in front of the church). It's also possible to drive – the main entrance to the park is at **Alberese**, where there's a visitors' centre – but the car park, next to the beach at Marina di Alberese, only has 240 places so the bus is probably the best option.

The history of the town can be seen in detail at the **Museo Archeologico e d'Arte della Maremma** and the **Museo d'Arte Sacra del Diocesi di Grosseto** (piazza Baccarini 3, 0564 488 750, closed Mon, admission €5).

Where to stay & eat

En route to Grosetto, **Le Milandre** (via Sense 23, 0564 900 683, closed Wed, average €18) near **Civitella Marittima** is a great little restaurant. The main room features reproductions of photos of Maremma, while outside there are tables overlooking the family's olive grove. In the town itself, the tiny **Trattoria Il Bavaro** (via Fucini 15, 0564 28673, closed Sun, average €16) has a roof terrace and serves Tuscan cuisine. The elegant **Buca San Lorenzo** (viale Manetti 1, 0564 25142, closed Sun, Mon, 2wks Jan & 2wks July, average €31) attracts the diamonds-and-pearls set of Grosseto. Coming from piazza Rosselli it's under the city walls to the right of

Fishermen on the rugged coast below **Monte Argentario**. *See p273.*

the gate. The delightfully quirky vegetarian **Pinzimonio** (via Garibaldi 52, 0564 20625, closed Sun) only serves five courses for €20 at dinner, but the food's great so bring an appetite. **Big Pizza** (via Novembre 9, 0564 23474, average €10) does spectacular pizzas and has a young, buzzy vibe.

It's unlikely that you'll want to stay overnight in Grosseto, but if you do, the tourist office (*see p274*) can recommend hotels. A much better bet accommodation-wise is to head to **Monte Argentario** (*see p273*) or **Talamone** (*see p272*), an attractive harbour town near the southern entrance to the Parco Naturale della Maremma.

Massa Marittima

Massa's position, together with its mineral wealth and fresh water supply, helped it to survive as an independent city state for 110 years before being taken over by Siena in 1335. Back then Massa dominated the high southern ranges of the Colline Metallifere, a rich source of the iron, copper and other minerals that were one of the economic driving forces behind the early Renaissance. But after the mines were closed in 1396 Massa's boom years were over. Half a millennium of neglect followed until a small-scale return to mining, along with the draining of the surrounding marshes, turned the tide in the middle of the 19th century. Today, Massa has preserved one of the most uniform examples of 13th-century town planning anywhere in Tuscany.

The **Duomo** harmoniously blends Romanesque and Gothic details and its bare stone interior includes a Baptistery, famous for its 13th-century bas-reliefs by Giroldo da Como.

In the second half of the 13th century the fountain was the hub of town life – and the saviour of the community when war and extensive surrounding social chaos forced the townsfolk to hole up for extended periods. Named Le Fonti dell'Abbondanza ('fountains of abundance'), the basins suffered neglect for several centuries before restoration work opened up the original source to allow the waters to flow once again. You can't actually see the fountain, but you can see, under the arches, a fresco that was only discovered and restored in 2000.

In the 13th-century **Palazzo del Podestà** on piazza Garibaldi is the interesting Museo Civico Archeologico (0566 902 289, closed Mon, admission €2), which has an Etruscan collection and a marvellous 1330 *Maestà* by Ambrogio Lorenzetti. Up via Moncini is the **Città Nuova** or 'new town' (the 14th-century bit rather than the 12th-/13th-century bit), which has a fine Sienese arch. You can climb the arch for €2.50 or walk around the side for equally excellent but free views over the town and countryside.

Another Massa draw is the **Balestro del Girifalco** festival on the fourth Sunday in May, the feast day of San Bernardino of Siena, who was born here. The Renaissance costumes are dazzling, the *bandieratori* (flag-throwers) are faultless and the final contest – when teams from the town's three *terzieri* attempt to shoot down a mechanical falcon with their crossbows – is a truly fascinating sight. The town also stages concerts in the square in August (the tourist office has details; *see p274*) and a photography festival (www.toscanafotofestival.it).

Where to stay & eat

If you fancy staying overnight, opt for the three-star **Sole** (corso Libertà 43, 0566 901 971, closed mid Jan-mid Feb, doubles €60-€85) in an old palazzo. As for food, walk past the cyclists supping beer at the *pizzerie* on the square to **Enoteca Grassini** (via della Libertà 1, 0566 940 149, closed Tue, average €17) for a plate of local food such as stewed wild boar with black olives. Even more atmospheric is **Da Tronca** (vicolo Porte 5, 0566 901 991, closed lunch, Wed, average €20), an *osteria* down a nearby side street serving distinctive regional fare.

Saturnia

The road to Saturnia is well worn by touring motorhome owners and others seeking regeneration in the small, sulphurous tributary of the Albenga. But there should be room for everyone and you'll find relaxing in the hot waters here sheer bliss once you've got accustomed to the steamy stench. You can pay through the nose for a luxurious experience at the thermal pools of the Hotel Terme (*below*), which offers, among many other things, mud treatments and massage, or follow the procession of camper vans further down the road in the direction of Manciano and bathe for free in the pretty **Cascate del Gorello** falls and pools, where the rocks are stained green. On a warm, clear night this is magical. According to legend, Saturn, to punish those who thought only of war, sent down a thunderbolt that split the earth open, causing steamy water to pour forth. In this liquid the disobedient earthlings found rejuvenation and became calm again.

Where to stay & eat

You won't get bored at **Hotel Terme** (0564 601 061, closed 2wks Jan, doubles €340-€392 incl breakfast), where you can work up a sweat in the gym, on the golf driving range or playing tennis.

Saturnia has several slightly expensive restaurants. Perhaps the pick is **Bacco e Cerere** (via Mazzini 4, 0564 601 235/ 601 805, closed Wed and 2wks Jan or Feb, average €40), which concentrates on the likes of wild boar, rabbit, steak and lamb. For something cheaper try exploring further up the road to Semproniano, another hill town with four eateries of its own.

In Montemerano, six kilometres (nearly four miles) south of Saturnia, the famous **Da Caino** (via Canonica 4, 0564 602 817, closed Wed, lunch Thur in low season, average €90) continues to win plaudits for its Tuscan cuisine. It has 20,000 bottles of wine in its cellar and three rooms should you wish to stay. A cheaper option is **Passaparola nel Antico Frantoio** (via dell Mura 21, 0564 602 835, closed Thur, 2wks July & 2wks Feb, average €27).

Manciano

The massive grey walls of Manciano loom up defensively out of the landscape, but its coat of arms bears an outstretched hand in a gesture of friendship. This is the administrative centre of the Maremma where you'll find a hospital and post office, and connecting buses between Grosseto and the surrounding Etruscan sights. Manciano is a quiet haven, which has views all over the surrounding countryside. It also offers the **Museum of Prehistory and Protohistory** (via Corsini, 0564 625 327, closed Mon, Sun afternoon, admission €2.80).

Il Poderino (0564 625 031, *agriturismo* rooms €41-€60) is a country inn just outside the town.

Pitigliano

Dubbed the 'eagle's nest' by the Etruscans, Pitigliano is an awesome sight. The town perches high on a plateau and the edges of three sides of it are flush with the sheer reddish tufa limestone cliffs making it look as though it were carved from one huge block of the stuff – indeed parts of it were. The dramatic drop into the valley below is accentuated by an immense aqueduct, built in 1545, that connects the lower and upper parts of town. The church of **Madonna delle Grazie** (1527), on an opposite hill as you approach, provides a great vantage point over the town and surrounding countryside.

The Orsinis built up the town's grandeur in the 14th century. They were preceded by the Aldobrancescas, who ruled over the Maremma for about 500 years. Both coats of arms are still on display in the Orsini family's palace courtyard on piazza Orsini.

The Jewish community that was attracted here by increasing Medici tolerance in the 16th century either left or was forced out during World War II. All that's left of it today – apart from four residents who returned here after the war – is a small Museum of Jewish History, housed in the former synagogue in via Zuccarelli, and a *pasticceria* around the corner, which still makes a local Jewish pastry called *sfratti* ('the evicted'). Just follow the delicious waft of fresh baking from down the passageway.

The **Museo Civico Archeologico** (piazza Orsini, for info call council on 0564 614 067, closed Mon, admission €2.60) has a small, but well-presented collection of Etruscan artefacts from the area.

Where to eat

Tucked away in an alleyway is the homely and award-winning **Il Tufo Allegro** (vicolo della Constituzione 2, 0564 616 192, closed Tue, Wed lunch, average €22); *see p37*. If you can't get in to Il Tufo, try a local trattoria such as **Il Grillo** (via Cavour 18, 0564 615 202, closed Tue and July, average €17), **La Chiave del Paradiso** (via Vignoli 209, 0564 616 823, closed Mon and mid Jan-late Feb, average €14) or **dell'Orso** (piazza San Gregorio VII 14-15, 0564 614 273, closed Thur in winter, average €18).

Sovana

North-west of Pitigliano, six and a half kilometres (four miles) by road, lies this now semi-abandoned but once important Etruscan town. Between the ninth and 12th centuries it was a thriving bishopric under the dominion of the wealthy Aldobrandini family. One of the clan's most famous scions, the great reforming pope Gregory VII (after whom the calendar is named), was born here in around 1020. There's a small museum of local history in the 13th-century Palazzo Pretorio, next door to the arched Loggetta del Capitano. At the other end of town, down a cobbled track lined with cypress trees, is the **Duomo**, a Lombard Romanesque structure with a cool, unfussy interior and a fine carved portal on the left side. Back in the centre medieval **Santa Maria** is a beautiful church. It's a blend of the Romanesque and Gothic, with a ciborium from the eighth or ninth century and a series of 15th-century Siena-school frescoes.

In a valley below the town to the west is one of the most completely preserved Etruscan necropolises, a series of tombs cut into the tufa walls of the Fosso Calesina. Among the tombs is the second century BC Tomba Ildebranda, complete with pedestal and sculpted columns.

Where to stay & eat

Sovana has two of the best places in the area to dine: **La Taverna Etrusca** (piazza del Pretorio 16, 0564 616 183, closed Wed, Jan and Feb, average €31), where you should try the wonderful lamb with globe artichokes; and **Scilla** (via Rodolfo Sidiero 1-3, 0564 616 531, closed Tue, average €25). Both have rooms should you find the village's sense of peace irresistible. A double with breakfast is €80 at La Taverna Etrusca, €92 at Scilla.

Sorano

This village of dark, greyish tufa perched precariously high above the Lente river as you head north-east from Sovana towards the Lazio border, is a dizzying sight. Under the Orsini empire Sorano was a defence post, but at times its geology proved more dangerous than its rampaging enemies. A series of deadly landslides encouraged a slow but steady exodus of people. **Masso Leopoldino**, a giant terraced tufa cliff, peers down on the town.

If you want to stay in a medieval Tuscan fortress, **Della Fortezza** (piazza Cairoli, 0564 632 010, closed Jan, Feb, doubles €72-€123) is comfortable and has amazing views.

Parco Naturale della Maremma

This beautiful, WWF-protected nature reserve, which encompasses Monti dell'Uccellina, has some great hikes. Birds, both migratory and resident, thrive here – ospreys, falcons, kingfishers, herons and the rare Knight of Italy can all be spotted. The terrain ranges from the mudflats and umbrella pines of the estuary to the untouched woodland of the hills.

Cars aren't allowed in the park (there's a large car park opposite the visitors' centre in Alberese, next to the main entrance). The visitor's centre (via Bersagliere 7-9, 0564 407 098, closed afternoons Nov-Apr) has stacks of helpful information, a long list of suggested trails and activities including canoeing and horse riding. One attraction is the wild and natural beach at Marina di Alberese, the best in mainland southern Tuscany. A train service runs from Grosseto to Marina di Alberese. From the station, take a bus or walk the four kilometres (2.5 miles) to the entrance.

The famous *butteri* (Maremma cowboys) put on a show for the public in Alberese on 1 May and 15 August . The park is open every day from 9am until one hour before sunset. Admission to the park is €5.50-€8.

Fields of sunshine near the hill town of **Pitigliano**. *See p270.*

Where to stay & eat

If you'd like to stay in the park, there are two lodges, which must be booked via the travel agent Poiana Viaggi on 0564 412 000.

There is a good restaurant with simple pastas, pizzas and cold meats in Alberese called **Mancini & Caoduro** (via del Fante 24, 0564 407 137, closed Tue and Nov-Feb, average €17), while at Alberese Scalo is **La Nuova Dispensa** (via Aurelia Vecchia, 0564 407321, closed Tue in winter and 2wks Jan, average €18), a simple restaurant with great food such as wild boar *cacciatora* ('hunter style' with tomato, herbs, garlic and wine) – booking advised. Fish restaurant **Da Remo** in Santa Maria di Rispecia (0564 405 014, closed Wed, average €30) is not much to look at but locals flock here for the quality of the cooking. Book ahead.

Talamone

Near the southern entrance to the park is the quiet, unspoilt town of Talamone, which has good accommodation. Friendly **Hotel Capo d'Uomo** (via Cala di Forno, 0564 887 077, closed Nov-Mar, doubles €119) is a three-star hotel overlooking the bay. In town there's **Telamonio** (piazza Garibaldi 4, 0564 887 008, closed Oct-Mar, doubles €49-€129).

La Buca di Nonno Ghigo (via Porta Garibaldi 1, 0564 887 067, closed Mon in winter, Nov, average €25) occupies a cute spot down a tiny street next to the city walls and offers all manner of wonderful fresh seafood.

Orbetello

In the middle of the most central of the three isthmuses that connect Monte Argentario to the mainland, Orbetello has remnants of Spanish fortifications dating from the 16th and 17th centuries when this was the capital of the Stato dei Presidi, a Spanish enclave on the Tuscan coast. There's a small antiquarium with some uninspiring Etruscan and Roman exhibits, and the cathedral has a Gothic façade, but Orbetello is really more about atmosphere than it is about sightseeing. Join the evening *struscio* (promenade up corso Italia) before dining on a plate of eels (fished from the lagoon) at one of the town's simple *trattorie*. **Osteria del Lupacante** (corso Italia 103, 0564 867 618, closed Tue in winter, average €25) also serves good spaghetti and shellfish dishes.

Of the town's three least expensive hotels the best is **Piccolo Parigi** (corso Italia 169, 0564 867 233, doubles €36-€62).

Ansedonia

This is the Beverly Hills of the Etruscan Riviera. Not much is left that really reflects its ancient history, though some Roman ruins from 170 BC overlook the villas with flower-draped walls, and the nearby Museo di Cosa displays artefacts from the area. Daily trains from Grosseto stop at Capalbio station; from there it's three kilometres (two miles) down to the beach alongside the picturesque Lago di Burano lagoon (now a WWF reserve).

The coastline stretching southward from Ansedonia offers 18 kilometres (11 miles) of beach, but there's an industrial plant looming through the haze at the far south end, so you're better off on the beaches north of Argentario or heading straight for an island.

Monte Argentario

A mountain rising abruptly from the sea, Monte Argentario is the Tuscan coast at its most rugged. If it looks as though it should be an island, that's because it was until the 18th century when the two long outer sand-spits created by the action of the tides finally reached the mainland. It has two attractive port towns, Porto Ercole and Porto Santo Stefano.

Porto Ercole

On the south-east corner of Argentario lies this exclusive town; the place where the painter Caravaggio died drunk on the beach in 1610. As with Orbetello and Santo Stefano, Easter and August holidays see this small bay full to the gills. The hotel with the best view in town is the three-star **Don Pedro** (via Panoramica 7, 0564 833 914, closed Oct-Mar, doubles €113.50-€139), which overlooks the harbour. The charismatic two-star **Hotel Marina** (lungomare Andrea Doria 23, 0564 833 055, doubles €67-€103.5) is more central and some rooms have balconies overlooking the harbour. If you can afford it, splash out at **Il Pellicano** (Sbarcatello village, 0564 833 801, closed Nov-Mar, doubles €300-€776) about three kilometres (two miles) out of town. With a private rocky beach, fabulous terraces overlooking the sea and the relaxed feel of a country house, it's one of the most glamorous and luxurious hotels in Italy. There are several seafood restaurants on Porto Ercole harbour and pizzeria **La Lanterna** at lungomare Doria 19 (0564 833 064, closed Thur, average €20).

Porto Santo Stefano

The place to get a ferry for the **Isola del Giglio** (*see p274*), this is also an atmospheric port where you'll find fishermen mending nets on the quay and fresh seafood stalls – although the vibe is more upmarket during the holidays when the yachting crowd arrives.

It's certainly worth pausing here for a meal, particularly at **Dal Greco** (via del Molo 1-2, 0564 814 885, closed Tue and Nov or Jan, average €45), a seafood restaurant with a terrace on the harbour. A little cheaper is **Il Moletto di Amato & Figli** (via del Molo, 0564 813 636, closed Wed and mid Jan-Feb, average €26), in a fantastic location on the end of the quay. A short walk from here, but removed from the hurly burly, is **Da Orlando** (via Breschi 3, 0564 812 788, closed Wed and Nov, Mon-Fri winter, average €35), which has a pretty terrace with an uninterrupted view across the bay. It's a fine place to savour the likes of spaghetti with big, juicy chunks of scampi in a tomato and herb sauce.

The seafront is lined with a string of bars. One of the hippest is **Il Buco** (Lungomare dei Navigatori 2, 0564 818 243) where the well-dressed and darkly tanned take their Camparis and Martinis. Join them if you dare.

The tourist office is at corso Umberto 55A (0564 814 208, closed afternoons in winter).

Beaches

There are two nice beaches making up the sand-spits that join Monte Argentario to the mainland – **La Giannella** to the north and **La Feniglia** to the south. Access to the former is from the main Talamone-Argentario road, look for any of the little pathways through the pines. To get to the latter you have to park at the western end. The further you walk, the less crowded it is. Both beaches have the odd paid *bagno*, but the rest is free. You can hire a bicycle and cycle through the protected pine woods behind La Feniglia. There's also a long, thin sandy beach between Talamone and Argentario on the Golfo di Talamone with great views of Argentario to the south and Talamone to the north. This is also the place to camp. You'll find sites in the pinewoods next to the beach all along this stretch.

Capalbio

Close to the Lazio border, **Capalbio** is a magnet for Rome's poets, musicians and politicians.

Il Giardino dei Tarocchi (0564 895 122, closed late Oct-mid May, admission €6.20-€10.50) is an amazing walled garden to the south-east of Capalbio, which was founded in 1976 by Anglo-American artist Niki de Saint Phalle. She created more than 20 massive sculptures of splinters of mirror, coloured tiles and sculpted stone to represent the main characters from the tarot deck: the High Priest and Priestess, the Moon, Sun and so on. Some of the sculptures house four-storey buildings, which you can enter. The artist herself made her home in the immense Empress for a while where she slept in the right breast and ate in the left.

Where to stay & eat

Trattoria la Torre da Carla (via Vittorio Emanuele 33, 0564 896 070/896 617, closed Thur, Mon-Fri winter, average €26) serves robust Tuscan cuisine and its terrace overlooks the forest where your *cinghiale* (wild boar) was probably shot. The renegade bandit Tiburzi ate here before he was strung up in 1896. His photo adorns one of the restaurant's walls.

Hotel Valle del Buttero (via Silone 21, 0564 896 097, doubles €40-€110) is a large three-star hotel. **Trattoria da Maria** (via Comunale 3, 0564 896 014, closed Tue spring-autumn, early Jan-early Feb, average €35) also rents double rooms (€52); call in advance. **Ghiaccio Bosco** (via della Sgrilla 4, 0564 896 539, doubles €75-€100) is a swish *agriturismo* with 15 pleasant rooms, well-tended grounds and a pool.

Resources

Tourist Information

Grosseto *Agenzia per il Turismo (APT), Viale Monterosa 206 (0564 462 611).* **Open** 8.30am-1.30pm, 3-6pm Mon-Fri; 8.30am-12.30pm Sat.
Massa Marritima *Ufficio Turistico, Via Todini 3 (0566 902 756/fax 0566 940 095).* **Open** *Winter* 9.30am-12.30pm, 3.30-6.30pm Mon-Sat. *Summer* also 10am-1pm Sun.
Pitigliano *Piazza Garibaldi 51 (0564 617 111).* **Open** 3-7pm Mon; 9.30am-1pm, 3.30-7pm Tue-Sat.
Saturnia *Consorzio L'altra Maremma, Piazza Vittorio Veneto 8 (0564 601 280/www.laltramaremma.it).* **Open** *Summer* 10.20am-1pm, 3-7pm Mon-Sat. *Winter* 10am-4.40pm Mon-Sat.

Getting there & around

By bus

There are about ten buses a day connecting Grosseto, the region's main town, and Siena (journey time 90mins). Buses leave from in front of Grosseto's train station. For further information on buses serving regional towns such as Piombino and Pitigliano call Rama on 0564 25215.

By car

The main coast road (E80/SS1) links Grosseto with Livorno to the north and the Maremma to the south. The SS223 is the main route down from Siena, though it's not well signposted in and around Siena. The region's most scenic road is the SS74, which branches inland off the SS1, north of Orbetello, and winds toward Manciano and Pitgliano.

By train

Grosseto is on the main train line between Rome and Pisa (90mins from Rome, 80mins from Pisa). Trains on this line also stop at Capalbio and Orbetello (for Monte Argentario) to the south, and San Vincenzo and Cecina to the north. A local train links Grosseto with Siena (2 hours).

The Islands

The Tuscan Islands can be a welcome antidote to the area's largely unremarkable coast, particularly tiny, tranquil Isola de Giglio west of Orbetello. Timing is everything, however. Both Elba and Giglio are crowded with beach junkies during Easter, July and August, but their idyllic sands and scenery are there all year and can be uncrowded even in temperate May, June and September. The islands and the sea in which they are set make up the Parco Nazionale Arcipelago Toscano, Europe's biggest protected marine park. For information call 0565 919 411 or you can visit www.islepark.it.

Isola del Giglio

A steep and winding road connects the three villages on this beautiful little island – Giglio Porto, where the ferry docks, Campese on the other side and Giglio Castello on the ridge between the two, with its medieval walls and steep narrow lanes. The main beach is at Campese but there are smaller ones dotted around.

Apart from chilling on the beach, two of the great pleasures here are exploring the virtually uninhabited south and indulging yourself nightly at one of the many good restaurants on the atmospheric quayside in Porto. Most of the hotels on the island are also in Porto and there are a number of rooms to let in local homes, as well.

Where to stay, eat & drink

Overlooking Giglio Porto, the three-star **Castello Monticello** (via Provinciale, 0564 809 252, closed Oct-Mar, doubles €44-€124) occupies a crenellated folly. For the ultimate sun and sea experience, head to **Pardini's Hermitage** (cala degli Alberi, 0564 809 034, closed Nov-Mar, doubles €105-€150 full board) in a secluded cove accessible only by foot or by boat. Don't worry, staff will fetch you.

While on the beach in Campese, have lunch at local stalwart **Tony's** (via della Torre 13, 0564 806 453, closed Nov) located on the north end of the beach below the tower. It can be relied upon for everything 'from a cappuccino to a lobster'. Pizzas start at €4.20. Meanwhile, tanned yachters and kids frequent **I Lombi Disco** at Giglio Castello (0564 806 001, closed Mon-Fri, Sun Sept-June, €7.80). This place also has a quieter piano bar that's open from 9.30pm.

A Tuscan idyll: the island of **Elba**.

Resources

Tourist Information

Via Provinciale 9 (0564 809 400/www.isoladel giglioufficioturistico.com). **Open** 9am-12.30pm, 4-6pm daily.

Elba

Part of the Tuscan archipelago, Elba is Italy's third largest island, with 142 kilometres (88 miles) of coastline. It boasts fantastic scenery across hills and bays with white sand and crystal clear waters at seemingly every corner. In this sense, at least, it makes a refreshing change from the rather prosaic coastline of mainland Tuscany. But be prepared for crowds in Easter, July and August when it can be unbearable and the resident population of 30,000 swells to almost a million. To catch the island at its best you should head there just out of season.

Portoferraio is the island's capital and the focus of Napoleonic interest . There's certainly plenty to see here if you can bear to drag yourself from the beach. Napoleon's town residence, the Palazzo dei Mulini, is worth a visit for its views and Empire-style furnishings, which are incongruous in this Mediterranean setting. However, more difficult to get to at more than six kilometres (nearly four miles) south-west of town, off the road for Marciana, is his summer retreat, the neo-classical Villa Napoleonica di San Martino.

Choosing between Elba's many village resorts can be a problem. Tiny **Viticcio** overlooks a pretty, secluded bay with some

Tuscany

rock and shingle to lay out on. Biodola has a terrific beach, but is dominated by large hotels and the inevitable parasols. Poggio has a good portion of free beach, but it can get very busy, while Marciana Marina is an attractive port town.

Up the hill, Marciana itself is one of two starting points for beginning an ascent of Monte Capanne. The village of Sant Andrea is relatively quiet and removed, although the beach is pretty tiny. The national park in the north-west is a walker's paradise. Marciana, Poggio and Sant Andrea are the main start-off points for hikes around the park and the relatively unexplored west part of the island. The tourist office has further information a good booklet with a list of trails.

Many of the villages on the south and south-western side of the island have good beaches ranging from rocks and shingle to smooth sand (like Chiessi, Pomonte, Fetovaia, Seccheto, Cavoli, Marina di Campo and Lacona). The pick of the beaches is Fetovaia, which is in a stunning sandy cove (despite the fact that it is half taken up by an array of dreaded sun-parasols).

The two main wine-producing areas of Elba are around Magazzini and Mola. Near the Magazzini is the pretty and friendly winery of **Monte Fabbrello** (Schiopparello village 30, 0565 933 324).

With all that clear water, diving is a popular pursuit around here, and there are numerous centres to satisfy under water urges. Two of the best places you'll find are: **Spiro Sub** (località La Foce 27, Marina di Campo, 0565 976 102); and, **Il Corsaro** (località Pareti, Capoliveri, 0565 935 066).

Where to stay, eat & drink

Rendez-Vous on Marciana Marina's buzzing piazza della Vittoria (piazza della Vittoria 1, 0565 99251, closed Wed in winter, average €31) does good grilled fish and steak, while the aesthetic hill town of Poggio is home to a restaurant with an amazing view called **Publius** (0565 99208, closed Mon in winter, Jan-Feb, average €25). In the upmarket port town of Porto Azzura you'll find **La Laterna** (via Vitaliani 5, Porto Azzuro, 0565 958 394, closed Mon, Dec-Jan, average €22) and **Delfino Verde** (0565 95197, closed Wed, Nov-Mar, average €18), which are two of the best-known seafood restaurants around.

Accommodation-wise, starting at the cheaper end of the scale, **Casa Lupi** on the outskirts of Marciana Marina (Ontanelli village, 0565 99143, closed Jan and Feb, doubles €26-€70) is one of the best one-star hotels on Elba. In Viticcio, stay at two star **Scoglio Bianco** (0565 939 036, closed Oct-Easter, doubles €42-€170 half board). More upmarket, in Fetovaia, three-star **Lo Scirocco** is clean, smart and well located (0565 988 033, closed Oct-Mar, doubles €49-€82). Or for two star try **Anna** (0565 988 032, doubles €26-€79).

Ottone is home to a huge camping and bungalow site called **Rosselba le Palme** (località Ottone, tel/fax 0565 933 101), which is one of the best on Elba, and a swish hotel and restaurant, **Villa Ottone** (località Ottone, 0565 933 042, doubles €80-€270). Both have access to the greyish sandy beach. Or, on the *agriturismo* tip, **Monte Fabbrello** (see *above*) has rooms at €45-€60, while apartments have a double bedroom and a double sofa-bed in the kitchen – the price for four people on this basis is €55, or €45 for two.

Resources

Tourist Information

Calata Italia 43, Portoferraio (0565 914 671/www.aptelba.it).

The other islands

The third largest Tuscan island, **Capraia**, is relatively undeveloped save for a few hotels in its small port town. It's mostly made up of national parkland, which will be of interest to ramblers and bird watchers. There's also a diving club and you can rent boats to tour the grottoes along its coast. Tourist information is at via Assunzione 2 (0586 905138, open 9am-12.30pm, 3.30-6pm summer only). There are ferries daily from Livorno with **Toremar** (0586 896113 at Livorno or 0586 905069 for the ticket office in Capraia).

Gorgona is a prison that can only be visited by permission – unless, that is, you're planning a longer stretch as an inmate. The same goes for **Pianosa**. **Montecristo** is completely out of bounds to all visitors.

The tourist office in Elba (*see above*) can supply any additional information on these islands should you need it.

Getting there

By boat

Toremar (0564 810 803/www.toremar.it) and **Maregiglio** (0564 812 920/www.maregiglio.it) have several sailings a day from Porto Santo Stefano. Most ferries run from Piombino to Portoferraio. There are frequent ferries every day. Ticket outlets for the ferry companies can be found at the port: **Moby** (0565 9361) and **Toremar** (0565 31100).

Directory

Getting Around	278
Resources A-Z	283
Italian Vocabulary	297
Art & Architecture Glossary	298
Further Reference	299
Index	300
Advertisers' Index	306

Directory

Getting Around

Arriving & leaving

By air

If you're travelling by air, you'll most likely land at Pisa's Galileo Galilei Airport, Bologna's Marconi Airport or the smaller, but nonetheless busy, Florence Vespucci Airport west of the city centre at Peretola.

Amerigo Vespucci, Florence

Vespucci Airport, Peretola (055 306 15/24hr flight info 055 306 1702/lost luggage 055 306 1302/ www.safnet.it).
A small airport handling more than 70 scheduled flights a day. About 5km (3 miles) west of central Florence, it's linked to the city by an airport bus service, the **Volainbus**, which runs half-hourly 6am-11.30pm, costs €4 and stops in the SITA bus station in via Santa Caterina da Siena 15 (*see p279*). Buy tickets on the bus. A taxi to central Florence costs about €16 (extra for luggage) at night and on public holidays. The journey takes about 20 minutes.

Galileo Galilei, Pisa

Galilei Airport (050 849 111/ flight info 050 500 707/www. pisa-airport.com).
South of Pisa and 84km (52 miles) west of Florence, this airport handles national and international scheduled and charter flights. To get to Florence by car take the Firenze-Pisa-Livorno dual carriageway (there's direct access at the airport), which goes to the west of the city. The direct train service to Florence's Santa Maria Novella station takes just over an hour. Buy tickets (€4.85 each way) at the info desk immediately to the right of arrivals in the main airport concourse. Train times are not co-ordinated with flight arrivals; they run roughly every hour 10.30am-5.45pm, with an inconvenient two-hour gap at lunchtime. After 5.45pm there are very few trains and none after about 10pm. There's another service to Florence via Lucca, but trains on this line are even less frequent and the journey time is nearly two hours. Check the departure board before taking the first train (fast trains usually leave from the platform on the left). Trains run further into the night from Pisa Centrale, with the last departure around 11.30pm. A taxi into Pisa costs about €8, and CPT bus 5 leaves for Pisa city centre and train station every quarter of an hour. Tickets and timetables are available at the info desk.

In the other direction the first train to Pisa airport from Florence Santa Maria Novella is at 11am, and trains run almost every hour 11am-5.05pm. For times outside these take the train for Pisa Centrale. There's a check-in facility on platform five for some flights (though not Ryanair or British Airways flights). The minimum check-in time is 15 minutes before your train to G.Galilei Airport is due to leave, five with only hand baggage, but there may be queues. Tickets cost €1 more than the normal fare if bought here. A flight info service is also provided (055 216 073).

Marconi, Bologna

Marconi Airport (051 647 9615).
Open 5am-midnight daily.
This is 10km (six miles) north-west of Bologna, with two terminals. Charter flights, Easyjet and British Airways fly here. There's a free shuttle bus between the terminals and an airport bus stops outside terminal A (arrivals); it leaves for Bologna train station every 15 minutes and costs €4.50. Get tickets from the machine in the terminal building or on board. The trip takes about 30 minutes, less at quiet times. A taxi to the station costs about €15.

From Bologna Centrale, trains to Florence are frequent and take anything from 50 to 90 minutes; ticket prices also vary. The fastest and most expensive trains are the Eurostars; tell the ticket vendor which train you want to catch. They run regularly 6.30am-9.45pm daily (7.15am-10.20pm back to Bologna from Florence). A single second-class ticket is €13.17. The Intercities are less regular, cost €10.75 and are reasonably fast. To travel on a Eurostar, reservations are always required. Be aware that Eurostar trains are often fully booked at weekends and during rush hour.

If you hire a car, the trip to Florence takes about 90 minutes, south on the A1.

Major airlines

Alitalia *055 27881/24hr booking service 848 865 642/www.alitalia.it.*
British Airways *199 712 266/ 050 501 838 (Pisa)/ www.britishairways.com.*
Easyjet *848 887 766/www.easyjet.co.uk.*
Meridiana *055 230 2334/ info & bookings 199 111 333/ www.meridiana.it.*
Ryanair *050 503 770/ www.ryanair.com.*

By rail

Train tickets can be bought from the ticket desks or cash-only vending machines in the station, from **Ticket Point** (*see p279*), from the official state railways website www.trenitalia.com, or from travel agents displaying the **FS** (Ferrovie dello Stato, state railways) logo. Before boarding a train in any Italian city, stamp (*convalidare*) your ticket and any supplements in the small yellow machines at the head of the platforms. Failure to do this will result in a fine payable on the train unless you go immediately to the train guard and ask him to validate your ticket.

Taxis serve Florence's main **Santa Maria Novella** station on a 24-hour basis and many city buses stop here. If you're travelling light, it's only a 15-minute walk into central Florence. Trains arriving during the night go to **Campo di Marte** station to the north-west of the city, where buses 67 and 70 also stop. Note that train strikes are common.

Campo di Marte

Via Mannelli, Outside the City Gates (055 235 4136/disabled assistance 055 235 2275). Bus 12, 70 (night).
Florence's main station when SMN is closed during the night. Many long-distance trains stop here. The ticket office is open 6.20am-9pm.

Santa Maria Novella

Piazza della Stazione, Santa Maria Novella (055 235 2061).
Open 4.15am-1.30am daily.
Information office 7am-9pm daily.
Ticket office 5.50am-10pm daily.
Map p314 A2.

Train information

892 021/www.trenitalia.com. **Open** 7.45am-5.15pm daily.
The centralised info service of the state railways (FS; *see p278*) provides details on national and international routes. Some English is spoken. You can also book and pay for tickets online.

Disabled enquiries

055 235 2275. **Open** 7am-9pm daily. English spoken.
The disabled assistance desk is on platform five at Santa Maria Novella (open 7am-9pm daily).

By bus

If you come to Florence by coach, you'll arrive at either the **SITA** or the **Lazzi** coach station, both offices are near Santa Maria Novella station. *See p278.*

Ticket Point Lazzi

Piazza Adua, Santa Maria Novella (055 215 155/www.lazzi.it). **Open** 9am-7pm Mon-Sat. **Credit** (train tickets only) AmEx, DC, MC, V. **Map** p314 A2.
Sells tickets for Lazzi, Eurolines coaches and Ferrovie dello Stato.

SITA

Via Santa Caterina da Siena, (information 800 373 760). **Map** p314 A2.
See also p281.

Public transport

Florence is a small city and while the council continues to consider subway and tram systems, its only public transport is the bus network. Run by **ATAF**, it covers most of the city. Strikes are regular, weekend and evening waiting times can be very long.

Information

ATAF

Information desk, Piazza della Stazione, opposite north-east exit of train station, Santa Maria Novella (freephone 800 424 500/www.ataf.net). **Open** 7am-1.15pm, 1.45-7.30pm Mon-Fri; 7.15am-1.15pm Sat.
The main ATAF information desk has English-speaking staff, but on the phone you may not be so lucky. At this office you can buy a variety of bus tickets and they also supply a booklet with details of all the major routes and fares.

Fares & tickets

Except on night buses (*see below*), all tickets must be bought in advance. Drivers cannot sell them. They're available from the ATAF office in piazza della Stazione (except for season tickets), a few machines, *tabacchi*, newsstands and bars displaying an orange ATAF sticker. When you board, stamp the ticket in one of the validation machines. If you are using a ticket for two consecutive journeys, stamp it on the first bus only, but keep it till you complete your journey, and if you go beyond the time limit, stamp another.

Plain-clothes inspectors circulate frequently and anyone without a valid ticket is fined €40 payable within 30 days at the main information office or in post offices.

60min ticket (*biglietto 60 minuti*) €1; valid for 1hr of travel on all buses.

Multiple ticket (*biglietto multiplo*) €3.90; 4 tickets, each valid for 60mins.

3-hour ticket (*biglietto 3 ore*) €1.80; valid for 3hrs.

24-hour ticket (*biglietto 24 ore*) €4; one-day pass that must be stamped at the beginning of the first journey.

Monthly pass (*abbonamento*) €31; €20.70 students. The ordinary pass can be bought without ID or photos from the ATAF office at Santa Maria Novella station, or from any of the normal outlets displaying an 'Abbonamenti ATAF' sign. For the student pass, go to the Ufficio Abbonamenti in piazza della Stazione (open 7.15am-1.15pm, 1.45-7.45pm Mon-Fri; 7.15am-1.15pm Sat). You will need to take ID and two passport photos.

Daytime services

Most ATAF routes run from 5.30am to 9pm with a frequency of between ten and 30 minutes. Don't take much notice of the timetables posted on many bus stops – on most routes they're over-optimistic to say the least. After 9pm, there are four night services (*see below*). The orange and white *fermata* (bus stops) list the main stops along the route. Each stop has its name indicated at the top.

Useful tourist routes

7 from Santa Maria Novella station, via Piazza San Marco to Fiesole
10 to and from Settignano
12, 13 circular routes via Santa Maria Novella station, piazza della Libertà, piazzale Michelangiolo and San Miniato.

About five years ago ATAF introduced a network of environmentally friendly electric buses, which runs four routes: **A**, **B**, and **C** plus a smaller version of the diesel buses, the **D**. Normal bus tickets or season tickets are valid. These routes are detailed in ATAF's booklet and marked on our map, *pp314-5*.

Night buses

Three bus routes operate until 12.30am/1am (67, 68 and 71). But only one (70) runs all night. The 70 leaves Santa Maria Novella every hour, passes through the centre of town, goes north, calls at Campo di Marte station and returns to Santa Maria Novella via a long, circular route. Tickets are usually available on board for €1.50, though you will need the correct change, and some drivers don't carry the tickets. So, it's always best to buy them first if possible.

Disabled services

New buses (grey and green) share routes 7,12, 13, 23, 27, 30 with the old (all orange), and are fully wheelchair accessible with an electric platform at the rear door. The small bus route D, which goes through the centre of town, is also fully equipped.

Transport in Tuscany

Having your own wheels is the most independent way of getting to, and meandering around, out-of-the-way places in Tuscany. It will also help you achieve more on better-worn paths, such as Chianti and the south of Siena province. On the down side, however, progress on winding country roads can be slow and parking in even the bigger towns is often difficult.

There are few parts of Tuscany that you can't reach via the bus network. A number of companies, including **Tra-in** (out of Siena) and **Lazzi** (out of Florence), operate around major towns and even the remotest parts of the region have a bus service. You can get just about everywhere with a bit of planning. Note that in most remote villages,

buses are timed to coincide with the school day, leaving early in the morning and returning at lunchtime.

The rail system is efficient too. One particularly helpful line, with regular services all day, links Florence with the cities to its west – from Prato to Lucca and continuing on to Viareggio or, alternatively, Pisa. There are also lots of small local lines.

Information

For train information, consult the Ferrovie dello Stato (**FS**, state railways) centralised service, which has an excellent website www.trenitalia.it (*see p278*). Major Tuscan bus companies include:
CAP *Via Nazionale 13, Santa Maria Novella, Florence (055 214 627/537).* **Map** p314 A2.
Lazzi *Piazza della Stazione 4, corner of Piazza Adua, Santa Maria Novella, Florence (055 351 061/www.lazzi.it).* **Map** p314 A2.
Rama *Via Topazo 12, Grosseto (0564 454 169).*
SITA *Via Santa Caterina da Siena 15, Santa Maria Novella, Florence (055 483 651/ticket office 055 21472/international 055 294 995).* **Map** p314 A2.
Tra-in *Piazza San Domenico, Siena (0577 204 111/www.comune.siena.it/train).*

Taxis

There are scandalously few taxis in Florence (almost half that of other European cities), so finding a cab can be a nightmare. This is especially during rush hour, at night or if there's a trade fair. Licensed cabs are white with yellow graphics, with a code name of a place plus ID number on the door; for example, Londra 6. If you have problems, make a note of this code.

You will find that it's practically impossible to flag a cab down in the street. So for important appointments, ma ke sure you book several hours before with a phone cab company. Not that this is necessarily a guarantee. You will sometimes be told that there are no cars available, and to call when you're ready to go).

Fares & surcharges

Taxis are expensive in Florence, but fares are standard. When the taxi arrives the meter should read €2.45 during the day, €4 on Sundays and public holidays, and €5.39 at night. The fare increases at a rate of 70c per kilometre. Lone women pay 10% less after 9pm – if you ask.

Phoning for a cab carries with it a surcharge of €1.71. There is an overall minimum fare of €3.65. Each item of luggage in the boot costs extra, and destinations beyond the official city limits (Fiesole, for example) cost considerably more. For details see the tariff card that cabs are legally obliged to display.

Taxi ranks

Ranks are indicated by a blue sign with TAXI written in white, but this is no guarantee any cars will be waiting, or will arrive in your lifetime. There are ranks in piazza della Repubblica, piazza della Stazione, piazza Santa Maria Novella, piazza del Duomo, piazza San Marco, piazza Santa Croce and piazza di Santa Trinità.

Phone cabs

When your call is answered, give the address where you want to be picked up, specifying if the street number is *nero* or *rosso* (*see p283*). If a cab is available, you will be given its code and a time; for example, *'Londra 6 in tre minuti'*. Otherwise, the operator will tell you to call back.
Taxi numbers 055 4390; 055 4798; 055 4242.

Driving in Florence

In a word: don't. Though it can be chaotic, Florence is easily walkable and the bus service is a good complement. The traffic is notorious, parts of the centre off limits and parking difficult and expensive.

The air quality is so poor that when pollution levels reach a certain limit, cars that use diesel or leaded fuel are banned from within a large radius of the city (though hire cars and cars with foreign plates are allowed access to hotels). Digital notices above the main roads into town give notice of these bans, and they are also announced on local radio and in the local papers.

In addition there are the permanent Traffic Free Zones (**ZTL**). These areas (lettered A-E) include the old city centre and are gradually expanding. Only residents or permit-holders can enter from 7.30am to 7.30pm, Monday to Saturday. This is usually extended in the summer to exclude cars from the centre in the evenings from Thursday or Friday to Sunday.

Breakdown services

It's advisable to join a national motoring organisation such as the AA or RAC in Britain or the AAA in the US before taking a car to Italy. They have reciprocal arrangements with the **Automobile Club d'Italia** (**ACI**), which will tell you what to do in case of a breakdown and provide useful general information on driving in Europe. Even for non-members, the ACI is the best number to call if you have any kind of breakdown – though you'll be charged, of course.

Automobile Club d'Italia (ACI)

Viale Amendola 36, Outside the City Gates (055 24861/24hr information in English 166 664 477/24hr emergency line 803 116). Bus 8, 12, 13 14, 31. **Open** 8.30am-1pm, 3-5.30pm Mon-Fri.
The ACI has English-speaking staff, and charges reasonable rates. Members of associated organisations are entitled to basic repairs free, and to other services at preferential rates.

Car pounds

If your car's not where you left it, it's probably been towed. Phone the municipal police (*vigili urbani*) on 055 32831, or the central car pound (Depositeria Comunale, via dell'Arcovata 6, open 24 hrs daily) on 055 308 249. Charges vary depending on where the car was left and the time lapsed between the towing and you fetching it. In the unlikely event your car was stolen (check that it has not been towed before pursuing this line of enquiry) and found it will be taken to via Circondaria 19, 055 328 3944.

Parking

Parking is a major problem and is severely restricted in the centre of town. Wheel clamping has been introduced and carries a hefty fine; if you find your car has been clamped, the number to call to have the clamp removed will be posted on the car.

In unrestricted areas parking is free in most side streets, while most main streets are strictly no-parking zones. No parking is allowed where you see *passo carrabile* (access at all times) and *sosta vietata* (no parking) signs. Disabled parking spaces are marked by yellow stripes. Blue lines indicate pay-parking; an attendant will issue you with a timed ticket, to return to them when you return to your car. A *Zona Rimozione* (tow-away area) sign at the end of a street is valid for its entire length.

Most streets are washed once every one or two weeks, usually in the small hours. Vehicles have to be removed or they will be towed or clamped. Signs tell you when cleaning takes place.

The safest place to leave a car is in one of the underground car parks (*parcheggi*), such as **Parterre** and **Piazza Stazione**, which both have surveillance cameras.

Garage Europa *Borgo Ognissanti 96, Santa Maria Novella (055 292 222).* **Open** 6am-2am daily. **Rates** €3 per hr; €30 per 24hrs; €96-€133 per wk. **Map** p314 B1.

Garage Lungarno *Borgo San Jacopo 10, Oltrarno (055 282 542).* **Open** 7am-midnight daily. **Rates** €3.50-€5 per hr; €22-€37 24hrs. **Map** p314 C3.

Parcheggio Parterre
Via Madonna delle Tosse 9, Outside the City Gates (055 500 1994). Bus 8, 17, 33. **Open** 24hrs daily. **Rates** €1.50 per hr; €15 per 24hrs; €55 per wk.
Just off piazza della Libertà.

Parcheggio Piazza Stazione
Via Alamanni 14/Piazza della Stazione 12-13, Santa Maria Novella (055 230 2655). **Open** 24hrs daily. **Rates** €2 per hr for 1st 2hrs, €3 per hr for subsequent hrs; €140,000 payable 5 days in advance. **Map** p314 A2.

Petrol

Most petrol stations sell unleaded petrol (*senza piombo*) and regular (*super*). Diesel fuel is *gasolio*. All offer a full service on weekdays; many offer a discount for self-service. Pump attendants don't expect tips.

There are petrol stations on most of the main roads leading out of town. Their normal opening hours are 7.30am-12.30pm, 3-7pm Monday to Saturday. There are no permanently staffed 24-hour petrol stations in Florence; the nearest are on the motorways. The following AGIP stations have 24-hour self-service machines that accept good-condition notes: via Bolognese, via Aretina, viale Europa, via Senese, and, via Baracca.

Roads

There are three motorways in Tuscany that you have to pay a toll to use. They are the *autostrade* **A1** (Rome-Florence-Bologna), **A11** (the coast-Lucca-Florence) and **A12** (Livorno-Genova). *Autostrade* are indicated by green road signs. As you drive on to one, you pick up a ticket from one of the toll booths; hand it in when you come off. As an idea of price, it costs €20 to drive the 270km (168 miles) from Rome to Florence. You can pay in cash, with a Viacard (a swipecard available from the ACI and newsagents) or by credit card.

Vehicle hire

Car hire

Branches of most major car hire companies are near the station, around borgo Ognissanti. Shop around for the best rates; prices given below are an indication, but they vary according to season (as do opening times).

Avis *Borgo Ognissanti 128r, Santa Maria Novella (055 213 629). Bus B.* **Open** 8am-7pm Mon-Sat; 9am-1pm Sun. **Credit** AmEx, DC, MC, V. **Map** p341 B1.
The cheapest grade B car costs around €160 for a (three-day) weekend and €238 for the week.
Branches: Peretola Airport (055 315 588); Pisa Airport (050 42028).

Europcar *Borgo Ognissanti 53-5, Santa Maria Novella (055 290 438/437). Bus B.* **Open** 8am-1pm, 2.30-7pm Mon-Fri; 8am-1pm Sat. **Credit** AmEx, DC, MC, V. **Map** p314 B1.
A Fiat Punto is €127.40 for a weekend and from €277.20 to €411.60 for a week. This branch is open on Sundays in summer.
Branches: Peretola Airport (055 318 609); Pisa Airport (050 41017).

Chauffeur-driven cars

Sunny Tuscany (055 400 652/0335 605 2001) provides chauffeur-driven cars for tours of Florence/Tuscany.

Golf carts

It might sound eccentric, but it's actually a very practical and pleasant way to see Florence. Golf cart hire costs €20 for three hours and €5 for each subsequent hour. The cost for the pick-up and delivery of the car is €10. For further information contact **S.A.V.E** on 055 713 1895/ 0339 871 9125.

Cycling

Cycling in Florence is a form of Russian roulette. There are cycle lanes on the main *viali* but that's no guarantee they'll only be used by bikes. Also, watch for roadside car doors being opened (a bad local habit).

Moped & bike hire

To hire a scooter or moped (*motorino*) you need a credit card, ID and cash deposit. Helmets must be worn on all mopeds. Cycle shops normally ask you to leave ID rather than a deposit.

Alinari

Via Guelfa 85r, San Lorenzo (055 280 500). **Open** 9.30am-1pm, 3-7.30pm Mon-Sat; 10am-1pm, 3-7pm Sun. **Credit** MC, V. **Map** p314/5 A3/4.
Scooter rental of a 50cc *motorino* for use of one person only is €28 per day; 125cc for one or two people is €55 per day. A current driver's licence is required.

Florence by Bike

Via San Zanobi 120r, San Lorenzo (055 488 992). **Open** *Mar-Oct* 9am-7.30pm daily. **Credit** AmEx, MC, V.
Bike hire costs €2.50 per hour, €12 per day. Guided tours are also available, and English is spoken.

Walking

Even if you're in a hurry, walking is the easiest and quickest way to get around this traffic-clogged city. Part of the historic centre (*centro storico*) is totally pedestrianised. Still, do be careful of bicycles and mopeds zooming up behind you. Don't be surprised if you meet two-wheeled vehicles coming the wrong way up a one-way street. What's more don't expect cars to stop instantly at lights, and do expect them to ignore red lights when making right turns from side streets.

Resources A-Z

Addresses

Addresses in Florence are numbered and colour-coded. Residential addresses are 'black' numbers (*nero*), and most commercial addresses are 'red' (*rosso*). This means that in any one street there can be two addresses of the same number, but different colours, sometimes far apart. Some houses are both shops and flats and could have two different numbers, one red and one black. Red numbers are followed by an 'r' when the address is written.

Age restrictions

In Italy there are official age restrictions, but it's very rare for anyone to be asked to show ID in bars or elsewhere, other than in gay bars and clubs. Beer and wine can legally be drunk in bars and pubs from the age of 16, spirits from 18. It's an offence to sell cigarettes to children under 16. Mopeds (50cc) can be driven from the age of 14; cars from 18; only those over 21 can hire a car.

Attitude & etiquette

In churches, women are expected to cover their arms and not wear anything daring. Meanwhile, shorts and vests are out for anyone. Most of the major museums and galleries forbid the taking of photos with flashes, and many even without. It's best to check at the ticket desk before you do.

Queues are a foreign concept, but in a crowded shop, customers know who is before them and who after, and usually respect that. In shops say *buongiorno* on entering and leaving. It's generally considered rude to walk in, look around and leave without asking for what you are looking for.

When addressing anyone except children it's important to use the appropriate title: *signora* for women; *signorina* for very young women; and *signore* for men.

Business

Conventions & conferences

Firenze Expo *Piazza Adua 1, San Lorenzo (055 26025/fax 055 211 830)*. **Map** p314 A2.
This centre includes Palazzo dei Congressi in the Fortezza da Basso and Centro degli Affari Firenze. It specialises in hosting international meetings and can accommodate large parties, anything between five and 1,000.

Couriers & shippers

DHL *199 199 345*. **Open** 24hrs daily. **Credit** AmEx, DC, MC, V.
Letters (up to 150g) cost €33.50 to the UK; €31.50 to the US (guaranteed delivery within 48 hours). A 5kg package is €110.50 to the UK (guaranteed delivery 24 hours); €123 to the US (guaranteed delivery within two to three days). Free same-day pick-up is offered – provided that you phone in your request before 3pm.

Federal Express *Freephone 800 123 800*. **Open** 8am-7pm Mon-Fri. **Credit** AmEx, DC, MC, V.
Sending letters (up to 500g) with Federal Express cost €42.95 to the UK, or €30.16 to the US. A 5kg package is €90.60 to the UK; €111.07 to the US. Federal Express's next-day service is guaranteed for all deliveries placed before 10am (except on Friday). They also offer free pick-up.

Mail Boxes Etc *Via della Scala 13r, Santa Maria Novella (055 268 173/fax 055 212 852/ www.mbec.com)*. **Open** 9am-1pm, 3.30-7pm Mon-Fri; 10am-1pm Sat. **Credit** AmEx, MC, V. **Map** p314 B2.
Various services offered, including packaging, shipping at good rates, and, of course, mailboxes (€46.48 for 3 months). Some staff at Mail Boxes Etc speak English.

SDA *Freephone 800 016 027/06 665 471 from mobiles/www.sda.it*. **No credit cards**.
This is the Italian post office courier service. Letters or documents up to 500g cost €34.09 to the UK; €28.41 to the US. A 5kg package costs €104.11 to the UK and €116.72 to the US.

UPS *Freephone 800 877 877/ www.ups.com*. **Open** 8am-7pm Mon-Fri; 8.30am-1pm Sat. **Credit** AmEx, MC, V.
With UPS letters are €44.29 to the UK and €34.68 to the US (guaranteed delivery by 10.30am the next day). A 5kg package costs €119.69 to the UK, €122.48 to the US (guaranteed delivery within two days). Free same-day pick-up is offered – provided that you phone in your request before 1pm.

Travel advice

For up-to-date information on travel to a specific country – including the latest news on safety and security, health issues, local laws and customs – contact your home country government's department of foreign affairs. Most have websites packed with useful advice for would-be travellers.

Australia
www.dfat.gov.au/travel

Republic of Ireland
www.irlgov.ie/iveagh

Canada
www.voyage.gc.ca

UK
www.fco.gov.uk/travel

New Zealand
www.mft.govt.nz/travel

USA
http://travel.state.gov

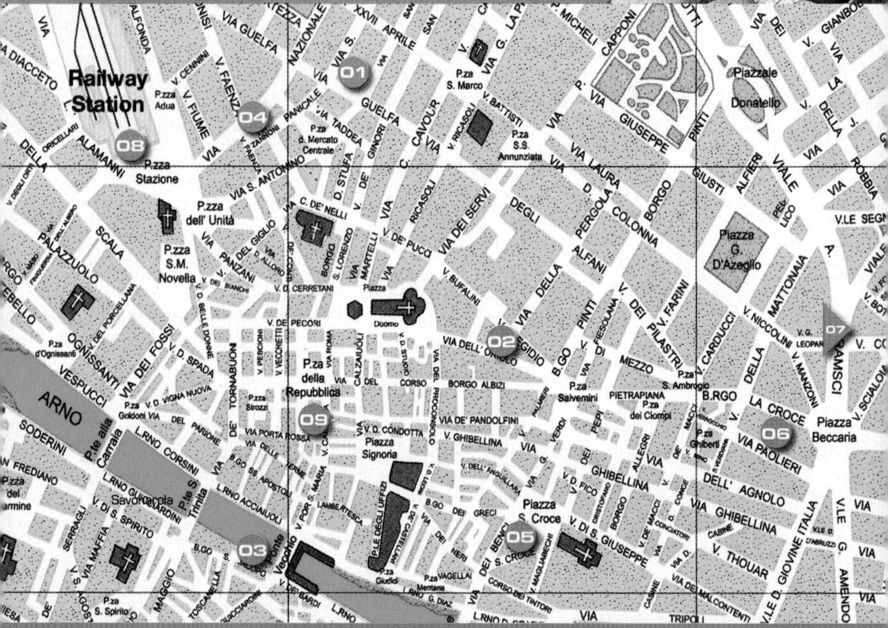

Packing & removals

Oli-Ca *Borgo SS Apostoli 27r, Duomo & Around (055 239 6917).* **Open** 9am-1pm, 3.30-7.30pm Mon-Fri; 9am-1pm Sat. **Map** p314 C3.
For full preparation (all materials and labour included) of a 70x40x 25cm box, the cost is €9. No mailing service, but the main post office is only two blocks away.

Translators & interpreters

Emynet *Lungarno Soderini 5/7/9r, Oltrarno (055 219 228/fax 055 218 992/emynet@emynet.com).* **Open** 9.30am-1.30pm, 3-7pm Mon-Fri. **Map** p314 C1.
Full written and spoken translations in 'all' languages.

Interpreti di Conferenza *Via Guelfa 116, San Lorenzo (055 475 165).* **Open** 9am-1pm Mon-Fri. **Map** p314 A2.
Interpreters for business meetings.

Useful organisations

Camera di Commercio Industria, Artigianato e Agricoltura (Chamber of Commerce), *Piazza Giudici 3, Duomo & Around (055 27951/ fax 055 279 5259).* **Open** 8am-3.30pm Mon-Fri. **Map** p315 C4.
Provides information on all elements of import/export and business in Italy, and on Italian trade fairs.

Commercial Office, British Consulate *Lungarno Corsini 2, Duomo & Around (055 289 556).* **Open** 9.30am-12.30pm, 2.30-4.30pm Mon-Fri. Telephone enquiries 9am-1pm, 2-5pm Mon-Fri. **Map** p314 C2.
Provides business advice and information to British nationals. Call for an appointment.

Commercial Office, United States of America Consulate *Lungarno A Vespucci 36/38/40 Outside the City Gates (055 211 676/283 780) Bus B.* **Open** 9am-12.30pm, 2-3.30pm Mon-Fri.

Consumer

Shops are unlikely to take back purchases for a refund, unless the goods are faulty. The best you can hope for is an exchange or credit note. If you feel hard done by, contact the organisation below.

Associazione Italiana per la Difesa Consumatori e Ambiente *Via Ricasoli 28, San Marco (055 216 180).* **Map** p315 A4.

Customs

EU nationals don't have to declare goods imported into or exported from Italy for their personal use, as long as they arrive from another EU country. US citizens should check their duty-free allowance on the way out. Random checks are made for drugs. For non-EU citizens the following import limits apply:

- 400 cigarettes or 200 small cigars or 100 cigars or 500g (17.6oz) of tobacco
- 1 litre of spirits (over 22% alcohol) or 2 litres of fortified wine (under 22%)
- 50 grams (1.76oz) of perfume.

There are no restrictions on the importation of cameras, watches or electrical goods. Visitors are also allowed to bring in up to €10,000 in cash.

Disabled

Disabled facilities are not great, but they are improving. All new public offices, bars, restaurants and hotels must be equipped with full disabled facilities. However, the standard of access varies greatly. Though some places have fully accessible rooms on upper floors, there is no lift wide enough to take a chair.

Many museums are wheelchair-accessible with lifts, ramps on steps and toilets for the disabled. Pavement corners in the centre of town are now sloped to allow for wheelchair access.

Most new buses are equipped with ramps and a wheelchair area (*see p279*). Trains that allow space for wheelchairs in the carriages and have disabled loos have a wheelchair logo on the outside, but there is no wheelchair access up the steep steps – call the information office for assistance (055 235 2275, English spoken). Taxis take wheelchairs, but tell them when you book. There are free disabled parking places throughout Florence, and disabled drivers displaying the sticker have access to pedestrian areas of the city. There are wheelchair-accessible toilets at Florence and Pisa airports and Santa Maria Novella train station, as well as in many of Florence's main sights.

The Provincia di Firenze produces a booklet (also in English) with disabled-aware descriptions (how many steps on each floor, wide doorways and so on) of venues across Florence province, available from tourist offices. For more info, call 800 437 631 (some English spoken). The official council website (www.comune.fi.it) also has useful sightseeing itineraries suitable for disabled visitors.

Drugs

Drug-taking is illegal in Italy and if you are caught in possession of drugs of any type, you may be taken before a magistrate.

If you can convince him or her that your stash was for purely personal use, then you may be let off with a fine or ordered to leave the country. Anything more than a tiny amount will push you into the criminal category: couriering or dealing can land you in prison for up to 20 years. It is an offence to buy or sell drugs, or to give them away. Sniffer dogs are a fixture at most ports of entry into Italy; customs police take a dim view of visitors entering with even the smallest quantities of narcotics, and they could be refused entry or arrested.

Electricity

Most wiring systems work on one electrical current, 220V, compatible with British and US-bought products. A few systems in old buildings are 125V. With US 110V equipment you will need a transformer. Buy two-pin travel plug converters before leaving, as they will be hard to find in Italy. Adapters for different Italian plugs can be bought at any electrical shop.

Embassies & consulates

There are no embassies in Florence. However, there are some consular offices, which offer limited services.

Australian Embassy *Via Alessandria 215, Suburbs-North, Rome (06 852 721).*

British Consulate *Lungarno Corsini 2, Duomo & Around (055 284 133/fax 055 219 112).* **Open** 9.30am-12.30pm, 2.30-4.30pm Mon-Fri. *Telephone enquiries* 9am-1pm, 2-5pm Mon-Fri. **Map** p314 C2.
Outside these hours, a message will tell you what to do.

Canadian Embassy *Via GB de Rossi 27, Suburbs-North, Rome (06 445 981).*

Irish Embassy *Piazza Campitelli 3, Ghetto, Rome (06 697 9121).*

New Zealand Embassy *Via Zara 28, Suburbs-North, Rome (06 441 7171).*

South African Consulate *Piazza dei Salterelli 1, Duomo & Around (055 281 863).* **Map** p314 C3.
No office. You have to call to make an appointment.

United States of America Consulate *Lungarno A Vespucci 38, Outside the City Gates (055 239 8276/fax 055 284 088). Bus B.* **Open** 9am-12.30pm, 2-3.30pm Mon-Fri.
In case of emergency call the above number and a message will refer you to the current emergency number.

Emergencies

Thefts or losses should be reported immediately at the nearest police station (*see p290*), where you should get a crime report for insurance purposes. You should report the loss of your passport to your embassy or consulate (*see above*). To prevent fraud, report the loss of a credit card or travellers' cheques to your credit card company (*see p290*) immediately.

Emergency numbers

Emergency services & state police *Polizia di stato* 113.
Police *Carabinieri* (English-speaking helpline) 112.
Fire service *Vigili del Fuoco* 115.
Ambulance *Ambulanza* 118.
Car breakdown Automobile Club d'Italia (ACI) 803 116.
City traffic police *Vigili Urbani* 055 32831.

Gay & lesbian

For HIV and AIDS services, *see p287.*

Azione Gay e Lesbica Circolo Finisterrae *c/o SMS Andrea del Sarto, Via Manara 12 (055 671 298).* **Open** 6-8pm Mon-Fri. Closed 3wks Aug.
Formerly part of ARCI Gay/Lesbica, this group has been independent since 1997. In addition to the Timida Godzilla parties it runs, it maintains a library and archive, facilitates HIV testing and provides community info.

IREOS-Queer Community Service Center *Via de' Serragli 3, Oltrano (055 216 907/ireos@freemail.it).* **Open** 5-8pm Mon-Thur, Sat. **Map** p341 C1/D1.
Formerly part of ARCI Gay/Lesbica, Ireos hosts a social open house every Wednesday evening, offers referrals for HIV testing, psychological counselling and self-help groups. It also organises hikes and outings. All Santa Maria Novella station buses pass nearby.

Queer Nation Holidays *Via del Moro 95r, Santa Maria Novella (055 265 4587/fax 055 265 4560/www.queernationholidays.com).* **Open** 9.30am-7.30 pm Mon-Fri, 10am-6pm Sat. **Credit** MC, V. **Map** p314 B2.
Queer Nation Holidays can organise individual and group travel. It also make referrals to other gay/lesbian organisations to aid the traveller.

Health

Emergency healthcare is available free for all travellers through the Italian national health system. EU citizens are entitled to most treatment for free, though many specialised medicines, examinations and tests will be charged for. To get treatment you need an E111 form (*see p288*). For hospital treatment, go to one of the casualty departments listed below. If you want to see a GP, go to the state health centre (**ASL**) for the district where you are staying, taking your E111 form with you. The ASLs are listed in the phone book and they usually open 9am-1pm and 2-7pm Monday to Friday.

Consulates (*see above*) can provide lists of English-speaking doctors, dentists and clinics, and they are also listed in the English Yellow Pages (available for purchase from larger bookshops and online at www.paginegialle.it).

Non-EU citizens are advised to take out private health insurance before they go.

Accident & emergency

If you need urgent medical care, it's best to go to the *pronto soccorso* (casualty) department of one of the hospitals listed below; they're open 24 hours daily, or call 118 for an ambulance (*ambulanza*).

To find a doctor on call in your area (emergencies only) call 118. For a night (8pm-8am) or all-day Sunday emergency doctor's home visit call the Guardia Medica for your area (west central Florence 055 287 788; east central Florence 055 233 9456).

Santa Maria Nuova *Piazza Santa Maria Nuova 1, Duomo & Around (055 27581).* **Map** p315 B4.
The most central hospital in Florence. There is also a 24-hour pharmacy directly outside.

Ospedale di Careggi *Viale Morgagni 85, Outside the City Gates (055 427 7111). Bus 2, 8, 14C.*

Ospedale Torregalli *Via Torregalli 3, Outside the City Gates (055 719 2447). Bus 83.*

Ospedale Meyer (Children) *Via Luca Giordano 13, Outside the City Gates (055 56621). Bus 11, 17.*

Ospedale Santa Maria Annunziata (known as Ponte a Nicchieri) *Via Antella 58, Bagno a Ripoli, Outside the City Gates (055 24961). Bus 32.*

Complementary medicine

Most pharmacies sell homeopathic and other complementary medicines, which are quite commonly used in Italy. Herbalists sell herbal but not homeopathic medicines; some can refer you to alternative health practitioners.

Ambulatorio Santa Maria Novella *Piazza Santa Maria Novella 24, Santa Maria Novella (055 280 143).* **Open** 3-7.30pm Mon; 9am-1pm, 3-7.30pm Tue-Fri. **No credit cards. Map** p314 B2.
Ambulatorio Santa Maria Novella is a large group practice where several homeopathic doctors have consulting rooms and offer a range of alternative health services. Some English is spoken. It's best to call first for an appointment.

Antica Farmacia Sodini *Via dei Banchi 18-20r, Santa Maria Novella (055 211 159).* **Open** 9am-1pm, 4pm-8pm Mon-Sat. **No credit cards. Map** p314 B2.
The English-speaking staff at this homeopathic pharmacy are very helpful. They carry a huge range of medicines and make up prescriptions as well as giving advice.

Contraception & abortion

Condoms and other forms of contraception are widely available in pharmacies and some supermarkets. If you need further assistance, the **Consultorio Familiare** (family-planning clinic) at your local ASL state health centre (in the phone book under **Azienda Sanitaria di Firenze**) provides free advice and information, though for an examination or prescription you need an E111 form or insurance. An alternative is to go to a private clinic like those run by AIED.

The morning-after pill is sold legally in Italy; it must be taken within 72 hours, and to obtain it you need to get a prescription, *see below*.

Abortion is legal in Italy and is performed in hospitals, but the private clinics listed below can give consultations and references.

Santa Chiara *Piazza Independenza 11, San Lorenzo (055 496 312/475 239).* **Open** 8am-7pm daily by appointment.
This private San Lorenzo clinic offers gynaecological examinations and physicals. Call for an appointment.

AIED *Via Ricasoli 10, San Marco (055 215 237).* **Open** 3-6.30pm Mon-Fri. **Map** p315 B4.
The clinics run by this private organisation provide help and information on contraception and related matters and medical care at low cost. Treatment is of a high standard and service is often faster than in state clinics. An examination will usually cost something in the region of €40 plus €15 compulsory membership, payable on the first visit and then valid for a year.

Dentists

The following dentists speak English. Call for an appointment.

Dr Maria Peltonen Portman *Via Teatina 2, Duomo & Around (055 218 594).* **Open** 9.30am-6.30pm Mon-Fri. **Map** p314 B3.

Dr Sandro Cosi *Via Pellicceria 10, Duomo & Around (055 214 238/ 0335 332 055).* **Open** 9am-1pm Mon-Fri. **Map** p314 C3.

Doctors

Dr Stephen Kerr *Via Porta Rossa 1, Duomo & Around (055 288 055/0335 836 1682).* **Open** *Surgery by appointment* 9am-1pm Mon-Fri. *Drop-in clinic* 3-5pm Mon-Fri. **Credit** AmEx, MC, V. **Map** p314 C3.
This English-speaking GP practises privately in Florence. He charges €30-€60 (standard charge €40) for a consultation in his surgery.

IAMAT (Associated Medical Studio) *Via Lorenzo il Magnifico 59, Outside the City Gates (24hr line 055 475 411). Bus 8, 13.* **Open** *Clinic* 11am-noon, 5-6pm Mon-Fri; 11am-noon Sat.
A private medical service that organises home visits by doctors. Catering particularly for foreigners, it will send an English-speaking GP or specialist out to you within an hour and a half for between €65 and €100. IAMAT also runs a clinic.

Hospitals

For emergencies, *see p286*.

One of the obvious anxieties involved with falling ill when you're abroad is the language problem. If you need a translator to help out at the hospital, contact:

AVO (Association of Hospital Volunteers) *055 425 0126 (24hrs)/234 4567 (24hrs).* **Open** office hours 4-6pm Mon, Wed, Fri; 10am-noon Tue, Thur.
A group of volunteer interpreters who help out with explanations to doctors and hospital staff in 22 languages. They also give support and advice.

Opticians

For eye-tests and prescription glasses and contact lenses, *see p147*.

Pharmacies

Pharmacies (*farmacia*), which are identified by a red or green cross hanging outside, function semi-officially as mini-clinics with staff able to give informal medical advice and suggest non-prescription medicines. Normal opening hours are 8.30am-1pm and 4-8pm Monday to Friday, 8.30am-1pm Saturday, but many central pharmacies are open all day. At other times there's a duty rota system. A list by the door of all pharmacies indicates the nearest one open outside normal hours, also published in local papers. At duty pharmacies there's a surcharge of €2.60 per client (not per item) when only the special duty counter is open – usually midnight-8.30am. The following pharmacies provide a 24-hour service without a supplement for night service.

Farmacia all'Insegna del Moro *Piazza San Giovanni 20r, Duomo & Around (055 211 343).* **Open** 24hrs daily. **Credit** V. **Map** p314 B3.
Some English spoken.

Farmacia Comunale no.13 *Inside Santa Maria Novella train station, Santa Maria Novella (055 216 761/055 289 435).* **Open** 24hrs daily. **No credit cards. Map** p314 A2.
English spoken.

Farmacia Molteni *Via Calzaiuoli 7r, Duomo & Around (055 215 472/289 490).* **Open** 24hrs daily. **Credit** AmEx, MC, V. **Map** p314 C3.
English spoken.

Prescriptions

Prescriptions are required for most medicines. Some prescription medicines are free, for others you will be charged the full price.

STDs, HIV & AIDS

Clinica Dermatologica *Piazza Brunelleschi 4, San Marco (055 275 8684).* **Open** 8am-noon Mon, Wed, Thur, Fri; 8-11am Tue, Sat. **Map** p315 A4.
Clinica Dermatologica carries out examinations, tests, treatment and counselling for all sexually transmitted diseases including HIV and AIDS. Some services are free,while others are state-subsidised. An examination costs €18.59. Some staff speak English.

AIDS centres

Ambulatorio Malattie Infettive, Ospedale di Careggi *Viale Morgagni, Outside the City Gates (055 427 9425/426). Bus 2, 8, 14C.* **Open** 9am-12.30pm, 3-6pm Mon-Fri; 9am-12.30pm Sat.
AIDS centre with info, advice and testing. Call ahead for an appointment. A little English is spoken.

Consultorio per la Salute Omosessuale *Via San Zanobi 54r, San Lorenzo (055 476 557).*

Run by the ARCI gay organisation, this centre provides various services relating to AIDS and HIV. Telephone counselling is offered from 4pm-8pm Monday to Friday, and counsellors are also available in person. AIDS tests are carried out on Wednesdays 4pm to 5.30pm. Staffed by volunteers, these services are free. English spoken.

Helplines

Alcoholics Anonymous *St James' Church, via Rucellai 9, Santa Maria Novella (055 294 417).* **Map** p314 A1.
This English-speaking branch of AA is affiliated to the American Episcopal Church. Meetings are held on Tuesdays and Thursdays at 1.30pm and Saturdays at 5pm. These are also open to anyone with drug-related problems.

Drogatel *Freephone 840 002 244.* **Open** 9am-8pm daily.
A national help centre for drug-related problems. It also gives advice on alcohol-related problems.

Samaritans *06 7045 4444/ 06 7045 4445.*
Staffed by native English-speakers.

ID

In Italy you are required by law to carry photo ID at all times. You will be asked to produce it if you're stopped by traffic police (who will demand your driving licence, which you must have on you whenever you are in charge of a motor vehicle). ID will also be required when you check into a hotel (and may be kept for the duration of your stay).

Insurance

EU nationals are entitled to reciprocal medical care in Italy, provided they have an E111 form. This form is widely available in the UK from health centres, post offices and Social Security offices. This will cover you for emergencies, but involves having to deal with the Italian state health system, which can, at times, be overwhelmingly frustrating. The E111 will only cover partial costs of medicines.

For short-term visitors it's really advisable to get private travel insurance to cover you for a broad number of evenutualities. Non-EU citizens should take out comprehensive medical insurance with a reputable company before leaving home.

Visitors should also take out adequate property insurance before setting off for Italy. If you rent a car, motorcycle or moped (unless your home insurance covers you), make sure you pay the extra for full insurance and sign the collision damage waiver before taking off.

Internet & email

Italy started late, but now it's going all out to catch up with the rest of the Western world in getting wired. Even most budget hotels will allow you to plug your modem into their phone system and the more upmarket establishments will probably have dataports in every bedroom. Some Italian phone plugs are different from US and UK versions, though in modern hotels the standard US Bell socket is often used. As usual, it's best to check in advance with your hotel.

A number of Italian providers offer free internet access. These include **Libero** (www.libero.it), **Tiscali** (www.tiscalinet.it), **Kataweb** (www.kataweb.com), **Telecom Italia** (www.tin.it) and **Wind** (www.inwind.it).

Internet access

There are internet points in all areas of the city centre, so you'll certainly never be stuck for somewhere to surf and check emails. Most places charge around €5 per hour, and there's often discounts offered for students. Remember to take ID though, as its needed to register, even as a guest user.

Internet Train *Via dei Benci 36r, Santa Croce (055 263 8555).* **Open** 10am-midnight Mon-Sat; 3-11pm Sun. **Credit** MC, V. **Map** p315 B5.
Internet Train was the first internet shop in Italy. It started off with four PCs and now has 14 shops in Florence. The chain has friendly English-speaking staff.

Intotheweb *Via de' Conti 23r, San Lorenzo (055 264 5628).* **Open** 10am-midnight daily. **Credit** MC, V. **Map** p314 B3.
Friendly centre with 18 PCs and Macs. It also sells international phone cards, sends and receives faxes and rents out mobile phones.

Netgate *Via Sant'Egidio 10r, Santa Croce (055 234 7967/www.thenetgate.it).* **Open** *Summer* 11am-9.45pm Mon-Sat. *Winter* 11am-9pm Mon-Sat; 2-8pm Sun. **Map** p315 B5.
A spacious work centre with 35 computers. For more branches, see the website.

Virtual Office *Via Faenza 49r, San Lorenzo (055 264 5560).* **Open** 10am-midnight Mon-Wed; 10am-1am Thur-Sat; noon-1am Sun. **Credit** MC, V. **Map** p314 A3.
Webcams on every PC, DVD players and a range of office services on offer, including shipping and money transfers. Also runs internet courses.

Language

English is spoken in many central shops, and all main hotels and restaurants, though in some family-run shops and restaurants, and in the smaller villages of Tuscany, it may be trickier to communicate. Taking a phrase book is a good idea. For basic Italian vocabulary, *see p297*.

Left luggage

There's a left luggage point in Santa Maria Novella train station on platform 16.

Legal help

Your first stop should be your embassy or consulate (*see p286*). Staff will be able to supply you with a comprehensive list of English-speaking lawyers.

Libraries

British Institute Library *Lungarno Guicciardini 9, Oltrarno (055 2677 8270/fax 055 2677 8252/library@britishinstitute.it).* **Open** 10am-6.30pm Mon-Fri. **Map** p314 C3.

The British Institute's library requires an annual membership fee (€56.50, students €38.50), but offers a reading room that overlooks the Arno, an extensive collection of art history books and Italian literature, and well-informed staff.

Kunsthistorisches Institut in Florenz *Via G Giusti 44, Santa Croce (055 249 111/fax 055 249 1155).* **Open** 9am-8pm Mon-Fri. **Map** p315 A6.

One of the largest collections of art history books in Florence is held by the German Institute and is available to students. You'll need a letter of presentation and a summary of your research project.

Biblioteca Marucelliana *Via Cavour 43-5, San Marco (055 27221/marucelliana@cesit1.unifi.it).* **Open** 9am-7pm Mon-Fri; 9am-1pm Sat. **Map** p315 A4.

A diverse range of books including some in English. ID is needed.

Lost property

For property lost anywhere other than in planes, trains and taxis, contact the council's lost property office (*below*). For lost passports, contact the police (*see p290*).

Ufficio Oggetti Ritrovati *Via Circondaria 19, Outside the City Gates (055 328 3942/3943). Bus 23, 33.* **Open** 9am-noon Mon-Sat.

Airports

Vespucci Airport: 055 306 1302; Pisa's **Galilei Airport**: 050 44325; Bologna's **Marconi Airport**: 051 647 9615.

Buses

Anything left on a bus should turn up at the lost property office (*see above*).

Trains

FS/Santa Maria Novella (SMN) Station *Interno Stazione SMN, Santa Maria Novella (055 235 2190).* **Open** 6am-midnight daily. **Map** p314 A2.

Articles found on state railways in the Florence area are sent to this office on platform 16, next to the left luggage. Minimal English.

Taxis

If you leave something in a cab, call the taxi company quoting the car's code (place name and number) if you can remember it. Or contact the *vigili urbani* police (055 212 290), where anything left in cabs will be taken by honest drivers.

Media

Magazines

Many newsstands sell *Time*, *Newsweek*, the *Economist* and glossy English-language magazines. For Italian-speakers, Italian magazines worth checking out are *Panorama* and *Espresso*, weekly current affairs and general interest rags whose full-frontal style covers do little justice to the high-level journalism and hot-issue coverage. There are also some useful booklets with listings of events in Florence:

Firenze Spettacolo

Monthly listings and local interest mag with an English-language section called Florencescope.

Florence Concierge Information

Found at tourist offices and most hotels, this freebie gives events, useful information, timetables and such like in English.

Newspapers

Foreign dailies

Many news-stands and newsagents sell foreign papers, which usually arrive the next day (the same evening in summer, except Sundays). You'll find the widest range around piazza del Duomo, piazza della Repubblica, via Tornabuoni and SMN station.

Italian dailies

Only one Italian in ten buys a daily newspaper, so the press has little of the clout of other European countries, and the paper is generally a simple vehicle for information rather than a forum of pressure for change. Most papers publish comprehensive listings for local events. Sports coverage in the dailies is extensive and thorough, but if you're not sated there are the mass-circulation sports papers **Corriere dello Sport** and **La Gazzetta dello Sport**.

La Nazione

Selling some 160,000 copies daily, this is the most popular newspaper in Tuscany. Founded in the mid 19th century by Bettino Ricasoli, it's also one of Italy's oldest. Basically right-wing and gossipy, it consists of three sections (national, sport and local). Each province has its own edition.

La Repubblica

One of the youngest of Italy's major papers. It's centre-left, with strong coverage of the Mafia and Vatican issues, but has an unfortunate tendency to pad the news section out with waffle and gossip. The Tuscan edition has about 20 pages dedicated to local and provincial news.

Il Giornale

Owned by the brother of Berlusconi it takes the expected government line. The Florence edition has a section dedicated to local news.

L'Unità

The media voice-piece for the far left.

Radio

Controradio (93.6 MHz)

Dub, hip hop, progressive, drum 'n' bass and indie rock feature heavily on this station.

Nova Radio (101.5 MHz)

No ads: run by volunteers and committed to social issues, Nova Radio broadcasts a very good mixture of jazz, soul, blues, reggae, world music, hip hop and rap.

Radio Diffusione Firenze (102.7 MHz)

Radio station playing mainstream pop, house and club music.

Radio Montebeni (108.5 MHz)

Classical music only.

Television

Italy has six major networks. Of these, three are Berlusconi-owned Mediaset channels; **Italia 6** shows familiar US series, Brazilian soaps, Japanese cartoons and adventure films; **Rete 4** spews out an awful lot of cheap gameshows and *Colombo* repeats but also shows top nature documentaries; and **Canale 5** is the top dog, with the best films, quiz shows, live shows and the most popular programme on Italian TV, the scandal-busting, satirical *Striscia la Notizia*. Programmes are riddled with ad breaks. **RAI** channels, which are also basically controlled by Berlusconi, are known for their better-quality programming but generally much less slick presenting, and there is still a relentless stream of quiz shows and high-kicking bikini-clad bimbettes. When these have bored you, there are numerous local stations featuring cleaning demos, dial-a-fortune-teller (surprisingly popular), prolonged adverts for slimming machines and late-night trashy soft porn.

Sky and **CNN** broadcast news in English in the early hours of the morning on **TMC**. The French channel Antenne 2 is also accessible in Tuscany.

Of the many satellite and cable TV subscription channels, the best are Stream and Telepiù. Some of their packages include BBC and major US channels.

Money

On 1 January 2002 the Italian lira made way for the **euro** (€), although some shops still pointedly accept old lire notes. There are euro banknotes for €5, €10, €20, €100, €200 and €500, and coins worth €1 and €2 plus 1, 2, 5, 10, 20 and 50 cents (c). €1 is equivalent to L1,936.27 old Italian lire. The introduction of the euro led to significant price increases in most sectors, and bare-faced speculation in some, although the ensuing furore and consumer strikes do appear to have 're-aligned' some prices to a degree.

ATMs

Most major banks have 24-hour cashpoint (Bancomat) machines, and the vast majority of these also accept cards with the Maestro and Cirrus symbols. To access the cashpoint lobby, you have to insert your card in the machine outside. Most machines will dispense a daily limit of €250. Your home bank will make a charge.

Banks

Bank opening hours are generally from 8.20am to 1.20pm and from 2.35pm to 3.35pm Monday to Friday. All banks are closed on public holidays and staff work reduced hours the day before a holiday, usually closing at around 11am.

Expect long queues even for simple transactions, and don't be surprised if the bank wants to photocopy your passport, driving licence and last exam essay as proof of ID. They even try to photocopy credit and debit cards in some banks – refuse if this happens. A small number of banks will give cash advances on credit cards, but it's always best to ask before joining the queue. Branches of most banks are found around piazza della Repubblica.

Bureaux de change

Changing your money in a bank usually gets you a better rate than in a private bureau de change (*cambio*) and will often be better than back home, but if you need to change money out of banking hours there's no shortage of *cambi*. Commission rates vary considerably: you can pay from nothing to €5 for each transaction. Watch out for 'No Commission' signs; the exchange rate at these places will almost certainly be worse. Main post offices also have exchange bureaux, where commission is €2.50 for all cash transactions (maximum €1,000). Travellers' cheques not accepted.

Some large hotels also offer an exchange service, but again, the rate is almost certainly worse than in a bank. Always take ID for any financial transaction. Many city-centre bank branches have automatic cash exchange machines, which accept notes in good condition in most currencies.

Agency Prime Link
Via Panicale 18r, San Lorenzo (055 291 275). **Open** 9.30am-1.30pm, 3-7pm daily. **Map** p314 A3.
The quickest if not the cheapest way to send money across the world.

American Express
Via Dante Alighieri 14r, Duomo & Around (055 50981). Bus 23. **Open** 9am-5.30pm Mon-Fri; 9am-12.30pm Sat. **Map** p315 B4.
Also has a travel agency.

Change Underground
Piazza della Stazione 14, interno 37, Santa Maria Novella (055 291 312). **Open** 9am-7pm Mon-Sat; 9am-1.30pm Sun in summer. **Map** p314 A2.
In the mall underneath the station.

Thomas Cook
Lungarno Acciaiuoli 4/8r, Duomo & Around (055 290 278). **Open** 9am-7pm Mon-Sat; 9.30am-5pm Sun. **Map** p314 C3.
One of the few exchange offices open on a Sunday. No commission for cash withdrawal via MasterCard or Visa.

Credit cards

Italians have an enduring fondness for cash, but nearly all hotels of two stars and above and most shops and restaurants now accept at least some of the major credit cards, though surprisingly few attractions do.

Lost/stolen

Most lines are freephone (800) numbers, have English-speaking staff and are open 24 hours daily.

American Express card emergencies 06 72282/gold card holders 06 722 807 385.
Diners Club 800 864 064
Eurocard/CartaSi (including MasterCard and Visa) 800 018 548
MasterCard 800 870 866
Visa 800 877 232

Tax

Sales tax (**IVA**) is applied to all purchases and services at 1%, 4% and 20% in an ascending scale of luxury, but is almost always included in the price given. At some luxury hotels it's added on, but prices will be clearly stated as *escluso IVA*.

By law, all non-EU residents are entitled to an IVA refund on purchases of €150 and over at shops participating in the 'Tax-free shopping' scheme, identified by a purple sticker. On presentation of your passport, they will give you a 'cheque' that can be cashed at the airport desk (look for signs after Customs) on your way home. You'll need to show your passport and the unused goods, and there's a three-month time limit. Sadly, IVA paid on hotel bills cannot be reclaimed.

Travellers' cheques

Travellers' cheques can be changed at all banks and bureaux de change but are only accepted as payment (in any major currency) by larger shops, hotels and restaurants.

Police

Italian police forces are divided into four colour-coded units. The *vigili urbani* and *polizia municipale* (municipal police) wear navy blue. The *vigili* deal with all traffic matters within the city, and the *polizia municipale* with petty crime. The two forces responsible for dealing with crime are the *polizia di stato* (state police), who also wear blue jackets but have pale grey trousers, and the normally black-clad *carabinieri*, part of the army. Their roles are essentially the same. The *guardia di finanza* (financial police) wear grey and have little to do with tourists.

In an emergency go to the nearest *carabinieri post* (*commissariato*) or police station (*questura*), in the phone book. If you have had something stolen, say you want to report a *furto*. A *denuncia* (statement) will be taken, which you'll need for an insurance claim. Lost or stolen passports should also be reported to your embassy or consulate.

Comando Provinciale Carabinieri *Borgo Ognissanti 48, Santa Maria Novella (055 2061).* **Open** 24hrs daily. **Map** p314 B1.
A *carabinieri post* near the town centre; the best place to report the loss or theft of personal property.

Questura Centrale
Via Zara 2, San Lorenzo (055 49771). **Open** 24hrs daily. *Ufficio Denuncie* 8.30am-8pm daily. To report a crime, go to the *Ufficio Denuncie*, where you will be asked to fill in a form.

Tourist Aid Police
Via Pietrapiana 24r, Santa Croce (055 203 911). **Open** 8.30am-7.30pm Mon-Fri; 8.30am-1.30pm Sat. **Map** p315 B6.
Interpreters are on hand to help report thefts, lost property and any other problems.

Postal services

Improvements have been made recently in Italy's notoriously unreliable postal service and you can now be more or less sure that the letter you sent will arrive in reasonable time, though some problems still remain with receiving mail from abroad.

Stamps (*francobolli*) can be bought at *tabacchi* or post offices. A letter or postcard of 20 grams or less to any EU destination costs 41c; to the US 52c. Most post boxes are red and have two slots, *Per la Città* (for Florence) and *Tutte le altre Destinazioni* (everywhere else). There are also blue post boxes with the EU star symbol for European Union mail only. A letter takes about five days to reach the UK, eight to the US. Mail can be sent *raccomandata* (registered €2.17 extra) or *assicurata* (insured for up to €51.65, costs €5.16) from post offices.

The new equivalent to first-class post (*posta prioritaria*) generally fulfils its delivery promise of within 24 hours in Italy, three days for EU countries and four or five for the rest of the world. A letter weighing 20 grams or less going to Italy or any EU country costs 62c by *posta prioritaria*; outside the EU the cost is 77c; and special stamps can be bought at post offices and *tabacchi*.

Heavier mail is charged according to weight. A one kilogram parcel to the UK costs €8.06 (air mail); €16.53 to the US. Italian postal charges are notoriously complicated, so be prepared for variations.

For guaranteed fast delivery, use a courier or the SDA Italian post office courier service (*see p283*).

Postal information *160.* **Open** 8am-7pm Mon-Fri; 8am-1pm Sat.
This phoneline (some English spoken) answers queries on the postal system. A call costs 30c.

Post offices

Local post offices (ufficio postale) in each district generally open from 8.15am to 1.30pm Monday to Friday and 8.15am to 12.30pm on Saturdays. The main post office has longer opening hours and a range of additional services.

Posta Centrale *Via Pellicceria 3, Duomo & Around (055 27361).* **Open** 8.15am-7pm Mon-Fri; 8.15am-12.30pm Sat. **Map** p315 A4.
This is the main city post office. A vast building on two floors, it's always busy and offers a full range of postal and telegram services.

Other post offices

Via Cavour 71A, San Marco (055 463 501). **Open** 8.15am-1.30pm Mon-Fri; 8.15am-12.30pm Sat. **Map** p314 C3.
Via Barbadori 37r, Oltrarno (055 288 175). **Open** 8.15am-1.30pm Mon-Fri; 8.15am-12.30pm Sat. **Map** p314 C3.

Poste restante

Poste restante (general delivery) letters (in Italian, *fermo posta*) should be sent to the main post office (*see above*), addressed to **Fermo Posta Centrale, Firenze**. You need a passport to collect mail and you may have to pay a small charge. Mail can also be sent to any **Mail Boxes Etc** branch (*see p283*).

Religion

There are Roman Catholic churches all over the city, and a few churches still sing mass. Catholic mass is held in English at Santa Maria del Fiore (the **Duomo**) on Saturday afternoons at 5pm and at the **Chiesa dell' Ospedale San Giovanni di Dio** (Borgo Ognissanti 20) on Sundays and holidays at 10am.

American Episcopal Church

St James, Via Rucellai 9, Santa Maria Novella (055 294 417). **Services** (in English) 9am, 11am Sun. **Map** p314 A1.

Anglican

St Mark's, Via Maggio 16, Oltrarno (055 294 764). **Services** 9am (Low Mass), 10.30am (Sung Mass) Sun; 6pm (Low Mass) Thur; 8pm (Low Mass) Fri. **Map** p314 C2.

Islamic

Associazione Islamica, Via Tagliamento 3A, Outside the City Gates (055 711 648). Bus 23, 31 (15mins from centre).

Jewish

Comunita Ebraica, Via Farini 4, Santa Croce (055 245 252). **Services** 8.30/8.45am Sat. Call for details of Fri & Sat evening services; times vary. **Map** p315 B6.

Methodist

Chiesa Metodista, Via dei Benci 9, Santa Croce. **Services** 11am Sun. **Map** p315 C4.

Safety & security

Crime is on the increase in Florence, causing great concern among residents, but for visitors the main risk is from pickpockets and bag-snatchers. Buses, shops, bars and other crowded areas are petty criminals' hunting grounds. As in any city, take the usual precautions:

- Don't keep wallets in back pockets. This is a pickpockets' favourite swipe, especially on buses and public transport.
- Wear shoulder bags diagonally and facing away from the road to minimise the risk of *scippi* – bag-snatching from mopeds.
- Never leave bags on tables or the backs of chairs in bars.
- Keep an eye on valuables while trying on clothes.

Also watch out for 'baby-gangs' of children who hang around the tourist spots and create a distraction by flapping newspaper or card while trying to slip their hands into bags or pockets. If you are approached, keep walking, keep calm and hang on to your valuables.

Serious street crime is rare in Florence, and it remains a relatively safe city to walk in, but take care at night. Stick to the main well-lit streets and, lone women particularly, avoid the station area.

Smoking

Cigarettes are on sale at *tabacchi* and *bar tabacchi*; both are recognisable by the blue/black and white sign outside. Smoking is not permitted in any public offices or on public transport. There is also a law that bans smoking in all public places without adequate air filtering, but this is widely ignored: you're likely to find people smoking in food shops, banks, even hospitals.

Study

With over 20 US university programmes and countless language schools and art courses, many of which have international reputations, the city's student population rivals its residents' at some times of the year. To study in Florence, you will need a *permesso di soggiorno per studio*. The same requirements apply as for the *permesso di soggiorno* (*see p296*), plus a guarantee that your medical bills will be paid (an E111 form will do), evidence that you can support yourself and a letter from the educational institution.

Art, design & restoration courses

Il Bisonte *Via San Niccolo 24, Oltrarno (055 234 7215).* **Map** p315 D5.

Located among the artisans' workshops in the former stables of Palazzo Serristori, il Bisonte has specialist courses and theoretical/practical seminars in the techniques of etching and printing by hand. Contact the school for a detailed programme of courses.

Charles H Cecil Studios
Borgo San Frediano 68, Oltrarno (tel/fax 055 285 102). **Map** p314 C1.
The church of San Rafaello Arcangelo was converted into a studio complex in the early 19th century. It now houses one of the more charismatic of Florence's art schools, Charles H Cecil Studios, which is heavily frequented by Brits. It gives a thorough training in the classical techniques of drawing and oil painting. Twice a week the school hosts life-drawing classes for the general public. For a bit of extra cash, models are always needed at the school either for portraits or as nude figure models.

L'Istituto per l'Arte e Il Restauro
Palazzo Spinelli, Borgo Santa Croce 10, Santa Croce (055 246 001/fax 055 234 3701/ www.spinelli.it). **Map** p315 C5.
Widely considered one of the best art restoration schools in Italy, Palazzo Spinelli offers a multitude of courses in the restoration of frescoes, paintings, furniture, gilt objects, ceramics, stone, paper and glass. Courses last between one and three years. One-month courses are held from July to September in the same disciplines.

Oro e Colore
Via della Chiesa 25, Oltrarno (tel/fax 055 229 040/www.oroecolore.com). **Map** p314 D1.
Month- to year-long courses in art restoration, gold leaf restoration and other techniques. No previous experience is needed; however, places on courses are limited and are all taught in Italian.

Studio Art Center International (SACI)
Via San Gallo 30, San Lorenzo (055 486 164/fax 55 486 230/info@saci-florence.org). **Map** p315 A4.
SACI offers five specific credit programmes for graduates and undergraduates. These include both academic and practical courses in the arts, ranging from museology to batik design. There is an entry requirement for certain courses.

Università Internazionale dell'Arte *Villa il Ventaglio, Via delle Forbici 24-6, Outside the City Gates (055 570 216/fax 055 570 508/www.vps.it/propart/uia). Bus 7.*
Courses at the university cover restoration and preservation, museum and gallery management and art criticism.

Language classes

There are no end of language and culture courses in Florence, including many intensive one- or two-month courses, which should provide an adequate everyday grasp of the language. Prices refer to a standard four-week course with four hours' tuition a day.

ABC Centro di Lingua e Cultura Italian
Via dei Rustici 7,Santa Croce (055 212 001/fax 055 212 112/ www.abcschool.com). **Price** €538. **Map** p315 C4.
Language teaching at six levels and preparatory courses for the entrance exam to the University of Florence.

British Institute
Piazza Strozzi 2, Duomo & Around (055 267 78200/fax 055 2677 8222/info@british institute.it/ www.britishinstitute.it). **Map** p314 B3.

Centro Linguistico Italiano Dante Alighieri
Piazza della Repubblica 5 (055 210 808/fax 055 287 828). **Price** €620, plus €80 enrolment fee. **Map** p315 D4.
Eleven language levels; opera and literature courses.

Library & Cultural Centre
Lungarno Guicciardini 9, Oltrarno (055 2677 8270). **Price** €805. **Map** p314 C2.
Short courses in Italian language, history of art, drawing and cooking.

Istituto Lorenzo de' Medici
Via Faenza 43, San Lorenzo (055 287 360/fax 055 239 8920/ldm @lorenzodemedici.it). **Price** €590. **Map** p314 A3.
Four different courses in Italian as well as classes in cooking, Italian cinema and art history.

Scuola Leonardo da Vinci
Via Bufalini 3, Duomo & Around (055 294 420/fax 055 294 820/www.scuolaleonardo.com). **Price** €500 plus €70 enrolment. **Map** p315 B4.
Versatile languages courses for all levels. Classes in history of art, fashion, drawing, design, cooking and wine are also on offer.

Scuola Machiavelli
Piazza Santo Spirito 4, Oltrarno (055 239 6966/280 800/www. centromachiavelli.it). **Price** €420 plus €30 enrolment fee. **Map** p314 D1.
One of the smaller language schools in the city, this co-op offers Italian, pottery, fresco, mosaic, *trompe l'œil* and book-binding classes.

Universities

To study alongside Florentine undergraduates, contact an Italian consulate to apply to do a *corso singolo*, or one year of study at the University of Florence. Register at the *Ufficio per Studenti Stranieri* at the beginning of November. The fees for a *corso singolo* (maximum five subjects) are approximately €1,100. To complete a degree course, you must have studied to university level. For details, see www.unifi.it. There are also exchange programmes for EU students.

Several US universities, including Georgetown, Middlebury, Sarah Lawrence, New York, Gonzaga and Syracuse, have Florence outposts open to students from any US university for the semester and summer courses.

Università di Firenze: Centro di Cultura per I Stranieri
Via Vittorio Emanuele 64, Outside the City Gates (055 472 139/www.unifi.it/ccs). Bus 4, 12 ,13, 25. **Open** 9am-noon Mon-Fri.
Offers language and cultural courses.

Useful organisations

Student Point *Viale Gramsci 9, Outside the City Gates (055 234 2857/fax 055 234 6212). Bus 8, 12, 13.* **Open** 2-6pm Mon, Wed, Fri.
The tourist board has established this office to help foreign students with orientation in Florence. Staff advise on accommodation, getting a ***permesso di soggiorno***, study courses, doctors and events.

Council of International Education Exchange (CIEE)
7 Custom House Street, 3rd Floor, Portland, Maine, ME 04101 (1 800 40/1 207 553 7600/fax 1 207 553 7699/www.ciee.org).

Institute of International Education *809 UN Plaza, New York, NY 10017-3580, USA (212 883 8200).*

Italian Cultural Institute
39 Belgrave Square, London SW1X 8NX, UK (0207 235 1461/ fax 0207 235 4618).

Telephones

Although competition has led to some price cuts, the biggest and most commonly used Italian telephone company, Telecom Italia, still operates one of the most expensive phone systems in Europe, particularly for international calls. Tariffs are higher if you're calling from a public phone and usually higher still from a hotel: you're usually better off buying an international phone card, though they don't offer anything approaching the same level of discount as in the UK and US. Calling from a phone centre costs the same as from a payphone, but is more convenient.

If you are staying for any length of time, there are numerous cheap phone companies that extremely competitive rates, for example Ultranet and Tele 2.

Dialling & codes

The international code for Italy is 39. To dial in from other countries, preface it with the exit code: 00 in the UK and 011 in the US. All normal Florence numbers begin with the area code 055. The code for Siena is 0577, for Pisa 050. As with all Italian codes these must always be used in full, even when you are calling from within the same area, and when dialling internationally.

To make an international call from Florence, dial 00, then the country code (Australia 61; Canada 1; Irish Republic 353; New Zealand 64; United Kingdom 44; United States 1), followed by the area code (for calls to the UK, omit the initial zero) and individual number. The same pattern works to mobile phones.

All numbers beginning 800 are free lines (*numero verde*). Until recently, these began 167: you may still find old-style numbers listed, in which case replace the prefix with 800 or call 12 – directory enquiries – for the new number. For numbers that begin 840 and 848 (147 and 148 until recently) you will be charged one unit only, regardless of where you're calling from or how long the call lasts. These numbers can be called from within Italy only; some only function within one phone district.

Public phones

Since the popular mobile phone revolution, many public phones in Florence have disappeared, especially in less central areas, and those that remain tend to be in areas where the traffic makes it impossible to hear. However, many bars have payphones. Most public phones only accept phone cards with magnetic strips (*schede telefoniche*); a few also accept major credit cards and on rare occasions some only accept coins. *Schede telefoniche* are available from *tabacchi*, some newsstands and some bars, as are the pre-paid phone cards offering access via an 800 number to both domestic and international calls.

To use a card phone, lift the receiver and wait for the tone, then insert the card (with the perforated corner torn off) and dial. To use a coin phone, lift the receiver and insert the minimum then dial. There are no beeps to warn you that your money is about to run out, so it's best to overdo the coins. Unused coins will be refunded, but change isn't given from half-used coins so keep small ones in hand.

Operator services

To make a reverse charge (collect) call, dial 170 for the international operator in Italy. To be connected to the operator in the country you want to call, dial 172 followed by a four-digit code for the country (hence 172 00 44 for the UK and 172 00 1 for the US) and you'll be connected directly to an operator in that country. If you are calling from a phone box, you will need to insert a coin, which will be refunded after your call.

The following services operate 24 hours daily (calls are charged):

Operator and **Italian directory enquiries** *12.*
International operator *170.*
International directory enquiries *176.*
Problems on national calls *182.*
Problems on international calls *176.*
Wake-up calls *114*; an automatic message will ask you to dial in the time you want your call, with four digits on a 24-hour clock, followed by your phone number.
Tourist information *110.*

Phone centres

Telecom Italia *Via Cavour 21r, San Lorenzo.* **Open** 8am-9.45pm daily. **Map** p315 A4.
At this Telecom Italia office, you are allocated a booth and can either use a phone card or pay cash at the desk after you have finished making all your calls. It also has phone books for all of Europe, information on telephone charges and phone cards.

Telephone directories

All hotels and most bars and restaurants have phone books and Yellow Pages (if they're not obviously on display, ask to see the *elenco telefonico* or *pagine gialle*). Telecom Italia has a useful website (www.telecomitalia.it) with an online directory enquiries service under Info 412.

Mobile phones

Italian mobile phone numbers begin with 3 (no zero).

Pay-as-you-go mobiles can be bought from any of the many phone shops from around €120, including the SIM card and €5 of calls. Top-up cards are available from all bar *tabacchi* and some news-stands; either call the number given on the card, or if the bar has the electronic top-up facility, tap in your phone number and the amount requested will be credited automatically.

Buying a mobile could be an option for longer or business stays or if you visit Italy frequently, since even if your UK mobile works here you will pay very inflated rates. One top-up has to be made at least every 11 months to keep the number active. Some internet points hire out phones. You could try **Intotheweb** or **Internet Train** (*see p288*).

The mobile phone shops below are centrally located:

Spazio Omnitel
Via Panzani 33r, Santa Maria Novella (055 267 0121). **Open** 3.30-7.30pm Mon; 9.30am-7.30pm Tue-Sat. **Credit** AmEx, MC, V. **Map** p314 B2.

Il Telefonino (TIM)
Via Pellicceria 3, Duomo & Around (055 239 6066). **Open** 9am-7pm Mon-Fri; 9am-1pm Sat. **Credit** AmEx, MC, V. **Map** p314 C3.

Faxes

Faxes can be sent from most large post offices (*see p291*), which charge per sheet sent. Rates are €1.30 per page in Italy or €5.10 for Europe. Faxes can also be sent from some photocopying outlets and internet points though at higher rates, and at most hotels.

Telegrams

These can be sent from main post offices. The telegraph office at the Posta Centrale (*see p291*) is open 8.30am-7pm Monday to Friday and 8.30am-12.30pm Saturday. Alternatively, you can dictate telegrams over the phone. Dial 186 from a private or hotel phone and a message in Italian will tell you to dial the number of the phone you're phoning from. You will then be passed to a telephonist who will take your message (some speak English).

Time

Italy is an hour ahead of London, six ahead of New York and eight behind Sydney. Clocks go forward an hour in spring and back in autumn, in line with other EU countries.

Tipping

The 10-15 per cent tip customary in many countries is considered generous in Florence. Locals sometimes leave a few coins on the counter when buying drinks at the bar and, depending on the standard of the restaurant, €1-€5 for the waiter after a meal. Many of the larger restaurants now include a 10-15 per cent service charge. Tips are not expected in smaller restaurants, although they are always appreciated. Taxi drivers will be surprised if you do more than round the fare up to the nearest €1.

Toilets

Florence has very few public loos. The most useful of them are in the Santa Maria Novella train station underpass (open 8am-8pm), Palazzo Vecchio, the Palazzo Pitti, the coach park to the west of Fortezza da Basso and piazzale Michelangiolo (open 11am-5pm). It's usually easiest to go to a bar (obliged by law to let you use its facilities). Ask for the *bagno*; in some bars you'll be given the key. Bar loos are often kept locked to discourage use by drug addicts.

Tourist information

To be sent an information pack in advance of your visit, get in touch with ENIT, the Italian tourist board (UK: 020 7498 1254/fax 020 7493 6695/ www.enit.it; US: 212 245 5618/fax 212 586 9249/www.italiantourism.com). Tell staff where and when you're going and any special interests.

Florence's provincial tourist board, the **Azienda Promozionale Turistica (APT)**, and the council-run **Ufficio Informazione Turistiche** have helpful multilingual staff who do their best to supply reliable information – not easy as museums and galleries tend to change their opening hours without telling them. There's no central information service for the Tuscany region; you have to contact the APT in each district (listed in this guide under the relevant area).

The English Yellow Pages, available from principal bookshops and online (www.paginegialle.it), lists English-speaking services and useful numbers. A good street map is available free from APT offices. Telecom Italia supplies subscribers with TuttoCittà, a detailed street atlas covering the whole urban area; most bars and hotels keep one.

APT *Via Portigiani 3, Outside the City Gates (055 597 8373).* **Open** 9am-1pm Mon-Sat.
This is the APT headquarters. The most central office, however, is at via Cavour 1r (open 8.15am-7.15pm Mon-Sat); there are also offices in Florence and Pisa airports. The APT provides information and brochures on attractions and events in Florence and the surrounding province (not all of Tuscany). As well as free maps, it publishes a brochure, *Firenze per i Giovani*, aimed at young people, with listings for language courses, internet services, clubs, bike hire, hostels and so on. APT provides hotel lists but not a booking service.
Branches: Via Cavour 1r, San Marco (055 290 832); Via Portigiani 3, Fiesole (055 5978 373).

Tourist Help Open *Easter-Sept* 8am-7pm daily.
This useful service is run by the *vigili urbani* from three vans, one in piazza della Repubblica, one in via Calziauoli and one just south of the Ponte Vecchio in via Guicciardini. APT personnel and the municipal police provide practical help and information. This is also where you can register any complaints you might have about abusive restaurant or hotel charges.

Ufficio Informazione Turistiche *Borgo Santa Croce 29r, Santa Croce (055 234 0444).* **Open** *Summer* 9am-7pm Mon-Sat; 9am-1.45pm Sun. *Winter* 9am-5pm Mon-Sat. **Map** p315 C5.
Run by the city of Florence, these offices provide all kinds of tourist information, free maps, restaurant and hotel lists.
Branch *Piazza della Stazione, Santa Maria Novella (055 212 245).*

Visas & immigration

Non-EU citizens and Britons require full passports to travel to Italy. EU citizens are permitted unrestricted access to Italy, and citizens of the US, Canada, Australia and New Zealand do not need visas for stays of up to three months. In theory, all visitors to Italy must declare their presence to the local police within eight days of arrival. If you are staying in a hotel, this will be done for you by the proprietors. If not, contact the Questura Centrale (*see p291*), the main police station, where they can give you advice along with all the requisite bureaucracy.

Weights & measures

Italy uses only the metric system; remember that all speed limits are in kilometres. One kilometre is equivalent to 0.62 mile (1 mile = 1.5km). Petrol, like other liquids, is measured in litres: one UK gallon = 4.54 litres; 1 US gallon = 3.79 litres). A kilogram is equivalent to 2.2 pounds (1lb = 0.45kg). Food is often sold in *ettos* (sometimes written *hg*); 1 *etto* = 100 grams (3.52 ounces), so in delicatessens, you should ask for multiples of *etti* (*un'etto, due etti*, etc).

What to take

Any prescription medicines should always be obtained before leaving, and should be enough to cover the entire period of your stay, as not all US and UK medicines are available in Italy, and even when they are, they can be more expensive.

When to go

Climate

The hills surrounding Florence mean that it can be cold and humid in winter and very hot and humid in the summer. In July and August, temperatures often soar to 40°C (104°F), and don't often fall below 30°C (86°F) between May and September. During the summer you should be sure to take the sun seriously – every year doctors in Florence warn about the number of visitors who are hospitalised with serious burns from spending too much time in the sun, going out in the middle of the day (Italians stay in whenever they can during the hottest hours) and not using high enough SPF suncreams. The short spring and autumn in Florence and Tuscany can be very warm, though it's not without the risk of rain, particularly in March, April and September. Between November and February you cannot rely on good weather, and don't be surprised if you come across either a week of rain, or crisp, bright (sometimes even warm) sunshine. For full climate information, *see below*.

Public holidays

On public holidays (*giorni festivi*) virtually all shops, banks and businesses are shut, though most bars and restaurants stay open so you will be able to eat and drink.

The public holidays are as follows: New Year's Day (*Capo d'anno*) 1 January; Epiphany (*La Befana*) 6 January; Easter Monday (*Lunedi Pasqua*); Liberation Day (*Venticinque Aprile*) 25 April; May Day (*Primo Maggio*) 1 May; Liberation Day 2 June; Florence Saints' Day (*San Giovanni*) 24 June; Feast of the Assumption (*Ferragosto*) 15 August; All Saints' (*Tutti Santi*) 1 November; Immaculate Conception (*Festa dell'Immacolata*) 8 December; Christmas Day (*Natale*) 25 December; Boxing Day (*Santo Stefano*) 26 December.

There is limited public transport on 1 May and Christmas afternoon. Holidays falling on a Saturday or Sunday are not celebrated the following Monday, but if a holiday falls on a Thursday or Tuesday many people make a long weekend of it, and take the intervening day off as well. Such a weekend is called a *ponte* (bridge). Beware of the *rientro* or homecoming when the roads are packed. Many people also disappear for a large chunk of August, when *chiuso per ferie*

Average monthly climate

Month	High temp	Low temp	Rainfall	Relative humidity
Jan	50° F (10°C)	30°F (-1°C)	2.5in (64.1mm)	75%
Feb	54°F (12°C)	34°F (1°C)	2.4in (61.5mm)	72%
Mar	59°F (15°C)	41°F (5°C)	2.7in (69.4mm)	72%
Apr	68°F (20°C)	46°F (8°C)	2.8in (70.5mm)	72%
May	75°F (24°C)	52°F (11°C)	2.9in (73.3mm)	71%
June	84°F (29°C)	57°F (14°C)	2.2in (56.4mm)	64%
July	93°F (34°C)	64°F (18°C)	1.3in (34.2mm)	66%
Aug	90°F (32°C)	57°F (14°C)	1.8in (46.9mm)	71%
Sep	82°F (28°C)	55°F (13°C)	3.3in (8.4mm)	76%
Oct	73°F (23°C)	52°F (11°C)	3.9in (99.1mm)	81%
Nov	61°F (16°C)	39°F (4°C)	4.1in (103.4mm)	81%
Dec	55°F (13°C)	39°F (4°C)	3.1in (79.4mm)	73%

(closed for holidays) signs appear in shops and restaurants, with the dates of closure. These closures are co-ordinated on a rota system by the city council, so there should be something open in each area at any given time. However, if you should find yourself in Florence, or many other Tuscan towns, on the *Ferragosto* (Feast of the Assumption; 15 August) the chances are that your only company will be other tourists wandering the baked streets in search of something to do or somewhere to eat. The Florentines desert the city like rats from a sinking ship and are likely to stay away for several days either side. You'll find the exceptions to this rule are holiday resorts such as coastal towns where, although shops and public offices may close, the infrastructure doesn't completely collapse.

For a calendar of Tuscany's traditional and modern festivals throughout the year, *see pp152-6.*

Women

Although it's not one of the worst places for women travellers Tuscany still has its hassles. Visiting women can feel daunted by the sheer volume of attention they receive, but most is friendly and men are unlikely to become pushy or aggressive if given the brush-off. It's normally a question of all talk and no action, but if ignoring unwanted advances doesn't work, using a few sharp words and a withering glance usually will. Be aware of who's around you – it's quite common to be followed by hopefuls. If things get too heavy, go into the nearest shop or bar and wait or ask for help. The notorious bum-pinching is uncommon, but not unknown, especially on buses. As in Anglo-Saxon countries, it's an assault and a criminal offence, and recent prosecutions and convictions show that it's taken seriously.

Network

Villa Rossa, piazza Savonarola 15, Outside the City Gates (Kelly Stevens 055 575 299/kelly.stevens@tin.it. Sahna Wicks 055 840 9751/wicks @katamail.com). Bus 10, 11, 13, 17.

A professional women's organisation geared mainly towards residents whose first language is English. It aims to improve communication, exchange ideas and information among the English-speaking community. Meetings are generally on the second Wednesday of the month. Annual fees are €35, which includes newsletter and mailings.

Women's health

Women who are suffering from gynaecological emergencies should head for the nearest *pronto soccorso* (accident & emergency) (*see p286*).

Tampons (*assorbenti interni*) and sanitary towels (*assorbenti esterni*) are cheaper in supermarkets, but you can also get them in pharmacies and some *tabacchi*.

Careggi hospital (*see p286*) has a clinic for women who have suffered a sexual assault, offering them examinations, treatment, counselling and liaison with the police. Some English is spoken.

For information on contraception, abortion and other health matters, *see p287.*

Clinica Ostetrica

Reparto Maternità, Ospedale di Careggi, Viale Morgagni, Outside the City Gates (055 427 7111/7493). Bus 2, 8, 14C. **Open** 24hrs daily.

Female victims of sexual assault should come Clinica Ostetrica for medical attention. Legal services and counselling are available 9am-1pm, 3pm-5pm Monday to Friday at the office at viale Santa Maria Maggiore 1, Careggi (055 284 752).

Working in Florence

Finding a job in Italy is not simple as one might hope it to be. The country's work market isn't particularly mobile. Most of the jobs that are available are connected to tourism in some way, although there are a few multinationals that occasionally advertise for native English-speakers. These can be a good opening.

The classified ads paper *La Pulce* has job listings, and it's worth looking in the local English-language press.

The bureaucracy involved isn't easy, either. Anyone intending to stay in Italy longer than three months has to acquire a bewildering array of papers in order to get a *permesso di soggiorno* (permit to stay), and if they plan to work, they'll also need a *permesso di soggiorno per lavoro*. While EU citizens should have no trouble getting documentation once they are in Italy, non-EU citizens on the other hand are advised to enquire at an Italian embassy or consulate in their own country before setting off for Italy with the hope of finding employment when they arrive.

All non-EU citizens and EU nationals who are working in Italy should register with the police within eight days of arrival and apply for their permits. There is a useful computer at the Questura Centrale (central police station) that prints out lists (in various languages) of the documents that you will need for every type of *permesso*. You can also get advice here. You will need a residency permit to perform certain transactions, including, for example, buying a car. To apply, contact your local *circoscrizione* office.

Administration & permit offices

Comune di Firenze (Florence council), Palazzo Vecchio & Piazza Signoria, Duomo & Around (switchboard 055 27681/freephone 800 831 133). **Open** 8.30am-1.30pm Mon-Wed, Fri, Sat; 8.30am-6.30pm Thur. **Map** p315 C4.

For residence enquiries, ask for the *Ufficio Circoscrizione*. Give your address, they will then give you the number you need to call to progress further with your application.

Questura Centrale (central police station)

Via Zara 2, San Lorenzo (055 49771). **Open** 24hrs daily. *Ufficio Stranieri* 8.30am-12.30pm Mon-Fri.

To apply for your documents, go to the *Ufficio Stranieri* (foreigners' section) where English-speaking staff are usually available to help. It's advisable to go early in the day to avoid the long queues that can form. There is a number system (take a ticket from the dispenser when you arrive) and applications are dealt with at one of eight desks.

Italian Vocabulary

Any attempt at speaking Italian will always be appreciated and is often necessary. Away from services such as tourist offices, hotels and restaurants popular with foreigners, the level of English is not very high. Wherever you are, the most important thing is making the effort, not whether or not your sentences are perfectly formed with an authentic accent. The key is just try and don't be shy.

When entering a shop or restaurant, it is the practice to announce your presence with *buongiorno* (*see p283*) or *buona sera*. Feel free to ask directions in the street as people often go out of their way to help.

Italian is spelled as it's pronounced and vice versa. Stresses usually fall on the penultimate syllable. There are three forms of the second person – the formal **lei** (used with strangers), the informal **tu**, and the plural form **voi**. Men and masculine nouns are accompanied by adjectives ending in 'o', women and female nouns by adjectives ending in 'a'. However, there are many nouns and adjectives that end in 'e'. These can be either masculine or feminine.

PRONUNCIATION

Vowels

a – as in **a**sk
e – like **a** in **a**ge (closed e) or **e** in s**e**ll (open e)
i – like **ea** in **ea**st
o – as in h**o**tel (closed o) or in h**o**t (open o)
u – as in b**oo**t

Consonants

c – before an a, o or u is like the **c** in **c**at
c – before an e or an i is like the **ch** in **ch**eck
ch – like the **c** in **c**at
g – before an a, o or u is like the **g** in **g**et
g – before an e or an i is like the **j** in **j**ig
gh – like the **g** in **g**et
gl – followed by an i is like **lli** in million
gn – like **ny** in ca**ny**on
qu – as in **qu**ick
r – is always rolled
s – has two sounds, as in **s**oap or **r**ose
sc – like the **sh** in **sh**ame
sch – like the **sc** in **sc**out
z –has two sounds, like **ts** and **dz**
Double consonants are always sounded more emphatically.

USEFUL PHRASES

hello and **goodbye** (informal) – *ciao*
good morning, good day – *buongiorno*
good afternoon, good evening – *buona sera*
I don't understand – *Non capisco/non ho capito*
Do you speak English? – *Parla inglese?*
please – *per favore*
thank you – *grazie*
you're welcome – *prego*
When does it open? – *Quando apre?*
Where is... ? – *Dov'è…?*
excuse me – *scusi* (polite), *scusa* (informal)
open – *aperto*
closed – *chiuso*
entrance – *entrata*
exit – *uscita*
left – *sinistra*;
right – *destra*
car – *macchina*;
bus – *autobus*;
train – *treno*
bus stop – *fermata dell'autobus*
ticket/s – *biglietto/i*
I would like a ticket to... – *Vorrei un biglietto per…*
postcard – *cartolina*
stamp – *francobollo*
glass – *bicchiere*
coffee – *caffè*
tea – *tè*
water – *acqua*
wine – *vino*
beer – *birra*
the bill – *conto*
single/twin/double bedroom – *camera singola/doppia/matrimoniale*
booking – *prenotazione*
Monday *lunedì*;
Tuesday *martedì*;
Wednesday *mercoledì*;
Thursday *giovedì*;
Friday *venerdì*;
Saturday *sabato*;
Sunday *domenica*
yesterday *ieri*;
today *oggi*;
tomorrow *domani*
morning *mattina*;
afternoon *pomeriggio*;
evening *sera*;
night *notte*;
weekend *fine settimana, weekend*

THE COME-ON

Do you have a light? – *Hai da accendere?*
What's your name? – *Come ti chiami?*
Would you like a drink? – *Vuoi bere qualcosa?*
Where are you from? – *Di dove sei?*
What are you doing here? – *Che fai qui?*
Do you have a boyfriend/girlfriend? – *Hai un ragazzo/una ragazza?*

THE BRUSH-OFF

I don't smoke – *Non fumo*
I'm married – *Sono sposato/a*
I'm tired – *Sono stanco/a*
I'm going home – *Vado a casa*
I have to meet a friend – *Devo andare a incontrare un amico/una amica*

INSULTS

shit – *merda*
idiot – *stronzo*
fuck off – *vaffanculo*
dickhead – *testa di cazzo*
What the hell are you doing? – *Che cazzo fai?*

NUMBERS & MONEY

0 *zero*; **1** *uno*; **2** *due*; **3** *tre*; **4** *quattro*; **5** *cinque*; **6** *sei*; **7** *sette*; **8** *otto*; **9** *nove*; **10** *dieci*; **11** *undici*; **12** *dodici*; **13** *tredici*; **14** *quattordici*; **15** *quindici*; **16** *sedici*; **17** *diciassette*; **18** *diciotto*; **19** *dicinnove*; **20** *venti*; **21** *ventuno*; **22** *ventidue*; **30** *trenta*; **40** *quaranta*; **50** *cinquanta*; **60** *sessanta*; **70** *settanta*; **80** *ottanta*; **90** *novanta*; **100** *cento*; **1,000** *mille*; **2,000** *duemilla*; **100,000** *centomila*; **1,000,000** *un milione*.
How much does it cost/is it? – *Quanto costa?/quant'è?*
Do you have any change? – *Ha da cambiare?*
Can you give me any discount? – *Si può fare uno sconto?*
Do you accept credit cards? – *Si accettano le carte di credito?*
Can I pay in pounds/dollars? – *Posso pagare in sterline/dollari?*
Can I have a receipt? – *Posso avere una ricevuta?*
Is service included? – *è compreso il servizio?*

Art & Architecture Glossary

Annunciation – depiction of the Virgin Mary being told by the Angel Gabriel that she will bear the son of God.
Attribute – object used in art to symbolise a particular person, often saints and martyrs.
Baldacchino – canopied structure, in paintings holding an enthroned Madonna and child.
Banderuola – small forked flag bearing an inscription, held in Renaissance art by angels or *putti*.
Baptistery – building for baptisms, usually octagonal to symbolise new beginnings, as seven is the number of completion and eight the start of a new cycle.
Baroque – sumptuous art and architectural style from the 17th to mid 18th centuries.
Byzantine – spiritual and religious art of the Byzantine Empire (fifth-15th centuries).
Campanile – bell tower.
Cartoon – full-scale sketch for painting or fresco.
Cenacolo – depiction of the Last Supper.
Chiaroscuro – painting or drawing technique using shades of black, grey and white to emphasise light and shade.
Classical – ancient Greek and Roman art and culture.
Corbel – brackets jutting from a roof.
Cupola – dome-shaped structure set on a larger dome or a roof.
Deposition – depiction of Christ taken down from the Cross.
Diptych – painting made of two panels.
Fresco – technique for wall painting where pigments bind with wet plaster.
Golden mean – Renaissance art theory with division of proportions by ratio of 8:13. Considered to create perfect harmony.
Gothic – architectural and artistic style of the late Middle Ages (from the 12th century) characterised by the integration of art forms, with pointed arches and an emphasis on line.
Grotesque – ornate artistic style derived from Roman underground painted rooms (*grotte*).
Hortus conclusus – garden around Madonna and child symbolising their uncontaminated world of perfection and contentment.
Iconography – study of subject and symbolism of works of art. For example, in Renaissance art: a **dog** symbolises faithfulness to a master, usually the Medici; an **egg** is a symbol of perfection; a **peacock** symbolises the Resurrection; a **giglio** (lily of Florence) is often found in Annunciations to symbolise the purity of the Madonna; a **sarcophagus** (stone or marble coffin) symbolises the death of an important person; and the colour **blue** sometimes symbolises divine peace
Illumination – miniature painted as an illustration for manuscripts.
Loggia – covered area with one or more sides open, with columns.
Lunette – half-moon painting or semicircular architectural space for decoration or window.
Madonna of Mercy – Madonna with her cloak open to give protection to those in need.
Maestà – depiction of the Madonna on a throne.
Mandorla – almond-shaped 'glory' surrounding depiction of holy person.
Mannerism – 15th-century Italian art movement, characterised by exaggerated perspective and scale, and complex compositions and poses.
Palazzo (*palazzi*) – large and/or important building, not necessarily a royal palace.
Panel – painting on wood.
Panneggio – style of folded and pleated drapery worn by figures in 15th- and 16th-century painting and sculpture.
Pietà – depiction of Christ lying across the Madonna's lap after the Crucifixion.
Pietra dura – inlaid gem mosaics.
Polyptych – painting composed of several panels.
Putto (*putti*) – small angelic naked boys, often depicted as attendants of Venus.
Relief – sculpted work with three-dimensional areas jutting out from a flat surface.
Renaissance – 14th to 16th century cultural movement based on the 'rebirth' of classical ideals and methods.
Romanesque – architectural style of the early Middle Ages (c500-1200), drawing on Roman Byzantine influences.
Secco – the finishing off or retouching of a fresco, carried out on the dried plaster (*intonaco*).
Sinopia – preparatory drawing for a fresco made with a red earth mix or the red paint itself
Tempera – pigment bound with egg, the main painting material from 12th to late 15th century, before oils took over.
Tondo – round painting or relief.
Triptych – painting composed of three panels.
Trompe l'œil – painting designed to give illusion of three-dimensional reality.
Vanitas – objects in art symbolising mortality, such as skulls, hourglasses and broken columns.
Votive – offering left as a prayer for good fortune or recovery from illness, usually as a painting or a silver model of the limb/organ to be cured.

Further Reference

Books

Non-fiction

Luigi Barzini *The Italians*
Dated yet hilarious portrait.
Julia Conaway Bondanella & Mark Musa *Introduction to the Major Italian Writers & Influential Thinkers of the Renaissance*
Famous names and a few surprises.
Thomas Campanello
A Defence of Galileo, the Mathematician from Florence
Life, times and influence of Florence's most famous heretic.
Leornardo Castellucci
Living in Tuscany
Account of restoration efforts that turned Tuscan abbeys, castles, villas and farmhouses into homes.
Paul Ginsbourg *A History of Contemporary Italy: Society and Politics 1943-1988*
Comprehensive modern history.
Frederick Hartt *The History of Italian Renaissance Art*
The definitive work.
Christopher Hibbert *The Rise and Fall of the House of Medici*
Very readable history tome.
Ross King *Brunelleschi's Dome: The Story of the Great Cathedral*
Fascinating account of the building of Florence's magnificent dome.
Monica Larner & Travis Neighbor *Living, Studying and Working in Italy*
Everything you need to know.
Mary McCarthy
The Stones of Florence
Loving portrait of Florence & its arts.
Iris Origo *Images and Shadows; The Merchant of Prato*
Autobiographical and biographical accounts of Florence and Tuscany.
Thomas Paloscia *Accadde in Toscana (Vol III)*
A beautifully illustrated who's who of Tuscany's contemporary artists.
Laura Raison
Tuscany: An Anthology
Collection of classic to contemporary writings and illustrations about Florence and Tuscany.
Leon Satkowski *Giorgio Vasari: Architect & Courtier*
Biography of the most famous Italian art chronicler.
Matthew Spender
Within Tuscany
A witty account of growing up in an unusual family in Tuscany.

Fiction

Italo Calvino *The Florentine*
One of Calvino's 'folktales' collections of short stories. Tells of the misery of a Florentine who has nothing to boast of and longs to travel.
Jack Dann
The Memory Cathedral – A Secret History of Leonardo da Vinci
Mystery and intrigue in 15th-century Florence.
Michael Dibdin *A Rich Full Death*
Amusing thriller with insight into 19th-century Florence.
Sarah Dunant
The Birth of Venus
Gender and art in Medici Florence.
EM Forster *A Room with a View; Where Angels Fear to Tread*
Social comedy from the master.
Robert Hellenga *The 16 Pleasures*
A young American woman goes to Florence and feels obliged to act out 16 'pleasures' from a book of erotica.
W Somerset Maugham
Up at the Villa
Temptation and fate in '30sFlorence.
Frances Mayes *Under the Tuscan Sun, Bella Tuscany*
Ubiquitous *Year in Provence*-style expat dreams and nightmares.
Magdalena Nabb
The Monster of Florence
Thriller based on a serial killer who murdered 16 campers in the 1980s.
Michael Ondaatje
The English Patient
Booker-winning novel turned Oscar-winning film, partly set in Tuscany.
Davina Sobell *Galileo's Daughter*
Study of Galileo's life in the context of his relationship with his daughter.
Sally Stewart
An Unexpected Harvest
London yuppie moves to Tuscany to help grandparents save family estate.

Food &wine

Leslie Forbes
A Table in Tuscany
Personal account of Tuscan food, with recipes from local restaurants.
Slow Food and Gambero Rosso
Italian Wines Guide
The English edition of reliable annual guide to Italian wines.

Film

The English Patient (1996)
Tragic World War II story starring Ralph Fiennes and Juliette Binoche, partly set in Tuscany.
Hannibal (2000)
Creepy sequel to *Silence of the Lambs* shows Anthony Hopkins' serial killer travelling to Florence.
Life is Beautiful
(La Vita e' Bella) (1997)
Roberto Benigni's bittersweet comedy, about wartime Arezzo.
Much Ado about Nothing (1993)
Kenneth Branagh's fanciful interpretation of Shakespeare's comedy, filmed in Tuscany.
Pinocchio (2002)
Roberto Benigni's latest, not-very-well-received film in which he plays an aged Pinocchio (the long-nosed puppet originates from Tuscany).
Portrait of a Lady (1996)
Nicole Kidman stars in adaptation of Henry James's story of a New World woman in Old World Italy.
A Room with a View (1985)
Merchant and Ivory flick in which Helena Bonham Carter learns of love and loss in 19th-century Florence.
Stealing Beauty (1995)
Bernardo Bertolucci's Tuscan-based film, which brought us Liv Tyler.
Tea with Mussolini (1998)
Judy Dench and Maggie Smith form part of an eccentric group of expat ladies in wartime Florence.
Up at the Villa (2000)
Sean Penn plays a cynical American who proves innocent in comparison to his European companions.

Music

Giacomo Puccini
Gianni Schicchi
Delightful comic one-act opera set in medieval Fucecchio, west of Florence.
Peter Ilich Tchaikovsky
Souvenir of Florence
String sextet written while the composer was living in via San Leonardo in Florence.

Websites

www.boxoffice.it Info and online booking for concerts and shows. Italian only.
www.comune.it Official council site with what's-on page, weather forecasts and useful info about visas, permits and tax.
www.cultura.toscana.it Official Regione Toscana site for info on museums, exhibitions and libraries throughout Tuscany.
www.fionline.it Shopping online, job search site and useful entertainment info.
www.firenze.vivacity.it
www.firenze.net Useful site with info on Florence and Tuscany cinemas, nightlife, music, art, traffic, weather plus a booking service for museums, hotels and farm holidays.
www.firenzespettacolo.it
The monthly listings mag website with constantly updated what's-on info, reviews and much more – you can even order a pizza here.
www.florenceonline.it/www.fol.it Useful info on health, travel, sports, hotel bookings and business.
www.lapulce.it Online version of the small-ads mag; free insertions.

Index

Note: page numbers in **bold** indicate section(s) giving key information on topic; *italics* indicate illustrations.

abbeys & monasteries
Badia a Coltibuono **227**, 232
Badia a Passignano 168, **225**
Badia di San Salvatore 261
Badia Fiesolana 27, *29*, **106**
Badia Fiorentina 75-76
Camaldoli Romualdo 262, *263*
Certosa del Galuzzo 106
Certosa di Pisa 209
Eremo di Calomini 252
Monte Oliveto Maggiore 230
San Galgano 168, **229**
Sant'Antimo 168, *230*, *231*, **234**
La Verna 262-263
Abetone 199
abortion 287
Accademia, gallery of 90
Accademia Bartolomeo Cristofori 168
Acciaiuoli family 11
accommodation **46-61**
Affittacamere (B&Bs) 46
agencies 62
farms **192**, 198
gay & lesbian B&Bs 166
self-catering 46, 62, 210
see also hostels; hotels
addresses 283
age restrictions 164, **283**
AIDS & HIV 287-288
airlines 278
airports 33, 207, **278**, 289
alabaster 210
Alberese 268, 271
Alberti, Leon Battista 28, **31**, 84, 85, 86, 234-235
Alcoholics Anonymous 288
Aldobrandini family 271
Alessandro de' Medici 12, **16**, 103, 242, 262
Allori, Cristofano 22-23
ambulance 286
Ammanati, Bartolommeo 28, 32, 73, 83, 99, 105
Angelico, Fra **23**, 93, 106, 204, 266
Anghiari 264-265
Ansedonia 272-273
antiques 84, 98, 132, 195, 208, 243, 257-258, 266
apartments 46, 62, 210
Apuan Alps 252
architecture **27-33**
features (illustrated) *30-31*
glossary of terms 298
Romanesque & Gothic 28-29
Renaissance 29-32
post-1600 32-33
Arena di Marte 161
Arezzo 191, **254-260**
accommodation 260
Anfiteatro Romano 257
churches **254-256**
Fortezza Medicea 257
Giostra del Saracino 153
gold jewellery 257, **259**
history 254
information & resources 260
map 255
museums 256-257
Piazza Grande *256*, 257
Il Prato (park) 257
restaurants & bars 258, 260
shops 257-258
transport 260
Arezzo Province 261-267
restaurants 36, 37
Argentario, Monte *269*, **273**
Arno, river 13, 18, 210
Arnolfo di Cambio 22, 28, 29, 67, 71, 79, 97, 196, 217
birthplace 227
art **21-23**
children's workshop 159
contemporary 162-163
courses 192, 292
glossary of terms 298
marble sculptors 249
non-Renaissance 22-23
Renaissance 21-23
supplies 150
tours 192
see also museums & galleries
Artigianato e Palazzo 152
Astor Caffè **126**, 163, **176**
Auditorium Flog 156, 165, **170**
Automobile Club 281
Azienda Promozionale Turistica (APT) 294

Baccio d'Agnolo 82
Baciocchi, Elisa 13, 238, 242, 250
Badia a Coltibuono **227**, 232
Badia a Passignano 168, **225**
Badia di San Salvatore a Soffena 261
Badia Fiesolana 27, *29*, **106**
Badia Fiorentina 75-76
Bagni di Lucca 250-251
Bagno Vignoni **234**, *235*
bags **139**, 140, 141, 150
Prada 137
bakeries **143-144**, 158-159
Bandinelli, Baccio 73
banking, history of **11**, 14-15
banks 290
Bardi family 11
Barga 251
Opera Festival 168
Bargello 22, 29, 75, **94-95**
bars 98, **126-131**, **176-180**
aperitivos 128
cocktails 177
gay & lesbian **164-165**, 166
live music 170-173
outdoor 179
sushi bar 130
see also wine bars
Bartolo di Fredi 227, 231, 265
Batignano Opera Festival **155**, 168
battles 212, 254
beaches 208, 209, 211, 248-249, 268, 271, 273, 274 275-276
beauty shops & salons 145-147
Beccafumi, Domenico 217, 219
Befana, La **156**, 158, 197
Bellosguardo 106
Benigni, Roberto 160, *161*
Bernini, Gian Lorenzo 217
Biblioteca Nazionale 94
bikes *see* cycling
Boboli Gardens *65*, 98, *98*, **99**, **100-101**, 159
Boccaccio, Giovanni 20, 195
Bolgheri 42, **211**
Bologna airport 278
Bonfire of the Vanities *see* Savonarola, Girolamo
bookbinding 148
bookshops 130, **133-134**, 158, 179, 182
Borgo San Jacopo 28, **98**
Borgo San Lorenzo 36, 196
Botticelli, Sandro 23, 72, 81-82, 85, 90, 92
Allegory of Spring 20
tomb 86
Bracciolini, Poggio 20
Brancacci Chapel 102
bridges **33**, 94
see also Ponte Santa Trinità; Ponte Vecchio
British Institute 160, 292
library 288-289
Bronzino, Il **22**, 80, 82, 89
Brunelleschi **22**, 28, 86, 90, 93, 95, 96, 99, 106
and Duomo 29, 68-69, 71
and San Lorenzo 29, 89
and Santo Spirito *27*, 29, 102
tomb 68
Buonconvento 230
Buontalenti, Bernardo 28, 32, 99
bureaux de change 290
buses **279-280**, 289
for buses to destinations outside Florence see individual places
business services 134, **283-285**

c

Caesar, Julius 7, 13, 238
cafés **126-131**, 158-159
calcio storico 73, 94, **153**
Camaldoli Romualdo 262, *263*
campsites **62**, 206, 208, 223, 273, 276
Canadian Island 159
canoeing 271
Canossa family 7
Canova, Antonio 101
Capalbio 41, **273-274**
Cappella dei Pazzi 29, **96-97**
Cappella di Montesiepi 229
Cappella Rucellai 85
Cappelle Medicee 87-88
Capraia 276
Caravaggio 82, 273
Carducci, Giosuè 211
Carmignano 193, **194**, 196
Carnevale 156
children's costumes 158
Viareggio **154-155**, **156**, 248
Carrara 249-250, *251*
cars & driving 25, **281-282**
breakdown services 281, 286
hire, petrol & parking 282
for routes to destinations outside Florence see individual places
Casa Buonarroti 95
Cascate del Gorello 270
Casciana Terme 209-210
Cascine, Parco delle 33, 85, **103**, **159**
markets 134
outdoor events 179
Casentino 261
cashpoints 290
Castagno, Andrea del 68, 69
Castelfranco di Sopra 261-262
Castellina 225
Castello di Brolio **227**, 232
Castello di Sorci *264*, 265
Castelnuovo Berardenga 227
Castelnuovo di Garfagnana **252**, 253
Castiglion Fiorentino 265-266
Holy Week 152
Castiglione della Pescaia 211
Cave di Maiano 181
Cecina 211
Cellini, Benvenuto 73-75
cemetery *103*, 105
Cenacolo del Conservatorio di Fuligno 88-89
Cenacolo di Andrea del Sarto 105
Cenacolo di Sant'Apollonia 89
Cenacolo di Santo Spirito 99
ceramics 147, *149*, 154, 194-195, 225, 265
museums 102, 257, 265
Certaldo Alto 193, **195-196**

Certosa del Galuzzo 106
Certosa di Pisa 209
Chamber of Commerce 285
Charles V, emperor 12, 16, 21, 31
Charles VIII, king 12, 21
Chianciano 237
Chianti (region) 191, **224-227**, 262
cycling tours 182
Chianti (wine) 40, 41, 43, **232-233**
Chianti Rufina 233
Chiardiluna 161
Chiesa Luterana 168
childcare 159
children's attractions 157-159
dance classes 187
parks & amusement parks 159
Pinocchio Park 198
play centres 159
restaurants 108-109, **158-159**
shops 158
swimming pools & camps 184
Chiostro dello Scalzo 89
Chiusi 237
chocolates 127, 129, 131, 143
Christmas **156**, 240
churches
dress etiquette 283
earliest 13
English mass 291
Gregorian chant 106
non-Catholic 103-104, 168, **291**
see also Duomo; Ognissanti; Orsanmichele; *and churches listed under saints' names, e.g.* San Lorenzo; Santa Croce. *For churches outside Florence see individual places.*
Cibrèo 94, **115**
Cimabue, Giovanni 21, **22**, 80, 97, 204
Cimitero degli Inglesi *103*, 105
cinemas 160-161
Clement VII, pope (Giulio de' Medici) 12, **16**
climate 295
climbing 181-182
clothes 135-141
leather 139
menswear 135, 137, **138**
repairs & alterations 141
clubs **174-176**, 248
discos 211, 245
gay & lesbian 165
live music 170-173
outdoor 179
cocktails 177
coffee etiquette 126
Colle di Val d'Elsa 227
Collezione Contini-Bonacossi 75, **76**
Collezione della Ragione 77
Collodi 198-199
Colonnata 250
Comunita Ebraica 291
concerts 167-169
conference centre 283
consulates 285, **286**
consumer advice 285
contraception 287
cookery schools 192
Corridorio Vasariano 75, **77**
corso dei Tintori 94
Cortona 266-267
Cosimo Il Vecchio **10**, **14**, 29-31, 79, 89, 93, 106
Cosimo I 12, **16**, 31, 32, 75, 77, 80, 99, 210
exhibition of clothes of 100
and Siena 212-213, 219
statue 73
costa di San Giorgio 104-105
costas 98
couriers 283
courses 187, **192**, **292-293**
crafts 98, 132
markets & fairs 152, 197, 208, 243, 264
credit cards 290
crime 24, 26, **291-292**
Cronaca, Il 28, 31
customs & duty-frees 285
cycling 25, **182**, 191, 238, 247, 252, 273, **282**
bike hire 182, 282
tours 159, **182**, **192**, 209, 282

d

dance 185-187
festivals 154, 156, **187**
Dante Alighieri 10, 20, 68, 71, 75, 76, 205, 262
memorials & statues 94, 97
museum 75, **77**
della Robbia, Andrea 90, 96, 241, 265
della Robbia, Giovanni 83, 197, *197*
della Robbia, Luca 71, 92, 96-97
dentists 287
department stores 134
Di Monte family 265
disabled access 279, **285**
diving 276
doctors 287
Dolce Vita 98, 128, **131**, 163, **178**
Dominicans 86, 93
Domenici, Leonardo 24
Domenico Veneziano 80
Donatello 21-22, 71, 73, 79, 89, 95, 97, 99, 193
Judith & Holofernes 73, 80
driving *see* cars & driving
drugs 26, **285**
helpline 288
dry-cleaners 138
Duccio di Buoninsegna 80, 219, 230
Duomo *24*, 28, 29, **67-71**
Baptistery 28, *69*, **71**
Campanile 29, **69**
Crypt of Santa Reparata 68
Cupola/Dome 68-69
museum 71
Duomo, area of 67-83
cafés & bars 123, 126-129, 170, 179, 180
clubs 171, 176
hotels 47-51
restaurant (Oliviero) 111
suggested walk 80-81

Elba 275-276
electricity 285-286
Eleonora di Toledo 80, 86, 99
exhibition of clothes of 100
embassies 286
emergencies 286
Eremo di Calomini 252
etiquette 283
Etruscans **6-7**, 105, 190, 210, 212, 220, 229, 236, 254, 266, 270, 271
architecture 27
and gold 259
museums 92, 210, 237, 242, 257, 265, 266, 269, 271
Populonia 211
ruins 27, 105, 265, 268
tombs 6, 211, 225, 270
euros 290
'evil eye' 244
exorcism 244

f

farm holidays 192
faxes 134, 150, 294
Ferdinando I **16-17**, 75, 93, 209
statue 90, *91*
Ferragamo 83, 135
Festa del Grillo 153
festivals & events **152-156**, 158, 193, 195, 197, 200, 208, 229, 234, 235-236, 240, 263, 265, 266, 270
dance 154, 156, **187**
film 161
gay & lesbian 166
theatre 187
see also Carnevale; music festivals; Palio
Fiesole 6, 13, 27, **105-106**
Badia Fiesolana 27, *29*, **106**
Estate Fiesolana **153**, 187
film festival 161
Scuola Musica 168
film **160-161**, 234, 299
fire service 286
Firenze Expo 283
Firenze Musei 65
Firenze Nova 25, 33
fitness 182-183
Fivizzano 253
Florence Province 193-196
flowers 141
shows & festivals 152, 195, 199, 240
Foiano della Chiana 265
food 34-39
aperitivos 128
cookery schools 192
local specialities 197, 205, 210, 220, 244, 253, 258
markets 87, 94, 98, 120, 134, 243
picnics, takeaways & deliveries 120, 144
shops 143-145
football 181
Forte dei Marmi 248
Forte di Belvedere (Forte di San Giorgio) 32, 98, **99**
cinema 161
Fortezza da Basso 32, **103**
Fosdinovo 252
frames 148
Francesco I **16**, 79, 80, 210
Franciscans 97, 262-263
funfair 159
Fuori Porta 105, **125**
furniture 148
restorers 98, 264

g

Gaddi, Taddeo 97, 266
Gaiole 227
Galilei, Galileo 12, 77, 204
tomb 97
Galleria dell'Accademia 90
galleries
contemporary 162-163
see also museums & galleries
Gallery Art Hotel 47
art galleries 163
Fusion Bar Shozan **127**, 128, 177
gardens
Garzoni 198-199
in Lucca & area 242, 243
Semplici 90
Tarocchi 273
Villa di Castello 105
see also Boboli Gardens; Cascine, Parco delle
Garfagnana **250-252**, 253
gates, city 87, 103, 105
gay & lesbian scene 164-166
organisations 164, 165, **286**
gelaterie see ice-cream
Gentile da Fabriano 80
Gentileschi, Artemisia 23
Judith and Holofernes 23, *23*, 82
Ghibellines *6*, **7-10**, 64, 72, 97
Ghiberti, Lorenzo 21, 68, 71, 79, 95
Ghirlandaio, Domenico 23, 80, 83, 85, 92, 93, 204, 227
Last Supper 85-86
and Santa Maria Novella 86
Giambologna **22**, 73, 75, 84, 90, 94-95, 96
gifts 133, 134, 143, 145, 147-148, 150
Giglio, Isola del 273, **274-275**
Giotto di Bondone 21, 22, 28, 29, 69, 77, 80, 85, 96
Crocifisso 86
Santa Croce frescoes 97
glassware **147**, 148, 227
gloves 139
golf 182
Gozzoli, Benozzo 89, 200
Gregorian chant 106
Greve in Chianti 41, **224**, *225*
Grosseto (town) **268-269**, 274
Grosseto Province 268-274
restaurants 36-37

Index

Grotta del Vento 252
Guelphs **7-10**, 72, 79, 82
guidebooks 133
gyms **182-183**, 184

hairdressers 146
health **286-288**, 295
  complementary treatments 146-147, 286-287
  shops 143, **145-146**
  women's 296
helplines 288
herbalists 145-146, 286-287
history 7-19
  key events 19
  20th century 16-18
  Arezzo 254
  Lucca 7, 10, **238-240**
  Siena 212-213
holidays, organised 192
holidays, public 295-296
Holy Week 152
homeware 147-148
horse racing 181
horse riding **183**, 271
hospitals 286, 287
hostels **62**, 206, 260
hotels **46-61**
  booking 47
  budget 50-51, 53, 56, 58-59
  moderate 50, 54-55, 56-57
  for hotels outside Florence see individual places
Humanism **20-21**, 93

Iacovino, Giuseppe 85
ice-cream 126, 129, 131, *132*, 143, 157
ice skating 183
ID 288
immigrants, attitudes to 26
immigration rules 295
inflatables 159
in-line skating 183
insurance 288
internet access 130, 133, **288**
interpreters 285
  medical 287
Islamic association 291
islands 274-276

Jacopo della Quercia 216, 217, 219, 240, 242, 264
jewellery 98, 132, 135, **138**, **140**
  gold (Arezzo) 257, **259**
  repairs 141
Jews 11, 18
jousting 153, 154, 197

key cutting 141
knives, bone-handled 196

language 288
  courses 192, 292
  vocabulary 297
laundrettes 138
leather goods **139**, 140, 141, 150
left luggage 288
legal help 288
Leo X, pope (Giovanni de' Medici) **12**, **15**, 89
Leonardo da Vinci 23, 82, 194, 264
Leopold II, Grand Duke 13-15
libraries 94, **288-289**
Lippi, Filippino 76, 81, 86, 90, 193, 241
Lippi, Filippo 23, 81, 89, 96, 101, 102, 193, 229
literature 299
Livorno 14, *191*, 191, **210-211**
  Effetto Venezia **155**, 210
  Fortezza Vecchia *209*, 210
  Parco Giochi Cavallino Matto (funfair) 159
  restaurants 36, 211
Livorno Province 208-211
Loggia dei Lanzi 22, **73-75**, *77*
Loggia del Pesce 94
Loggia di San Paolo 84
Lorenzetti, Ambrogio 216, 217, 219, 229, 269
Lorenzetti, Pietro 216, 219, 230, 266
Lorenzo 'Il Magnifico' **10-12**, **14-15**, 21, 31, 83
  tomb 88
Loro Ciuffenna 261-262
lost property 289
Lucca 191, **238-247**
  accommodation 246-247
  cafés & bars 245-246
  churches 240-241
  history 7, 10, **238-240**
  information & resources 247
  map 239
  museums 241-242
  parks & gardens 243
  restaurants 244-245
  shops 243-244
  Torre Guinigi *243*, 243
  transport 247
  villas 242
  walls 238, 242-243
Lucca Province 248-253
Lucignano 265
luggage 140
Lunigiana 252-253

Macchiaioli 23
magazines 289
Maggio Musicale Fiorentino 152
Manciano 270
Mannerism 22
marathon 156
Maremma 190, 191, **268-274**
WWF nature reserve 271-272
Marina di Pisa 208
Marini, Marino 23, 85, 197
markets 87, 98, 103, **134**, 153
  antiques & junk 94, 98, 134, 195, 243, 257-258
  ceramics 195
  crafts 152, 197, 206, 264
  food 87, 94, 98, 120, 134, 243
  in Arezzo 257-258
  in Lucca 243
  in Pisa 206
  in Siena 219
martial arts 182
Martini, Simone 217, 231
Masaccio **22**, 80, 102, 204
  Trínita *84*, 86
Masolino da Panicale 77, 80, 102
Massa-Carrara 248-253
Massa Marittima **269-270**, 274
medical care *see* health
Medici family 10-12, **14-17**, 32, 79, 80, 89, 99, 103, 104-105, 167, 204, 271
  and banking 11
  coat of arms 193
  tombs 87-88, 89
  Alessandro 12, **16**, 103, 242, 262
  Anna Maria 12, **17**
  Catherine 15
  Cosimo Il Vecchio **10**, **14**, 29-31, 79, 89, 93, 106
  Cosimo I *see* Cosimo I
  Cosimo II 12, **17**, 83
  Cosimo III **17**, 92, 253
  Ferdinando I **16-17**, 75, 90, *91*, 93, 209
  Ferdinando II 17
  Francesco I **16**, 79, 80, 210
  Gian Gastone 12, **17**
  Giovanni *see* Leo X
  Giovanni di Bicci 14
  Giuliano, Duke of Nemours 12, **15**
  Giulio *see* Clement VII
  Lorenzo *see* Lorenzo 'Il Magnifico'
  Lorenzo, Duke of Urbino 12, **15**
  Piero di Lorenzo 11, 12, **15**
  Piero 'Il Gottoso' 14
Mercato Centrale 87, 120, **134**
  Nerbone (trattoria) 112
Mercato delle Pulci 134
Mercato di Santi Ambrogio 94, 120, **134**
Mercato Nuovo **75**, 134
Michelangelo 21, 22, 23, 31-32, 71, 79, 82, 89
  Bacchus Drunk 94
  and Cappelle Medicee 87-88
  and Carrara marble 250
  Casa Buonarroti works 95
  David 73, 73, **90**
  life 86, 106
  and Siena 217
  tomb 97
Michelozzo 28, 29-31, 89, 93, 193, 236
Michelucci, Giovanni 33, 84, 197
Mille Miglia 152
mobile phones 293-294
monasteries *see* abbeys & monasteries
money 290
Montalcino (town) 230-231
  tourist information 234
Montalcino (wine) 40, 41, 42-43, 230, 231, **233**
Montanelli, Giuseppe 14
Monte Argentario *269*, **273**
Monte Oliveto Maggiore 230
Monte San Savino 265
Montecatini Terme 166, 191, **198**, *199*, 199
Montefioralle 37, **224**
Montelupo 193, **194-195**
Montepulciano (town) 235-237
Montepulciano (wine) 40, 41, **233**
Monterchi 263-264
moped hire 282
mosaic craft 93
motor racing 181
  vintage cars 152
motorbike racing 181
Mugello 193, 196
Museo Archeologico *92*, **92**, 157
Museo Archeologico (Fiesole) 105
Museo Bandini 105
Museo Bardini 99
Museo Casa di Dante 75, **77**
Museo dei Ragazzi **77**, 157
Museo del Cenacolo di Andrea del Sarto 105
Museo dell'Antica Casa Fiorentina 83
Museo dell'Opera del Duomo 71
Museo dell'Opera di Santa Croce 96-97
Museo di Antropologia e Etnologia 95
Museo di Arte e Storia Ebraica 97
Museo di Bigallo 71-72
Museo di Casa Siviero 99
Museo di Firenze com'era 95-96
Museo di Geologia e Paleontologia **92**, 157
Museo di Mineralogia e Lithologia 92
Museo di San Marco 93
Museo di Storia della Scienza 75, **77-79**, 157
Museo Diocesano di Santo Stefano al Ponte 77
Museo Ferragamo 82, **83**
Museo Fiorentino di Preistoria 95
Museo Horne 31, **96**
Museo Marino Marini 85
Museo Stibbert **104**, 157
museums & galleries 64-66
  booking 65
  free week 152
  anthropology/ethnology 95
  archaeology: Museo Archeologico *92*, **92**, 157; Museo Fiorentino di Preistoria 95
  art (contemporary) 162-163
  art (historic): Accademia 90; Bargello 22, 29, 75, **94-95**; Casa Buonarroti 95; Collezione Contini-

Bonacossi 75, **76**; Galleria del Palatina 23, **101-102**; Museo Bandini 105; Museo Bardini 99; Museo del Cenacolo di Andrea del Sarto 105; Museo di Bigallo 71-72; Museo di San Marco 93; Museo Marino Marini 85; Spedale degli Innocenti 90, **92**; *see also* Uffizi
art (modern): Collezione della Ragione 77; Galleria d'Arte Moderna 23, **100**
ceramics see under ceramics
children's 77, **157**
clothes: Museo del Costume **100**, 157; Museo Ferragamo 82, **83**
Dante 77
eclectic: Museo Horne 31, **96**; Museo Stibbert **104**, 157
Etruscan see under Etruscans
geology: Museo di Geologia e Paleontologia **92**, 157; Museo di Mineralogia e Lithologia 92
Jewish 97
local history 95-96
natural history: Natural History Museum of the University of Pisa 209; La Specola **102**, 157
religion: Museo dell'Opera del Duomo 71; Museo dell'Opera di Santa Croce 96-97; Museo Diocesano di Santo Stefano al Ponte 77
science: Museo di Storia della Scienza 75, **77-79**, 157
silver 102
transport: Museo delle Carrozze 102
for museums outside Florence see individual places
music, live
classical concerts 167-169
rock, roots & jazz venues 126, 130, **170-173**, 174, 176, 179, 180, 206
see also music festivals
music, recorded 299
shops 149, 172
music festivals 152, 153, 154, 155, 156, **168**, 229, 240, 251, 265, 270
blues 197
jazz 251, 266
world music 156
music tours 192

Napoleon Bonaparte 13, 32, 275
nature reserves 211, 252, 271-272, 273, 274
Negroni 128, 163, **180**
New Year **156**, 200
newspapers 289
northern Florence 103-105

Oasi di Bolgheri 211
Officina Move Bar 180
film shows 160
Ognissanti 85-86
Oltrarno **98-102**, 132
cafés & bars 131, 124-125, 170
hotels 56-59
restaurants 116-119
opening hours 66, 133
opera 167-169
festivals 155, 168
Opificio delle Pietre Dure 93
opticians **147**, 258
Orbetello 36-37, **272**
Orsanmichele 28, 75, **79**
Museo di 79
Orsini family 270, 271
outside the city gates 103-106
cafés & bars 125, 131
clubs 170, 171, 173
hotels 58-61
restaurants 120-122

p

Palasport 171
Palazzo Bartolini-Salimbeni 82
Palazzo Davanzati 82, 83
Palazzo dell'Arte della Lana 72, 75
Palazzo Medici-Riccardi 29-31, **89**
Palazzo Pitti 32, 98, **99-102**
Boboli Gardens *65*, 98, *98*, **99**, **100-101**, 159
Galleria d'Arte Moderna 23, **100**
Galleria del Palatina & Appartamenti Reali 23, **101-102**
Museo degli Argentini 102
Museo del Costume **100**, 157
Museo delle Carrozze 102
Museo delle Porcellane 102
Palazzo Rucellai 31, **84-85**
Palazzo Strozzi 82, **83**
Palazzo Vecchio 22, 29, *30*, 72, **79-80**
Palio
Magliano in Toscana 152
Siena *153*, **155**, 213, **222**
Panzano in Chianti 224-225
paper 98, **148**, 150
Parco Carraia 159
Parco Orecchiella 252
Parco Preistorico 159
Parigi, Pietro 97
parks 159
see also Cascine; gardens
pasticcerie 130, 131, **144**
Pazzi family 11
Pelago 156
perfumes 145-146
Perugino 88-89, 90
Peruzzi family 11
Pescia 199
Petrarch 20
pharmacies 146, **287**
photocopying 134, 150
photography
bookshop (Alinari) 133
festival 270
restrictions 283
supplies/processing **149**, 150
piazza dei Ciompi 94
piazza del Carmine 18, **98**
piazza del Limbo 82
piazza dell'Unità 96
piazza della Libertà 32, **104**
piazza della Repubblica 27, 33, **67**
piazza della Signoria 27, **72-82**
piazza Santa Croce 94
piazza Santa Maria Novella 84, 86
piazza Santa Trinità 82
piazza Santissima Annunziata 90
piazza Santo Spirito **98**, 99, 102, 134
outdoor events 179
piazzale Michelangelo 33, 98, **106**
picnics **120**, 157
Piedmont, kingdom of 15-16
Pienza 234-235
Piero della Francesca **23**, 80-81, 254, 256, 263
pietra dura 93
Pietrasanta 249
Pieve di Romena *261*, 262
Pinocchio 198
Pinturicchio 217
Piombino 211
Pisa 7, 10, 14, 191, **200-207**, 238
accommodation 206-207
airport 207, **278**
cafés & bars 206
Campo dei Miracoli 200-204
churches 203-204, 205
festivals **154**, 200
gay & lesbian scene 166
harbour excavations 200
information & resources 200, **207**
Leaning Tower 200, *201*, **204**, **207**
map 202-203
museums 204
music, theatre & dance 206
Orto Botanico 204
piazza dei Cavalieri 204-205
restaurants 205-206
shops & markets 206
transport 207
Pisa Province 208-211
Pisano, Andrea 69, 71
Pisano, Giovanni 197, 204, 217
Pisano, Nicola 21, 200, 217
Pistoia 166, 185, 191, 193, **197-198**
Giardino Zoologico 159
Giostra dell'Orso **154**, 197
tourist information 199
transport 199
Pistoia Province 197-199
Pitigliano 41, **270-271**, *272*
restaurants 37, 271
tourist information 274
Pitti Imagine 162
Pitti Palace *see* Palazzo Pitti
Pius II, pope 217, 219, 234-235
pizzas 111, 115, 119, 122, 159
takeaway 120, *121*, 143, 144
Poggi, Giuseppe 28, 32, 33, 106
Poggibonsi 227
police 286, **290-291**, 296
politics 24-25
Pollaiuolo, Antonio 81
Ponte alle Grazie 94
Ponte Santa Trinità 18, 32, 33, **82-83**
Ponte Vecchio *30*, 32, **75**, 132
Pontormo, Jacopo da **22**, 93, 102, 194, 242
Pontremoli 253
pool 183
Poppi 262
populo grasso 10
Populonia 211
Porto Ercole 273
Porto Santo Stefano 273
postal services 291
telegrams 294
Prato 31, 185, 191, **193-194**
Centro Per L'Arte Contemporanea 162, 194
Duomo 193, *195*
tourist information 196
Prato Province 193-196
property 26
prostitution 26
pubs **176-180**, 211
Puccini, Giacomo 241, **248**
Casa Natale 241
Opera Festival **155**, 168

Radda 225-227
Radicofacini 237
radio 289
Raggio Verde 161
railways **278-279**, 281
left luggage 288
lost property 289
station architecture 32, 33, 84, 197
for trains to destinations outside Florence see individual places
Raphael 101, 102
Rassegna Internazionale Musica dei Popoli 156
records & CDs 133, **149**, **172**
refectories
Andrea del Sarto 105
Conservatorio di Fuligno 88
Sant'Apollonia 89
Santo Spirito 99
removals 285
Renaissance 20-23, 29-32
residence permits 296
restaurants 98, **108-122**
best (Florence) 108
best countryside 36-37

bills 109-110
children's 197-198
Chinese 111, 120, 194
fish 36-37, 120, 122, 227, 249, 252, 272, 273
Indian 122
kosher 116
menus 38-39, 109
vegetarian food 109, 112, 116, 119, 208, 269
see also cafés; food; pizzas; *rosticcerie*; wine bars; *and individual places outside Florence*
restaurant-bars 177
restoration 98, 264
courses 292
Rex Caffé 128, 163, **180**
Rificolona, La 158
Rinascente 134
La Terrazza (café) 129
Robbia family *see* della Robbia
Roman remains **13**, 73, 241, 272-273
in Arezzo 254, **257**
in Duomo 68
Santa Trinità column 82
Teatro Romano, Fiesole 105
Romans 7, **13**, 27, 238, 250
literature 20
Rosai, Ottone 23
Roselle 268
Rossellino, Antonio 106
Rossellino, Bernardo 97, 106, 217, 235
Rosso Fiorentino **22**, 82, 89, 93, 101, 210
rosticcerie 120, **144**
Rucellai family 84-85, 86
running 184
Russian Orthodox Church 103-104

S

St James's American Church 158
San Casciano dei Bagni (spa) 237
San Domenico (hamlet) 106
San Filippo Neri 32
San Frediano 32
San Frediano (district) 98
San Gaetana 32
San Galgano abbey 168, **229**
San Gimignano (town) 41, 191, **227-229**
festivals 152, 156, 229
San Giorgio alla Costa 32
San Giovanni Battista 33
San Leonardo in Arcetri 105
San Lorenzo 29, 32, **89**
San Lorenzo, area of 87-89
cafés & bars 123-124, 130, 170
hotels 53-54
market **134**, 157
restaurants 112
San Marco 23, **93**
San Marco, area of **90-93**, 170
cafés & bars 130
hotels 54-55
vegetarian restaurant 112
San Miniato (town) **208**, 211
San Miniato al Monte 28, *30*, 105, **106**
San Niccolò (district) 98
San Pancrazio 85
San Quirico d'Orcia (town) 234
San Remigio 28
San Vincenzo (town) 211
Sangallo, Antonio da, the Elder 236, 257, 265
Sangallo, Antonio da, the Younger 103, 210
Sangallo, Giuliano da 28, 31, 194
sanitary towels 296
Sano di Pietro 231, 234, 236
Sansepolcro **263**, 267
Sant'Antimo abbey 168, *230*, *231*, **234**
Santa Croce 18, 28, 94, *95*, **97**
Santa Croce, area of 94-97
cafés & bars 124, 130-131
clubs 171
hotels 55-56
leather goods 139
restaurants 112-116
Santa Felicità 102
Santa Maria del Carmine 102
Santa Maria Maddalena dei Pazzi 31, **97**
Santa Maria Novella 22, 28, 31, 84, **86**
Santa Maria Novella, area of **84-86**, 171
cafés & bars 129-130
hotels 51-53
restaurants 111
station 33, 84, 197, **278**
Santa Trinità 82, **83**
Santissima Annunziata 31, **93**
Santissimi Apostoli 28, **83**
Santo Spirito *27*, 29, 31, **102**
Cenacolo di 99
Santo Spirito (district) 98
Sarteano 237
Sarto, Andrea del 89, 93, 101, 105
Saschali-Teatro di Firenze 173
Saturnia **270**, 274
saunas 166, **183**
Savonarola, Girolamo **12**, 21, 72, 79, 89, 93
Savoy Hotel 47-49
L'Incontro (bar) 129
Scarperia 193, **196**
scooter hire 282
Scoppio del Carro 152
Settembre Musica 156
Settignano 106
Settimana dei Beni Culturali 152
sexual assault 296
Sfilata dei Canottieri 156
shippers 150, 283
shoes 139, **141**
Ferragamo 83, 135
repairs 140-141
shops 132-150
the best 133
children's 158
etiquette 283
opening hours 133
in Arezzo 257-258
in Lucca 243-244
in Pisa 206
in Siena 219
see also individual products
Siena 191, **212-223**
accommodation 221-223
combined tickets 213
contrade 212, **222**
churches 216-217
Duomo & museum *216*, 216-217
Estate Musicale Chigiana 168
Fortezza Medicea & Enoteca Italiana 219, 220
history 7, 10, 18, **212-213**
information & resources 223
map 214-215
monuments 219
museums 217-219
Palazzo Pubblico 213, *220*
Palio *153*, **155**, 213, **222**
piazza del Campo 212, *213*, **213**
restaurants 220-221
shops 219
Torre del Mangia 216
transport 223
Siena Province 224-237
south-east of Siena 230-237
west of Siena 227-228
see also Chianti
sights, the best 66, 190
Signorelli, Luca 230, 265, 266
signoria 10, 79
Siviero, Rodolfo 99
skating 183
skiing 199
smoking 292
Soderini, Piero 12
Sodomo, Il 217, 219, 230
Soffici, Ardengo 23
Sorano 271
southern Florence 106
Sovana 41, **271**
Spadolini, Guido 33
spas 198, 209-210, **226**, 234, 237, 250-251, 270
Specola, La **102**, 157
Spedale degli Innocenti 90, **92**
sports 181-184
see also specific activities
squash 184
Stadio Artemio Franchi 33, **181**
Stadio Comunale 105
stationery 98, 148, **150**
Stazione Leopolda **173**, 187
STDs 287
Stibbert, Fredrick 104
Strozzi family 83
students 292-293
organisations & advice 293
travel centre 150
supermarkets 145
swimming 184
Synagogue 97

tabacchi 292
tabernacles 64, 72, 85, 88, 96
Taddeo di Bartoli 217, 236
Talamone 269, **272**
Talenti, Francesco 69, 79
tampons 296
tax 133, **290**
taxis **281**, 289
Teatro Cantiere Florida **185**, 186, *187*
Teatro del Maggio Musicale Fiorentino (formerly Teatro Comunale) *167*, **168-169**, 185, **186**, 187
Teatro della Limonaia 186
Teatro della Pergola 168, **169**, 185, **186**
Teatro di Rifredi 186
Teatro Goldoni **169**, **185**, 186
Teatro Puccini 186
Teatro Studio di Scandicci 186
Teatro Verdi 168, **169**
telephones 293-294
television 289
Tempo Reale 169
Tenax 165, **173**, **176**
tennis 184
textiles 148, 264-265
theatre 185-187
ticket agencies 150
time, local 294
tipping 294
Tirrenia 209
Titian 82, 101
toiletries 145-146
toilets 294
Torre del Lago 166, **248**
opera festival **155**, 248
Torre della Pagliazza 27-28
tourist information 66, **294**
tours 77, **66**, **192**
cycling 159, **182**, **192**, 209, 282
walking 181
towers, medieval 27-28
toys 158
translators 285
transport 25, **278-282**
for travel to destinations outside Florence see individual places
travel advice 283
gay & lesbian 286
travel agents 150
trotting 181
truffles 143, 208
Tuscany **190-276**
best sights 190
Tuscany, southern 268-276

U

Uccello, Paolo 22-23, 68, 77, 81, 86, 193
Ugo, Margrave of Tuscany 75-76
Ufficio Informazione Turistiche 294
Uffizi 18, 22-23, 26, 32, 75, **80-82**
universities 292-293

Vagli di Sotto 252
Val d'Ambra 262
Valdarno 261
Valdichiana 261

Valtiberina 261
Vasari, Giorgio 21, 28, 32, 68, 77, 79, 80, 83, 86, 94, 97, 102, 262
Lives of the Most EminentPainters 21, 22, 254
museum 256-257
and Pisa 204
Wedding Feast of Ahasuerus and Esther 257
Vecchietta 235, 236
Verna, La 262-263
Verrocchio, Andrea del 23, 82
Versilia 166, **248-250**
Vespucci family 85
via degli Alfani 88
via dei Fossi 84, 132
via dei Tornabuoni **82-83**, 88, 132, 135-137
via della Spada 85
via Francigena (pilgrim route) 208, 212, 217, 234, 238, 252, 253
via Maggio 98, 132
via Ricasoli 90, **96**
via Vigna Nuova 84, 135-137
Viareggio 248-249
Carnevale **154-155**, **156**, 248
gay & lesbian scene 166
tourist information 250
video rental 150
views 66, 99, 105, 106, 129
Villa Bellosguardo 106
Villa della Petraia 104-105
Villa di Castello 105
Villa Medici 106
villas 32, **242**
Vinci 193, **194**, 196
visas 295
Volpaia 225
Volterra **210**, 211

walking 191, **282**
guided treks 181, **192**, 209
information on trekking 182
natural parks 252, 271, 276
tours of Florence 66
walks, suggested
Boboli Gardens 100-101
Duomo & around 80-81
Fiesole & around 106
south of the river 104-105
walls, city 28, 32
weather 295
websites, useful 299
weights & measures 295
Willa 75-76
windsurfing 211
wine & wineries **40-43**, 109, 194, **232-233**, 244, 276
Cantina Aperte 153, 232
Enoteca Italiana 220
shops 143, **145**
tours 43
wine bars 98, **123-125**
in Arezzo 258, 260
Women's Day 152
women's safety & services 296
bookshop 134
work 296
World War II **17-18**, 33, 77, 83, 94, 99, 200, 209, 210, 271

zoo 159
Zuccari, Federico 68

Restaurants in Florence

Alla Vecchia Bettola 116
Alle Murate 112
Arte Gaia 120
Baldovino 112
Beccofino 116
Bibe 121
Casalinga, La 116
Cavolo Nero 116
Cibreino *109*, 115
Cibrèo 115
Da Mario 112
Da Ruggero 122
Da Sergio 112
Enoteca Pinchiorri 115
Finisterrae 115, *117*
Funiculì 111
Fuor d'Acqua 122
Garga 111
Guscio, Il 117
Latini, I 111
Nerbone 112
Nin Hao 111
Oliviero 111
Omero 122
Osteria dei Benci 115
Osteria Santo Spirito 119
Pane e Vino 119
Pizzaiuolo, Il 115
Ruth's 116
Sabatino 119
Salaam Bombay 122
Salumeria, Vini, Trattoria 116
Santa Lucia 122
Santo Bevitore, Il 119
Simon Boccanegra 116
Targa 122
Tarocchi, I 119
Trattoria del Carmine 119
Trattoria 4 Leoni *113*, 119
Vegetiariano, Il 112
Zibibbo 122

Cafés & bars in Florence

All'Antico Vinaio 124
Amerini 129
Angels 128, 177
Apollo 176
Art Bar 176
Astor Caffè 126, 176
Bar Curtatone 129
Bar Perseo 126
Boccadama 124
BZF – Bizzeffe Vallecchi 130
Cabiria 176
Caffè, Il 177
Caffè Cibreo 130
Caffè Concerto Paszkowski 126
Caffè degli Artigiani 131
Caffè dei Macci 130
Caffè Italiano 126, *127*
Caffè la Torre 170, 177
Caffè Megara 129
Caffè Ricchi 128, 131
Caffè Rivoire 126
Caffèllatte 130
Caffetteria Piansa 131
Cantinetta del Verrazzano 123
Capocaccia 128, 129, 177
Casa del Vino 123, *125*
Chalet Fontana 131
Chiaroscuro 127
Colle Bereto 127
Coquinarius 127
Dolce Vita 128, 131, 178
Enoteca Baldovino 124
Enoteca de'Giraldi 124
Enotria 125
Fiddler's Elbow 178
Finisterrae 177
Fratellini, I 123
Frescobaldi Wine Bar 123, *125*
Fuori Porta 125
Fusian Bar Shozan 127, 128, 177
Gelateria dei Neri 131
Giacosa Roberto Cavalli 129
Gilli 127
Giubbe Rosse 127
Gold 129
Hemingway 131
Incontro 129
James Joyce 179
JJ Cathedral Pub 179
Latteria Moggi 129
Lido 179
Loggia degli Albizi, La 131
Loonees 179
Mayday Lounge Café 179
Montecaria 179
Nabucco 130
Nannini Coffee Shop 130
Negroni 128, 180
Officina Move Bar 180
Perche' No! 129
Pitti Gola e Cantina 124
Porfirio Rubirosa 130, 180
Rex Caffè 128, 180
Rifrullo, Il 131
Robiglio 130
Rose's 130, 177
Rotonda, La 180
Sèsame 177
Slowly 128, *178*, 180
Sugar e Spice 129
Terrazza, La 129
Vivoli 131
Volpi e L'Uva, Le 124
William Pub 180
Zanobini 124
Zoe 180
Zona 15 130, 177

Accommodation in Florence

Abaco 53
Alessandra 50
Annalena 56
Aprile 51
B&B Borgo Pinti 54
B&B Piazza Signoria 49
Bavaria 56
Beacci Tornabuoni 49
Bellettini 54
Bencistà 58
Casci 50
Cimabue 60
Classic Hotel 60
Dali 49
Dei Mori 50
Excelsior 51
Gallery Art Hotel 47
Grand Hotel 51
Grand Hotel Minerva 53
Guelfo Bianco 49
Helvetia & Bristol 47
Hermitage 49
Hostel Archi Rossi 62
Hotel Boboli 56
Hotel Continentale 47
Hotel delle Arti 54
Hotel Maxim 50
Hotel Orchidea 56
Istituto Gould 58
J & J 55
J K Place 53
Liana 55
Locanda degli Artisti 53
Loggiato dei Serviti *51*, 54
Lungarno 56
Morandi alla Crocetta 55
Ostello per la Giovent 62
Palazzo Castiglioni 53
Palazzo Magnani Feroni 56, *57*
Pensionato Pio X 58
Relais degli Uffizi 50
Relais Marignolle 58
Residence Johanna 61
Residence Johanna Cinque Giornate 61
Residenza Johlea Uno & Due 55
Santa Monaca 62
Savoy 47
Scaletta 57
Scoti 50
Sorelle Bandini 57
Stanze di Santa Croce *54*, 55
Torre Guelfa 50
Villa Belvedere 60
Villa La Massa 59
Villa Poggio San Felice 60
Villa San Michele 60

Advertisers' Index

Please refer to the relevant sections for contact details

Telecom Italia **IFC**

In Context

Scuola del Cuoio **4**
Telecom Italia Mobile **8,9**

Accommodation

Milligan & Milligan **44**
Hotel Cellai **48**
Centro Machiavelli **48**
Hotel Casci **48**
Slowly Café **52**

Sightseeing

The British Institute of Florence **70**
Odeon Cinema **74**
Residenza Pucci **74**
Antica Torre Tornabuoni **74**
Caffè San Carlo **78**

Restaurants

Trattoria/Enoteca Baldovino **110**
Ristorante Beccofino **114**
Finisterrae **114**
Zona 15 **118**
Enoteca Boccadama **118**

Shops & Services

Il Bisonte **136**
Misuri **142**
The Gold Market **142**

Tuscany

Borgo Tre Rose **188**
B&B Bianchi **218**
Dulcis in Fundo **218**
The Informer **218**
Time Out City Guides **228**

Directory

Direct Line Travel Insurance **280**
Hotel Connect **280**
Internet Train **284**

APT Firenze/Florence Tourist Office **IBC**

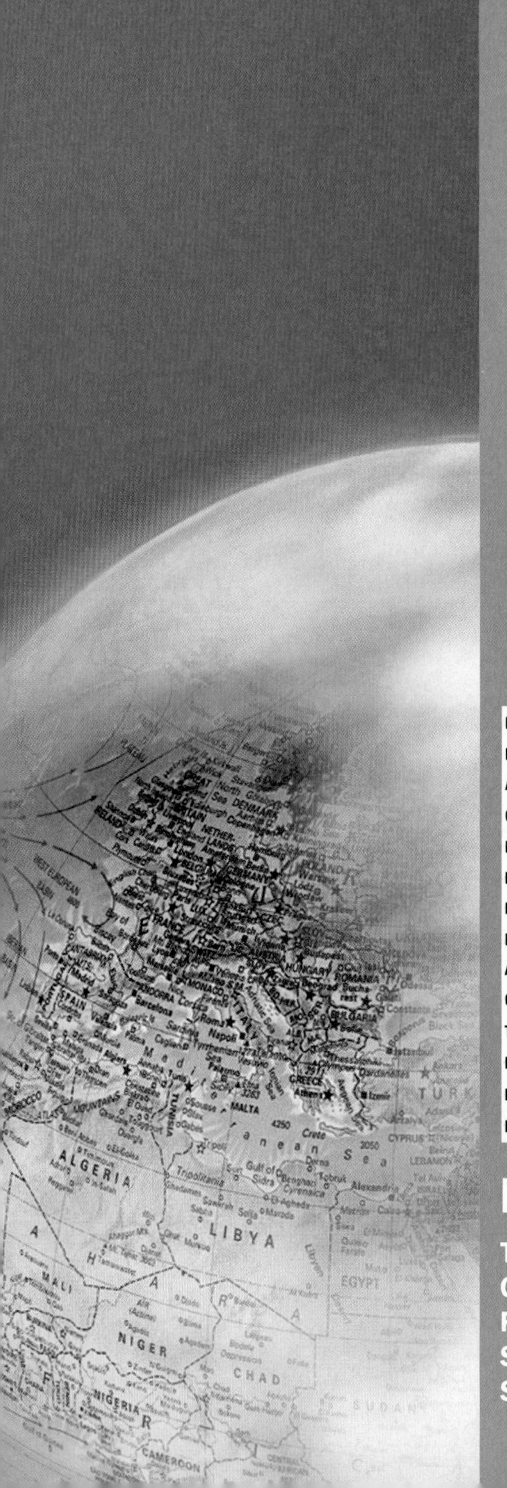

Regional border	- - - -
Province border	— — —
Autostrade	
City wall	
Place of interest and/or entertainment	
Railway station	
Park	
Hospital/university	
Ancient site	
Car park	P
Tourist information	*i*
Pedestrianised area	
Bus routes	*12, 13*
Electric bus routes	A

Maps

Tuscany 308
Greater Florence 311
Florence Overview 312
Street Maps 314
Street Index 316

LIGURIA
EMILIA-ROMAGNA
Massa-Carrara
pp248-53
Lunigiana
Pontrémoli
A15
63
Fivizzano
Aulla
Parco dell' Orecchiella
Garfagnana
445
12
1
Fosdinovo
LA SPEZIA
Alpi Apuane
Castelnuovo di Garfagnana
Abetone
Carrara
Colonnata
Isolasanta
Massa
Barga
Riviera della Versilia
Forte dei Marmi
Fornovolasco
Val di Lima
Pistoia
pp197-9
Bagni di Lucca
Pietrasanta
Lucca
pp248-53
PISTOIA
A12
Pescia
Collodi
Montecatini Terme
Viareggio
LUCCA
pp238-47
Torre del Lago Puccini
Monsummano Terme
A11
Vinci
Empoli
San Miniato
PISA
pp200-7
Cascina
67
Montopoli in Val D'Ano
Terricciola
LIVORNO
Casciana Terme
439
Pisa
pp208-11
Rosignano
Volterra
Vada
68
Cecina
TOS
(TUS
1
San Vincenzo
Livorno
Golfo di Baratti
pp208-11
Massa Maritima
Populonia
Piombino
Vetulonia
Portoferraio
322
Elba
p275
MAR LIGURE
Bastia
Corse (Corsica)
Capraia
Pianosa
Montecristo
Giglio
p274
AUSTRIA
SWITZERLAND
HUNGARY
SLOVENIA
CROATIA
Milan
Venice
Bologna
Genoa
BOSNIA AND HERCEGOVINA
SERBIA
Firenze (Florence)
Rimini
Livorno
Pisa
Siena
MONTENEGRO
Bastia
ITALY
CORSICA
ROME
ALBANIA
Naples
SARDINIA
SICILY
0
40 km
0
20 miles

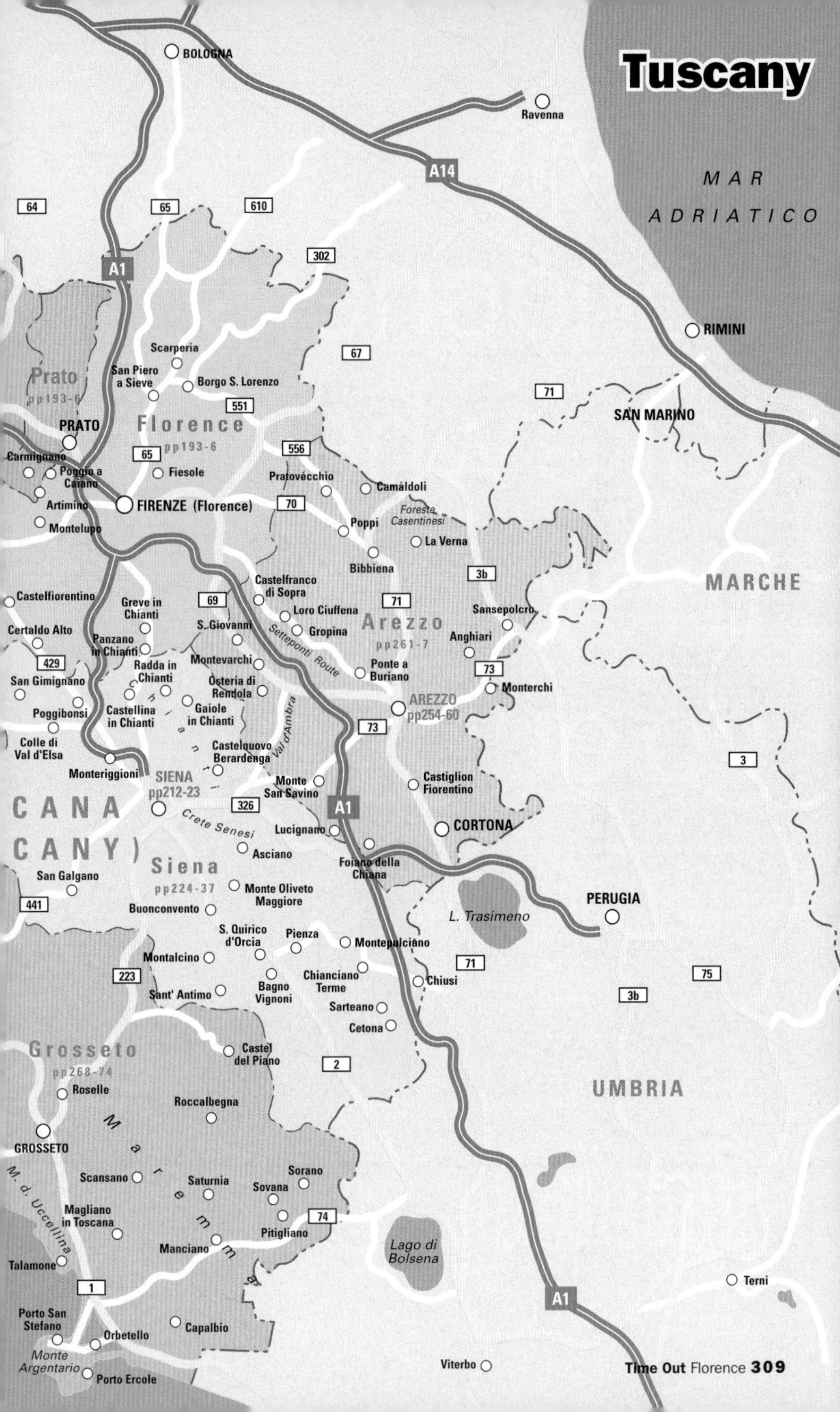
Tuscany
BOLOGNA
Ravenna
A14
MAR ADRIATICO
64
65
610
302
A1
RIMINI
67
71
SAN MARINO
Scarperia
San Piero a Sieve
Borgo S. Lorenzo
551
Prato pp193-6
PRATO
Florence pp193-6
65
556
Carmignano
Poggio a Caiano
Fiesole
Pratovécchio
Camàldoli
Artimino
FIRENZE (Florence)
70
Foreste Casentinesi
Montelupo
Poppi
La Verna
Bibbiena
3b
MARCHE
Castelfranco di Sopra
Castelfiorentino
Greve in Chianti
69
71
Loro Ciuffena
Sansepolcro
Certaldo Alto
S. Giovanni
Arezzo pp261-7
Gropina
Panzano in Chianti
Setteponti Route
Anghiari
429
Montevarchi
Radda in Chianti
Ponte a Buriano
73
San Gimignano
Osteria di Rendola
Monterchi
Chianti
Gaiole in Chianti
Castellina in Chianti
AREZZO pp254-60
Poggibonsi
Val d'Ambra
73
Colle di Val d'Elsa
3
Castelnuovo Berardenga
Castiglion Fiorentino
Monteriggioni
SIENA pp212-23
Monte San Savino
326
A1
Crete Senesi
Lucignano
CORTONA
Asciano
Siena pp224-37
Foiano della Chiana
San Galgano
PERUGIA
Monte Oliveto Maggiore
441
Buonconvento
L. Trasimeno
S. Quirico d'Orcia
Pienza
Montepulciano
Montalcino
Chianciano Terme
71
223
Bagno Vignoni
Chiusi
75
Sant' Antimo
3b
Sarteano
Cetona
Grosseto pp268-74
Castel del Piano
2
Roselle
UMBRIA
Roccalbegna
Maremma
GROSSETO
M. d. Uccellina
Sorano
Scansano
Saturnia
Sovana
Magliano in Toscana
74
Pitigliano
Manciano
Lago di Bolsena
Talamone
1
Terni
A1
Porto San Stefano
Orbetello
Capalbio
Monte Argentario
Porto Ercole
Viterbo

Greater Florence

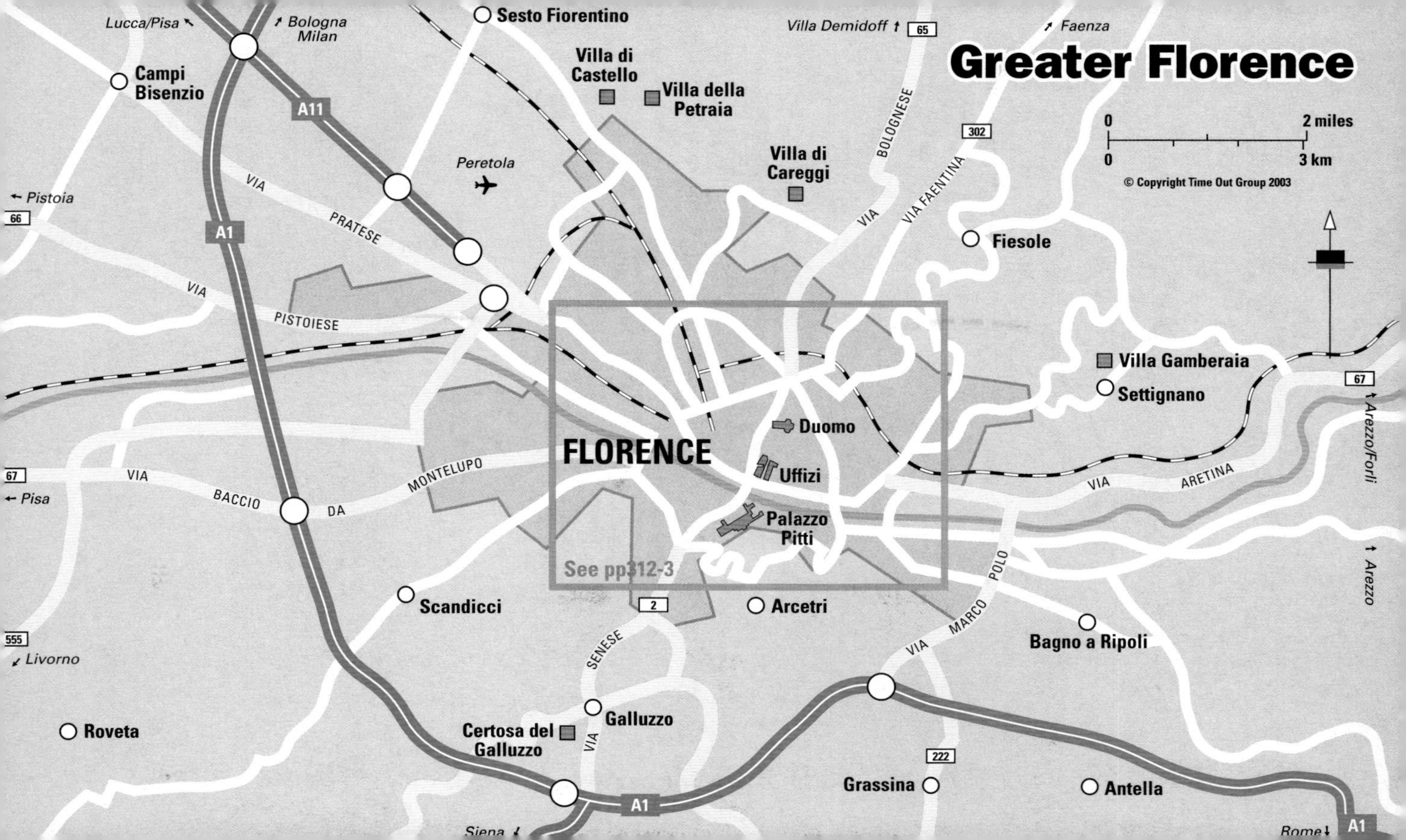

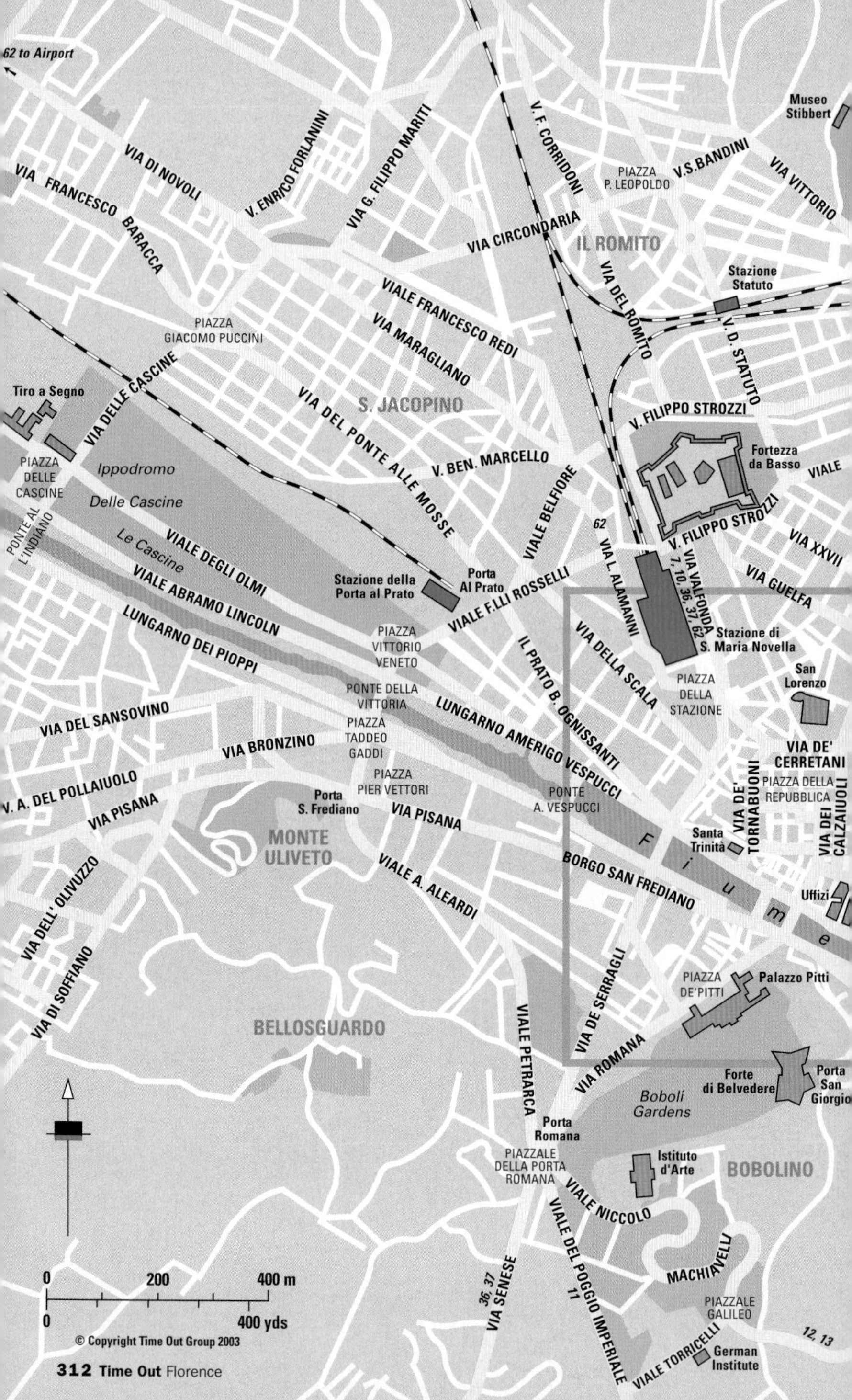
62 to Airport
Museo Stibbert
VIA DI NOVOLI
VIA FRANCESCO BARACCA
V. ENRICO FORLANINI
VIA G. FILIPPO MARITI
V. F. CORRIDONI
PIAZZA P. LEOPOLDO
V.S.BANDINI
VIA VITTORIO
VIA CIRCONDARIA
IL ROMITO
VIA DEL ROMITO
Stazione Statuto
V. D. STATUTO
VIALE FRANCESCO REDI
VIA MARAGLIANO
PIAZZA GIACOMO PUCCINI
S. JACOPINO
VIA DEL PONTE ALLE MOSSE
V. FILIPPO STROZZI
Fortezza da Basso
VIALE
Tiro a Segno
VIA DELLE CASCINE
PIAZZA DELLE CASCINE
Ippodromo
Delle Cascine
V. BEN. MARCELLO
VIALE BELFIORE
PONTE AL L'INDIANO
Le Cascine
VIALE DEGLI OLMI
VIALE ABRAMO LINCOLN
Stazione della Porta al Prato
Porta Al Prato
VIALE F.LLI ROSSELLI
62
VIA L. ALAMANNI
VIA VALFONDA
7, 10, 36, 37, 62
VIA XXVII
VIA GUELFA
LUNGARNO DEI PIOPPI
PIAZZA VITTORIO VENETO
VIA DELLA SCALA
Stazione di S. Maria Novella
PIAZZA DELLA STAZIONE
San Lorenzo
IL PRATO B. OGNISSANTI
PONTE DELLA VITTORIA
LUNGARNO AMERIGO VESPUCCI
VIA DEL SANSOVINO
PIAZZA TADDEO GADDI
VIA BRONZINO
VIA DE' CERRETANI
PIAZZA DELLA REPUBBLICA
V. A. DEL POLLAIUOLO
PIAZZA PIER VETTORI
PONTE A. VESPUCCI
VIA DE' TORNABUONI
VIA DEI CALZAIUOLI
VIA PISANA
Porta S. Frediano
VIA PISANA
MONTE ULIVETO
Santa Trinità
VIALE A. ALEARDI
BORGO SAN FREDIANO
Fiume
Uffizi
VIA DELL' OLIVUZZO
VIA DI SOFFIANO
PIAZZA DE'PITTI
Palazzo Pitti
VIA DE SERRAGLI
BELLOSGUARDO
VIALE PETRARCA
VIA ROMANA
Forte di Belvedere
Porta San Giorgio
Boboli Gardens
Porta Romana
PIAZZALE DELLA PORTA ROMANA
Istituto d'Arte
BOBOLINO
VIALE NICCOLO
VIALE DEL POGGIO IMPERIALE
11
MACHIAVELLI
36, 37
VIA SENESE
0
200
400 m
0
400 yds
PIAZZALE GALILEO
12, 13
VIALE TORRICELLI
German Institute

Florence Overview
7 To Fiesole
To Fiesole
10 to Settignano
VIA BOLOGNESE
VIA FAENTINA
VIA FRANCESCO
EMANUELE
VIA SAN DOMENICO
PIAZZA
DELLE CURE
VIA XX SETTEMBRE
V. DON G. MINZONI
VIALE ALESSANDRO VOLTA
V. AUGUSTO RIGHI
7
PIAZZA
DELLA LIBERTÀ
Russian
Church
SAN LAVAGNINI
Porta
San Gallo
VIALE DEI MILLE
V. CALATAFIMI
PIAZZA
V. FARDELLA
DI TORREARSA
V. GIACOMO MATTEOTTI
V. MANFREDO FANTI
Stadio
Comunale
VIA D. ARTISTI
VIA MASACCIO
V. PASQUALE PAOLI
VIA CAMILLO CAVOUR
VIALE EDMONDO DE AMICIS
APRILE
FILAROC
PIAZZA
SAN MARCO
Giardino
della
Gherardesca
English
Cemetery
PIAZZA
DONATELLO
10
VIALE MALTA
VIA DELLA COLONNA
VIA DEGLI ALFANI
VIA GABRIELE D'ANNUNZ
Duomo
Cenacolo
di Andrea del
Sarteo
Psychiatric
Hospital
V. DEL PROCONSOLO
PIAZZA
C. BECCARIA
Porta
Alla Croce
VIA VINCENZO GIOBERTI
PIAZZA
L.B. ALBERTI
VIA ARETINA
VIA PIAGENTINA
V. G. LANZA
MADONNONE
V. QUINTINO SELLA
LUNG. ALDO MORO
PONTE ALLE
GRAZIE
LUNG. D. ZECCA VECCHIA
L. DEL TEMPIO
LUNGARNO C. COLOMBO
LUNG. B. CELLINI
Porta
San Niccolò
Porta
San Miniato
PONTE SAN
NICCOLÒ
Arno
PONTE G. DA
VERRAZZANO
LUNG. FRANCESCO FERRUCCI
PIAZZA
RAVENNA
See pp314-5
PIAZZALE
MICHELANGIOLO
PIAZZA
F. FERRUCCI
VIA DI VILLAMAGNA
12, 13
V. COLUCCIO SALUTATI
RICORBOLI
VIALE DONATO GIANNOTTI
VIA DI RIPOLI
VIALE GALILEO
San Miniato
al Monte
12, 13
VIALE MICHELANGIOLO
VIA ERBOSA
V. TRAVERSARI
VIALE EUROPA

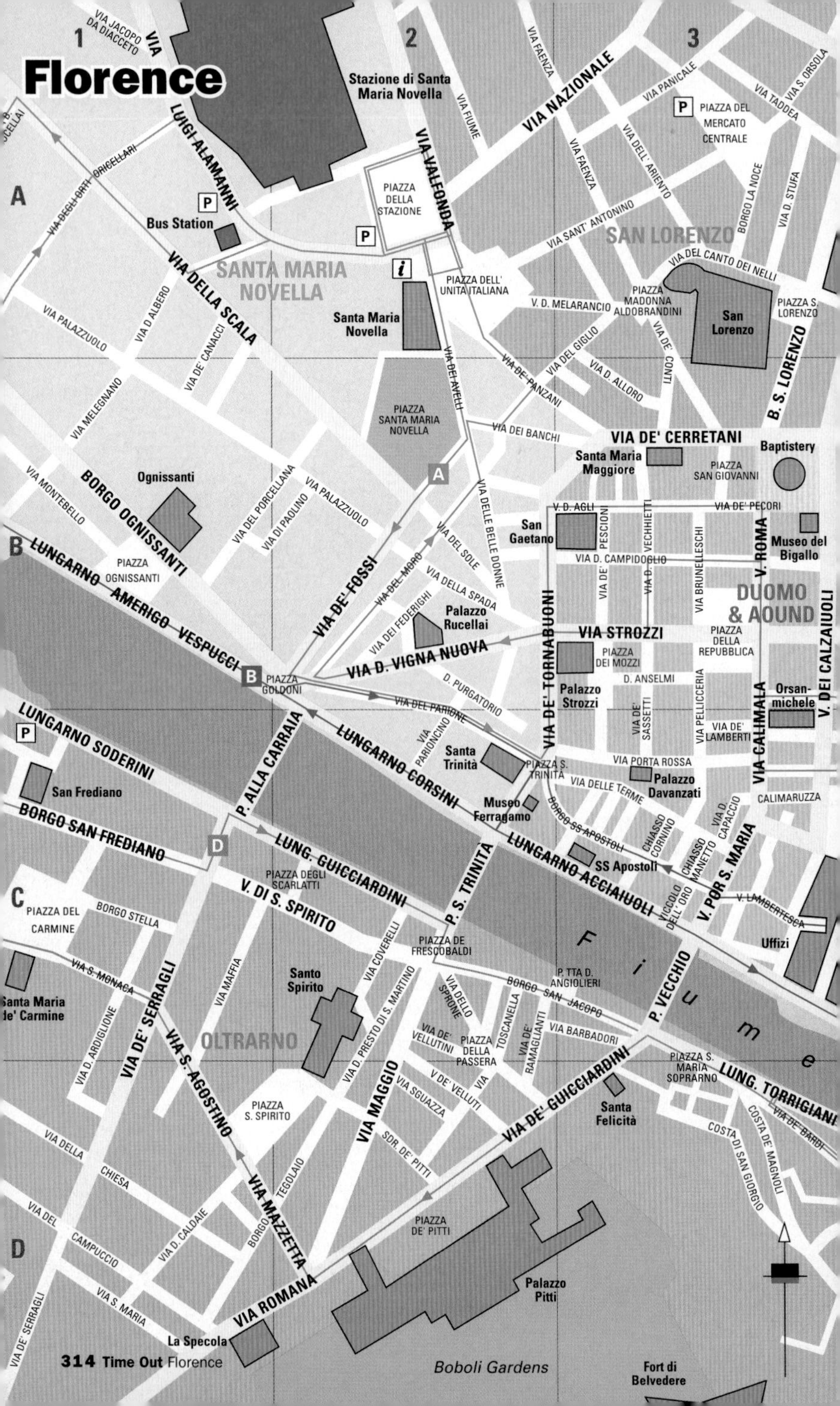
Florence
1
2
3
A
B
C
D
Stazione di Santa Maria Novella
Bus Station
Piazza della Stazione
Santa Maria Novella
Piazza Santa Maria Novella
Piazza dell' Unità Italiana
Santa Maria Novella
Ognissanti
Piazza Ognissanti
San Lorenzo
Piazza del Mercato Centrale
Piazza Madonna Aldobrandini
Piazza S. Lorenzo
Baptistery
Piazza San Giovanni
Santa Maria Maggiore
San Gaetano
Museo del Bigallo
Duomo & Aound
Palazzo Rucellai
Piazza dei Mozzi
Piazza della Repubblica
Palazzo Strozzi
Orsanmichele
Piazza Goldoni
Santa Trinità
Piazza S. Trinità
Palazzo Davanzati
Museo Ferragamo
SS Apostoli
Uffizi
San Frediano
Piazza degli Scarlatti
Piazza del Carmine
Piazza de Frescobaldi
Santo Spirito
Santa Maria de' Carmine
Oltrarno
Piazza della Passera
P. tta d. Angiolieri
Piazza S. Maria Soprarno
Santa Felicità
Piazza S. Spirito
Piazza de' Pitti
Palazzo Pitti
La Specola
Boboli Gardens
Fort di Belvedere
Fiume
Via Nazionale
Via Valfonda
Via Luigi Alamanni
Via della Scala
Borgo Ognissanti
Lungarno Amerigo Vespucci
Via de' Fossi
Via d. Vigna Nuova
Via Strozzi
Via de' Tornabuoni
Via de' Cerretani
B. S. Lorenzo
V. Roma
Via Calimala
V. dei Calzaiuoli
Lungarno Soderini
Borgo San Frediano
P. alla Carraia
Lungarno Corsini
Lung. Guicciardini
V. di S. Spirito
P. S. Trinità
Lungarno Acciaiuoli
V. Por S. Maria
P. Vecchio
Lung. Torrigiani
Via de' Guicciardini
Via Maggio
Via de' Serragli
Via S. Agostino
Via Mazzetta
Via Romana
Via Jacopo da Diacceto
Via Faenza
Via Fiume
Via Panicale
Via Taddea
Via S. Orsola
Via dell' Ariento
Borgo la Noce
Via d. Stufa
Via Sant' Antonino
Via del Canto dei Nelli
V. d. Melarancio
Via de' Conti
Via del Giglio
Via d. Alloro
Via de' Panzani
Via dei Banchi
Via degli Orti Oricellari
Via Palazzuolo
Via d. Albero
Via de' Canacci
Via Melegnano
Via dell'Avelli
Via delle Belle Donne
Via Montebello
Via del Porcellana
Via di Paolino
Via del Sole
Via del Moro
Via della Spada
Via dei Federighi
V. d. Agli
Via de' Pecori
Via de' Pescioni
Via d. Vecchietti
Via Brunelleschi
Via d. Campidoglio
D. Anselmi
D. Purgatorio
Via del Parione
Via Parioncino
Via de' Sassetti
Via Pellicceria
Via de' Lamberti
Via Porta Rossa
Via delle Terme
Calimaruzza
Borgo SS Apostoli
Chiasso Cornino
Chiasso Manetto
Via d. Capaccio
V. Lambertesca
Viccolo dell'Oro
Borgo Stella
Via S. Monaca
Via Maffia
Via Coverelli
Via d. Presto di S. Martino
Via dello Sprone
Borgo San Jacopo
Via Barbadori
Via de' Vellutini
Toscanella
Via de' Ramaglianti
V de' Velluti
Via Sguazza
Sdr. de' Pitti
Via d. Ardiglione
Via della Chiesa
Via del Campuccio
Via d. Caldaie
Borgo Tegolaio
Via S. Maria
Via de' Serragli
Costa di San Giorgio
Costa de' Magnoli
Via de' Bardi

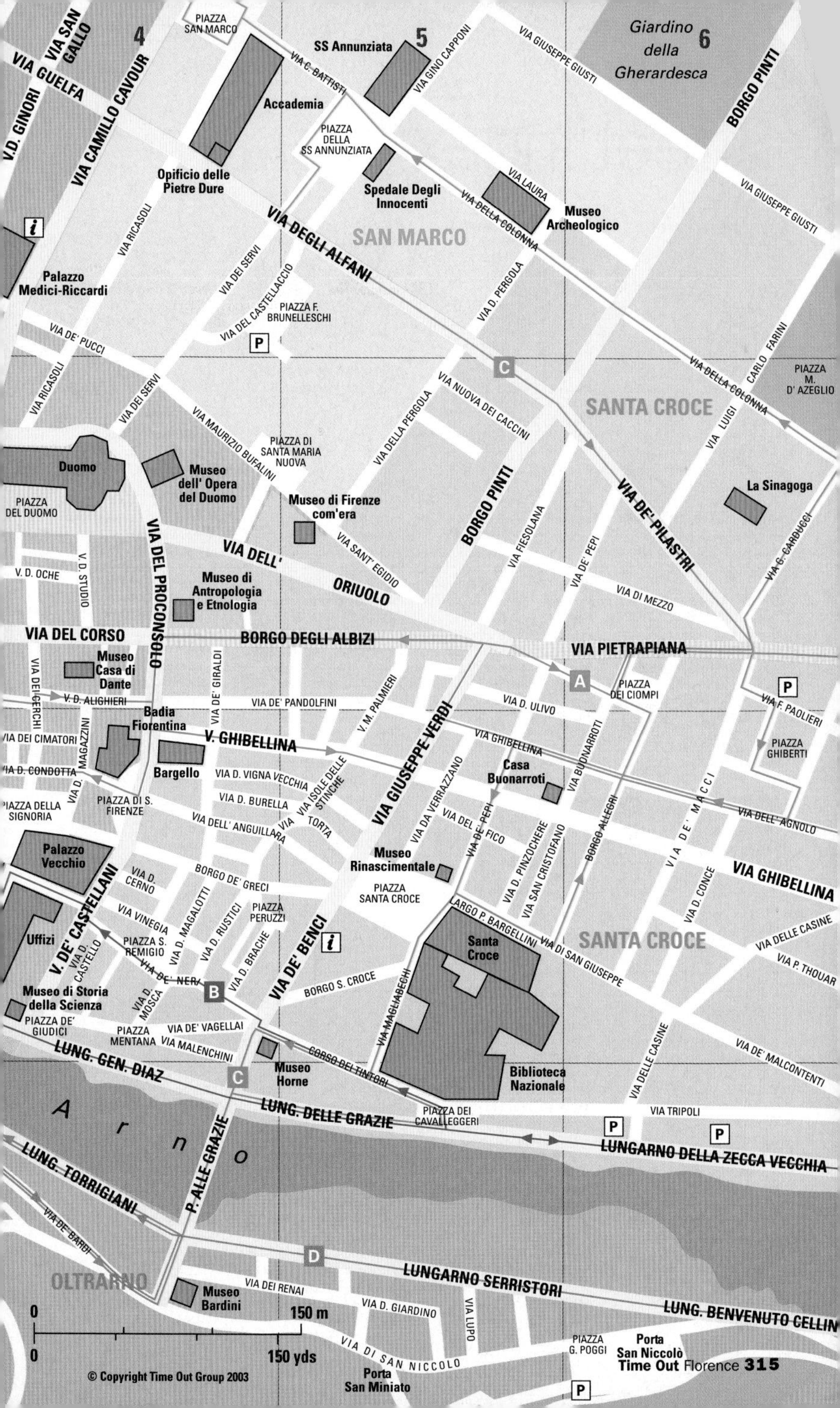

PIAZZA SAN MARCO
4
5
6
Giardino della Gherardesca
VIA SAN GALLO
VIA GUELFA
V.D. GINORI
VIA CAMILLO CAVOUR
Accademia
SS Annunziata
VIA C. BATTISTI
VIA GINO CAPPONI
VIA GIUSEPPE GIUSTI
BORGO PINTI
PIAZZA DELLA SS ANNUNZIATA
Opificio delle Pietre Dure
Spedale Degli Innocenti
VIA LAURA
VIA DELLA COLONNA
Museo Archeologico
VIA RICASOLI
VIA DEGLI ALFANI
SAN MARCO
Palazzo Medici-Riccardi
VIA DEI SERVI
VIA DEL CASTELLACCIO
PIAZZA F. BRUNELLESCHI
VIA D. PERGOLA
VIA DE' PUCCI
VIA CARLO FARINI
PIAZZA M. D'AZEGLIO
SANTA CROCE
VIA NUOVA DEI CACCINI
VIA DELLA PERGOLA
VIA MAURIZIO BUFALINI
PIAZZA DI SANTA MARIA NUOVA
VIA LUIGI
Duomo
Museo dell' Opera del Duomo
PIAZZA DEL DUOMO
Museo di Firenze com'era
BORGO PINTI
VIA DE' PILASTRI
La Sinagoga
VIA SANT' EGIDIO
VIA FIESOLANA
VIA DE' PEPI
VIA G. CARDUCCI
VIA DELL' ORIUOLO
V. D. OCHE
V. D. STUDIO
VIA DEL PROCONSOLO
Museo di Antropologia e Etnologia
VIA DI MEZZO
VIA DEL CORSO
BORGO DEGLI ALBIZI
VIA PIETRAPIANA
Museo Casa di Dante
PIAZZA DEI CIOMPI
VIA DEI CERCHI
V. D. ALIGHIERI
VIA DE' GIRALDI
VIA DE' PANDOLFINI
V. M. PALMIERI
VIA D. ULIVO
VIA F. PAOLIERI
Badia Fiorentina
VIA DEI CIMATORI
V. GHIBELLINA
VIA GIUSEPPE VERDI
VIA GHIBELLINA
PIAZZA GHIBERTI
VIA D. CONDOTTA
MAGAZZINI
Bargello
VIA D. VIGNA VECCHIA
VIA ISOLE DELLE STINCHE
Casa Buonarroti
VIA BUONARROTI
PIAZZA DELLA SIGNORIA
PIAZZA DI S. FIRENZE
VIA D. BURELLA
VIA DA VERRAZZANO
VIA DE' MACCI
VIA DELL' AGNOLO
VIA DELL' ANGUILLARA
VIA TORTA
VIA DEL FICO
VIA DE' PEPI
Palazzo Vecchio
Museo Rinascimentale
VIA D. PINZOCHERE
VIA SAN CRISTOFANO
BORGO ALLEGRI
VIA GHIBELLINA
VIA D. CERNO
BORGO DE' GRECI
PIAZZA SANTA CROCE
VIA D. CONCE
V. DE' CASTELLANI
VIA VINEGIA
VIA D. MAGALOTTI
VIA D. RUSTICI
PIAZZA PERUZZI
LARGO P. BARGELLINI
Uffizi
VIA D. CASTELLO
PIAZZA S. REMIGIO
VIA D. BRACHE
VIA DE' BENCI
Santa Croce
VIA DI SAN GIUSEPPE
SANTA CROCE
VIA DELLE CASINE
VIA P. THOUAR
VIA DE' NERI
B
Museo di Storia della Scienza
VIA D. MOSCA
BORGO S. CROCE
VIA MAGLIABECHI
PIAZZA DE' GIUDICI
PIAZZA MENTANA
VIA DE' VAGELLAI
VIA MALENCHINI
VIA DE' MALCONTENTI
LUNG. GEN. DIAZ
Museo Horne
CORSO DEI TINTORI
VIA DELLE CASINE
C
Biblioteca Nazionale
LUNG. DELLE GRAZIE
PIAZZA DEI CAVALLEGGERI
VIA TRIPOLI
Arno
LUNGARNO DELLA ZECCA VECCHIA
LUNG. TORRIGIANI
P. ALLE GRAZIE
VIA DE' BARDI
D
LUNGARNO SERRISTORI
OLTRARNO
Museo Bardini
VIA DEI RENAI
VIA D. GIARDINO
VIA LUPO
LUNG. BENVENUTO CELLIN
0
150 m
150 yds
VIA DI SAN NICCOLO
PIAZZA G. POGGI
Porta San Niccolò
Porta San Miniato
A
P
i

Street Index to map pages 314-315

Acciaiuoli, Lungarno - C2/3
Agli, Via D. - B3
Agnolo, Via Dell' - C6
Agostino, Via Sant' - C1/D1
Alamanni, Via Luigi - A1
Albero, Via D. - A1
Albizi, Borgo Degli - B4/5
Alfani, Via Degli - A4/5
Alighieri, Via D. - B4
Allegri, Borgo - C6
Alloro, Via D. - B3
Anguillara, Via Dell' - C4/5
Annunziata, Piazza Della SS - A5
Anselmi, Via D. - B3
Ardiglione, Via D. - C1/D1
Ariento, Via Dell' - A3
Avelli, Via Dei - A2/B2
Azeglio, Piazza M. D' - B6

Banchi, Via Dei - B2
Barbadori, Via - C2/3
Bardi, Via De' - D3/4
Battisti, Via C. - A5
Belle Donne, Via Delle - B2
Benci, Via De' - C4/5
Brache, Via D. - C4
Brunelleschi, Via - B3
Buonarroti, Via - C6
Burella, Via D. - C4

Caldaie, Via D. - D1
Calimala, Via - B3/C3
Calimaruzza - C3
Calzaiuoli, Via Dei - B3/C3
Campidoglio, Via D. - B3
Campuccio, Via Del - D1
Canacci, Via De' - A1/B1
Canto Dei Nelli, Via Del - A3
Capaccio, Via D. - C3
Capponi, Via Gino - A5
Carducci, Via G. - B6
Carmine, Piazza Del - C1
Casine, Via Delle - C6/D6
Castellaccio, Via Del - A4
Castellani, Via De' - C4
Castello, Via D. - C4
Cavalleggeri, Piazza Dei - D5
Cavour, Via Camillo - A4
Cellini, Lung. Benvenuto - D6
Cerchi, Via Dei - B4/C4
Cerno, Via D. - C4
Cerretani, Via De' - B3
Chiesa, Via Della - D1
Cimatori, Via Dei - C4
Ciompi, Piazza Dei - B6
Colonna, Via Della - A5/6/B6
Conce, Via D. - C6
Condotta, Via D. - C4
Conti, Via De' - A3/B3
Cornino, Chiasso - C3
Corsini, Lungarno - C2
Corso Dei Tintori - C5/D5
Corso, Via Del - B4
Costa De' Magnoli - D3
Costa Di San Giorgio - D3
Coverelli, Via - C2
Croce, Borgo La - C5

Duomo, Piazza Del - B4

Faenza, Via - A2/3
Farini, Via Luigi Carlo - A6/B6
Federighi, Via Dei - B2
Fico, Via Del - C5
Fiesolana, Via - B5
Fiume, Via - A2
Fossi, Via De' - B2

Gen. Diaz, Lung. - C4/D4
Ghibellina, Via - C4/5/6
Ghiberti, Piazza - C6
Giardino, Via D. - D5
Giglio, Via Del - A3
Ginori, Via D. - A4
Giraldi, Via De' - B4/C4
Giuseppe Giusti, Via - A5/6
Giuseppe Verdi, Via - B5/C5
Goldoni, Piazza - B2
Grazie, Lung. Delle - D4/5
Grazie, Ponte Alle - D4
Greci, Borgo De' - C4/5
Guelfa, Via - A4
Guicciardini, Lung. - C2
Guicciardini, Via De' - D2/3

Jacopo Da Diacceto, Via - A1

La Noce, Borgo - A3
Lambertesca, Via - C3
Lamberti, Via De' - C3
Laura, Via - A5/6

Macci, Via De' - C6
Maffia, Via - C1
Magalotti, Via D. - C4
Magazzini, Via D. - C4
Maggio, Via - C2/D2
Magliabechi, Via - C5
Malcontenti, Via De' - C6/D6
Malenchini, Via - C4
Manetto, Chiasso - C3
Maurizio Bufalini, Via - B4
Mazzetta, Via - D1/2
Melarancio, Via D. - A2/3
Melegnano, Via - B1
Mentana, Piazza - C4
Mercato Centrale, Piazza Del - A3
Mezzo, Via Di - B6
Montebella, Via - B1
Moro, Via Del - B2
Mozzi, Piazza Dei - B3

Nazionale, Via - A2/C2
Neri, Via De' - C4
Nuova Dei Caccini, Via - B5

Oche, Via D. - B4
Ognissanti, Piazza - B1
Ognissanti, Borgo - B1
Oriuolo, Via Dell' - B4/5
Orti Oricellari, Via Degli - A1

Palazzuolo, Via - A1/B1/2
Palmieri, Via M. - B5/C5
Pandolfini, Via De' - B4/5
Panicale, Via - A3
Panzani, Via De' - B2/3
Paolieri, Via F. - B6/C6
Paolino, Via Di - B1/2
Parioncino, Via - C2
Parione, Via Del - B2/C2
Passer, Piazza Della - C2
Pecori, Via De' - B3
Pellicceria, Via - B3/C3
Pepi, Via De' - B6/C5
Pergola, Via D. - A5
Pergola, Via Della - B5
Peruzzi, Piazza - C4
Pescioni, Via De' - B3
Pietrapiana, Via - B6
Pilastri, Via De' - B6
Pinti, Borgo - A6
Pinti, Borgo - B5
Pinzochere, Via D. - C5
Pitti, Piazza De' - D2
Poggi, Piazza G. - D6
Ponte Alla Carraia - C1/2
Por S. Maria, Via - C3
Porcellana, Via Del - B1/2
Porta Rossa, Via - C3
Presto Di S. Martino, Via Di - C2/D2
Proconsolo, Via Del - B4
Pucci, Via De' - A4
Purgatorio, Via D. - B2/C2

Ramaglianti, Via De' - C2
Renai, Via Dei - D4/5
Repubblica, Piazza Della - B3
Ricasoli, Via - A4
Roma, Via - B3
Romana, Via - D1
Rucellai, Via B. - A1
Rustici, Via D. - C4

San Cristofano, Via - C5
San Egidio, Via - B5
San Frediano, Borgo - C1
San Gallo, Via - A4
San Giovanni, Piazza - B3
San Giuseppe, Via Di - C5/6
San Jacopo, Borgo - C2/3
San Lorenzo, Borgo - A3/B3
San Marco, Piazza - A4
San Niccolo, Via Di - D4/5
San Spirito, Piazza - D1/2
Sant' Antonino, Via - A3
Sant' Orsola, Via - A3
Santa Croce, Piazza - C5
Santa Maria Novella, Piazza - B2
Santa Maria Novella, Piazza di - B4/5
Santa Maria, Via - D1
Santa Monaca, Via - C1
Santa Trinità, Piazza - C2
Santo Spirito, Via Di - C1/2
Sassetti, Via De' - B3/C3
Scala, Via Della - A1/B2
Serragli, Via De' - C1/D1
Serristori, Lungarno - D5
Servi, Via Dei - A4
Sguazza, Via - D2
Signoria, Piazza Della - C4
Soderini, Lungarno - B1/C1
Sole, Via Del - B2
Sprone, Via Dello - C2
SS Apostoli, Borgo - C3
Stazione, Piazza Della - A2
Stella, Borgo - C1
Stinche, Via Isole delle - C5
Strozzi, Via - B3
Studio, Via D. - B4
Stufa, Via D. - A3

Taddea, Via - A3
Tegolaio, Borgo - D1/2
Terme, Via Delle - C3
Thouar, Via P. - C6
Tornabuoni, Via De' - B2/C2
Torrigiani, Lung. - C3/D3/4
Torta, Via - C5
Toscanella, Via - C2/D2
Trinità, P. S. - C2
Tripoli, Via - D6

Ulivo, Via D. - B5
Unita Italiana, Piazza Dell' - A2

Vagellai, Via De' - C4
Valfonda, Via - A2
Vecchio, P. - C3
Vechhietti, Via D. - B3
Velluti, Via De' - D2
Vellutini, Via De' - C2
Verrazzano, Via Da - C5
Vespucci, Lungarno Amerigo - B1
Vigna Nuova, Via D. - B2
Vigna Vecchia, Via D. - C4/5
Vinegia, Via - C4

Zecca Vecchia, Lungarno Della - D6